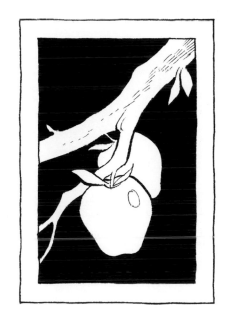

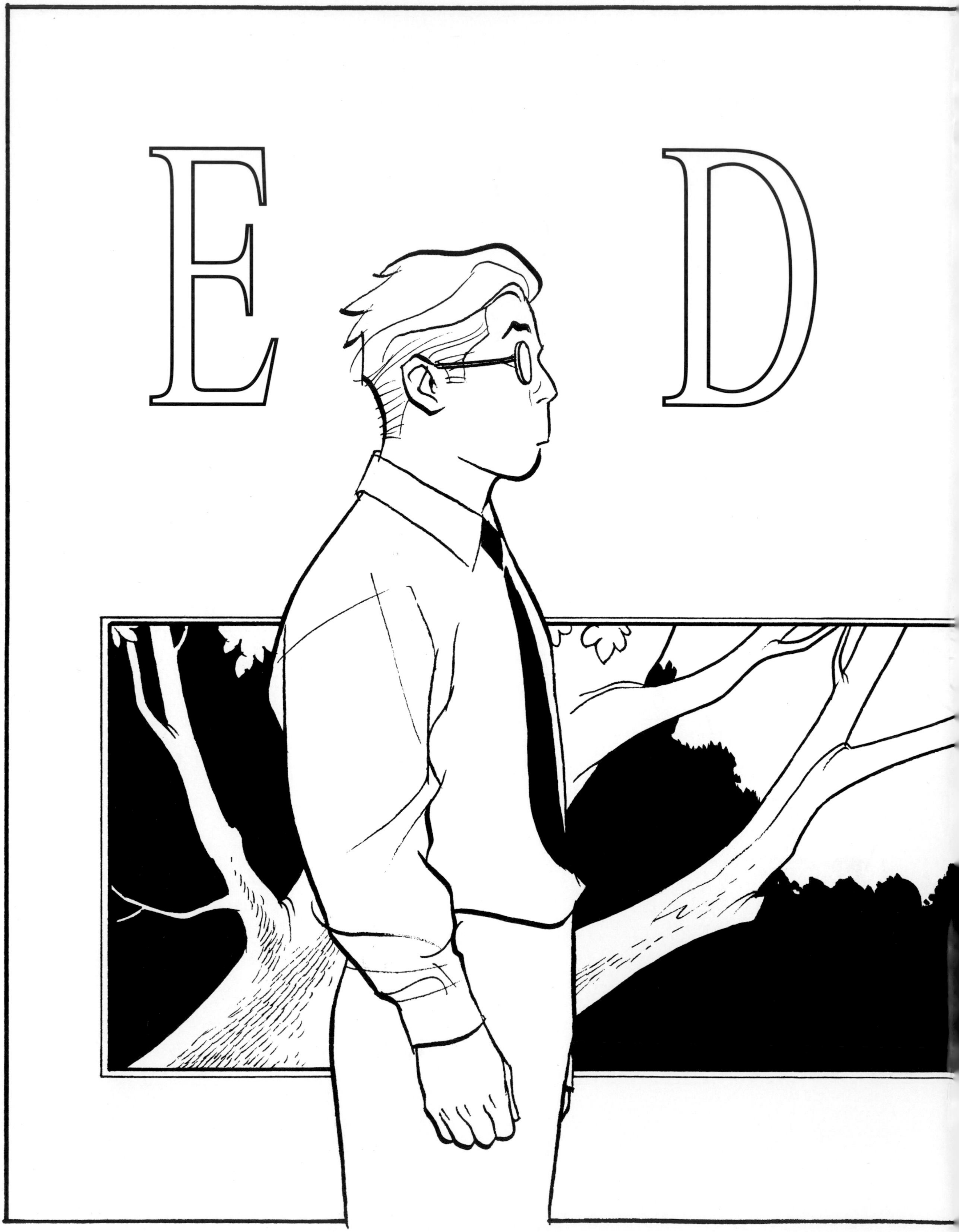
E D

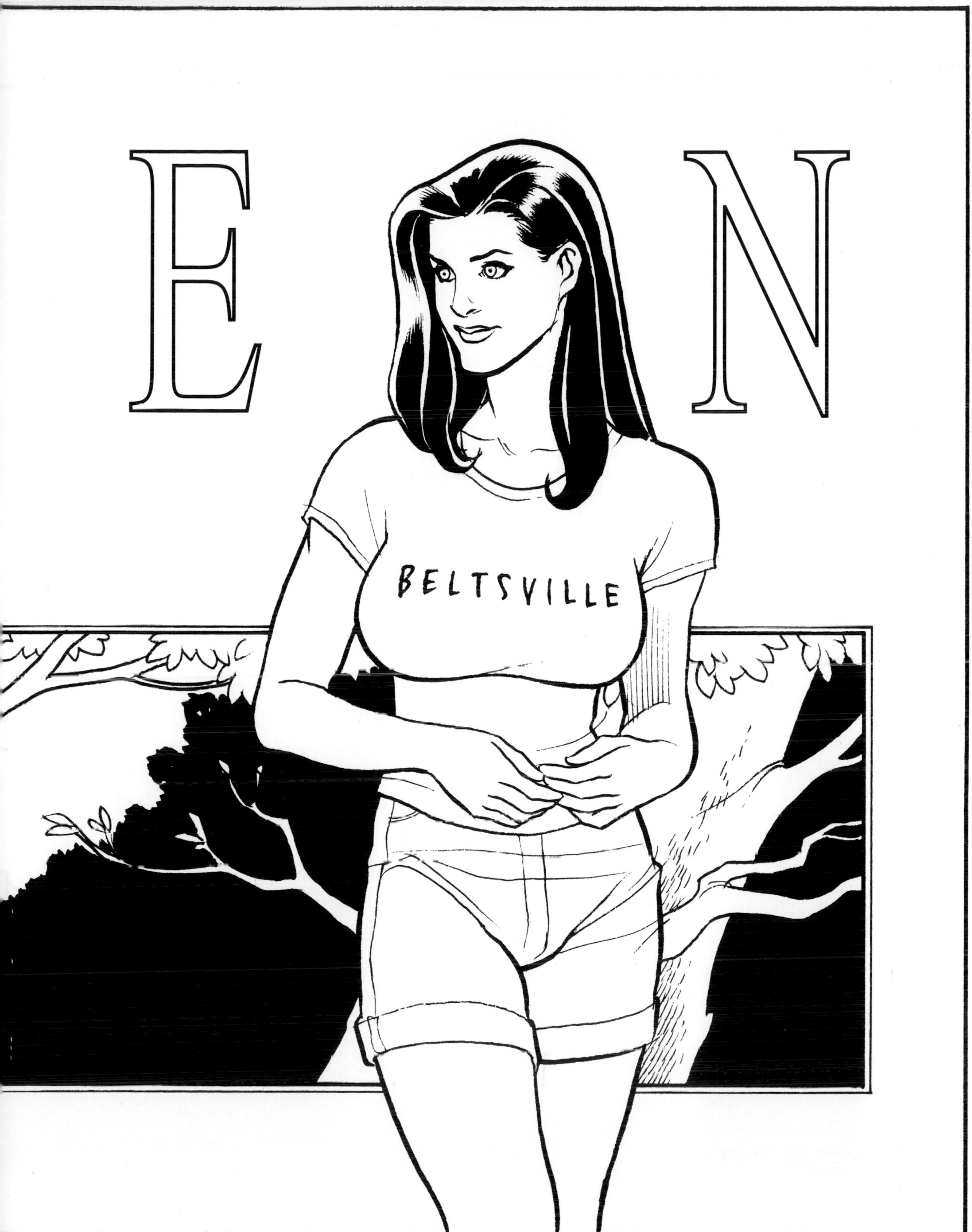
E
N
BELTSVILLE

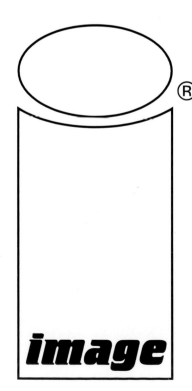

image comics

Jim Valentino	Publisher
Doug Griffith	Art Director
Brent Braun	Director of Production
Eric Stephenson	Director of Marketing
Brett Evans	Graphic Designer
Traci Hale	Controller/Foreign Licensing
Cyndie Espinoza	Accounting Assistant
Sean O'Brien	Inventory Controller

Liberty Meadows: Eden Book1, First Printing. Published by Image Comics, 1071 N. Batavia St., Suite A, Orange, CA 92867.

LIBERTY MEADOWS

EDEN

VOLUME ONE

CHO
©1999

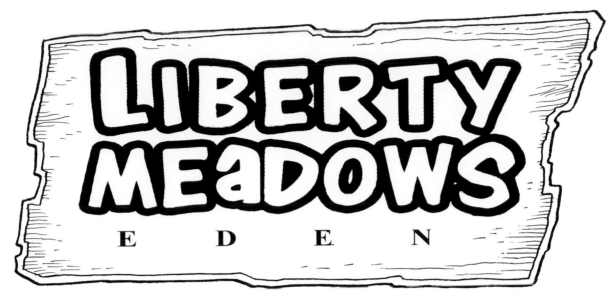

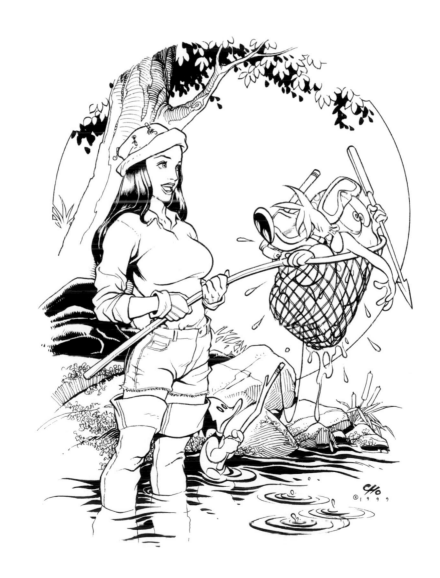

FRANK CHO

Dedicated to my daughter, Emily. Who gave me the courage to take the next step.

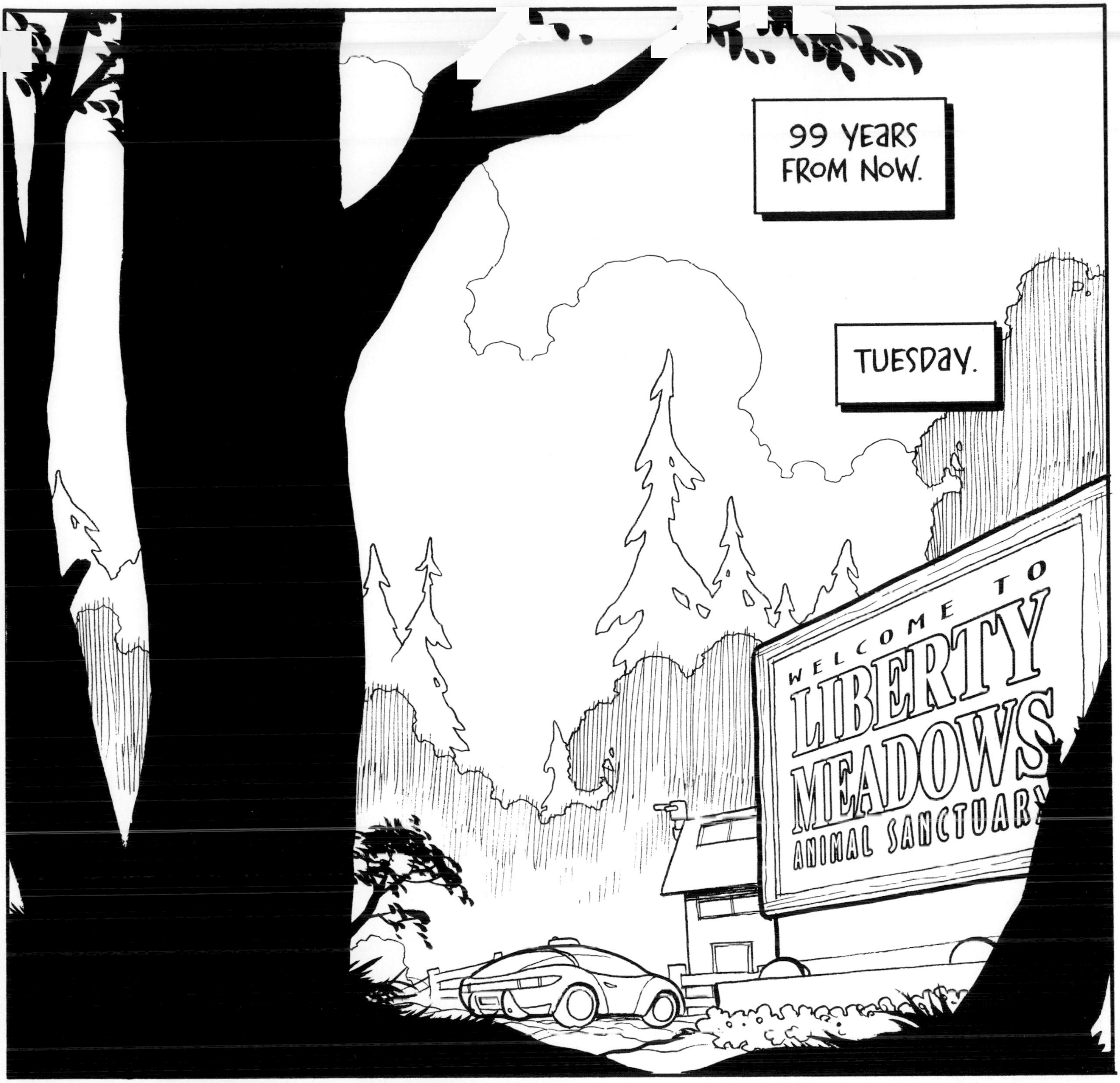
99 YEARS FROM NOW.
TUESDAY.
WELCOME TO
LIBERTY MEADOWS
ANIMAL SANCTUARY

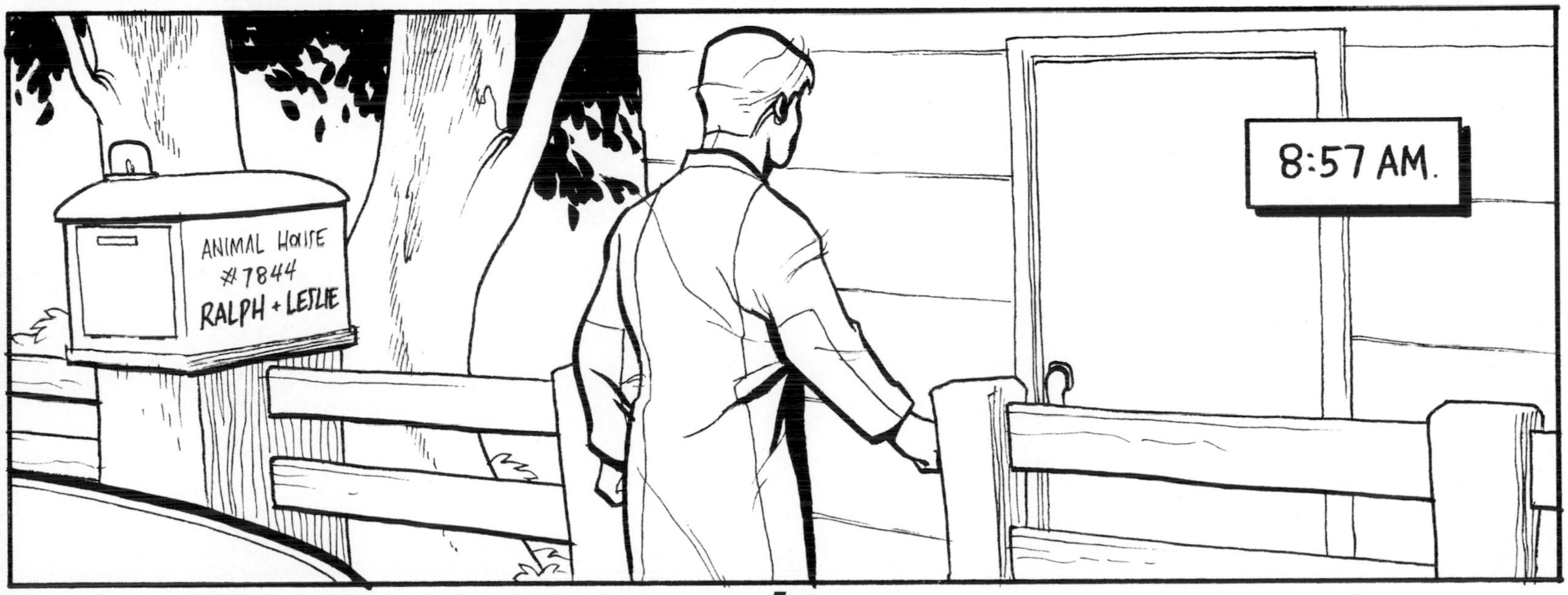
8:57 AM.
ANIMAL HOUSE
#7844
RALPH + LESLIE

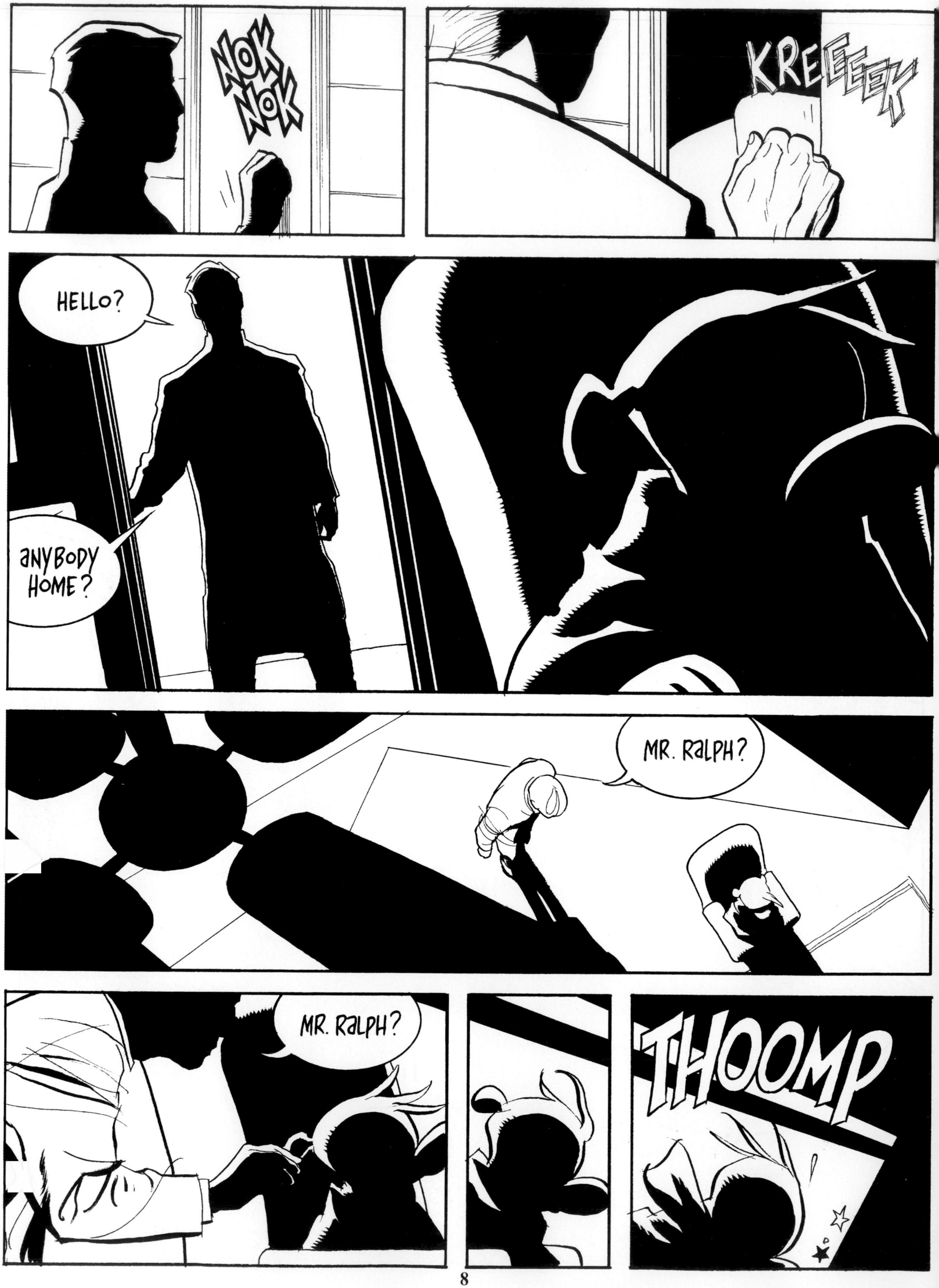
NOK NOK
KREEEEK
HELLO?
anybody HOME?
MR. RalPH?
MR. RalPH?
THOOMP

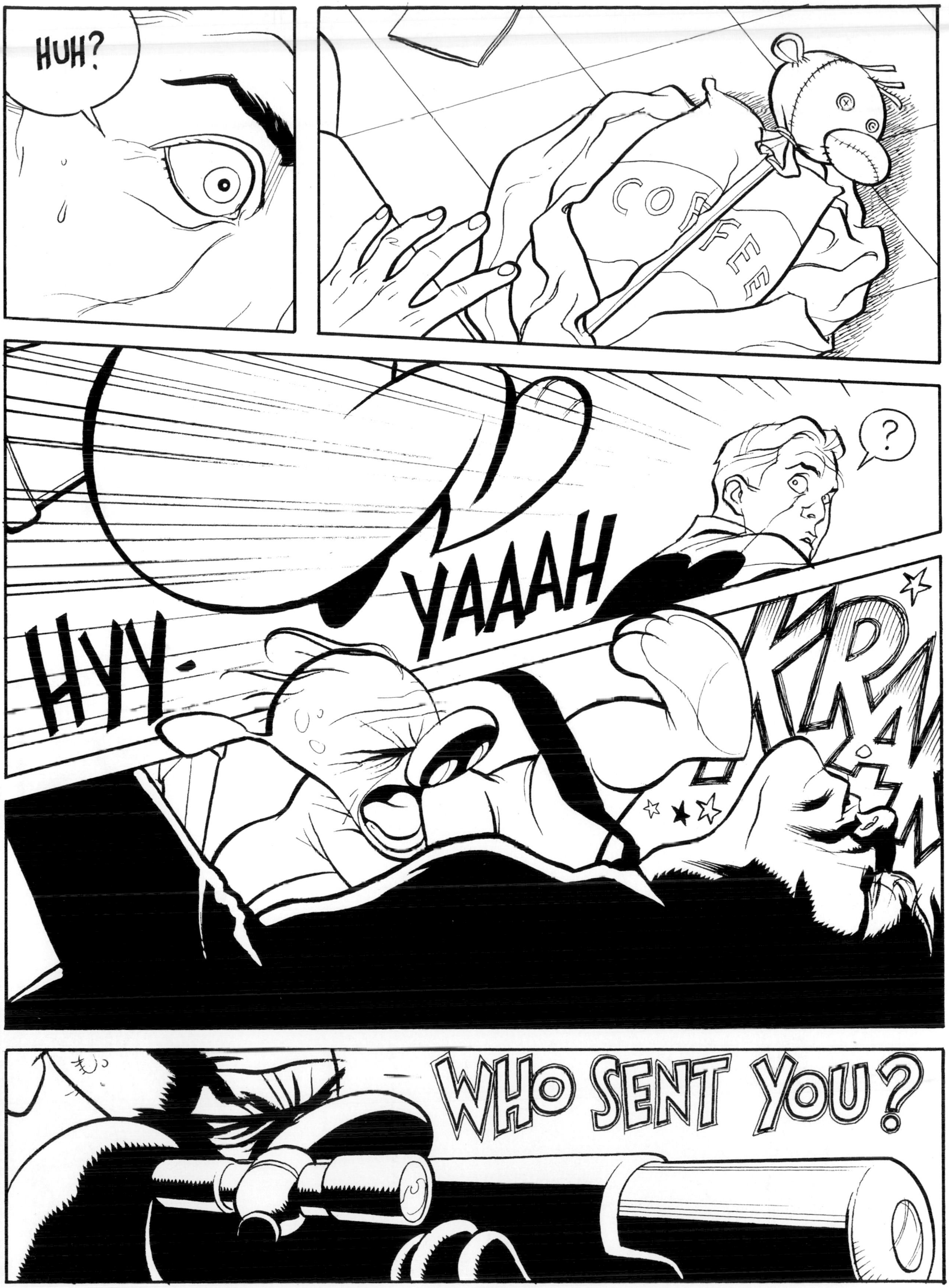
HUH?
COFFEE
?
HYY-YAAAH
KRA
WHO SENT YOU?

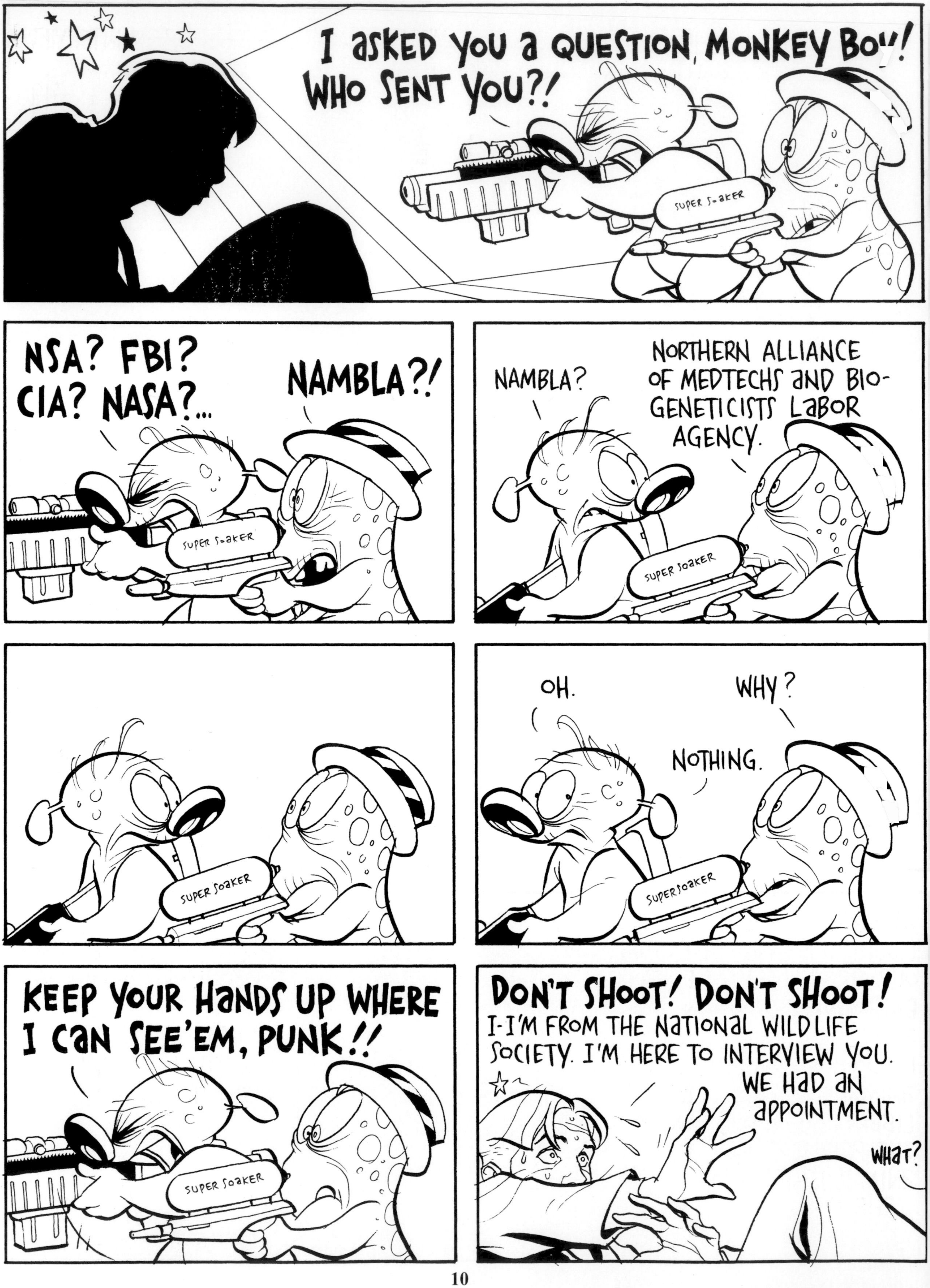
I ASKED YOU A QUESTION, MONKEY BOY! WHO SENT YOU?!
SUPER SOAKER
NSA? FBI? CIA? NASA?...
NAMBLA?!
SUPER SOAKER
NAMBLA?
NORTHERN ALLIANCE OF MEDTECHS AND BIO-GENETICISTS LABOR AGENCY.
SUPER SOAKER
SUPER SOAKER
OH.
WHY?
NOTHING.
SUPER SOAKER
KEEP YOUR HANDS UP WHERE I CAN SEE'EM, PUNK!!
SUPER SOAKER
DON'T SHOOT! DON'T SHOOT! I-I'M FROM THE NATIONAL WILDLIFE SOCIETY. I'M HERE TO INTERVIEW YOU. WE HAD AN APPOINTMENT.
WHAT?

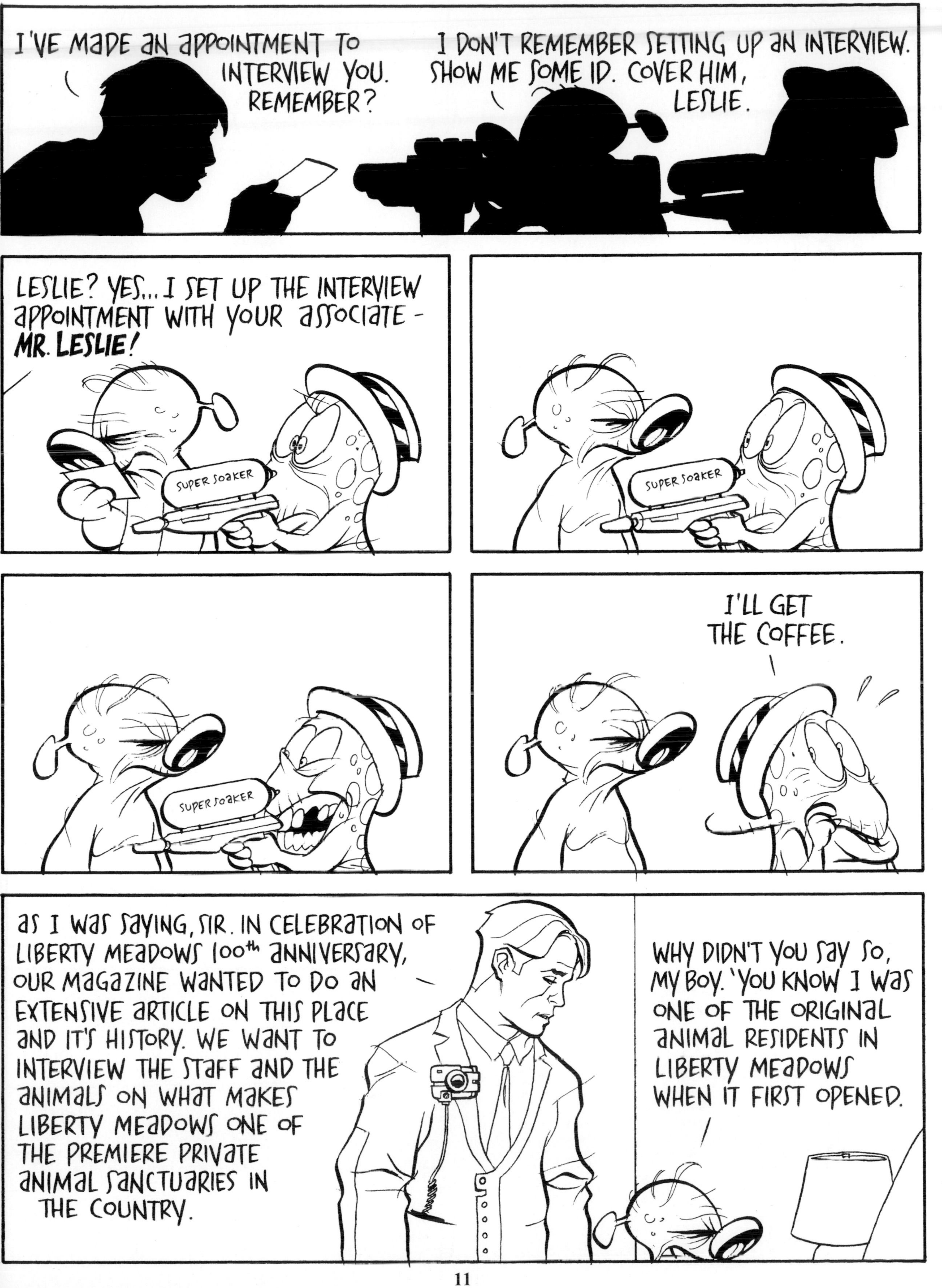
I'VE MADE AN APPOINTMENT TO INTERVIEW YOU. REMEMBER?
I DON'T REMEMBER SETTING UP AN INTERVIEW. SHOW ME SOME ID. COVER HIM, LESLIE.
LESLIE? YES... I SET UP THE INTERVIEW APPOINTMENT WITH YOUR ASSOCIATE - MR. LESLIE!
SUPER SOAKER
SUPER SOAKER
SUPER SOAKER
I'LL GET THE COFFEE.
AS I WAS SAYING, SIR. IN CELEBRATION OF LIBERTY MEADOWS 100th ANNIVERSARY, OUR MAGAZINE WANTED TO DO AN EXTENSIVE ARTICLE ON THIS PLACE AND IT'S HISTORY. WE WANT TO INTERVIEW THE STAFF AND THE ANIMALS ON WHAT MAKES LIBERTY MEADOWS ONE OF THE PREMIERE PRIVATE ANIMAL SANCTUARIES IN THE COUNTRY.
WHY DIDN'T YOU SAY SO, MY BOY. 'YOU KNOW I WAS ONE OF THE ORIGINAL ANIMAL RESIDENTS IN LIBERTY MEADOWS WHEN IT FIRST OPENED.

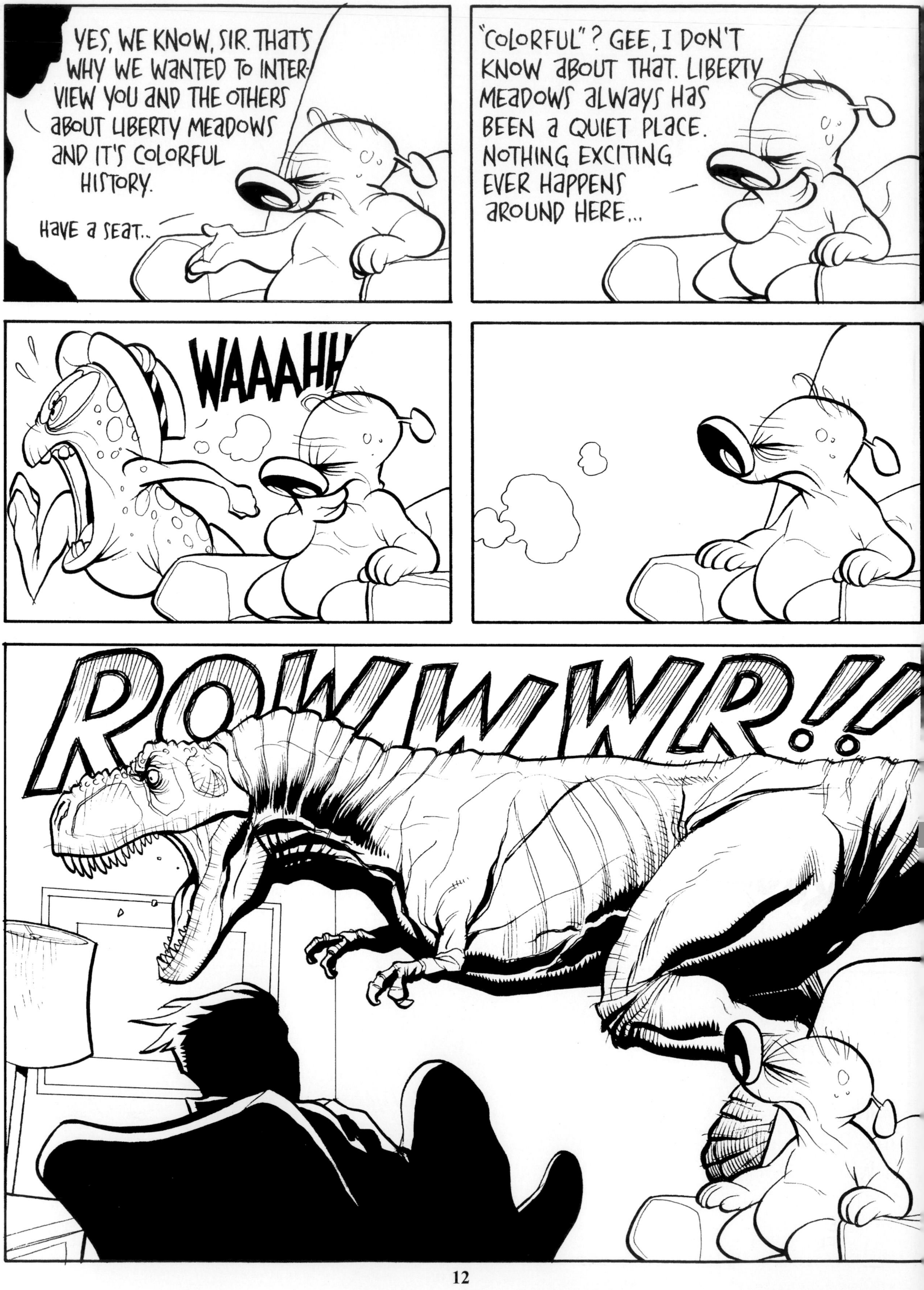
YES, WE KNOW, SIR. THAT'S WHY WE WANTED TO INTERVIEW YOU AND THE OTHERS ABOUT LIBERTY MEADOWS AND IT'S COLORFUL HISTORY.
HAVE A SEAT..
"COLORFUL"? GEE, I DON'T KNOW ABOUT THAT. LIBERTY MEADOWS ALWAYS HAS BEEN A QUIET PLACE. NOTHING EXCITING EVER HAPPENS AROUND HERE...
WAAAHH
ROWWWR!!

EXCUSE ME.

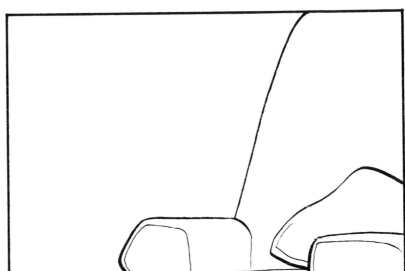

BLAM BLAM! D'OH! KABOOM CRAASH! ZOW

BANG! MOOOOO!

I'VE TOLD YOU NOT TO TOUCH THE QUANTUM CHRONOMATRIX UNTIL I'VE STABLIZED THE FIELDS.

MAN, ALL YOUR MACHINES HAVE THE SAME DESIGN. I THOUGHT IT WAS THE "COFFEE MAKER."

GRR. WE'LL TALK LATER.

HERE'S YOUR COFFEE, SON.

OKAY, NOW WHERE WAS I?

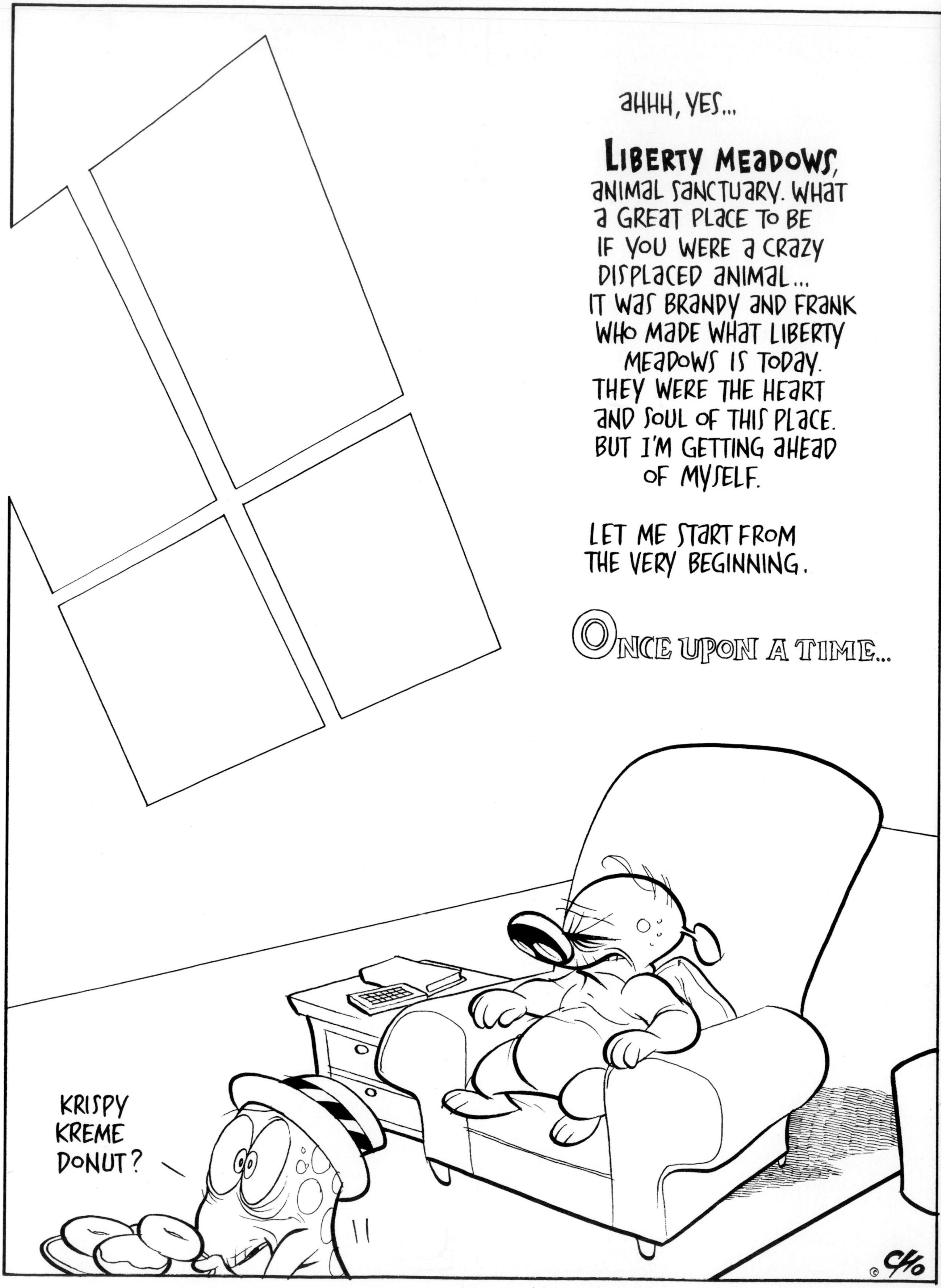
AHHH, YES...
LIBERTY MEADOWS, ANIMAL SANCTUARY. WHAT A GREAT PLACE TO BE IF YOU WERE A CRAZY DISPLACED ANIMAL... IT WAS BRANDY AND FRANK WHO MADE WHAT LIBERTY MEADOWS IS TODAY. THEY WERE THE HEART AND SOUL OF THIS PLACE. BUT I'M GETTING AHEAD OF MYSELF.
LET ME START FROM THE VERY BEGINNING.
ONCE UPON A TIME...
KRISPY KREME DONUT?
© CHO

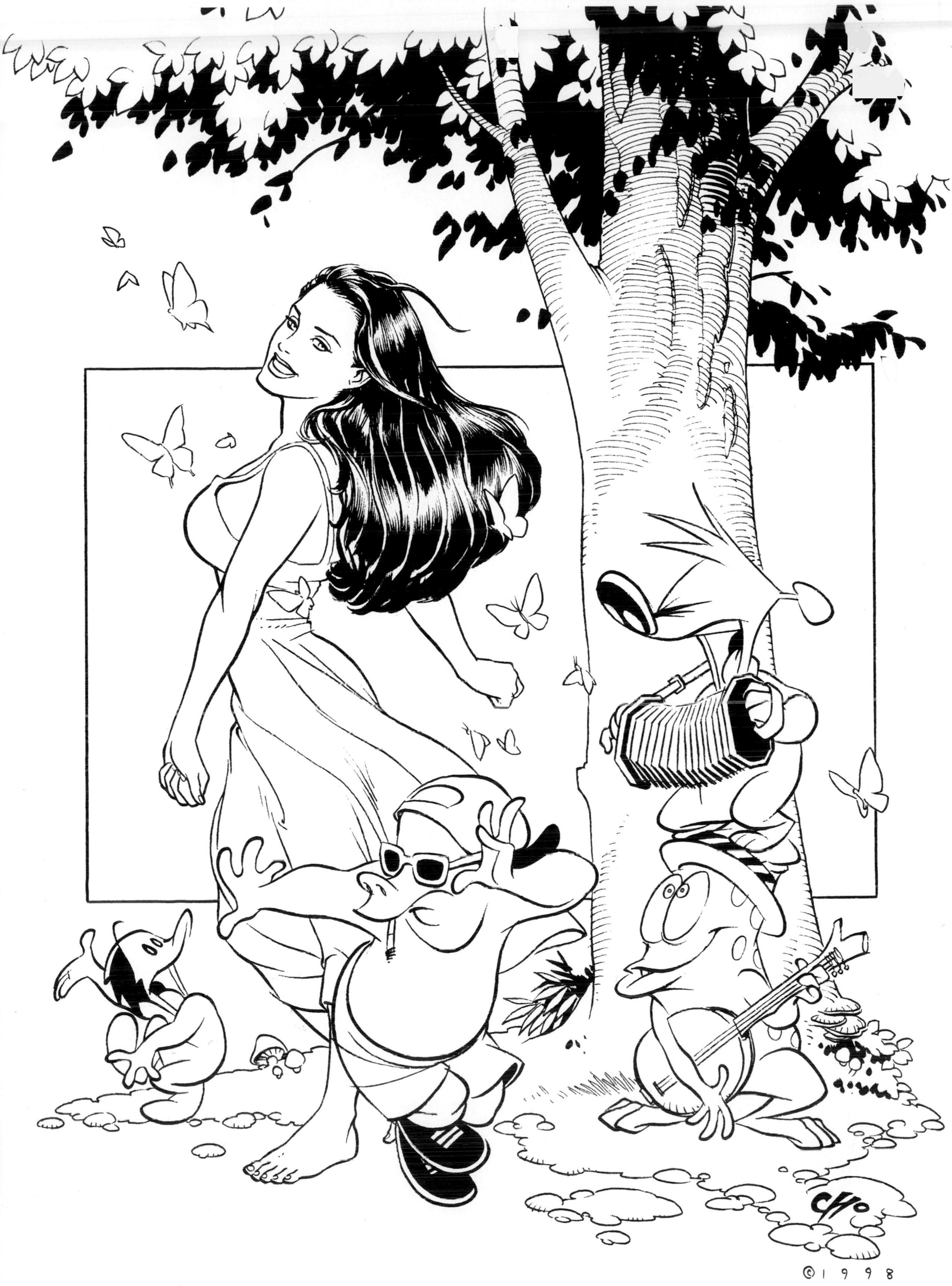
CHO
©1998

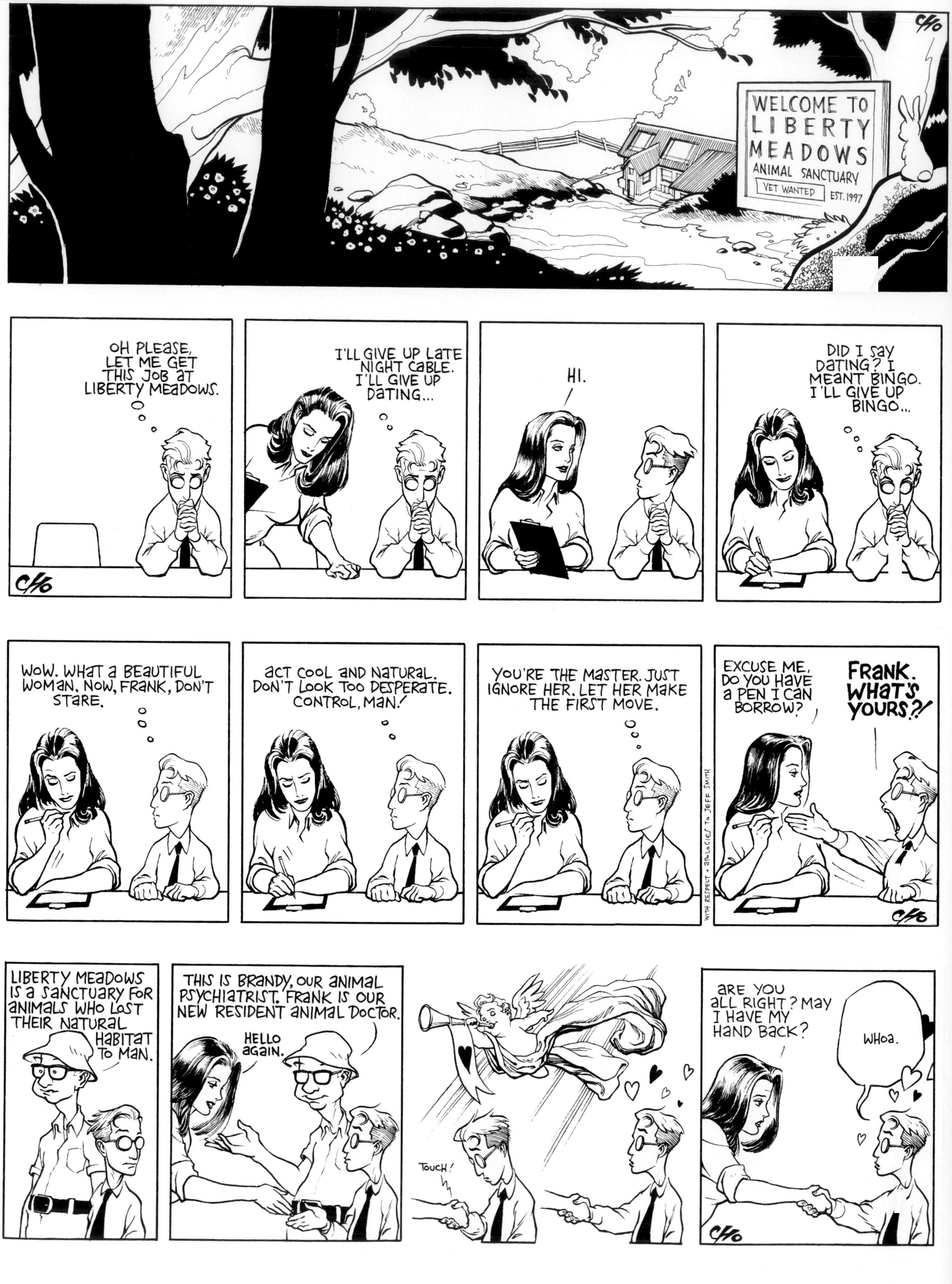
CHO
WELCOME TO LIBERTY MEADOWS ANIMAL SANCTUARY
VET WANTED
EST. 1997
CHO
OH PLEASE, LET ME GET THIS JOB AT LIBERTY MEADOWS.
I'LL GIVE UP LATE NIGHT CABLE. I'LL GIVE UP DATING...
HI.
DID I SAY DATING? I MEANT BINGO. I'LL GIVE UP BINGO...
WOW. WHAT A BEAUTIFUL WOMAN. NOW, FRANK, DON'T STARE.
ACT COOL AND NATURAL. DON'T LOOK TOO DESPERATE. CONTROL, MAN!
YOU'RE THE MASTER. JUST IGNORE HER. LET HER MAKE THE FIRST MOVE.
WITH RESPECT + APOLOGIES TO JEFF SMITH
EXCUSE ME. DO YOU HAVE A PEN I CAN BORROW?
FRANK. WHAT'S YOURS?!
CHO
LIBERTY MEADOWS IS A SANCTUARY FOR ANIMALS WHO LOST THEIR NATURAL HABITAT TO MAN.
THIS IS BRANDY, OUR ANIMAL PSYCHIATRIST. FRANK IS OUR NEW RESIDENT ANIMAL DOCTOR.
HELLO AGAIN.
TOUCH!
ARE YOU ALL RIGHT? MAY I HAVE MY HAND BACK?
WHOA.
CHO

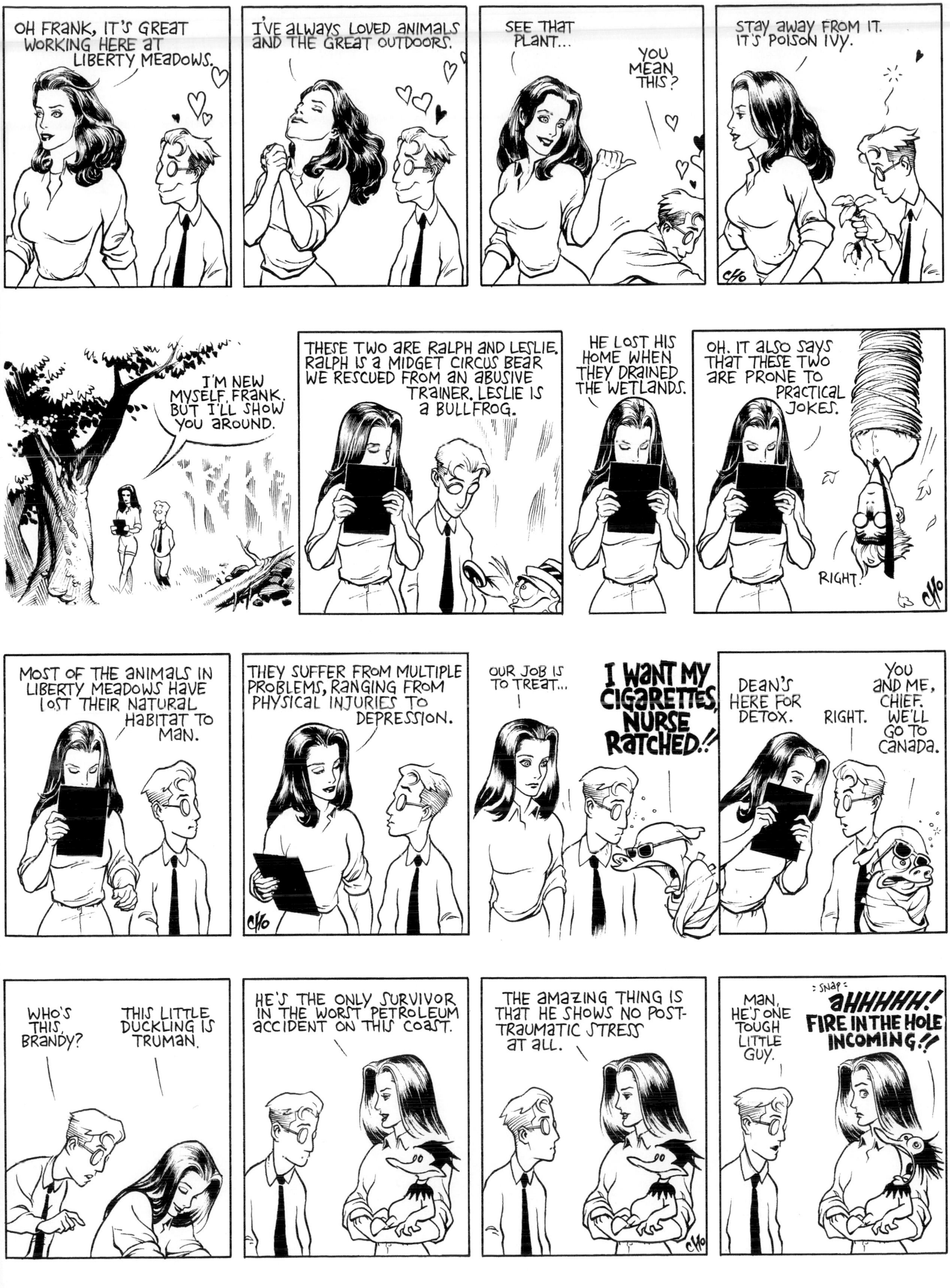
OH FRANK, IT'S GREAT WORKING HERE AT LIBERTY MEADOWS.
I'VE ALWAYS LOVED ANIMALS AND THE GREAT OUTDOORS.
SEE THAT PLANT...
YOU MEAN THIS?
STAY AWAY FROM IT. IT'S POISON IVY.
CHO
I'M NEW MYSELF, FRANK. BUT I'LL SHOW YOU AROUND.
THESE TWO ARE RALPH AND LESLIE. RALPH IS A MIDGET CIRCUS BEAR WE RESCUED FROM AN ABUSIVE TRAINER. LESLIE IS A BULLFROG.
HE LOST HIS HOME WHEN THEY DRAINED THE WETLANDS.
OH. IT ALSO SAYS THAT THESE TWO ARE PRONE TO PRACTICAL JOKES.
RIGHT.
CHO
MOST OF THE ANIMALS IN LIBERTY MEADOWS HAVE LOST THEIR NATURAL HABITAT TO MAN.
THEY SUFFER FROM MULTIPLE PROBLEMS, RANGING FROM PHYSICAL INJURIES TO DEPRESSION.
CHO
OUR JOB IS TO TREAT...
I WANT MY CIGARETTES, NURSE RATCHED!!
DEAN'S HERE FOR DETOX.
RIGHT.
YOU AND ME, CHIEF. WE'LL GO TO CANADA.
WHO'S THIS, BRANDY?
THIS LITTLE DUCKLING IS TRUMAN.
HE'S THE ONLY SURVIVOR IN THE WORST PETROLEUM ACCIDENT ON THIS COAST.
THE AMAZING THING IS THAT HE SHOWS NO POST-TRAUMATIC STRESS AT ALL.
CHO
MAN, HE'S ONE TOUGH LITTLE GUY.
SNAP
AHHHHH! FIRE IN THE HOLE INCOMING!!

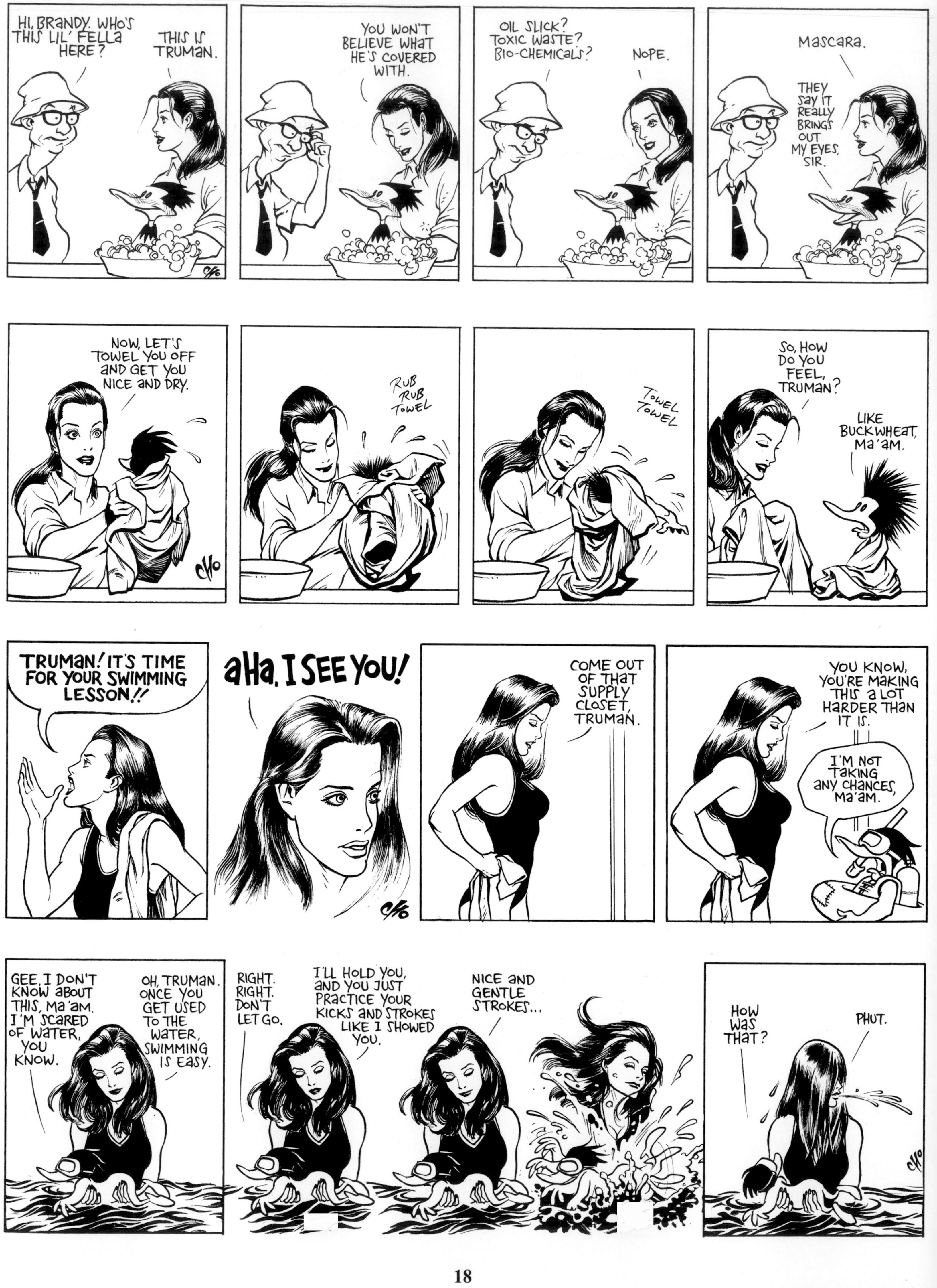
HI, BRANDY. WHO'S THIS LIL' FELLA HERE?
THIS IS TRUMAN.
YOU WON'T BELIEVE WHAT HE'S COVERED WITH.
OIL SLICK? TOXIC WASTE? BIO-CHEMICALS?
NOPE.
MASCARA.
THEY SAY IT REALLY BRINGS OUT MY EYES, SIR.
NOW, LET'S TOWEL YOU OFF AND GET YOU NICE AND DRY.
RUB RUB TOWEL
TOWEL TOWEL
SO, HOW DO YOU FEEL, TRUMAN?
LIKE BUCKWHEAT, MA'AM.
TRUMAN! IT'S TIME FOR YOUR SWIMMING LESSON!!
AHA, I SEE YOU!
COME OUT OF THAT SUPPLY CLOSET, TRUMAN.
YOU KNOW, YOU'RE MAKING THIS A LOT HARDER THAN IT IS.
I'M NOT TAKING ANY CHANCES, MA'AM.
GEE, I DON'T KNOW ABOUT THIS, MA'AM. I'M SCARED OF WATER, YOU KNOW.
OH, TRUMAN. ONCE YOU GET USED TO THE WATER, SWIMMING IS EASY.
RIGHT. RIGHT. DON'T LET GO.
I'LL HOLD YOU, AND YOU JUST PRACTICE YOUR KICKS AND STROKES LIKE I SHOWED YOU.
NICE AND GENTLE STROKES...
HOW WAS THAT?
PHUT.

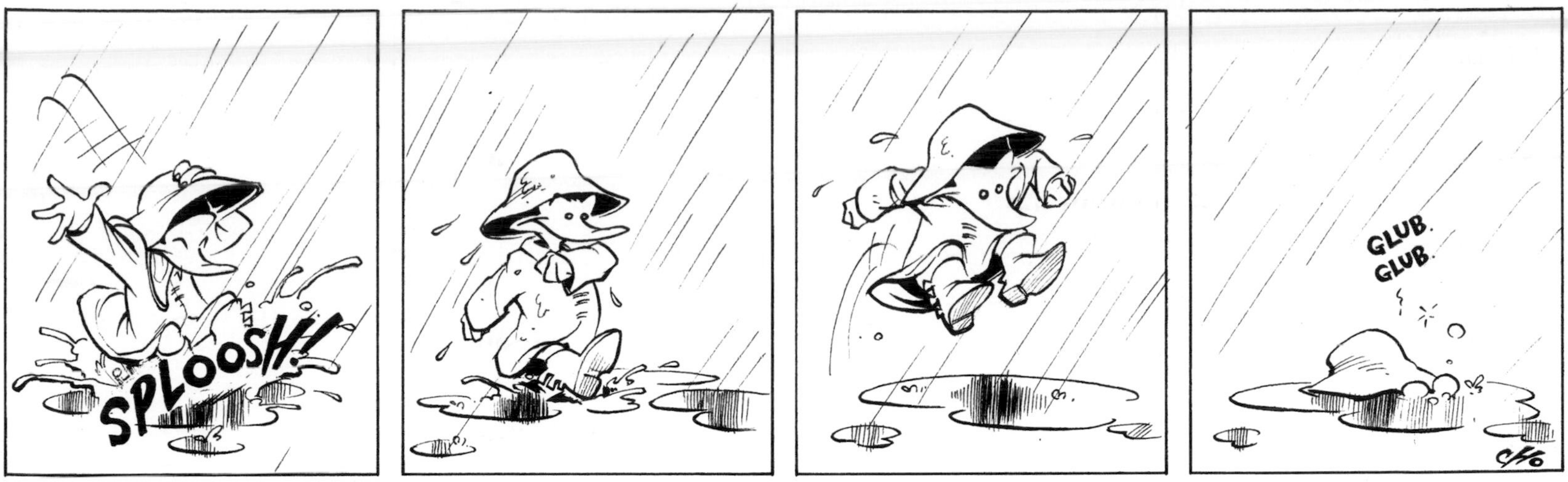
SPLOOSH!
GLUB.
GLUB.
CHO

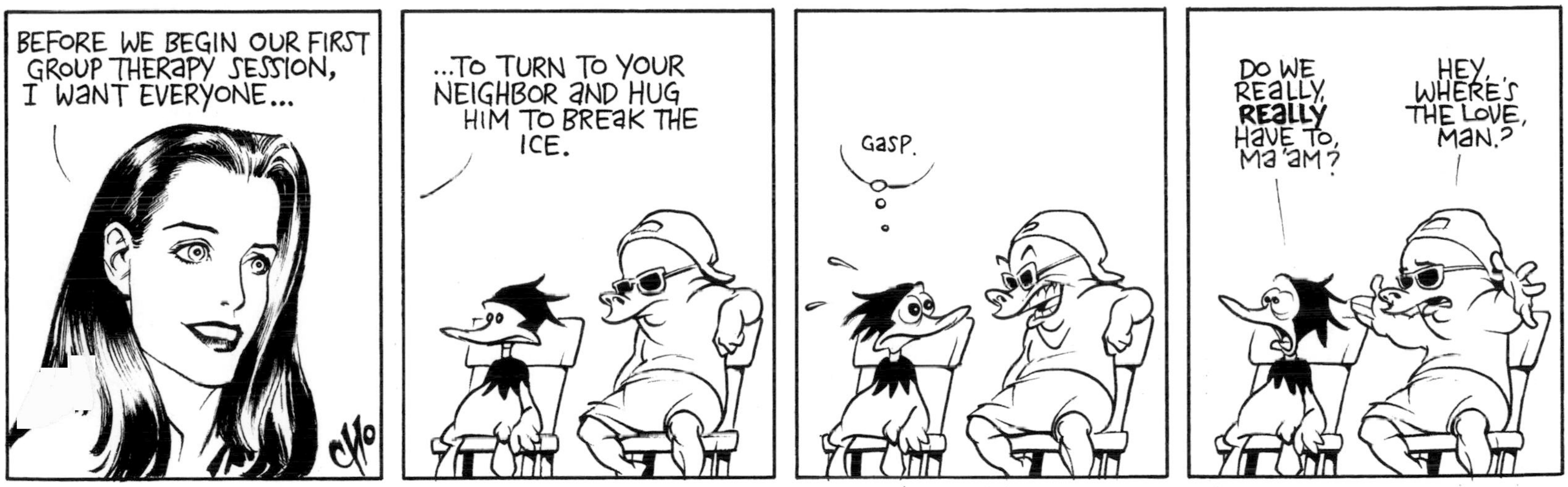
BEFORE WE BEGIN OUR FIRST GROUP THERAPY SESSION, I WANT EVERYONE...
CHO
...TO TURN TO YOUR NEIGHBOR AND HUG HIM TO BREAK THE ICE.
GASP.
DO WE REALLY, REALLY HAVE TO, MA'AM?
HEY, WHERE'S THE LOVE, MAN.?

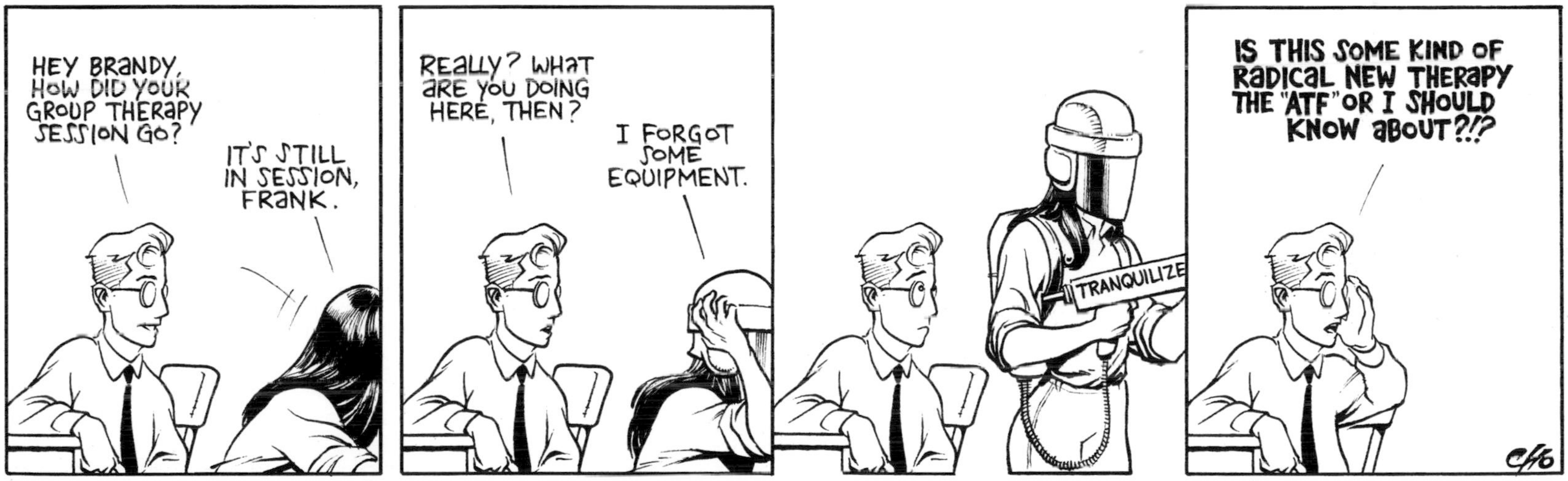
HEY BRANDY, HOW DID YOUR GROUP THERAPY SESSION GO?
IT'S STILL IN SESSION, FRANK.
REALLY? WHAT ARE YOU DOING HERE, THEN?
I FORGOT SOME EQUIPMENT.
TRANQUILIZE
IS THIS SOME KIND OF RADICAL NEW THERAPY THE "ATF" OR I SHOULD KNOW ABOUT?!?
CHO

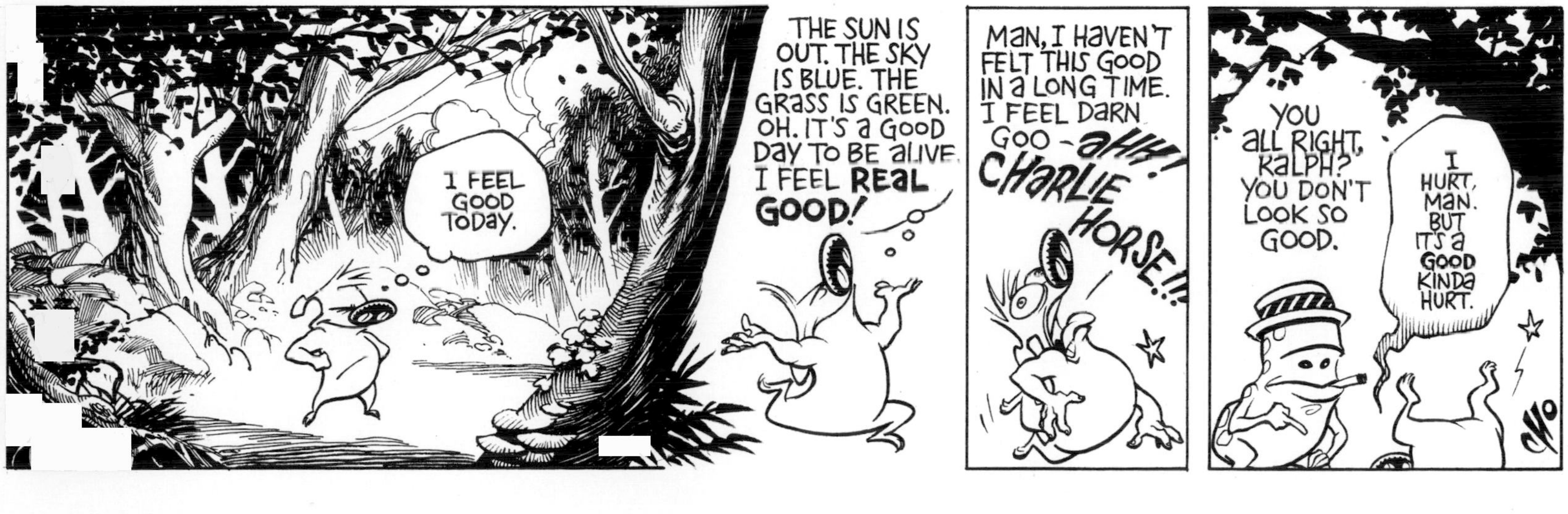
I FEEL GOOD TODAY.
THE SUN IS OUT. THE SKY IS BLUE. THE GRASS IS GREEN. OH. IT'S A GOOD DAY TO BE ALIVE. I FEEL REAL GOOD!
MAN, I HAVEN'T FELT THIS GOOD IN A LONG TIME. I FEEL DARN GOO - AHH! CHARLIE HORSE!!!
YOU ALL RIGHT, RALPH? YOU DON'T LOOK SO GOOD.
I HURT, MAN. BUT IT'S A GOOD KINDA HURT.
CHO

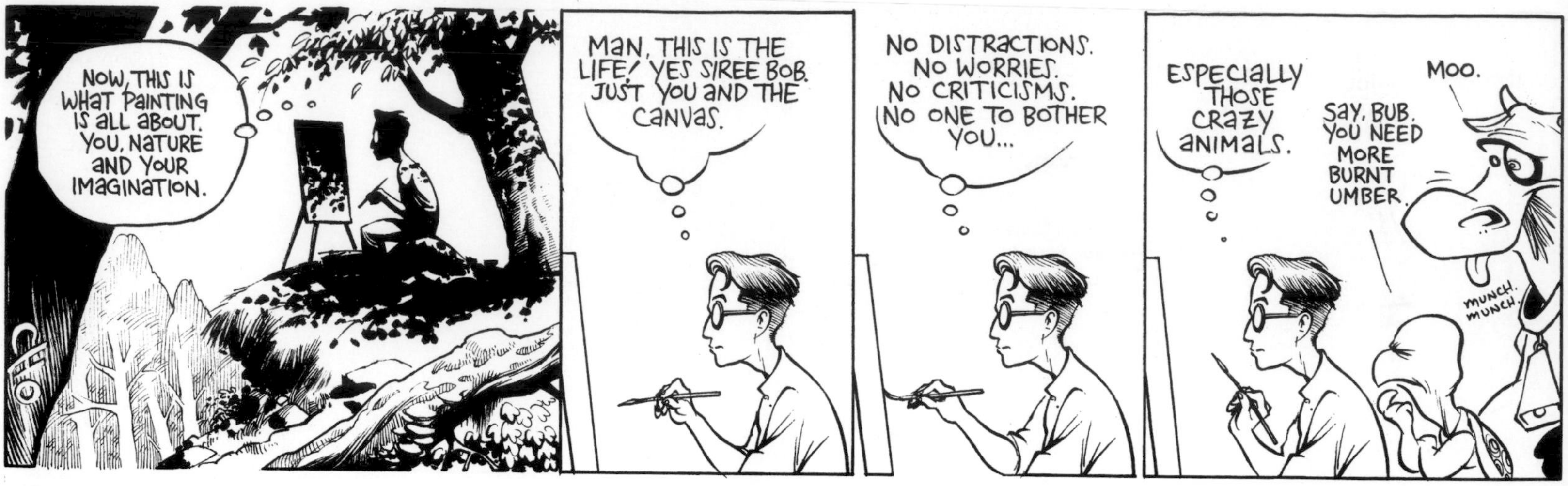
NOW, THIS IS WHAT PAINTING IS ALL ABOUT. YOU, NATURE AND YOUR IMAGINATION.
MAN, THIS IS THE LIFE! YES SIREE BOB. JUST YOU AND THE CANVAS.
NO DISTRACTIONS. NO WORRIES. NO CRITICISMS. NO ONE TO BOTHER YOU...
ESPECIALLY THOSE CRAZY ANIMALS.
MOO.
SAY, BUB. YOU NEED MORE BURNT UMBER.
MUNCH. MUNCH.

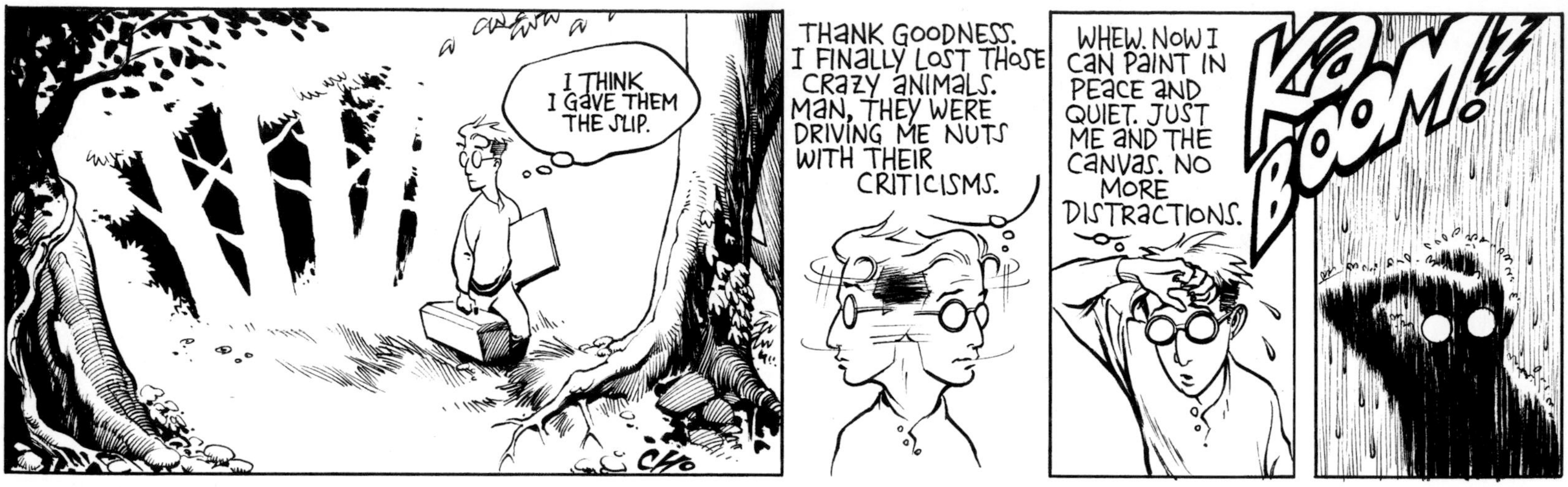
I THINK I GAVE THEM THE SLIP.
THANK GOODNESS. I FINALLY LOST THOSE CRAZY ANIMALS. MAN, THEY WERE DRIVING ME NUTS WITH THEIR CRITICISMS.
WHEW. NOW I CAN PAINT IN PEACE AND QUIET. JUST ME AND THE CANVAS. NO MORE DISTRACTIONS.
KA BOOM!

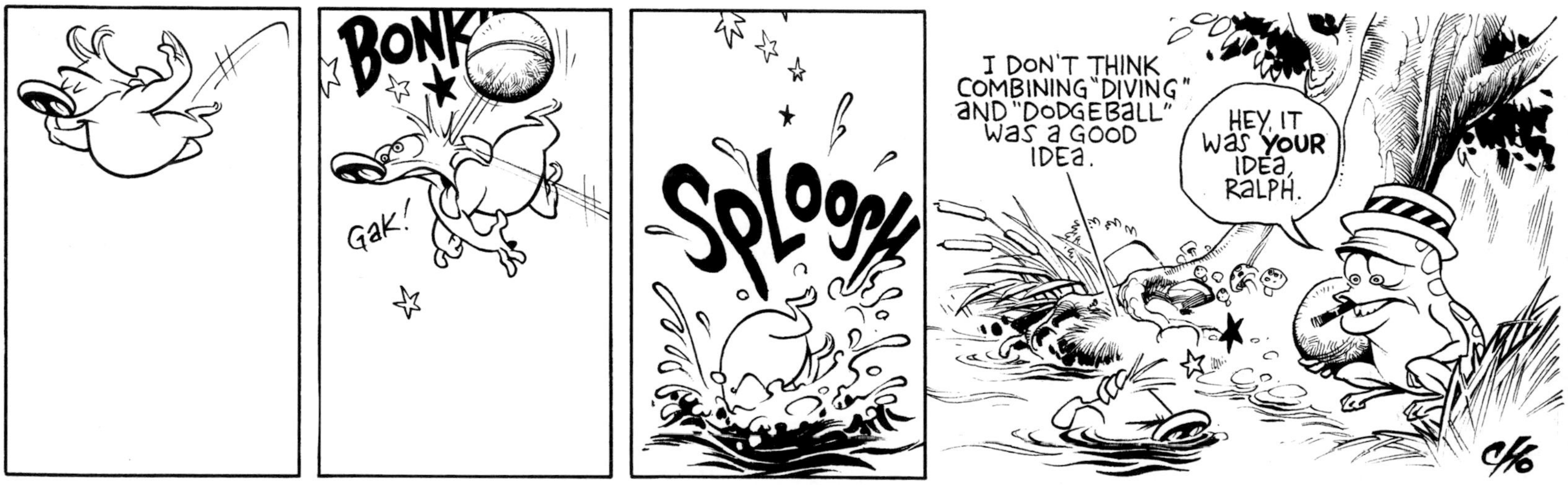
BONK!
GAK!
SPLOOSH
I DON'T THINK COMBINING "DIVING" AND "DODGEBALL" WAS A GOOD IDEA.
HEY, IT WAS **YOUR** IDEA, RALPH.

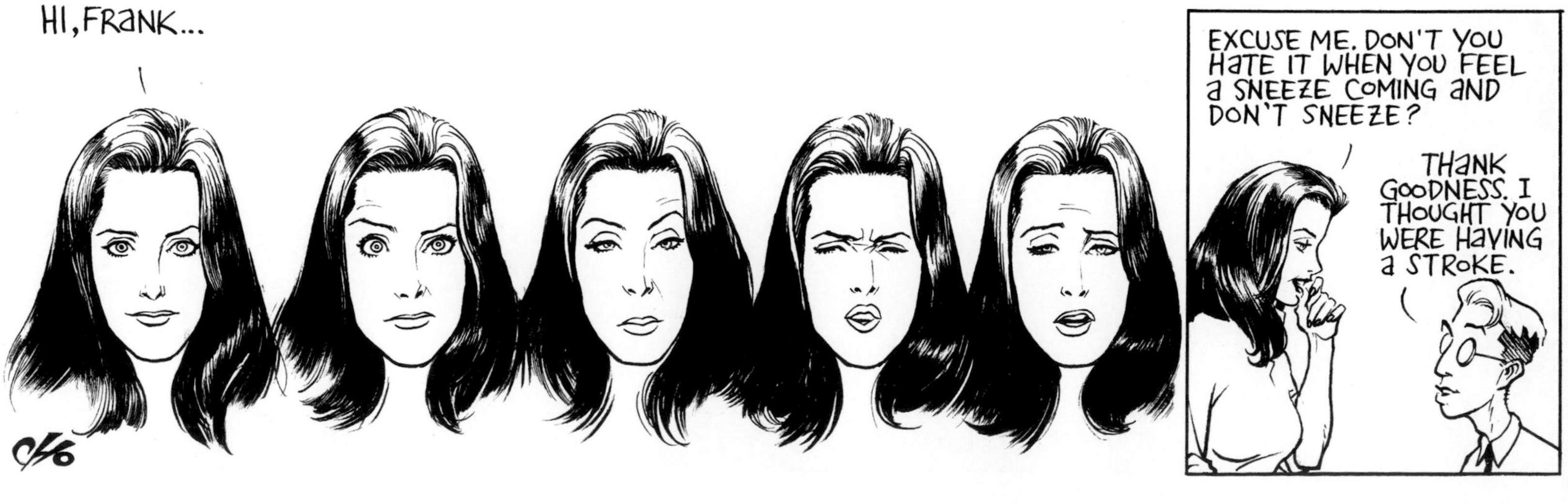
HI, FRANK...
EXCUSE ME. DON'T YOU HATE IT WHEN YOU FEEL A SNEEZE COMING AND DON'T SNEEZE?
THANK GOODNESS. I THOUGHT YOU WERE HAVING A STROKE.

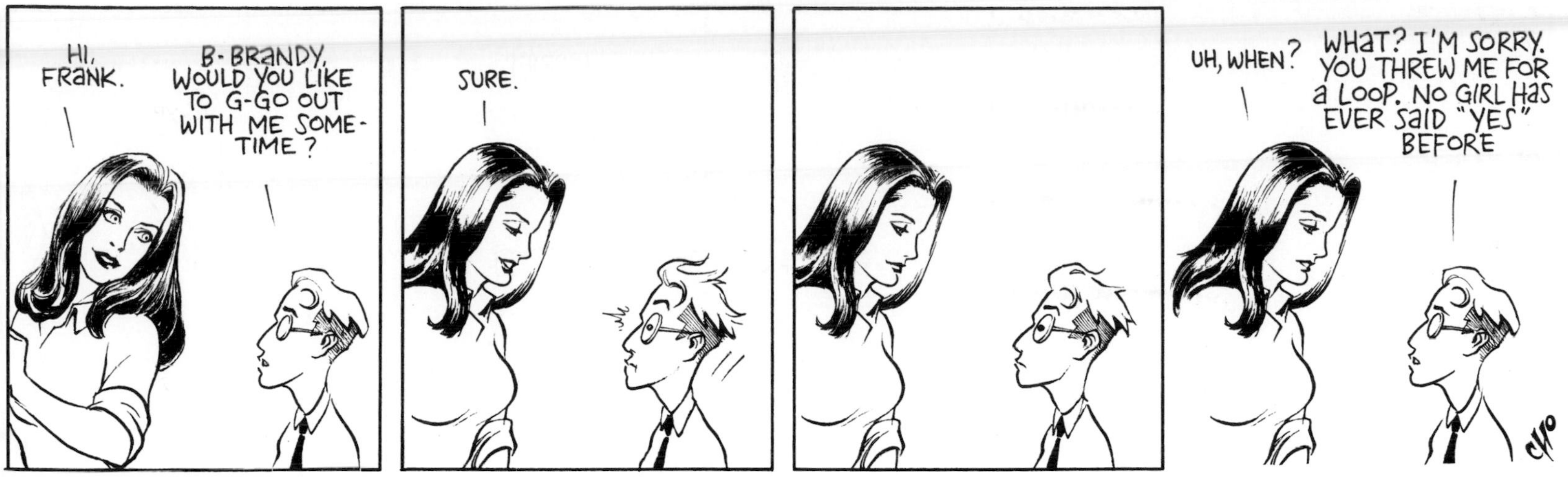
HI, FRANK.
B-BRANDY, WOULD YOU LIKE TO G-GO OUT WITH ME SOME-TIME?
SURE.
UH, WHEN?
WHAT? I'M SORRY. YOU THREW ME FOR A LOOP. NO GIRL HAS EVER SAID "YES" BEFORE
CHO

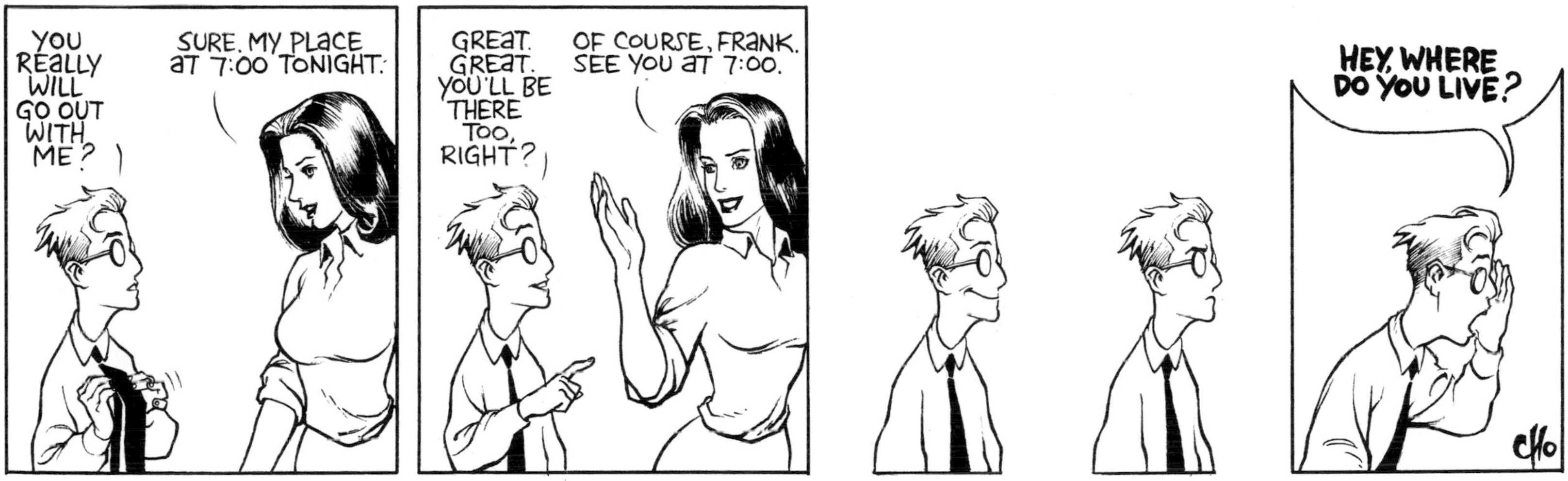
YOU REALLY WILL GO OUT WITH ME?
SURE. MY PLACE AT 7:00 TONIGHT.
GREAT. GREAT. YOU'LL BE THERE TOO, RIGHT?
OF COURSE, FRANK. SEE YOU AT 7:00.
HEY, WHERE DO YOU LIVE?
CHO

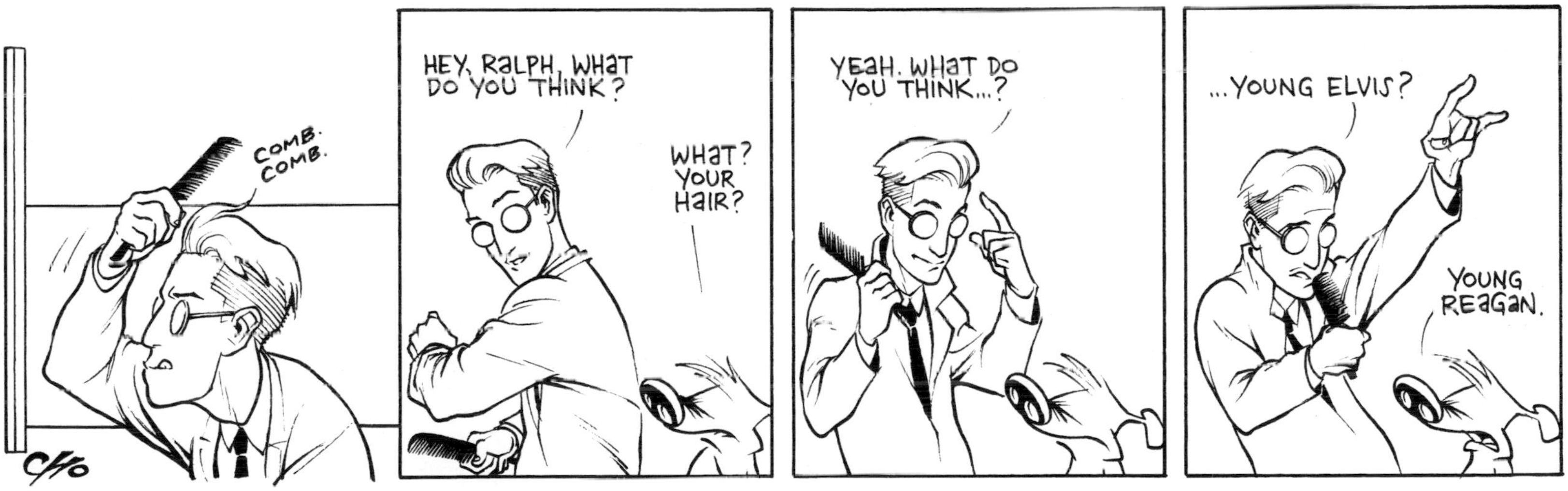
COMB. COMB.
CHO
HEY, RALPH, WHAT DO YOU THINK?
WHAT? YOUR HAIR?
YEAH. WHAT DO YOU THINK...?
...YOUNG ELVIS?
YOUNG REAGAN.

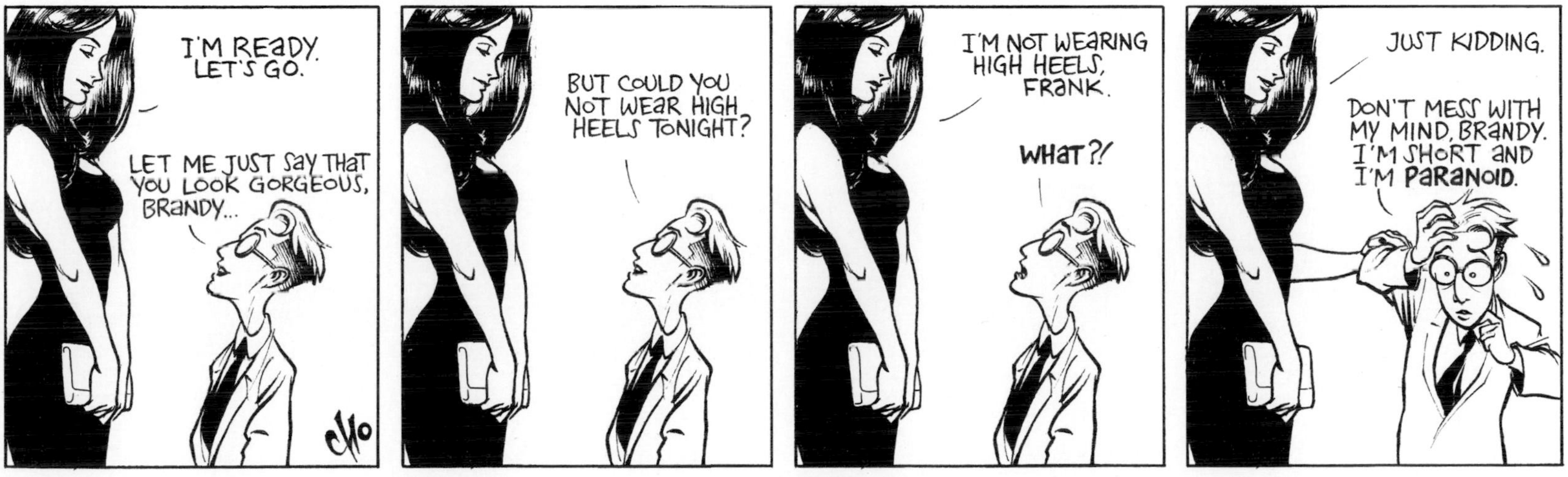
I'M READY. LET'S GO.
LET ME JUST SAY THAT YOU LOOK GORGEOUS, BRANDY...
CHO
BUT COULD YOU NOT WEAR HIGH HEELS TONIGHT?
I'M NOT WEARING HIGH HEELS, FRANK.
WHAT?!
JUST KIDDING.
DON'T MESS WITH MY MIND, BRANDY. I'M SHORT AND I'M PARANOID.

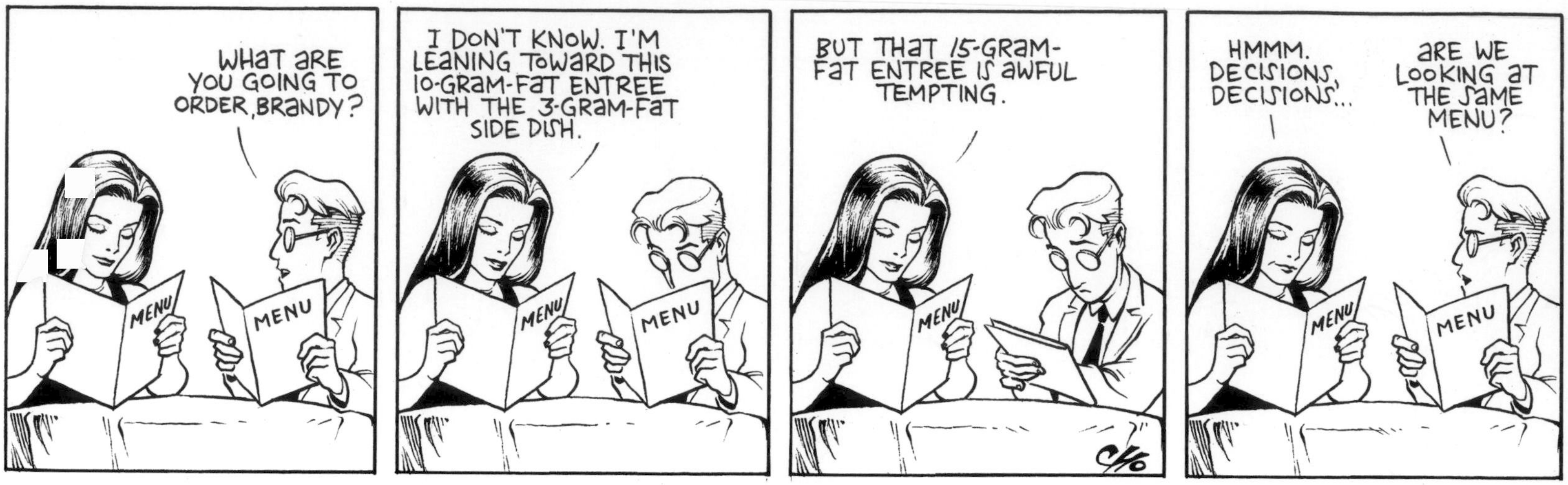
WHAT ARE YOU GOING TO ORDER, BRANDY?
I DON'T KNOW. I'M LEANING TOWARD THIS 10-GRAM-FAT ENTREE WITH THE 3-GRAM-FAT SIDE DISH.
MENU
BUT THAT 15-GRAM-FAT ENTREE IS AWFUL TEMPTING.
HMMM. DECISIONS, DECISIONS...
ARE WE LOOKING AT THE SAME MENU?
CHO

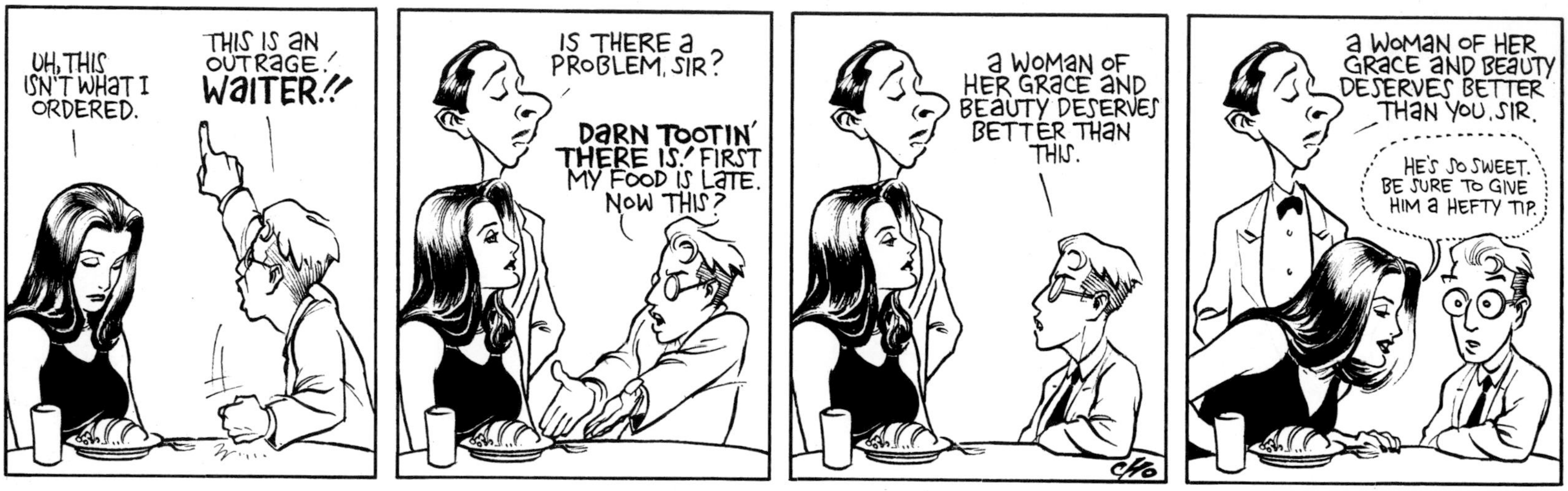
UH, THIS ISN'T WHAT I ORDERED.
THIS IS AN OUTRAGE! WAITER!!
IS THERE A PROBLEM, SIR?
DARN TOOTIN' THERE IS! FIRST MY FOOD IS LATE. NOW THIS?
A WOMAN OF HER GRACE AND BEAUTY DESERVES BETTER THAN THIS.
A WOMAN OF HER GRACE AND BEAUTY DESERVES BETTER THAN YOU, SIR.
HE'S SO SWEET. BE SURE TO GIVE HIM A HEFTY TIP.
CHO

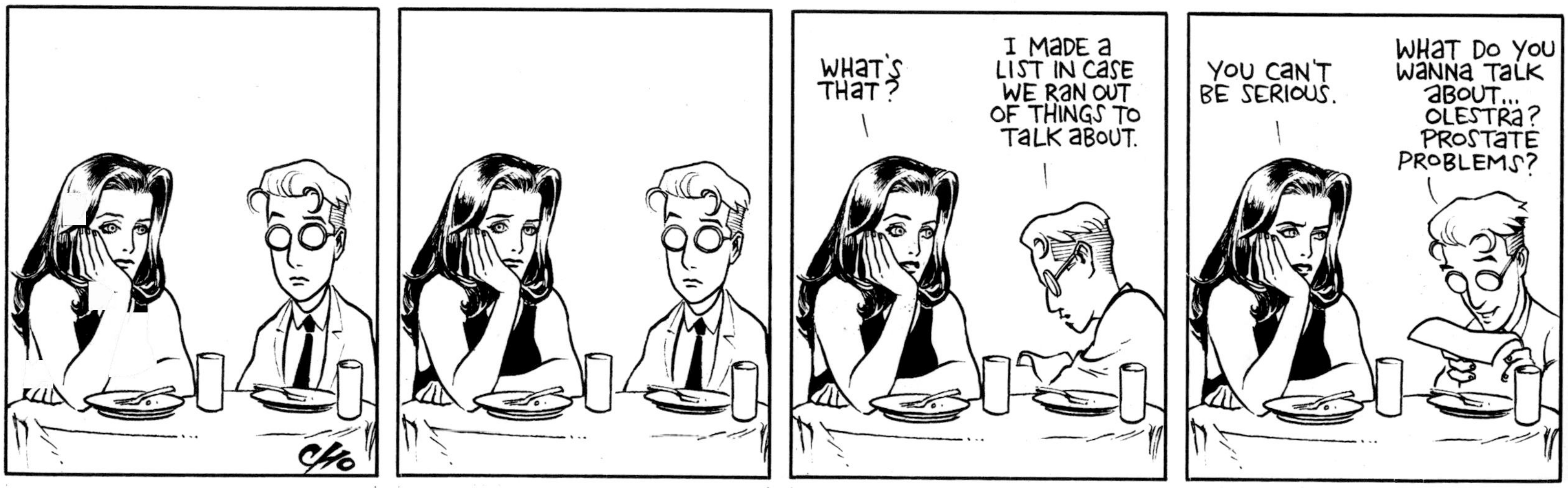
WHAT'S THAT?
I MADE A LIST IN CASE WE RAN OUT OF THINGS TO TALK ABOUT.
YOU CAN'T BE SERIOUS.
WHAT DO YOU WANNA TALK ABOUT... OLESTRA? PROSTATE PROBLEMS?
CHO

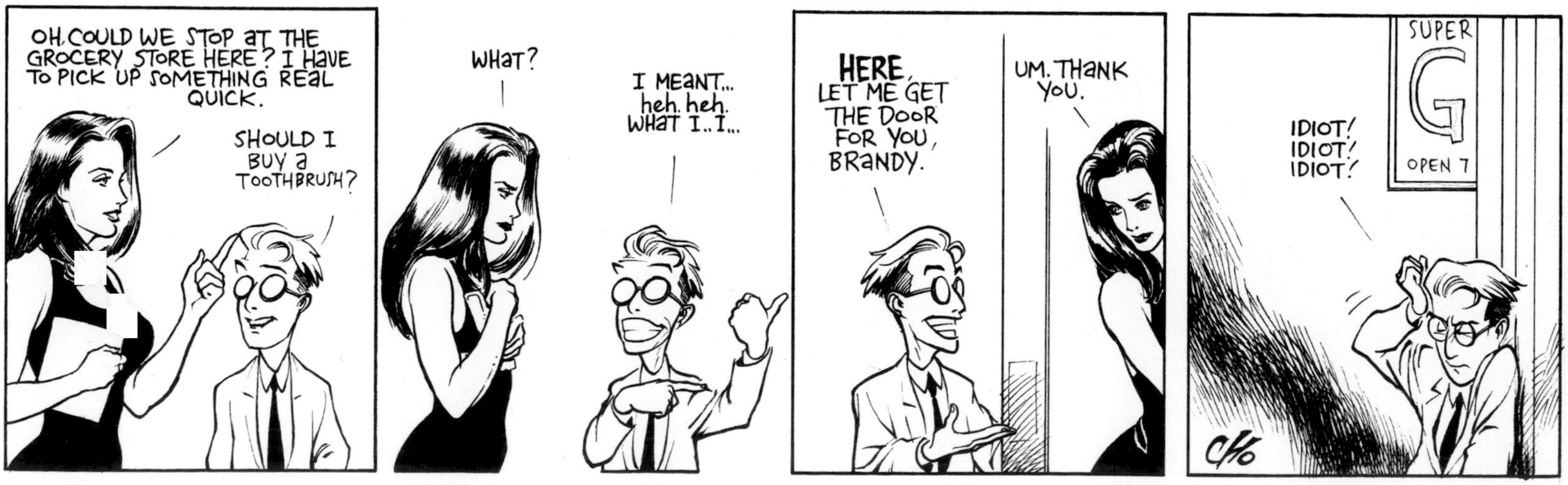
OH, COULD WE STOP AT THE GROCERY STORE HERE? I HAVE TO PICK UP SOMETHING REAL QUICK.
SHOULD I BUY A TOOTHBRUSH?
WHAT?
I MEANT... heh. heh. WHAT I.. I...
HERE, LET ME GET THE DOOR FOR YOU, BRANDY.
UM. THANK YOU.
SUPER G OPEN 7
IDIOT! IDIOT! IDIOT!
CHO

SO THIS IS THE WIMP YOU DUMPED ME FOR, HUH BRANDY?
LEAVE US ALONE, ERIC...
TOINK! TOINK!
HEY!
CHO
QUIT SHOVING, YOU GORILLA!
WHAP.
GOOD GOOGALY MOOGALY! I THINK I FRACTURED MY HAND.
DID YOU JUST HIT ME?
NO... MAYBE.
RUN, FRANK! RUN!!
HELP! CALL 911!! CALL THE POLICE! PLEASE HURRY!!
MY EX-BOYFRIEND'S BEATING MY DATE TO A PULP! CALL THE POLICE!!!
OH NO. ERIC, NO! NOT HIS SPINE! DROP THE CART!!
EXPRESS LANE 10 ITEMS OR LESS
UM. CLEAN-UP ON AISLE 4.
CHO
OFFICERS! HELP! MY EX-BOYFRIEND IS BEATING MY DATE TO A PULP!
CLICK.
CHO
BAD BOYS! BAD BOYS! WHATCHA GONNA DO...
THANKS FOR A WONDERFUL EVENING, BRANDY.
Y-YOU'RE VERY SPECIAL. I'D R-REALLY LIKE TO SEE YOU AGAIN SOON...
SO... UM... UNTIL NEXT... TIME... UH...
CHO
BRANDY?

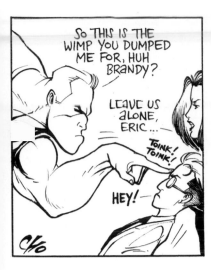

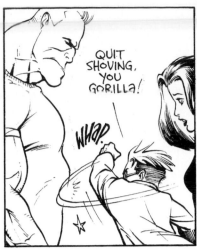

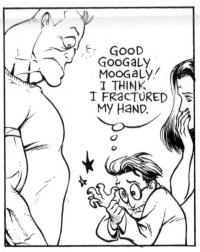

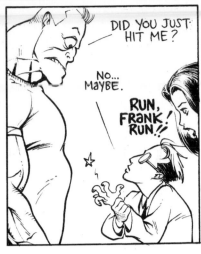

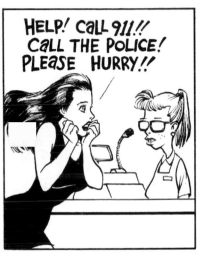

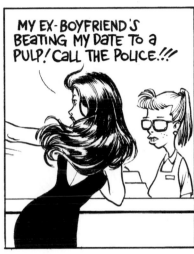

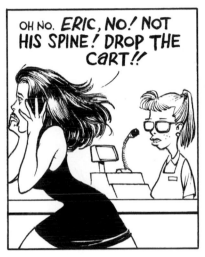

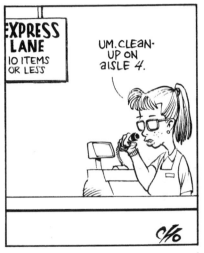

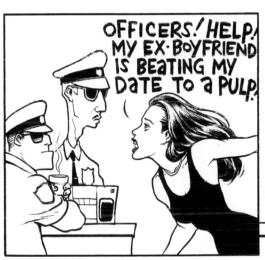

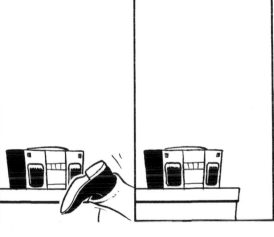

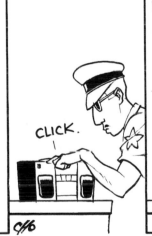

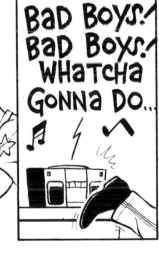

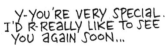

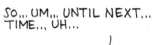

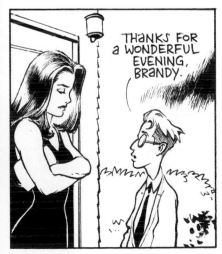

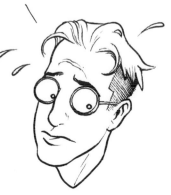

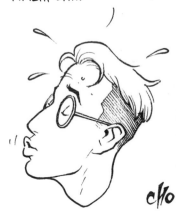

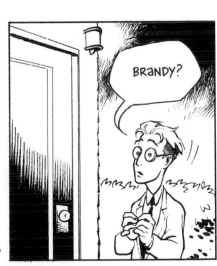

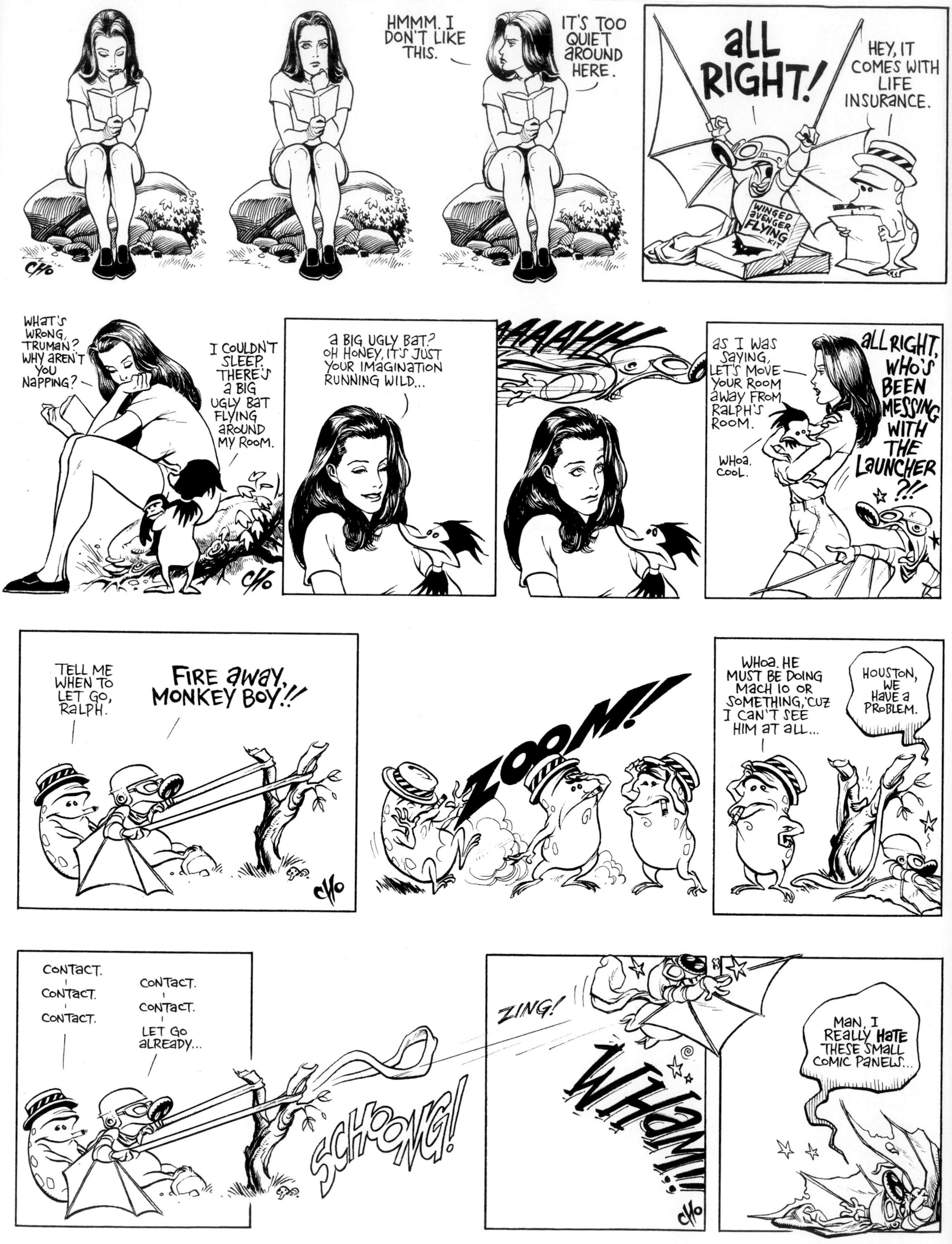

HMMM. I DON'T LIKE THIS.
IT'S TOO QUIET AROUND HERE.
ALL RIGHT!
HEY, IT COMES WITH LIFE INSURANCE.
WINGED AVENGER FLYING KIT
WHAT'S WRONG, TRUMAN? WHY AREN'T YOU NAPPING?
I COULDN'T SLEEP. THERE'S A BIG UGLY BAT FLYING AROUND MY ROOM.
A BIG UGLY BAT? OH HONEY, IT'S JUST YOUR IMAGINATION RUNNING WILD...
AAAAHH
AS I WAS SAYING, LET'S MOVE YOUR ROOM AWAY FROM RALPH'S ROOM.
ALL RIGHT, WHO'S BEEN MESSING WITH THE LAUNCHER?!!
WHOA. COOL.
TELL ME WHEN TO LET GO, RALPH.
FIRE AWAY, MONKEY BOY!!!
ZOOM!!
WHOA. HE MUST BE DOING MACH 10 OR SOMETHING, 'CUZ I CAN'T SEE HIM AT ALL...
HOUSTON, WE HAVE A PROBLEM.
CONTACT. CONTACT. CONTACT.
CONTACT. CONTACT. LET GO ALREADY...
SCHOONG!
ZING!
WHAM!!!
MAN, I REALLY HATE THESE SMALL COMIC PANELS...

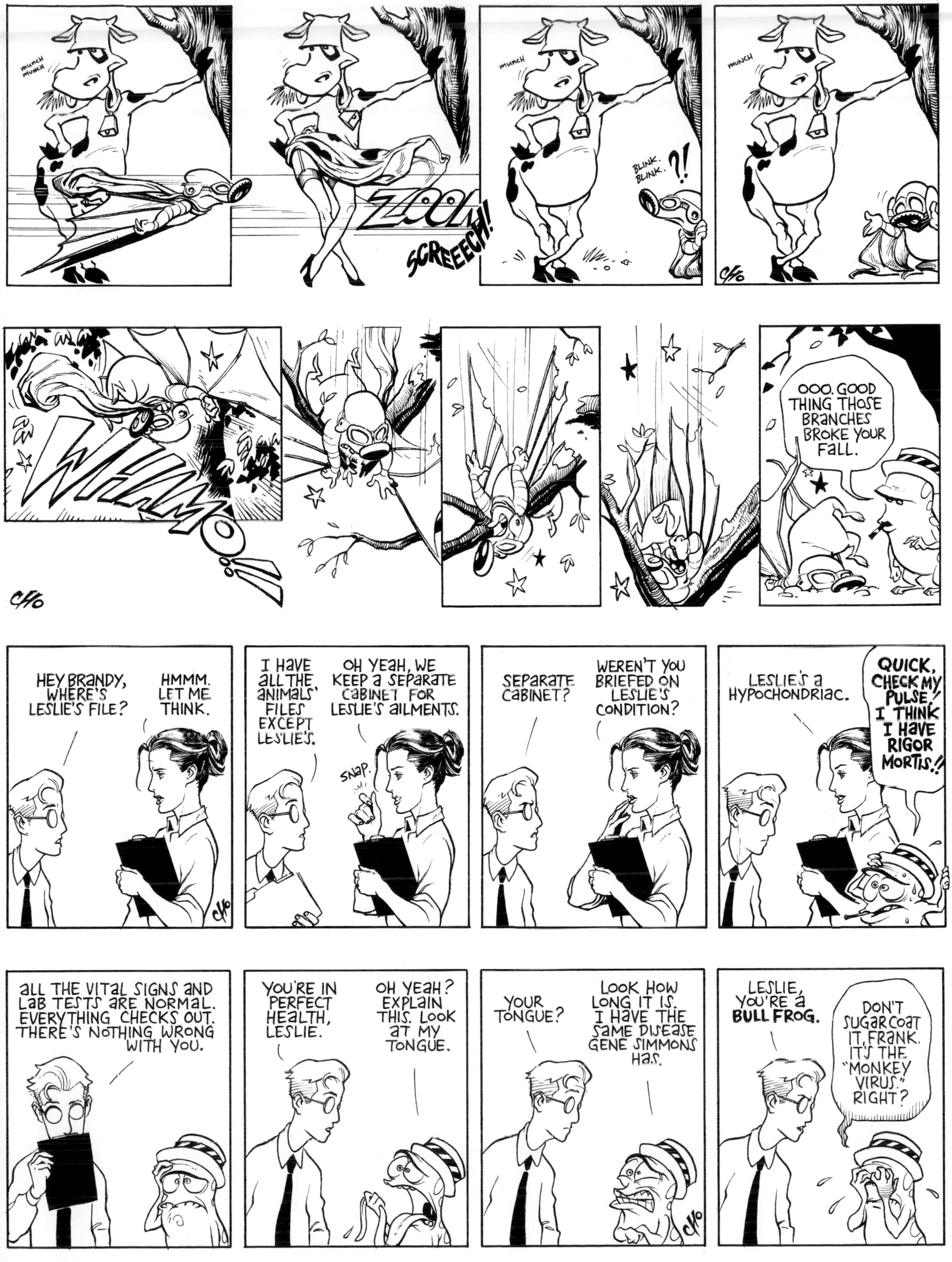
MUNCH MUNCH
ZOOM
SCREEECH!
MUNCH
BLINK. BLINK.
?!
MUNCH
CHO
WHAM
O!!
CHO
OOO. GOOD THING THOSE BRANCHES BROKE YOUR FALL.
HEY BRANDY, WHERE'S LESLIE'S FILE?
HMMM. LET ME THINK.
CHO
I HAVE ALL THE ANIMALS' FILES EXCEPT LESLIE'S.
OH YEAH, WE KEEP A SEPARATE CABINET FOR LESLIE'S AILMENTS.
SNAP.
SEPARATE CABINET?
WEREN'T YOU BRIEFED ON LESLIE'S CONDITION?
LESLIE'S A HYPOCHONDRIAC.
QUICK, CHECK MY PULSE! I THINK I HAVE RIGOR MORTIS!!
ALL THE VITAL SIGNS AND LAB TESTS ARE NORMAL. EVERYTHING CHECKS OUT. THERE'S NOTHING WRONG WITH YOU.
YOU'RE IN PERFECT HEALTH, LESLIE.
OH YEAH? EXPLAIN THIS. LOOK AT MY TONGUE.
YOUR TONGUE?
LOOK HOW LONG IT IS. I HAVE THE SAME DISEASE GENE SIMMONS HAS.
CHO
LESLIE, YOU'RE A BULL FROG.
DON'T SUGARCOAT IT, FRANK. IT'S THE "MONKEY VIRUS." RIGHT?

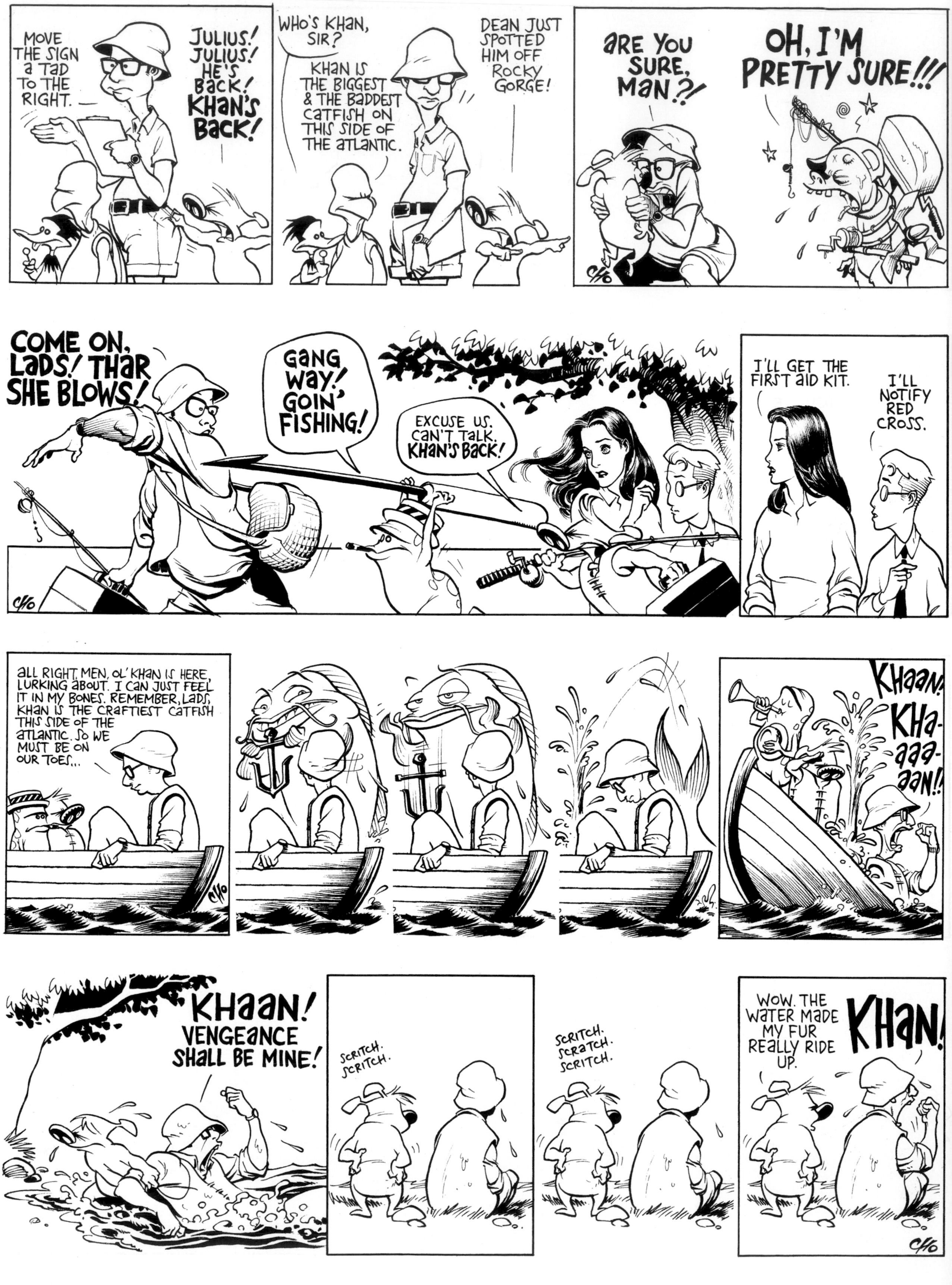
MOVE THE SIGN A TAD TO THE RIGHT.
JULIUS! JULIUS! HE'S BACK! KHAN'S BACK!
WHO'S KHAN, SIR?
KHAN IS THE BIGGEST & THE BADDEST CATFISH ON THIS SIDE OF THE ATLANTIC.
DEAN JUST SPOTTED HIM OFF ROCKY GORGE!
ARE YOU SURE, MAN?!
OH, I'M PRETTY SURE!!!
CHO
COME ON, LADS! THAR SHE BLOWS!
GANG WAY! GOIN' FISHING!
EXCUSE US. CAN'T TALK. KHAN'S BACK!
CHO
I'LL GET THE FIRST AID KIT.
I'LL NOTIFY RED CROSS.
ALL RIGHT, MEN, OL' KHAN IS HERE, LURKING ABOUT. I CAN JUST FEEL IT IN MY BONES. REMEMBER, LADS, KHAN IS THE CRAFTIEST CATFISH THIS SIDE OF THE ATLANTIC. SO WE MUST BE ON OUR TOES...
CHO
KHAAN! KHA-AAA-AAN!!
KHAAN! VENGEANCE SHALL BE MINE!
SCRITCH. SCRITCH.
SCRITCH. SCRATCH. SCRITCH.
WOW. THE WATER MADE MY FUR REALLY RIDE UP.
KHAN!
CHO

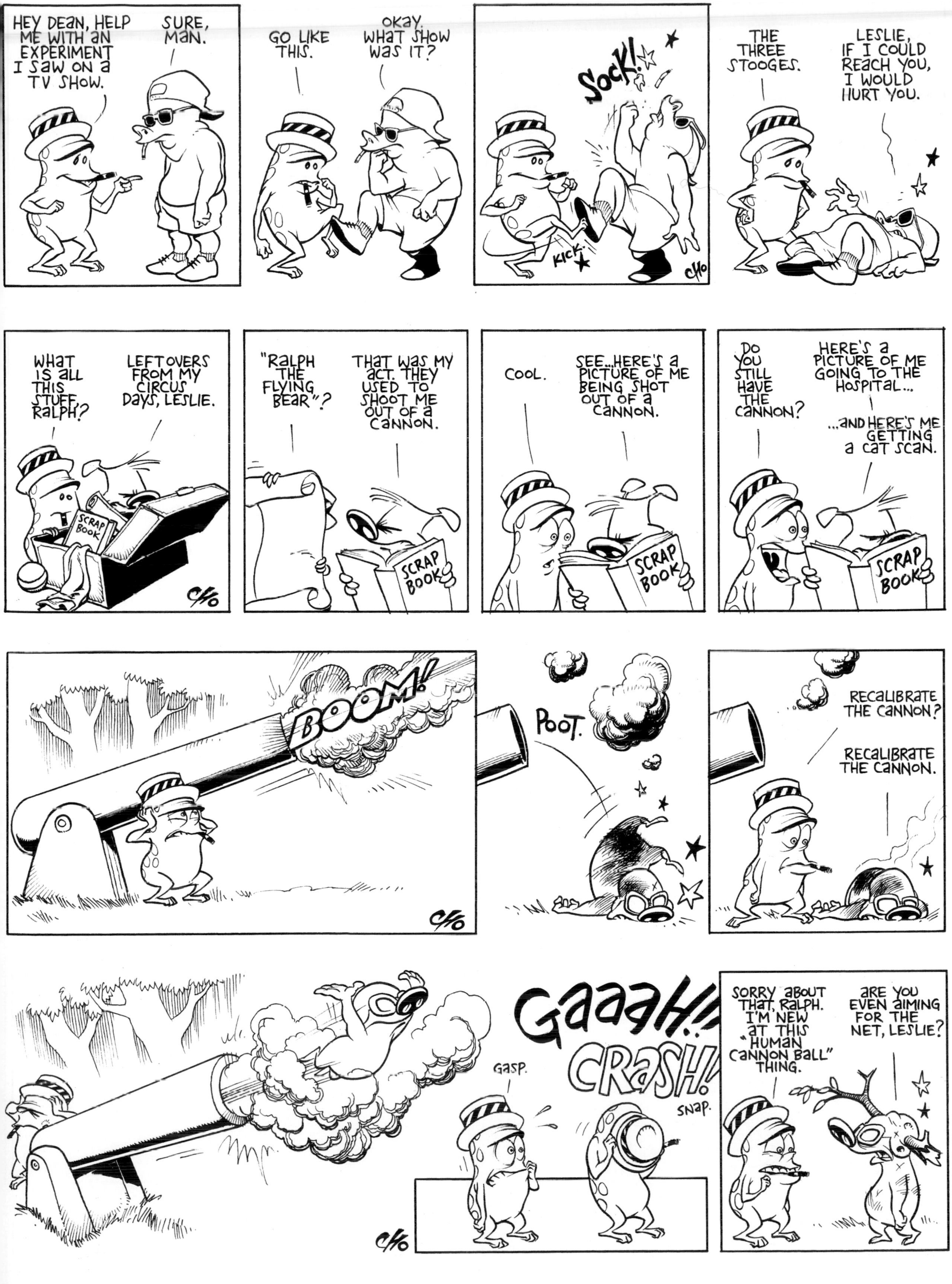
HEY DEAN, HELP ME WITH AN EXPERIMENT I SAW ON A TV SHOW.
SURE, MAN.
GO LIKE THIS.
OKAY. WHAT SHOW WAS IT?
SOCK!
KICK.
THE THREE STOOGES.
LESLIE, IF I COULD REACH YOU, I WOULD HURT YOU.
WHAT IS ALL THIS STUFF, RALPH?
LEFTOVERS FROM MY CIRCUS DAYS, LESLIE.
SCRAP BOOK
"RALPH THE FLYING BEAR"?
THAT WAS MY ACT. THEY USED TO SHOOT ME OUT OF A CANNON.
SCRAP BOOK
COOL.
SEE...HERE'S A PICTURE OF ME BEING SHOT OUT OF A CANNON.
SCRAP BOOK
DO YOU STILL HAVE THE CANNON?
HERE'S A PICTURE OF ME GOING TO THE HOSPITAL...
...AND HERE'S ME GETTING A CAT SCAN.
SCRAP BOOK
BOOM!
POOT.
RECALIBRATE THE CANNON?
RECALIBRATE THE CANNON.
GAAAH!!
CRASH!
GASP.
SNAP.
SORRY ABOUT THAT, RALPH. I'M NEW AT THIS "HUMAN CANNON BALL" THING.
ARE YOU EVEN AIMING FOR THE NET, LESLIE?

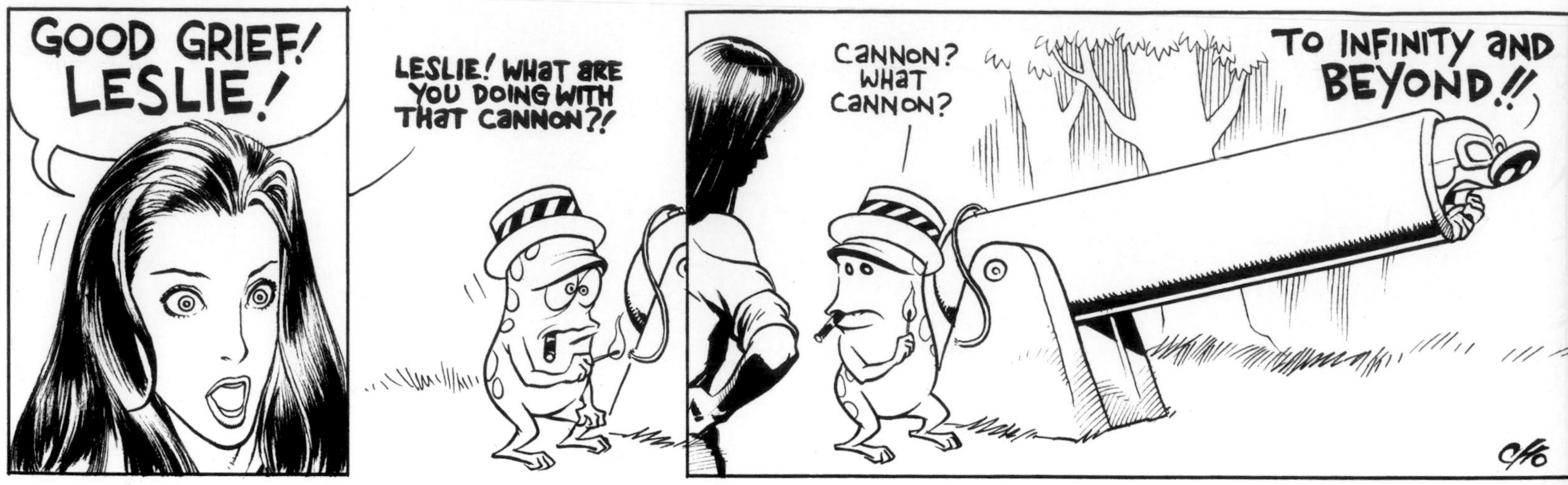
GOOD GRIEF! LESLIE!
LESLIE! WHAT ARE YOU DOING WITH THAT CANNON?!
CANNON? WHAT CANNON?
TO INFINITY AND BEYOND!!
CHO

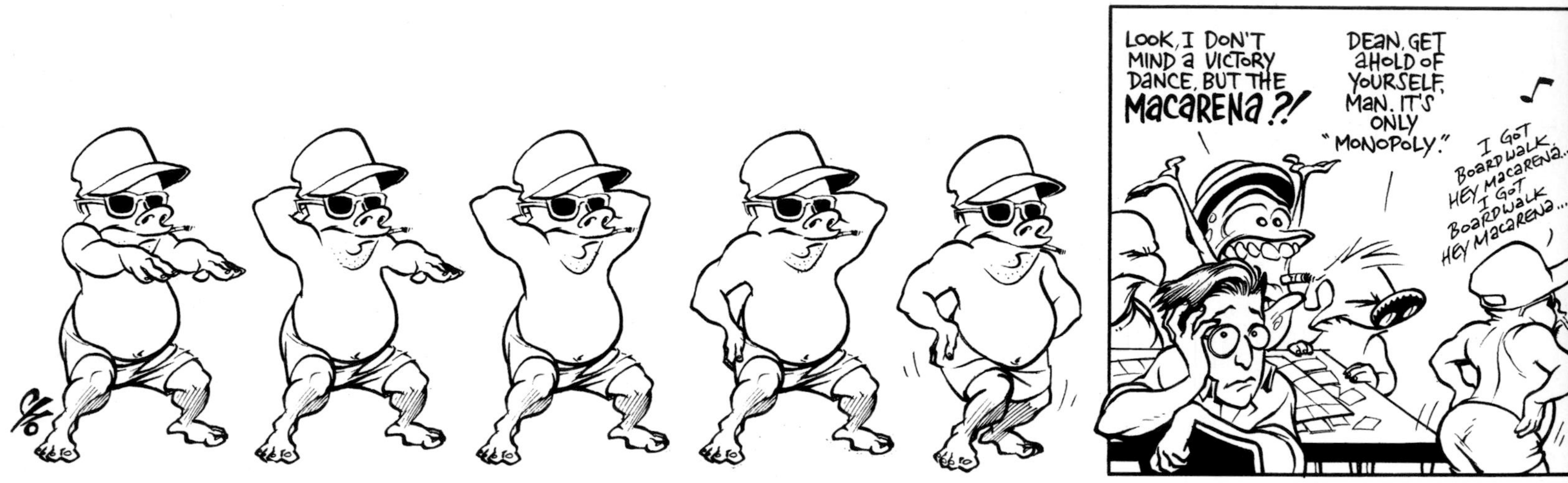
CHO
LOOK, I DON'T MIND A VICTORY DANCE, BUT THE MACARENA?!
DEAN, GET AHOLD OF YOURSELF, MAN. IT'S ONLY "MONOPOLY."
I GOT BOARDWALK HEY MACARENA... I GOT BOARDWALK HEY MACARENA...

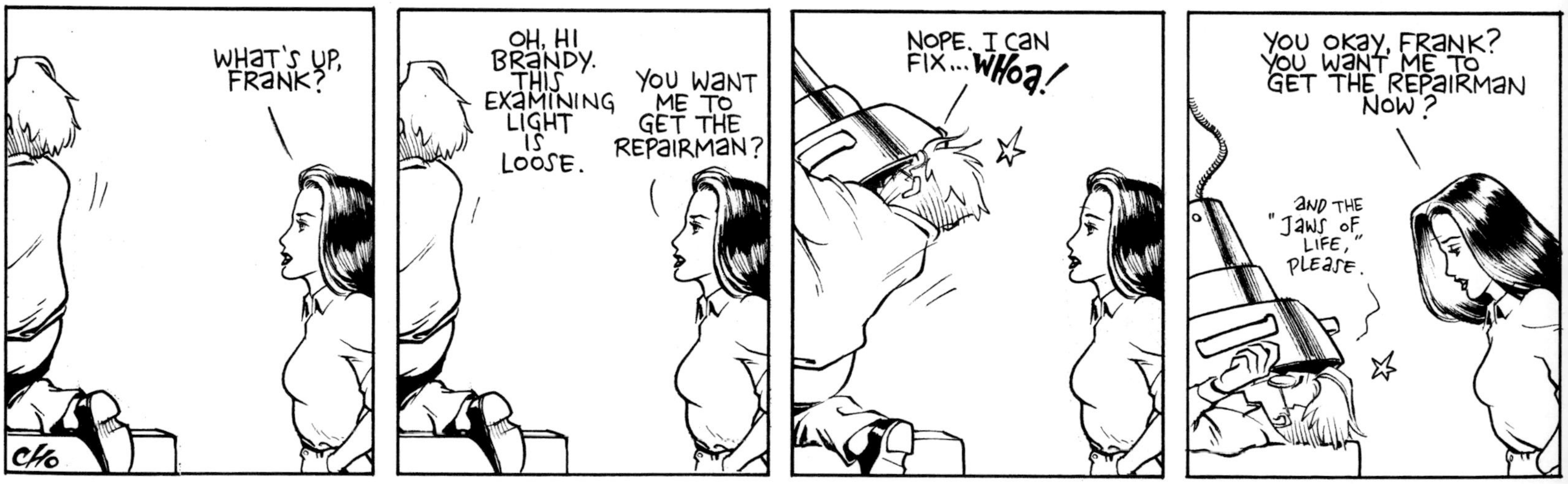
WHAT'S UP, FRANK?
CHO
OH, HI BRANDY. THIS EXAMINING LIGHT IS LOOSE.
YOU WANT ME TO GET THE REPAIRMAN?
NOPE. I CAN FIX... WHOA!
YOU OKAY, FRANK? YOU WANT ME TO GET THE REPAIRMAN NOW?
AND THE "JAWS OF LIFE," PLEASE.

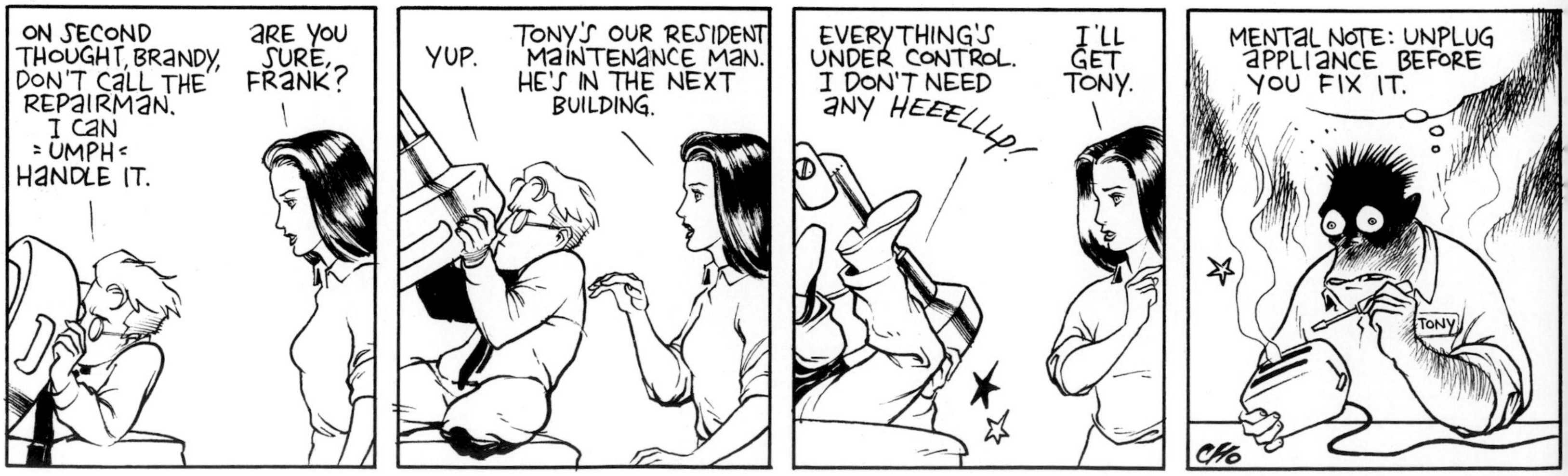
ON SECOND THOUGHT, BRANDY, DON'T CALL THE REPAIRMAN. I CAN =UMPH= HANDLE IT.
ARE YOU SURE, FRANK?
YUP.
TONY'S OUR RESIDENT MAINTENANCE MAN. HE'S IN THE NEXT BUILDING.
EVERYTHING'S UNDER CONTROL. I DON'T NEED ANY HEEELLLP!
I'LL GET TONY.
MENTAL NOTE: UNPLUG APPLIANCE BEFORE YOU FIX IT.
TONY
CHO

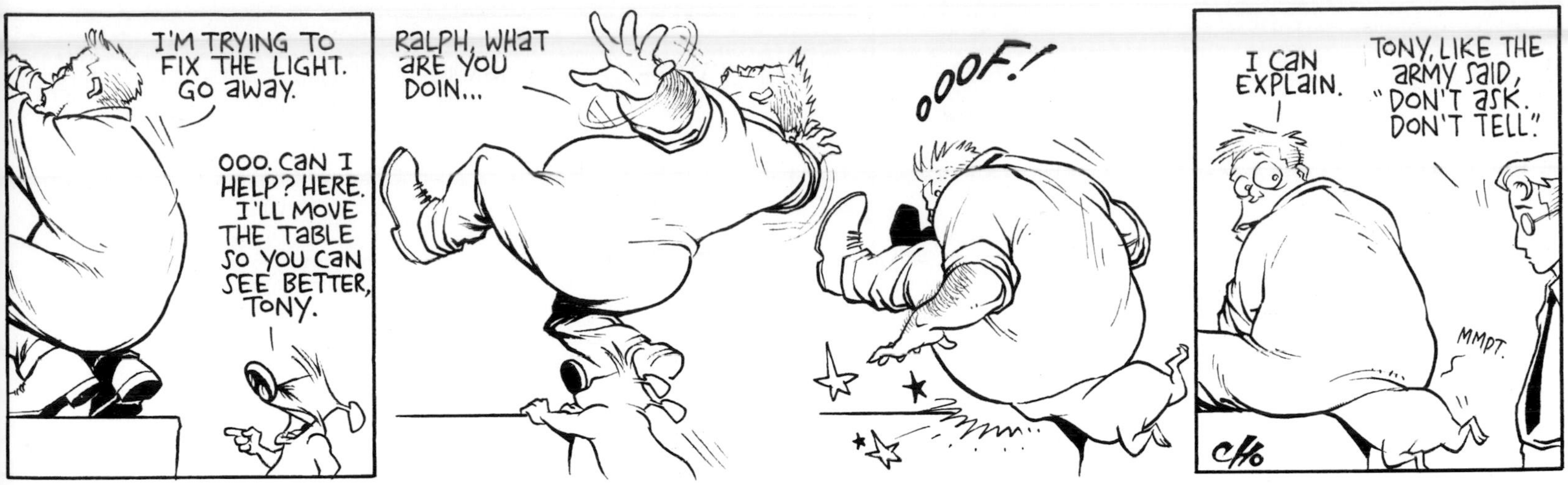
I'M TRYING TO FIX THE LIGHT. GO AWAY.
OOO. CAN I HELP? HERE. I'LL MOVE THE TABLE SO YOU CAN SEE BETTER, TONY.
RALPH, WHAT ARE YOU DOIN...
OOOF!
I CAN EXPLAIN.
TONY, LIKE THE ARMY SAID, "DON'T ASK. DON'T TELL."
MMPT.
CHO

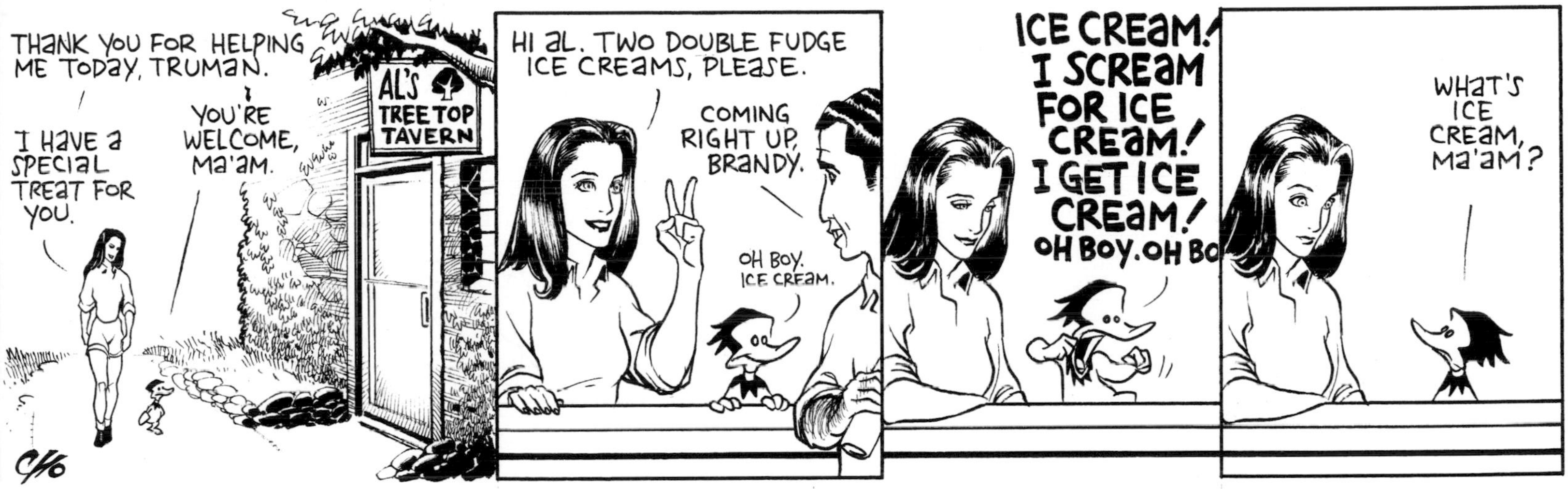
THANK YOU FOR HELPING ME TODAY, TRUMAN.
YOU'RE WELCOME, MA'AM.
I HAVE A SPECIAL TREAT FOR YOU.
AL'S TREE TOP TAVERN
CHO
HI AL. TWO DOUBLE FUDGE ICE CREAMS, PLEASE.
COMING RIGHT UP, BRANDY.
OH BOY. ICE CREAM.
ICE CREAM! I SCREAM FOR ICE CREAM! I GET ICE CREAM! OH BOY. OH BO
WHAT'S ICE CREAM, MA'AM?

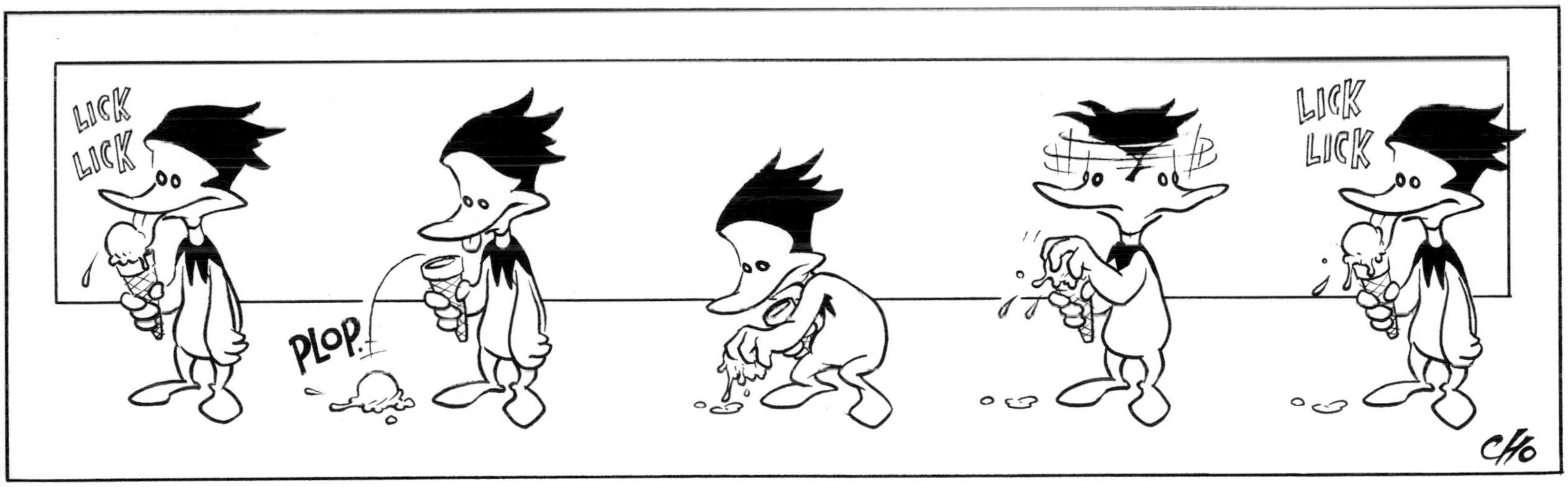
LICK LICK
PLOP.
LICK LICK
CHO

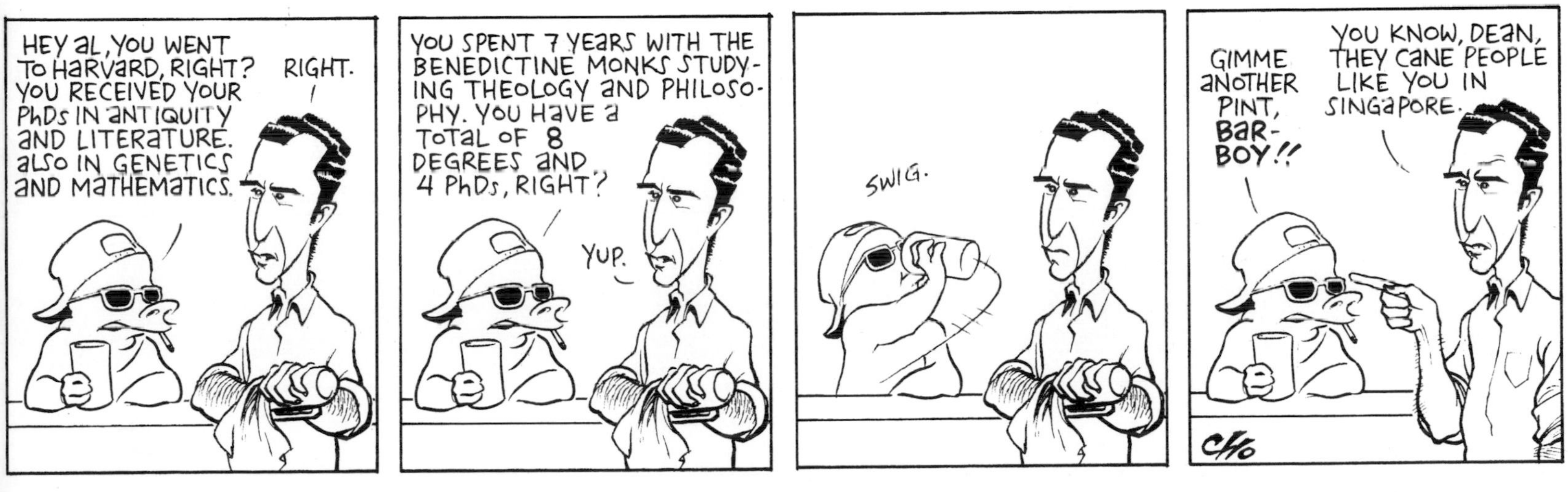
HEY AL, YOU WENT TO HARVARD, RIGHT? YOU RECEIVED YOUR PhDs IN ANTIQUITY AND LITERATURE. ALSO IN GENETICS AND MATHEMATICS.
RIGHT.
YOU SPENT 7 YEARS WITH THE BENEDICTINE MONKS STUDYING THEOLOGY AND PHILOSOPHY. YOU HAVE A TOTAL OF 8 DEGREES AND 4 PhDs, RIGHT?
YUP.
SWIG.
GIMME ANOTHER PINT, BAR-BOY!!
YOU KNOW, DEAN, THEY CANE PEOPLE LIKE YOU IN SINGAPORE.
CHO

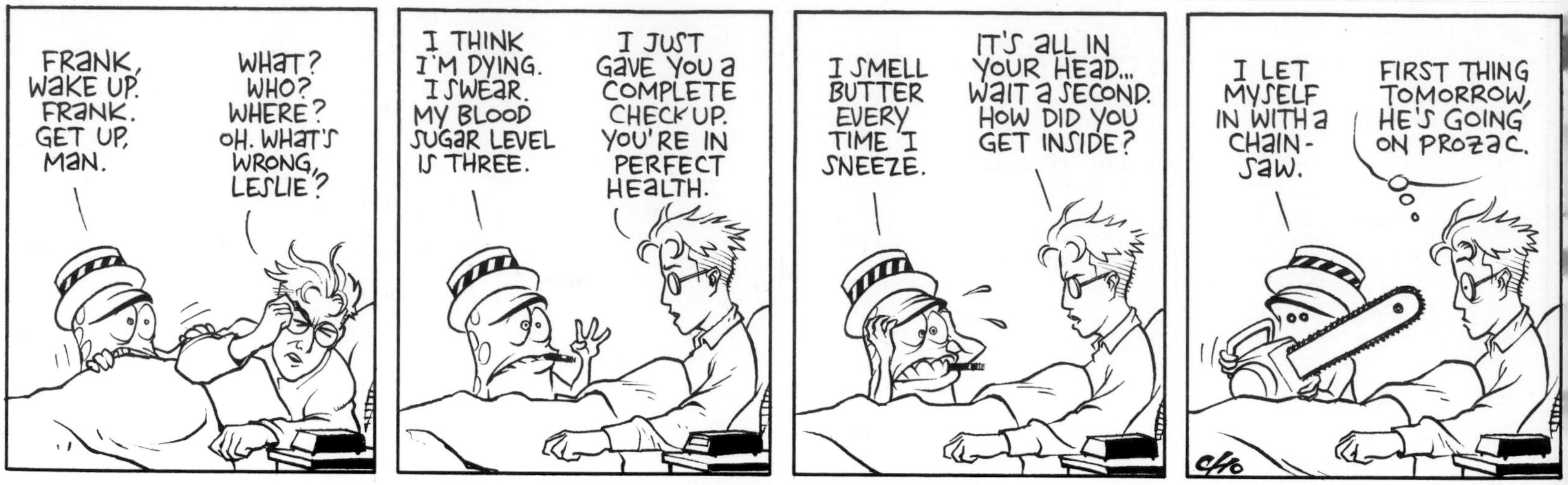
FRANK, WAKE UP. FRANK. GET UP, MAN.
WHAT? WHO? WHERE? OH. WHAT'S WRONG, LESLIE?
I THINK I'M DYING. I SWEAR. MY BLOOD SUGAR LEVEL IS THREE.
I JUST GAVE YOU A COMPLETE CHECK UP. YOU'RE IN PERFECT HEALTH.
I SMELL BUTTER EVERY TIME I SNEEZE.
IT'S ALL IN YOUR HEAD... WAIT A SECOND. HOW DID YOU GET INSIDE?
I LET MYSELF IN WITH A CHAIN-SAW.
FIRST THING TOMORROW, HE'S GOING ON PROZAC.
CHO

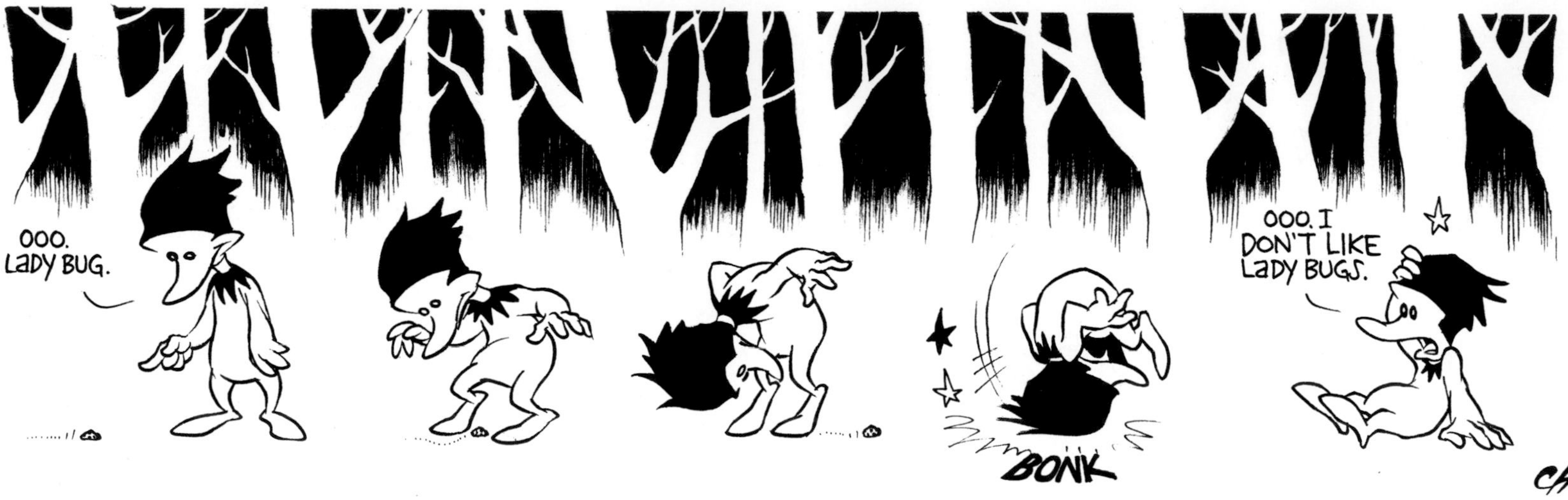
OOO. LADY BUG.
BONK
OOO. I DON'T LIKE LADY BUGS.
CHO

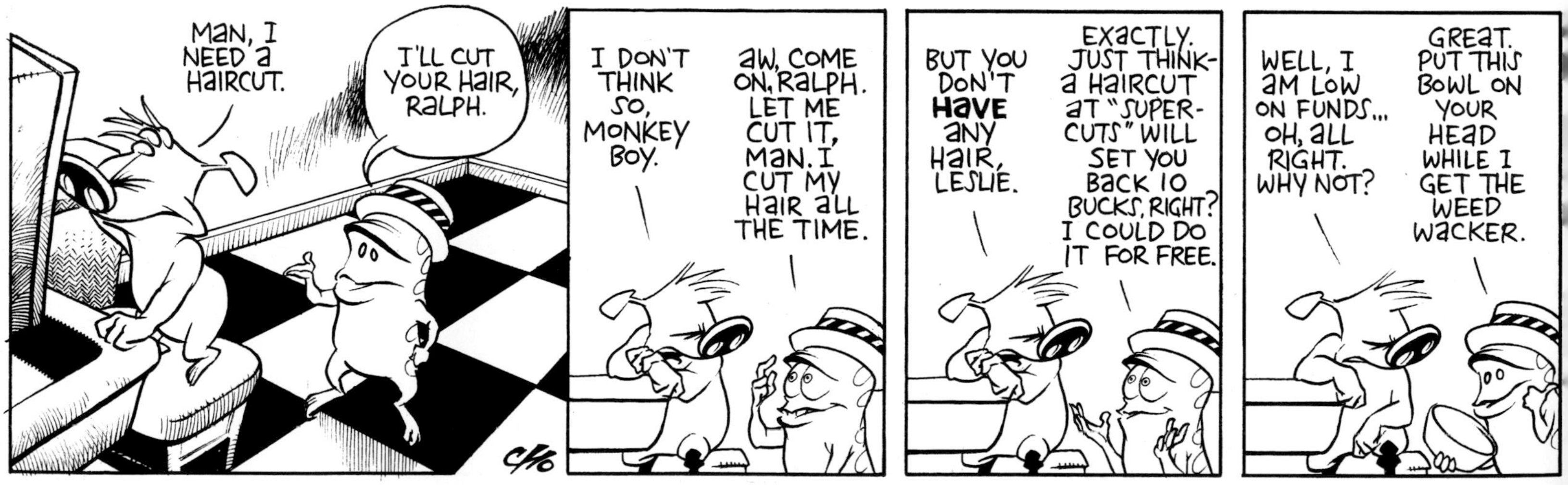
MAN, I NEED A HAIRCUT.
I'LL CUT YOUR HAIR, RALPH.
CHO
I DON'T THINK SO, MONKEY BOY.
AW, COME ON, RALPH. LET ME CUT IT, MAN. I CUT MY HAIR ALL THE TIME.
BUT YOU DON'T **HAVE** ANY HAIR, LESLIE.
EXACTLY. JUST THINK- A HAIRCUT AT "SUPER-CUTS" WILL SET YOU BACK 10 BUCKS, RIGHT? I COULD DO IT FOR FREE.
WELL, I AM LOW ON FUNDS... OH, ALL RIGHT. WHY NOT?
GREAT. PUT THIS BOWL ON YOUR HEAD WHILE I GET THE WEED WACKER.

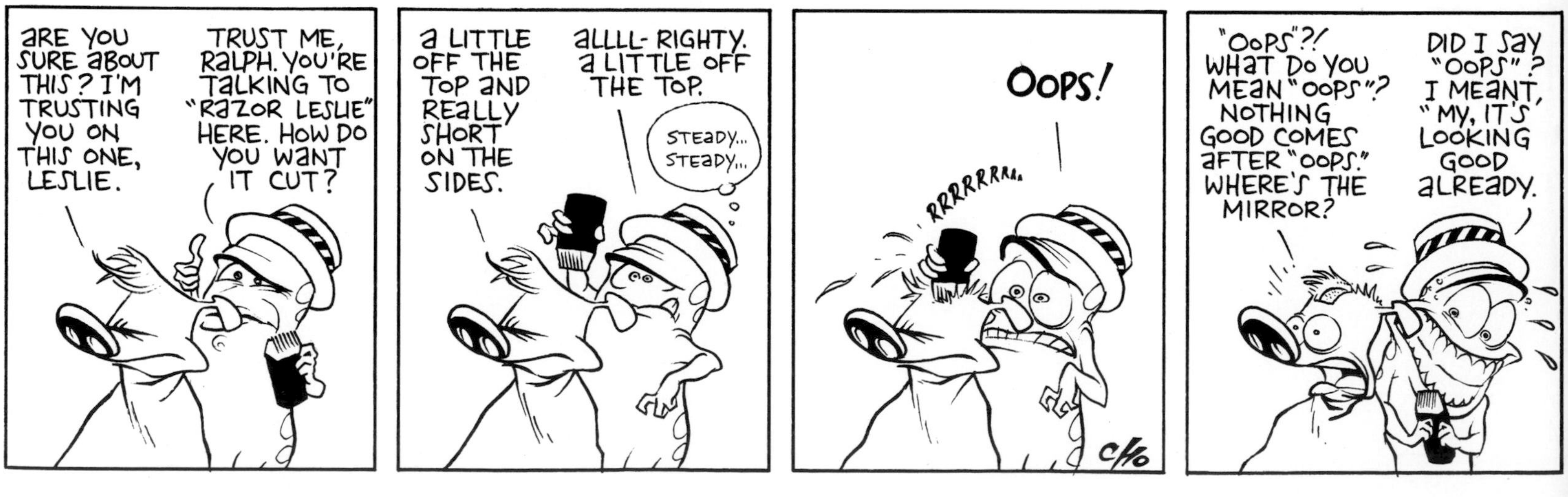
ARE YOU SURE ABOUT THIS? I'M TRUSTING YOU ON THIS ONE, LESLIE.
TRUST ME, RALPH. YOU'RE TALKING TO "RAZOR LESLIE" HERE. HOW DO YOU WANT IT CUT?
A LITTLE OFF THE TOP AND REALLY SHORT ON THE SIDES.
ALLLL-RIGHTY. A LITTLE OFF THE TOP.
STEADY... STEADY...
RRRRRRRR...
OOPS!
CHO
"OOPS"?! WHAT DO YOU MEAN "OOPS"? NOTHING GOOD COMES AFTER "OOPS." WHERE'S THE MIRROR?
DID I SAY "OOPS"? I MEANT, "MY, IT'S LOOKING GOOD ALREADY."

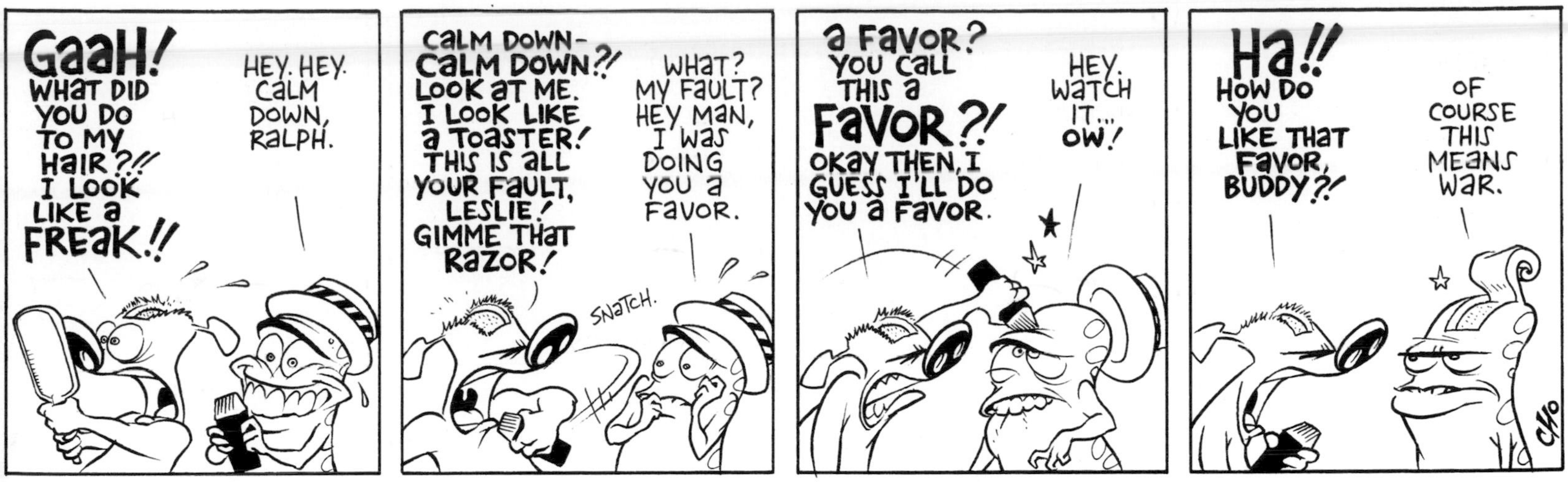
GAAH! WHAT DID YOU DO TO MY HAIR?!! I LOOK LIKE A FREAK!!
HEY. HEY. CALM DOWN, RALPH.
CALM DOWN - CALM DOWN?! LOOK AT ME. I LOOK LIKE A TOASTER! THIS IS ALL YOUR FAULT, LESLIE! GIMME THAT RAZOR!
WHAT? MY FAULT? HEY MAN, I WAS DOING YOU A FAVOR.
SNATCH.
A FAVOR? YOU CALL THIS A FAVOR?! OKAY THEN, I GUESS I'LL DO YOU A FAVOR.
HEY. WATCH IT... OW!
HA!! HOW DO YOU LIKE THAT FAVOR, BUDDY?!
OF COURSE THIS MEANS WAR.
CHO

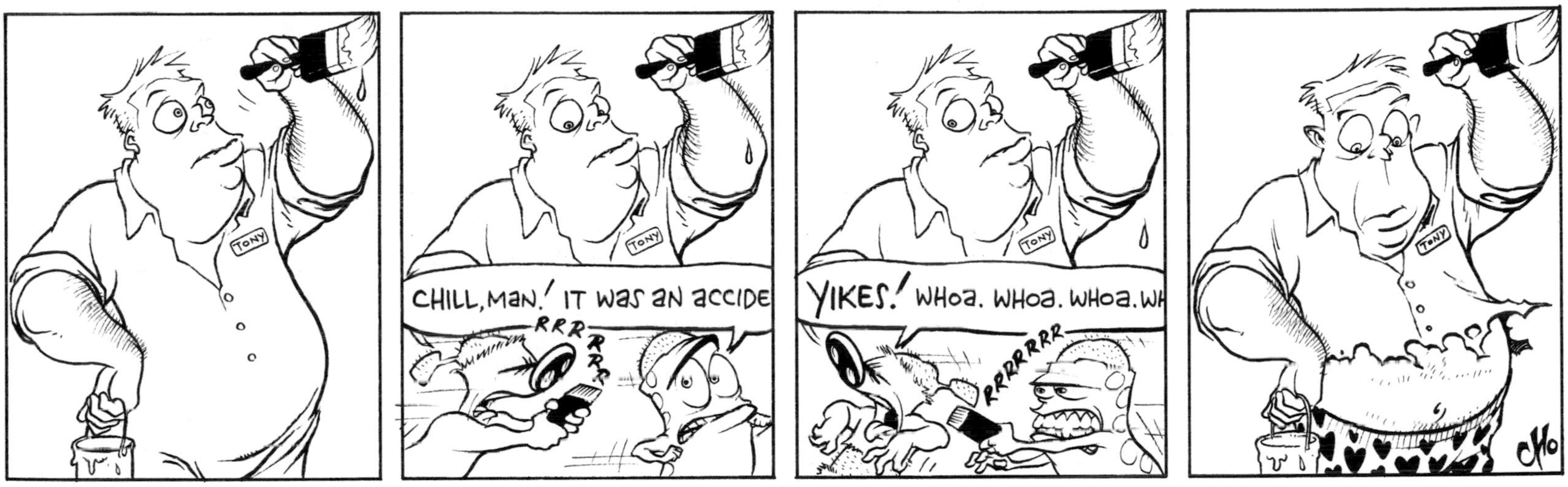
TONY
CHILL, MAN! IT WAS AN ACCIDE
RRRRRR
YIKES! WHOA. WHOA. WHOA. WH
RRRRRRR
CHO

LIBERTY MEADOWS SALUTES FRANCE:

LEARN FRENCH AS YOU READ THE COMICS. AMAZE YOUR FRIENDS AND FAMILY!

(NOW WITH SUBTITLES)

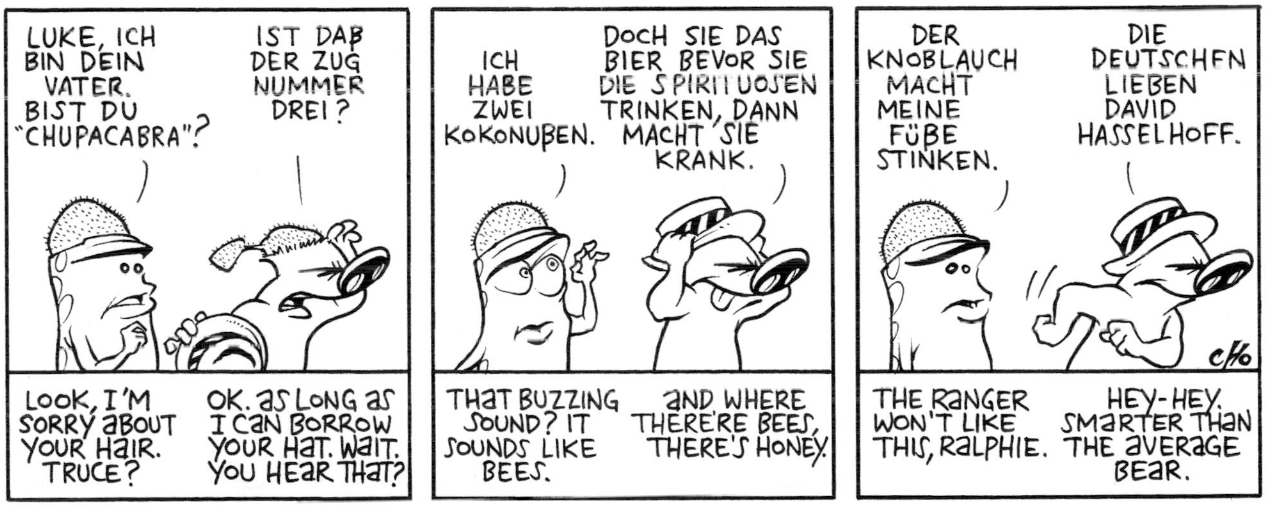
LUKE, ICH BIN DEIN VATER. BIST DU "CHUPACABRA"?
IST DAß DER ZUG NUMMER DREI?
LOOK, I'M SORRY ABOUT YOUR HAIR. TRUCE?
OK. AS LONG AS I CAN BORROW YOUR HAT. WAIT. YOU HEAR THAT?
ICH HABE ZWEI KOKONUßEN.
DOCH SIE DAS BIER BEVOR SIE DIE SPIRITUOSEN TRINKEN, DANN MACHT SIE KRANK.
THAT BUZZING SOUND? IT SOUNDS LIKE BEES.
AND WHERE THERE'RE BEES, THERE'S HONEY.
DER KNOBLAUCH MACHT MEINE FÜßE STINKEN.
DIE DEUTSCHEN LIEBEN DAVID HASSELHOFF.
THE RANGER WON'T LIKE THIS, RALPHIE.
HEY-HEY. SMARTER THAN THE AVERAGE BEAR.
CHO

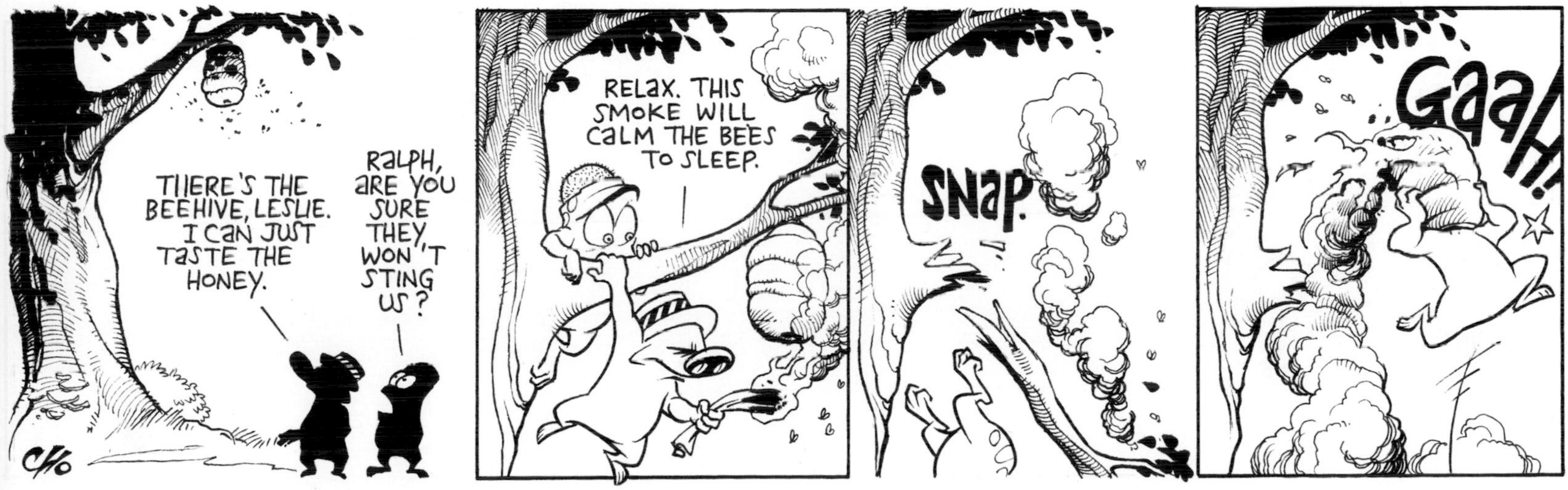
THERE'S THE BEEHIVE, LESLIE. I CAN JUST TASTE THE HONEY.
RALPH, ARE YOU SURE THEY WON'T STING US?
RELAX. THIS SMOKE WILL CALM THE BEES TO SLEEP.
SNAP.
GAAH!
CHO

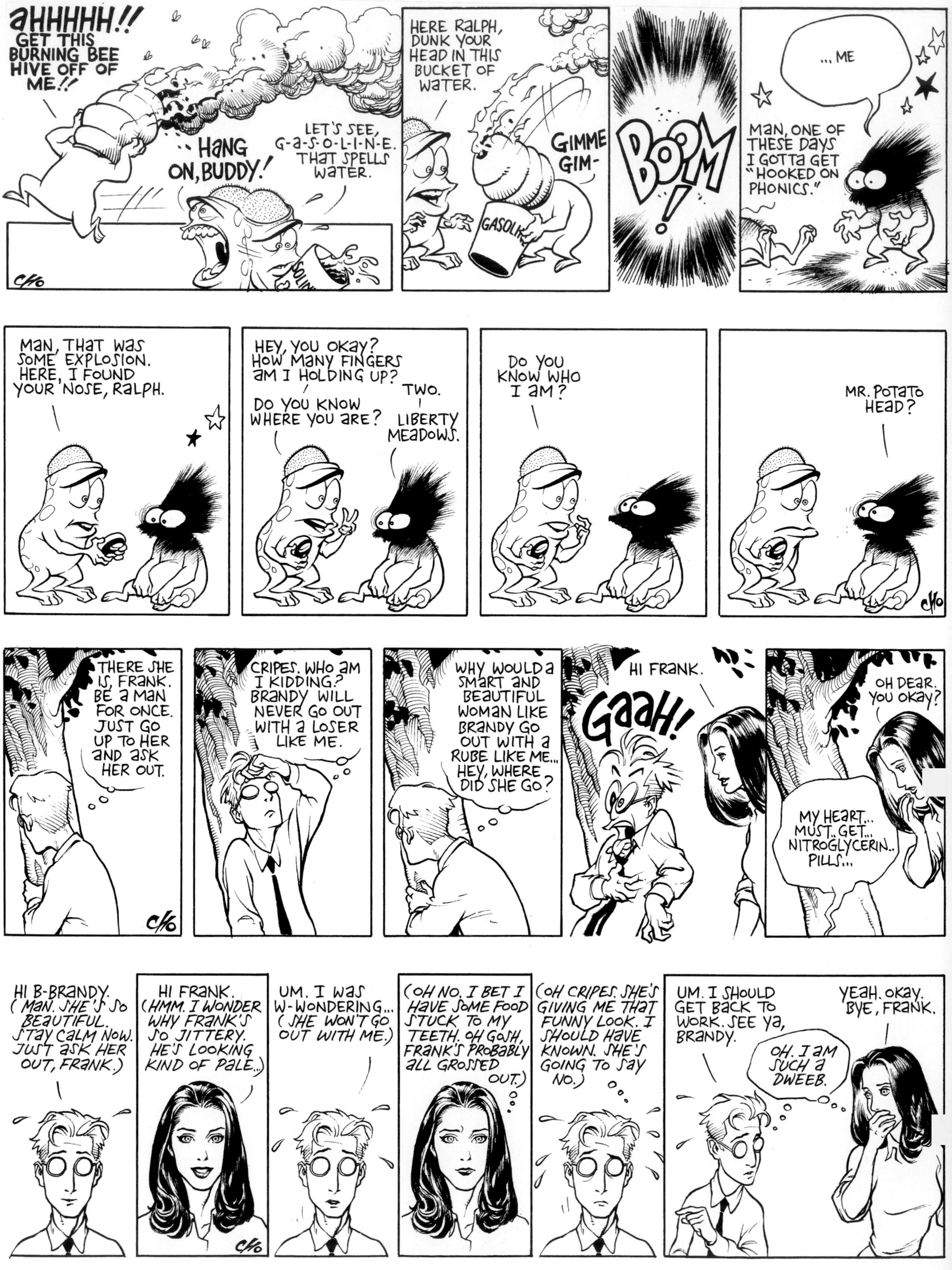
AHHHHH!! GET THIS BURNING BEE HIVE OFF OF ME!!
HANG ON, BUDDY!
LET'S SEE, G-A-S-O-L-I-N-E. THAT SPELLS WATER.
HERE RALPH, DUNK YOUR HEAD IN THIS BUCKET OF WATER.
GIMME GIM-
GASOLI
BOOM!
... ME
MAN, ONE OF THESE DAYS I GOTTA GET "HOOKED ON PHONICS."
MAN, THAT WAS SOME EXPLOSION. HERE, I FOUND YOUR NOSE, RALPH.
HEY, YOU OKAY? HOW MANY FINGERS AM I HOLDING UP?
TWO.
DO YOU KNOW WHERE YOU ARE?
LIBERTY MEADOWS.
DO YOU KNOW WHO I AM?
MR. POTATO HEAD?
THERE SHE IS, FRANK. BE A MAN FOR ONCE. JUST GO UP TO HER AND ASK HER OUT.
CRIPES. WHO AM I KIDDING? BRANDY WILL NEVER GO OUT WITH A LOSER LIKE ME.
WHY WOULD A SMART AND BEAUTIFUL WOMAN LIKE BRANDY GO OUT WITH A RUBE LIKE ME... HEY, WHERE DID SHE GO?
HI FRANK.
GAAH!
OH DEAR. YOU OKAY?
MY HEART... MUST.. GET... NITROGLYCERIN.. PILLS...
HI B-BRANDY. (MAN. SHE'S SO BEAUTIFUL. STAY CALM NOW. JUST ASK HER OUT, FRANK.)
HI FRANK. (HMM. I WONDER WHY FRANK'S SO JITTERY. HE'S LOOKING KIND OF PALE...)
UM. I WAS W-WONDERING... (SHE WON'T GO OUT WITH ME.)
(OH NO. I BET I HAVE SOME FOOD STUCK TO MY TEETH. OH GOSH, FRANK'S PROBABLY ALL GROSSED OUT.)
(OH CRIPES. SHE'S GIVING ME THAT FUNNY LOOK. I SHOULD HAVE KNOWN. SHE'S GOING TO SAY NO.)
UM. I SHOULD GET BACK TO WORK. SEE YA, BRANDY.
YEAH. OKAY. BYE, FRANK.
OH. I AM SUCH A DWEEB.

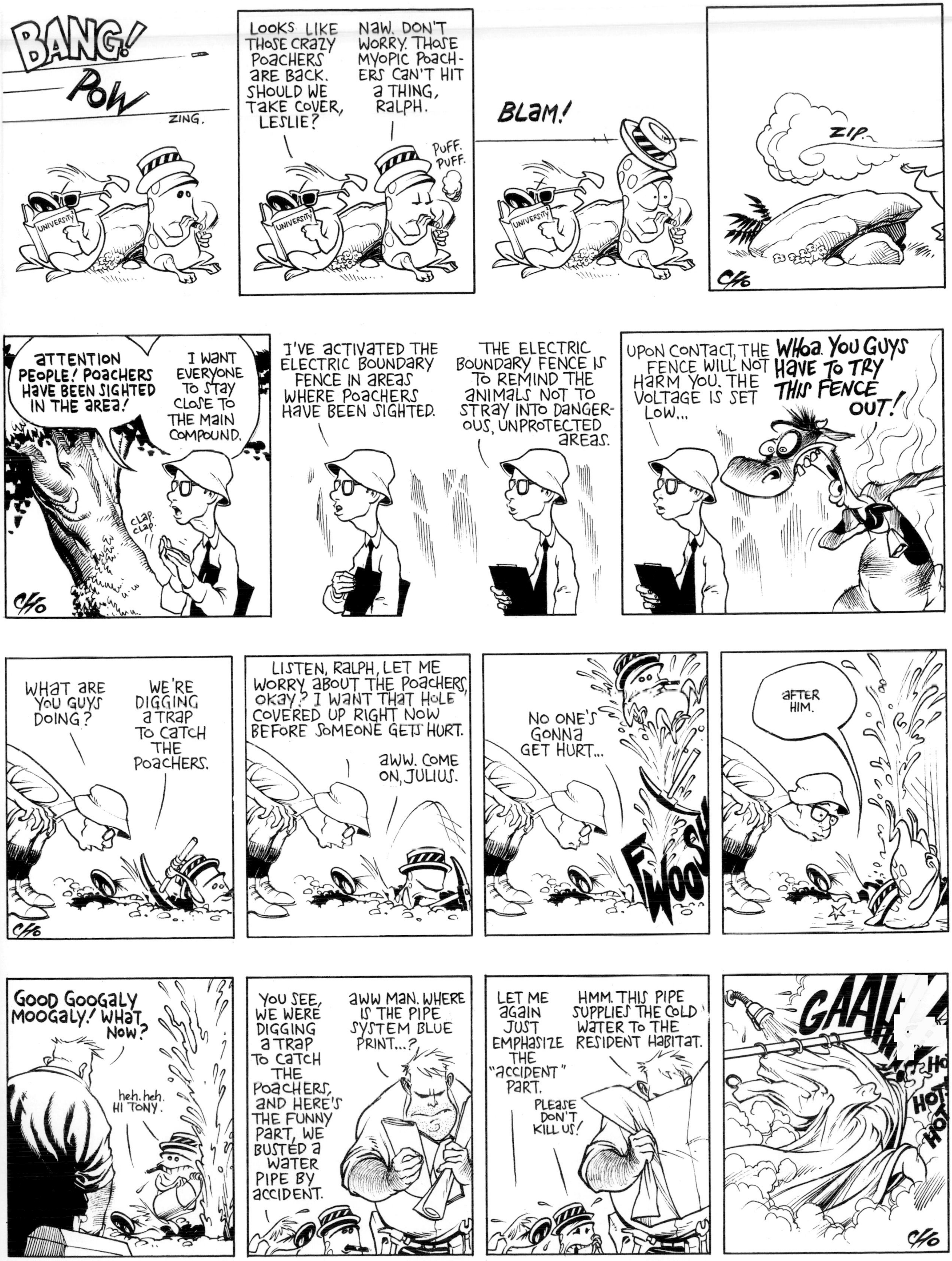
BANG!
POW
ZING.
UNIVERSITY
LOOKS LIKE THOSE CRAZY POACHERS ARE BACK. SHOULD WE TAKE COVER, LESLIE?
NAW. DON'T WORRY. THOSE MYOPIC POACHERS CAN'T HIT A THING, RALPH.
PUFF. PUFF.
BLAM!
ZIP.
ATTENTION PEOPLE! POACHERS HAVE BEEN SIGHTED IN THE AREA!
I WANT EVERYONE TO STAY CLOSE TO THE MAIN COMPOUND.
CLAP. CLAP.
I'VE ACTIVATED THE ELECTRIC BOUNDARY FENCE IN AREAS WHERE POACHERS HAVE BEEN SIGHTED.
THE ELECTRIC BOUNDARY FENCE IS TO REMIND THE ANIMALS NOT TO STRAY INTO DANGEROUS, UNPROTECTED AREAS.
UPON CONTACT, THE FENCE WILL NOT HARM YOU. THE VOLTAGE IS SET LOW...
WHOA. YOU GUYS HAVE TO TRY THIS FENCE OUT!
WHAT ARE YOU GUYS DOING?
WE'RE DIGGING A TRAP TO CATCH THE POACHERS.
LISTEN, RALPH, LET ME WORRY ABOUT THE POACHERS, OKAY? I WANT THAT HOLE COVERED UP RIGHT NOW BEFORE SOMEONE GETS HURT.
AWW. COME ON, JULIUS.
NO ONE'S GONNA GET HURT...
FWOOSH
AFTER HIM.
GOOD GOOGALY MOOGALY! WHAT NOW?
HEH. HEH. HI TONY.
YOU SEE, WE WERE DIGGING A TRAP TO CATCH THE POACHERS, AND HERE'S THE FUNNY PART, WE BUSTED A WATER PIPE BY ACCIDENT.
AWW MAN. WHERE IS THE PIPE SYSTEM BLUE PRINT...?
LET ME AGAIN JUST EMPHASIZE THE "ACCIDENT" PART.
HMM. THIS PIPE SUPPLIES THE COLD WATER TO THE RESIDENT HABITAT.
PLEASE DON'T KILL US!
GAA
HOT HOT HOT

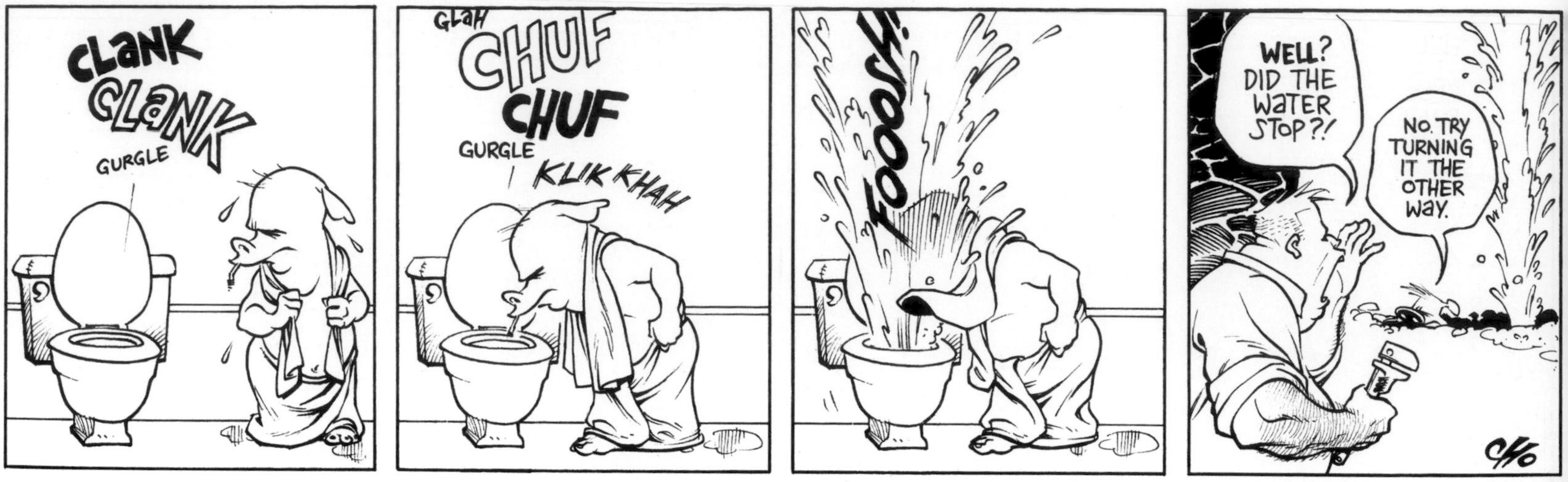
CLANK
CLANK
GURGLE
GLAH
CHUF
CHUF
GURGLE
KLIK KHAH
FOOOSH!
WELL? DID THE WATER STOP?!
NO. TRY TURNING IT THE OTHER WAY.
CHO

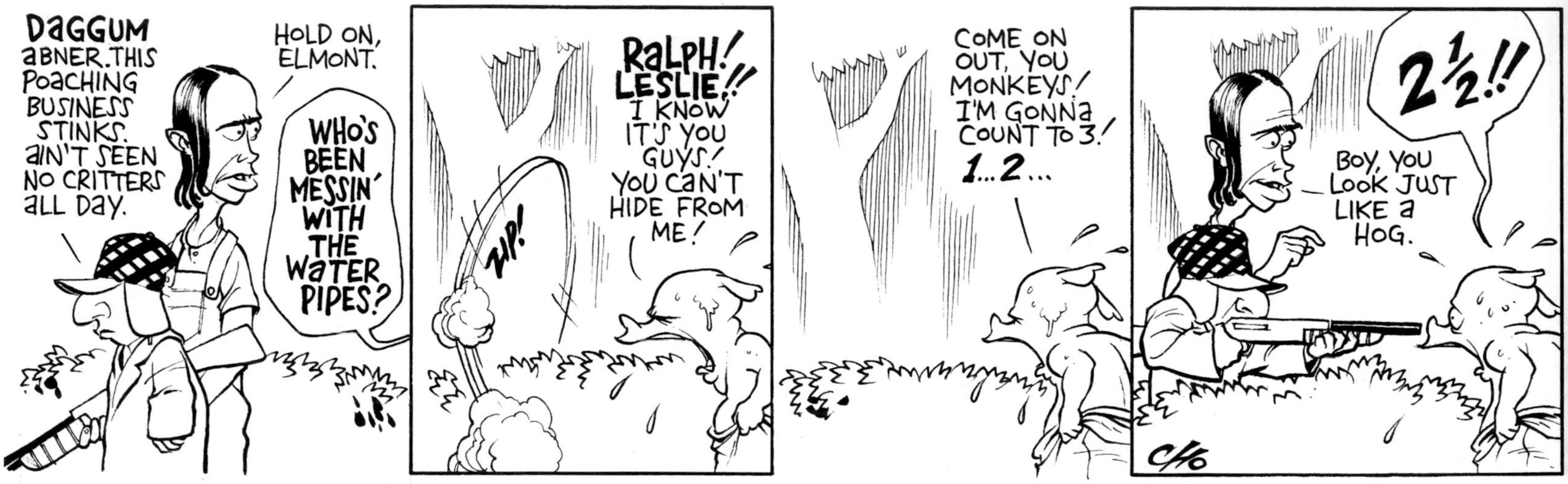
DAGGUM ABNER. THIS POACHING BUSINESS STINKS. AIN'T SEEN NO CRITTERS ALL DAY.
HOLD ON, ELMONT.
WHO'S BEEN MESSIN' WITH THE WATER PIPES?
ZIP!
RALPH! LESLIE!! I KNOW IT'S YOU GUYS! YOU CAN'T HIDE FROM ME!
COME ON OUT, YOU MONKEYS! I'M GONNA COUNT TO 3! 1...2...
2 1/2!!
BOY, YOU LOOK JUST LIKE A HOG.
CHO

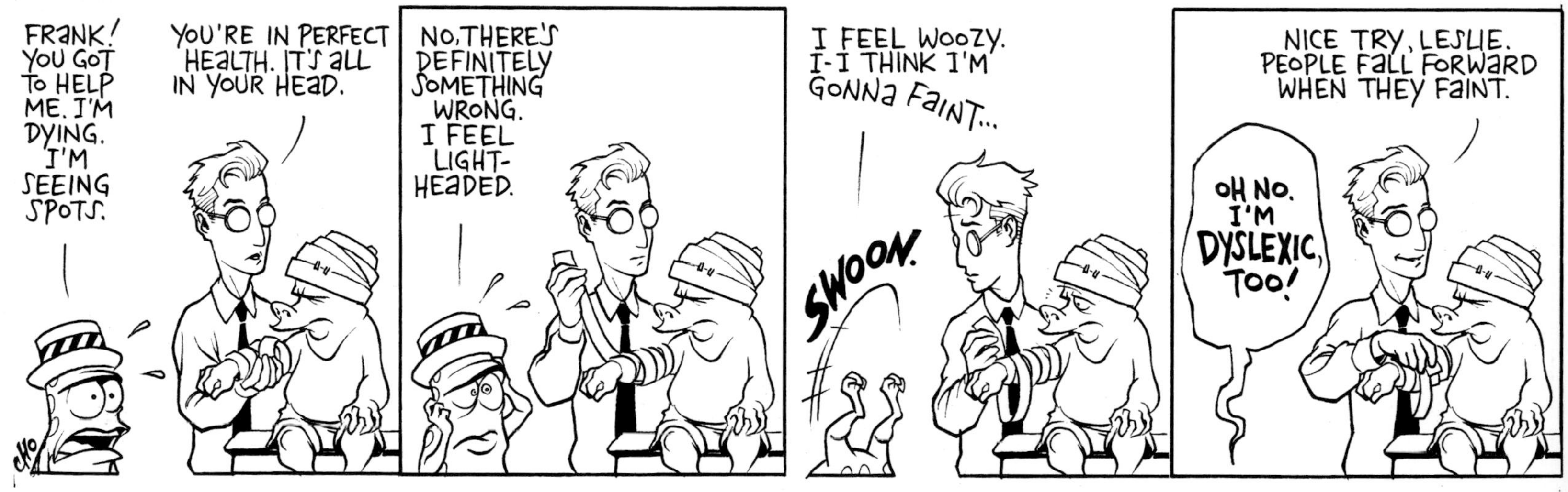
FRANK! YOU GOT TO HELP ME. I'M DYING. I'M SEEING SPOTS.
YOU'RE IN PERFECT HEALTH. IT'S ALL IN YOUR HEAD.
CHO
NO, THERE'S DEFINITELY SOMETHING WRONG. I FEEL LIGHT-HEADED.
I FEEL WOOZY. I-I THINK I'M GONNA FAINT...
SWOON.
NICE TRY, LESLIE. PEOPLE FALL FORWARD WHEN THEY FAINT.
OH NO. I'M DYSLEXIC, TOO!

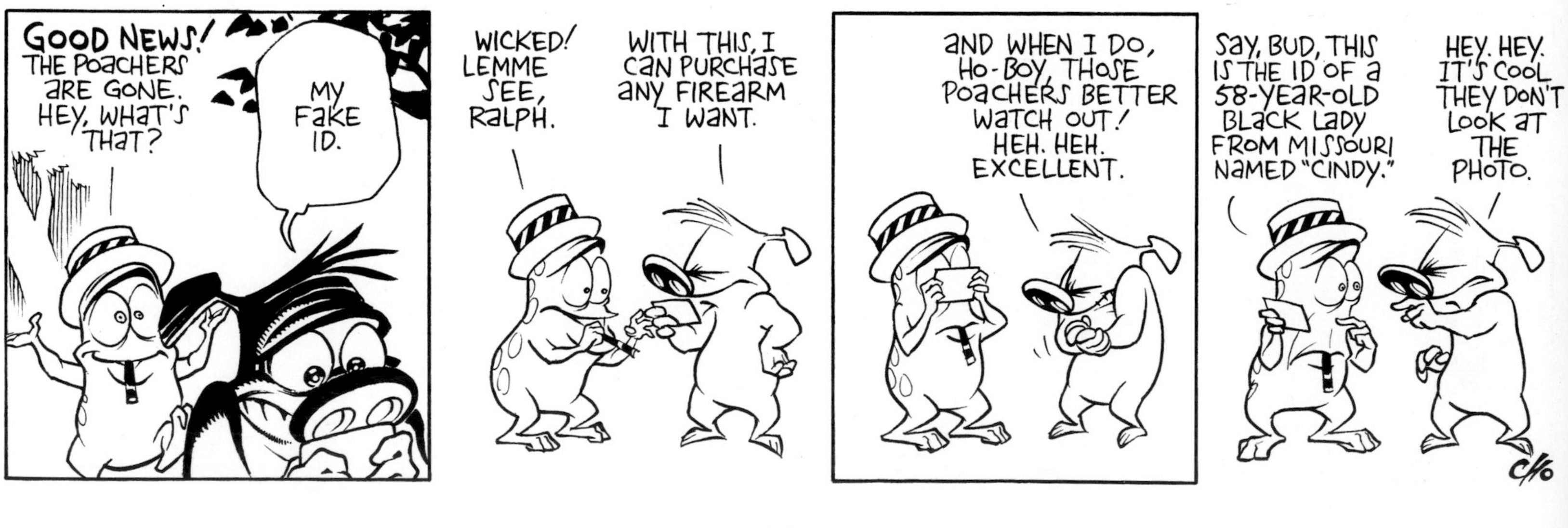
GOOD NEWS! THE POACHERS ARE GONE. HEY, WHAT'S THAT?
MY FAKE ID.
WICKED! LEMME SEE, RALPH.
WITH THIS, I CAN PURCHASE ANY FIREARM I WANT.
AND WHEN I DO, HO-BOY, THOSE POACHERS BETTER WATCH OUT! HEH. HEH. EXCELLENT.
SAY, BUD, THIS IS THE ID OF A 58-YEAR-OLD BLACK LADY FROM MISSOURI NAMED "CINDY."
HEY. HEY. IT'S COOL. THEY DON'T LOOK AT THE PHOTO.
CHO

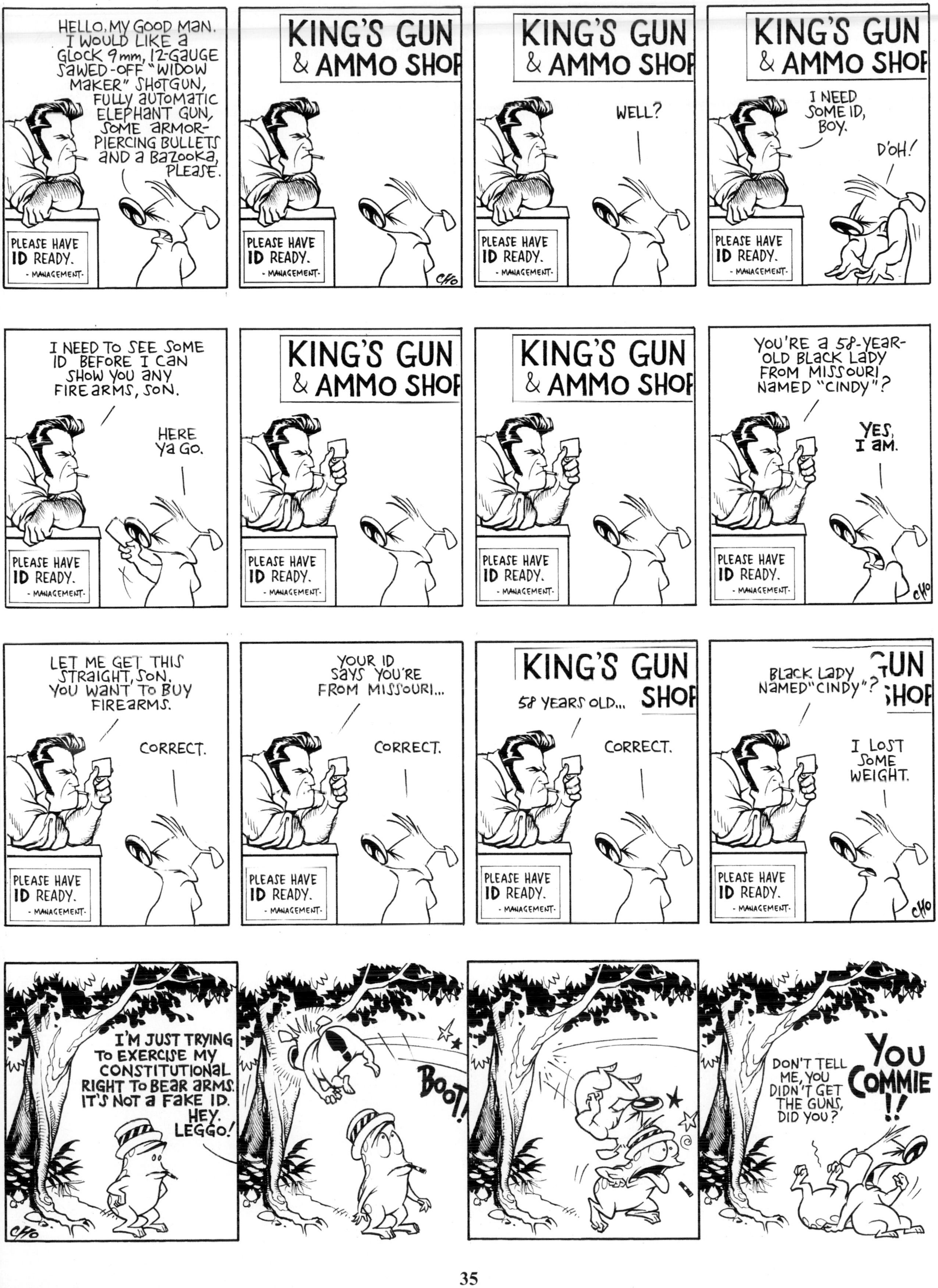

HELLO, MY GOOD MAN. I WOULD LIKE A GLOCK 9mm, 12-GAUGE SAWED-OFF "WIDOW MAKER" SHOTGUN, FULLY AUTOMATIC ELEPHANT GUN, SOME ARMOR-PIERCING BULLETS AND A BAZOOKA, PLEASE.
PLEASE HAVE ID READY. - MANAGEMENT -
KING'S GUN & AMMO SHOP
PLEASE HAVE ID READY. - MANAGEMENT -
KING'S GUN & AMMO SHOP
WELL?
PLEASE HAVE ID READY. - MANAGEMENT -
KING'S GUN & AMMO SHOP
I NEED SOME ID, BOY.
D'OH!
PLEASE HAVE ID READY. - MANAGEMENT -
I NEED TO SEE SOME ID BEFORE I CAN SHOW YOU ANY FIREARMS, SON.
HERE YA GO.
PLEASE HAVE ID READY. - MANAGEMENT -
KING'S GUN & AMMO SHOP
PLEASE HAVE ID READY. - MANAGEMENT -
KING'S GUN & AMMO SHOP
PLEASE HAVE ID READY. - MANAGEMENT -
YOU'RE A 58-YEAR-OLD BLACK LADY FROM MISSOURI NAMED "CINDY"?
YES, I AM.
PLEASE HAVE ID READY. - MANAGEMENT -
LET ME GET THIS STRAIGHT, SON. YOU WANT TO BUY FIREARMS.
CORRECT.
PLEASE HAVE ID READY. - MANAGEMENT -
YOUR ID SAYS YOU'RE FROM MISSOURI...
CORRECT.
PLEASE HAVE ID READY. - MANAGEMENT -
KING'S GUN SHOP
58 YEARS OLD...
CORRECT.
PLEASE HAVE ID READY. - MANAGEMENT -
BLACK LADY NAMED "CINDY"?
I LOST SOME WEIGHT.
PLEASE HAVE ID READY. - MANAGEMENT -
I'M JUST TRYING TO EXERCISE MY CONSTITUTIONAL RIGHT TO BEAR ARMS. IT'S NOT A FAKE ID. HEY. LEGGO!
BOOT!
DON'T TELL ME, YOU DIDN'T GET THE GUNS, DID YOU?
YOU COMMIE!!

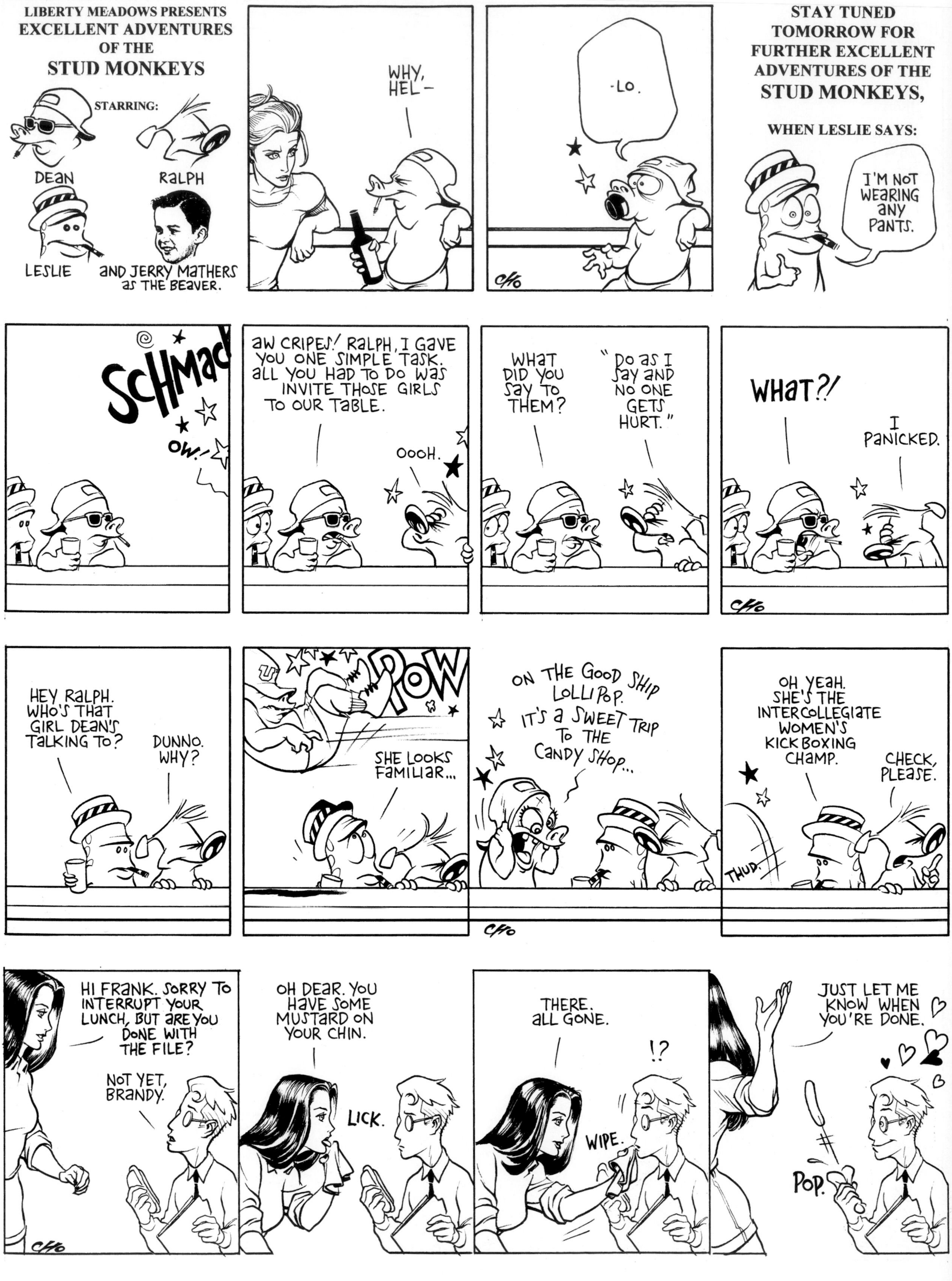
LIBERTY MEADOWS PRESENTS
EXCELLENT ADVENTURES OF THE
STUD MONKEYS
STARRING:
DEAN
RALPH
LESLIE
AND JERRY MATHERS AS THE BEAVER.
WHY, HEL–
-LO.
STAY TUNED TOMORROW FOR FURTHER EXCELLENT ADVENTURES OF THE
STUD MONKEYS,
WHEN LESLIE SAYS:
I'M NOT WEARING ANY PANTS.
SCHMAC
OW!
AW CRIPES! RALPH, I GAVE YOU ONE SIMPLE TASK. ALL YOU HAD TO DO WAS INVITE THOSE GIRLS TO OUR TABLE.
OOOH.
WHAT DID YOU SAY TO THEM?
"DO AS I SAY AND NO ONE GETS HURT."
WHAT?!
I PANICKED.
HEY RALPH. WHO'S THAT GIRL DEAN'S TALKING TO?
DUNNO. WHY?
POW
SHE LOOKS FAMILIAR...
ON THE GOOD SHIP LOLLIPOP. IT'S A SWEET TRIP TO THE CANDY SHOP...
OH YEAH. SHE'S THE INTERCOLLEGIATE WOMEN'S KICKBOXING CHAMP.
CHECK, PLEASE.
THUD.
HI FRANK. SORRY TO INTERRUPT YOUR LUNCH, BUT ARE YOU DONE WITH THE FILE?
NOT YET, BRANDY.
OH DEAR. YOU HAVE SOME MUSTARD ON YOUR CHIN.
LICK.
THERE. ALL GONE.
!?
WIPE.
JUST LET ME KNOW WHEN YOU'RE DONE.
POP.

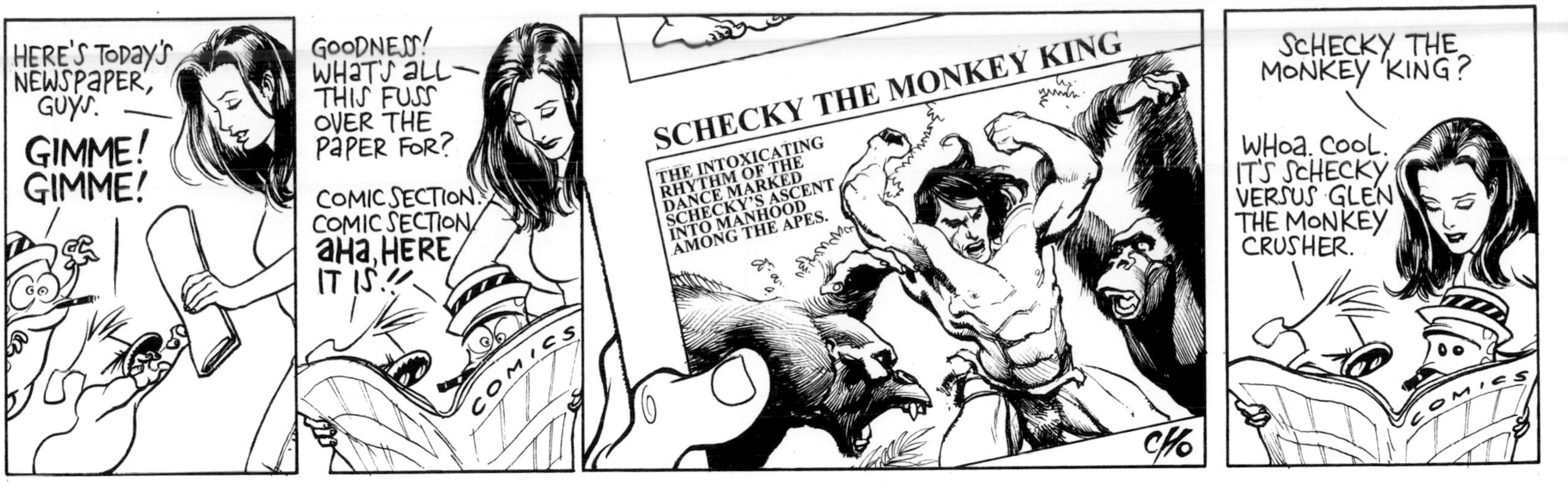
HERE'S TODAY'S NEWSPAPER, GUYS.
GIMME! GIMME!
GOODNESS! WHAT'S ALL THIS FUSS OVER THE PAPER FOR?
COMIC SECTION. COMIC SECTION. AHA, HERE IT IS!!
COMICS
SCHECKY THE MONKEY KING
THE INTOXICATING RHYTHM OF THE DANCE MARKED SCHECKY'S ASCENT INTO MANHOOD AMONG THE APES.
SCHECKY THE MONKEY KING?
WHOA. COOL. IT'S SCHECKY VERSUS GLEN THE MONKEY CRUSHER.
COMICS

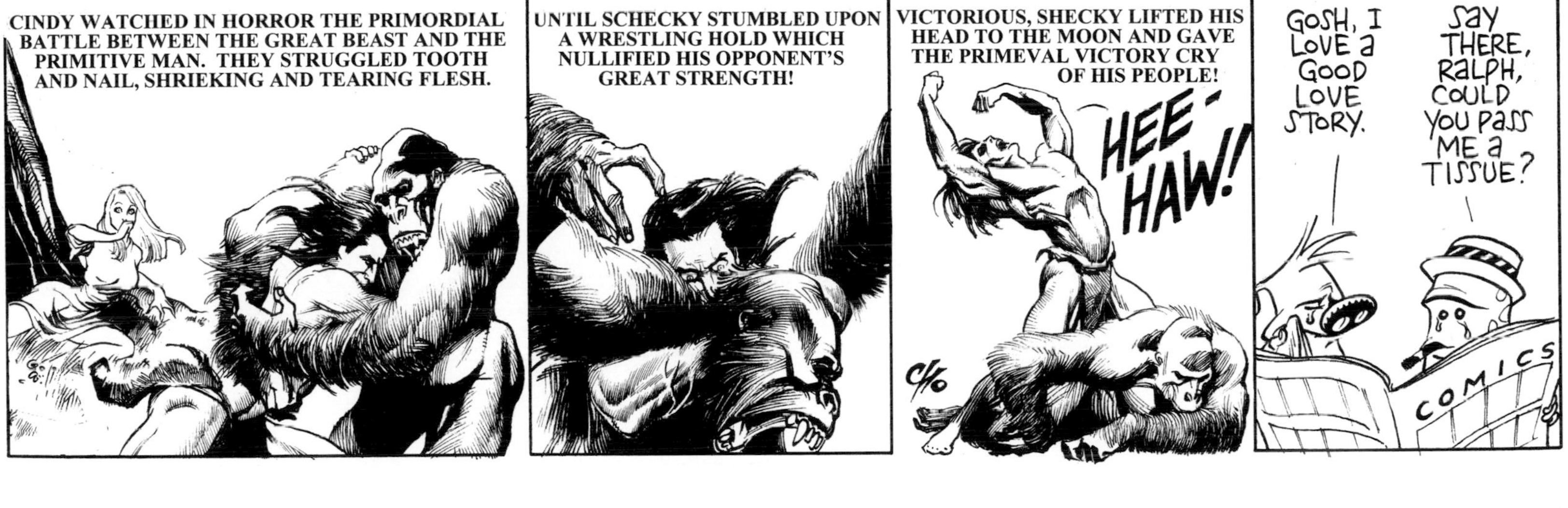
CINDY WATCHED IN HORROR THE PRIMORDIAL BATTLE BETWEEN THE GREAT BEAST AND THE PRIMITIVE MAN. THEY STRUGGLED TOOTH AND NAIL, SHRIEKING AND TEARING FLESH.
UNTIL SCHECKY STUMBLED UPON A WRESTLING HOLD WHICH NULLIFIED HIS OPPONENT'S GREAT STRENGTH!
VICTORIOUS, SHECKY LIFTED HIS HEAD TO THE MOON AND GAVE THE PRIMEVAL VICTORY CRY OF HIS PEOPLE!
HEE-HAW!
GOSH, I LOVE A GOOD LOVE STORY.
SAY THERE, RALPH, COULD YOU PASS ME A TISSUE?
COMICS

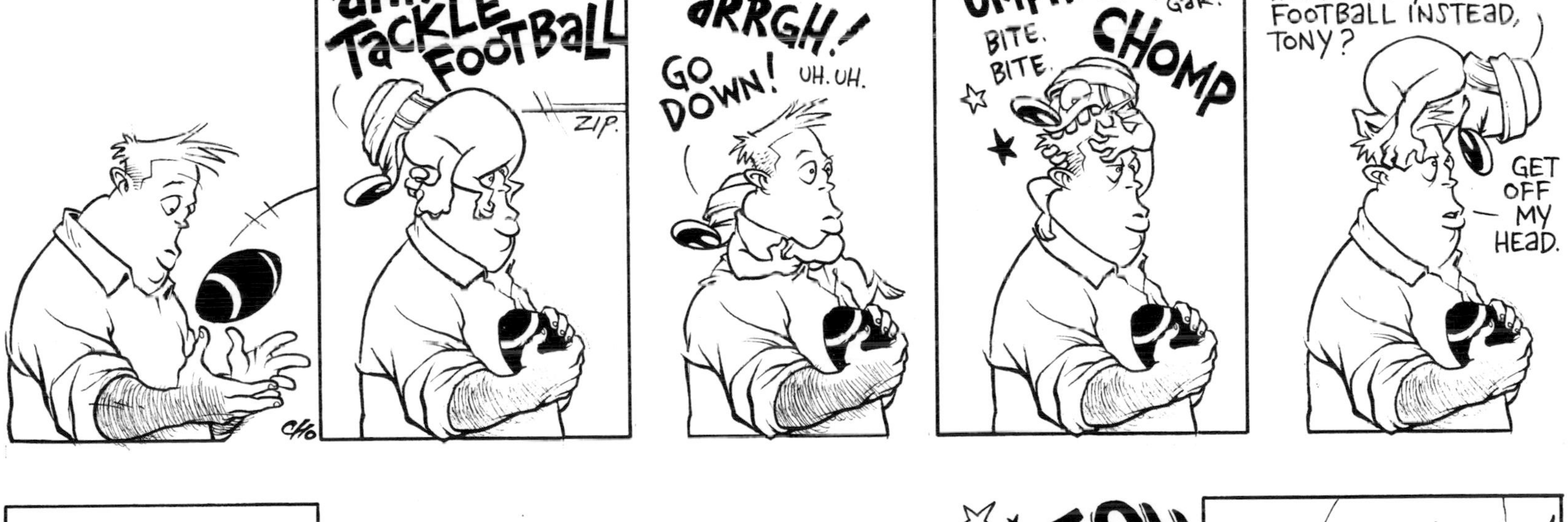
AHHHH!!
TACKLE FOOTBALL
ZIP.
ARRGH!
GRRR.
GO DOWN!
UH. UH.
UMPH. UMPH.
GAK.
BITE. BITE.
CHOMP
WANNA PLAY "TOUCH" FOOTBALL INSTEAD, TONY?
GET OFF MY HEAD.

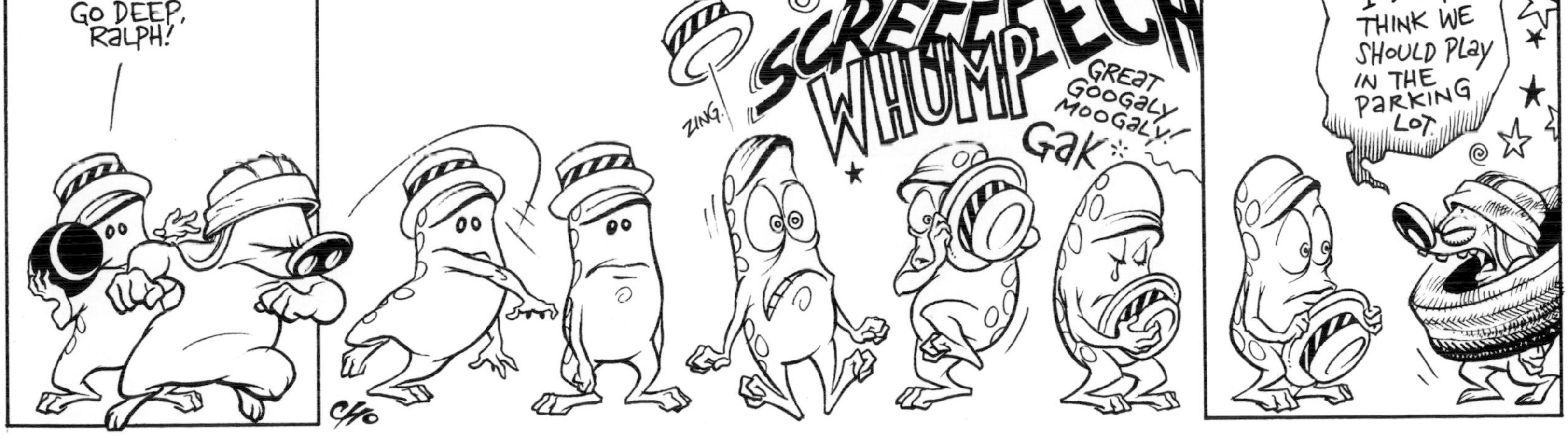
GO DEEP, RALPH!
ZING.
SCREEEEECH
WHUMP
GREAT GOOGALY MOOGALY!
GAK
I DON'T THINK WE SHOULD PLAY IN THE PARKING LOT.

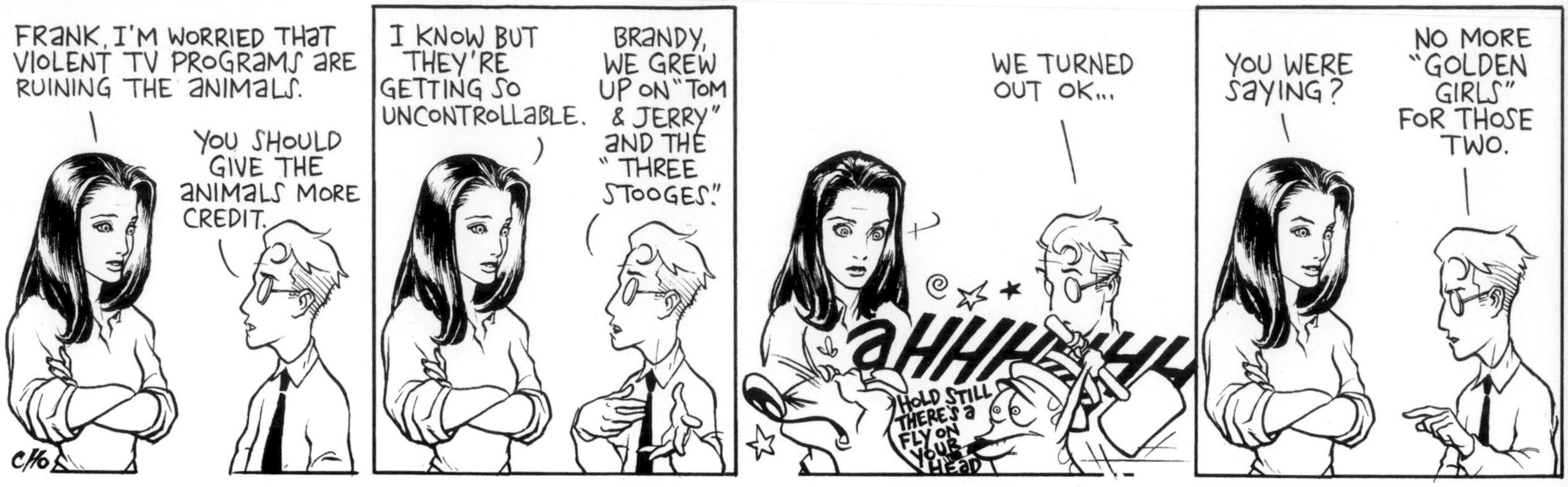
FRANK, I'M WORRIED THAT VIOLENT TV PROGRAMS ARE RUINING THE ANIMALS.
YOU SHOULD GIVE THE ANIMALS MORE CREDIT.
I KNOW BUT THEY'RE GETTING SO UNCONTROLLABLE.
BRANDY, WE GREW UP ON "TOM & JERRY" AND THE "THREE STOOGES."
WE TURNED OUT OK...
AHHHHHHH
HOLD STILL THERE'S A FLY ON YOUR HEAD
YOU WERE SAYING?
NO MORE "GOLDEN GIRLS" FOR THOSE TWO.

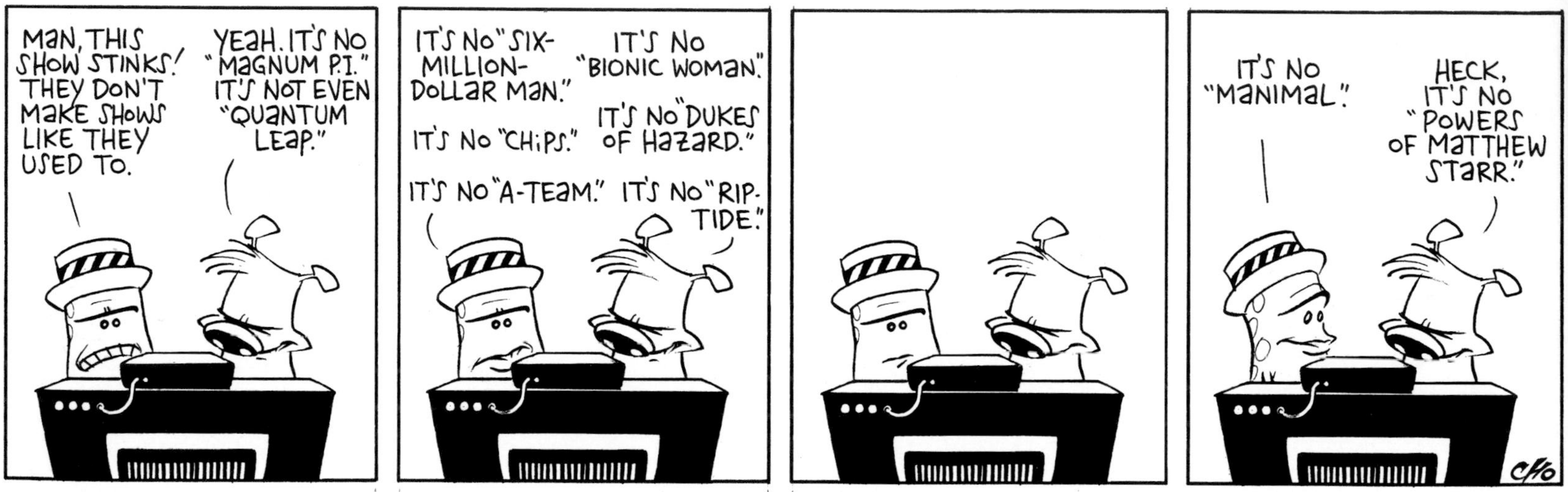
MAN, THIS SHOW STINKS! THEY DON'T MAKE SHOWS LIKE THEY USED TO.
YEAH. IT'S NO "MAGNUM P.I." IT'S NOT EVEN "QUANTUM LEAP."
IT'S NO "SIX-MILLION-DOLLAR MAN."
IT'S NO "BIONIC WOMAN."
IT'S NO "CHIPS."
IT'S NO "DUKES OF HAZARD."
IT'S NO "A-TEAM."
IT'S NO "RIP-TIDE."
IT'S NO "MANIMAL."
HECK, IT'S NO "POWERS OF MATTHEW STARR."

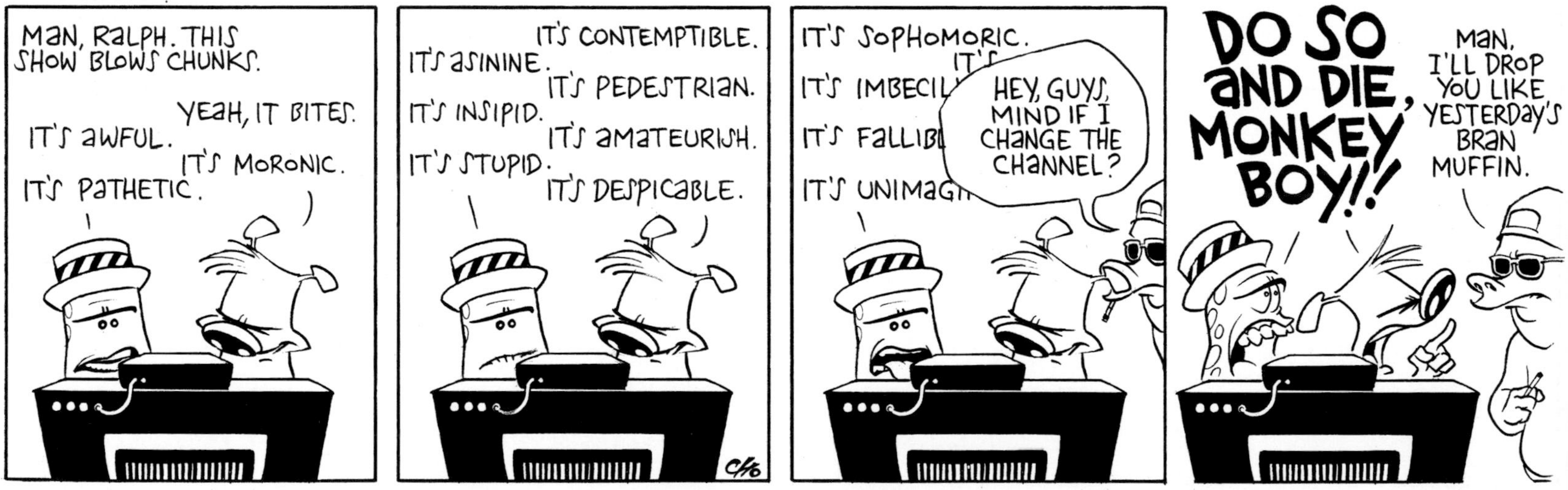
MAN, RALPH. THIS SHOW BLOWS CHUNKS.
YEAH, IT BITES.
IT'S AWFUL.
IT'S MORONIC.
IT'S PATHETIC.
IT'S CONTEMPTIBLE.
IT'S ASININE.
IT'S PEDESTRIAN.
IT'S INSIPID.
IT'S AMATEURISH.
IT'S STUPID.
IT'S DESPICABLE.
IT'S SOPHOMORIC.
HEY, GUYS, MIND IF I CHANGE THE CHANNEL?
DO SO AND DIE, MONKEY BOY!!!
MAN, I'LL DROP YOU LIKE YESTERDAY'S BRAN MUFFIN.

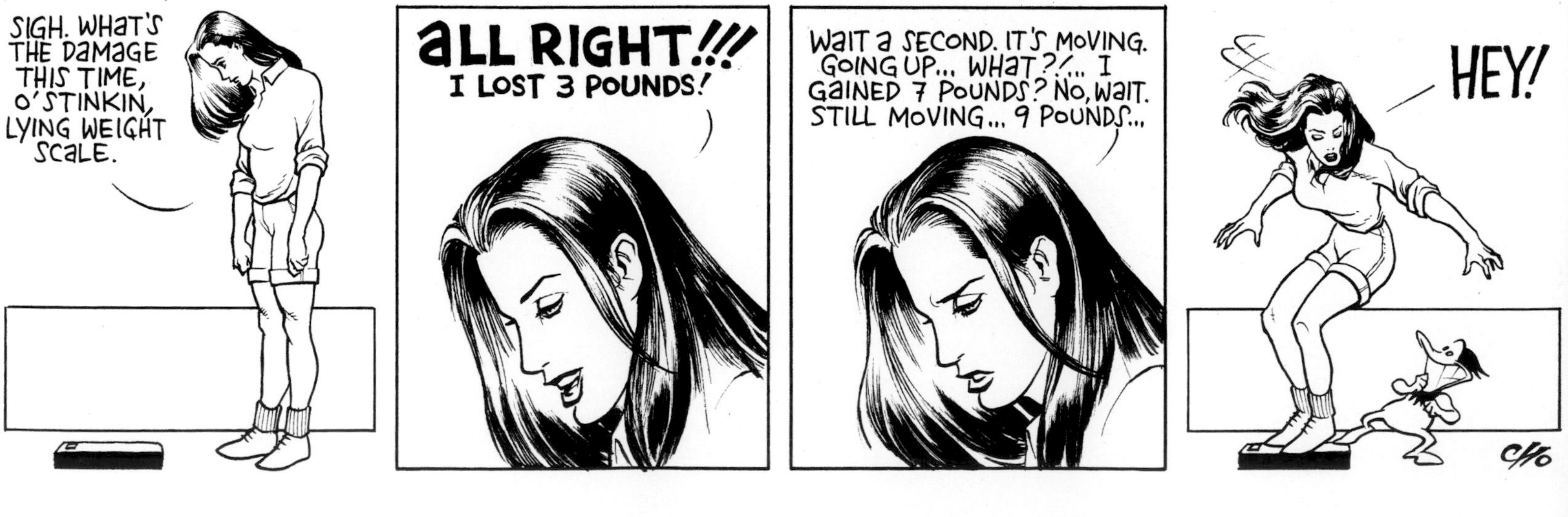
SIGH. WHAT'S THE DAMAGE THIS TIME, O'STINKIN, LYING WEIGHT SCALE.
ALL RIGHT!!! I LOST 3 POUNDS!
WAIT A SECOND. IT'S MOVING. GOING UP... WHAT?!... I GAINED 7 POUNDS? NO, WAIT. STILL MOVING... 9 POUNDS...
HEY!

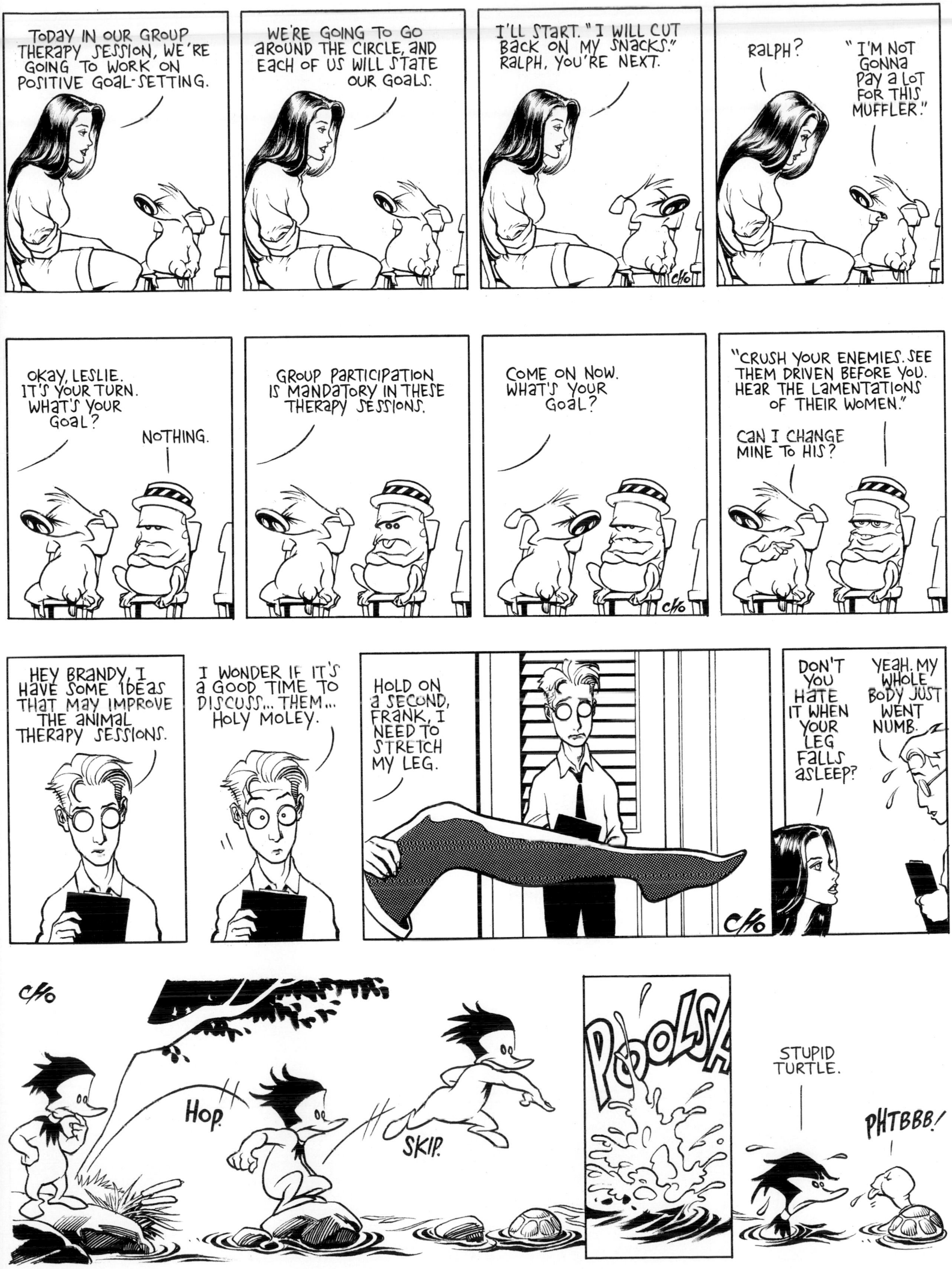
TODAY IN OUR GROUP THERAPY SESSION, WE'RE GOING TO WORK ON POSITIVE GOAL-SETTING.
WE'RE GOING TO GO AROUND THE CIRCLE, AND EACH OF US WILL STATE OUR GOALS.
I'LL START. "I WILL CUT BACK ON MY SNACKS." RALPH, YOU'RE NEXT.
RALPH?
"I'M NOT GONNA PAY A LOT FOR THIS MUFFLER."
OKAY, LESLIE. IT'S YOUR TURN. WHAT'S YOUR GOAL?
NOTHING.
GROUP PARTICIPATION IS MANDATORY IN THESE THERAPY SESSIONS.
COME ON NOW. WHAT'S YOUR GOAL?
"CRUSH YOUR ENEMIES. SEE THEM DRIVEN BEFORE YOU. HEAR THE LAMENTATIONS OF THEIR WOMEN."
CAN I CHANGE MINE TO HIS?
HEY BRANDY, I HAVE SOME IDEAS THAT MAY IMPROVE THE ANIMAL THERAPY SESSIONS.
I WONDER IF IT'S A GOOD TIME TO DISCUSS... THEM... HOLY MOLEY.
HOLD ON A SECOND, FRANK, I NEED TO STRETCH MY LEG.
DON'T YOU HATE IT WHEN YOUR LEG FALLS ASLEEP?
YEAH. MY WHOLE BODY JUST WENT NUMB.
HOP
SKIP
POOLSH
STUPID TURTLE.
PHTBBB!

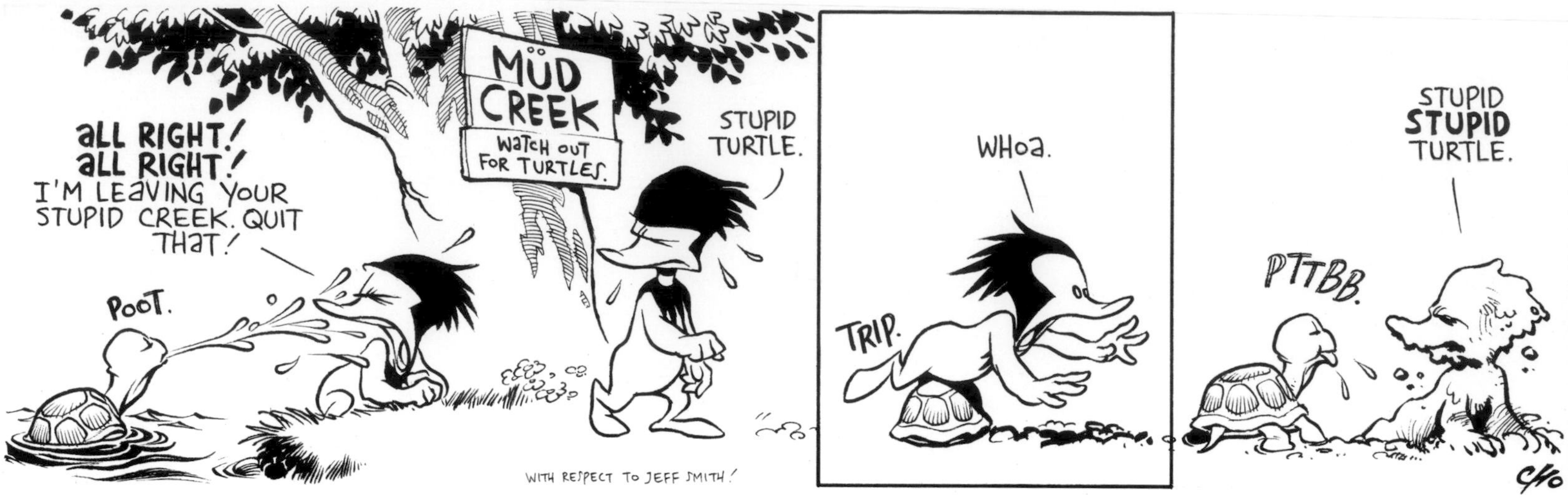
MÜD CREEK
WATCH OUT FOR TURTLES.
ALL RIGHT! ALL RIGHT! I'M LEAVING YOUR STUPID CREEK. QUIT THAT!
POOT.
STUPID TURTLE.
WITH RESPECT TO JEFF SMITH!
WHOA.
TRIP.
PTTBB.
STUPID STUPID TURTLE.
CHO

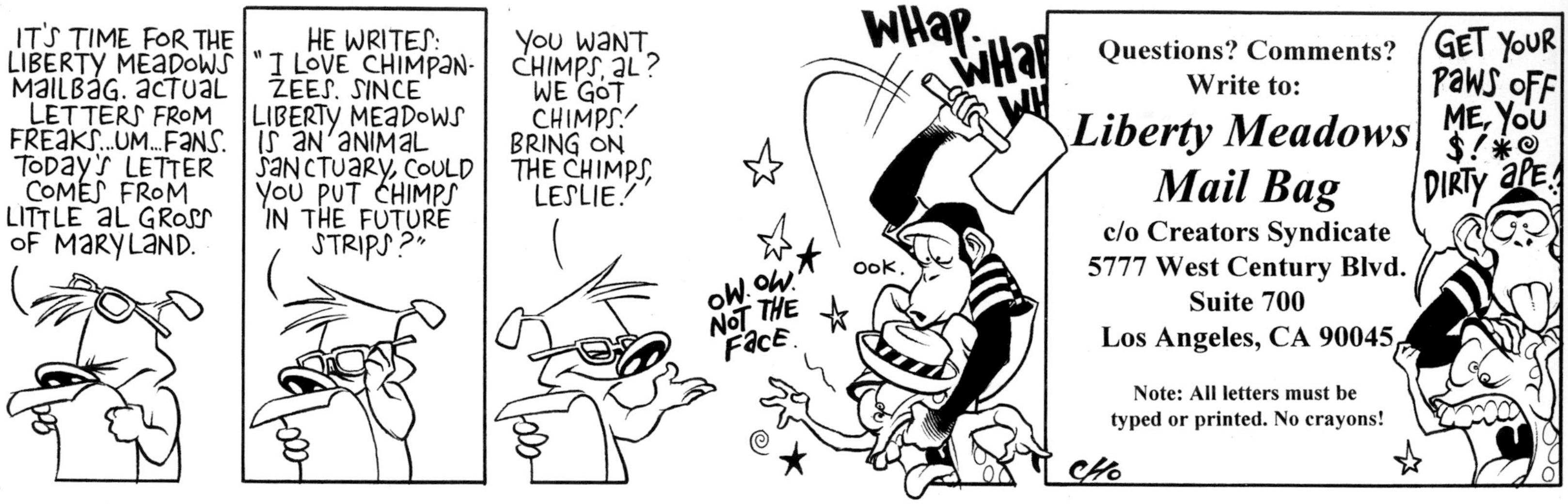
IT'S TIME FOR THE LIBERTY MEADOWS MAILBAG. ACTUAL LETTERS FROM FREAKS...UM...FANS. TODAY'S LETTER COMES FROM LITTLE AL GROSS OF MARYLAND.
HE WRITES: "I LOVE CHIMPANZEES. SINCE LIBERTY MEADOWS IS AN ANIMAL SANCTUARY, COULD YOU PUT CHIMPS IN THE FUTURE STRIPS?"
YOU WANT CHIMPS, AL? WE GOT CHIMPS! BRING ON THE CHIMPS, LESLIE!
WHAP. WHAP WH
OOK.
OW. OW. NOT THE FACE.
Questions? Comments?
Write to:
Liberty Meadows
Mail Bag
c/o Creators Syndicate
5777 West Century Blvd.
Suite 700
Los Angeles, CA 90045
Note: All letters must be typed or printed. No crayons!
GET YOUR PAWS OFF ME, YOU $!*@ DIRTY APE!
CHO

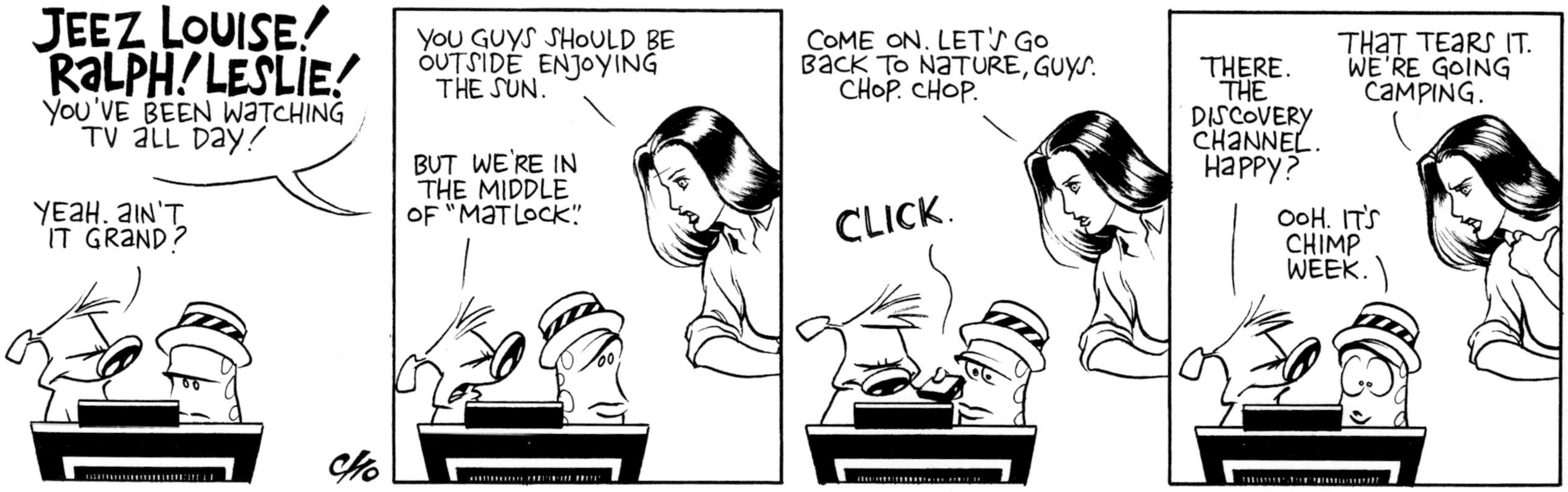
JEEZ LOUISE! RALPH! LESLIE! YOU'VE BEEN WATCHING TV ALL DAY!
YEAH. AIN'T IT GRAND?
CHO
YOU GUYS SHOULD BE OUTSIDE ENJOYING THE SUN.
BUT WE'RE IN THE MIDDLE OF "MATLOCK."
COME ON. LET'S GO BACK TO NATURE, GUYS. CHOP. CHOP.
CLICK.
THERE. THE DISCOVERY CHANNEL. HAPPY?
THAT TEARS IT. WE'RE GOING CAMPING.
OOH. IT'S CHIMP WEEK.

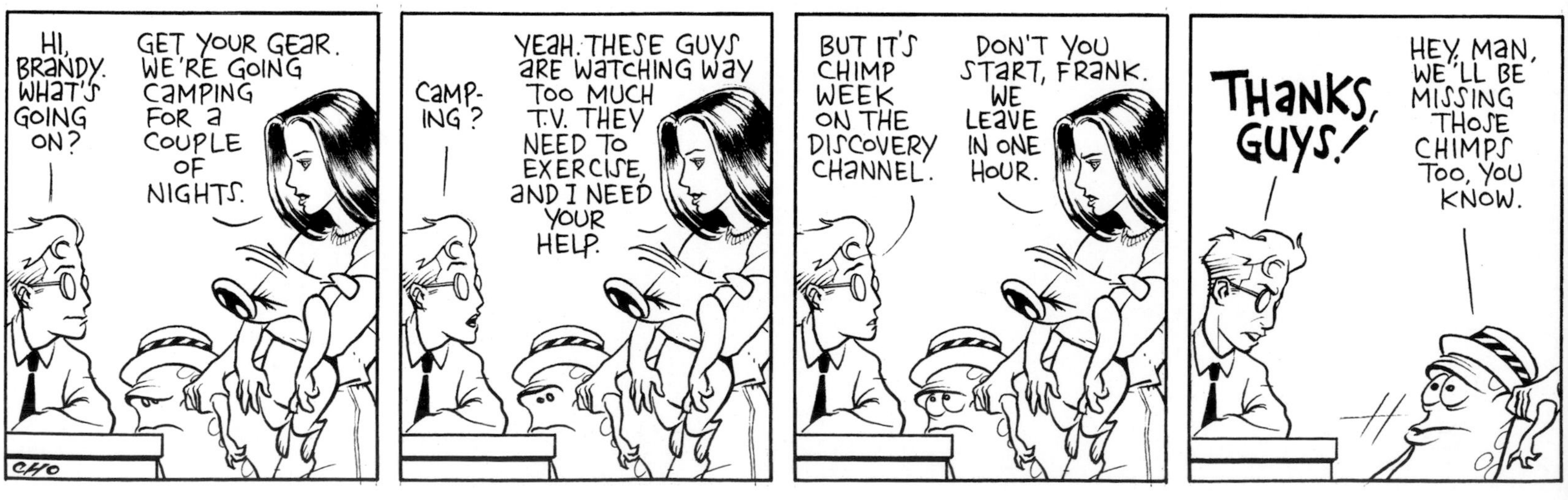
HI, BRANDY. WHAT'S GOING ON?
GET YOUR GEAR. WE'RE GOING CAMPING FOR A COUPLE OF NIGHTS.
CHO
CAMPING?
YEAH. THESE GUYS ARE WATCHING WAY TOO MUCH T.V. THEY NEED TO EXERCISE, AND I NEED YOUR HELP.
BUT IT'S CHIMP WEEK ON THE DISCOVERY CHANNEL.
DON'T YOU START, FRANK. WE LEAVE IN ONE HOUR.
THANKS, GUYS!
HEY, MAN, WE'LL BE MISSING THOSE CHIMPS TOO, YOU KNOW.

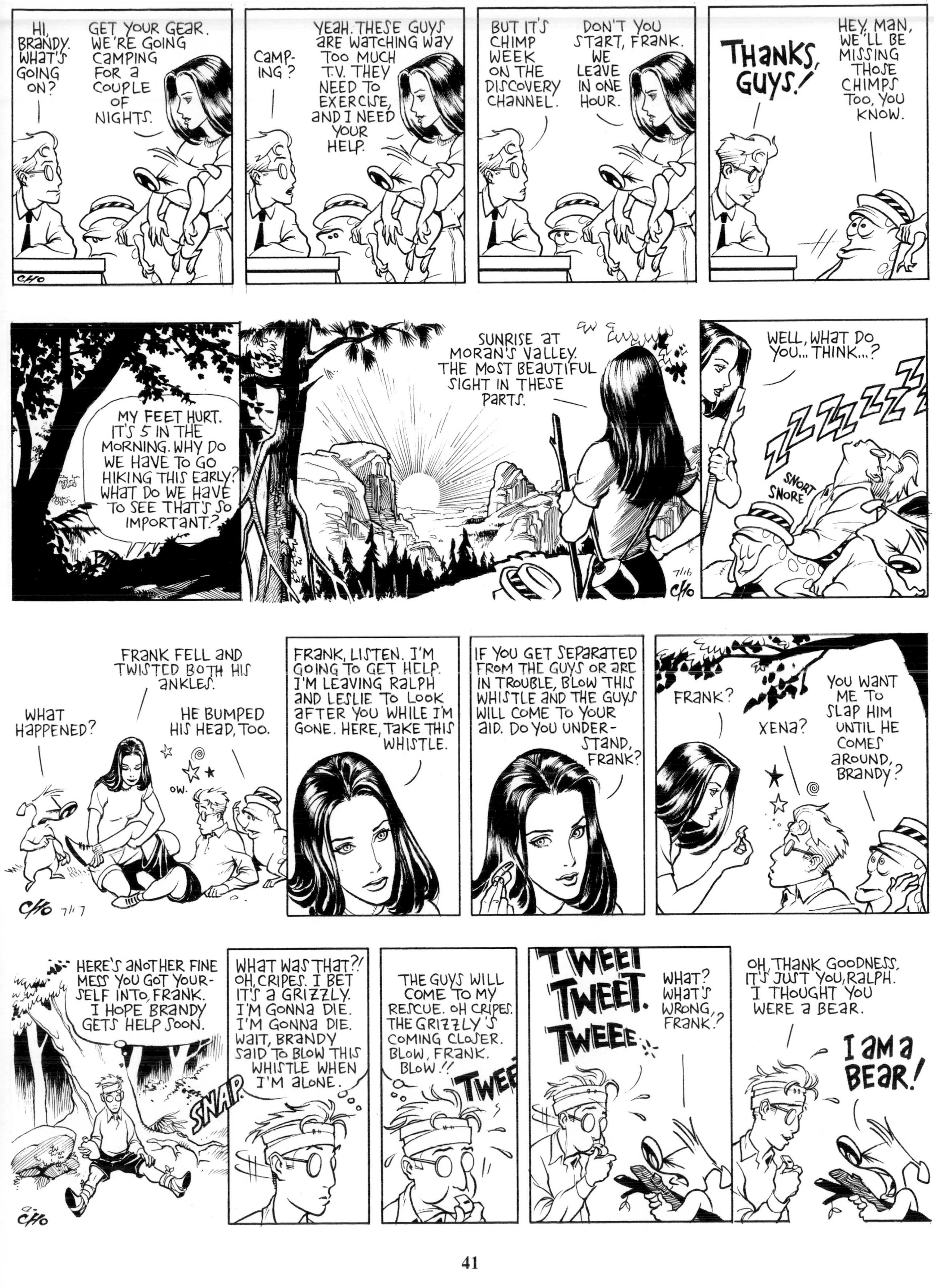
HI, BRANDY. WHAT'S GOING ON?
GET YOUR GEAR. WE'RE GOING CAMPING FOR A COUPLE OF NIGHTS.
CAMP-ING?
YEAH. THESE GUYS ARE WATCHING WAY TOO MUCH T.V. THEY NEED TO EXERCISE, AND I NEED YOUR HELP.
BUT IT'S CHIMP WEEK ON THE DISCOVERY CHANNEL.
DON'T YOU START, FRANK. WE LEAVE IN ONE HOUR.
THANKS, GUYS!
HEY, MAN, WE'LL BE MISSING THOSE CHIMPS TOO, YOU KNOW.
CHO
MY FEET HURT. IT'S 5 IN THE MORNING. WHY DO WE HAVE TO GO HIKING THIS EARLY? WHAT DO WE HAVE TO SEE THAT'S SO IMPORTANT?
SUNRISE AT MORAN'S VALLEY. THE MOST BEAUTIFUL SIGHT IN THESE PARTS.
WELL, WHAT DO YOU... THINK...?
ZZZZZZZ
SNORT
SNORE
7/6
CHO
WHAT HAPPENED?
FRANK FELL AND TWISTED BOTH HIS ANKLES.
HE BUMPED HIS HEAD, TOO.
OW.
CHO 7/7
FRANK, LISTEN. I'M GOING TO GET HELP. I'M LEAVING RALPH AND LESLIE TO LOOK AFTER YOU WHILE I'M GONE. HERE, TAKE THIS WHISTLE.
IF YOU GET SEPARATED FROM THE GUYS OR ARE IN TROUBLE, BLOW THIS WHISTLE AND THE GUYS WILL COME TO YOUR AID. DO YOU UNDERSTAND, FRANK?
FRANK?
XENA?
YOU WANT ME TO SLAP HIM UNTIL HE COMES AROUND, BRANDY?
HERE'S ANOTHER FINE MESS YOU GOT YOURSELF INTO, FRANK. I HOPE BRANDY GETS HELP SOON.
SNAP.
CHO
WHAT WAS THAT?! OH, CRIPES. I BET IT'S A GRIZZLY. I'M GONNA DIE. I'M GONNA DIE. WAIT, BRANDY SAID TO BLOW THIS WHISTLE WHEN I'M ALONE.
THE GUYS WILL COME TO MY RESCUE. OH CRIPES. THE GRIZZLY'S COMING CLOSER. BLOW, FRANK. BLOW!!
TWEE
TWEET TWEET. TWEEE
WHAT? WHAT'S WRONG, FRANK?
OH, THANK GOODNESS, IT'S JUST YOU, RALPH. I THOUGHT YOU WERE A BEAR.
I AM A BEAR!

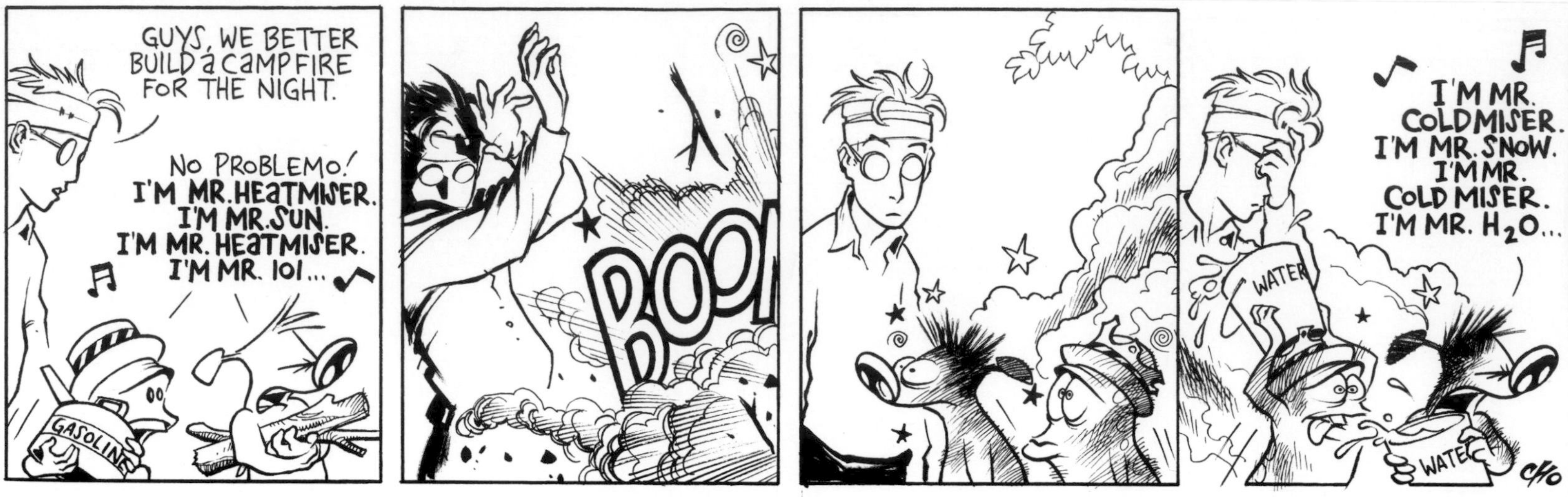
GUYS, WE BETTER BUILD A CAMPFIRE FOR THE NIGHT.
NO PROBLEMO! I'M MR. HEATMISER. I'M MR. SUN. I'M MR. HEATMISER. I'M MR. 101...
GASOLINE
BOOM
I'M MR. COLDMISER. I'M MR. SNOW. I'M MR. COLD MISER. I'M MR. H_2O...
WATER
WATE
CHO

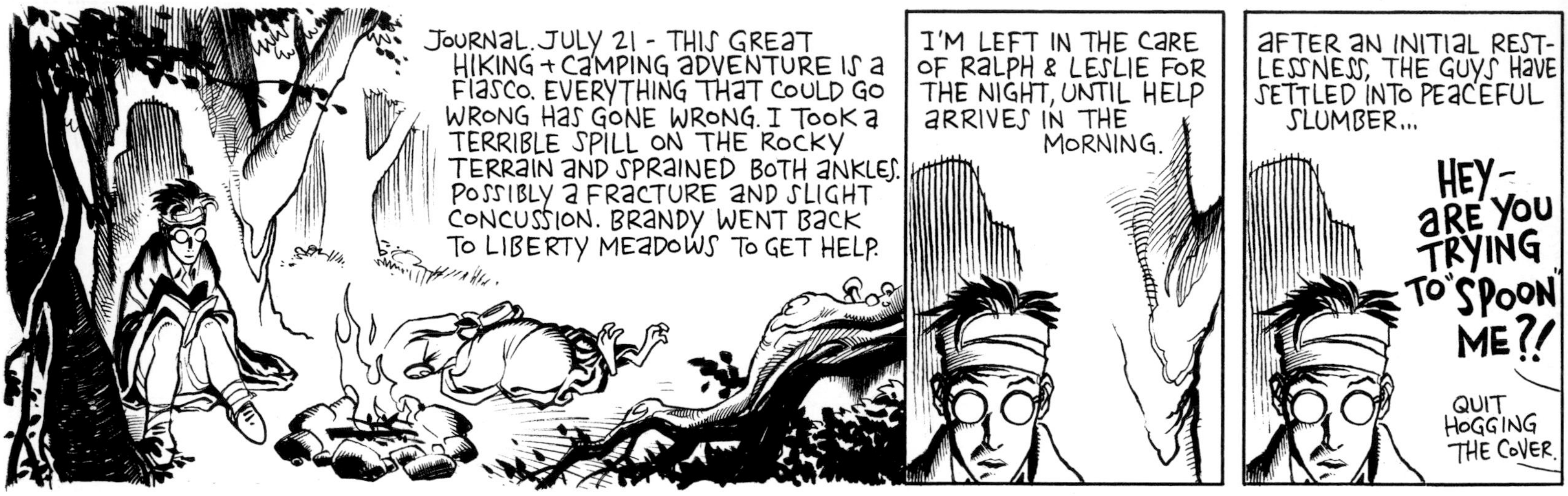
JOURNAL. JULY 21 - THIS GREAT HIKING + CAMPING ADVENTURE IS A FIASCO. EVERYTHING THAT COULD GO WRONG HAS GONE WRONG. I TOOK A TERRIBLE SPILL ON THE ROCKY TERRAIN AND SPRAINED BOTH ANKLES. POSSIBLY A FRACTURE AND SLIGHT CONCUSSION. BRANDY WENT BACK TO LIBERTY MEADOWS TO GET HELP.
I'M LEFT IN THE CARE OF RALPH & LESLIE FOR THE NIGHT, UNTIL HELP ARRIVES IN THE MORNING.
AFTER AN INITIAL RESTLESSNESS, THE GUYS HAVE SETTLED INTO PEACEFUL SLUMBER...
HEY- ARE YOU TRYING TO "SPOON" ME?!
QUIT HOGGING THE COVER.

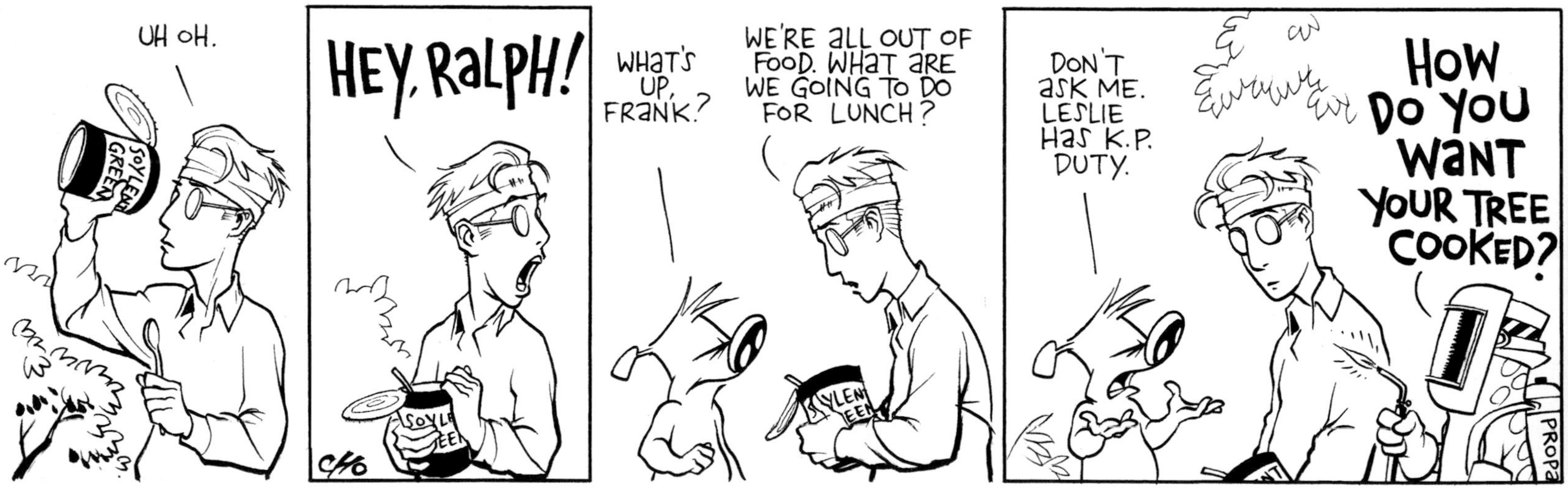
UH OH.
SOYLENT GREEN
HEY, RALPH!
CHO
WHAT'S UP, FRANK?
WE'RE ALL OUT OF FOOD. WHAT ARE WE GOING TO DO FOR LUNCH?
DON'T ASK ME. LESLIE HAS K.P. DUTY.
HOW DO YOU WANT YOUR TREE COOKED?
PROPA

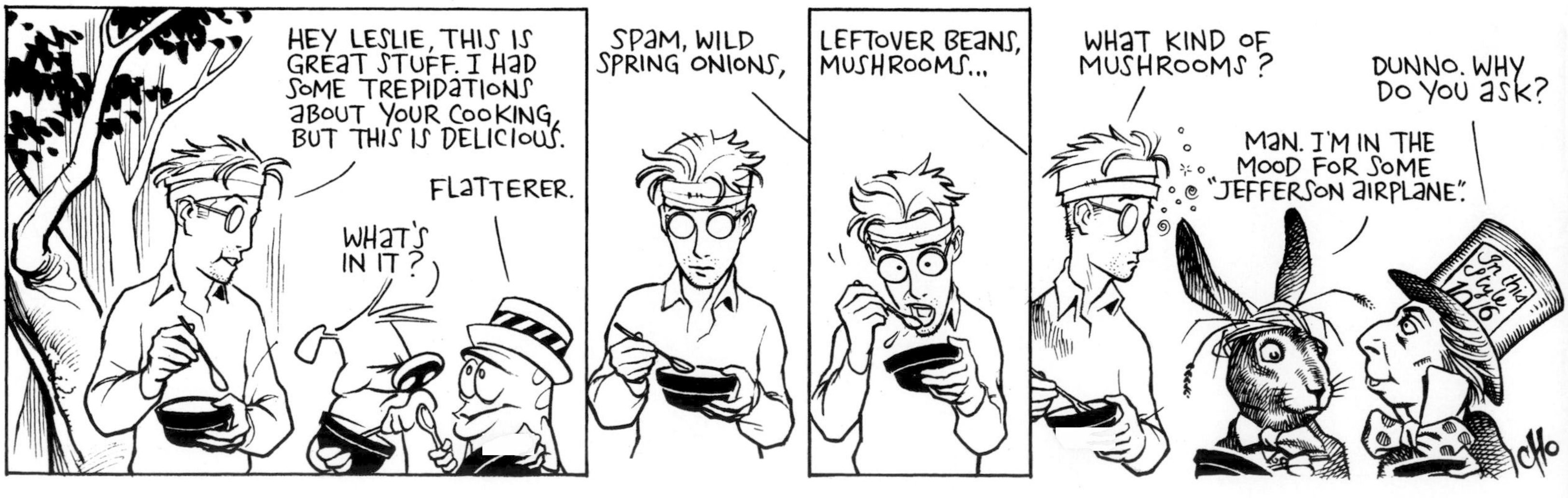
HEY LESLIE, THIS IS GREAT STUFF. I HAD SOME TREPIDATIONS ABOUT YOUR COOKING, BUT THIS IS DELICIOUS.
FLATTERER.
WHAT'S IN IT?
SPAM, WILD SPRING ONIONS,
LEFTOVER BEANS, MUSHROOMS...
WHAT KIND OF MUSHROOMS?
DUNNO. WHY DO YOU ASK?
MAN. I'M IN THE MOOD FOR SOME "JEFFERSON AIRPLANE".
CHO

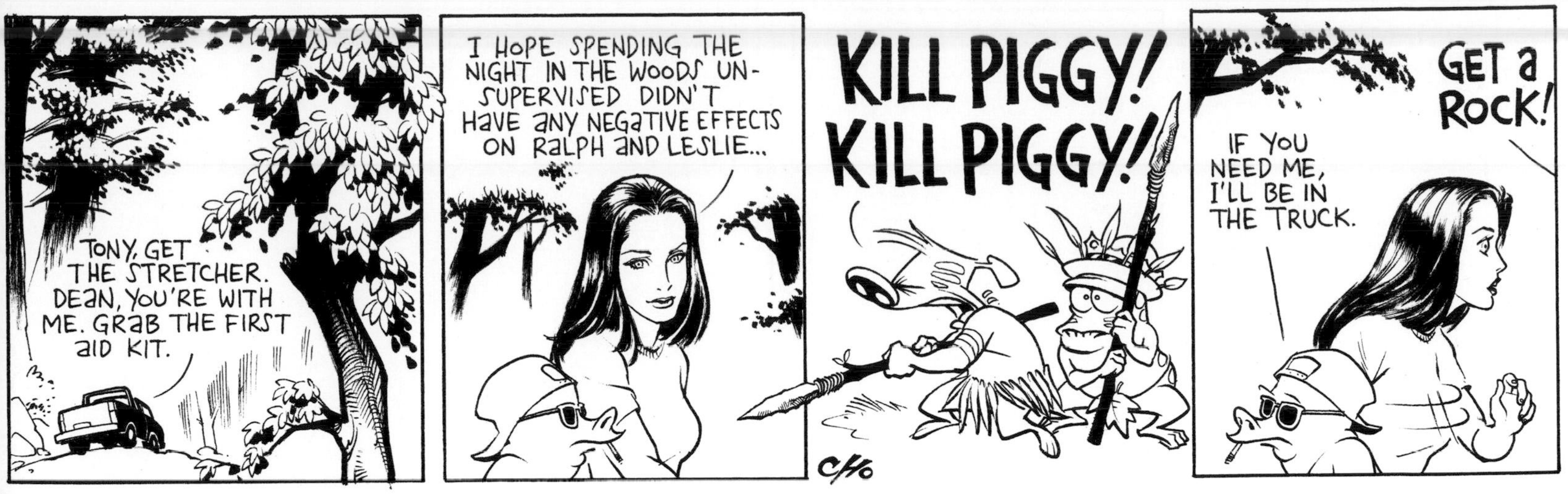
TONY, GET THE STRETCHER. DEAN, YOU'RE WITH ME. GRAB THE FIRST AID KIT.
I HOPE SPENDING THE NIGHT IN THE WOODS UN-SUPERVISED DIDN'T HAVE ANY NEGATIVE EFFECTS ON RALPH AND LESLIE...
KILL PIGGY! KILL PIGGY!
IF YOU NEED ME, I'LL BE IN THE TRUCK.
GET A ROCK!
CHO

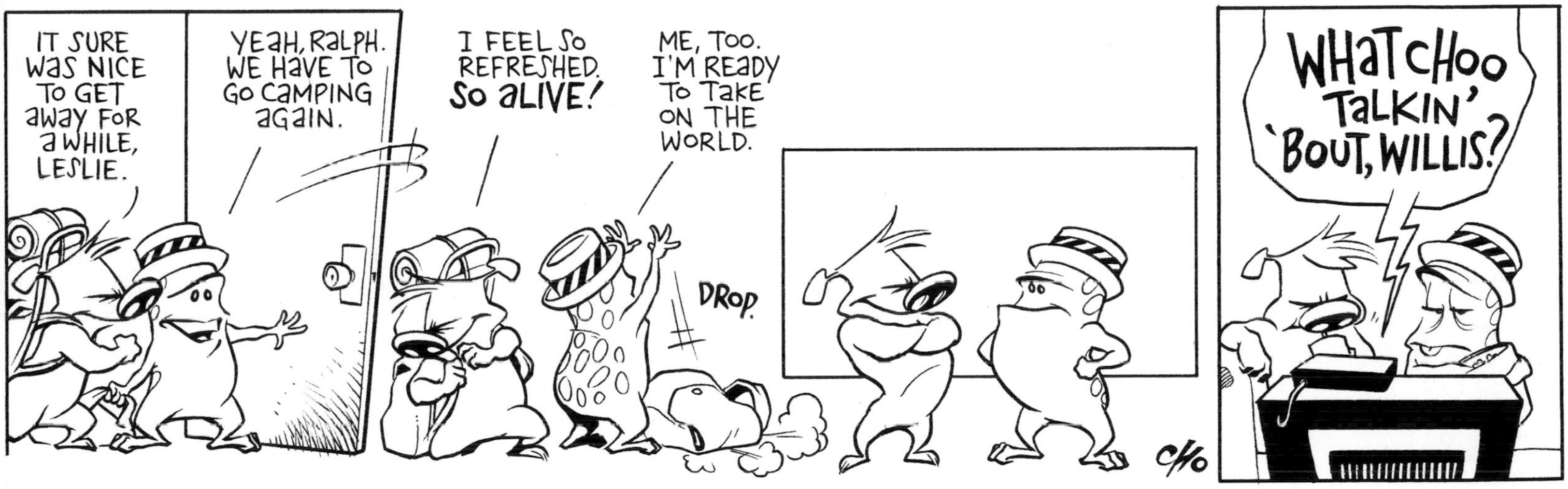
IT SURE WAS NICE TO GET AWAY FOR A WHILE, LESLIE.
YEAH, RALPH. WE HAVE TO GO CAMPING AGAIN.
I FEEL SO REFRESHED. SO ALIVE!
ME, TOO. I'M READY TO TAKE ON THE WORLD.
DROP
CHO
WHATCHOO TALKIN' 'BOUT, WILLIS?

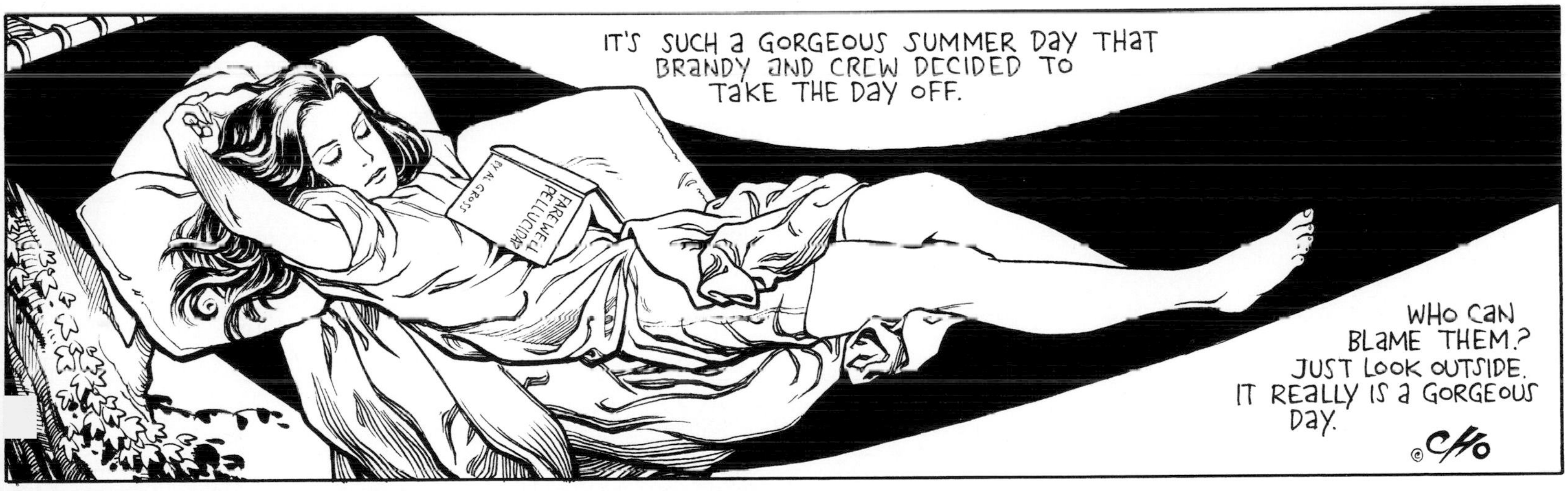
IT'S SUCH A GORGEOUS SUMMER DAY THAT BRANDY AND CREW DECIDED TO TAKE THE DAY OFF.
FAREWELL PELLUCIDAR
WHO CAN BLAME THEM? JUST LOOK OUTSIDE. IT REALLY IS A GORGEOUS DAY.
© CHO

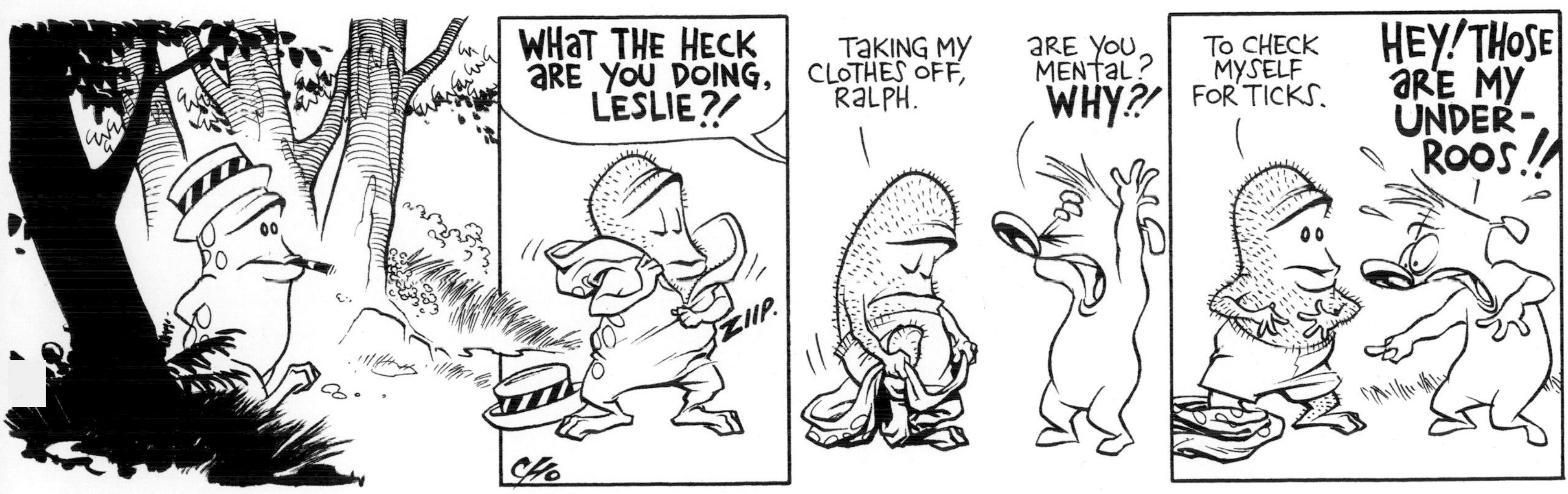
WHAT THE HECK ARE YOU DOING, LESLIE?!
ZIIP.
CHO
TAKING MY CLOTHES OFF, RALPH.
ARE YOU MENTAL? WHY?!
TO CHECK MYSELF FOR TICKS.
HEY! THOSE ARE MY UNDER-ROOS!!

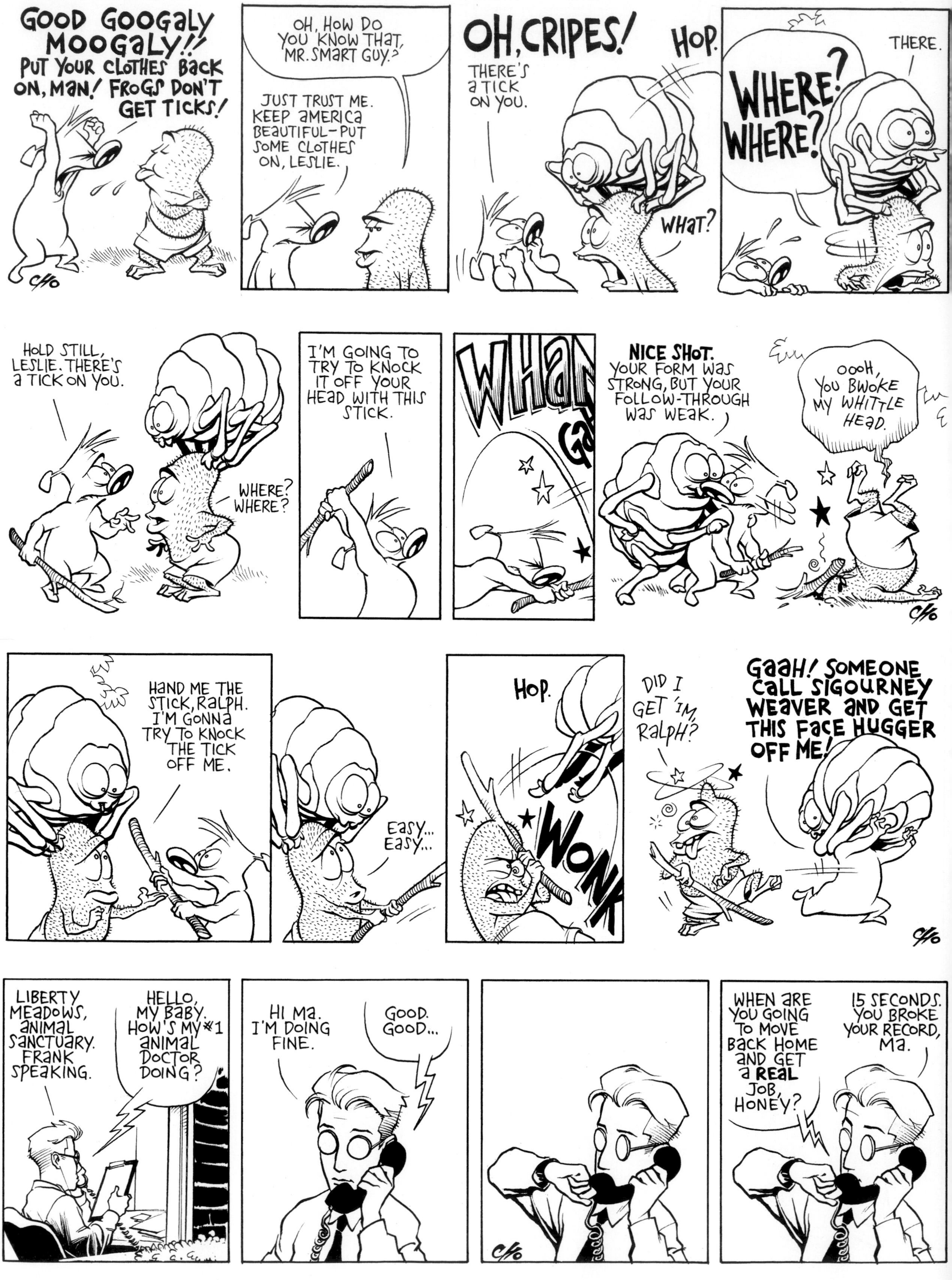
GOOD GOOGALY MOOGALY!! PUT YOUR CLOTHES BACK ON, MAN! FROGS DON'T GET TICKS!
CHO
OH, HOW DO YOU KNOW THAT, MR. SMART GUY?
JUST TRUST ME. KEEP AMERICA BEAUTIFUL—PUT SOME CLOTHES ON, LESLIE.
OH, CRIPES!
THERE'S A TICK ON YOU.
HOP.
WHAT?
THERE.
WHERE? WHERE?
HOLD STILL, LESLIE. THERE'S A TICK ON YOU.
WHERE? WHERE?
I'M GOING TO TRY TO KNOCK IT OFF YOUR HEAD WITH THIS STICK.
WHAP
NICE SHOT. YOUR FORM WAS STRONG, BUT YOUR FOLLOW-THROUGH WAS WEAK.
OOOH, YOU BWOKE MY WHITTLE HEAD.
CHO
HAND ME THE STICK, RALPH. I'M GONNA TRY TO KNOCK THE TICK OFF ME.
EASY... EASY...
HOP.
WONK
DID I GET 'IM, RALPH?
GAAH! SOMEONE CALL SIGOURNEY WEAVER AND GET THIS FACE HUGGER OFF ME!
CHO
LIBERTY MEADOWS, ANIMAL SANCTUARY. FRANK SPEAKING.
HELLO, MY BABY. HOW'S MY #1 ANIMAL DOCTOR DOING?
HI MA. I'M DOING FINE.
GOOD. GOOD...
CHO
WHEN ARE YOU GOING TO MOVE BACK HOME AND GET A REAL JOB, HONEY?
15 SECONDS. YOU BROKE YOUR RECORD, MA.

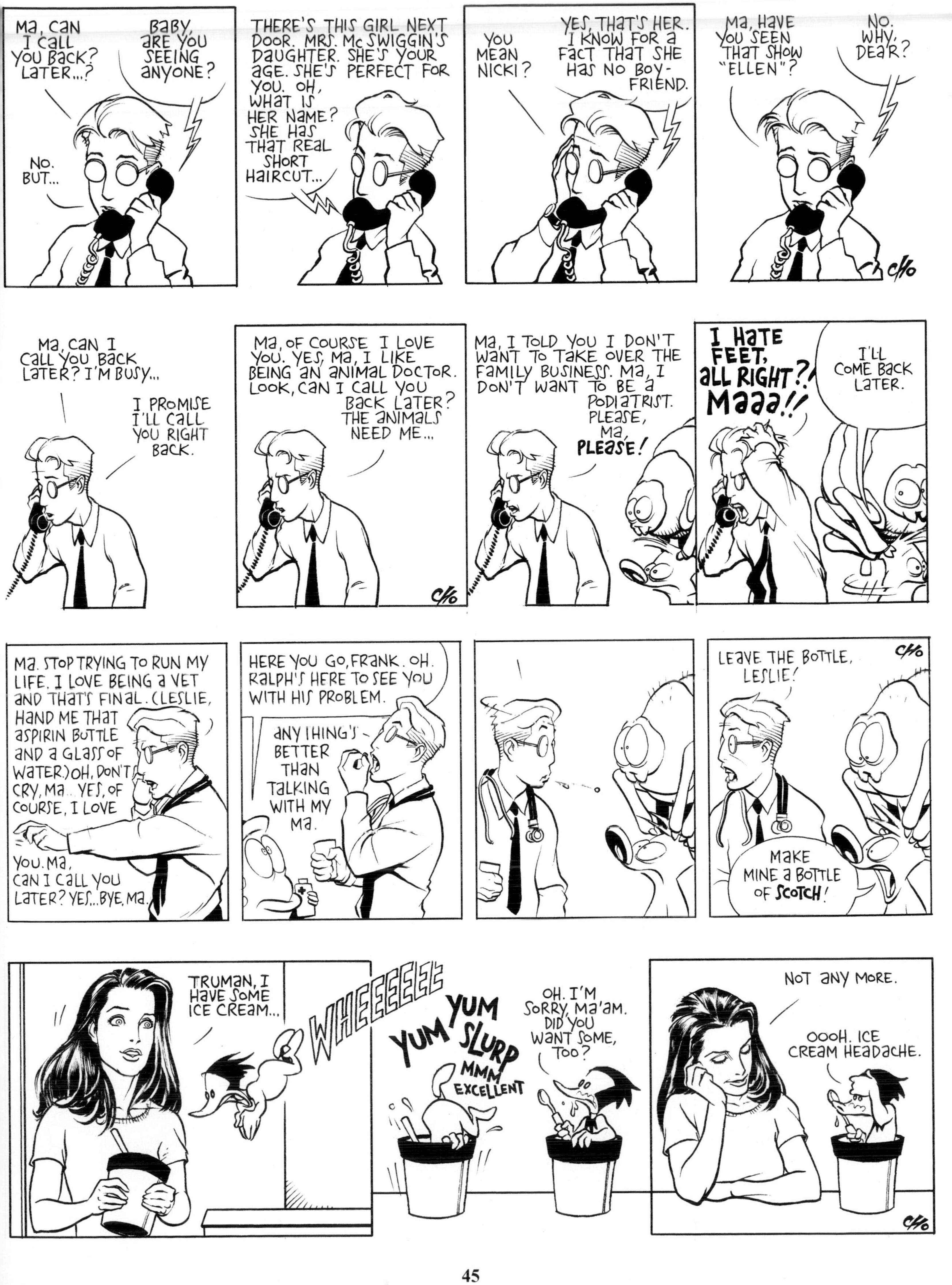
MA, CAN I CALL YOU BACK? LATER...?
BABY, ARE YOU SEEING ANYONE?
NO. BUT...
THERE'S THIS GIRL NEXT DOOR. MRS. McSWIGGIN'S DAUGHTER. SHE'S YOUR AGE. SHE'S PERFECT FOR YOU. OH, WHAT IS HER NAME? SHE HAS THAT REAL SHORT HAIRCUT...
YOU MEAN NICKI?
YES, THAT'S HER. I KNOW FOR A FACT THAT SHE HAS NO BOY-FRIEND.
MA, HAVE YOU SEEN THAT SHOW "ELLEN"?
NO. WHY, DEAR?
CHO
MA, CAN I CALL YOU BACK LATER? I'M BUSY...
I PROMISE I'LL CALL YOU RIGHT BACK.
MA, OF COURSE I LOVE YOU. YES, MA, I LIKE BEING AN ANIMAL DOCTOR. LOOK, CAN I CALL YOU BACK LATER? THE ANIMALS NEED ME...
CHO
MA, I TOLD YOU I DON'T WANT TO TAKE OVER THE FAMILY BUSINESS. MA, I DON'T WANT TO BE A PODIATRIST. PLEASE, MA, PLEASE!
I HATE FEET, ALL RIGHT?! MAAA!!
I'LL COME BACK LATER.
MA. STOP TRYING TO RUN MY LIFE. I LOVE BEING A VET AND THAT'S FINAL. (LESLIE, HAND ME THAT ASPIRIN BOTTLE AND A GLASS OF WATER.) OH, DON'T CRY, MA... YES, OF COURSE, I LOVE YOU. MA, CAN I CALL YOU LATER? YES... BYE, MA.
HERE YOU GO, FRANK. OH. RALPH'S HERE TO SEE YOU WITH HIS PROBLEM.
ANYTHING'S BETTER THAN TALKING WITH MY MA.
CHO
LEAVE THE BOTTLE, LESLIE!
MAKE MINE A BOTTLE OF SCOTCH!
TRUMAN, I HAVE SOME ICE CREAM...
WHEEEEEEE
YUM YUM SLURP
MMM EXCELLENT
OH. I'M SORRY, MA'AM. DID YOU WANT SOME, TOO?
NOT ANY MORE.
OOOH. ICE CREAM HEADACHE.
CHO

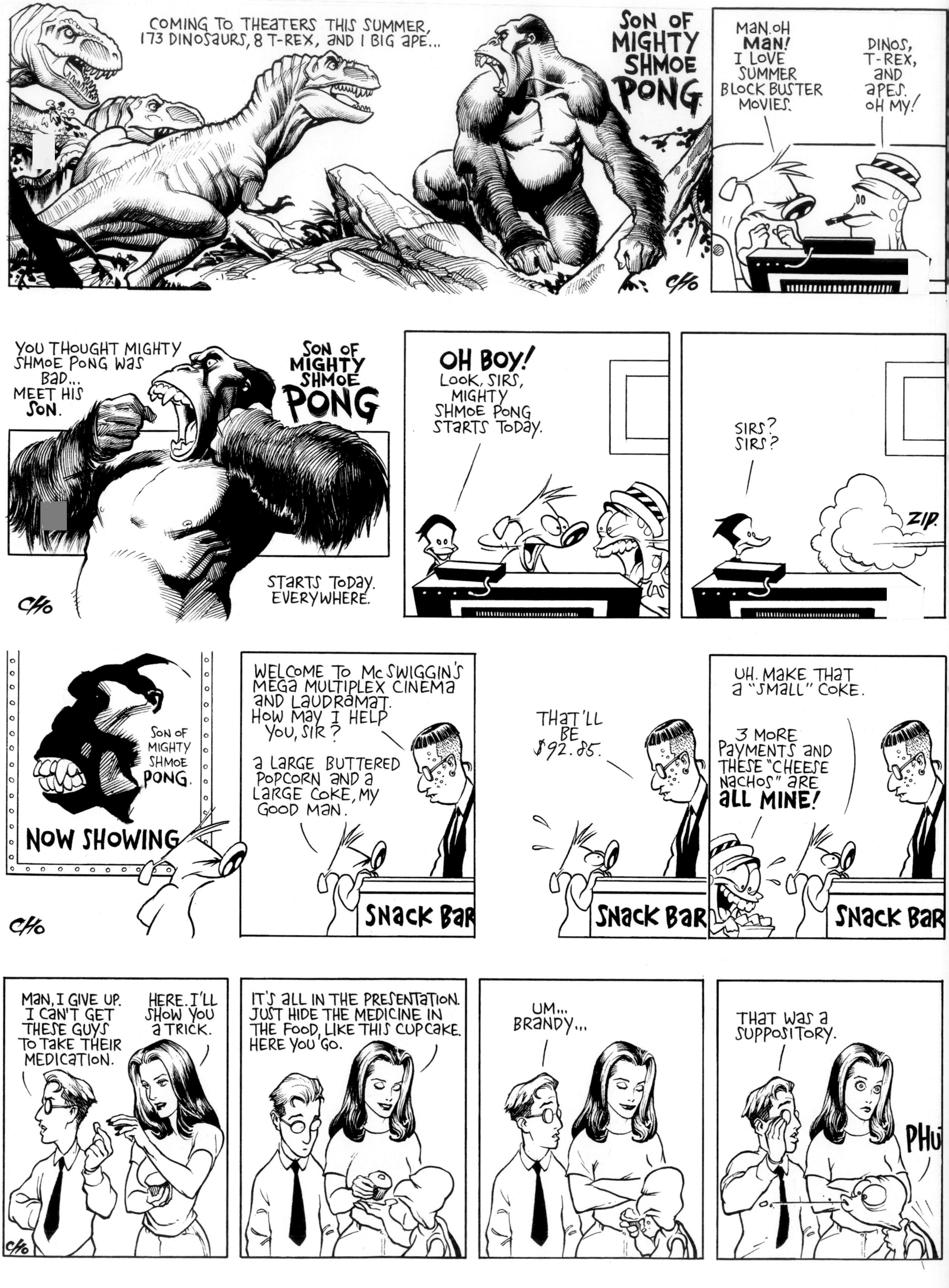
COMING TO THEATERS THIS SUMMER, 173 DINOSAURS, 8 T-REX, AND 1 BIG APE...
SON OF MIGHTY SHMOE PONG
MAN, OH MAN! I LOVE SUMMER BLOCK BUSTER MOVIES.
DINOS, T-REX, AND APES. OH MY!
YOU THOUGHT MIGHTY SHMOE PONG WAS BAD... MEET HIS SON.
SON OF MIGHTY SHMOE PONG
STARTS TODAY. EVERYWHERE.
OH BOY! LOOK, SIRS, MIGHTY SHMOE PONG STARTS TODAY.
SIRS? SIRS?
ZIP.
SON OF MIGHTY SHMOE PONG.
NOW SHOWING
WELCOME TO McSWIGGIN'S MEGA MULTIPLEX CINEMA AND LAUDRAMAT. HOW MAY I HELP YOU, SIR?
A LARGE BUTTERED POPCORN AND A LARGE COKE, MY GOOD MAN.
SNACK BAR
THAT'LL BE $92.85.
SNACK BAR
UH. MAKE THAT A "SMALL" COKE.
3 MORE PAYMENTS AND THESE "CHEESE NACHOS" ARE ALL MINE!
SNACK BAR
MAN, I GIVE UP. I CAN'T GET THESE GUYS TO TAKE THEIR MEDICATION.
HERE. I'LL SHOW YOU A TRICK.
IT'S ALL IN THE PRESENTATION. JUST HIDE THE MEDICINE IN THE FOOD, LIKE THIS CUPCAKE. HERE YOU GO.
UM... BRANDY...
THAT WAS A SUPPOSITORY.
PHU

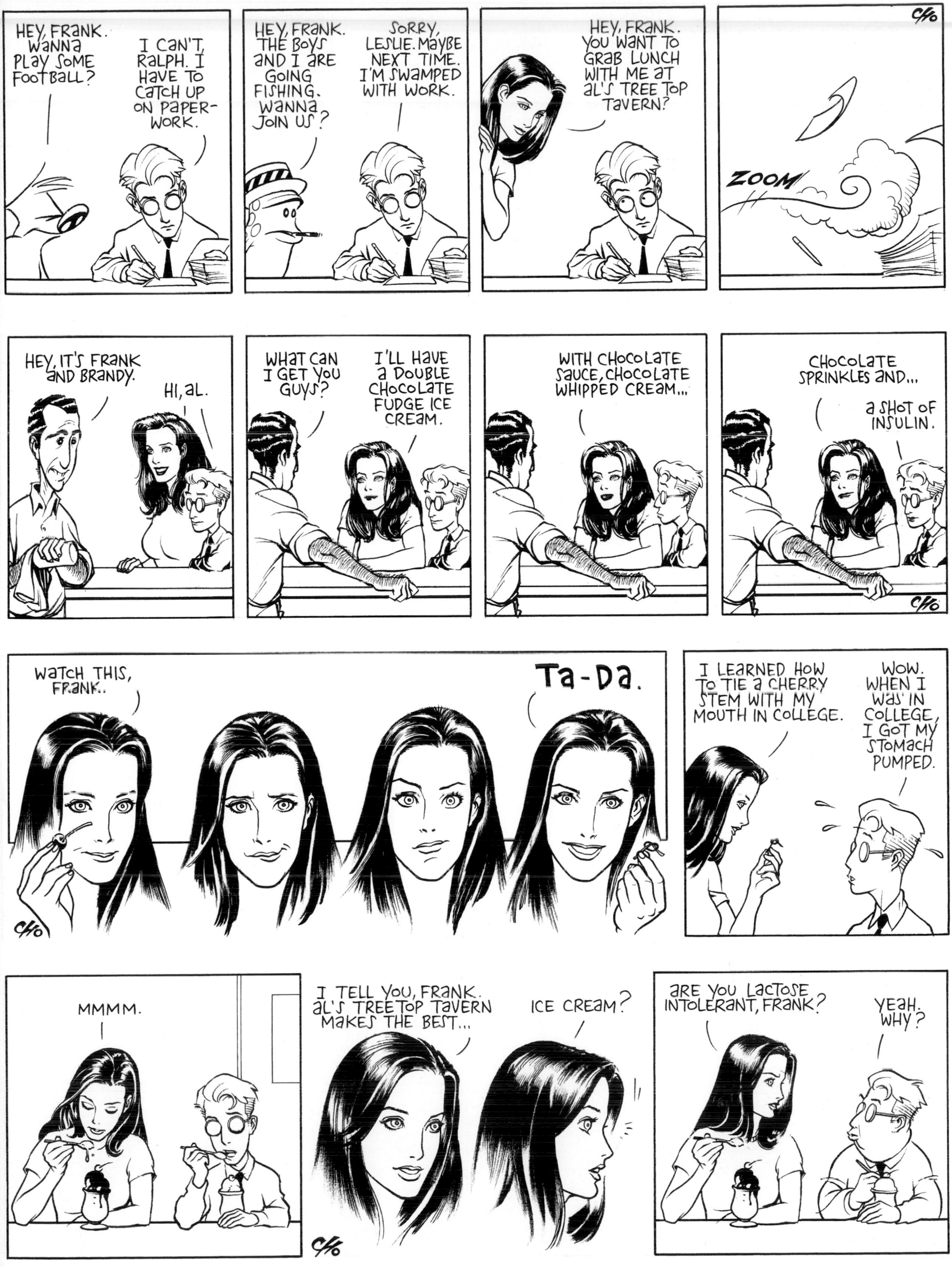
HEY, FRANK. WANNA PLAY SOME FOOTBALL?
I CAN'T, RALPH. I HAVE TO CATCH UP ON PAPER-WORK.
HEY, FRANK. THE BOYS AND I ARE GOING FISHING. WANNA JOIN US?
SORRY, LESLIE. MAYBE NEXT TIME. I'M SWAMPED WITH WORK.
HEY, FRANK. YOU WANT TO GRAB LUNCH WITH ME AT AL'S TREE TOP TAVERN?
ZOOM
HEY, IT'S FRANK AND BRANDY.
HI, AL.
WHAT CAN I GET YOU GUYS?
I'LL HAVE A DOUBLE CHOCOLATE FUDGE ICE CREAM.
WITH CHOCOLATE SAUCE, CHOCOLATE WHIPPED CREAM...
CHOCOLATE SPRINKLES AND...
A SHOT OF INSULIN.
WATCH THIS, FRANK..
TA-DA.
I LEARNED HOW TO TIE A CHERRY STEM WITH MY MOUTH IN COLLEGE.
WOW. WHEN I WAS IN COLLEGE, I GOT MY STOMACH PUMPED.
MMMM.
I TELL YOU, FRANK. AL'S TREETOP TAVERN MAKES THE BEST...
ICE CREAM?
ARE YOU LACTOSE INTOLERANT, FRANK?
YEAH. WHY?

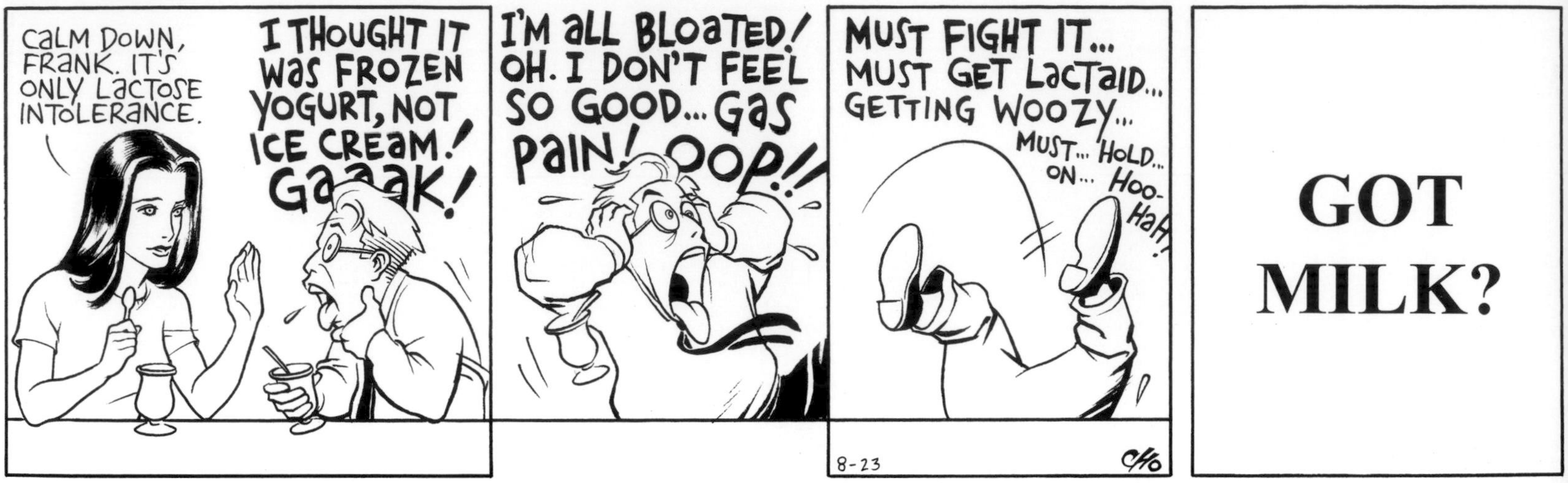
CALM DOWN, FRANK. IT'S ONLY LACTOSE INTOLERANCE.
I THOUGHT IT WAS FROZEN YOGURT, NOT ICE CREAM! GAAAK!
I'M ALL BLOATED! OH. I DON'T FEEL SO GOOD... GAS PAIN! OOP!!
MUST FIGHT IT... MUST GET LACTAID... GETTING WOOZY...
MUST... HOLD... ON... HOO-HAH!
8-23
CHO
GOT MILK?

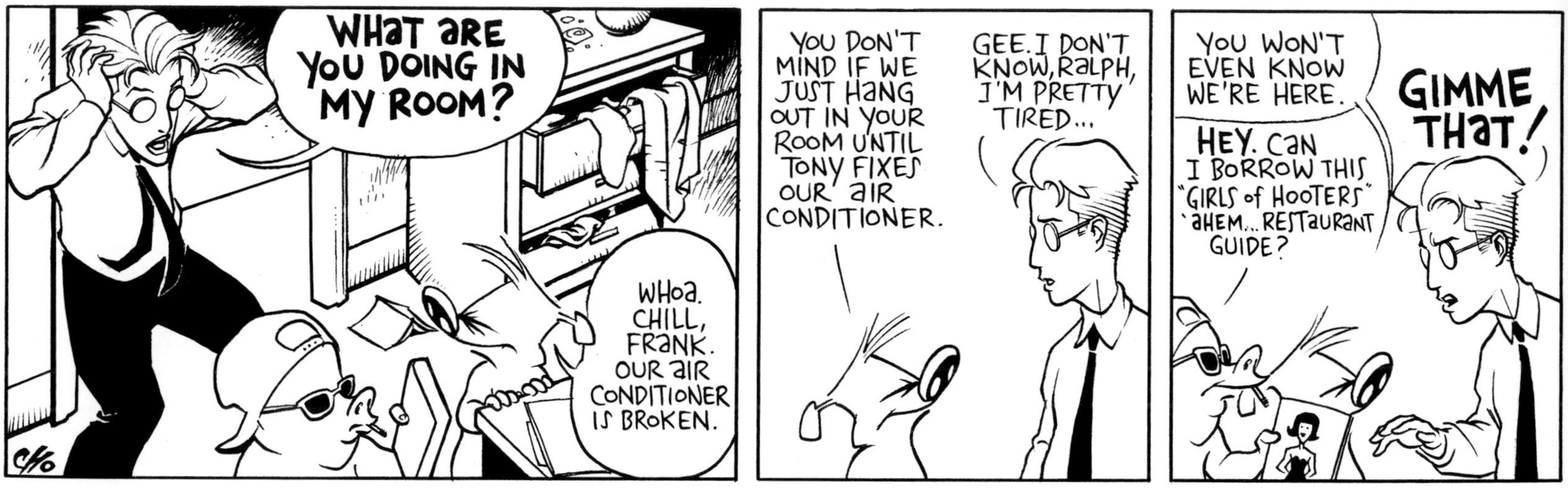
WHAT ARE YOU DOING IN MY ROOM?
WHOA. CHILL, FRANK. OUR AIR CONDITIONER IS BROKEN.
CHO
YOU DON'T MIND IF WE JUST HANG OUT IN YOUR ROOM UNTIL TONY FIXES OUR AIR CONDITIONER.
GEE. I DON'T KNOW, RALPH, I'M PRETTY TIRED...
YOU WON'T EVEN KNOW WE'RE HERE.
HEY. CAN I BORROW THIS "GIRLS OF HOOTERS" AHEM... RESTAURANT GUIDE?
GIMME THAT!

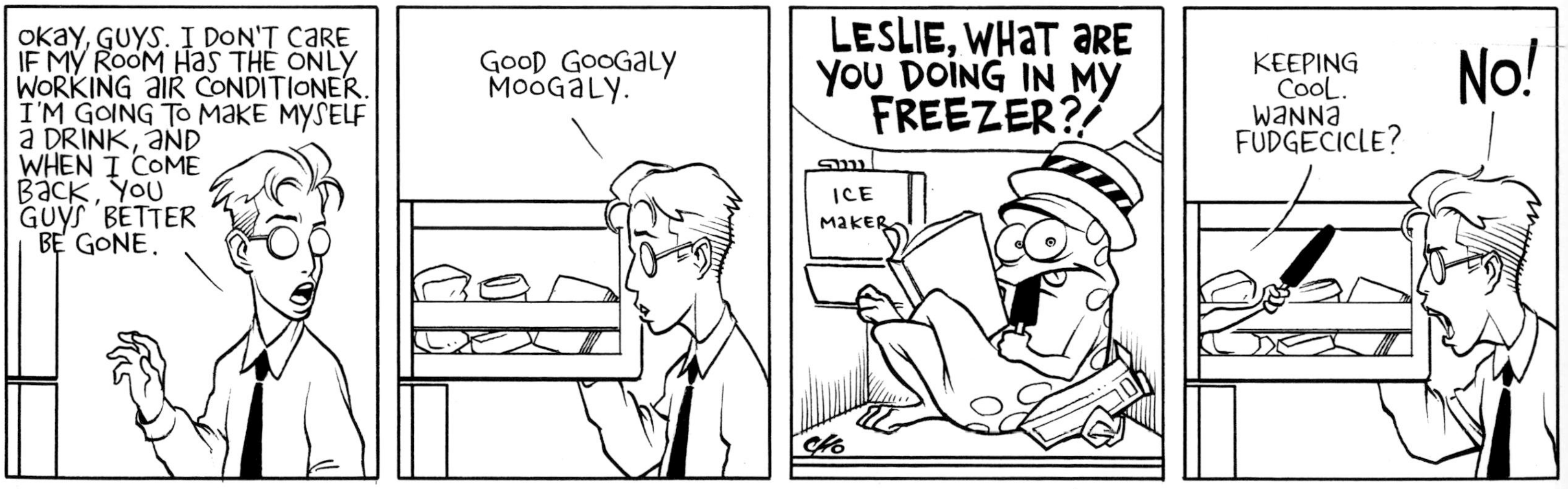
OKAY, GUYS. I DON'T CARE IF MY ROOM HAS THE ONLY WORKING AIR CONDITIONER. I'M GOING TO MAKE MYSELF A DRINK, AND WHEN I COME BACK, YOU GUYS BETTER BE GONE.
GOOD GOOGALY MOOGALY.
LESLIE, WHAT ARE YOU DOING IN MY FREEZER?!
ICE MAKER
CHO
KEEPING COOL. WANNA FUDGECICLE?
NO!

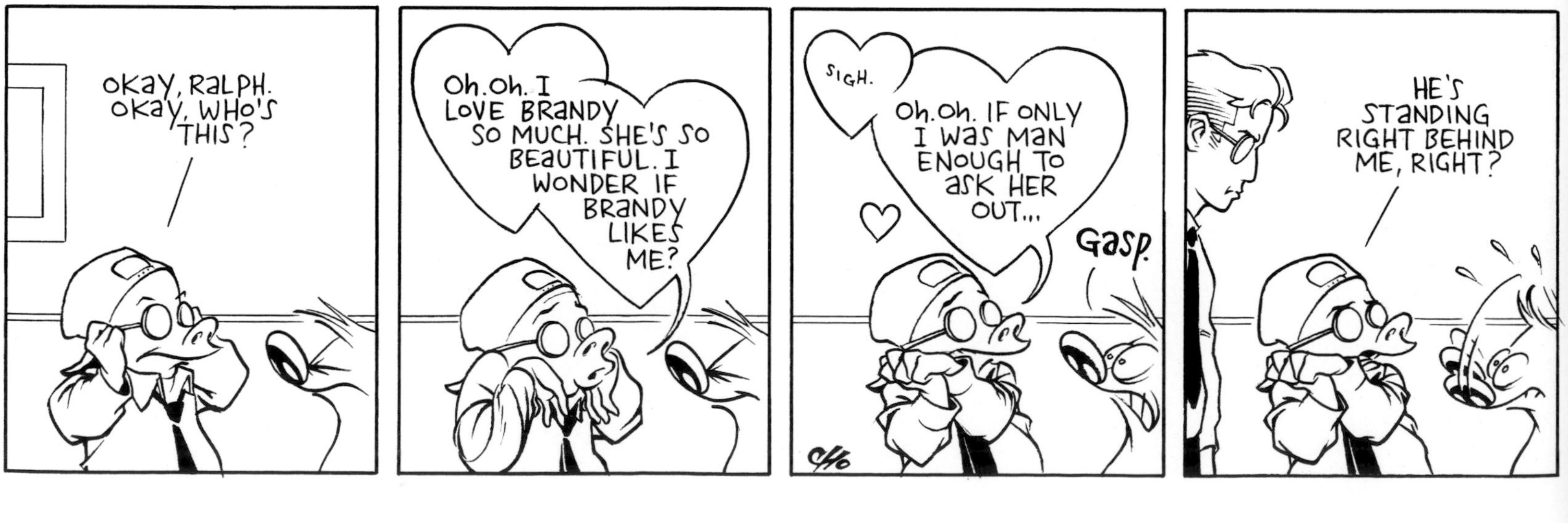
OKAY, RALPH. OKAY, WHO'S THIS?
OH. OH. I LOVE BRANDY SO MUCH. SHE'S SO BEAUTIFUL. I WONDER IF BRANDY LIKES ME?
SIGH.
OH. OH. IF ONLY I WAS MAN ENOUGH TO ASK HER OUT...
GASP.
CHO
HE'S STANDING RIGHT BEHIND ME, RIGHT?

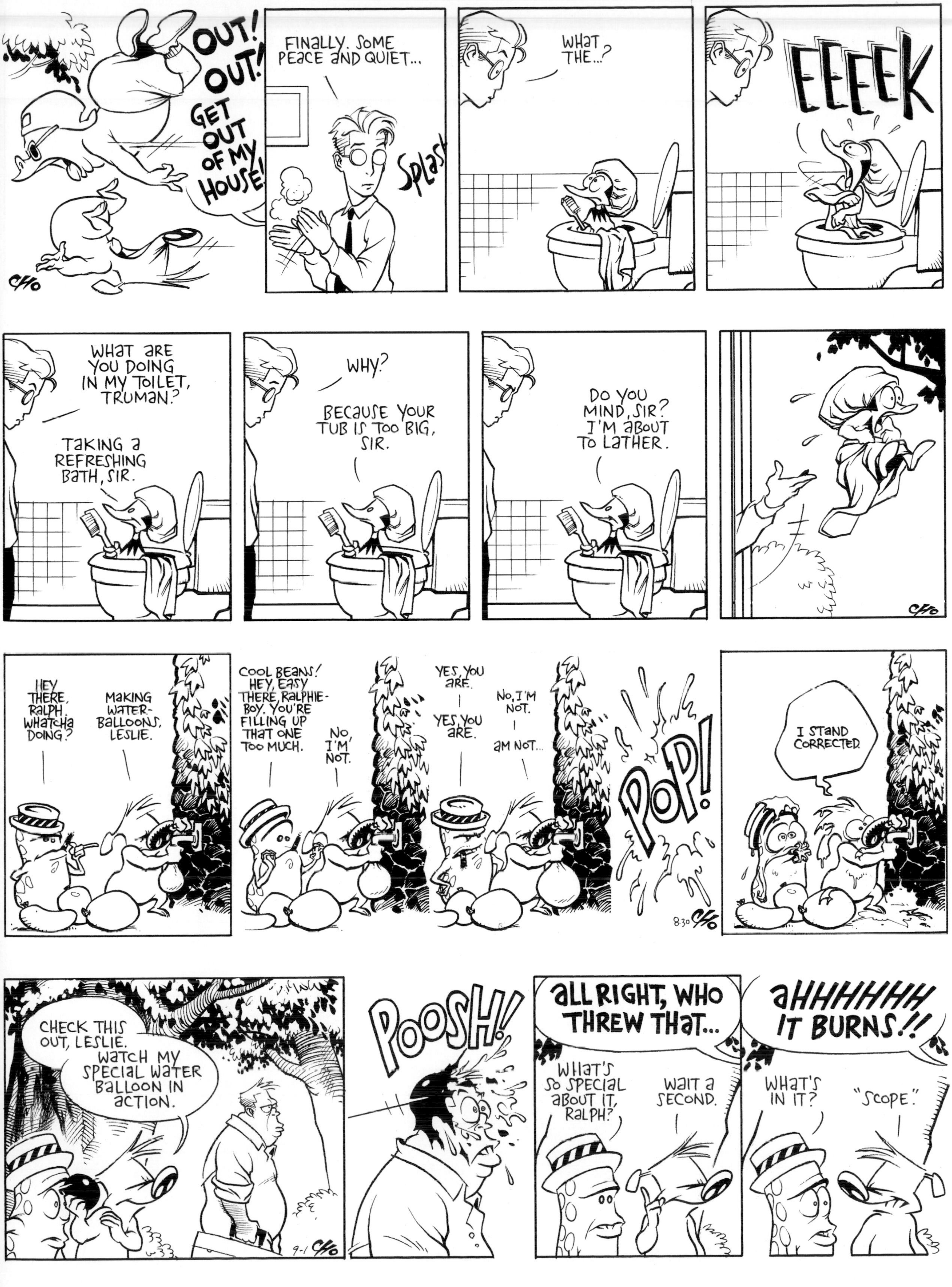
OUT! OUT! GET OUT OF MY HOUSE!
CHO
FINALLY. SOME PEACE AND QUIET...
SPLASH
WHAT THE...?
EEEEK
WHAT ARE YOU DOING IN MY TOILET, TRUMAN?
TAKING A REFRESHING BATH, SIR.
WHY?
BECAUSE YOUR TUB IS TOO BIG, SIR.
DO YOU MIND, SIR? I'M ABOUT TO LATHER.
CHO
HEY THERE, RALPH. WHATCHA DOING?
MAKING WATER-BALLOONS, LESLIE.
COOL BEANS! HEY, EASY THERE, RALPHIE-BOY. YOU'RE FILLING UP THAT ONE TOO MUCH.
NO, I'M NOT.
YES, YOU ARE.
NO, I'M NOT.
YES, YOU ARE.
AM NOT...
POP!
8-30 CHO
I STAND CORRECTED.
CHECK THIS OUT, LESLIE.
WATCH MY SPECIAL WATER BALLOON IN ACTION.
9-1 CHO
POOSH!
ALL RIGHT, WHO THREW THAT...
WHAT'S SO SPECIAL ABOUT IT, RALPH?
WAIT A SECOND.
AHHHHHH IT BURNS!!
WHAT'S IN IT?
"SCOPE."

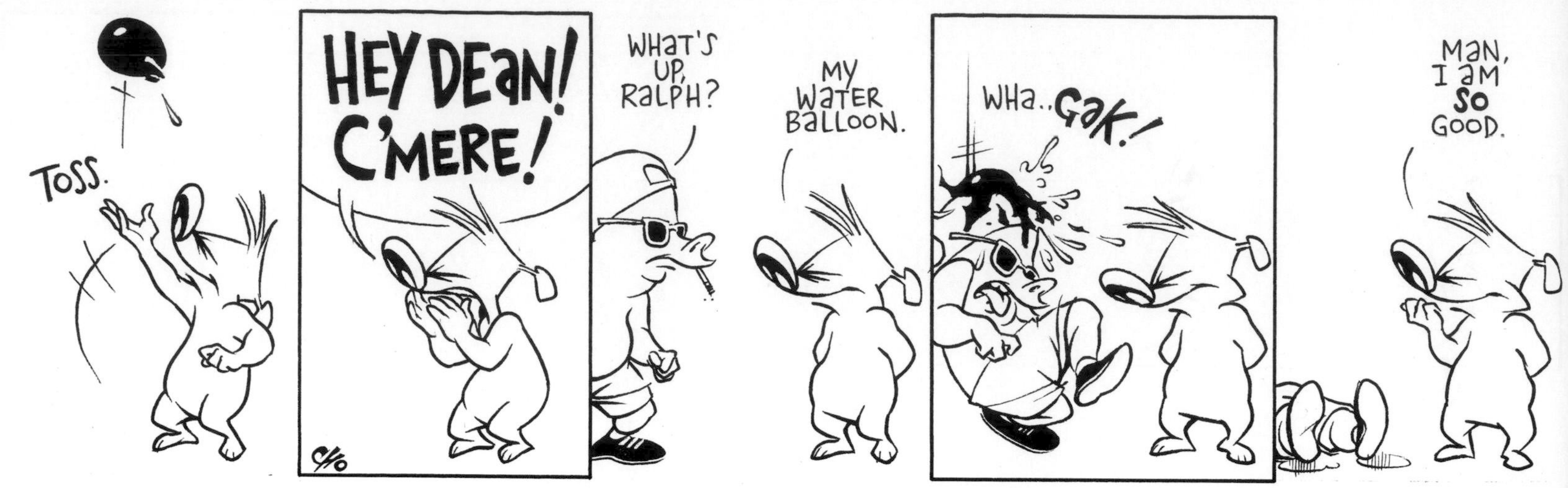
TOSS.
HEY DEAN! C'MERE!
WHAT'S UP, RALPH?
MY WATER BALLOON.
WHA.. GAK!
MAN, I AM SO GOOD.
CHO

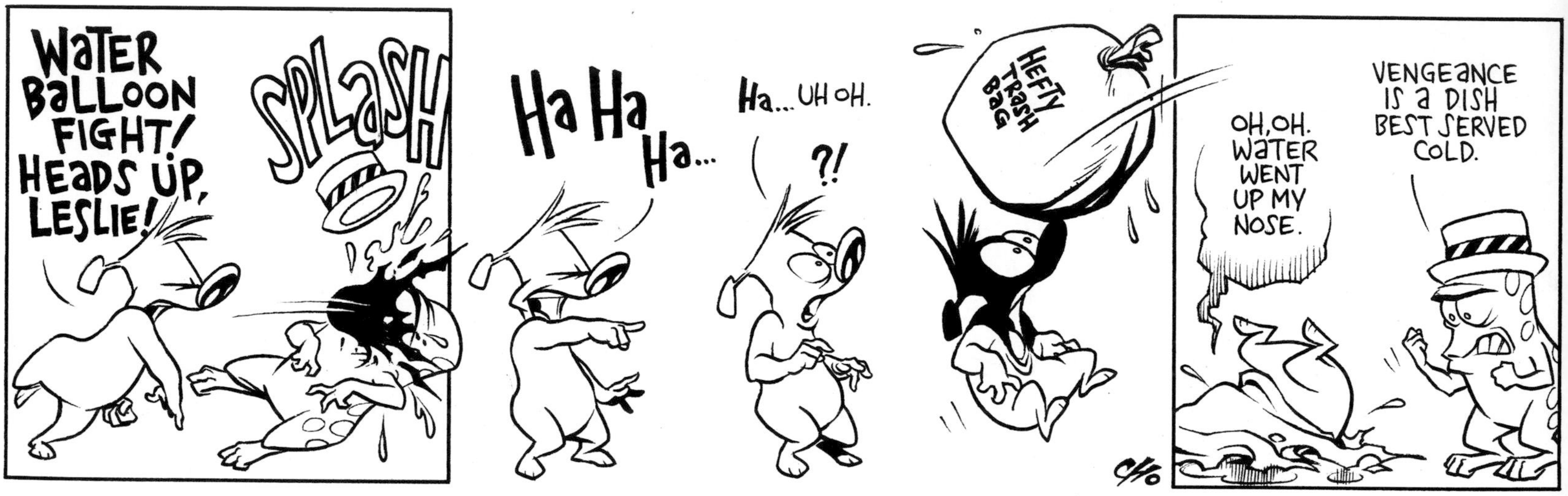
WATER BALLOON FIGHT! HEADS UP, LESLIE!
SPLASH
HA HA HA...
HA... UH OH.
?!
HEFTY TRASH BAG
OH, OH. WATER WENT UP MY NOSE.
VENGEANCE IS A DISH BEST SERVED COLD.
CHO

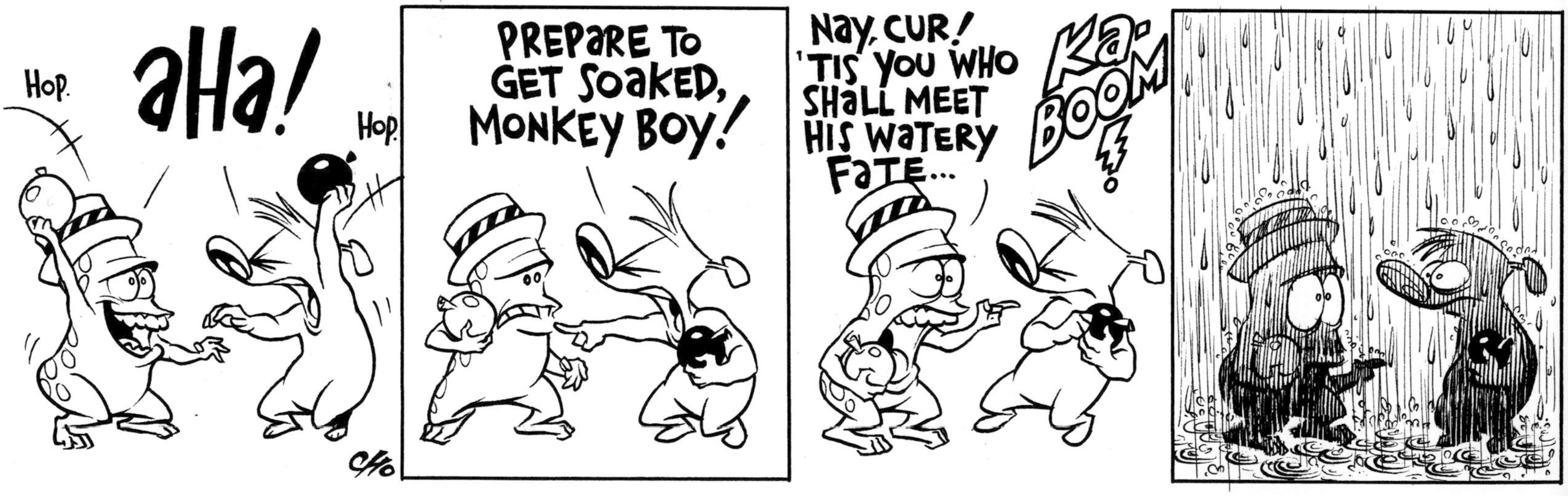
HOP.
AHA!
HOP.
PREPARE TO GET SOAKED, MONKEY BOY!
NAY, CUR! 'TIS YOU WHO SHALL MEET HIS WATERY FATE...
KA-BOOM
CHO

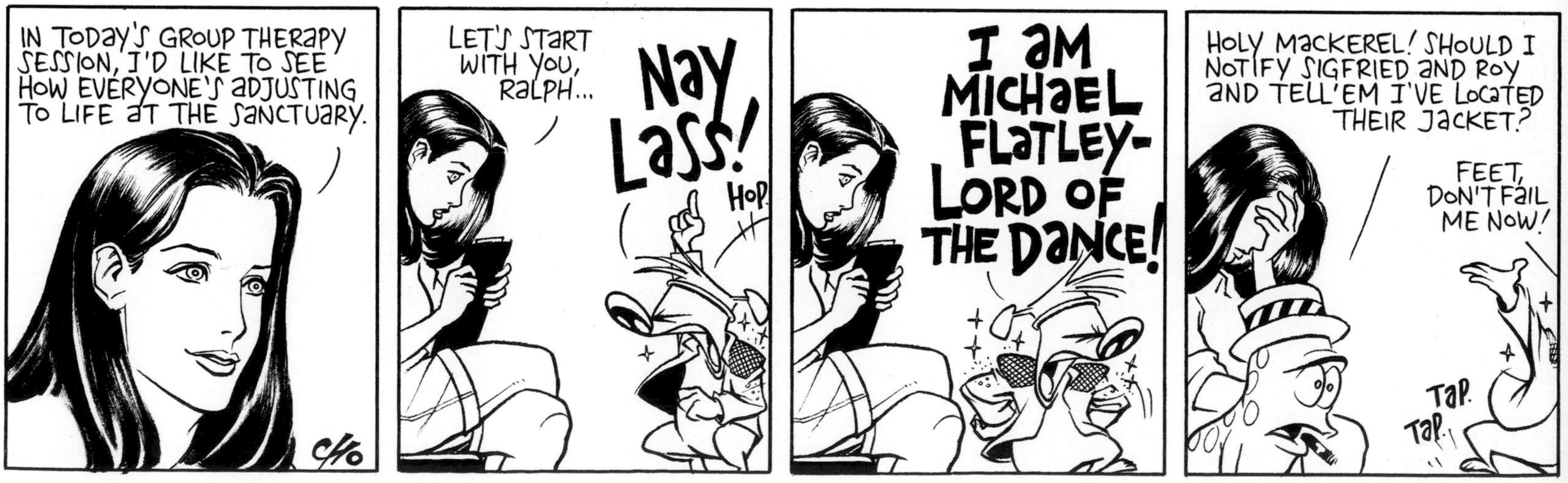
IN TODAY'S GROUP THERAPY SESSION, I'D LIKE TO SEE HOW EVERYONE'S ADJUSTING TO LIFE AT THE SANCTUARY.
LET'S START WITH YOU, RALPH...
NAY LASS!
HOP.
I AM MICHAEL FLATLEY- LORD OF THE DANCE!
HOLY MACKEREL! SHOULD I NOTIFY SIGFRIED AND ROY AND TELL'EM I'VE LOCATED THEIR JACKET?
FEET, DON'T FAIL ME NOW!
TAP. TAP.
CHO

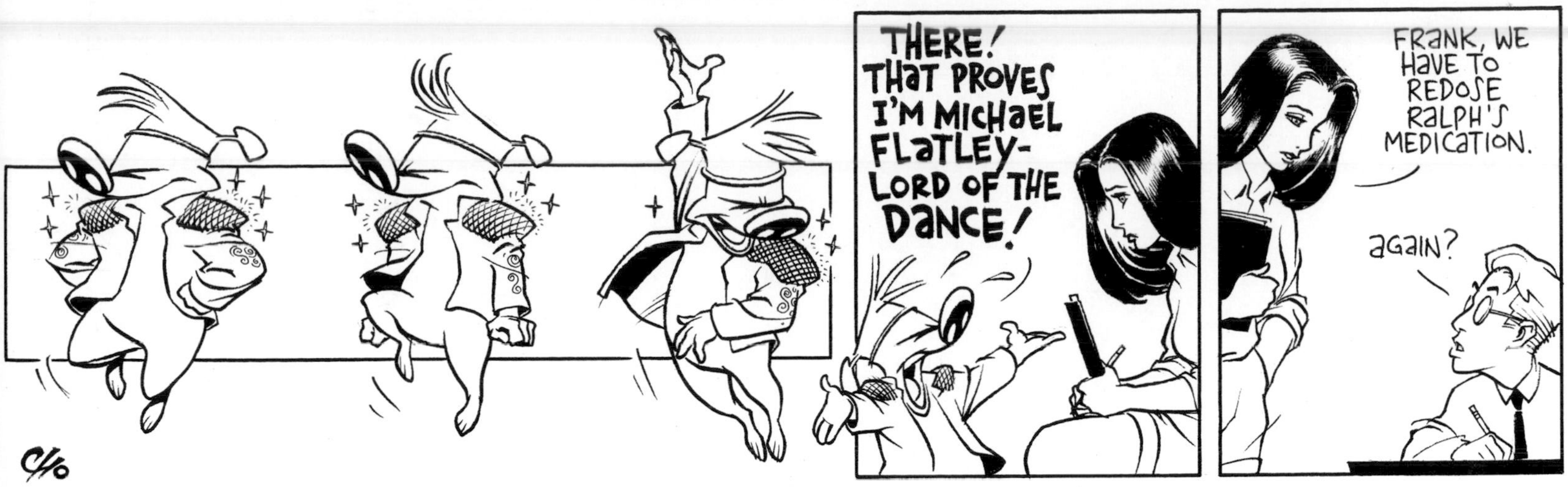
THERE! THAT PROVES I'M MICHAEL FLATLEY- LORD OF THE DANCE!
FRANK, WE HAVE TO REDOSE RALPH'S MEDICATION.
AGAIN?

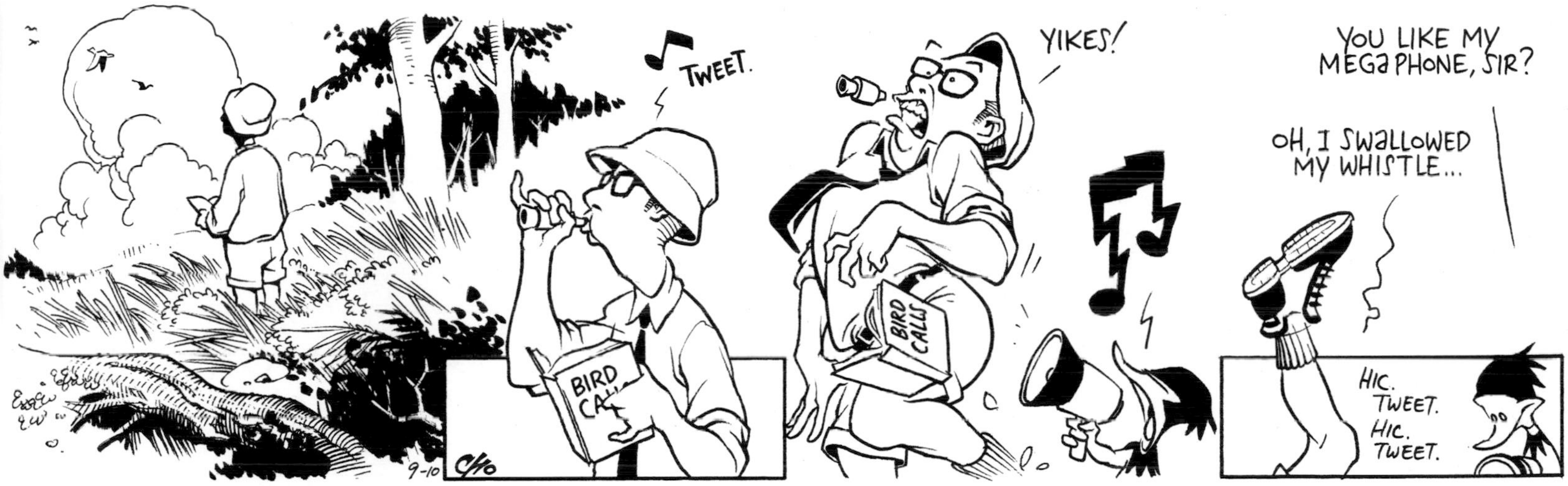
TWEET.
BIRD CALLS
YIKES!
BIRD CALLS
YOU LIKE MY MEGAPHONE, SIR?
OH, I SWALLOWED MY WHISTLE...
HIC. TWEET. HIC. TWEET.

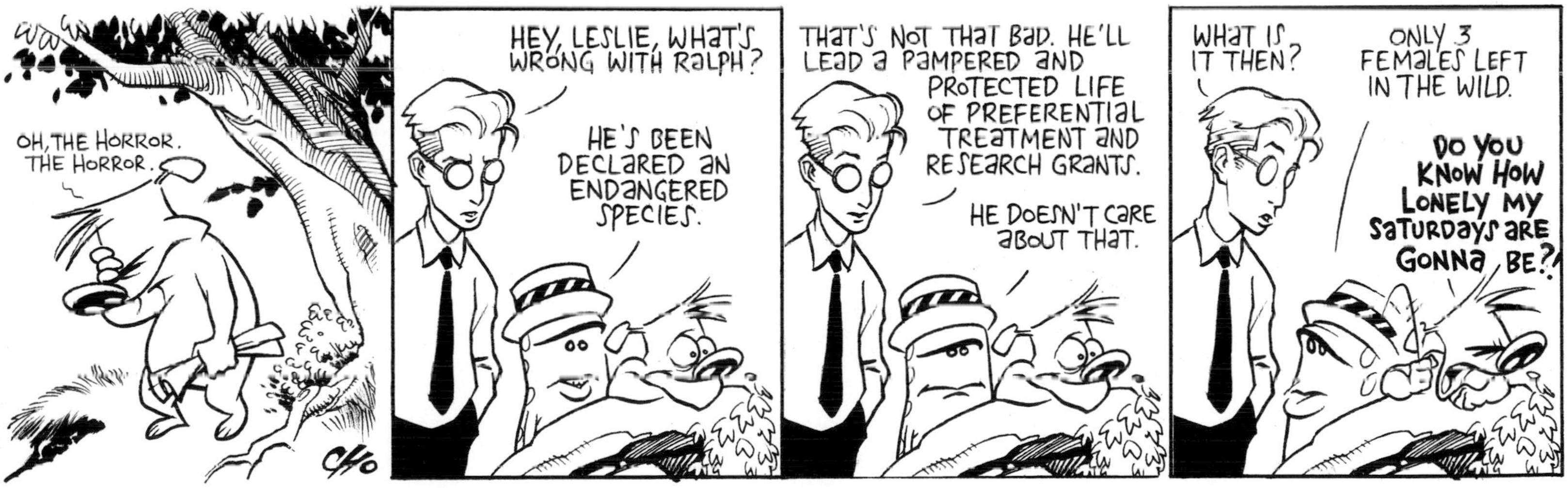
OH, THE HORROR. THE HORROR.
HEY, LESLIE, WHAT'S WRONG WITH RALPH?
HE'S BEEN DECLARED AN ENDANGERED SPECIES.
THAT'S NOT THAT BAD. HE'LL LEAD A PAMPERED AND PROTECTED LIFE OF PREFERENTIAL TREATMENT AND RESEARCH GRANTS.
HE DOESN'T CARE ABOUT THAT.
WHAT IS IT THEN?
ONLY 3 FEMALES LEFT IN THE WILD.
DO YOU KNOW HOW LONELY MY SATURDAYS ARE GONNA BE?!

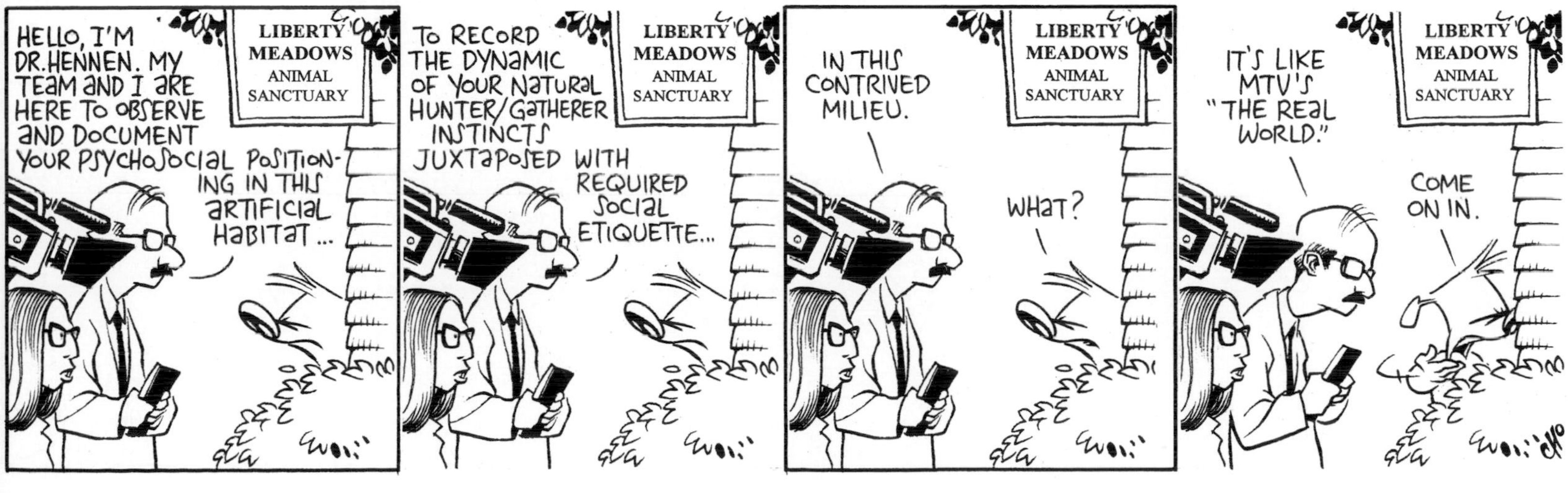
LIBERTY MEADOWS ANIMAL SANCTUARY
HELLO, I'M DR. HENNEN. MY TEAM AND I ARE HERE TO OBSERVE AND DOCUMENT YOUR PSYCHOSOCIAL POSITIONING IN THIS ARTIFICIAL HABITAT...
TO RECORD THE DYNAMIC OF YOUR NATURAL HUNTER/GATHERER INSTINCTS JUXTAPOSED WITH REQUIRED SOCIAL ETIQUETTE...
IN THIS CONTRIVED MILIEU.
WHAT?
IT'S LIKE MTV'S "THE REAL WORLD."
COME ON IN.

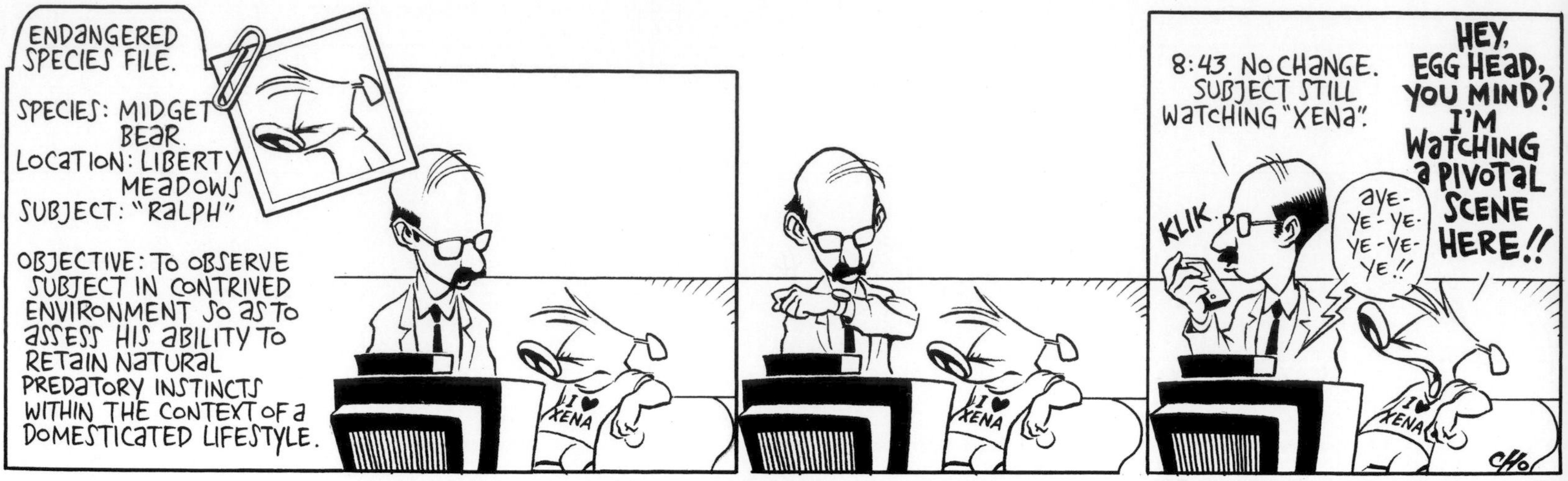
ENDANGERED SPECIES FILE.
SPECIES: MIDGET BEAR.
LOCATION: LIBERTY MEADOWS
SUBJECT: "RALPH"
OBJECTIVE: TO OBSERVE SUBJECT IN CONTRIVED ENVIRONMENT SO AS TO ASSESS HIS ABILITY TO RETAIN NATURAL PREDATORY INSTINCTS WITHIN THE CONTEXT OF A DOMESTICATED LIFESTYLE.
I ♥ XENA
I ♥ XENA
8:43. NO CHANGE. SUBJECT STILL WATCHING "XENA".
KLIK
AYE-YE-YE-YE-YE-YE!!
HEY, EGG HEAD, YOU MIND? I'M WATCHING A PIVOTAL SCENE HERE!!
I ♥ XENA

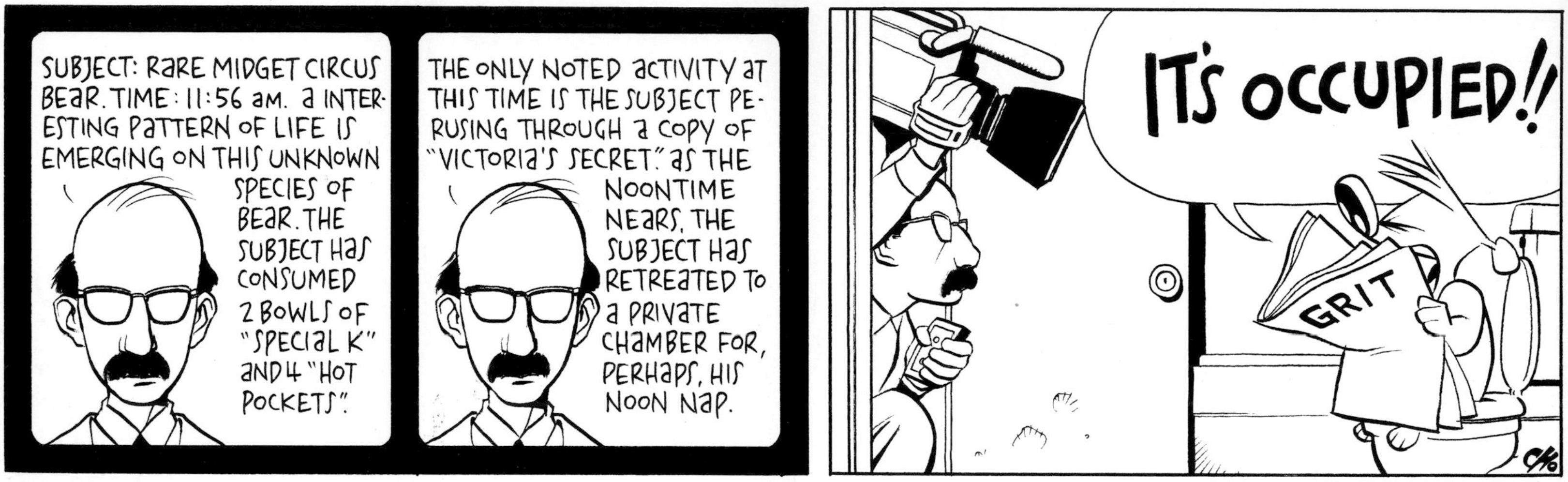
SUBJECT: RARE MIDGET CIRCUS BEAR. TIME: 11:56 AM. A INTERESTING PATTERN OF LIFE IS EMERGING ON THIS UNKNOWN SPECIES OF BEAR. THE SUBJECT HAS CONSUMED 2 BOWLS OF "SPECIAL K" AND 4 "HOT POCKETS".
THE ONLY NOTED ACTIVITY AT THIS TIME IS THE SUBJECT PERUSING THROUGH A COPY OF "VICTORIA'S SECRET" AS THE NOONTIME NEARS, THE SUBJECT HAS RETREATED TO A PRIVATE CHAMBER FOR, PERHAPS, HIS NOON NAP.
IT'S OCCUPIED!!
GRIT

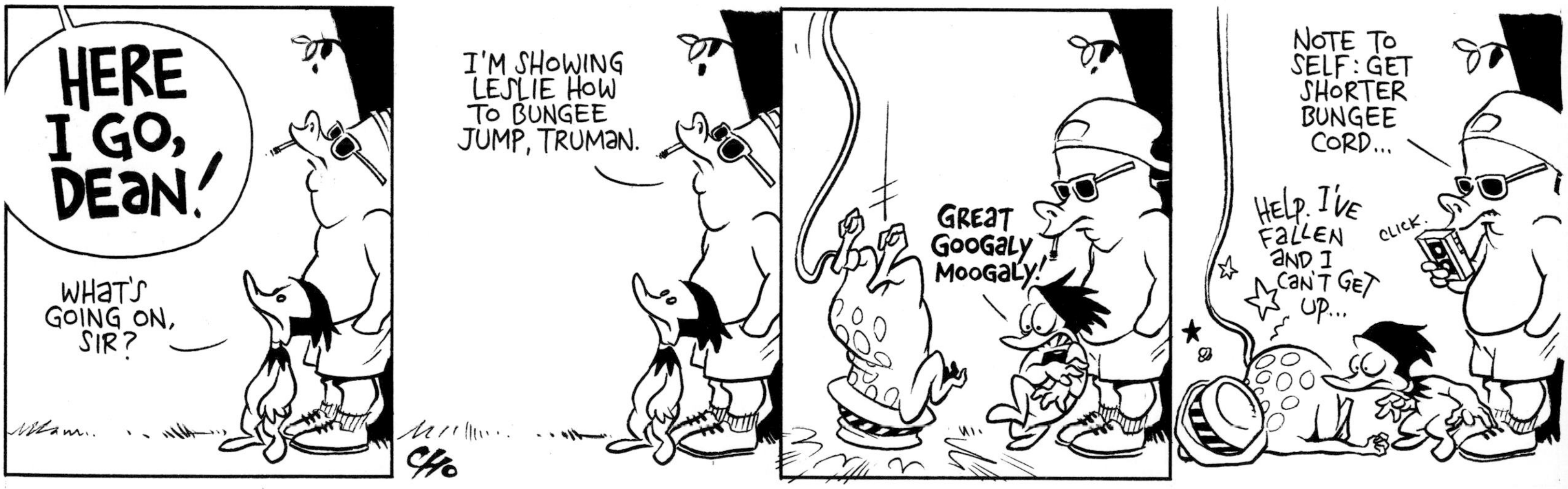
HERE I GO, DEAN!
WHAT'S GOING ON, SIR?
I'M SHOWING LESLIE HOW TO BUNGEE JUMP, TRUMAN.
GREAT GOOGALY MOOGALY!
NOTE TO SELF: GET SHORTER BUNGEE CORD...
HELP. I'VE FALLEN AND I CAN'T GET UP...
CLICK.

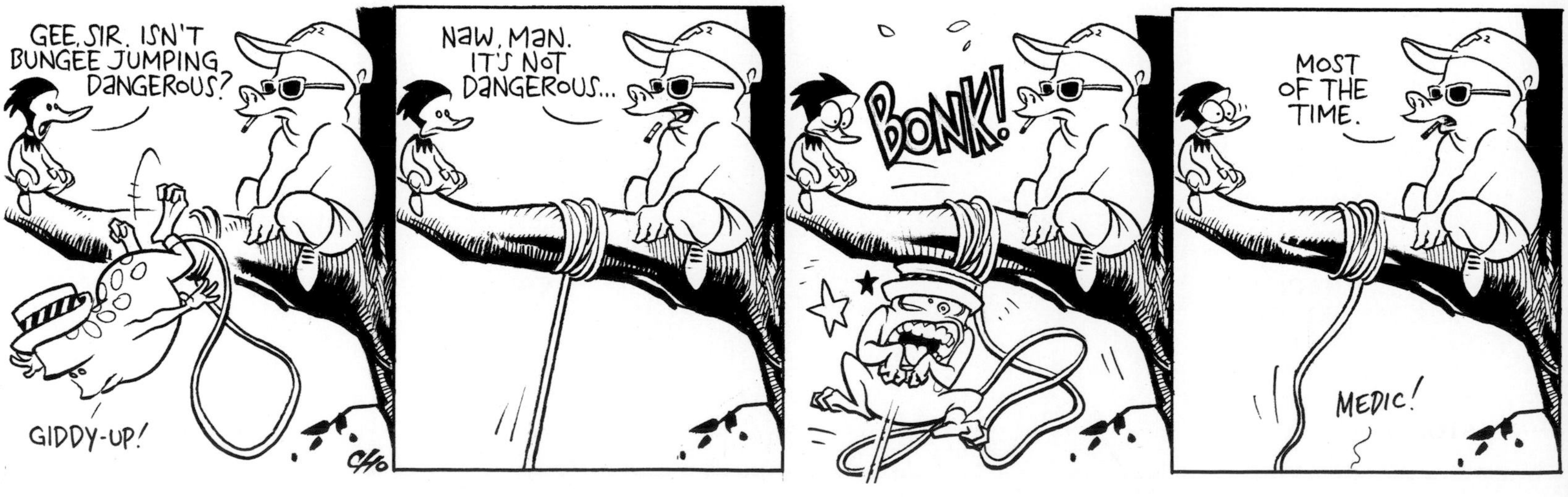
GEE, SIR. ISN'T BUNGEE JUMPING DANGEROUS?
GIDDY-UP!
NAW, MAN. IT'S NOT DANGEROUS...
BONK!
MOST OF THE TIME.
MEDIC!

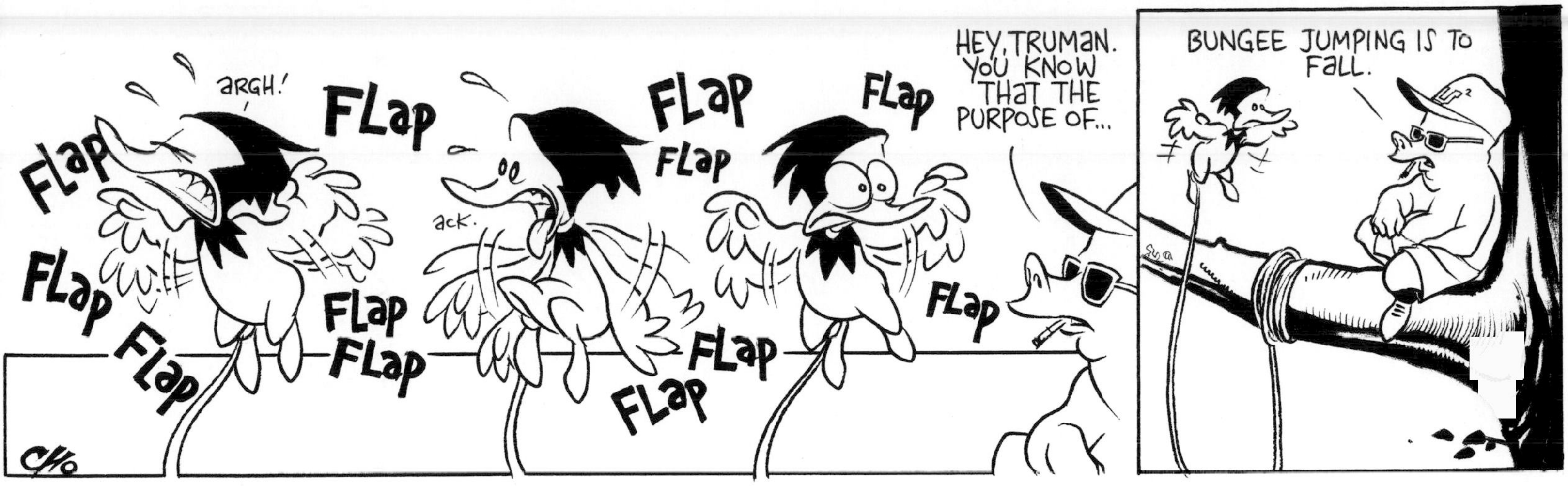

ARGH!
FLAP FLAP FLAP FLAP FLAP FLAP
ACK.
FLAP FLAP FLAP FLAP FLAP FLAP FLAP
HEY, TRUMAN. YOU KNOW THAT THE PURPOSE OF...
BUNGEE JUMPING IS TO FALL.
CHO

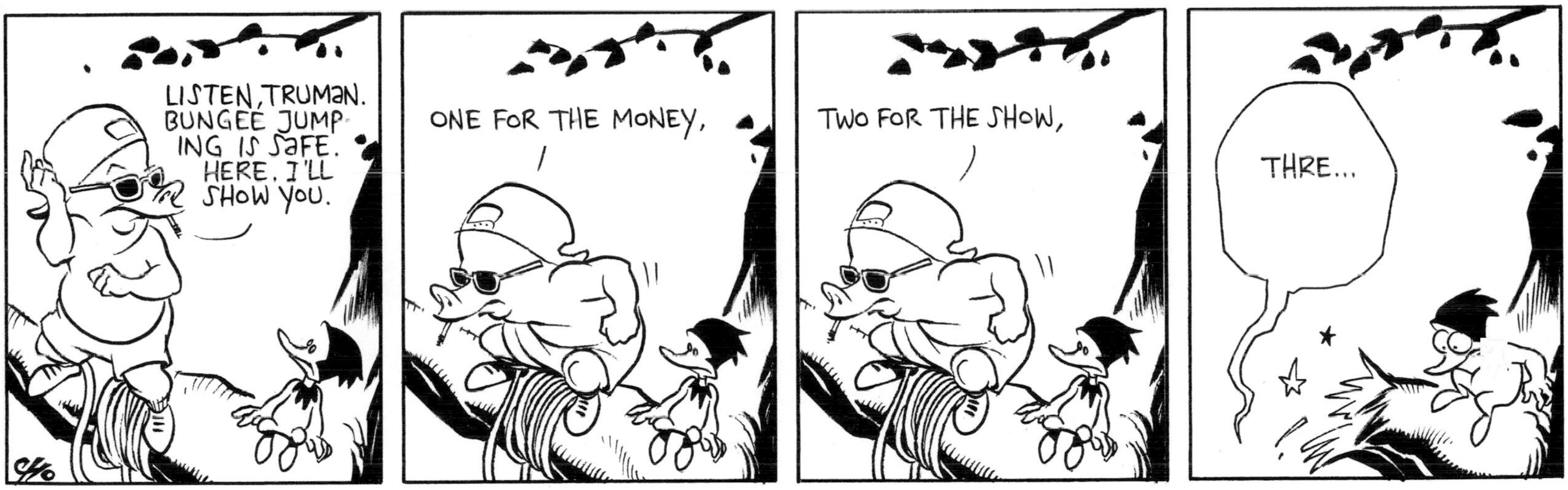

LISTEN, TRUMAN. BUNGEE JUMPING IS SAFE. HERE. I'LL SHOW YOU.
ONE FOR THE MONEY,
TWO FOR THE SHOW,
THRE...
CHO

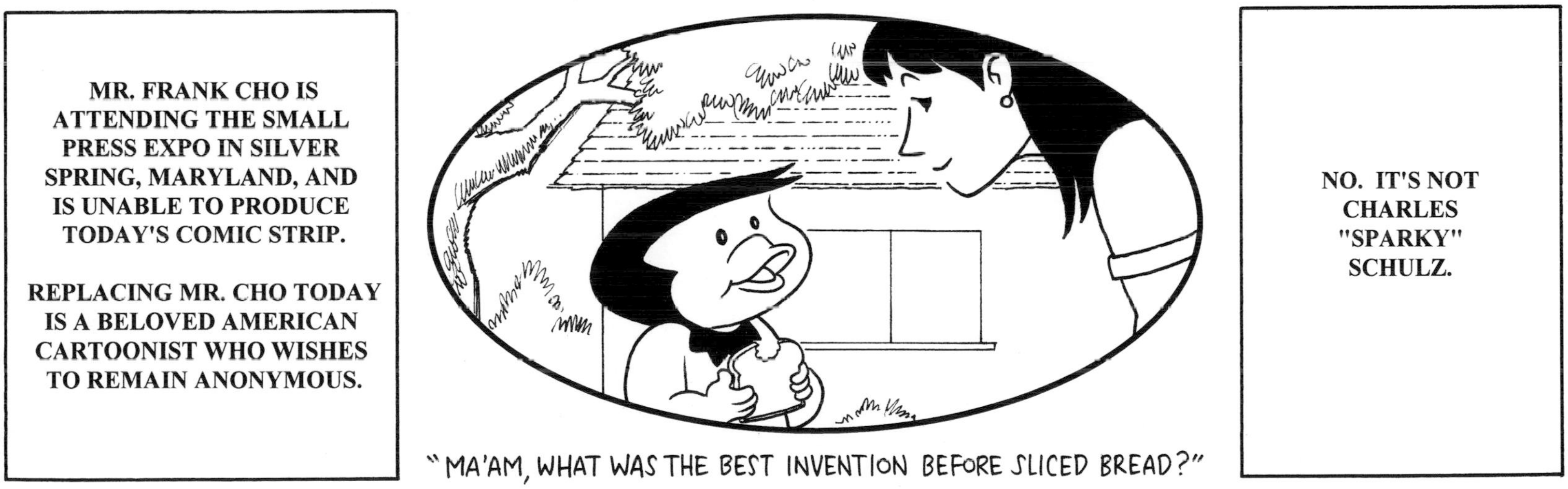

MR. FRANK CHO IS ATTENDING THE SMALL PRESS EXPO IN SILVER SPRING, MARYLAND, AND IS UNABLE TO PRODUCE TODAY'S COMIC STRIP.
REPLACING MR. CHO TODAY IS A BELOVED AMERICAN CARTOONIST WHO WISHES TO REMAIN ANONYMOUS.
"MA'AM, WHAT WAS THE BEST INVENTION BEFORE SLICED BREAD?"
NO. IT'S NOT CHARLES "SPARKY" SCHULZ.

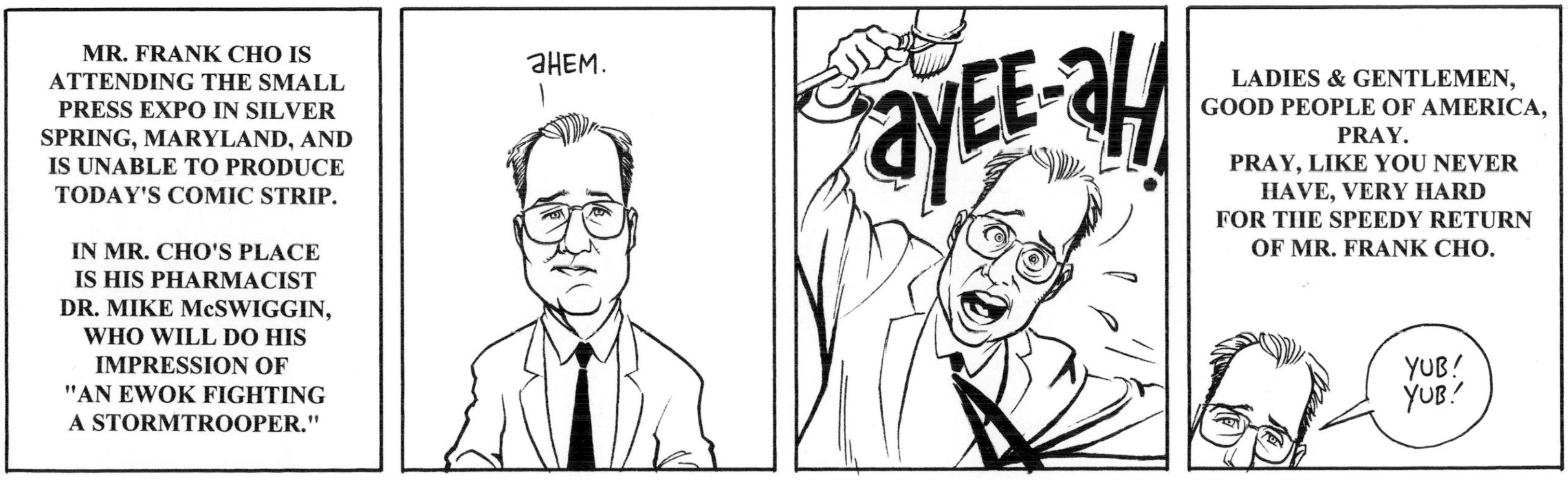

MR. FRANK CHO IS ATTENDING THE SMALL PRESS EXPO IN SILVER SPRING, MARYLAND, AND IS UNABLE TO PRODUCE TODAY'S COMIC STRIP.
IN MR. CHO'S PLACE IS HIS PHARMACIST DR. MIKE McSWIGGIN, WHO WILL DO HIS IMPRESSION OF "AN EWOK FIGHTING A STORMTROOPER."
AHEM.
AYEE-AH!
LADIES & GENTLEMEN, GOOD PEOPLE OF AMERICA, PRAY. PRAY, LIKE YOU NEVER HAVE, VERY HARD FOR THE SPEEDY RETURN OF MR. FRANK CHO.
YUB! YUB!

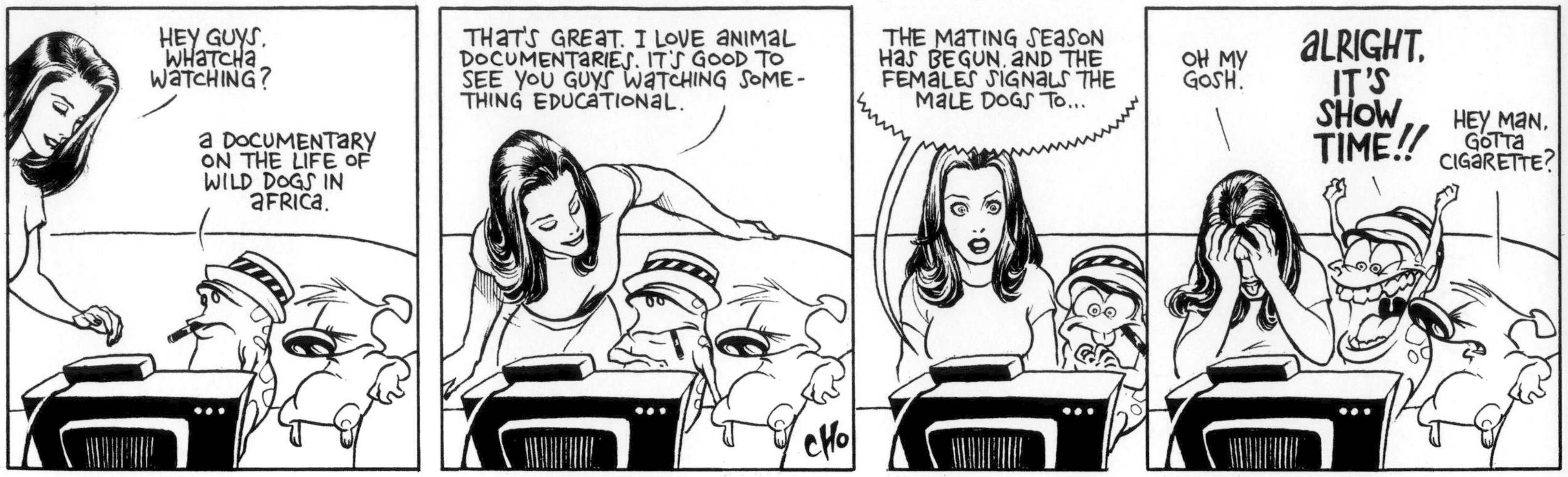
HEY GUYS. WHATCHA WATCHING?
A DOCUMENTARY ON THE LIFE OF WILD DOGS IN AFRICA.
THAT'S GREAT. I LOVE ANIMAL DOCUMENTARIES. IT'S GOOD TO SEE YOU GUYS WATCHING SOMETHING EDUCATIONAL.
THE MATING SEASON HAS BEGUN, AND THE FEMALES SIGNALS THE MALE DOGS TO...
OH MY GOSH.
ALRIGHT. IT'S SHOW TIME!!
HEY MAN, GOTTA CIGARETTE?
CHO

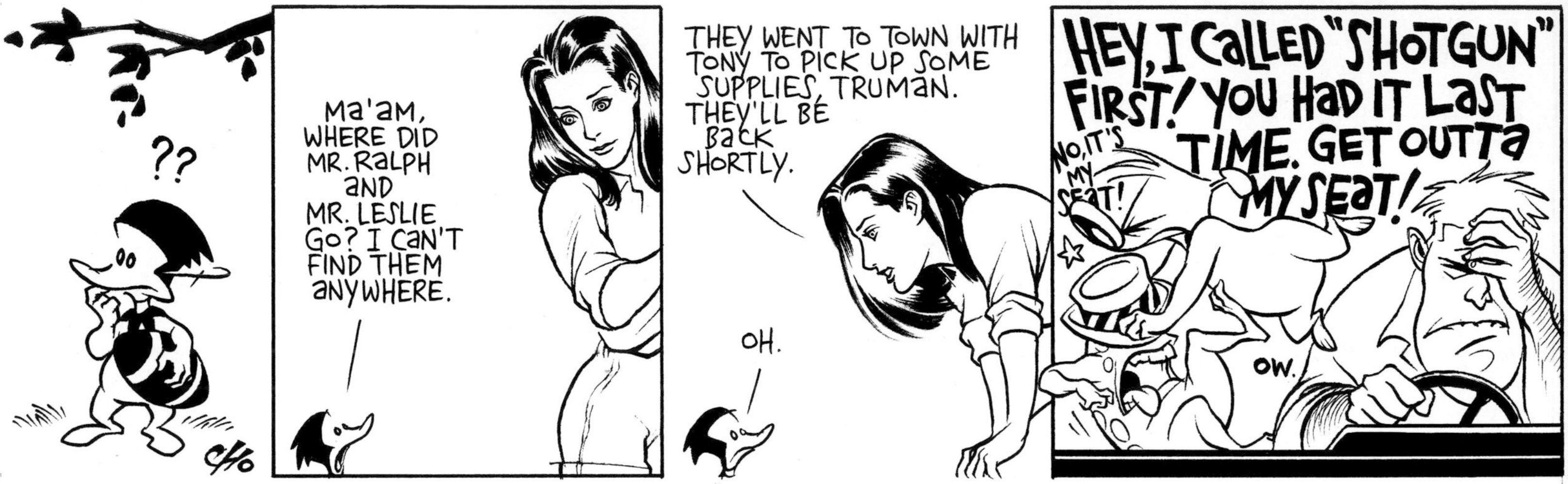
??
CHO
MA'AM, WHERE DID MR. RALPH AND MR. LESLIE GO? I CAN'T FIND THEM ANYWHERE.
THEY WENT TO TOWN WITH TONY TO PICK UP SOME SUPPLIES, TRUMAN. THEY'LL BE BACK SHORTLY.
OH.
HEY, I CALLED "SHOTGUN" FIRST! YOU HAD IT LAST TIME. GET OUTTA MY SEAT!
NO, IT'S MY SEAT!
OW.

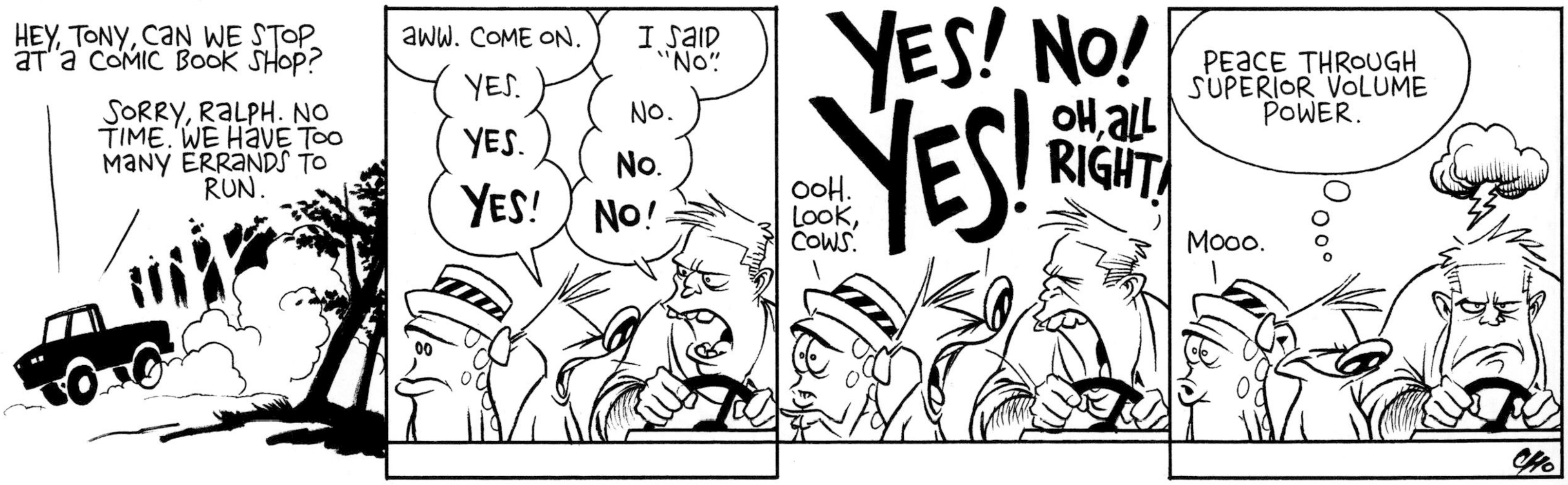
HEY, TONY, CAN WE STOP AT A COMIC BOOK SHOP?
SORRY, RALPH. NO TIME. WE HAVE TOO MANY ERRANDS TO RUN.
AWW. COME ON.
YES.
YES.
YES!
I SAID "NO".
NO.
NO.
NO!
YES! NO!
YES!
OH, ALL RIGHT!
OOH. LOOK, COWS.
PEACE THROUGH SUPERIOR VOLUME POWER.
MOOO.
CHO

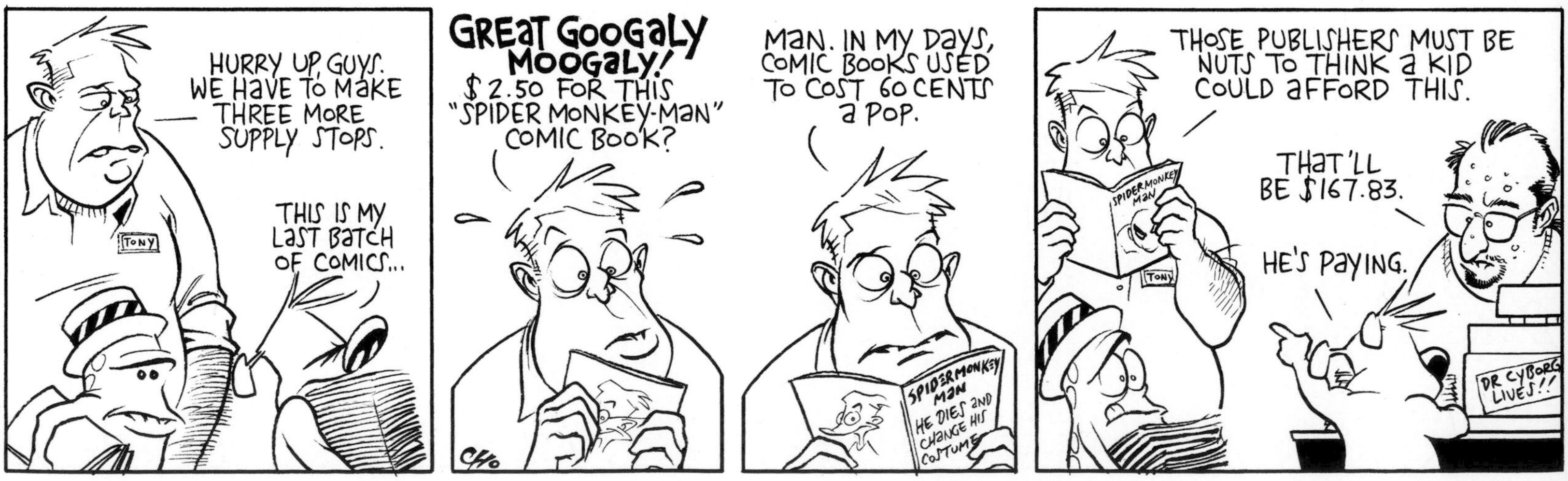
HURRY UP, GUYS. WE HAVE TO MAKE THREE MORE SUPPLY STOPS.
TONY
THIS IS MY LAST BATCH OF COMICS...
GREAT GOOGALY MOOGALY! $2.50 FOR THIS "SPIDER MONKEY-MAN" COMIC BOOK?
CHO
MAN. IN MY DAYS, COMIC BOOKS USED TO COST 60 CENTS A POP.
SPIDER MONKEY MAN
HE DIES AND CHANGE HIS COSTUME
THOSE PUBLISHERS MUST BE NUTS TO THINK A KID COULD AFFORD THIS.
SPIDER MONKEY MAN
TONY
THAT'LL BE $167.83.
HE'S PAYING.
DR CYBORG LIVES!!

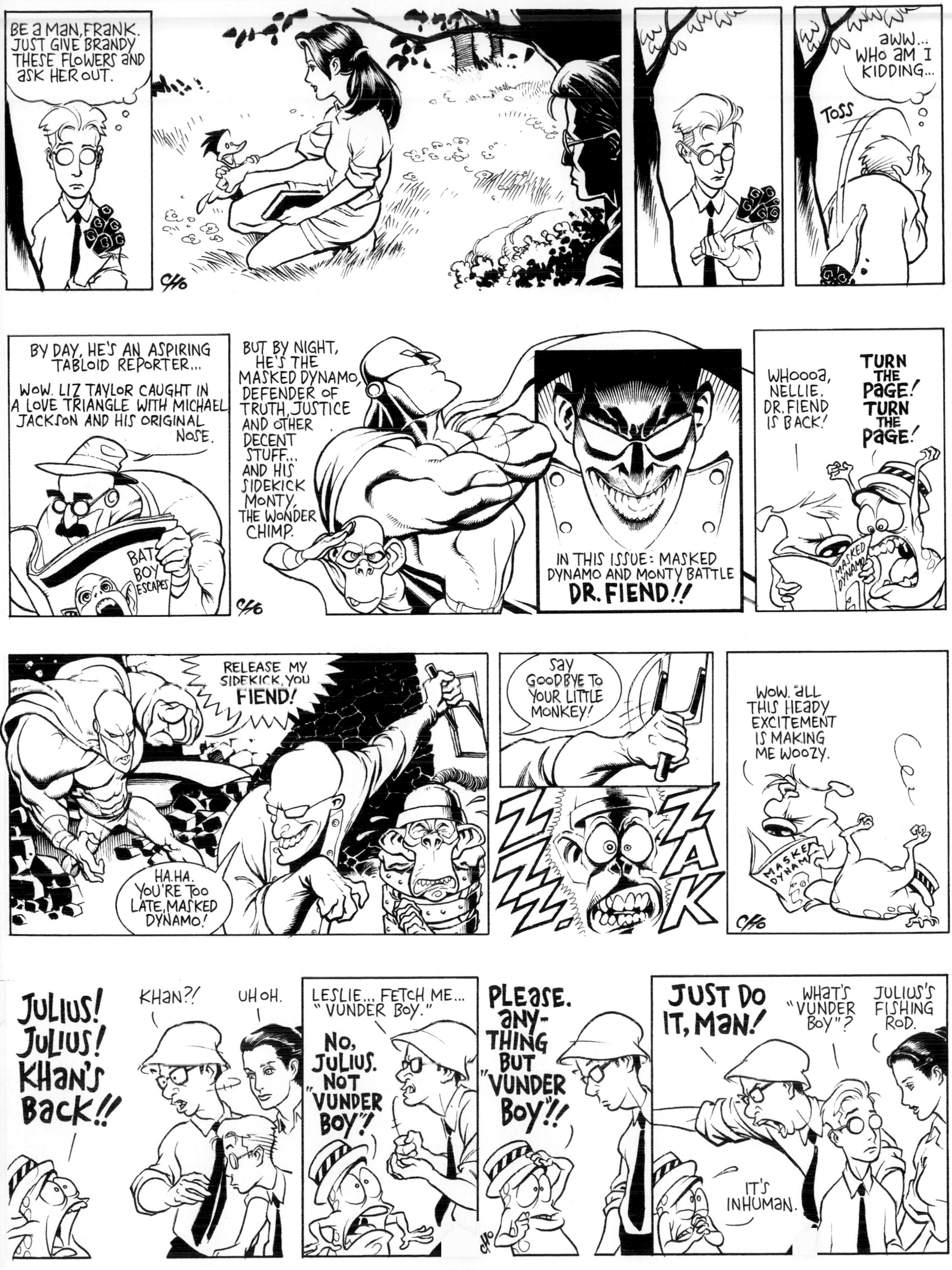
BE a MAN, FRANK. JUST GIVE BRANDY THESE FLOWERS and ask HER OUT.
aww... WHO am I KIDDING...
TOSS
BY DAY, HE'S AN ASPIRING TABLOID REPORTER...
WOW. LIZ TAYLOR CAUGHT IN A LOVE TRIANGLE WITH MICHAEL JACKSON AND HIS ORIGINAL NOSE.
BAT BOY ESCAPES
BUT BY NIGHT, HE'S THE MASKED DYNAMO, DEFENDER OF TRUTH, JUSTICE AND OTHER DECENT STUFF... AND HIS SIDEKICK MONTY, THE WONDER CHIMP.
IN THIS ISSUE: MASKED DYNAMO AND MONTY BATTLE DR. FIEND!!
WHOOOa, NELLIE. DR. FIEND IS BACK!
TURN THE PaGE! TURN THE PaGE!
RELEASE MY SIDEKICK, YOU FIEND!
HA.HA. YOU'RE TOO LATE, MASKED DYNAMO!
Say GOODBYE TO YOUR LITTLE MONKEY!
ZZZ. ZAK
WOW. aLL THIS HEaDY EXCITEMENT IS MAKING ME WOOZY.
JULIUS! JULIUS! KHaN'S Back!!
KHaN?!
UH OH.
LESLIE... FETCH ME... "VUNDER BOY."
NO, JULIUS. NOT "VUNDER BOY"!
PLEaSE. aNY-THING BUT "VUNDER BOY"!!
JUST DO IT, MaN!
WHaT'S "VUNDER BOY"?
JULIUS'S FISHING ROD.
IT'S INHUMaN.

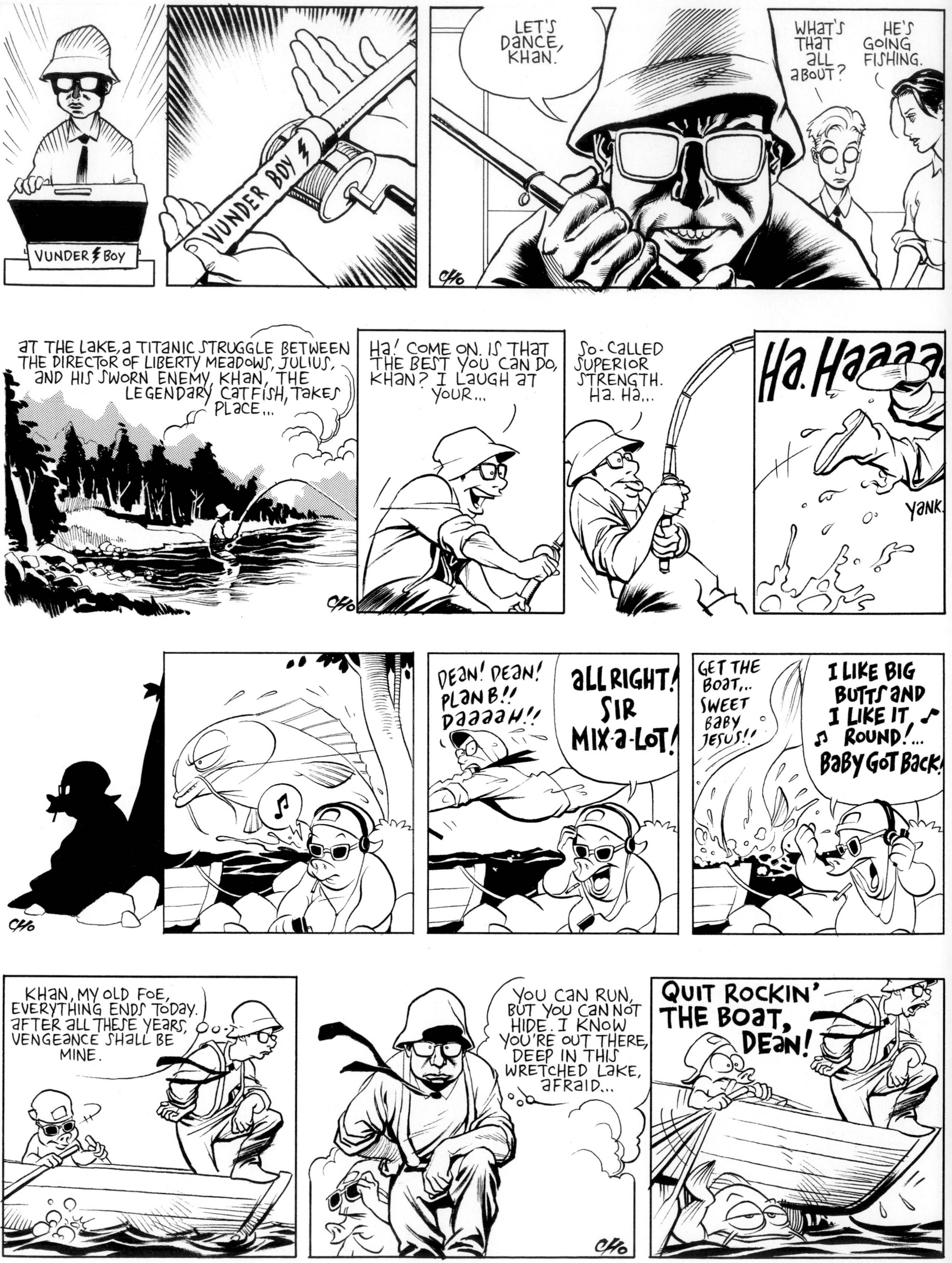
VUNDER BOY
VUNDER BOY
LET'S DANCE, KHAN.
WHAT'S THAT ALL ABOUT?
HE'S GOING FISHING.
CHO
AT THE LAKE, A TITANIC STRUGGLE BETWEEN THE DIRECTOR OF LIBERTY MEADOWS, JULIUS, AND HIS SWORN ENEMY, KHAN, THE LEGENDARY CATFISH, TAKES PLACE...
CHO
HA! COME ON. IS THAT THE BEST YOU CAN DO, KHAN? I LAUGH AT YOUR...
SO-CALLED SUPERIOR STRENGTH. HA. HA...
HA. HAAAAA
YANK
CHO
DEAN! DEAN! PLAN B!! DAAAAH!!
ALL RIGHT! SIR MIX-A-LOT!
GET THE BOAT... SWEET BABY JESUS!!
I LIKE BIG BUTTS AND I LIKE IT ROUND!... BABY GOT BACK!
KHAN, MY OLD FOE, EVERYTHING ENDS TODAY. AFTER ALL THESE YEARS, VENGEANCE SHALL BE MINE.
YOU CAN RUN, BUT YOU CAN NOT HIDE. I KNOW YOU'RE OUT THERE, DEEP IN THIS WRETCHED LAKE, AFRAID...
CHO
QUIT ROCKIN' THE BOAT, DEAN!

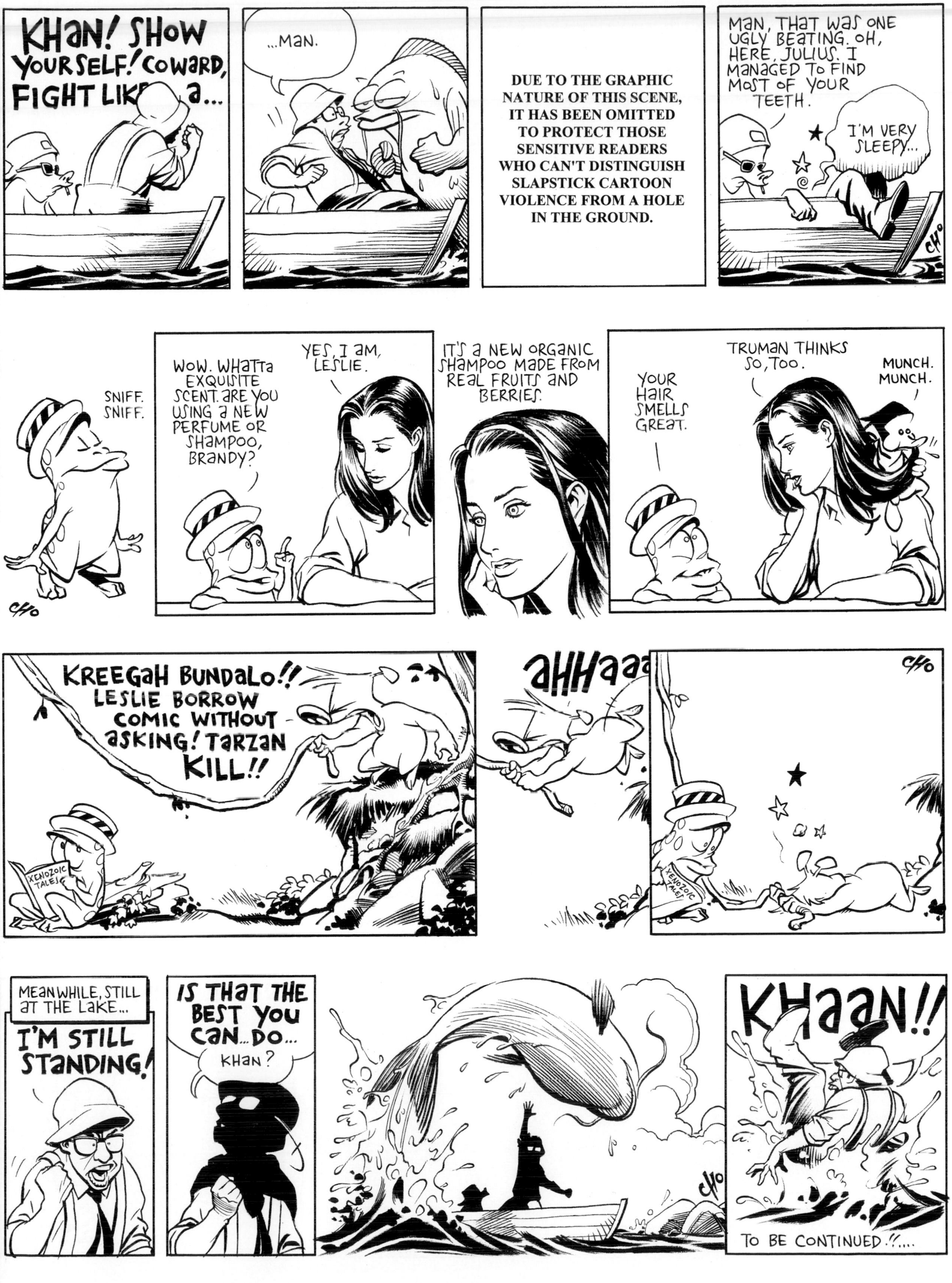
KHAN! SHOW YOURSELF! COWARD, FIGHT LIKE a...
...MAN.
DUE TO THE GRAPHIC NATURE OF THIS SCENE, IT HAS BEEN OMITTED TO PROTECT THOSE SENSITIVE READERS WHO CAN'T DISTINGUISH SLAPSTICK CARTOON VIOLENCE FROM A HOLE IN THE GROUND.
MAN, THAT WAS ONE UGLY BEATING. OH, HERE, JULIUS. I MANAGED TO FIND MOST OF YOUR TEETH.
I'M VERY SLEEPY...
CHO
SNIFF. SNIFF.
CHO
WOW. WHATTA EXQUISITE SCENT. ARE YOU USING A NEW PERFUME OR SHAMPOO, BRANDY?
YES, I AM, LESLIE.
IT'S A NEW ORGANIC SHAMPOO MADE FROM REAL FRUITS AND BERRIES.
YOUR HAIR SMELLS GREAT.
TRUMAN THINKS SO, TOO.
MUNCH. MUNCH.
KREEGAH BUNDALO!! LESLIE BORROW COMIC WITHOUT ASKING! TARZAN KILL!!
XENOZOIC TALES
AHHAAA
CHO
XENOZOIC TALES
MEANWHILE, STILL AT THE LAKE...
I'M STILL STANDING!
IS THAT THE BEST YOU CAN...DO...
KHAN?
CHO
KHAAN!!
TO BE CONTINUED!!...

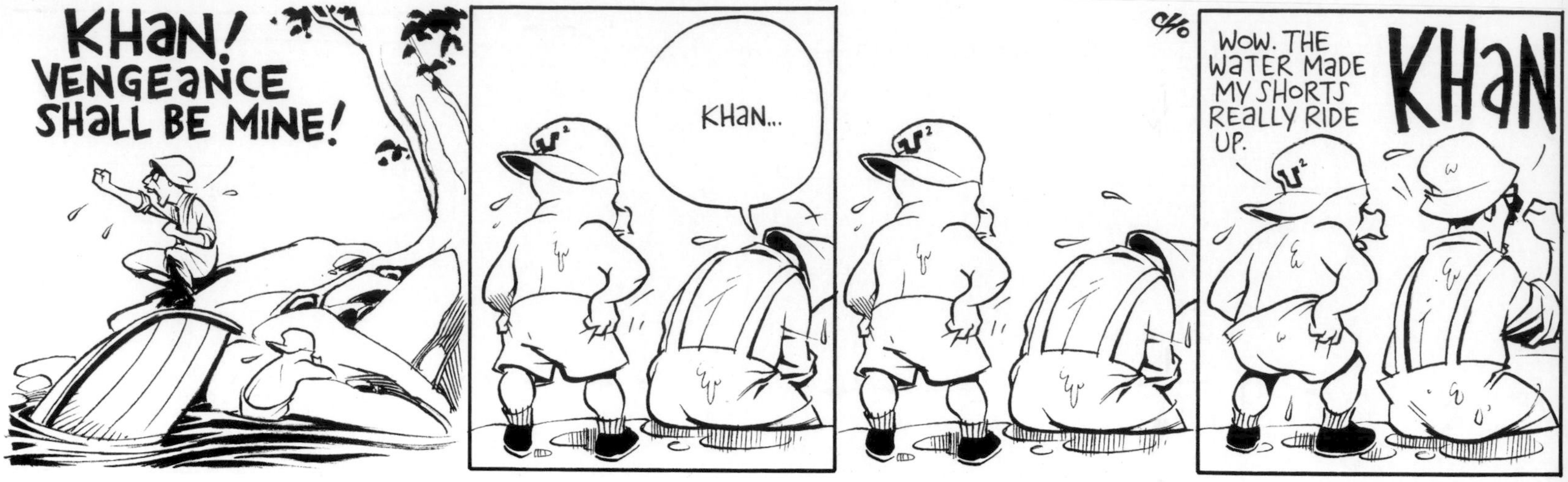
KHAN! VENGEANCE SHALL BE MINE!
KHAN...
WOW. THE WATER MADE MY SHORTS REALLY RIDE UP.
KHAN

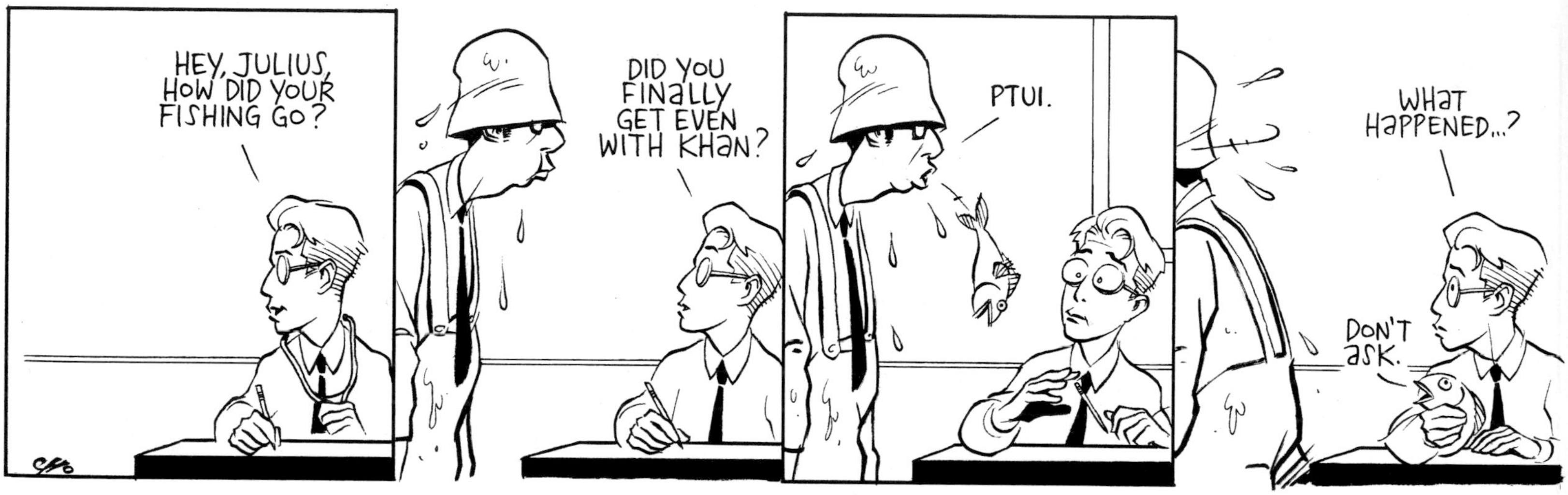
HEY, JULIUS, HOW DID YOUR FISHING GO?
DID YOU FINALLY GET EVEN WITH KHAN?
PTUI.
WHAT HAPPENED...?
DON'T ASK.

CORRECTION:

MANY READERS CONTINUE TO COMPLAIN ABOUT OUR AUGUST 11TH STRIP WHICH DEPICTED RALPH SUFFERING FROM TICK INFESTATION.

ASTUTE READERS CORRECTLY POINTED OUT THAT AN ACTUAL TICK HAS 8 LEGS WHILE OUR VERSION HAD ONLY 6.

IN RESPONSE TO THIS EMBARRASSING ERROR WE PRESENT THE TICK, HIMSELF, WITH A PERSONAL STATEMENT . . .

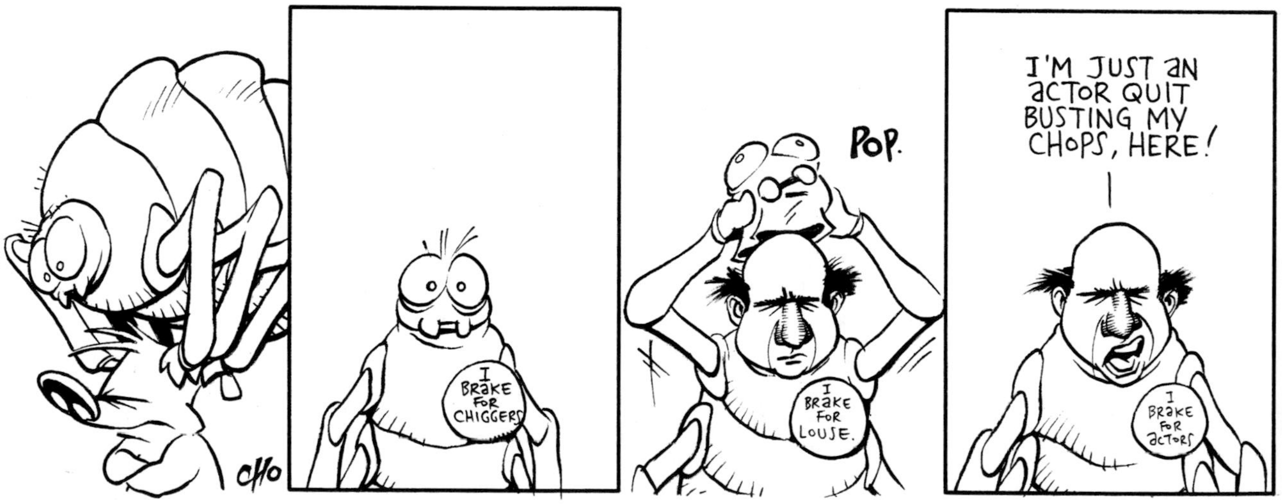
I BRAKE FOR CHIGGERS
POP.
I BRAKE FOR LOUSE.
I'M JUST AN ACTOR QUIT BUSTING MY CHOPS, HERE!
I BRAKE FOR ACTORS

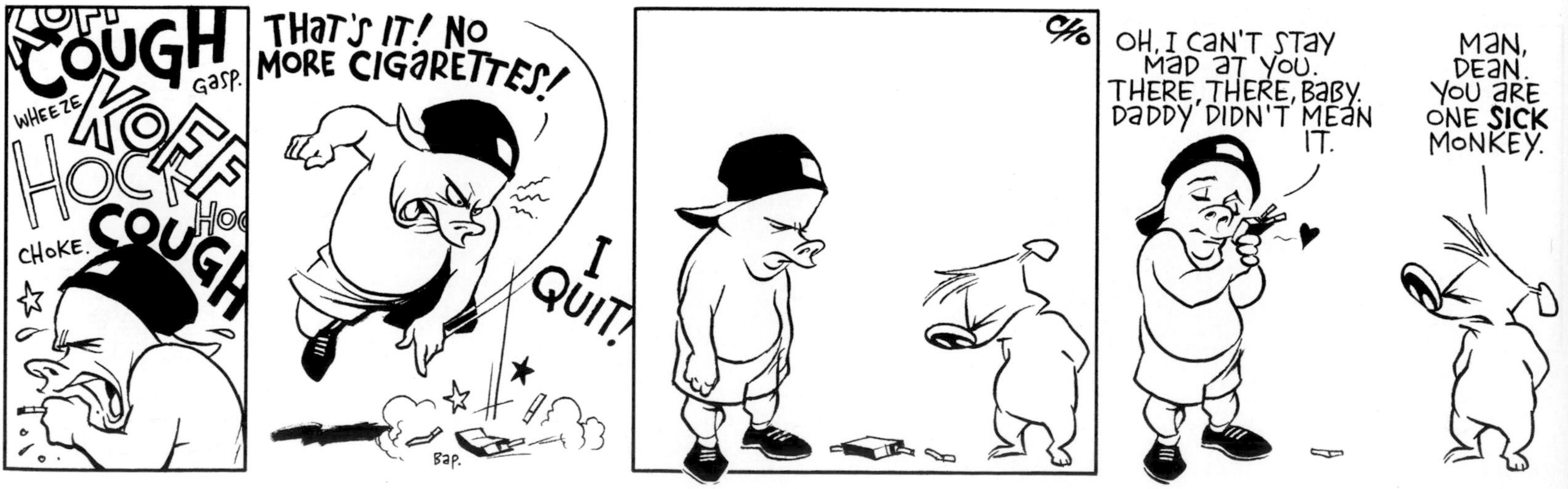
COUGH
GASP.
WHEEZE
KOFF
HOCK
CHOKE.
COUGH
THAT'S IT! NO MORE CIGARETTES!
I QUIT!
BAP.
OH, I CAN'T STAY MAD AT YOU. THERE, THERE, BABY. DADDY DIDN'T MEAN IT.
MAN, DEAN. YOU ARE ONE SICK MONKEY.

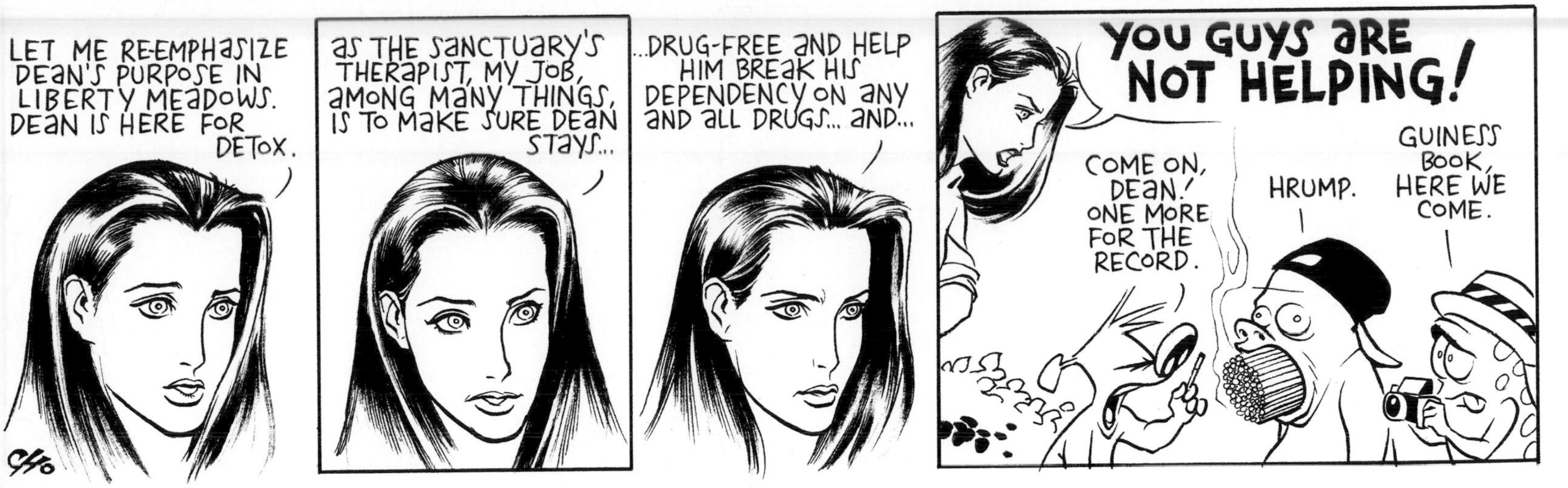
LET ME RE-EMPHASIZE DEAN'S PURPOSE IN LIBERTY MEADOWS. DEAN IS HERE FOR DETOX.
AS THE SANCTUARY'S THERAPIST, MY JOB, AMONG MANY THINGS, IS TO MAKE SURE DEAN STAYS...
...DRUG-FREE AND HELP HIM BREAK HIS DEPENDENCY ON ANY AND ALL DRUGS... AND...
YOU GUYS ARE NOT HELPING!
COME ON, DEAN! ONE MORE FOR THE RECORD.
HRUMP.
GUINESS BOOK, HERE WE COME.
CHO

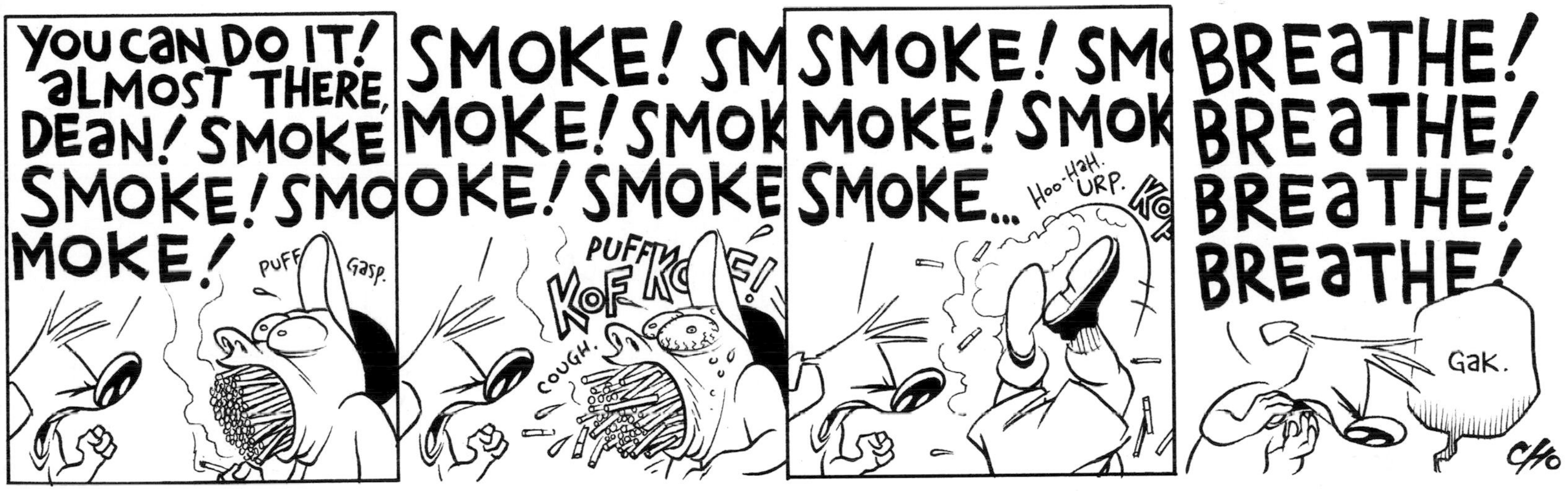
YOU CAN DO IT! ALMOST THERE, DEAN! SMOKE SMOKE! SMOKE!
PUFF
GASP.
SMOKE! SMOKE! SMOKE! SMOKE!
PUFF
KOF KOF!
COUGH.
SMOKE! SMOKE! SMOKE...
HOO-HAH.
URP.
KOF
BREATHE! BREATHE! BREATHE! BREATHE!
GAK.
CHO

ATTENTION
No actors or animals were hurt during the filming of the following sequence, except for one stunt monkey named Roy.

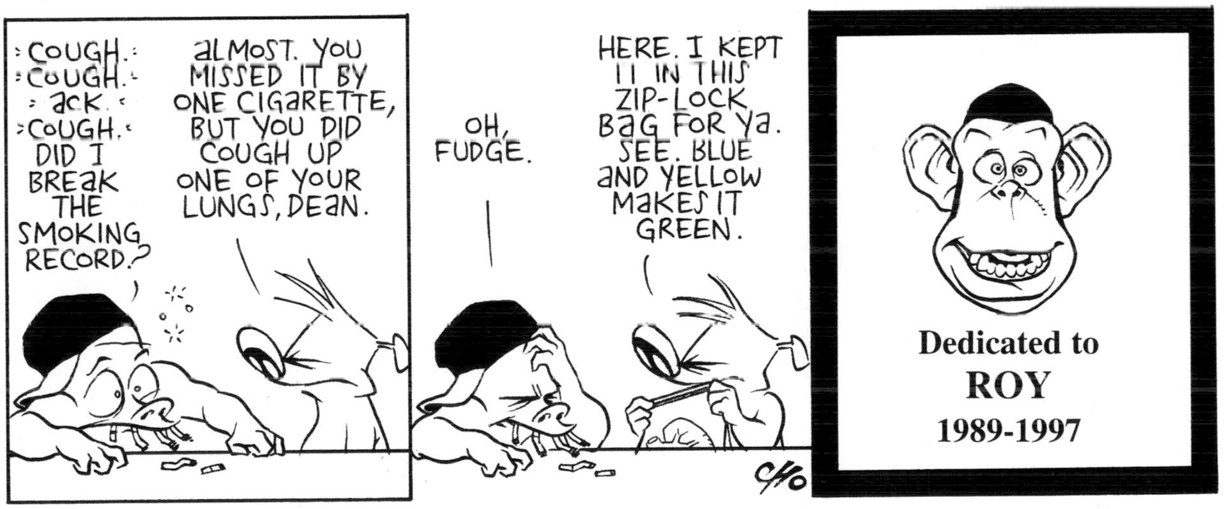
COUGH. COUGH. ACK. COUGH. DID I BREAK THE SMOKING RECORD?
ALMOST. YOU MISSED IT BY ONE CIGARETTE, BUT YOU DID COUGH UP ONE OF YOUR LUNGS, DEAN.
OH, FUDGE.
HERE. I KEPT IT IN THIS ZIP-LOCK BAG FOR YA. SEE. BLUE AND YELLOW MAKES IT GREEN.
CHO
Dedicated to
ROY
1989-1997

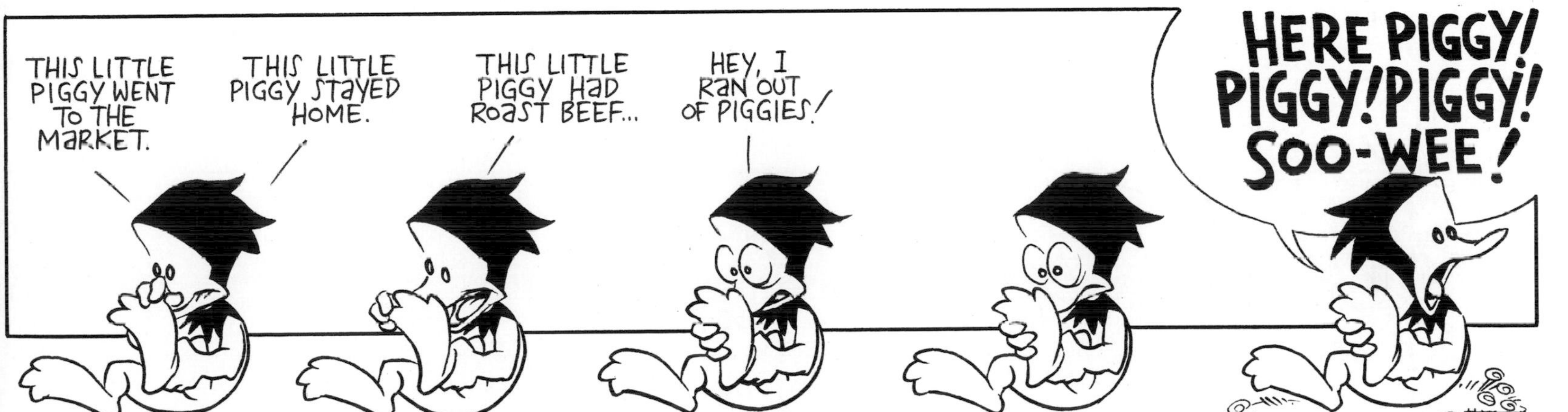
THIS LITTLE PIGGY WENT TO THE MARKET.
THIS LITTLE PIGGY STAYED HOME.
THIS LITTLE PIGGY HAD ROAST BEEF...
HEY, I RAN OUT OF PIGGIES!
HERE PIGGY! PIGGY! PIGGY! SOO-WEE!
CHO

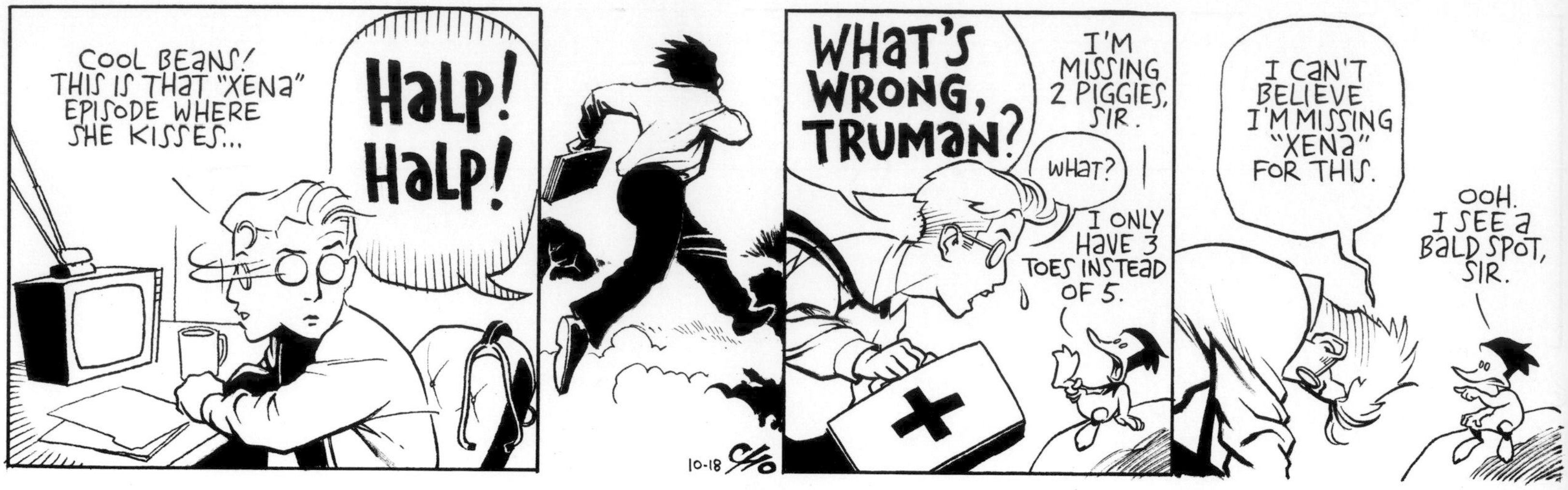
COOL BEANS! THIS IS THAT "XENA" EPISODE WHERE SHE KISSES...
HALP! HALP!
WHAT'S WRONG, TRUMAN?
I'M MISSING 2 PIGGIES, SIR.
WHAT?
I ONLY HAVE 3 TOES INSTEAD OF 5.
I CAN'T BELIEVE I'M MISSING "XENA" FOR THIS.
OOH. I SEE A BALD SPOT, SIR.
10-18

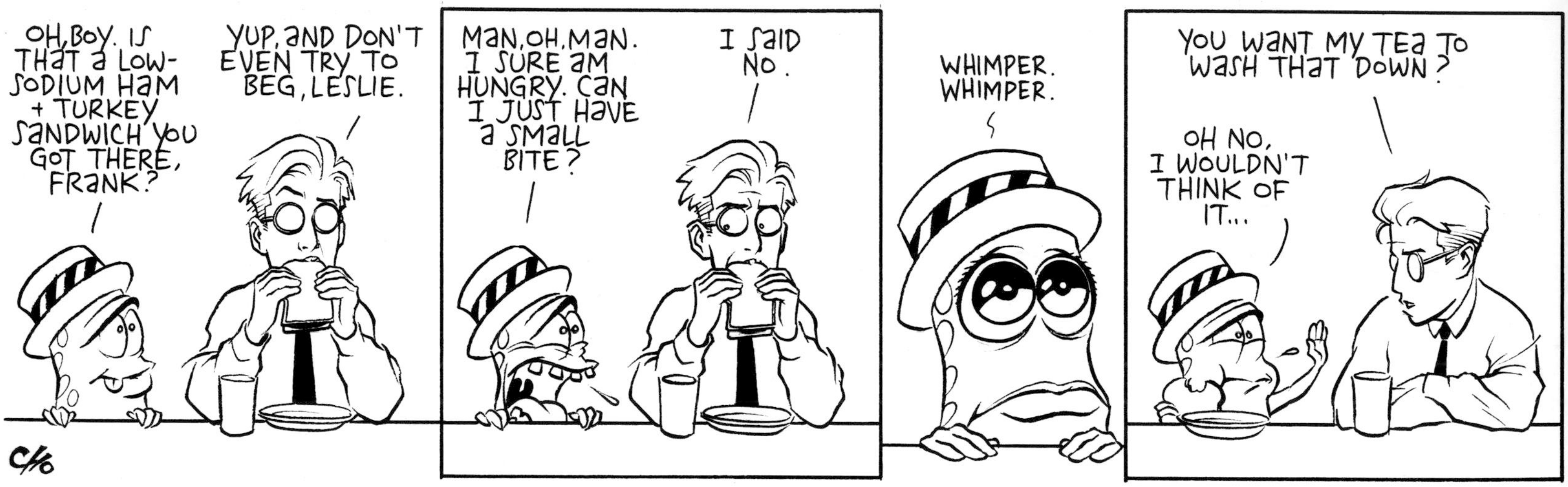
OH, BOY. IS THAT A LOW-SODIUM HAM + TURKEY SANDWICH YOU GOT THERE, FRANK?
YUP, AND DON'T EVEN TRY TO BEG, LESLIE.
MAN, OH, MAN. I SURE AM HUNGRY. CAN I JUST HAVE A SMALL BITE?
I SAID NO.
WHIMPER. WHIMPER.
YOU WANT MY TEA TO WASH THAT DOWN?
OH NO, I WOULDN'T THINK OF IT...

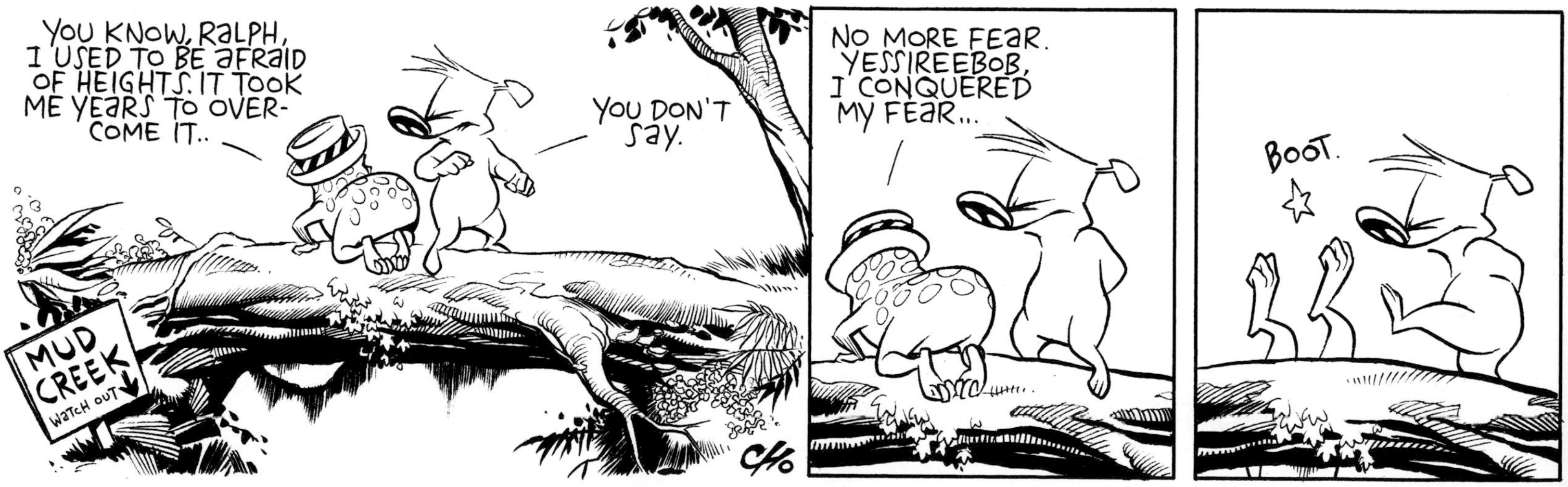
YOU KNOW, RALPH, I USED TO BE AFRAID OF HEIGHTS. IT TOOK ME YEARS TO OVER-COME IT..
YOU DON'T SAY.
MUD CREEK
WATCH OUT
NO MORE FEAR. YESSIREEBOB, I CONQUERED MY FEAR...
BOOT.

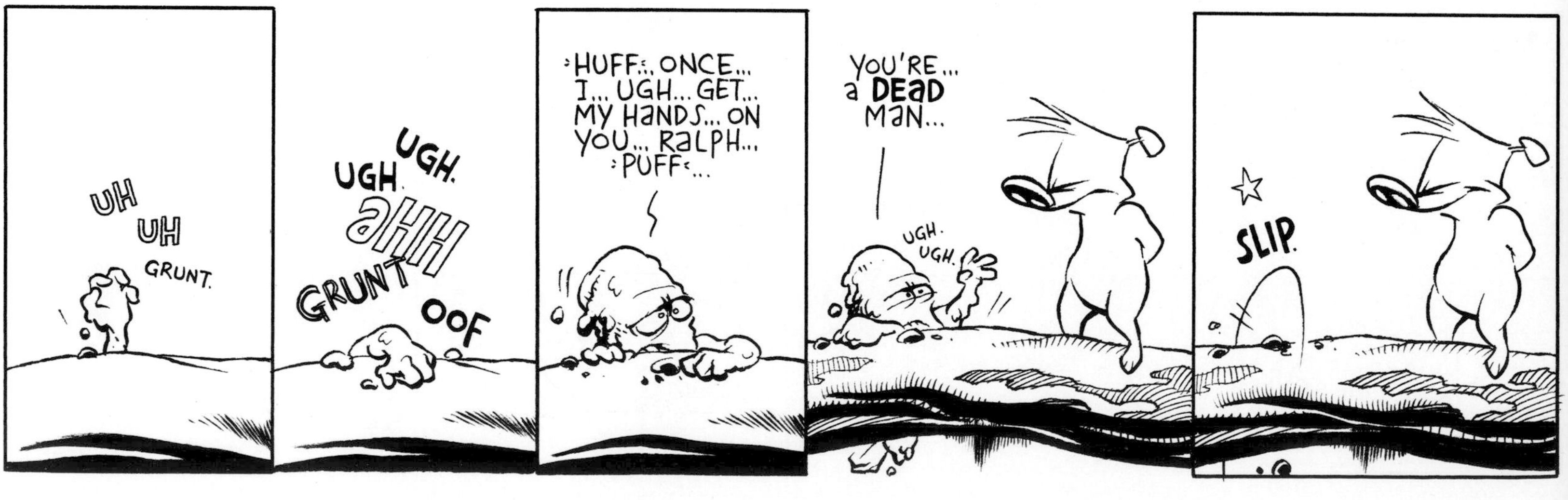
UH
UH
GRUNT.
UGH
UGH.
AHH
GRUNT
OOF
:HUFF:.. ONCE... I... UGH... GET... MY HANDS... ON YOU... RALPH... :PUFF:...
YOU'RE... A DEAD MAN...
UGH. UGH.
SLIP.

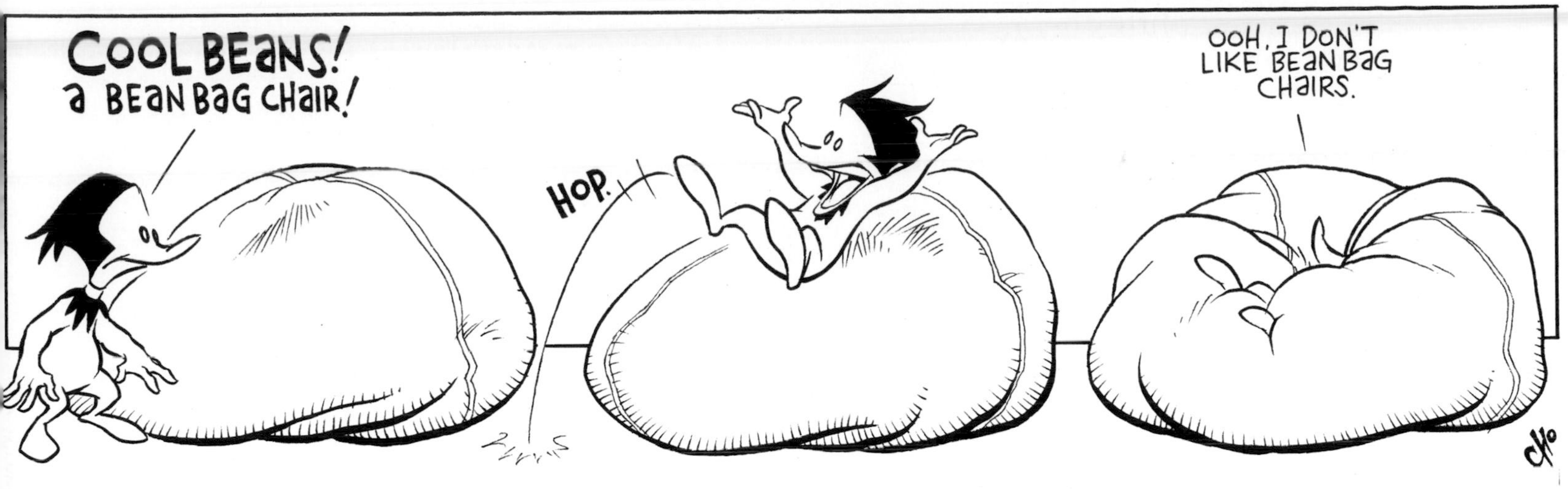
COOL BEANS!
a BEAN BAG CHAIR!
HOP.
OOH, I DON'T LIKE BEAN BAG CHAIRS.

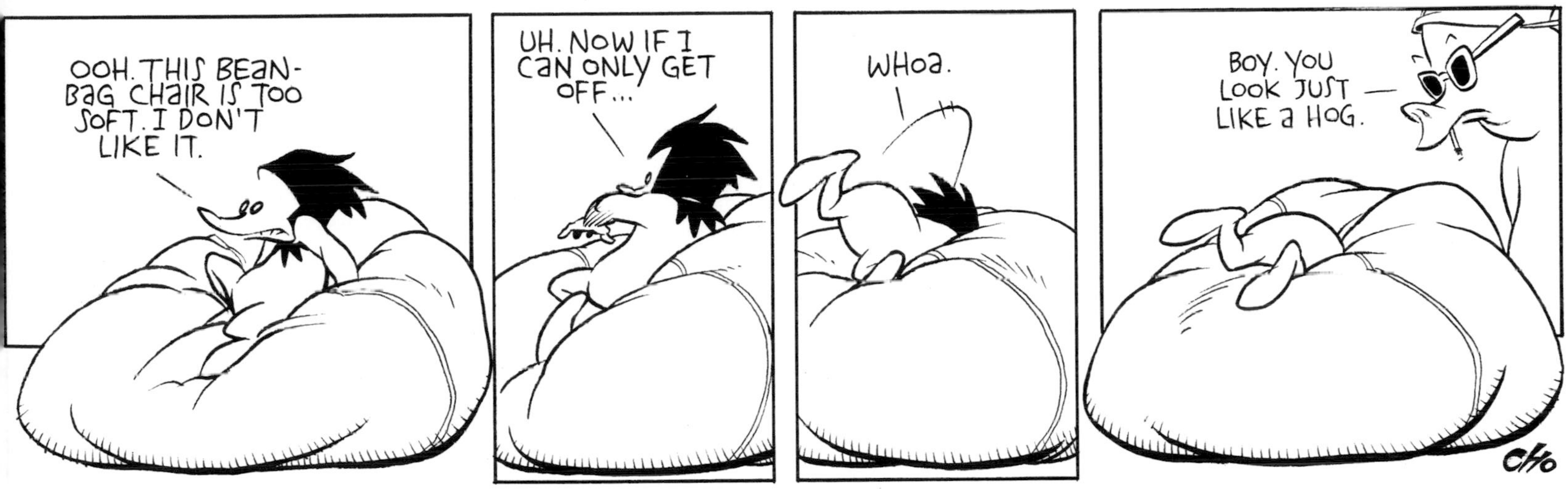
OOH. THIS BEAN-BAG CHAIR IS TOO SOFT. I DON'T LIKE IT.
UH. NOW IF I CAN ONLY GET OFF...
WHOA.
BOY. YOU LOOK JUST LIKE A HOG.

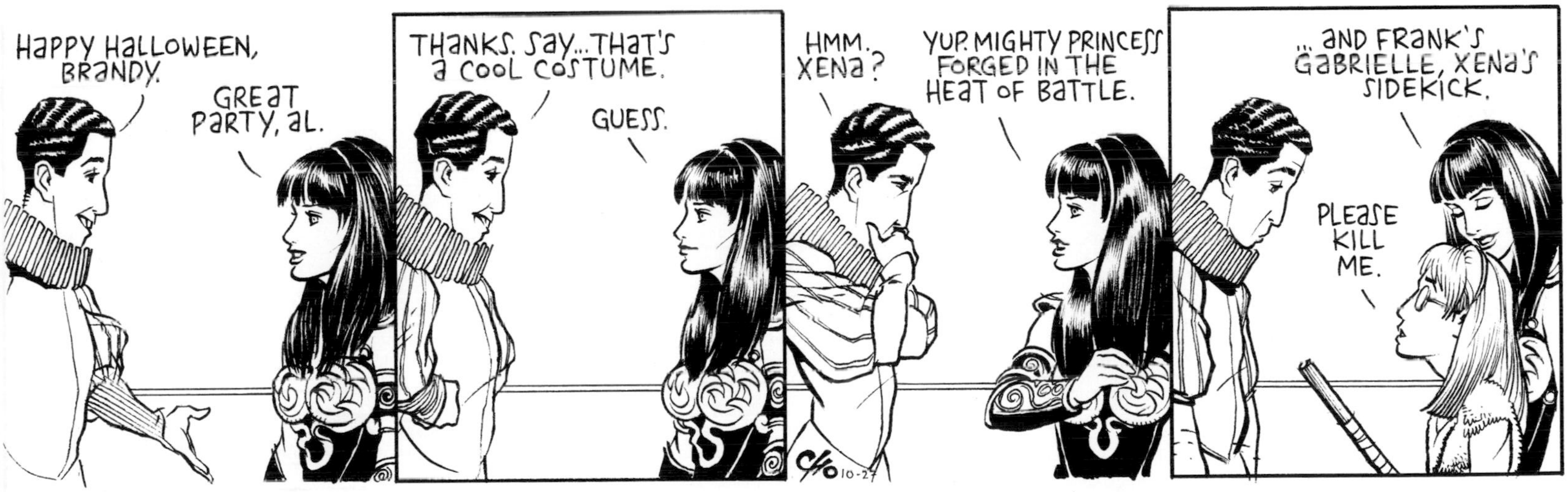
HAPPY HALLOWEEN, BRANDY.
GREAT PARTY, AL.
THANKS. SAY...THAT'S A COOL COSTUME.
GUESS.
HMM. XENA?
YUP. MIGHTY PRINCESS FORGED IN THE HEAT OF BATTLE.
...AND FRANK'S GABRIELLE, XENA'S SIDEKICK.
PLEASE KILL ME.

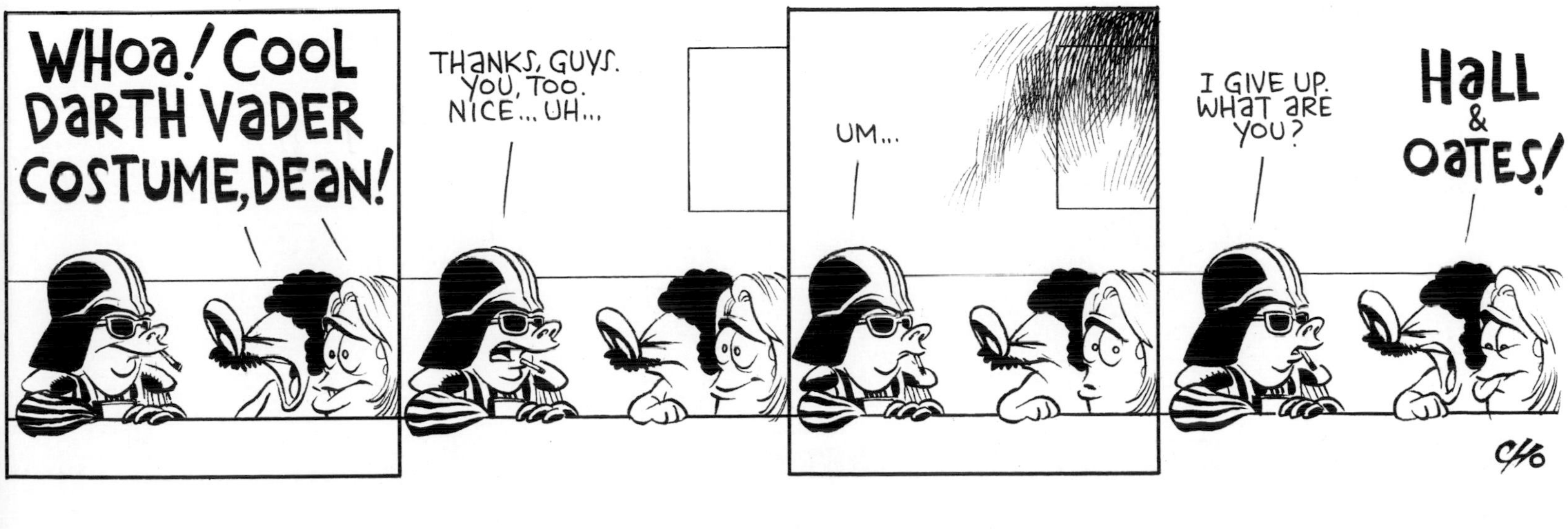
WHOA! COOL DARTH VADER COSTUME, DEAN!
THANKS, GUYS. YOU, TOO. NICE... UH...
UM...
I GIVE UP. WHAT ARE YOU?
HALL & OATES!

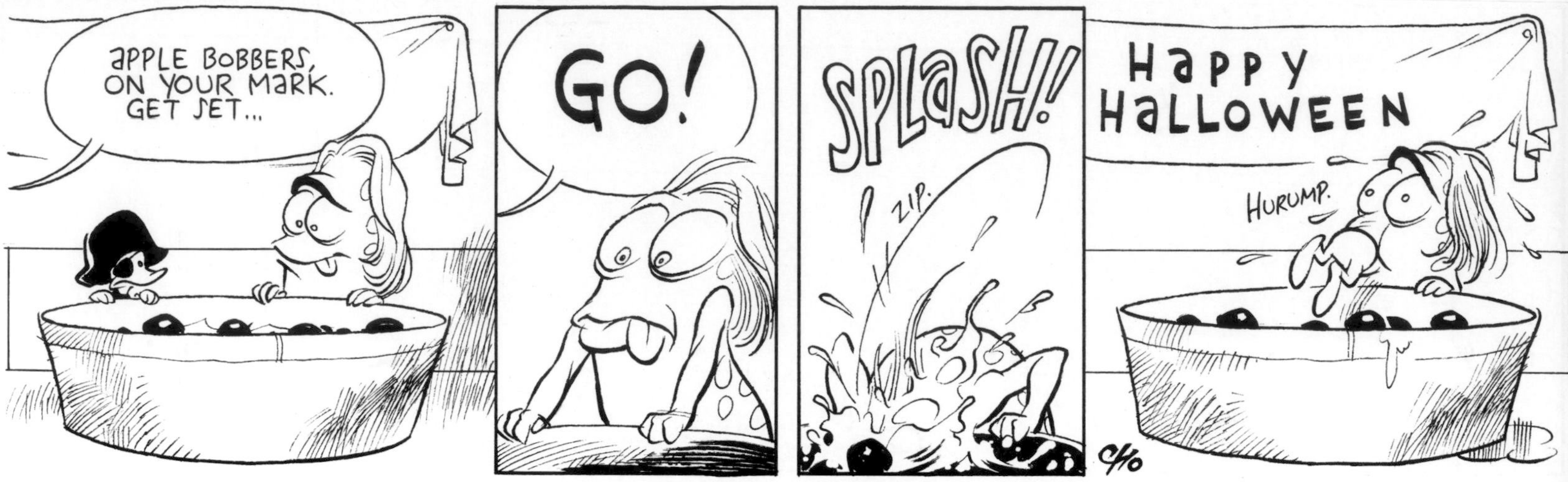
APPLE BOBBERS, ON YOUR MARK. GET SET...
GO!
SPLASH!
ZIP.
HAPPY HALLOWEEN
HURUMP.

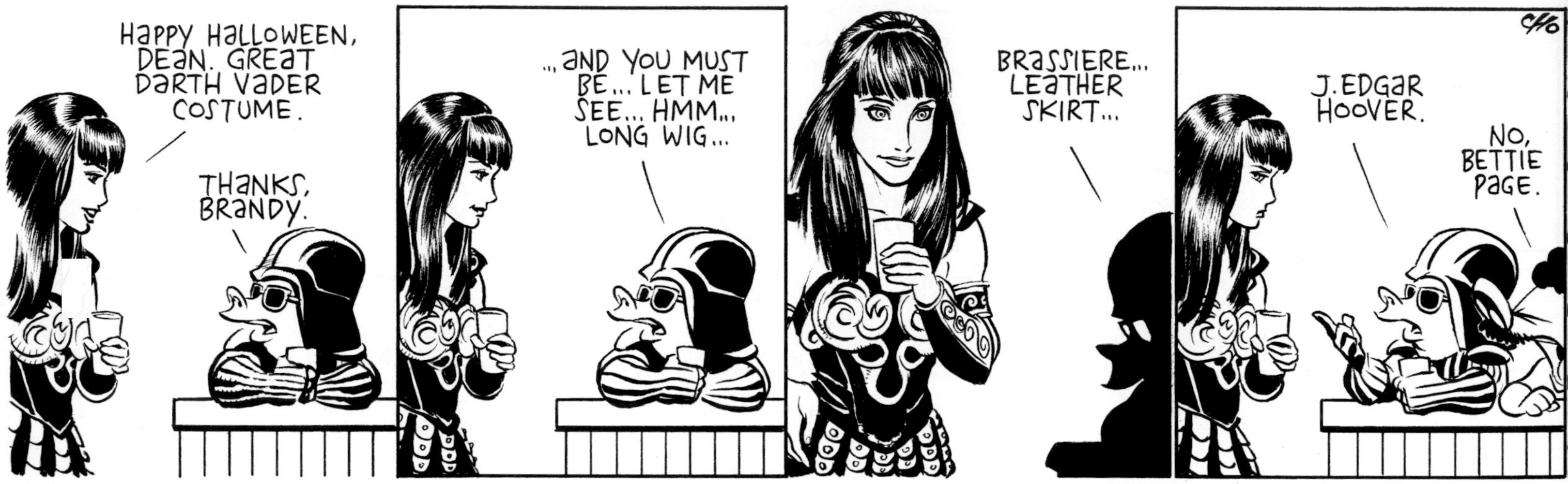
HAPPY HALLOWEEN, DEAN. GREAT DARTH VADER COSTUME.
THANKS, BRANDY.
...AND YOU MUST BE... LET ME SEE... HMM... LONG WIG...
BRASSIERE... LEATHER SKIRT...
J. EDGAR HOOVER.
NO, BETTIE PAGE.

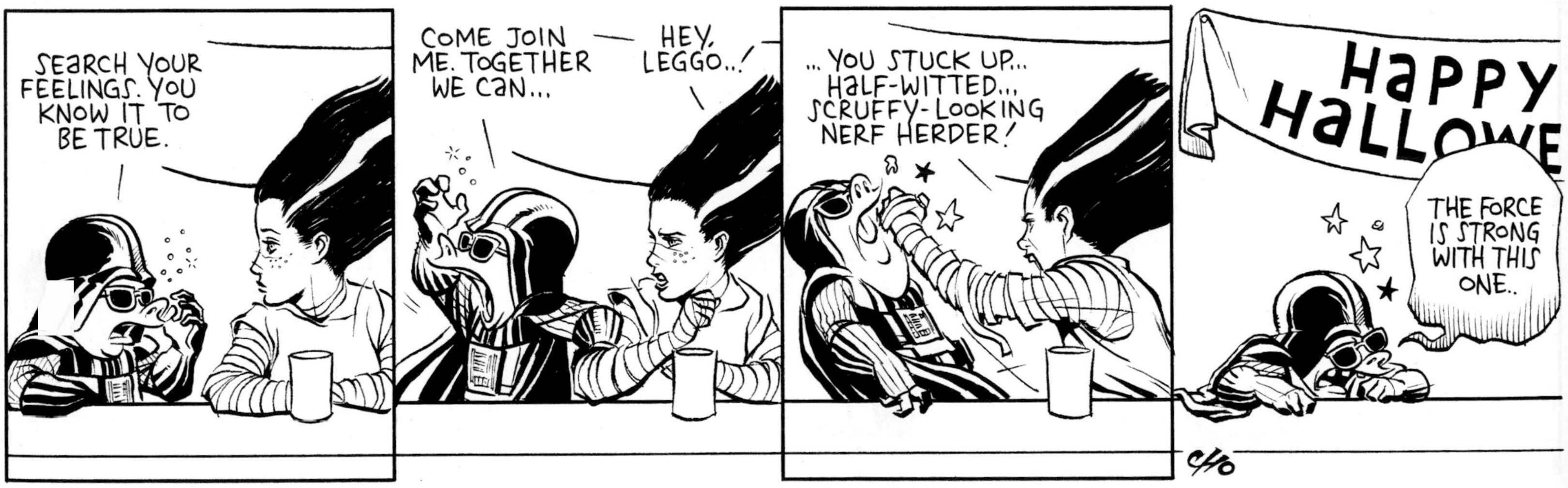
SEARCH YOUR FEELINGS. YOU KNOW IT TO BE TRUE.
COME JOIN ME. TOGETHER WE CAN...
HEY, LEGGO..!
...YOU STUCK UP.. HALF-WITTED... SCRUFFY-LOOKING NERF HERDER!
HAPPY HALLOWE
THE FORCE IS STRONG WITH THIS ONE..

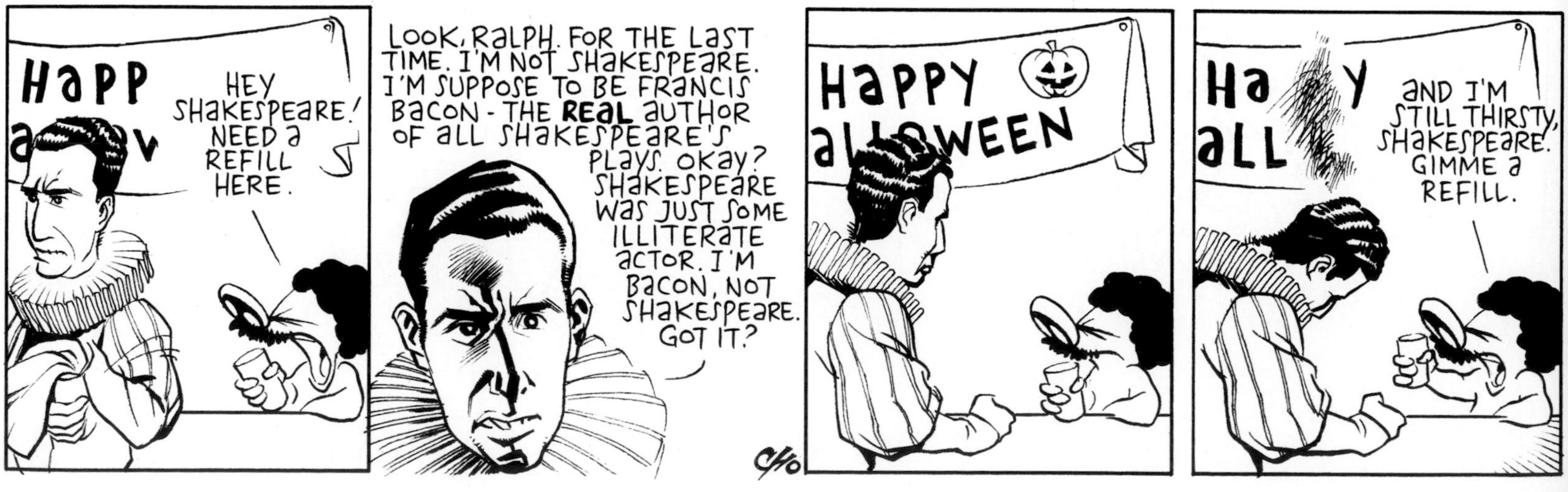
HAPP
HEY SHAKESPEARE! NEED A REFILL HERE.
LOOK, RALPH. FOR THE LAST TIME. I'M NOT SHAKESPEARE. I'M SUPPOSE TO BE FRANCIS BACON - THE **REAL** AUTHOR OF ALL SHAKESPEARE'S PLAYS. OKAY? SHAKESPEARE WAS JUST SOME ILLITERATE ACTOR. I'M BACON, NOT SHAKESPEARE. GOT IT?
HAPPY
ALLOWEEN
AND I'M STILL THIRSTY, SHAKESPEARE. GIMME A REFILL.

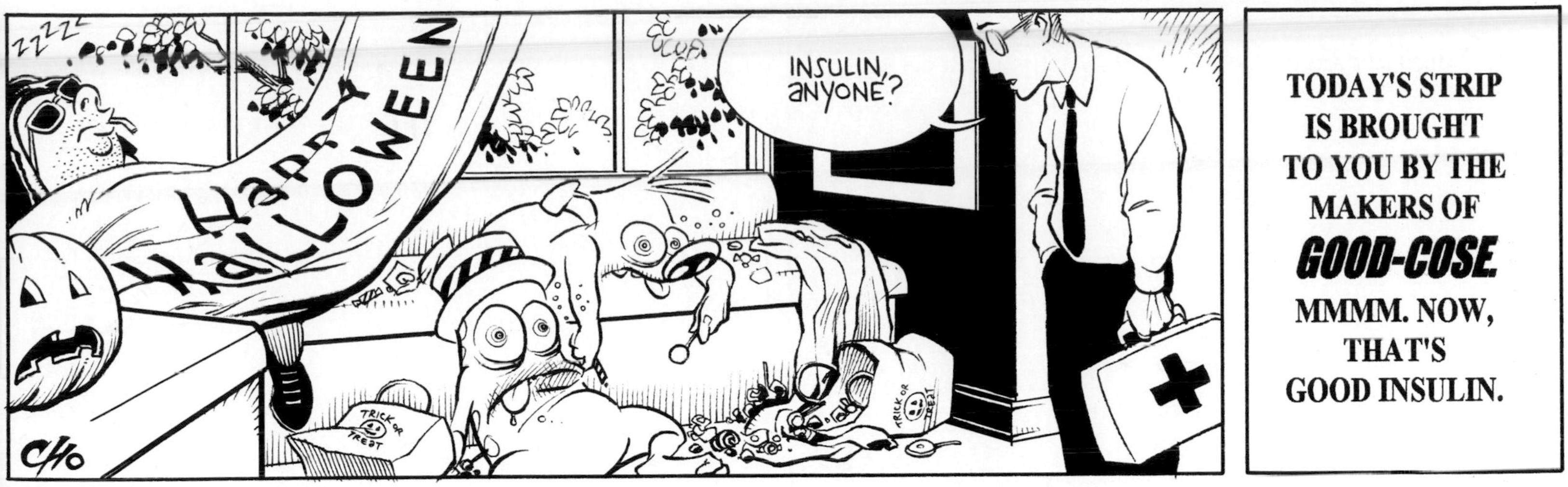
HAPPY HALLOWEEN
ZZZZZ
TRICK OR TREAT
INSULIN, ANYONE?
TODAY'S STRIP IS BROUGHT TO YOU BY THE MAKERS OF
GOOD-COSE.
MMMM. NOW, THAT'S GOOD INSULIN.

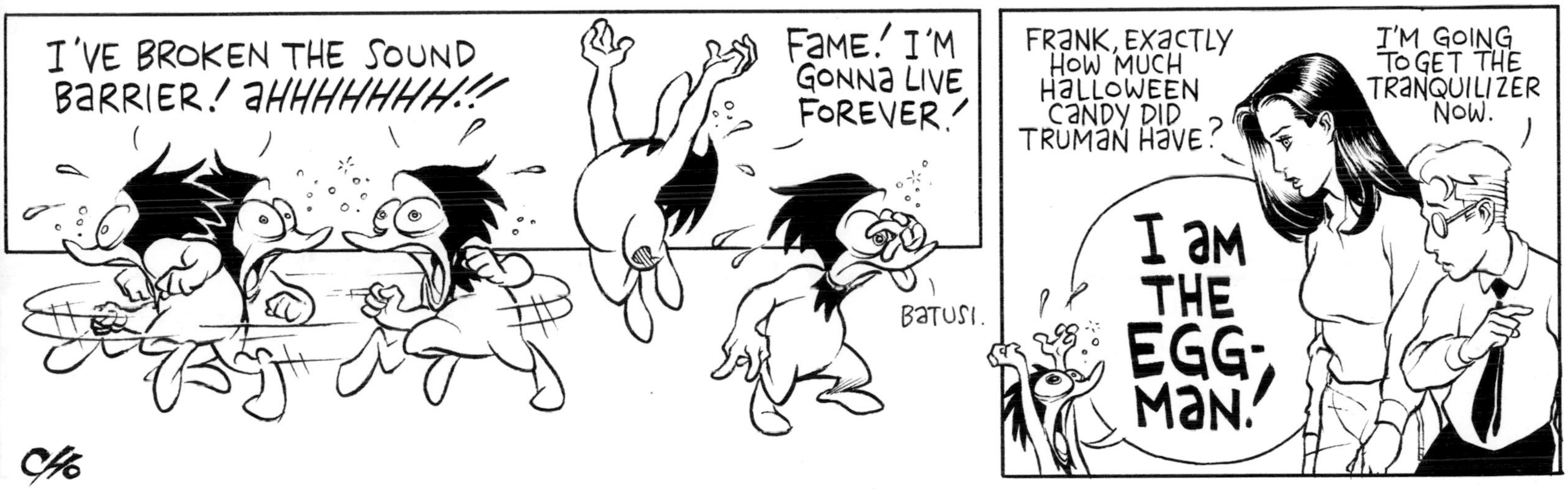
I'VE BROKEN THE SOUND BARRIER! AHHHHHHH!!!
FAME! I'M GONNA LIVE FOREVER!
BATUSI.
FRANK, EXACTLY HOW MUCH HALLOWEEN CANDY DID TRUMAN HAVE?
I'M GOING TO GET THE TRANQUILIZER NOW.
I AM THE EGG-MAN!

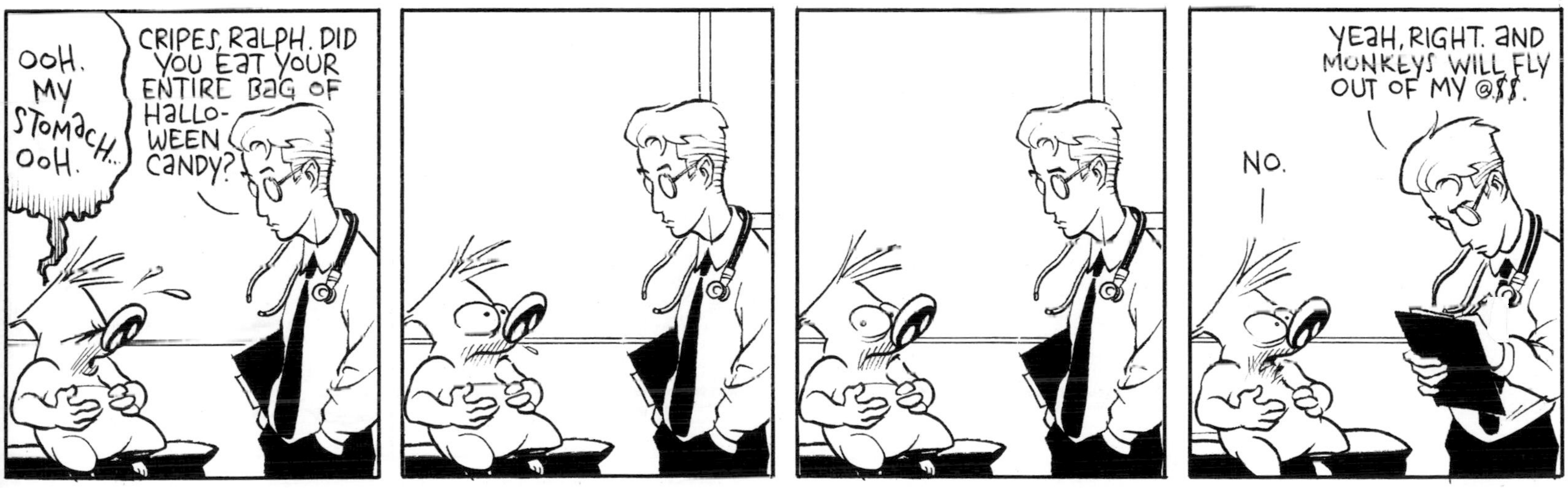
OOH. MY STOMACH... OOH.
CRIPES, RALPH. DID YOU EAT YOUR ENTIRE BAG OF HALLOWEEN CANDY?
NO.
YEAH, RIGHT. AND MONKEYS WILL FLY OUT OF MY @$$.

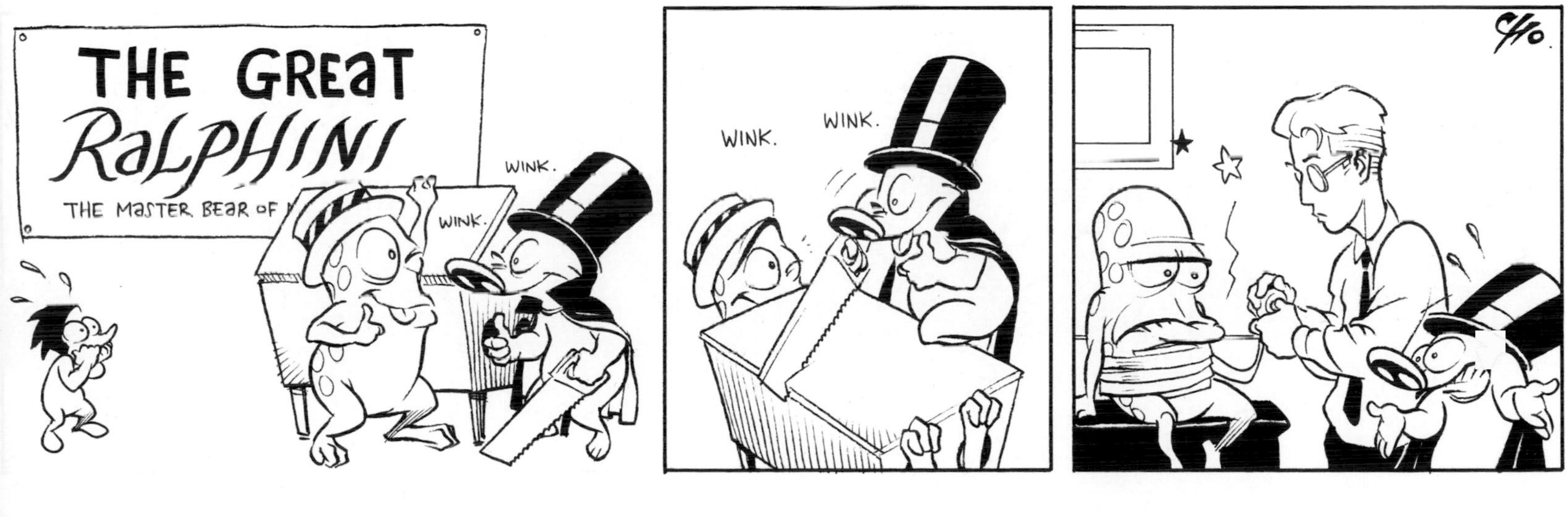
THE GREAT RALPHINI
THE MASTER BEAR OF
WINK.
WINK.
WINK.
WINK.

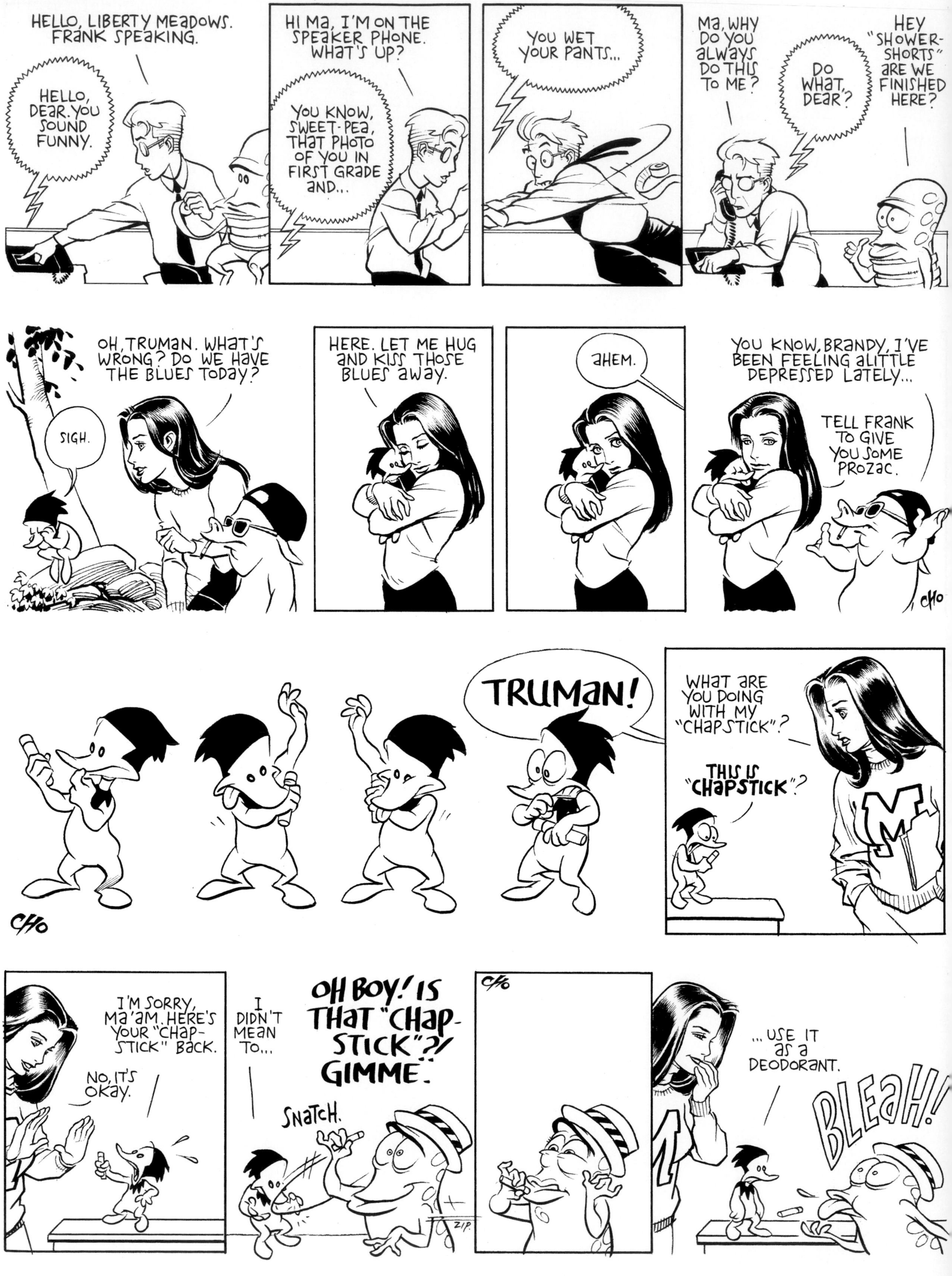
HELLO, LIBERTY MEADOWS. FRANK SPEAKING.
HELLO, DEAR. YOU SOUND FUNNY.
HI MA, I'M ON THE SPEAKER PHONE. WHAT'S UP?
YOU KNOW, SWEET-PEA, THAT PHOTO OF YOU IN FIRST GRADE AND...
YOU WET YOUR PANTS...
MA, WHY DO YOU ALWAYS DO THIS TO ME?
DO WHAT, DEAR?
HEY "SHOWER-SHORTS" ARE WE FINISHED HERE?
OH, TRUMAN. WHAT'S WRONG? DO WE HAVE THE BLUES TODAY?
SIGH.
HERE. LET ME HUG AND KISS THOSE BLUES AWAY.
AHEM.
YOU KNOW, BRANDY, I'VE BEEN FEELING ALITTLE DEPRESSED LATELY...
TELL FRANK TO GIVE YOU SOME PROZAC.
CHO
CHO
TRUMAN!
WHAT ARE YOU DOING WITH MY "CHAPSTICK"?
THIS IS "CHAPSTICK"?
I'M SORRY, MA'AM. HERE'S YOUR "CHAP-STICK" BACK.
NO, IT'S OKAY.
I DIDN'T MEAN TO...
OH BOY! IS THAT "CHAP-STICK"?! GIMME.
SNATCH.
ZIP.
CHO
...USE IT AS A DEODORANT.
BLEAH!

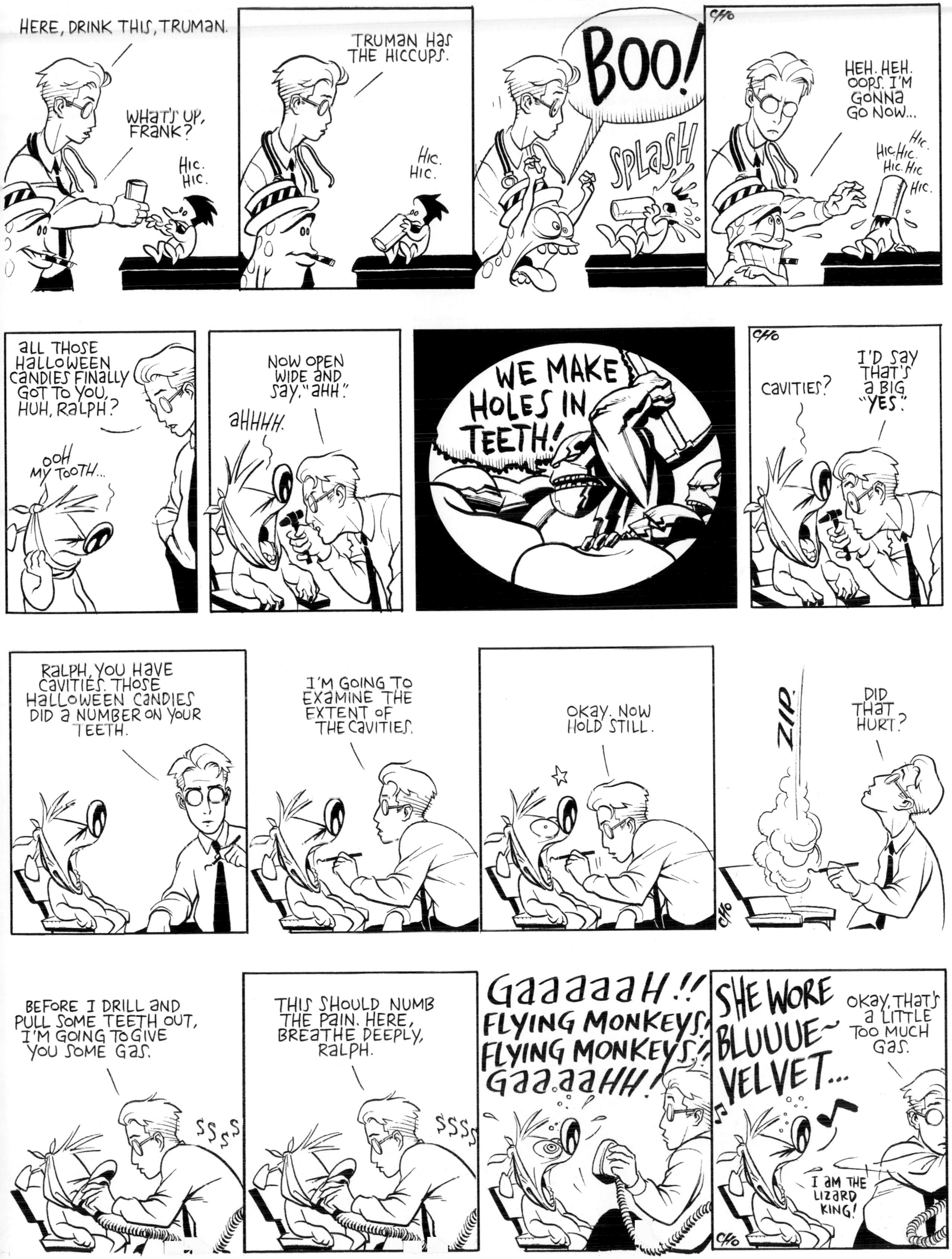

HERE, DRINK THIS, TRUMAN.
WHAT'S UP, FRANK?
HIC. HIC.
TRUMAN HAS THE HICCUPS.
HIC. HIC.
BOO!
SPLASH
HEH. HEH. OOPS. I'M GONNA GO NOW...
HIC. HIC. HIC. HIC. HIC HIC.
ALL THOSE HALLOWEEN CANDIES FINALLY GOT TO YOU, HUH, RALPH?
OOH MY TOOTH...
NOW OPEN WIDE AND SAY, "AHH."
AHHHH.
WE MAKE HOLES IN TEETH!
CAVITIES?
I'D SAY THAT'S A BIG "YES".
RALPH, YOU HAVE CAVITIES. THOSE HALLOWEEN CANDIES DID A NUMBER ON YOUR TEETH.
I'M GOING TO EXAMINE THE EXTENT OF THE CAVITIES.
OKAY. NOW HOLD STILL.
ZIP.
DID THAT HURT?
BEFORE I DRILL AND PULL SOME TEETH OUT, I'M GOING TO GIVE YOU SOME GAS.
SSSS
THIS SHOULD NUMB THE PAIN. HERE, BREATHE DEEPLY, RALPH.
SSSS
GAAAAAH!! FLYING MONKEYS! FLYING MONKEYS!! GAAAAHH!
SHE WORE BLUUUE~ VELVET...
OKAY, THAT'S A LITTLE TOO MUCH GAS.
I AM THE LIZARD KING!

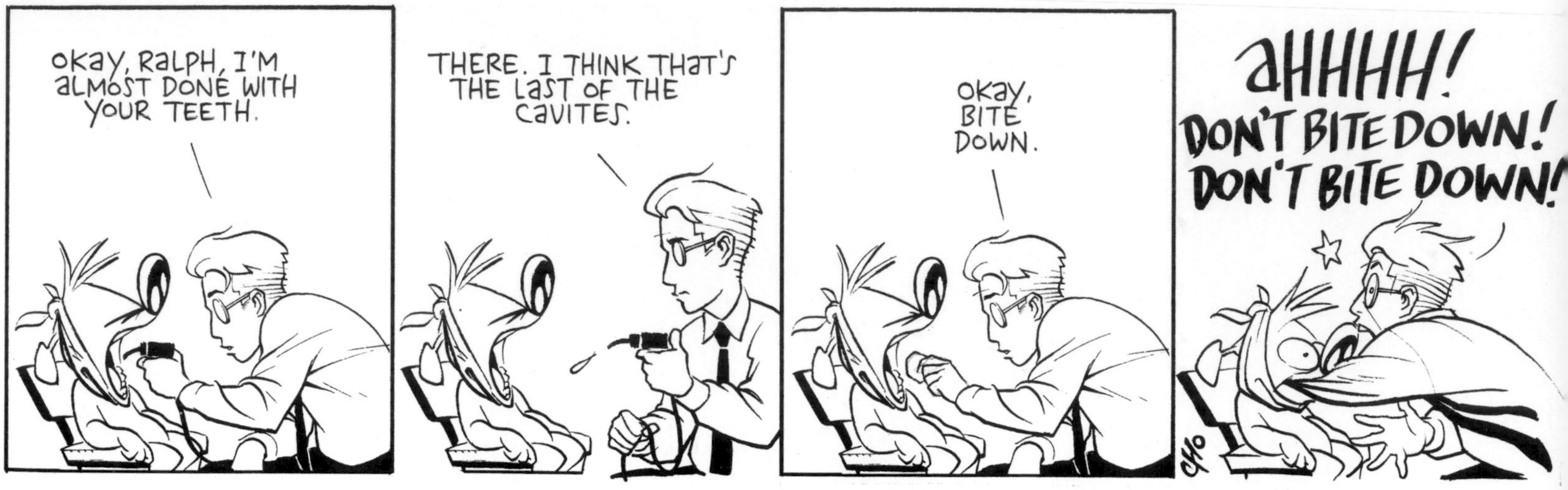
OKAY, RALPH, I'M ALMOST DONE WITH YOUR TEETH.
THERE. I THINK THAT'S THE LAST OF THE CAVITIES.
OKAY, BITE DOWN.
AHHHH!
DON'T BITE DOWN! DON'T BITE DOWN!
CHO

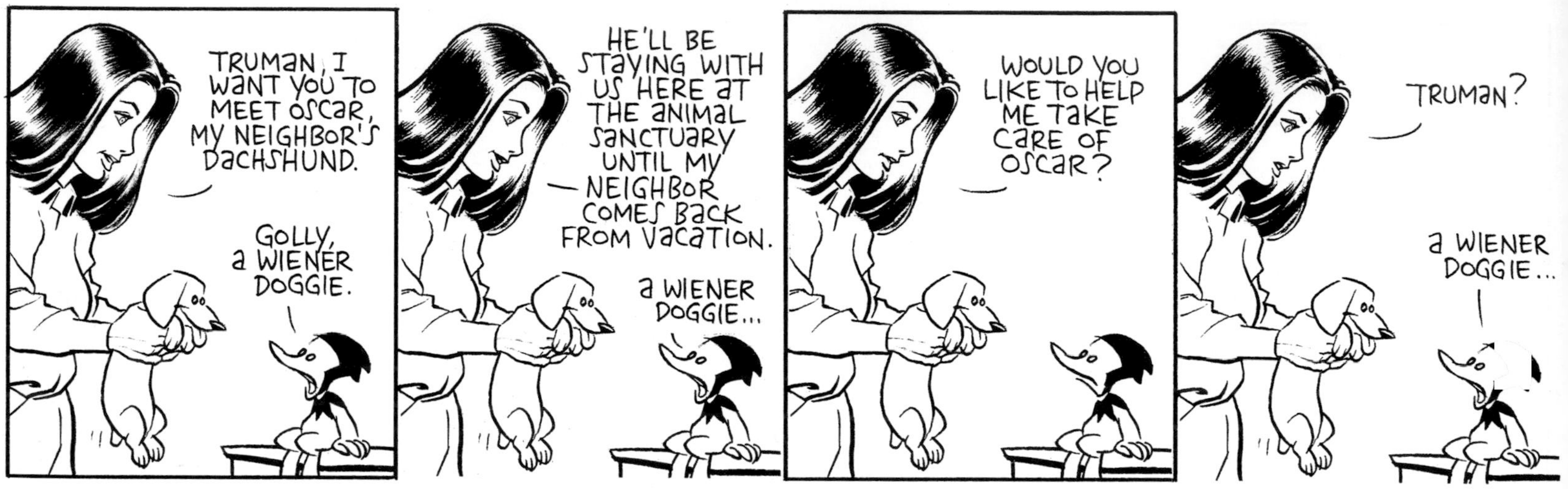
TRUMAN, I WANT YOU TO MEET OSCAR, MY NEIGHBOR'S DACHSHUND.
GOLLY, A WIENER DOGGIE.
HE'LL BE STAYING WITH US HERE AT THE ANIMAL SANCTUARY UNTIL MY NEIGHBOR COMES BACK FROM VACATION.
A WIENER DOGGIE...
WOULD YOU LIKE TO HELP ME TAKE CARE OF OSCAR?
TRUMAN?
A WIENER DOGGIE...

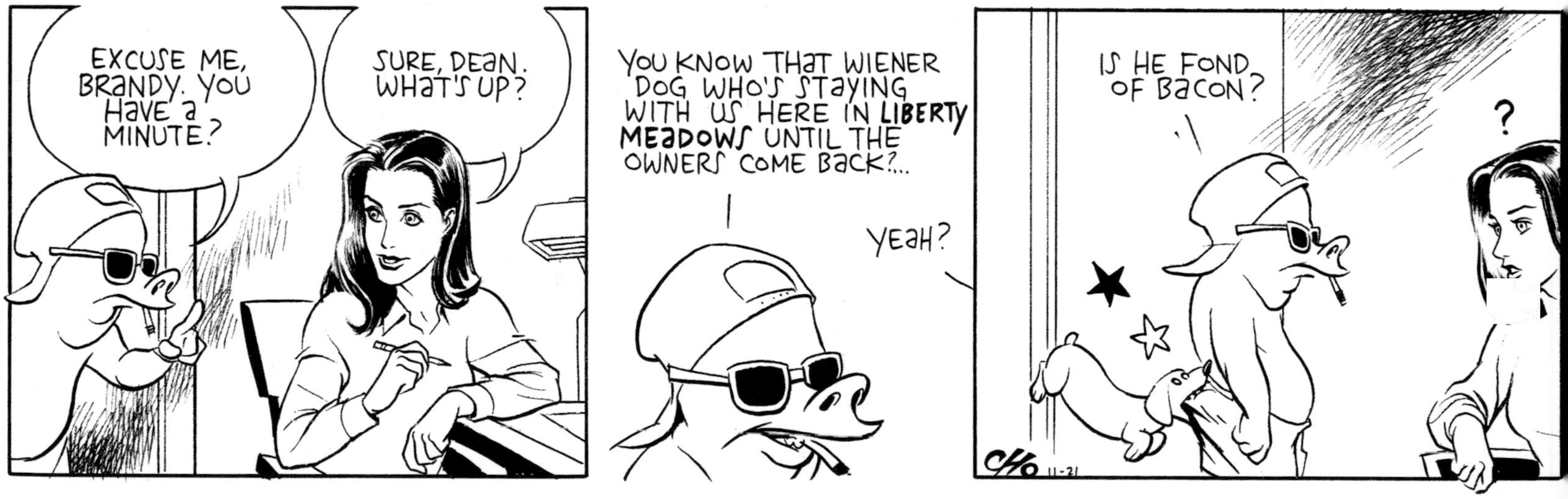
EXCUSE ME, BRANDY. YOU HAVE A MINUTE?
SURE, DEAN. WHAT'S UP?
YOU KNOW THAT WIENER DOG WHO'S STAYING WITH US HERE IN LIBERTY MEADOWS UNTIL THE OWNERS COME BACK?...
YEAH?
IS HE FOND OF BACON?
?
CHO 11-21

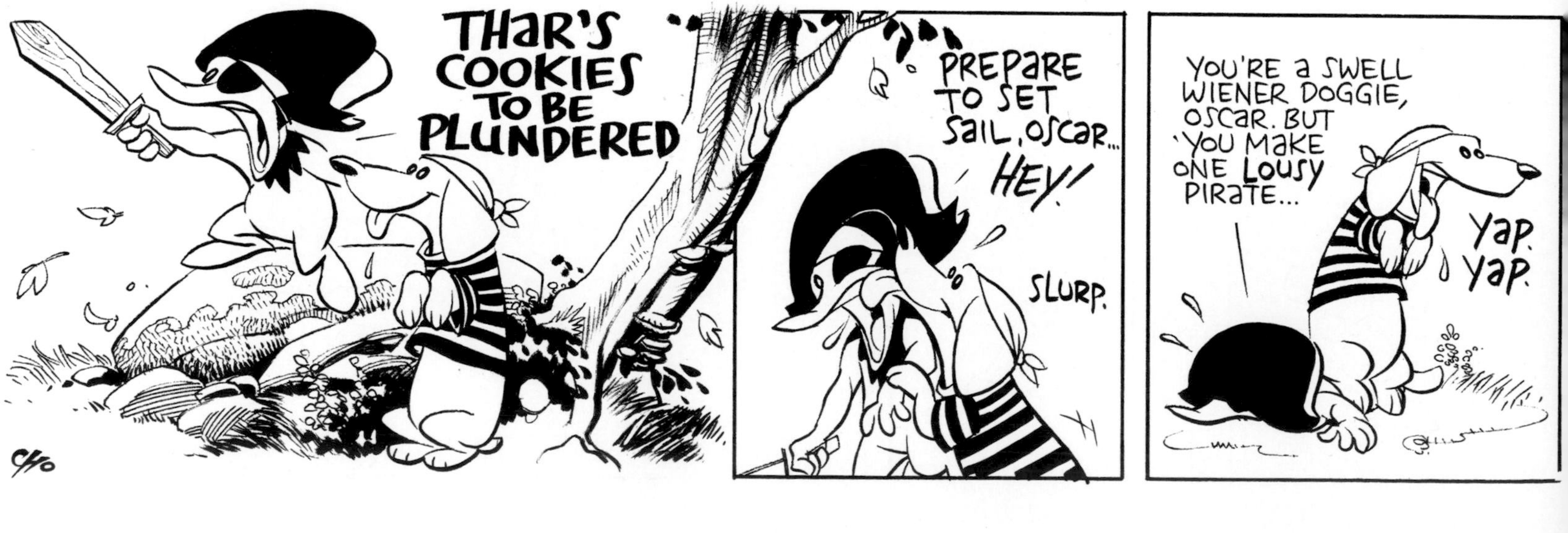
THAR'S COOKIES TO BE PLUNDERED
PREPARE TO SET SAIL, OSCAR...
HEY!
SLURP.
YOU'RE A SWELL WIENER DOGGIE, OSCAR. BUT YOU MAKE ONE LOUSY PIRATE...
YAP. YAP.
CHO

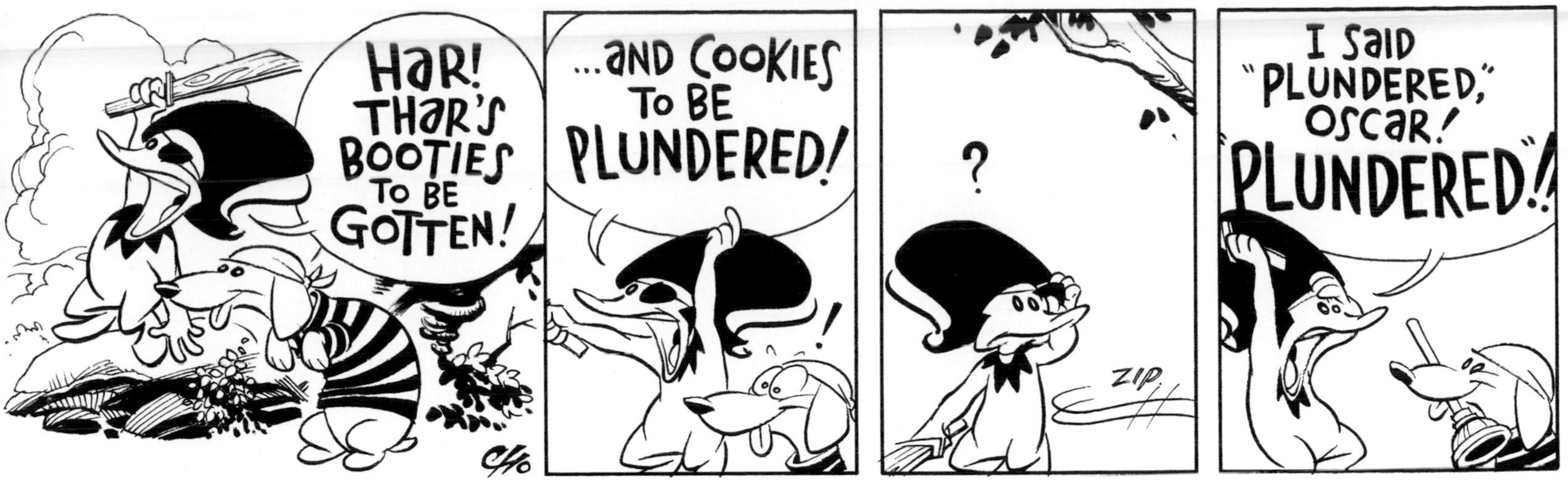
HAR! THAR'S BOOTIES TO BE GOTTEN!
...AND COOKIES TO BE PLUNDERED!
!
?
ZIP
I SAID "PLUNDERED," OSCAR! "PLUNDERED"!!

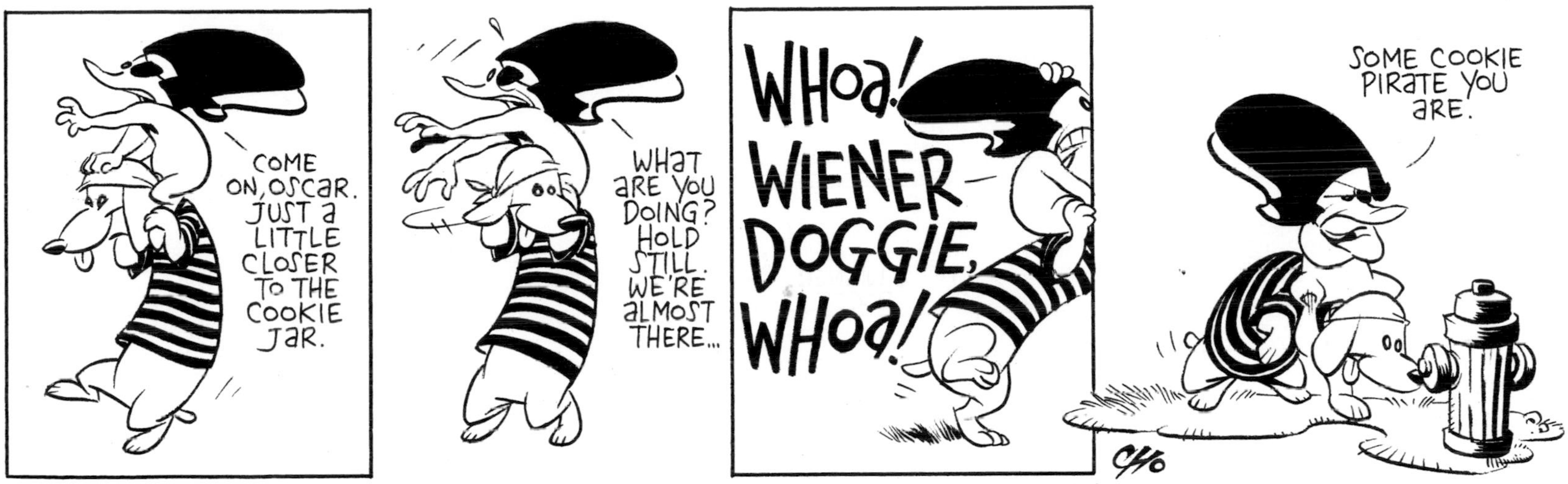
COME ON, OSCAR. JUST A LITTLE CLOSER TO THE COOKIE JAR.
WHAT ARE YOU DOING? HOLD STILL. WE'RE ALMOST THERE...
WHOA! WIENER DOGGIE, WHOA!
SOME COOKIE PIRATE YOU ARE.

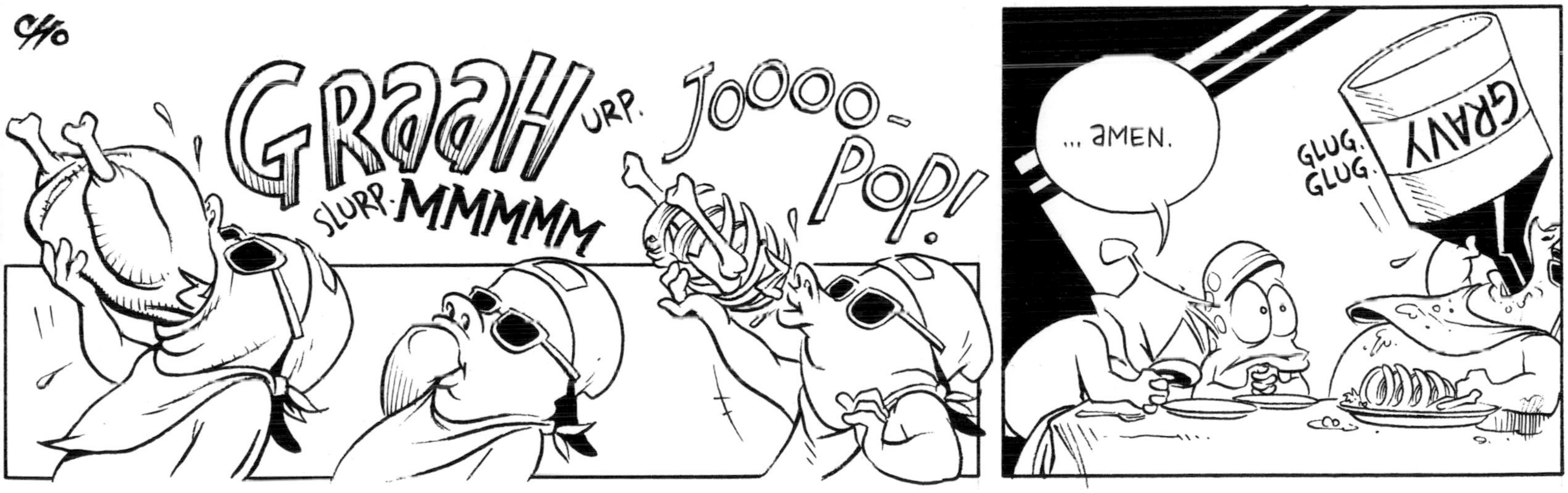
GRAAH
URP.
SLURP. MMMMMM
JOOOO-POP!
...AMEN.
GLUG. GLUG.
GRAVY

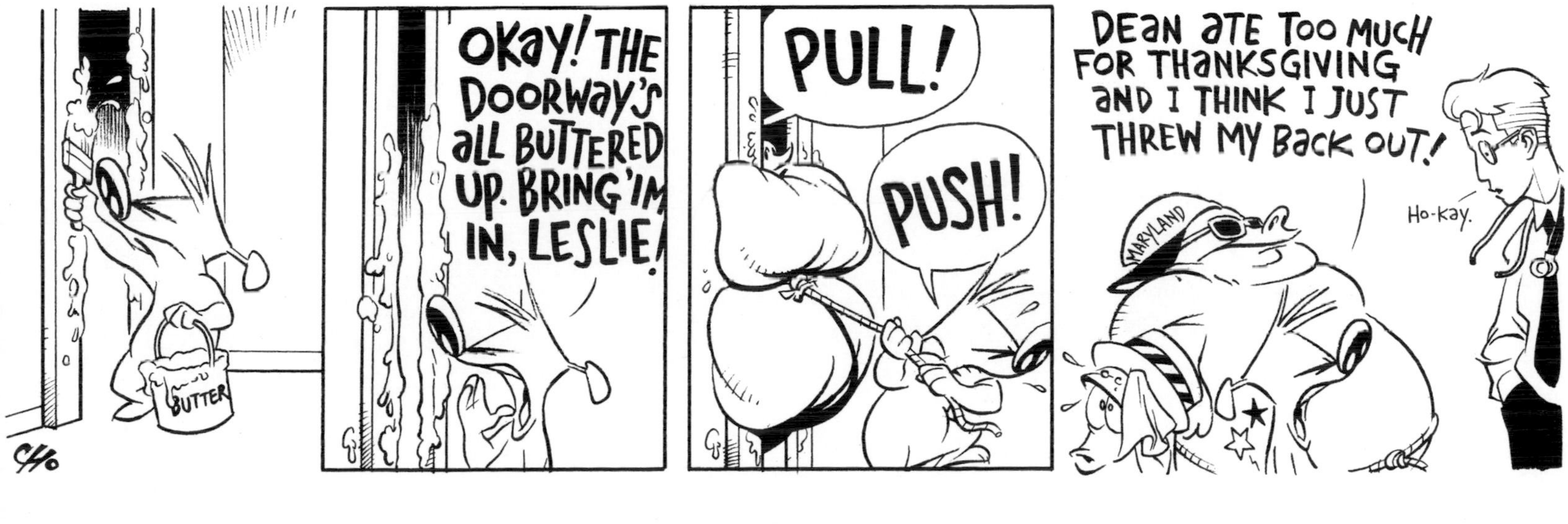
BUTTER
OKAY! THE DOORWAY'S ALL BUTTERED UP. BRING 'IM IN, LESLIE!
PULL!
PUSH!
DEAN ATE TOO MUCH FOR THANKSGIVING AND I THINK I JUST THREW MY BACK OUT!
HO-KAY.
MARYLAND

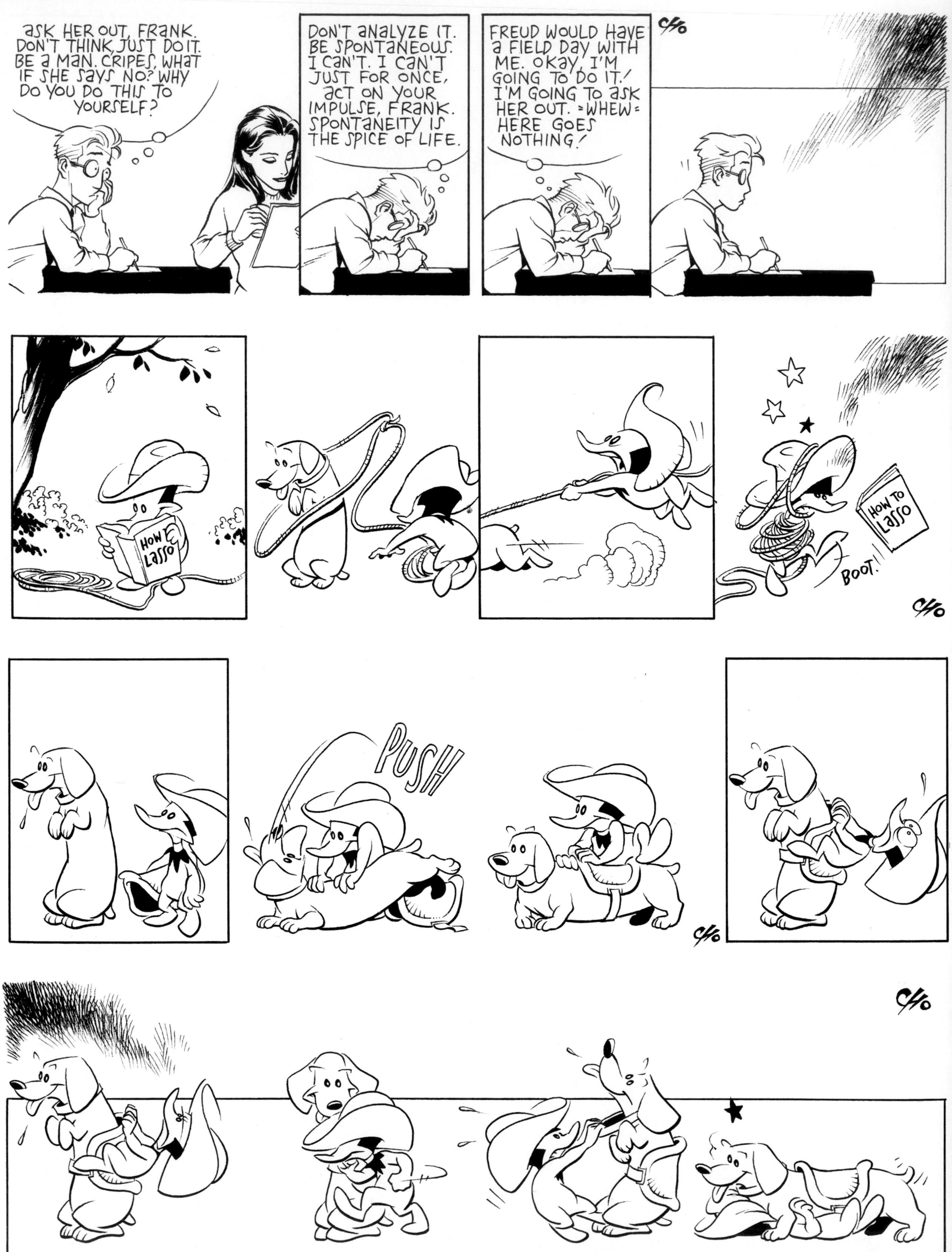
ASK HER OUT, FRANK. DON'T THINK, JUST DO IT. BE A MAN. CRIPES, WHAT IF SHE SAYS NO? WHY DO YOU DO THIS TO YOURSELF?
DON'T ANALYZE IT. BE SPONTANEOUS. I CAN'T. I CAN'T JUST FOR ONCE, ACT ON YOUR IMPULSE, FRANK. SPONTANEITY IS THE SPICE OF LIFE.
FREUD WOULD HAVE A FIELD DAY WITH ME. OKAY, I'M GOING TO DO IT! I'M GOING TO ASK HER OUT. =WHEW= HERE GOES NOTHING!
CHO
HOW LASSO
HOW TO LASSO
BOOT!
CHO
PUSH
CHO
CHO

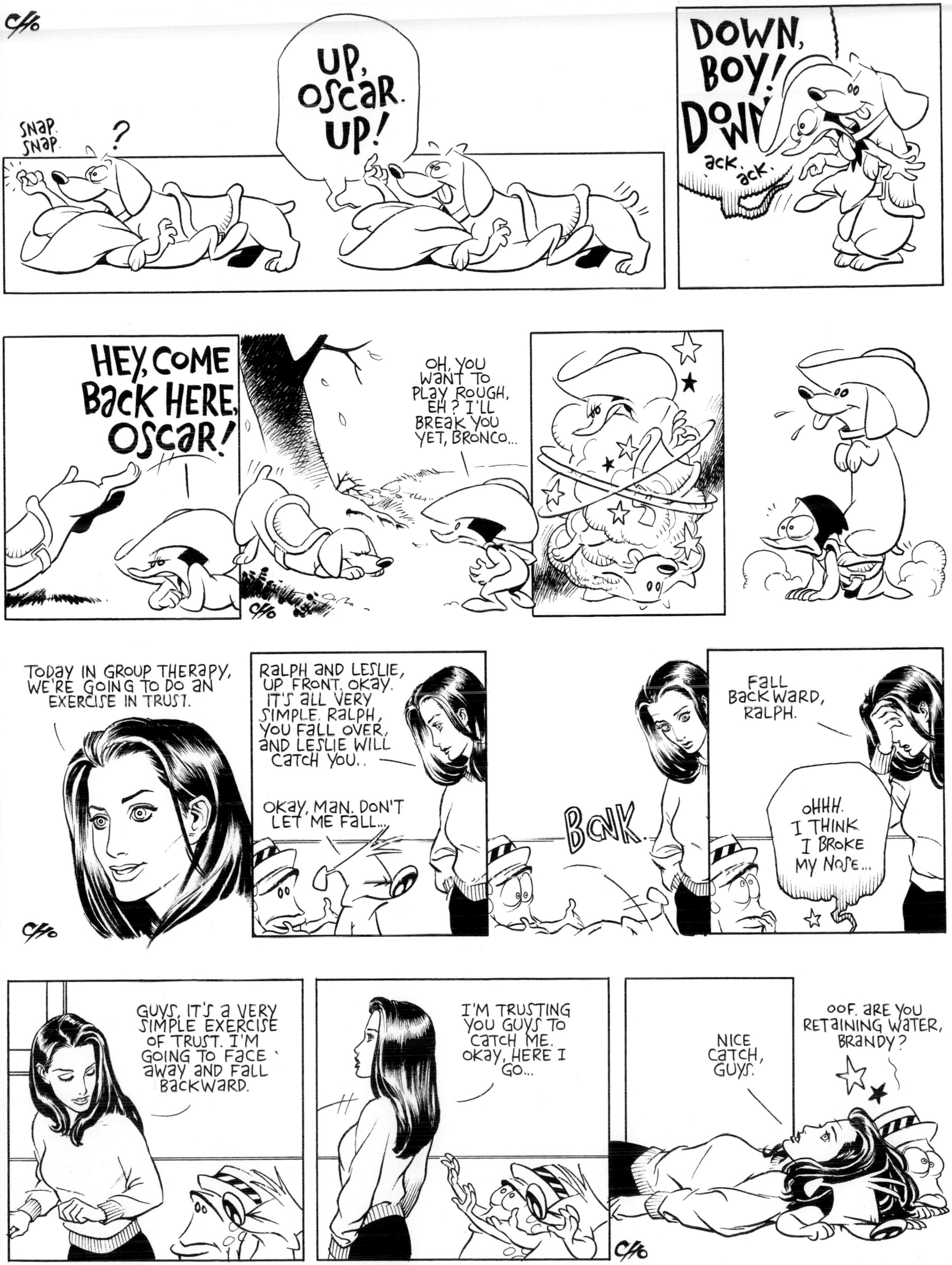
SNAP. SNAP.
?
UP, OSCAR. UP!
DOWN, BOY! DOWN
ack. ack.
HEY, COME BACK HERE, OSCAR!
OH, YOU WANT TO PLAY ROUGH, EH? I'LL BREAK YOU YET, BRONCO...
TODAY IN GROUP THERAPY, WE'RE GOING TO DO AN EXERCISE IN TRUST.
RALPH AND LESLIE, UP FRONT. OKAY. IT'S ALL VERY SIMPLE. RALPH, YOU FALL OVER, AND LESLIE WILL CATCH YOU..
OKAY, MAN. DON'T LET ME FALL...
BONK.
FALL BACKWARD, RALPH.
OHHH. I THINK I BROKE MY NOSE...
GUYS, IT'S A VERY SIMPLE EXERCISE OF TRUST. I'M GOING TO FACE AWAY AND FALL BACKWARD.
I'M TRUSTING YOU GUYS TO CATCH ME. OKAY, HERE I GO...
NICE CATCH, GUYS.
OOF. ARE YOU RETAINING WATER, BRANDY?

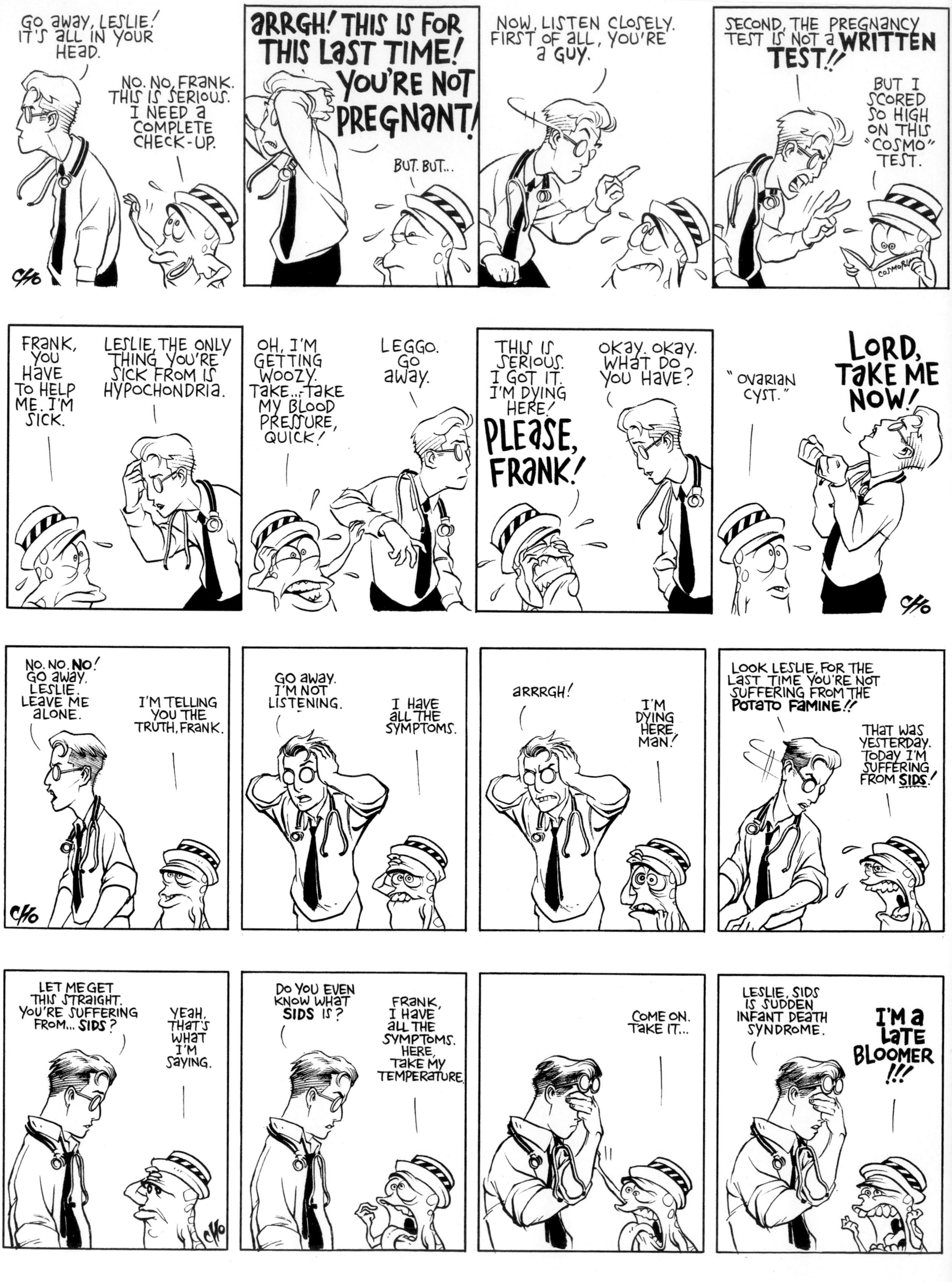
GO AWAY, LESLIE! IT'S ALL IN YOUR HEAD.
NO. NO, FRANK. THIS IS SERIOUS. I NEED A COMPLETE CHECK-UP.
CHO
ARRGH! THIS IS FOR THIS LAST TIME! YOU'RE NOT PREGNANT!
BUT. BUT...
NOW, LISTEN CLOSELY. FIRST OF ALL, YOU'RE A GUY.
SECOND, THE PREGNANCY TEST IS NOT A WRITTEN TEST!!
BUT I SCORED SO HIGH ON THIS "COSMO" TEST.
FRANK, YOU HAVE TO HELP ME. I'M SICK.
LESLIE, THE ONLY THING YOU'RE SICK FROM IS HYPOCHONDRIA.
OH, I'M GETTING WOOZY. TAKE... TAKE MY BLOOD PRESSURE, QUICK!
LEGGO. GO AWAY.
THIS IS SERIOUS. I GOT IT. I'M DYING HERE! PLEASE, FRANK!
OKAY. OKAY. WHAT DO YOU HAVE?
"OVARIAN CYST."
LORD, TAKE ME NOW!
CHO
NO. NO. NO! GO AWAY. LESLIE. LEAVE ME ALONE.
I'M TELLING YOU THE TRUTH, FRANK.
CHO
GO AWAY. I'M NOT LISTENING.
I HAVE ALL THE SYMPTOMS.
ARRRGH!
I'M DYING HERE, MAN!
LOOK LESLIE, FOR THE LAST TIME YOU'RE NOT SUFFERING FROM THE POTATO FAMINE!!
THAT WAS YESTERDAY. TODAY I'M SUFFERING FROM SIDS!
LET ME GET THIS STRAIGHT. YOU'RE SUFFERING FROM... SIDS?
YEAH, THAT'S WHAT I'M SAYING.
CHO
DO YOU EVEN KNOW WHAT SIDS IS?
FRANK, I HAVE ALL THE SYMPTOMS. HERE, TAKE MY TEMPERATURE.
COME ON. TAKE IT...
LESLIE, SIDS IS SUDDEN INFANT DEATH SYNDROME.
I'M A LATE BLOOMER!!!

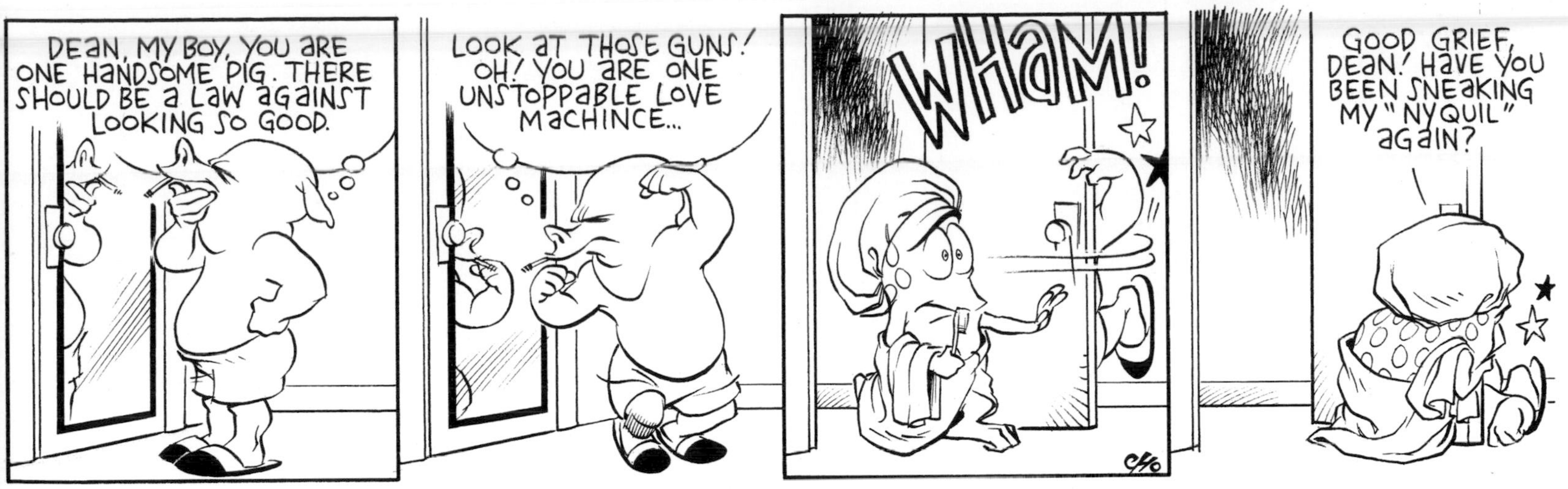
DEAN, MY BOY, YOU ARE ONE HANDSOME PIG. THERE SHOULD BE A LAW AGAINST LOOKING SO GOOD.
LOOK AT THOSE GUNS! OH! YOU ARE ONE UNSTOPPABLE LOVE MACHINCE...
WHAM!
GOOD GRIEF, DEAN! HAVE YOU BEEN SNEAKING MY "NYQUIL" AGAIN?
CHO

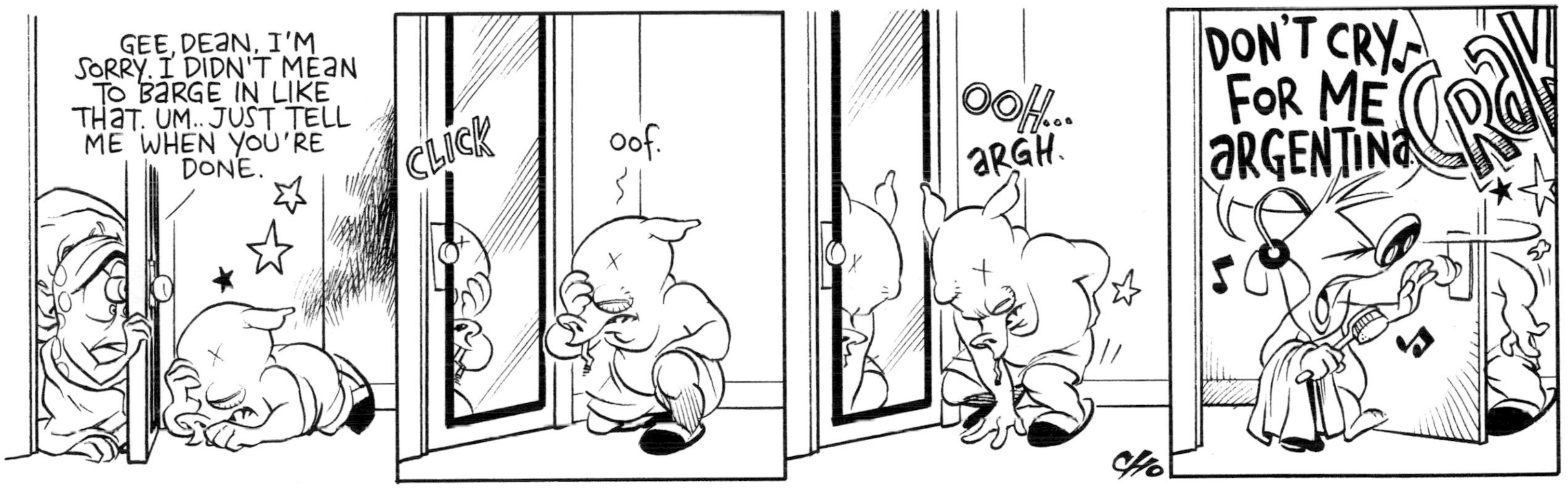
GEE, DEAN, I'M SORRY. I DIDN'T MEAN TO BARGE IN LIKE THAT. UM.. JUST TELL ME WHEN YOU'RE DONE.
CLICK
oof.
OOH... ARGH.
DON'T CRY FOR ME ARGENTINA
CHO

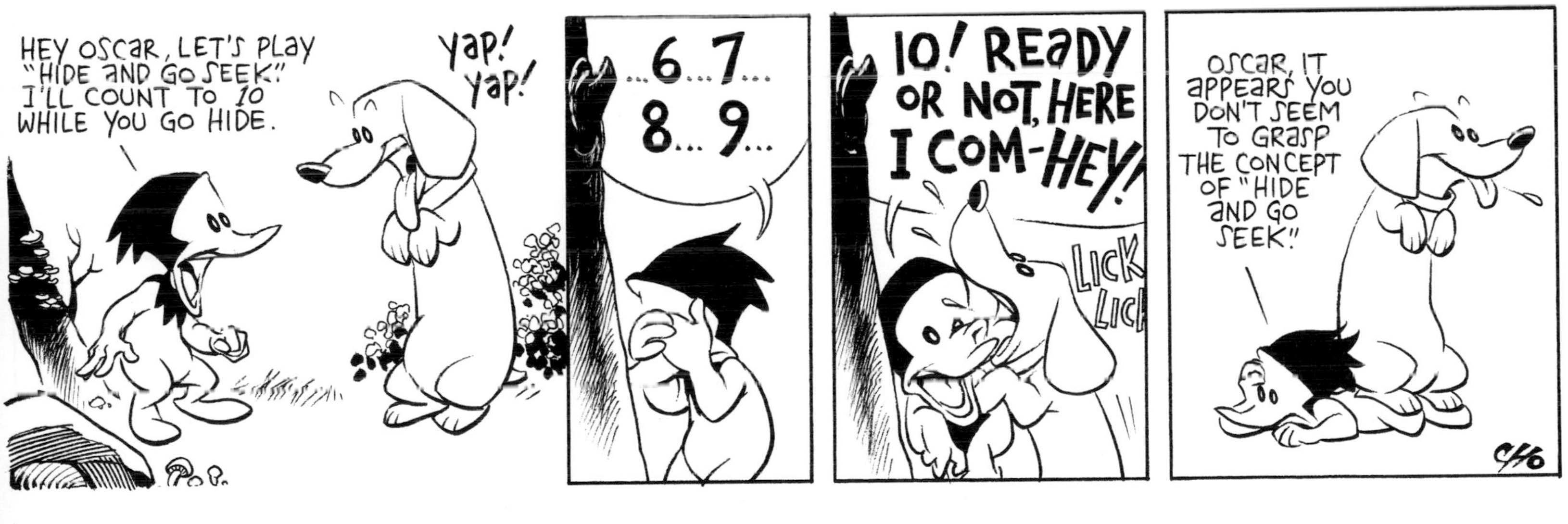
HEY OSCAR, LET'S PLAY "HIDE AND GO SEEK!" I'LL COUNT TO 10 WHILE YOU GO HIDE.
YAP! YAP!
...6...7... 8...9...
10! READY OR NOT, HERE I COM-HEY!
LICK LICK
OSCAR, IT APPEARS YOU DON'T SEEM TO GRASP THE CONCEPT OF "HIDE AND GO SEEK."
CHO

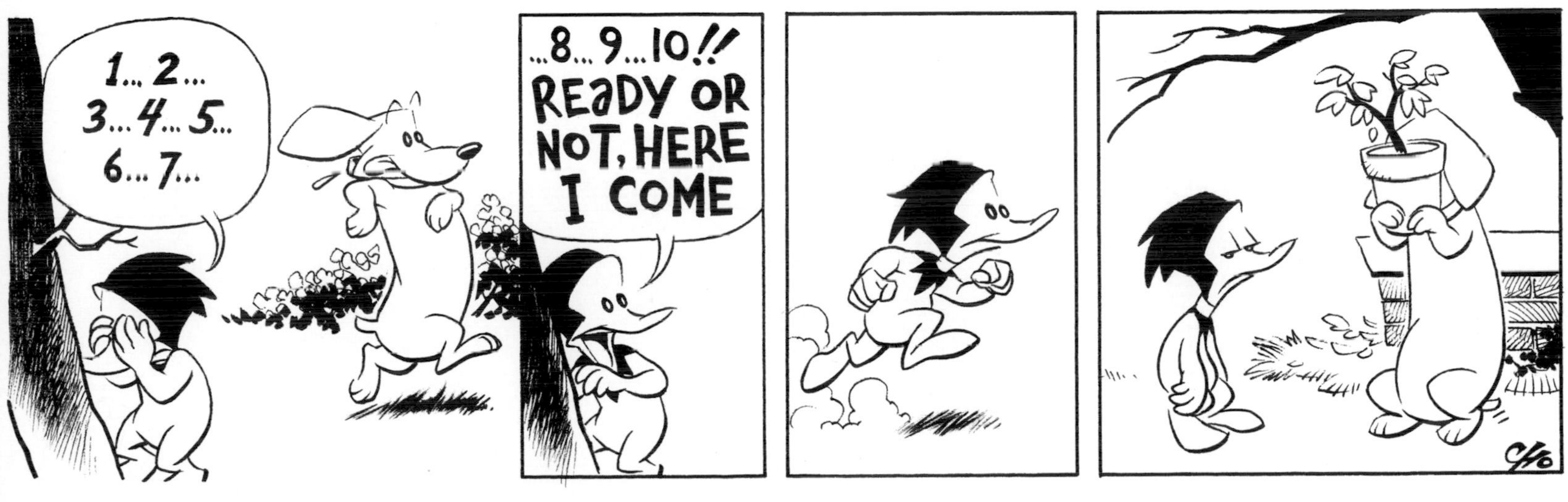
1... 2... 3... 4... 5... 6... 7...
...8... 9... 10!! READY OR NOT, HERE I COME
CHO

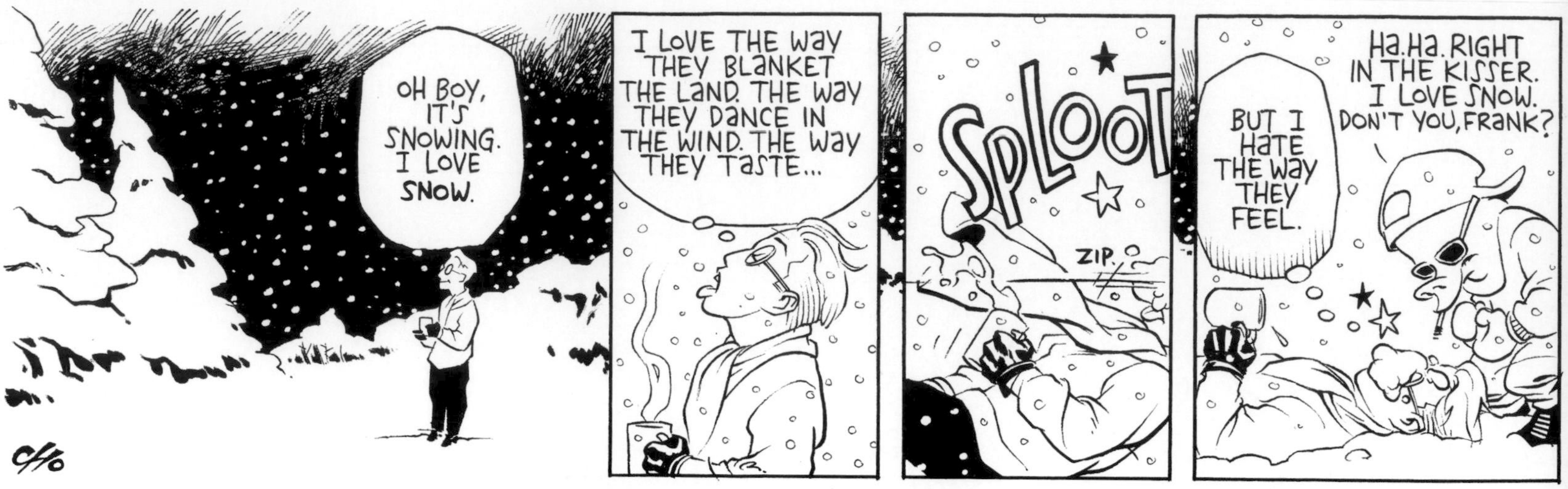
OH BOY, IT'S SNOWING. I LOVE SNOW.
I LOVE THE WAY THEY BLANKET THE LAND. THE WAY THEY DANCE IN THE WIND. THE WAY THEY TASTE...
SPLOOT
ZIP
HA.HA. RIGHT IN THE KISSER. I LOVE SNOW. DON'T YOU, FRANK?
BUT I HATE THE WAY THEY FEEL.

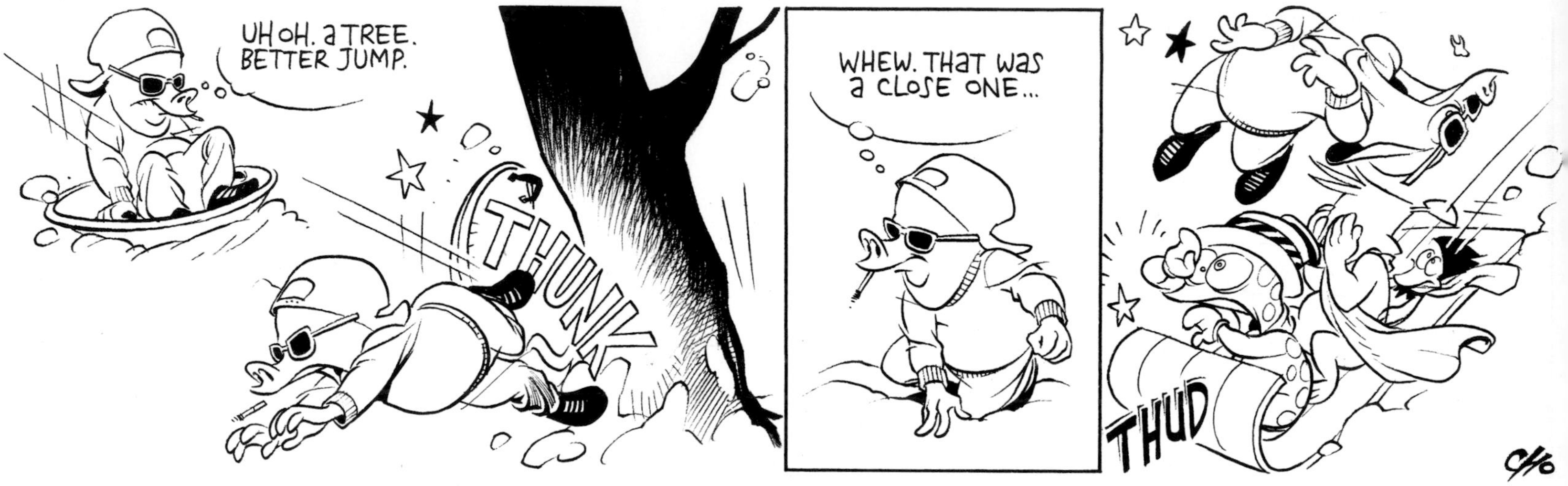
UH OH. A TREE. BETTER JUMP.
THUNK
WHEW. THAT WAS A CLOSE ONE...
THUD

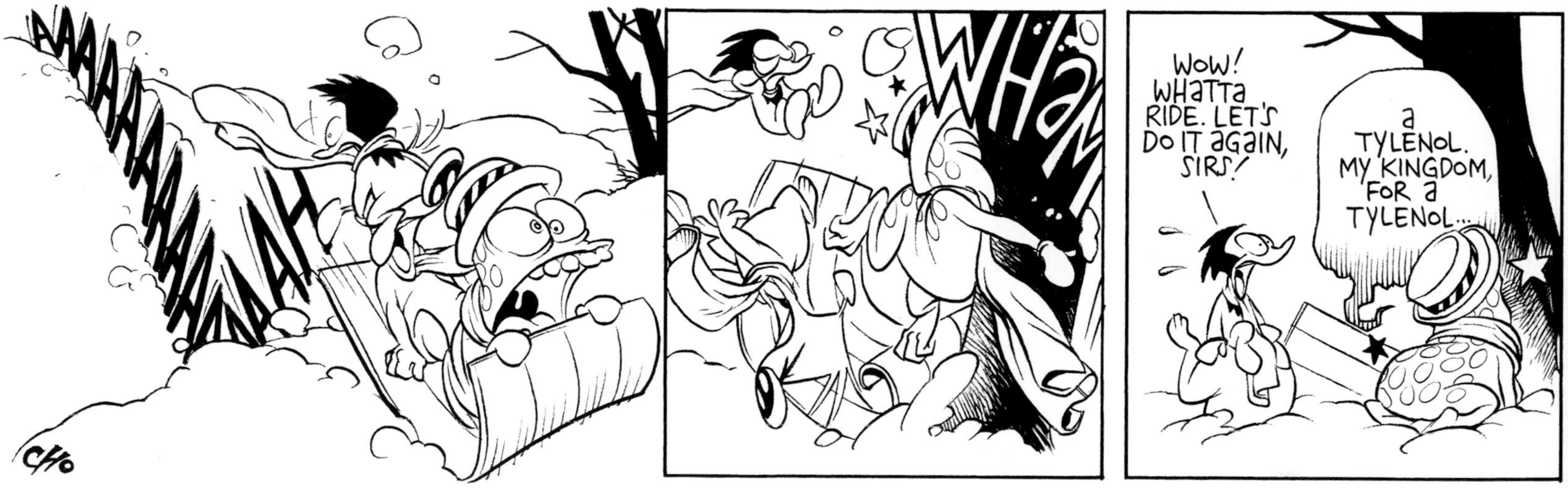
AAAAAAAAAAAAAAAH
WHAM
WOW! WHATTA RIDE. LET'S DO IT AGAIN, SIRS!
A TYLENOL. MY KINGDOM, FOR A TYLENOL...

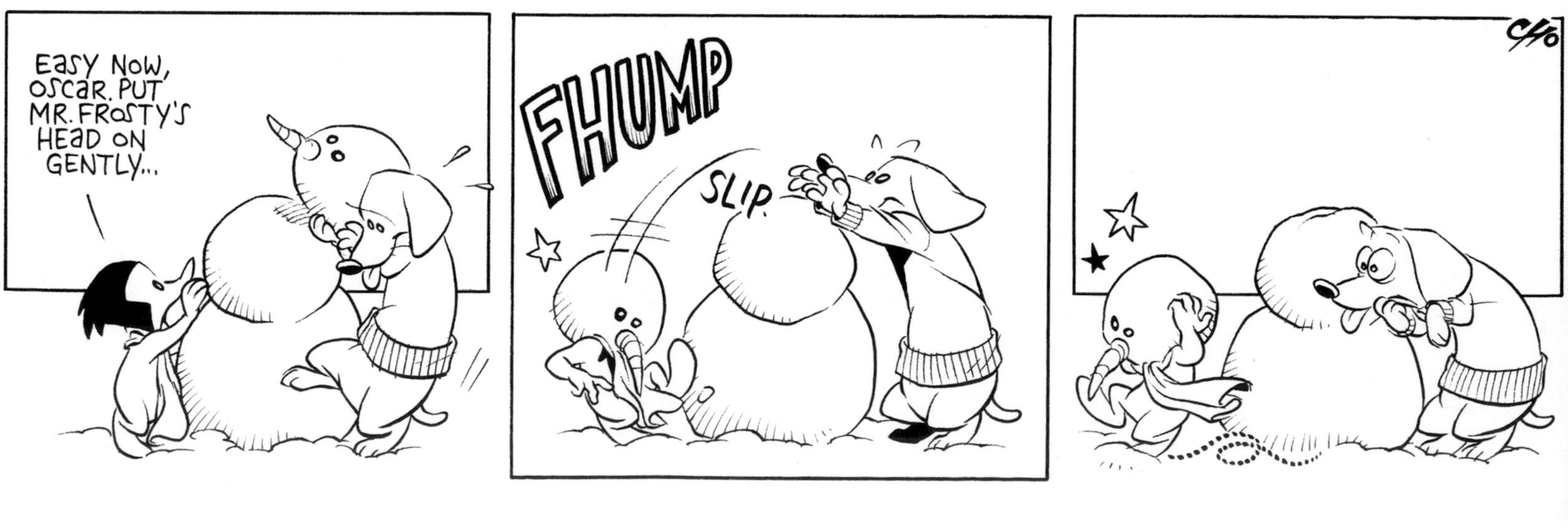
EASY NOW, OSCAR. PUT MR. FROSTY'S HEAD ON GENTLY...
FHUMP
SLIP

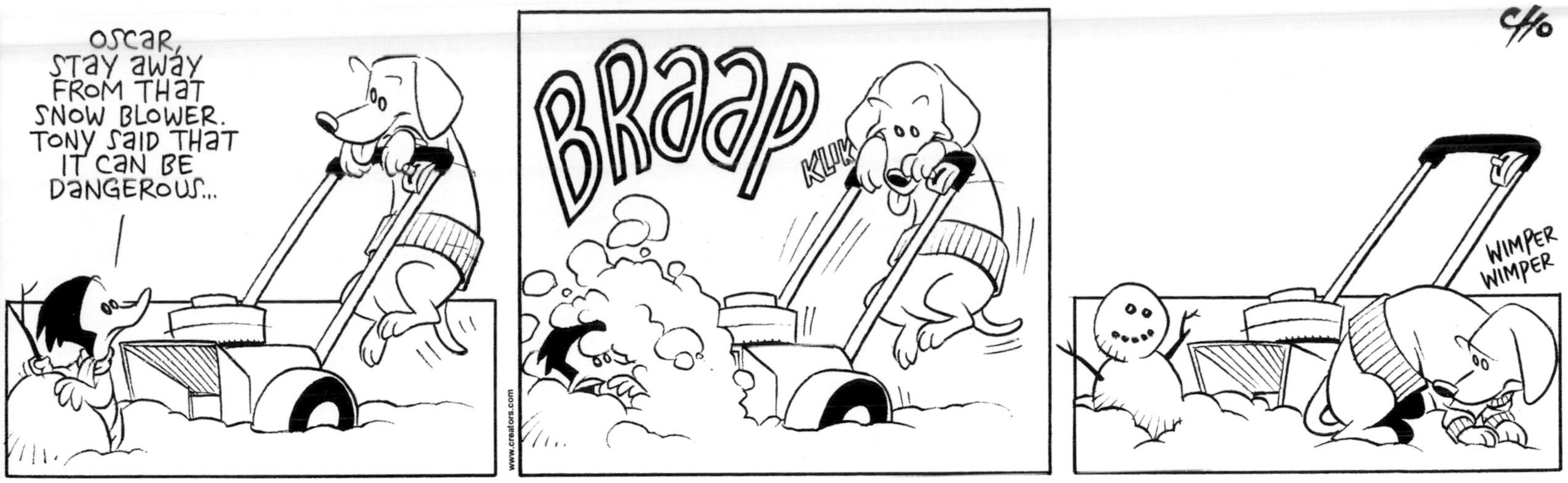
OSCAR, STAY AWAY FROM THAT SNOW BLOWER. TONY SAID THAT IT CAN BE DANGEROUS...
BRAAP
KLIK
WIMPER WIMPER
www.creators.com

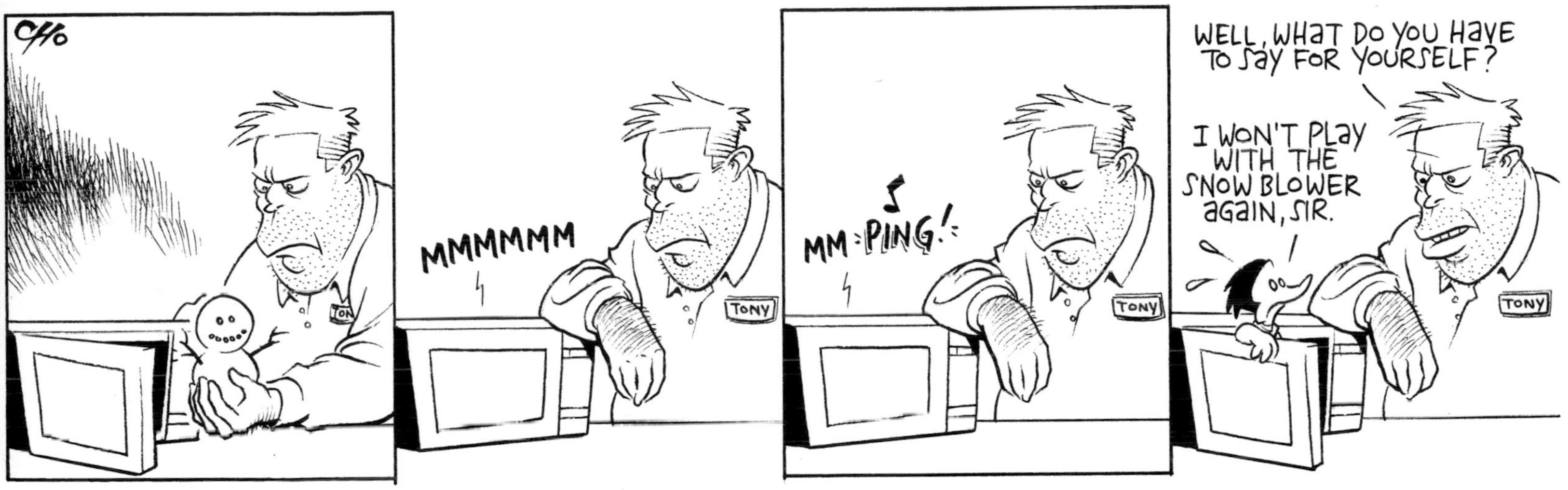
TONY
MMMMMM
MM PING!
WELL, WHAT DO YOU HAVE TO SAY FOR YOURSELF?
I WON'T PLAY WITH THE SNOW BLOWER AGAIN, SIR.

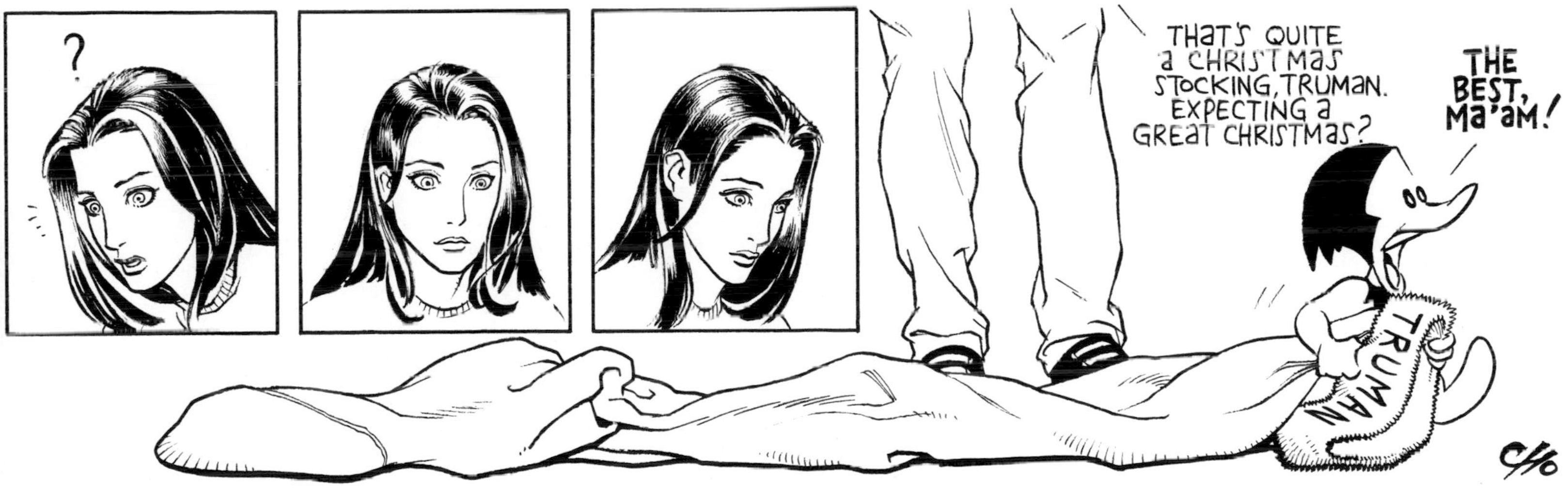
?
THAT'S QUITE A CHRISTMAS STOCKING, TRUMAN. EXPECTING A GREAT CHRISTMAS?
THE BEST, MA'AM!
TRUMAN

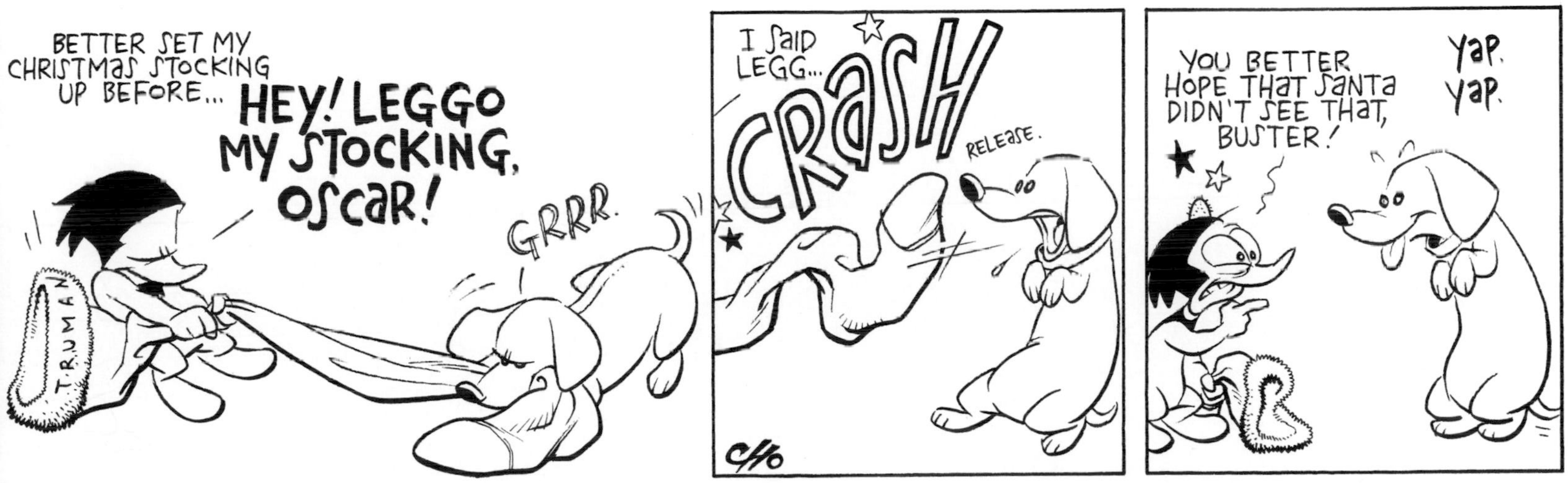
BETTER SET MY CHRISTMAS STOCKING UP BEFORE...
HEY! LEGGO MY STOCKING, OSCAR!
GRRR.
TRUMAN
I SAID LEGG...
CRASH
RELEASE.
YOU BETTER HOPE THAT SANTA DIDN'T SEE THAT, BUSTER!
YAP. YAP.

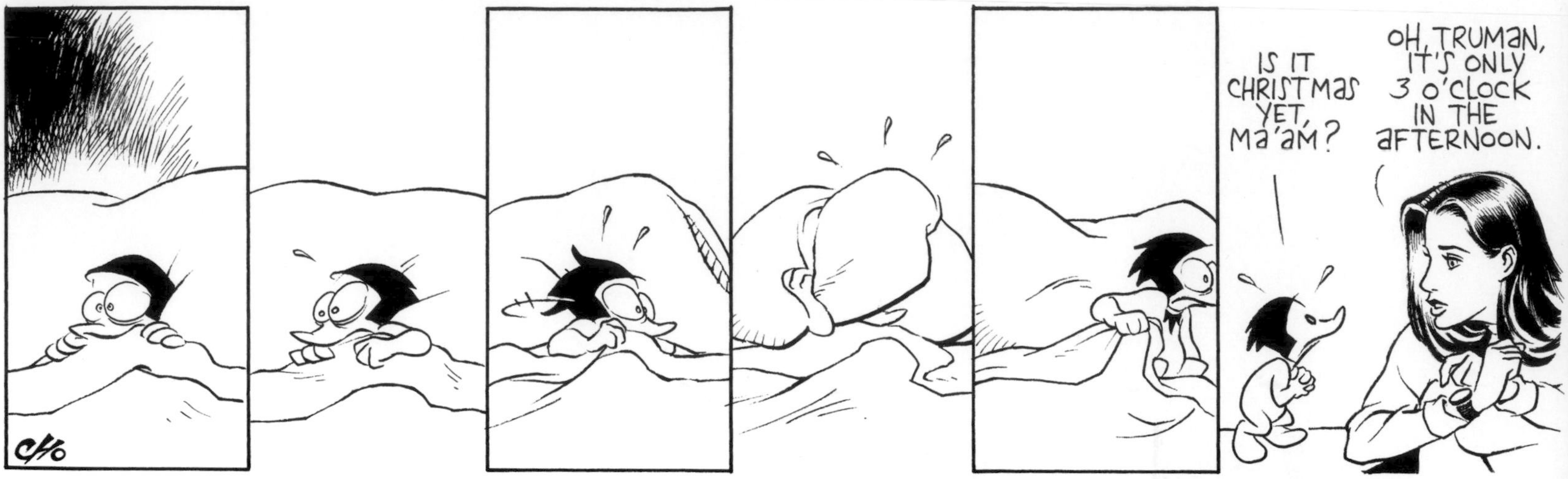
CHO
IS IT CHRISTMAS YET, MA'AM?
OH, TRUMAN, IT'S ONLY 3 O'CLOCK IN THE AFTERNOON.

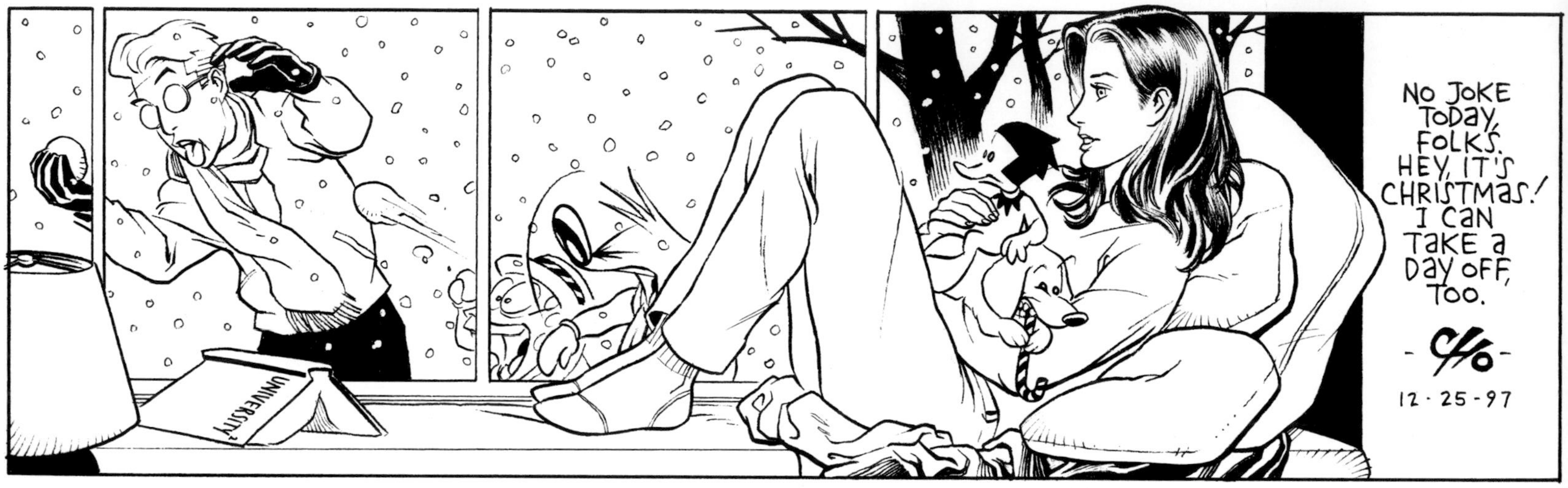
UNIVERSITY
NO JOKE TODAY, FOLKS. HEY, IT'S CHRISTMAS! I CAN TAKE A DAY OFF, TOO.
CHO
12 · 25 · 97

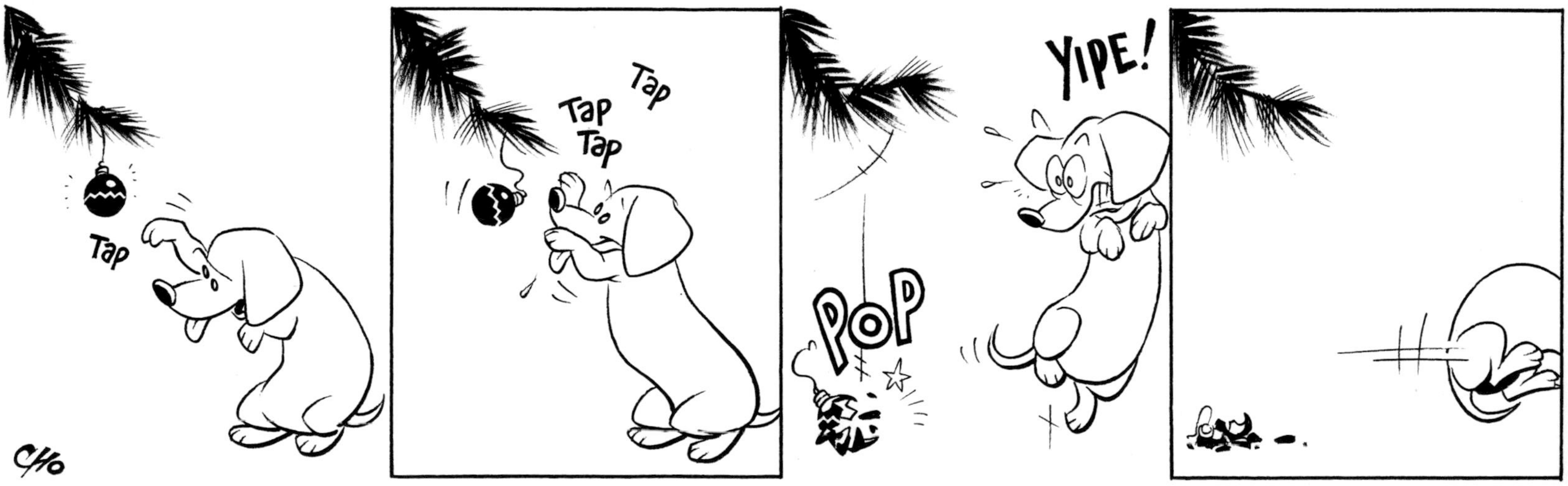
CHO
TAP
TAP
TAP
TAP
POP
YIPE!

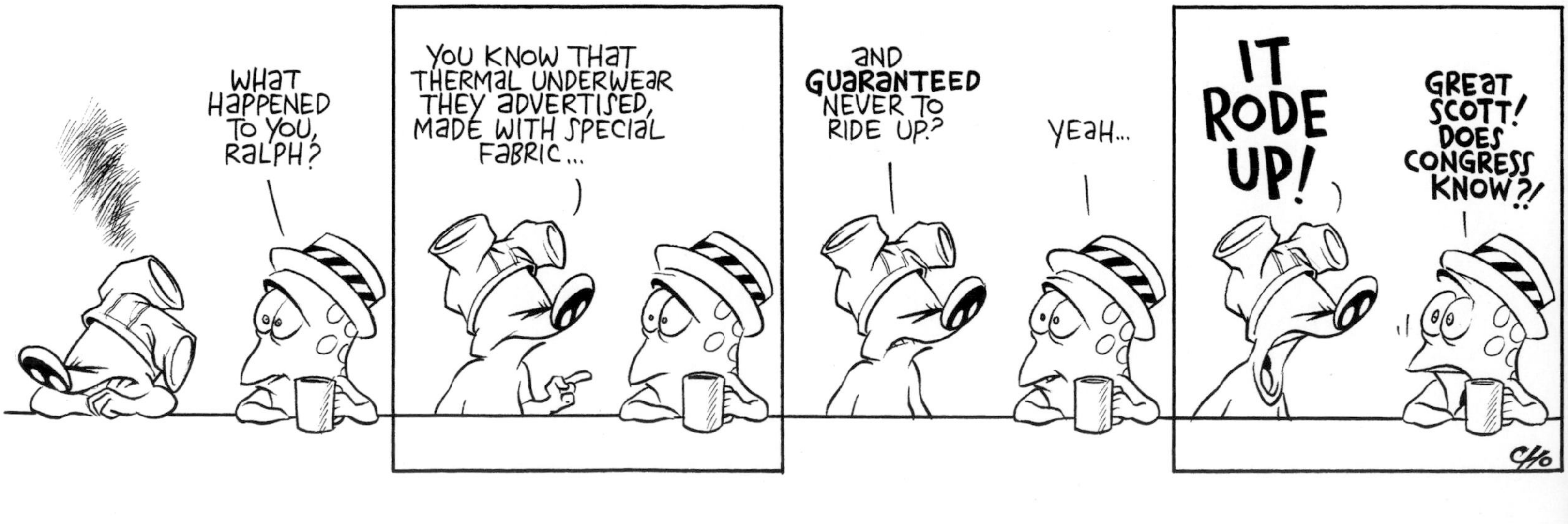
WHAT HAPPENED TO YOU, RALPH?
YOU KNOW THAT THERMAL UNDERWEAR THEY ADVERTISED, MADE WITH SPECIAL FABRIC...
AND GUARANTEED NEVER TO RIDE UP?
YEAH...
IT RODE UP!
GREAT SCOTT! DOES CONGRESS KNOW?!
CHO

Intermission...

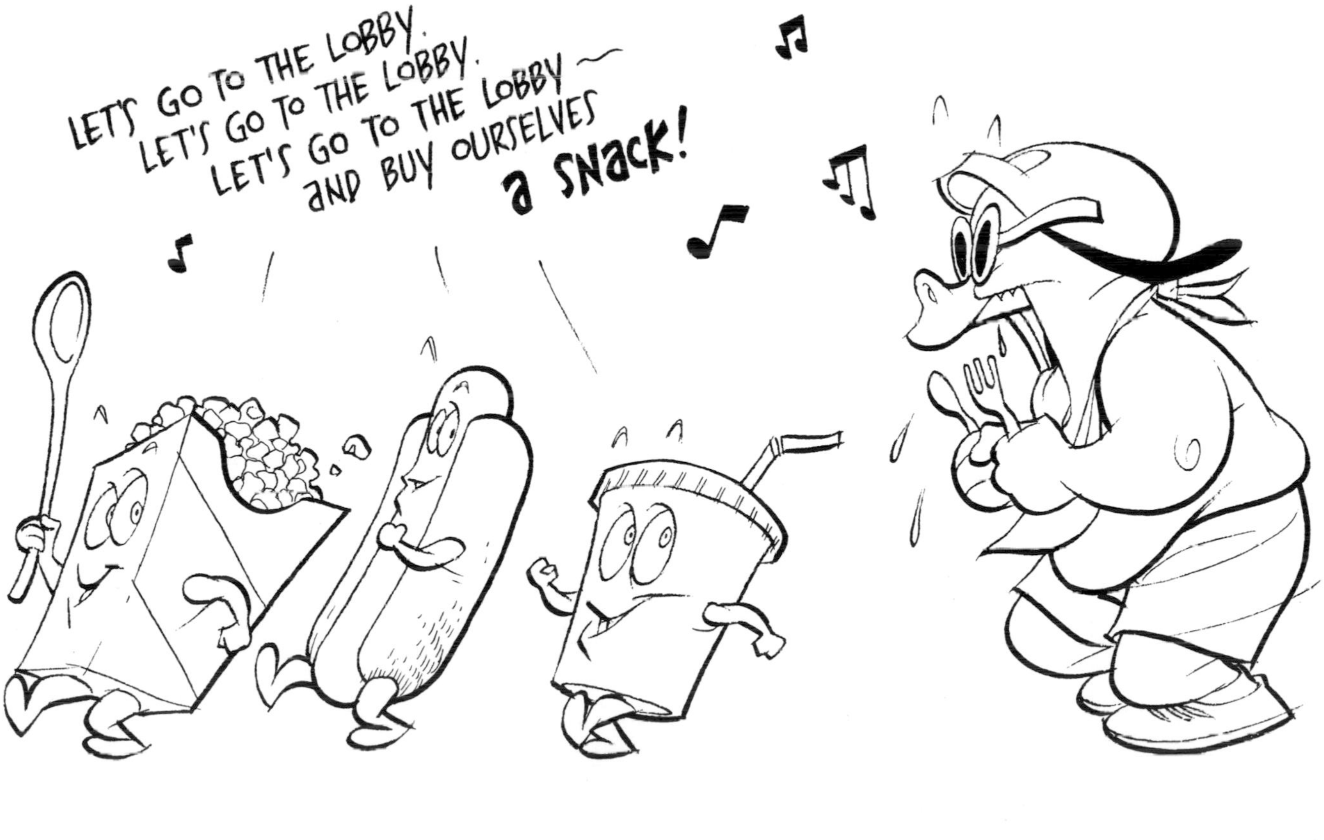

LET'S GO TO THE LOBBY.
LET'S GO TO THE LOBBY.
LET'S GO TO THE LOBBY
AND BUY OURSELVES
A SNACK!

And now back to the show.

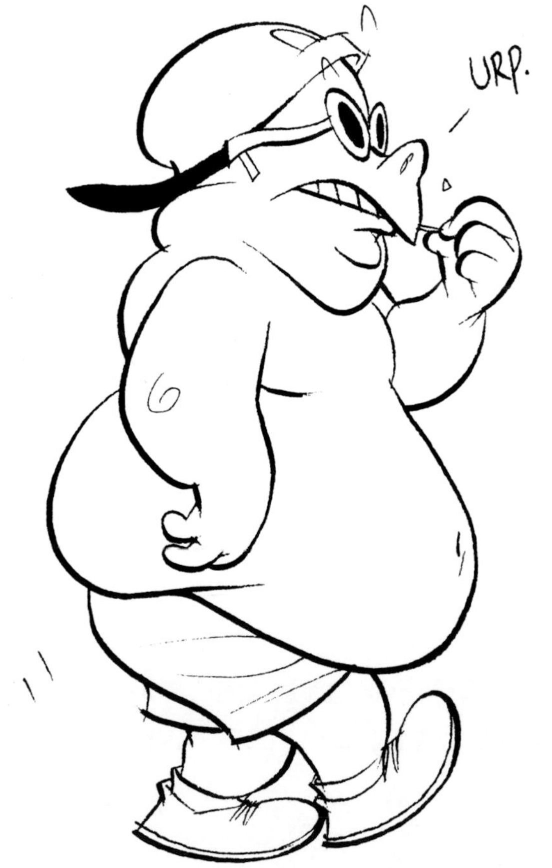
URP.

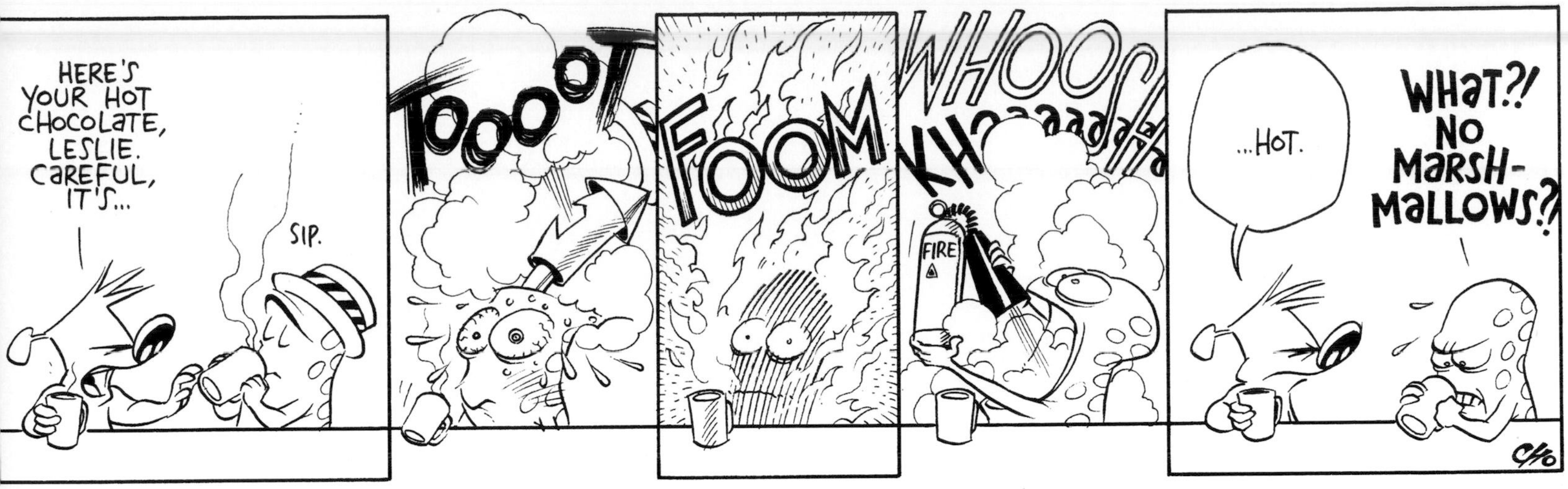
HERE'S YOUR HOT CHOCOLATE, LESLIE. CAREFUL, IT'S...
SIP.
TOOOOT
FOOM
WHOOSH
KHaaaaaah
FIRE
...HOT.
WHAT?! NO MARSH-MALLOWS?!

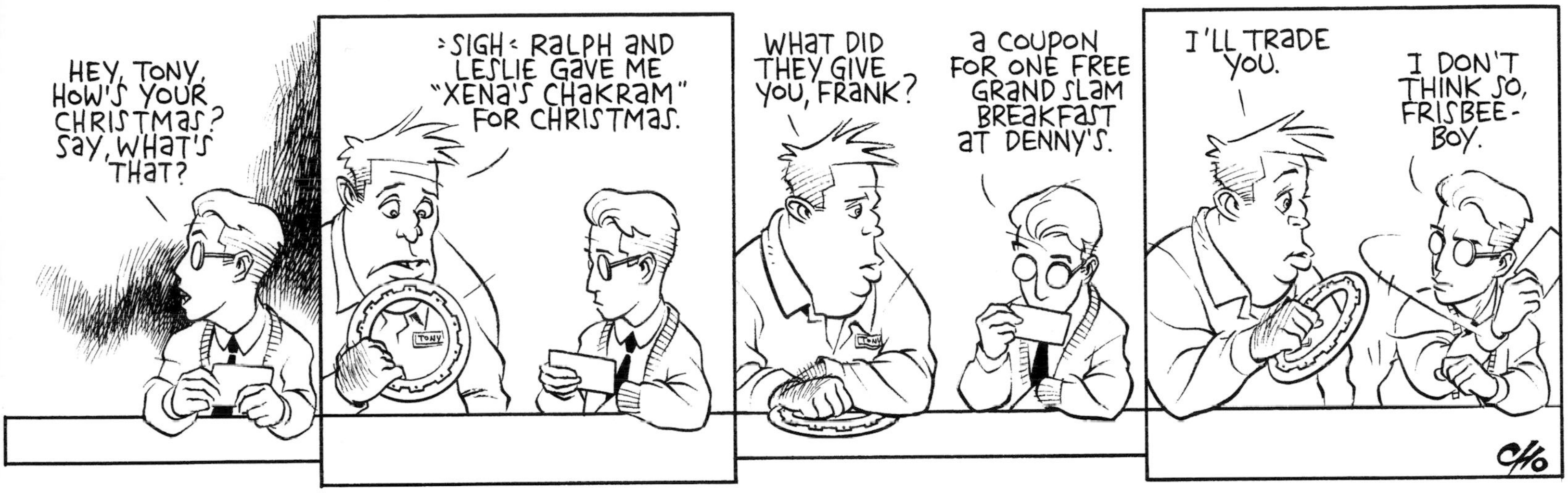
HEY, TONY, HOW'S YOUR CHRISTMAS? SAY, WHAT'S THAT?
:SIGH: RALPH AND LESLIE GAVE ME "XENA'S CHAKRAM" FOR CHRISTMAS.
TONY
WHAT DID THEY GIVE YOU, FRANK?
A COUPON FOR ONE FREE GRAND SLAM BREAKFAST AT DENNY'S.
I'LL TRADE YOU.
I DON'T THINK SO, FRISBEE-BOY.

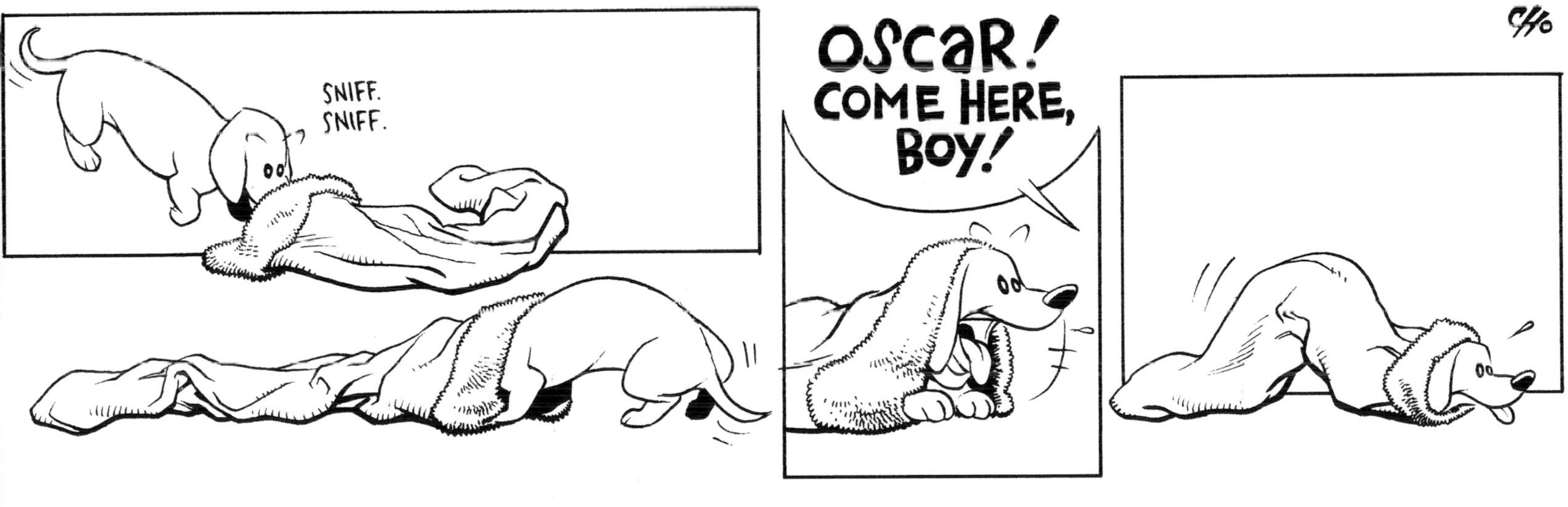
SNIFF. SNIFF.
OSCAR! COME HERE, BOY!

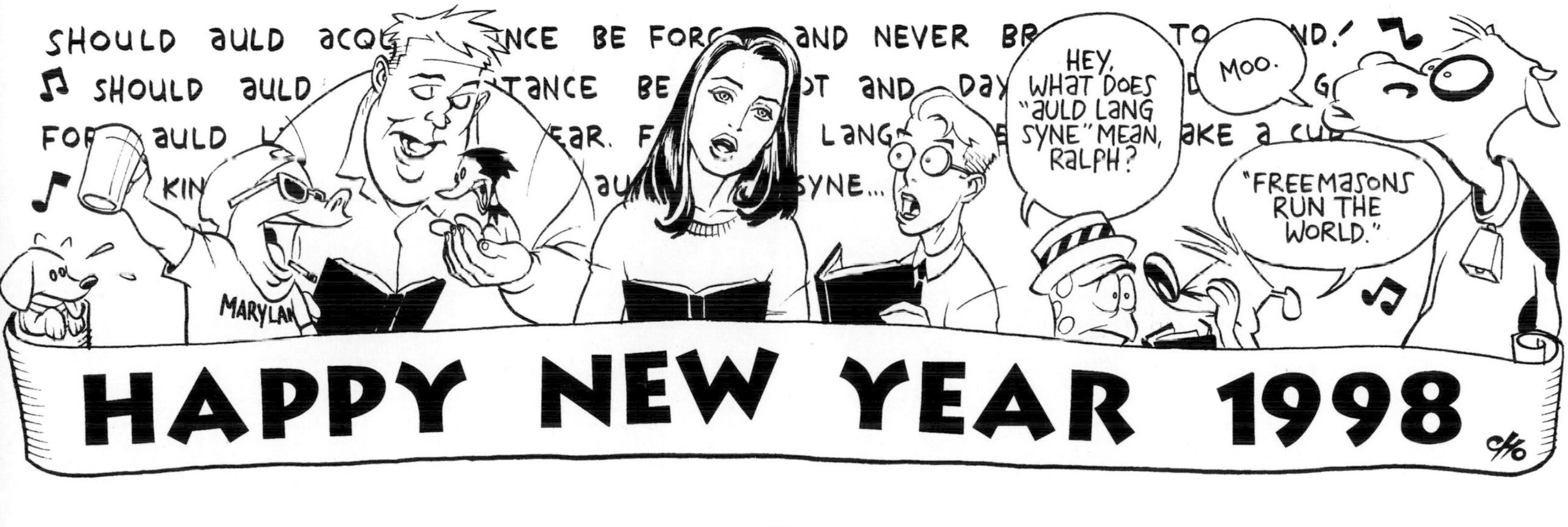
SHOULD AULD ACQ NCE BE FOR AND NEVER BR TO ND!
SHOULD AULD TANCE BE OT AND DAY
FOR AULD EAR. F LANG AKE A CU
KIN AU SYNE...
HEY, WHAT DOES "AULD LANG SYNE" MEAN, RALPH?
MOO.
"FREEMASONS RUN THE WORLD."
MARYLAN
HAPPY NEW YEAR 1998

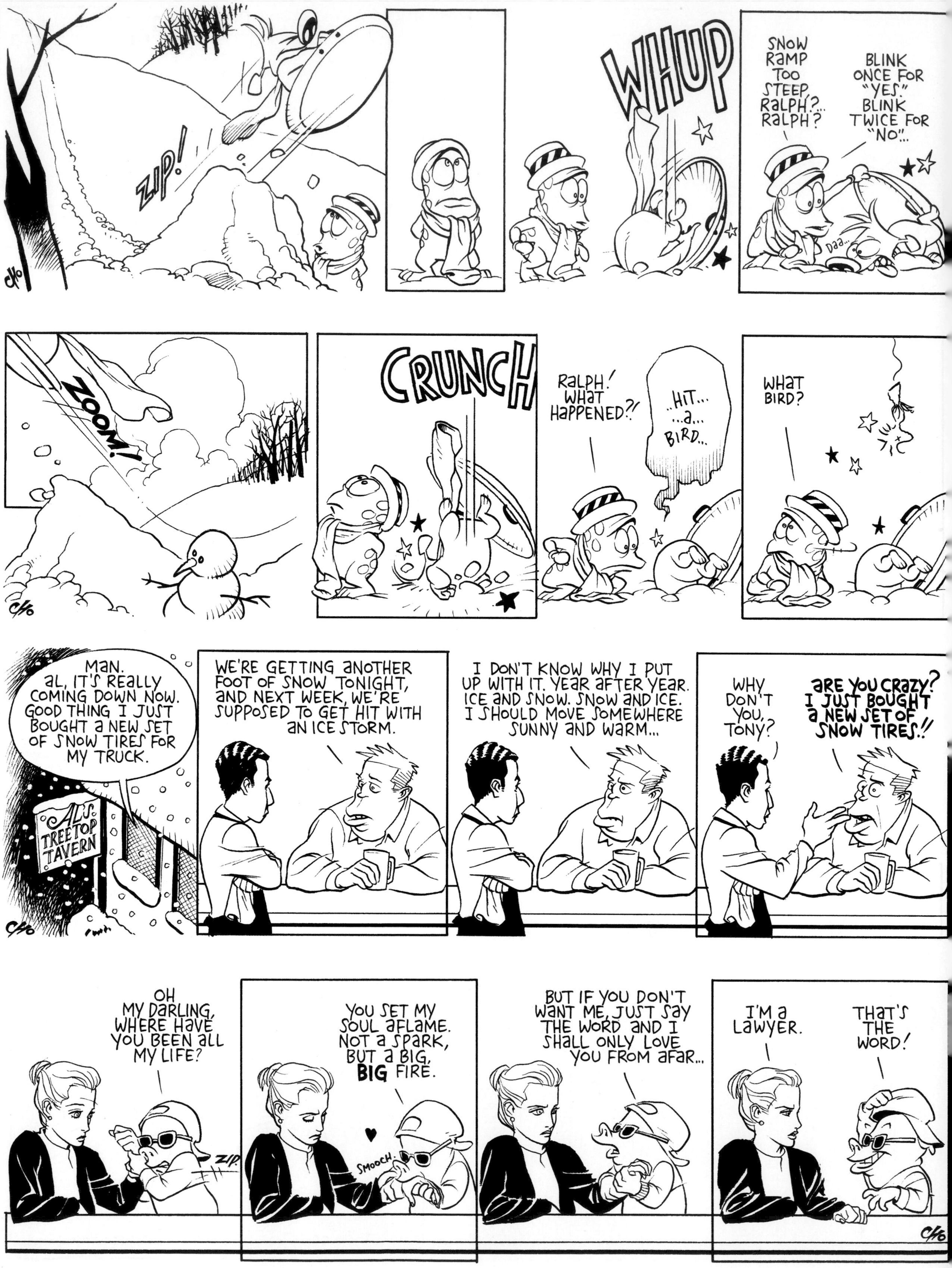
ZIP!
WHUP
SNOW RAMP TOO STEEP, RALPH?... RALPH?
BLINK ONCE FOR "YES." BLINK TWICE FOR "NO"...
DAA...
ZOOM!
CRUNCH
RALPH! WHAT HAPPENED?!
..HIT... ...A... BIRD...
WHAT BIRD?
MAN. AL, IT'S REALLY COMING DOWN NOW. GOOD THING I JUST BOUGHT A NEW SET OF SNOW TIRES FOR MY TRUCK.
AL'S TREETOP TAVERN
WE'RE GETTING ANOTHER FOOT OF SNOW TONIGHT, AND NEXT WEEK, WE'RE SUPPOSED TO GET HIT WITH AN ICE STORM.
I DON'T KNOW WHY I PUT UP WITH IT. YEAR AFTER YEAR. ICE AND SNOW. SNOW AND ICE. I SHOULD MOVE SOMEWHERE SUNNY AND WARM...
WHY DON'T YOU, TONY?
ARE YOU CRAZY? I JUST BOUGHT A NEW SET OF SNOW TIRES!!
OH MY DARLING, WHERE HAVE YOU BEEN ALL MY LIFE?
ZIP.
YOU SET MY SOUL AFLAME. NOT A SPARK, BUT A BIG, BIG FIRE.
SMOOCH.
BUT IF YOU DON'T WANT ME, JUST SAY THE WORD AND I SHALL ONLY LOVE YOU FROM AFAR...
I'M A LAWYER.
THAT'S THE WORD!

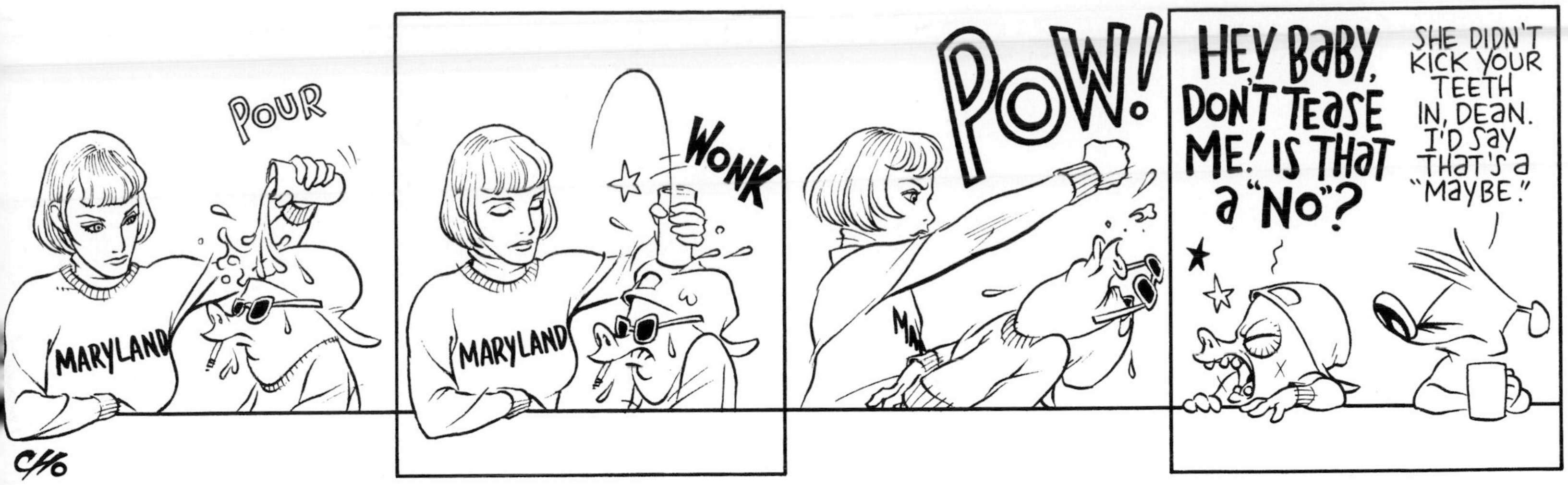
POUR
MARYLAND
WONK
MARYLAND
POW!
HEY BABY, DON'T TEASE ME! IS THAT a "NO"?
SHE DIDN'T KICK YOUR TEETH IN, DEAN. I'D SAY THAT'S a "MAYBE."
CHO

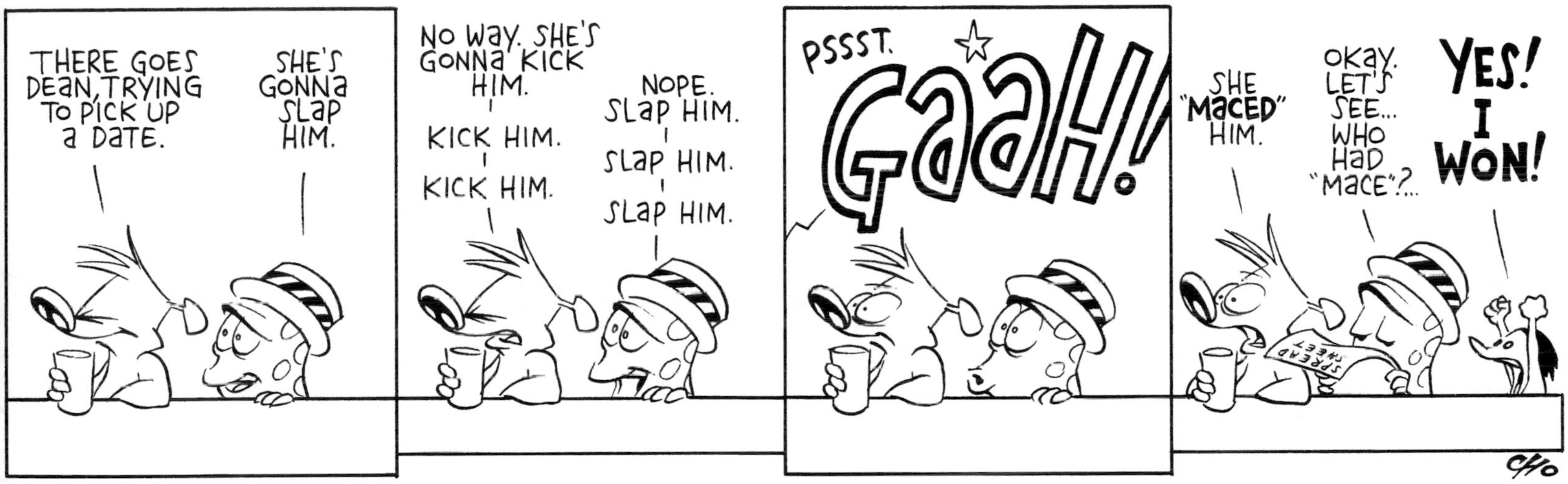
THERE GOES DEAN, TRYING TO PICK UP a DATE.
SHE'S GONNA SLAP HIM.
NO WAY. SHE'S GONNA KICK HIM.
NOPE. SLAP HIM.
KICK HIM.
SLAP HIM.
KICK HIM.
SLAP HIM.
PSSST.
GaaH!
SHE "MACED" HIM.
OKAY. LET'S SEE... WHO HAD "MACE"?...
YES! I WON!
SPREAD SHEET
CHO

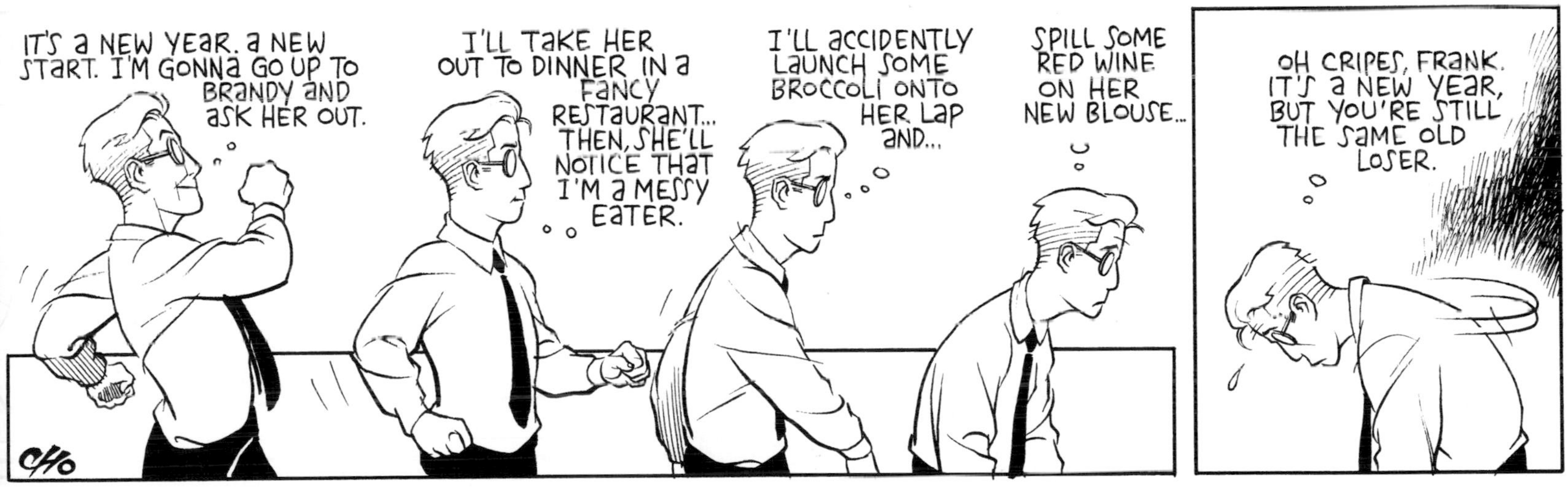
IT'S a NEW YEAR. a NEW START. I'M GONNA GO UP TO BRANDY AND ASK HER OUT.
I'LL TAKE HER OUT TO DINNER IN a FANCY RESTAURANT... THEN, SHE'LL NOTICE THAT I'M a MESSY EATER.
I'LL ACCIDENTLY LAUNCH SOME BROCCOLI ONTO HER LAP AND...
SPILL SOME RED WINE ON HER NEW BLOUSE...
OH CRIPES, FRANK. IT'S a NEW YEAR, BUT YOU'RE STILL THE SAME OLD LOSER.
CHO

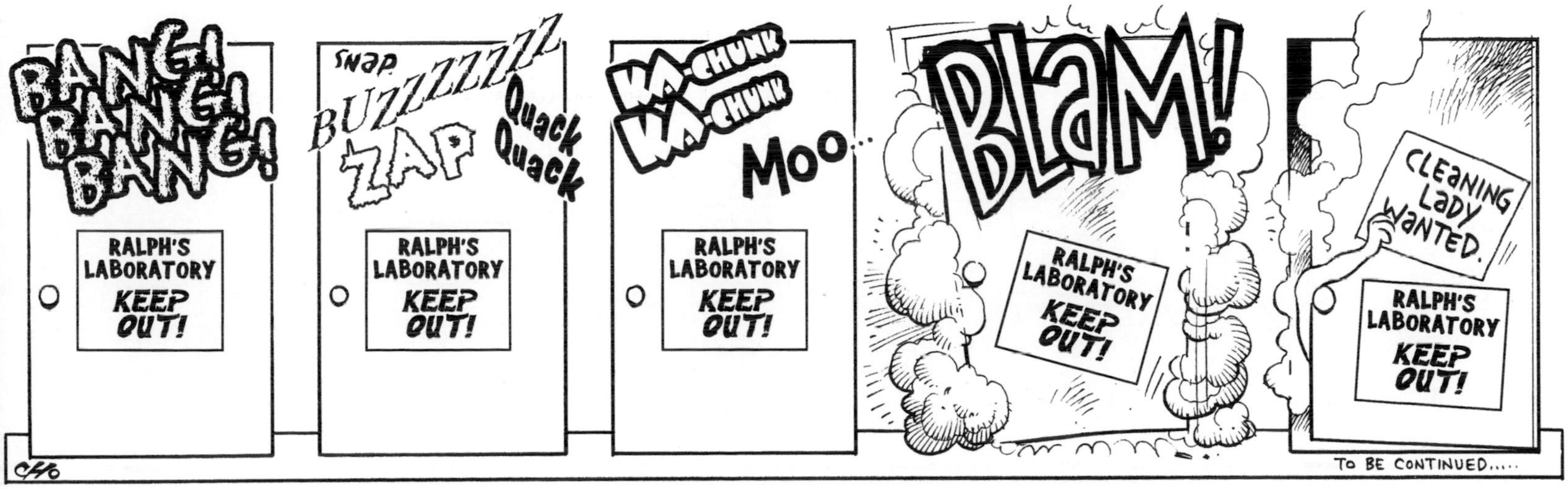
BANG! BANG! BANG!
RALPH'S LABORATORY KEEP OUT!
SNAP
BUZZZZZZZ
ZAP
QUACK QUACK
RALPH'S LABORATORY KEEP OUT!
KA-CHUNK KA-CHUNK
MOO...
RALPH'S LABORATORY KEEP OUT!
BLAM!
RALPH'S LABORATORY KEEP OUT!
CLEANING LADY WANTED.
RALPH'S LABORATORY KEEP OUT!
TO BE CONTINUED.....
CHO

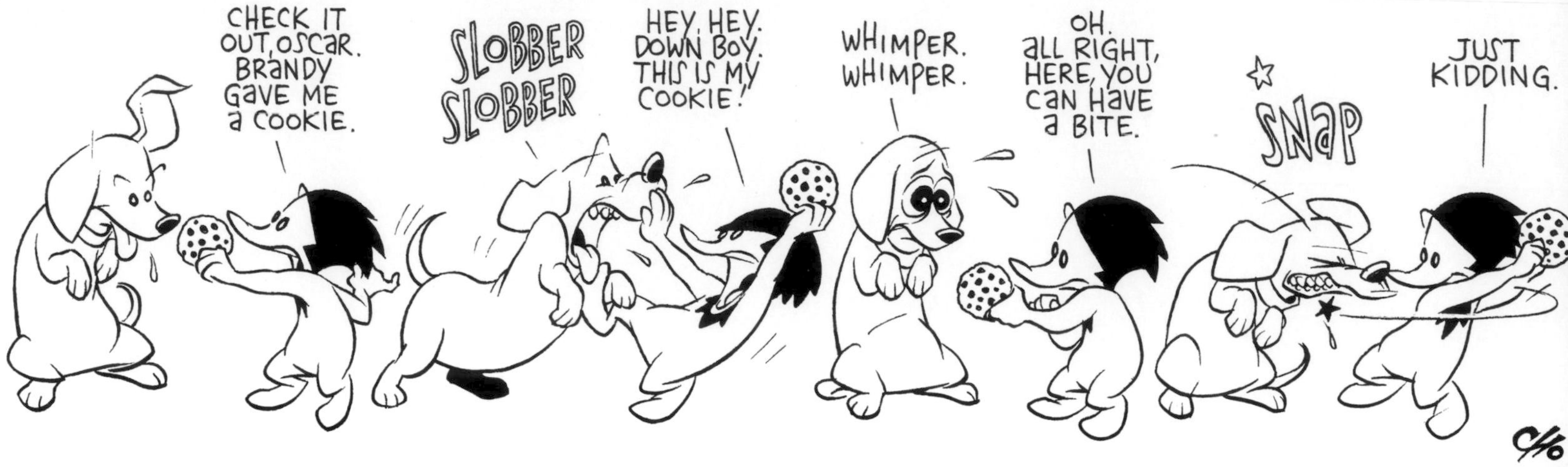
CHECK IT OUT, OSCAR. BRANDY GAVE ME A COOKIE.
SLOBBER SLOBBER
HEY, HEY. DOWN BOY. THIS IS MY COOKIE!
WHIMPER. WHIMPER.
OH. ALL RIGHT, HERE, YOU CAN HAVE A BITE.
SNAP
JUST KIDDING.
CHO

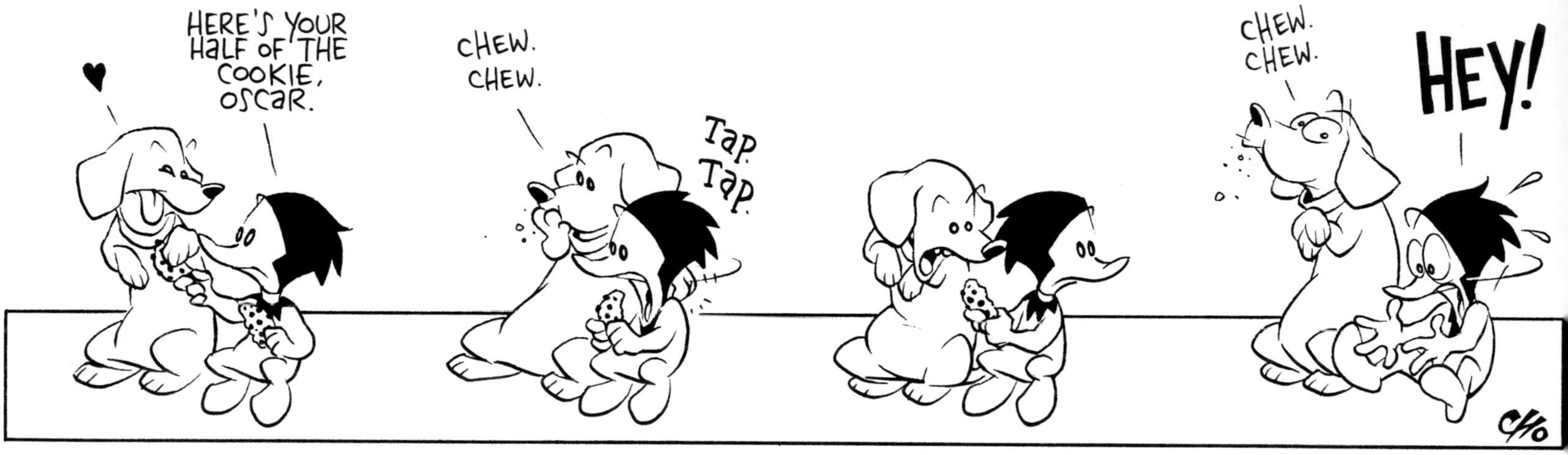
HERE'S YOUR HALF OF THE COOKIE, OSCAR.
CHEW. CHEW.
TAP TAP
CHEW. CHEW.
HEY!
CHO

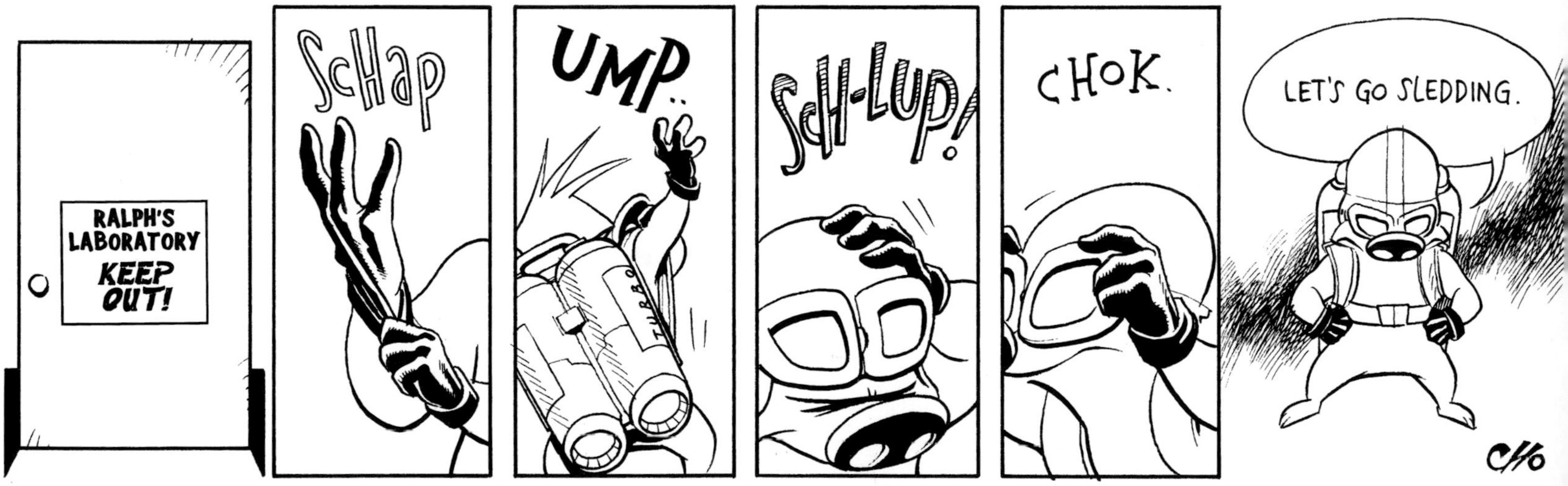
RALPH'S LABORATORY
KEEP OUT!
SCHAP
UMP..
SCH-LUP!
CHOK.
LET'S GO SLEDDING.
CHO

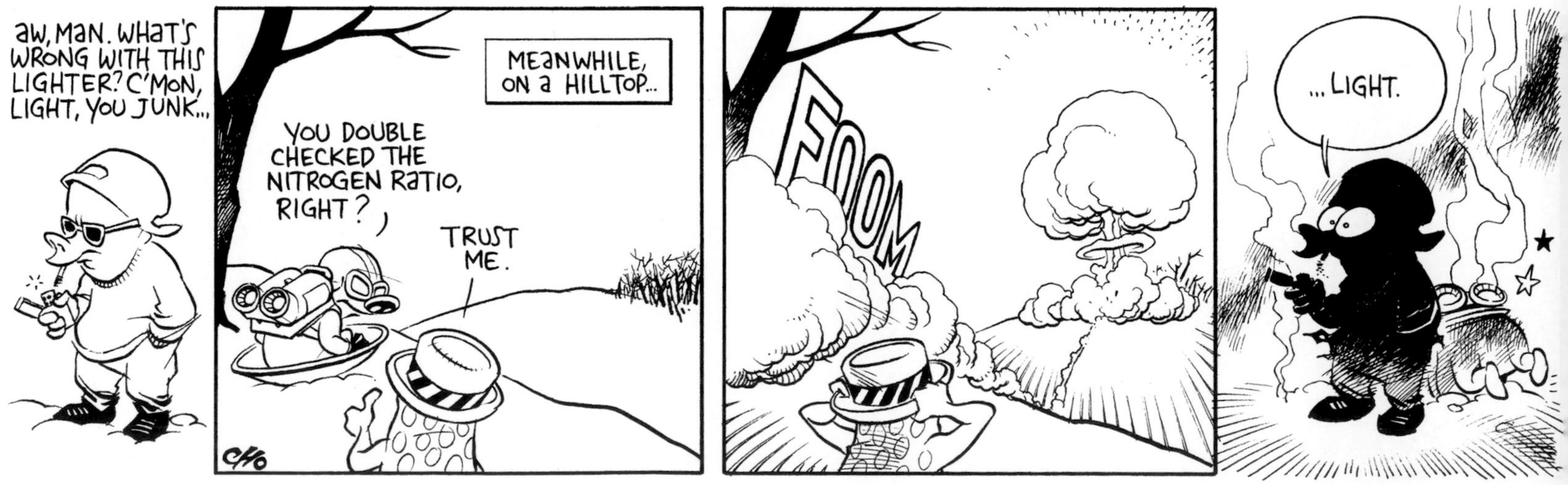
AW, MAN. WHAT'S WRONG WITH THIS LIGHTER? C'MON, LIGHT, YOU JUNK...
MEANWHILE, ON A HILLTOP...
YOU DOUBLE CHECKED THE NITROGEN RATIO, RIGHT?
TRUST ME.
CHO
FOOM
...LIGHT.

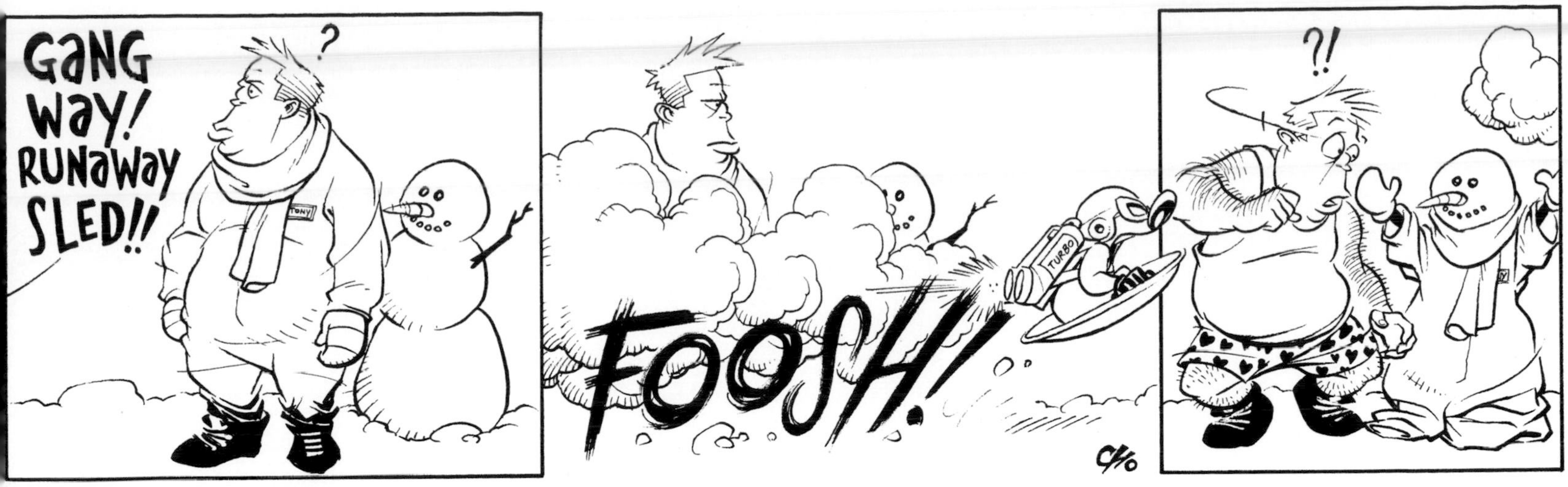
GANG WAY! RUNAWAY SLED!!
?
TONY
FOOSH!
TURBO
?!

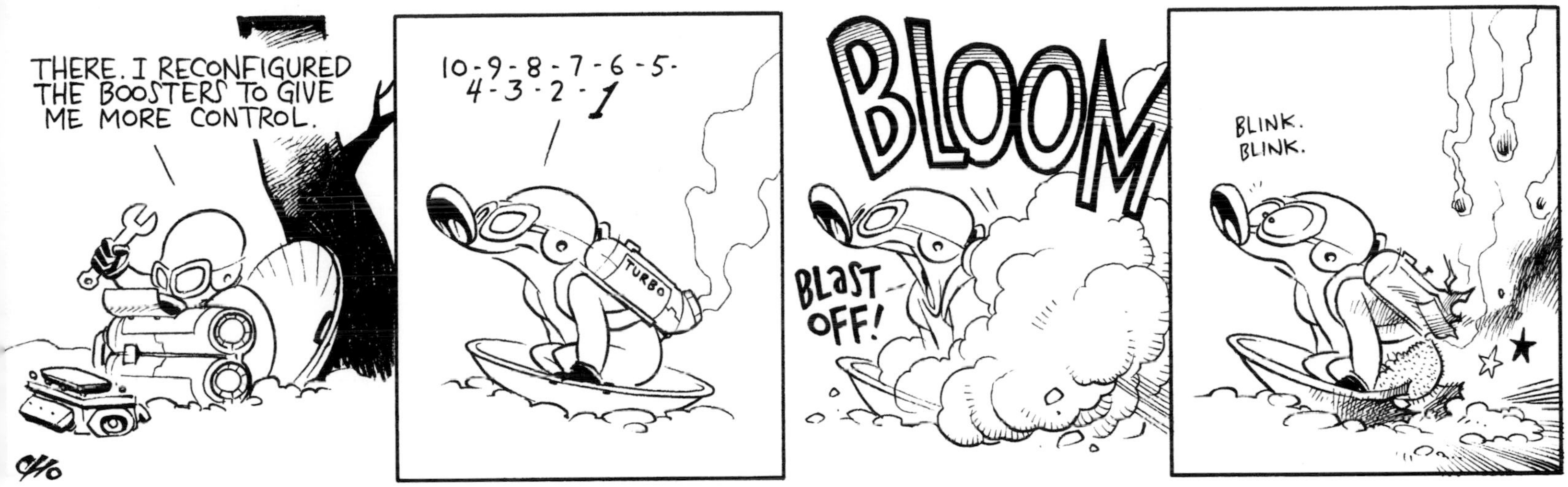
THERE. I RECONFIGURED THE BOOSTERS TO GIVE ME MORE CONTROL.
10-9-8-7-6-5-4-3-2-1
TURBO
BLOOM
BLAST OFF!
BLINK. BLINK.

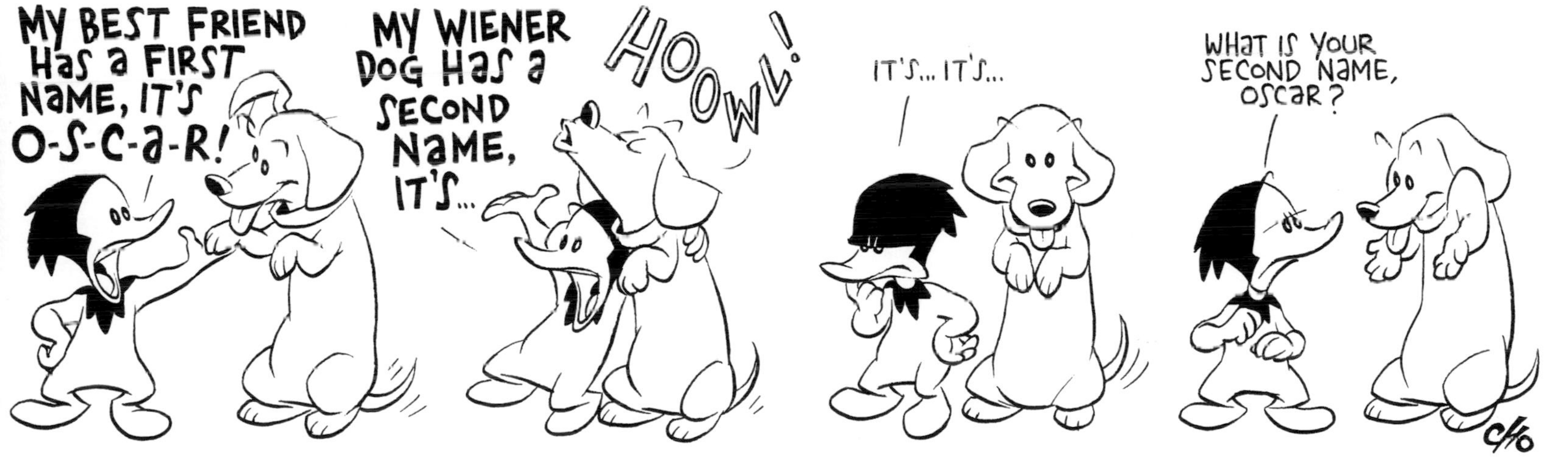
MY BEST FRIEND HAS A FIRST NAME, IT'S O-S-C-A-R!
MY WIENER DOG HAS A SECOND NAME, IT'S...
HOOWL!
IT'S... IT'S...
WHAT IS YOUR SECOND NAME, OSCAR?

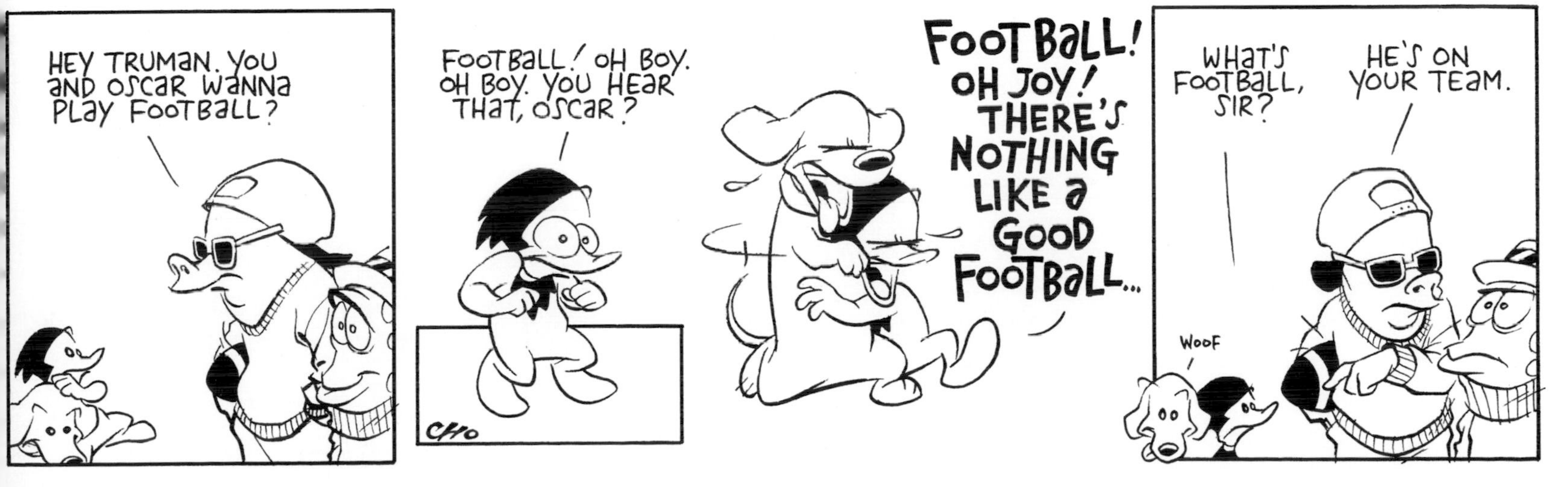
HEY TRUMAN. YOU AND OSCAR WANNA PLAY FOOTBALL?
FOOTBALL! OH BOY. OH BOY. YOU HEAR THAT, OSCAR?
FOOTBALL! OH JOY! THERE'S NOTHING LIKE A GOOD FOOTBALL...
WHAT'S FOOTBALL, SIR?
HE'S ON YOUR TEAM.
WOOF

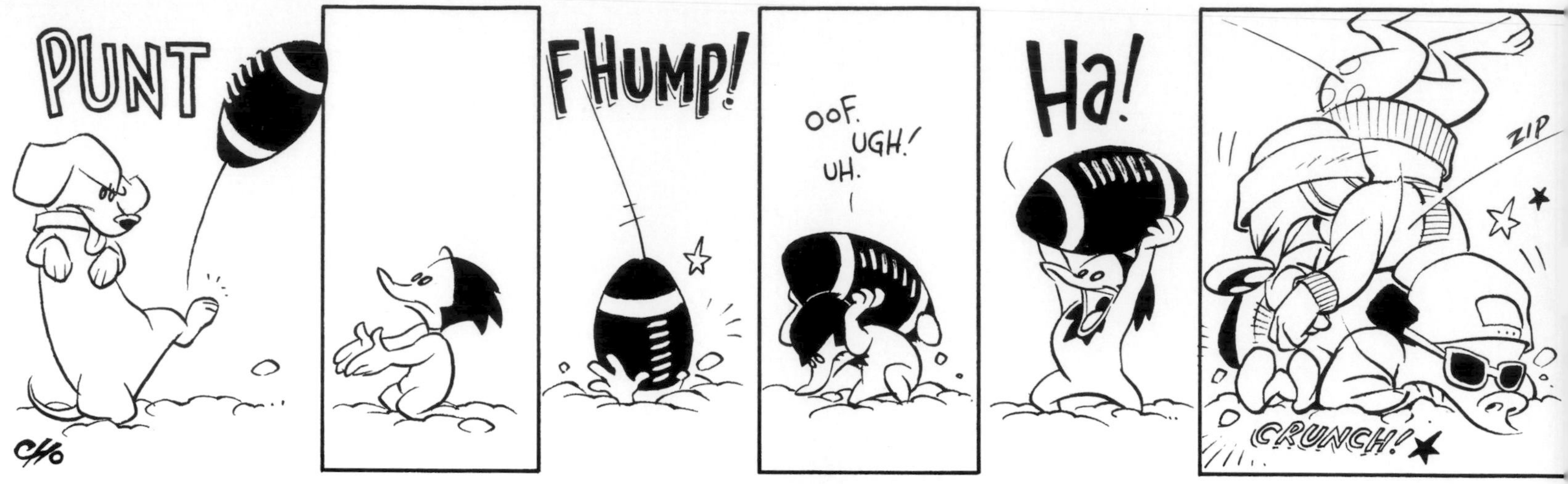
PUNT
FHUMP!
OOF.
UGH!
UH.
Ha!
ZIP
CRUNCH!

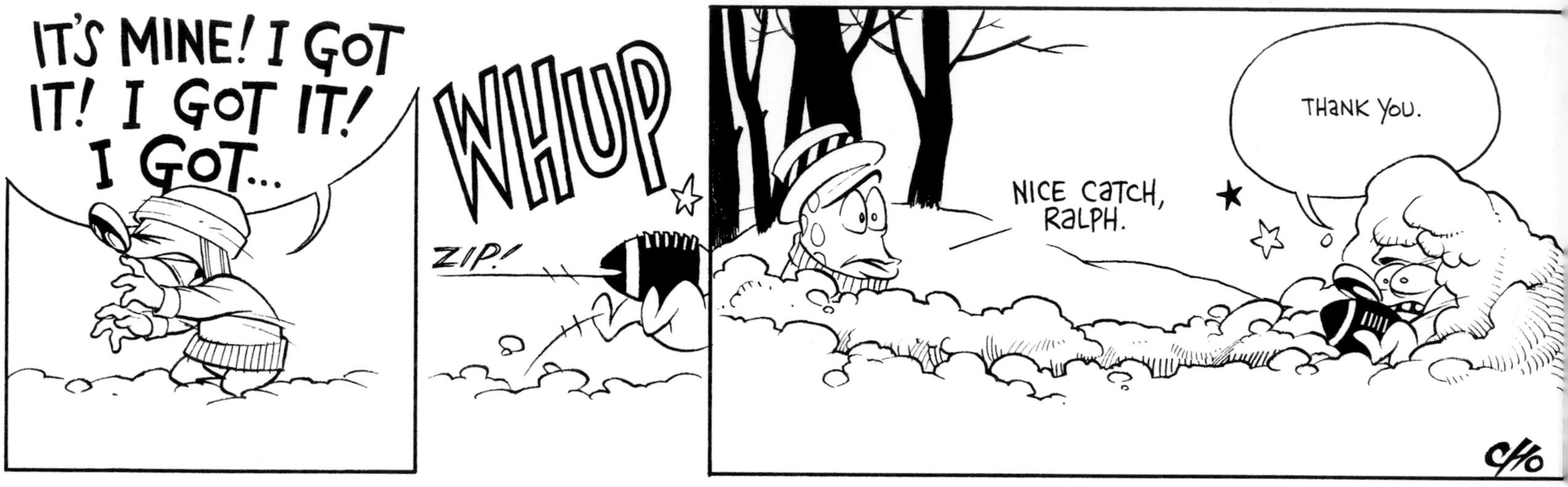
IT'S MINE! I GOT IT! I GOT IT! I GOT...
WHUP
ZIP!
NICE CATCH, RALPH.
THANK YOU.

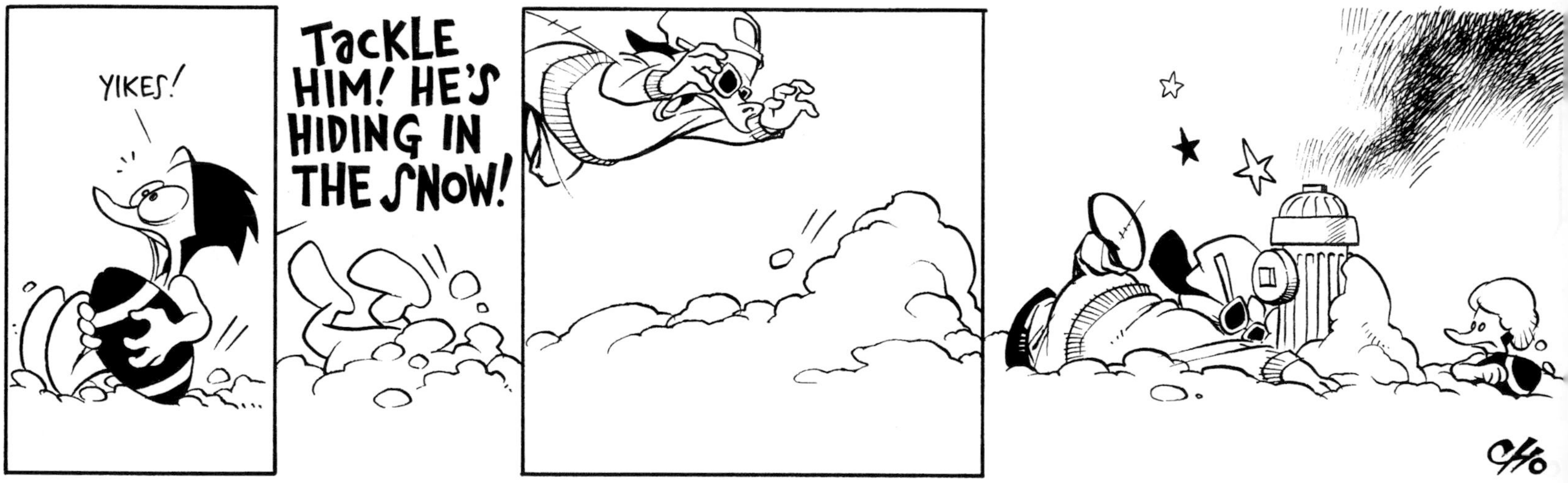
YIKES!
TACKLE HIM! HE'S HIDING IN THE SNOW!

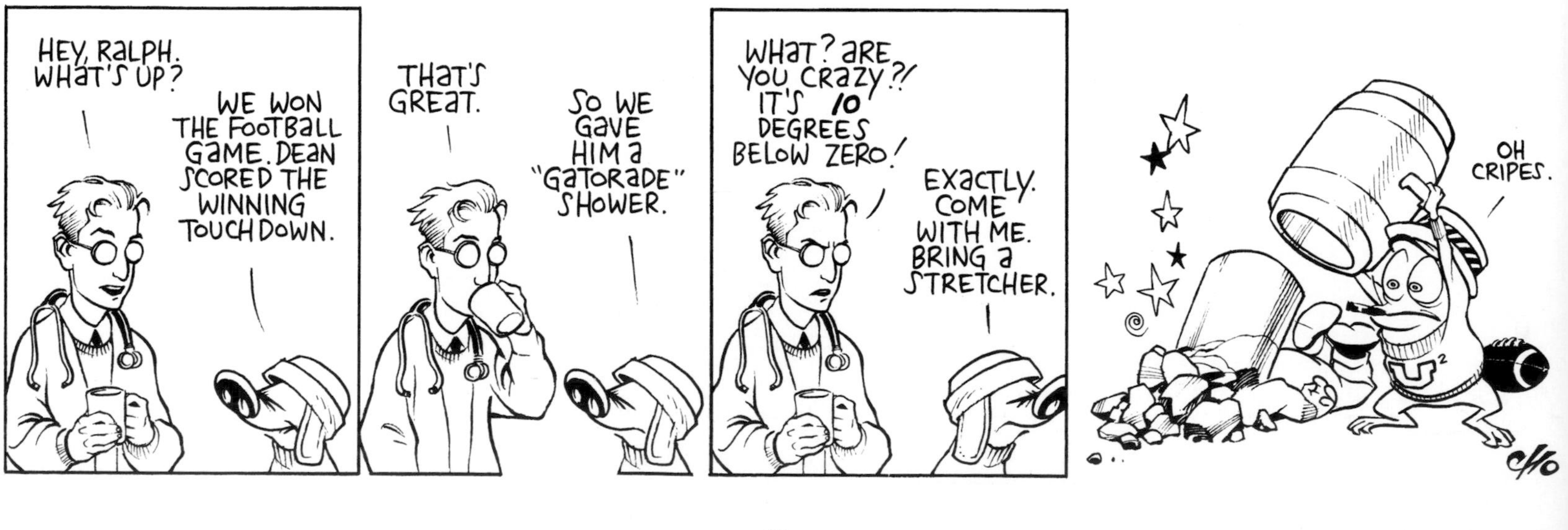
HEY, RALPH. WHAT'S UP?
WE WON THE FOOTBALL GAME. DEAN SCORED THE WINNING TOUCHDOWN.
THAT'S GREAT.
SO WE GAVE HIM A "GATORADE" SHOWER.
WHAT? ARE YOU CRAZY?! IT'S 10 DEGREES BELOW ZERO!
EXACTLY. COME WITH ME. BRING A STRETCHER.
OH CRIPES.

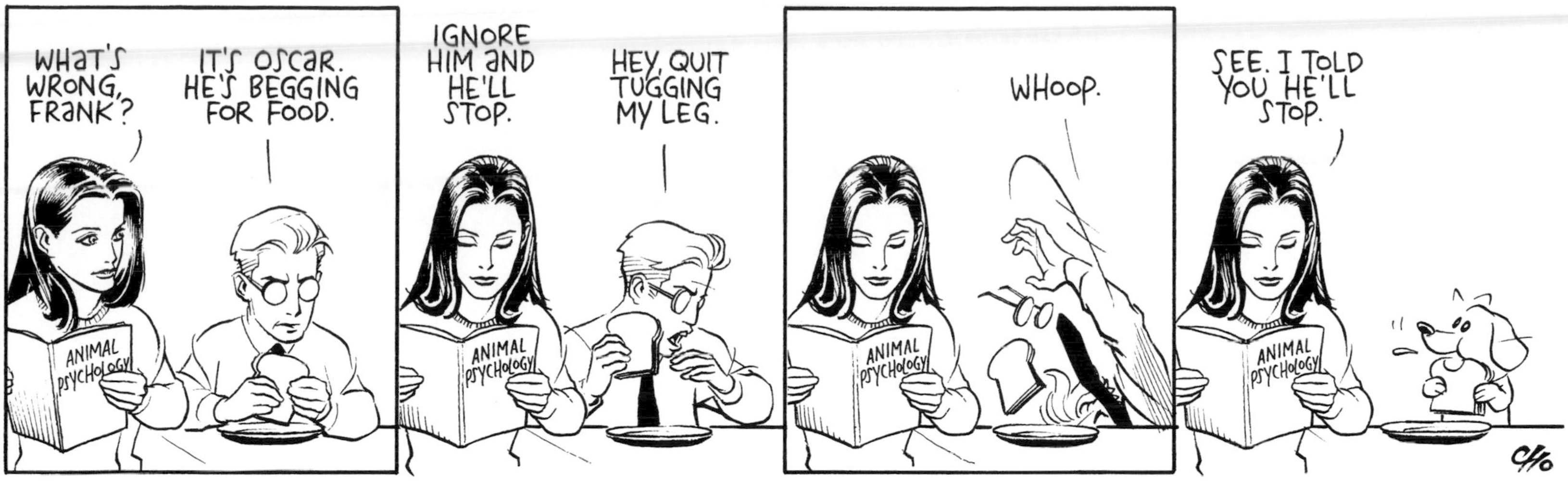
WHAT'S WRONG, FRANK?
IT'S OSCAR. HE'S BEGGING FOR FOOD.
ANIMAL PSYCHOLOGY
IGNORE HIM AND HE'LL STOP.
HEY, QUIT TUGGING MY LEG.
WHOOP.
SEE. I TOLD YOU HE'LL STOP.
CHO

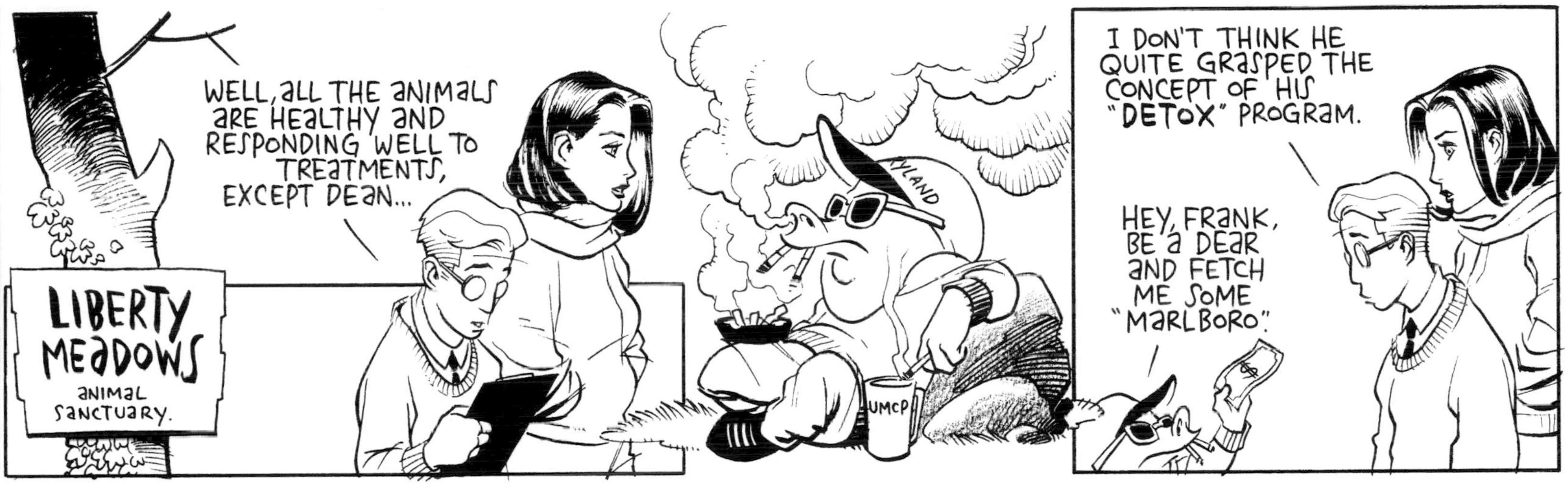
LIBERTY MEADOWS
ANIMAL SANCTUARY.
WELL, ALL THE ANIMALS ARE HEALTHY AND RESPONDING WELL TO TREATMENTS, EXCEPT DEAN...
UMCP
I DON'T THINK HE QUITE GRASPED THE CONCEPT OF HIS "DETOX" PROGRAM.
HEY, FRANK, BE A DEAR AND FETCH ME SOME "MARLBORO".

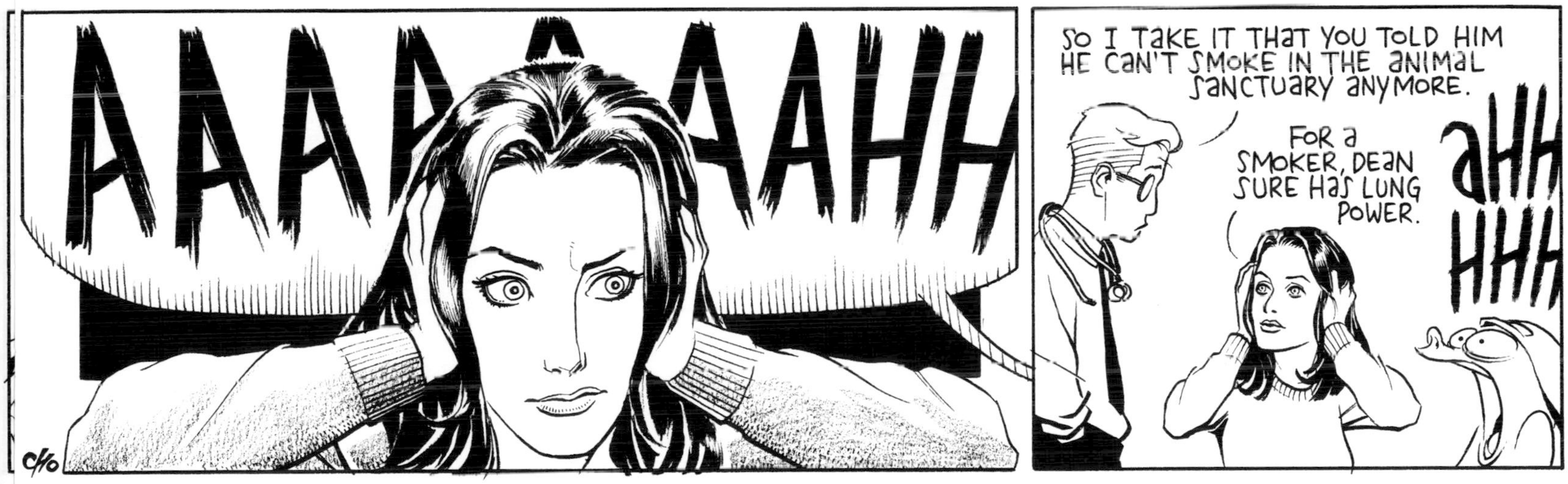
AAAAAAAHH
CHO
SO I TAKE IT THAT YOU TOLD HIM HE CAN'T SMOKE IN THE ANIMAL SANCTUARY ANYMORE.
FOR A SMOKER, DEAN SURE HAS LUNG POWER.
AHHHHH

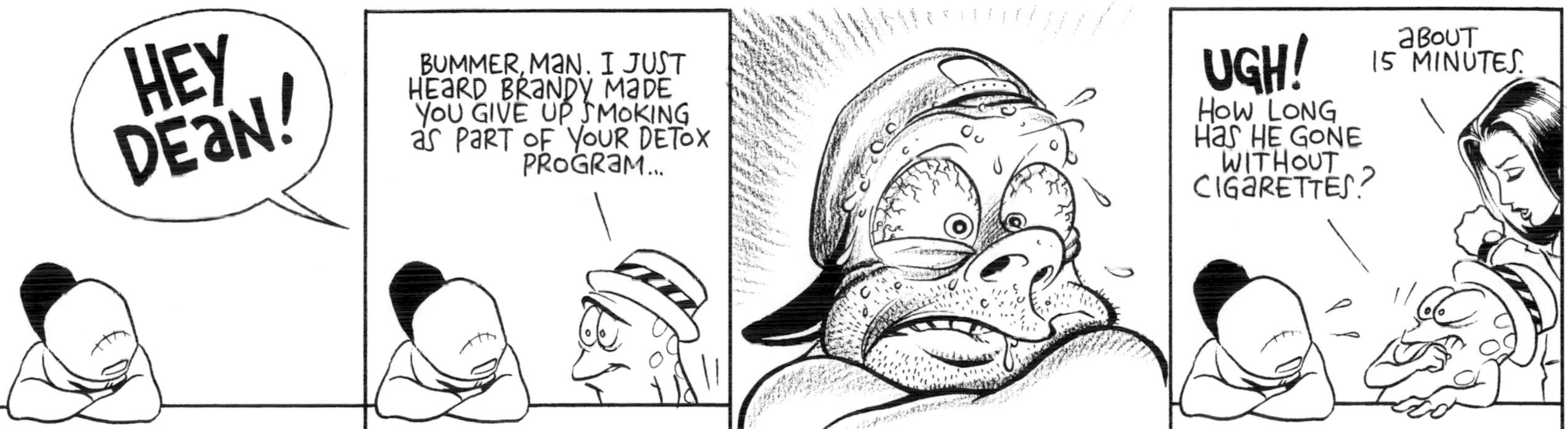
HEY DEAN!
BUMMER, MAN. I JUST HEARD BRANDY MADE YOU GIVE UP SMOKING AS PART OF YOUR DETOX PROGRAM...
UGH!
HOW LONG HAS HE GONE WITHOUT CIGARETTES?
ABOUT 15 MINUTES.
CHO

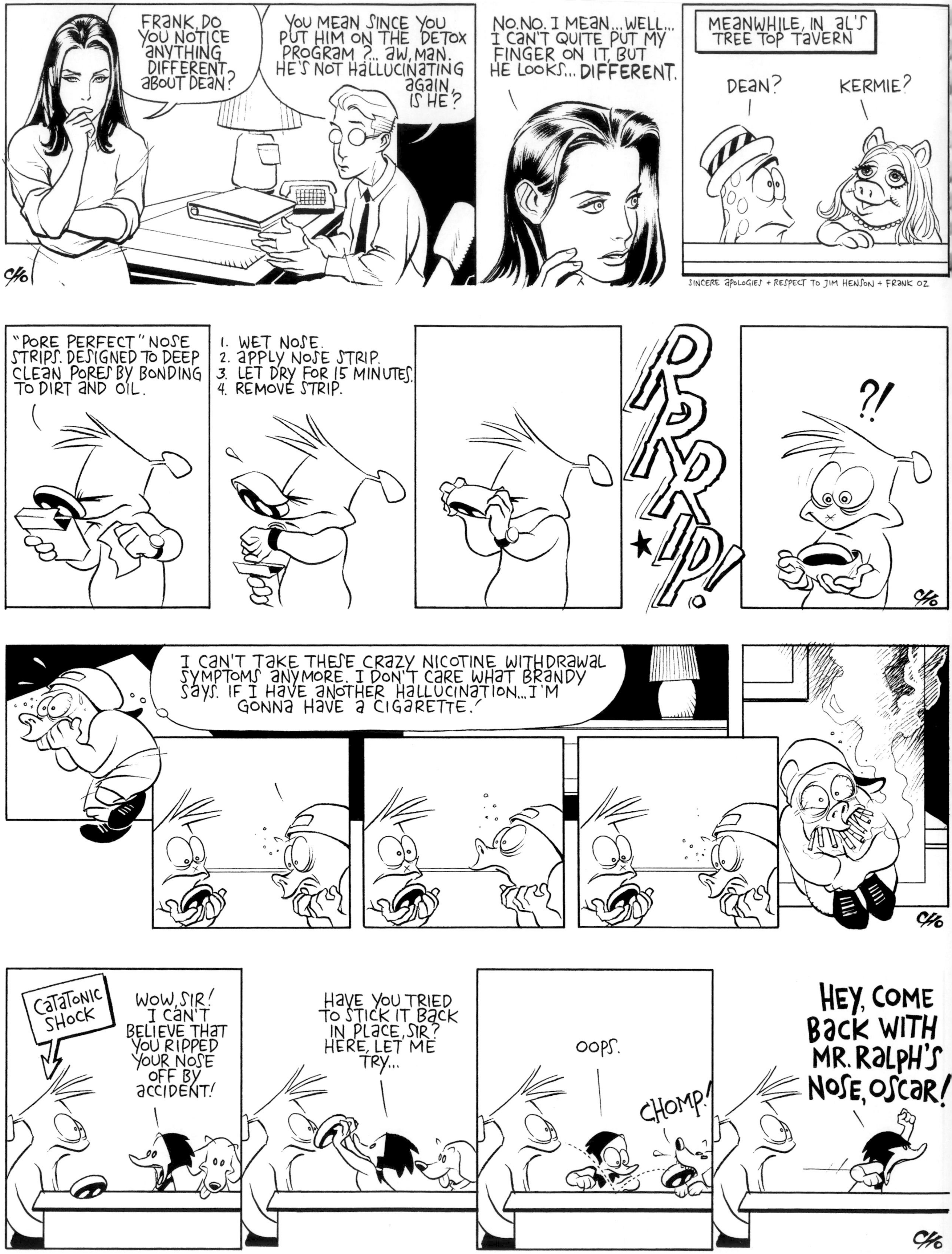
FRANK, DO YOU NOTICE ANYTHING DIFFERENT ABOUT DEAN?
YOU MEAN SINCE YOU PUT HIM ON THE DETOX PROGRAM?... AW, MAN. HE'S NOT HALLUCINATING AGAIN, IS HE?
NO. NO. I MEAN... WELL... I CAN'T QUITE PUT MY FINGER ON IT, BUT HE LOOKS... DIFFERENT.
MEANWHILE, IN AL'S TREE TOP TAVERN
DEAN?
KERMIE?
SINCERE APOLOGIES + RESPECT TO JIM HENSON + FRANK OZ
"PORE PERFECT" NOSE STRIPS. DESIGNED TO DEEP CLEAN PORES BY BONDING TO DIRT AND OIL.
1. WET NOSE.
2. APPLY NOSE STRIP.
3. LET DRY FOR 15 MINUTES.
4. REMOVE STRIP.
RRRIP!
?!
I CAN'T TAKE THESE CRAZY NICOTINE WITHDRAWAL SYMPTOMS ANYMORE. I DON'T CARE WHAT BRANDY SAYS. IF I HAVE ANOTHER HALLUCINATION... I'M GONNA HAVE A CIGARETTE.
CATATONIC SHOCK
WOW, SIR! I CAN'T BELIEVE THAT YOU RIPPED YOUR NOSE OFF BY ACCIDENT!
HAVE YOU TRIED TO STICK IT BACK IN PLACE, SIR? HERE, LET ME TRY...
OOPS.
CHOMP!
HEY, COME BACK WITH MR. RALPH'S NOSE, OSCAR!

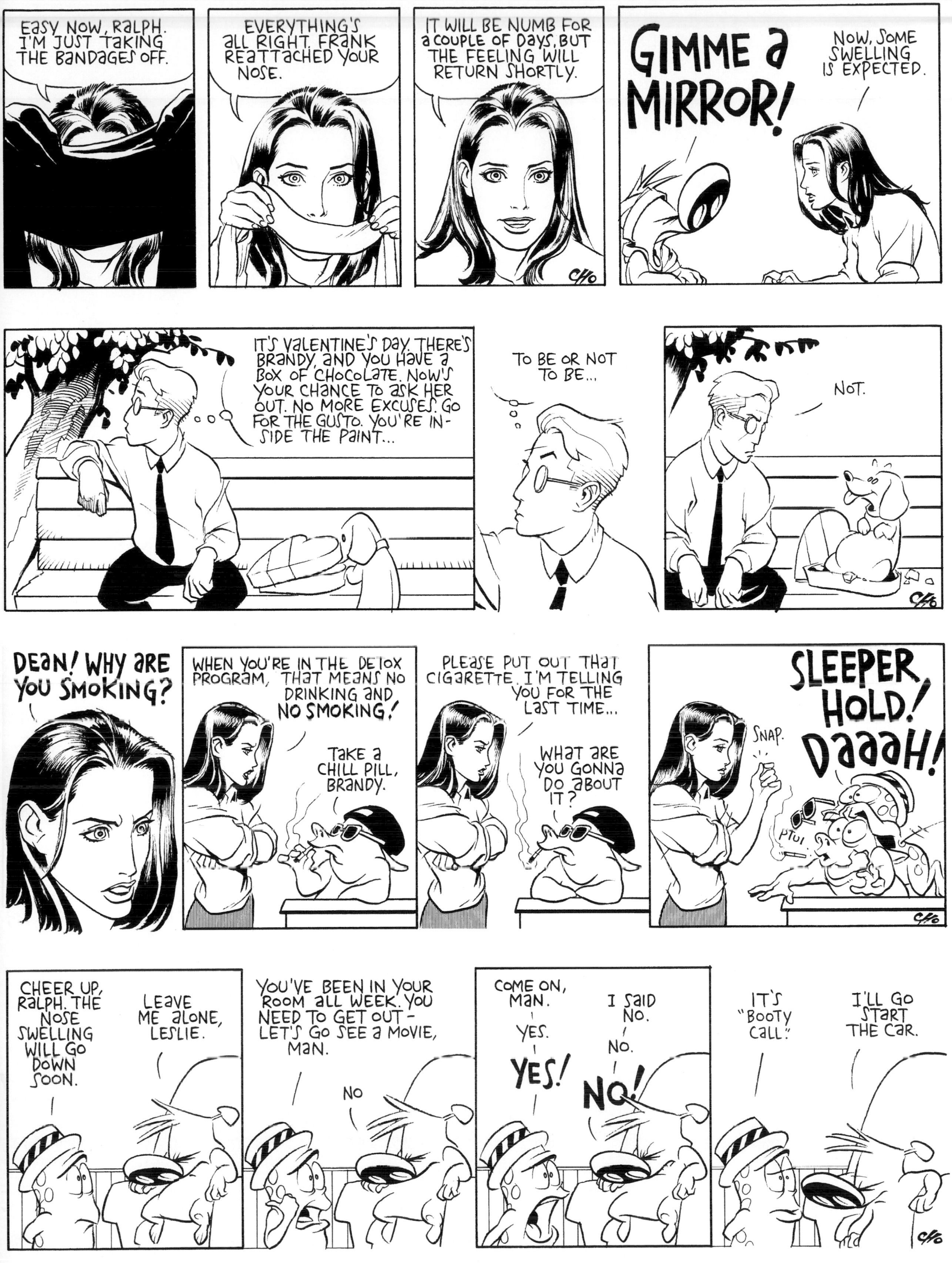
EASY NOW, RALPH. I'M JUST TAKING THE BANDAGES OFF.
EVERYTHING'S ALL RIGHT. FRANK REATTACHED YOUR NOSE.
IT WILL BE NUMB FOR A COUPLE OF DAYS, BUT THE FEELING WILL RETURN SHORTLY.
GIMME A MIRROR!
NOW, SOME SWELLING IS EXPECTED.
CHO
IT'S VALENTINE'S DAY. THERE'S BRANDY, AND YOU HAVE A BOX OF CHOCOLATE. NOW'S YOUR CHANCE TO ASK HER OUT. NO MORE EXCUSES. GO FOR THE GUSTO. YOU'RE INSIDE THE PAINT...
TO BE OR NOT TO BE...
NOT.
CHO
DEAN! WHY ARE YOU SMOKING?
WHEN YOU'RE IN THE DETOX PROGRAM, THAT MEANS NO DRINKING AND NO SMOKING!
TAKE A CHILL PILL, BRANDY.
PLEASE PUT OUT THAT CIGARETTE. I'M TELLING YOU FOR THE LAST TIME...
WHAT ARE YOU GONNA DO ABOUT IT?
SLEEPER HOLD! DAAAH!
SNAP.
PTUI
CHO
CHEER UP, RALPH. THE NOSE SWELLING WILL GO DOWN SOON.
LEAVE ME ALONE, LESLIE.
YOU'VE BEEN IN YOUR ROOM ALL WEEK. YOU NEED TO GET OUT - LET'S GO SEE A MOVIE, MAN.
NO
COME ON, MAN.
I SAID NO.
YES.
NO.
YES!
NO!
IT'S "BOOTY CALL."
I'LL GO START THE CAR.
CHO

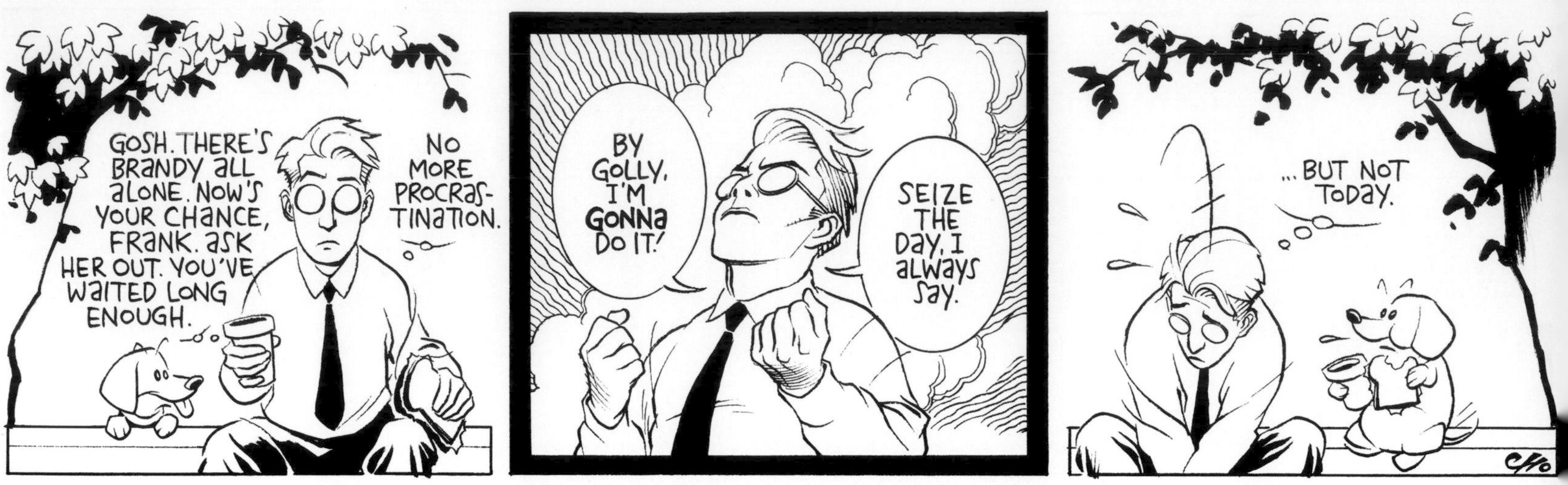
GOSH. THERE'S BRANDY ALL ALONE. NOW'S YOUR CHANCE, FRANK. ASK HER OUT. YOU'VE WAITED LONG ENOUGH.
NO MORE PROCRAS-TINATION.
BY GOLLY, I'M **GONNA** DO IT!
SEIZE THE DAY, I ALWAYS SAY.
... BUT NOT TODAY.
CHO

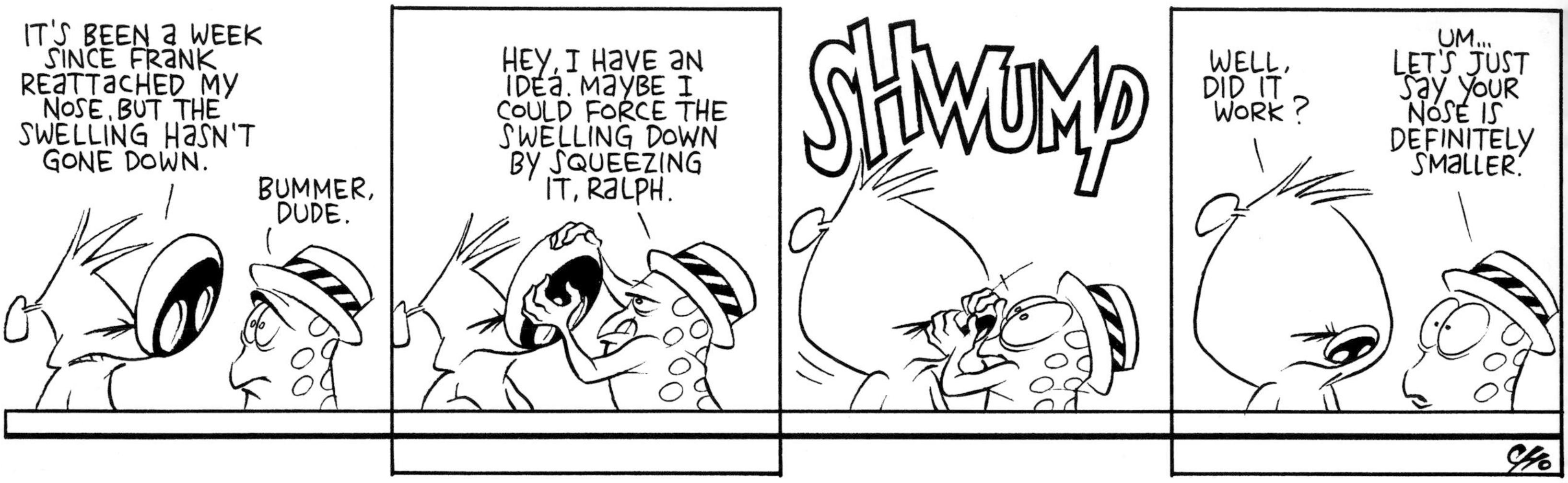
IT'S BEEN A WEEK SINCE FRANK REATTACHED MY NOSE, BUT THE SWELLING HASN'T GONE DOWN.
BUMMER, DUDE.
HEY, I HAVE AN IDEA. MAYBE I COULD FORCE THE SWELLING DOWN BY SQUEEZING IT, RALPH.
SHWUMP
WELL, DID IT WORK?
UM... LET'S JUST SAY YOUR NOSE IS DEFINITELY SMALLER.
CHO

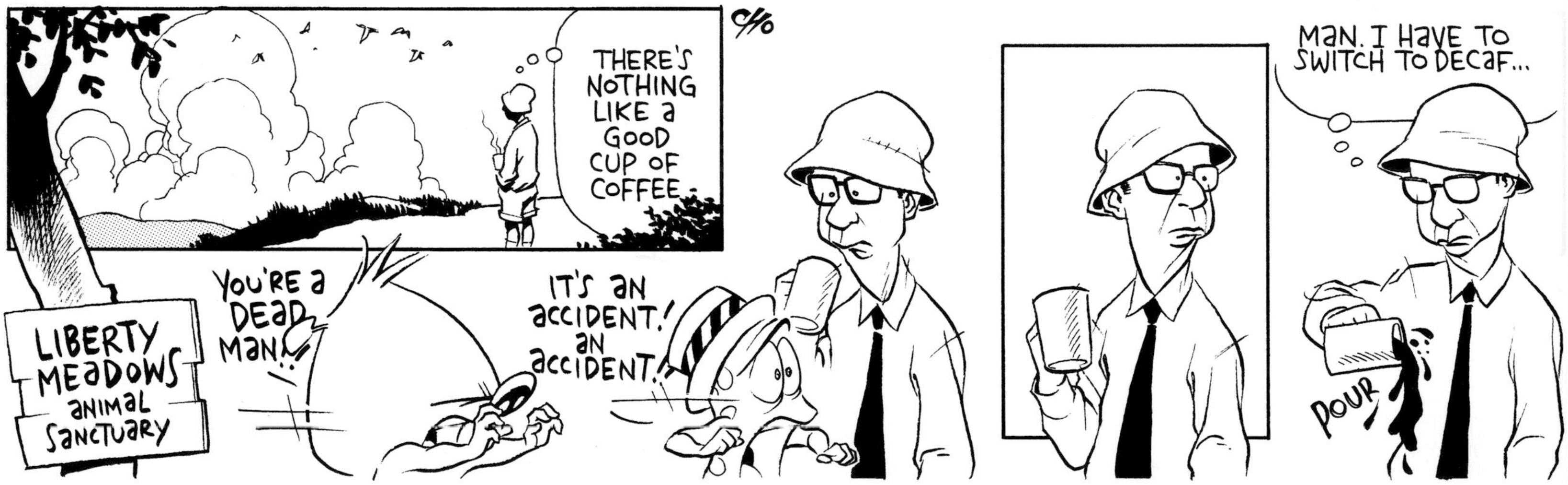
THERE'S NOTHING LIKE A GOOD CUP OF COFFEE.
CHO
YOU'RE A DEAD MAN!
IT'S AN ACCIDENT! AN ACCIDENT!
LIBERTY MEADOWS animal sanctuary
MAN. I HAVE TO SWITCH TO DECAF...
POUR

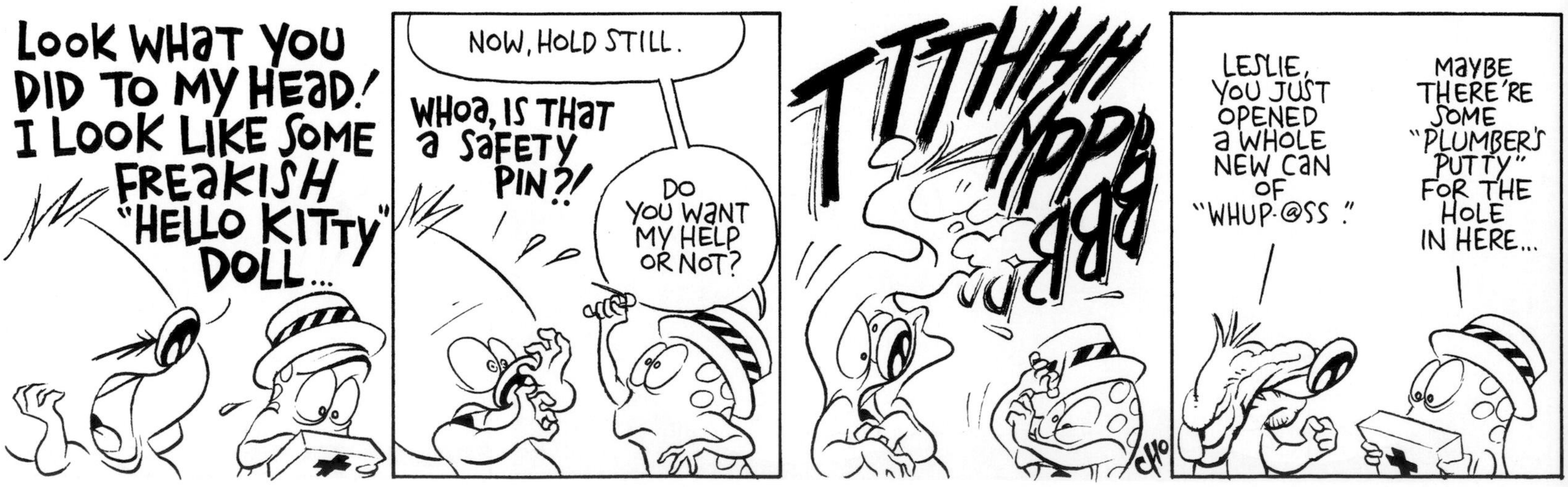
LOOK WHAT YOU DID TO MY HEAD! I LOOK LIKE SOME FREAKISH "HELLO KITTY" DOLL...
NOW, HOLD STILL.
WHOA, IS THAT A SAFETY PIN?!
DO YOU WANT MY HELP OR NOT?
TTTHHHH
LESLIE, YOU JUST OPENED A WHOLE NEW CAN OF "WHUP-@SS."
MAYBE THERE'RE SOME "PLUMBER'S PUTTY" FOR THE HOLE IN HERE...
CHO

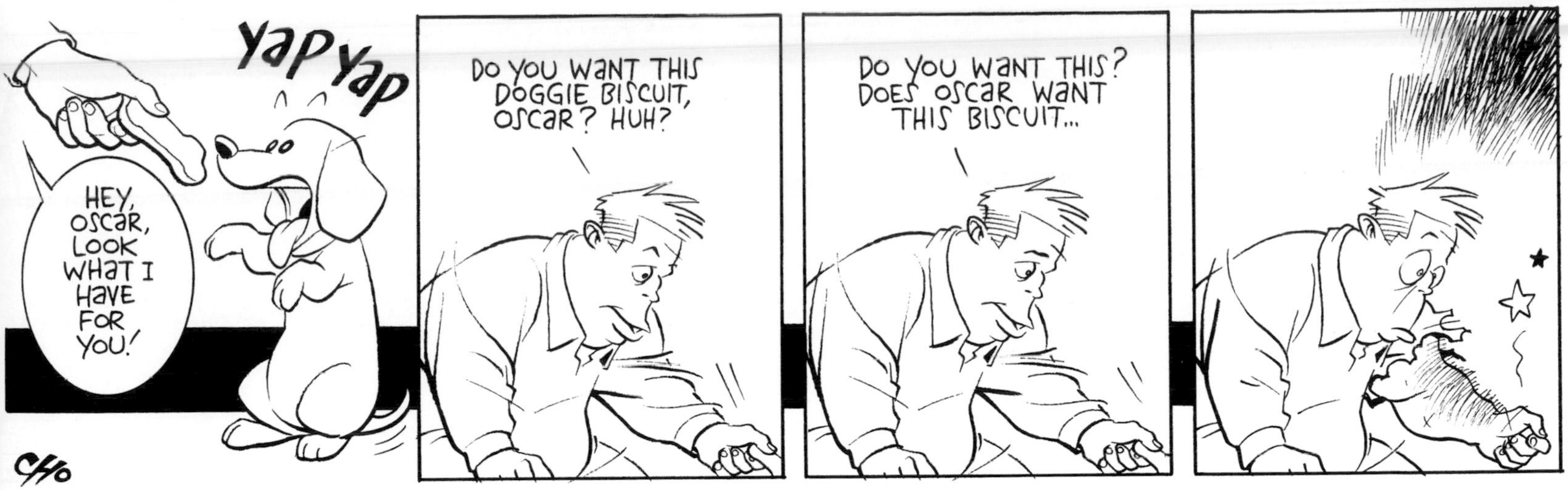
YAP YAP
HEY, OSCAR, LOOK WHAT I HAVE FOR YOU!
DO YOU WANT THIS DOGGIE BISCUIT, OSCAR? HUH?
DO YOU WANT THIS? DOES OSCAR WANT THIS BISCUIT...
CHO

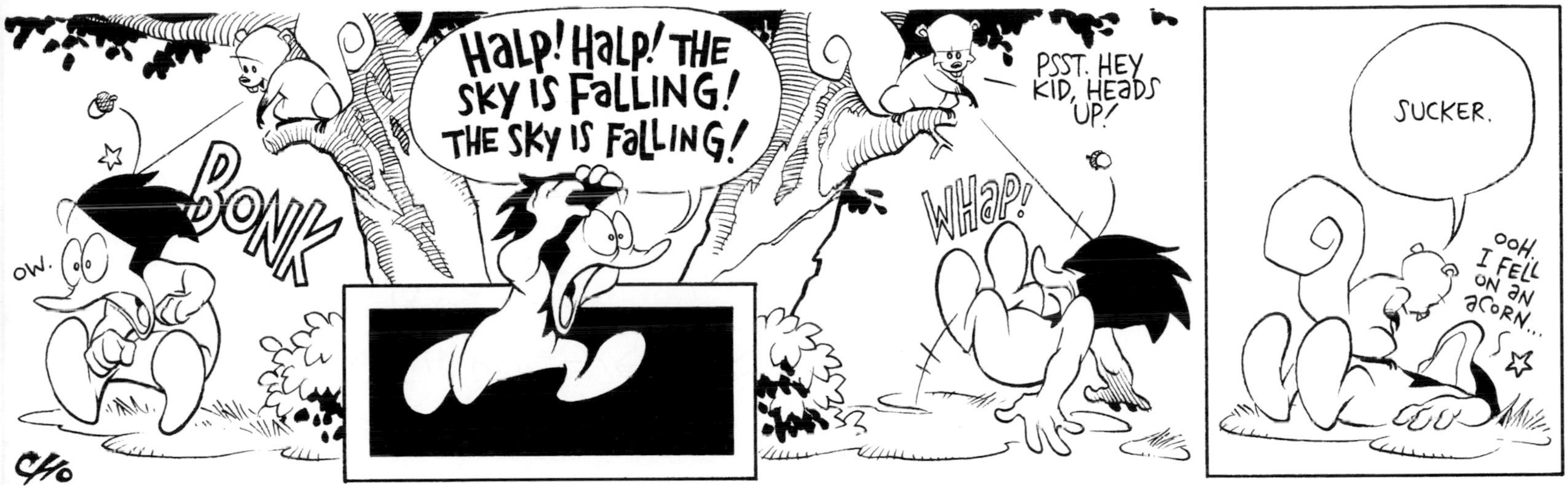
BONK
OW.
HALP! HALP! THE SKY IS FALLING! THE SKY IS FALLING!
PSST. HEY KID, HEADS UP!
WHAP!
SUCKER.
OOH, I FELL ON AN ACORN...
CHO

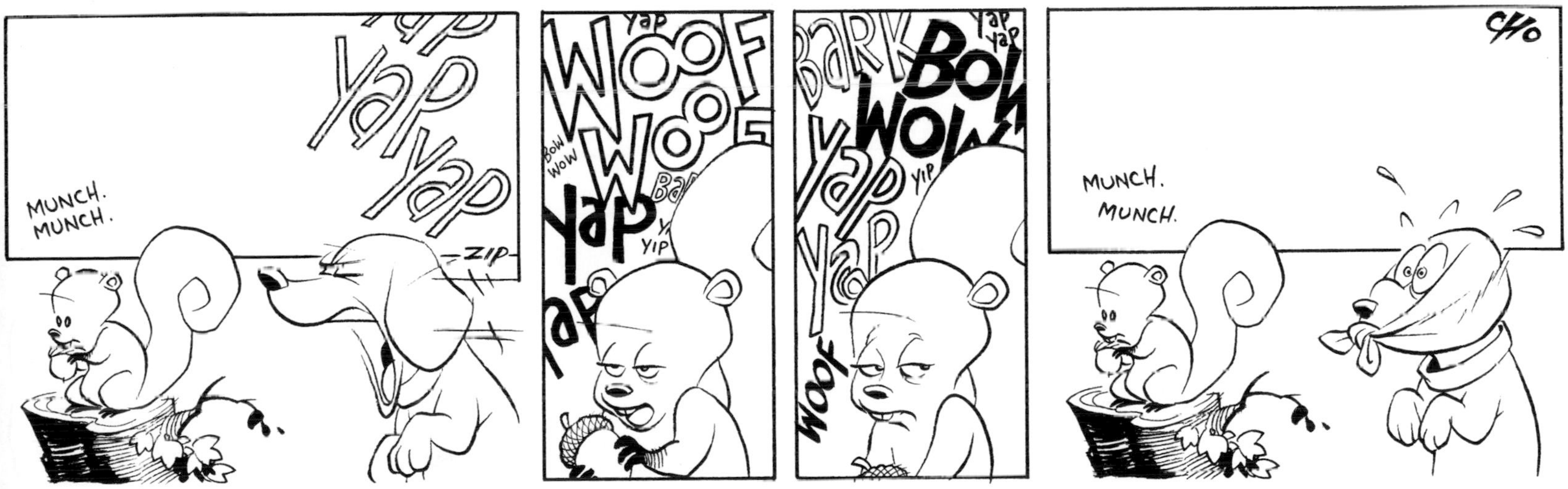
YAP YAP YAP YAP
ZIP
MUNCH. MUNCH.
WOOF WOOF
BOW WOW
YAP
YIP
BARK
BOW WOW
YAP YAP
YIP
WOOF
CHO
MUNCH. MUNCH.

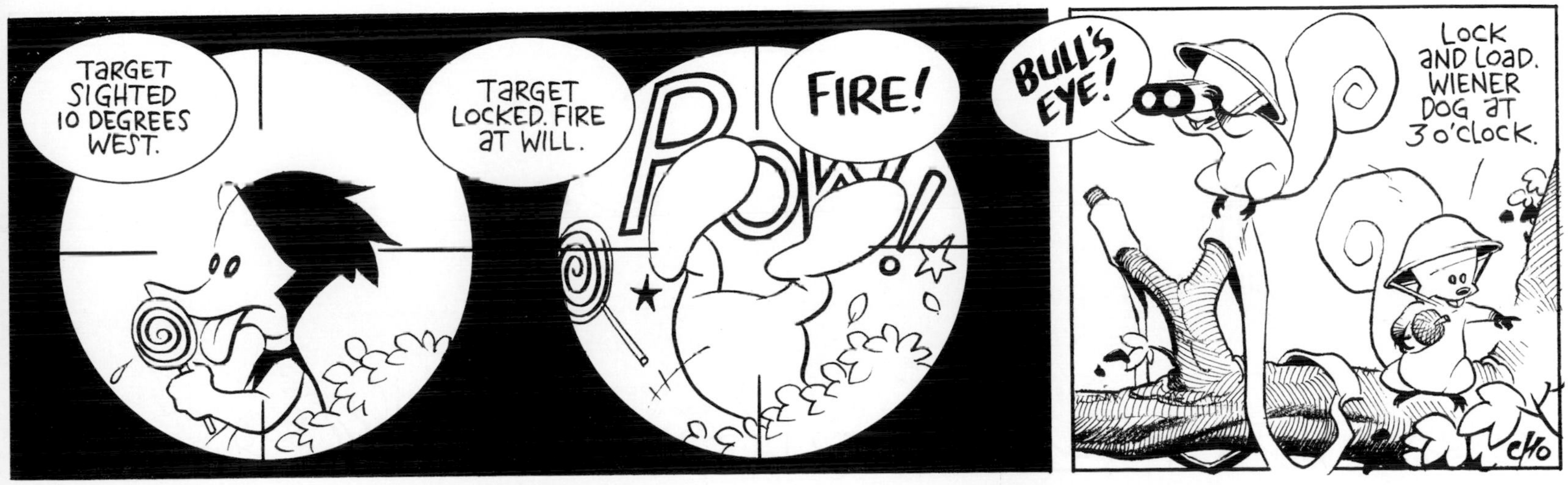
TARGET SIGHTED 10 DEGREES WEST.
TARGET LOCKED. FIRE AT WILL.
FIRE!
POW!
BULL'S EYE!
LOCK AND LOAD. WIENER DOG AT 3 O'CLOCK.
CHO

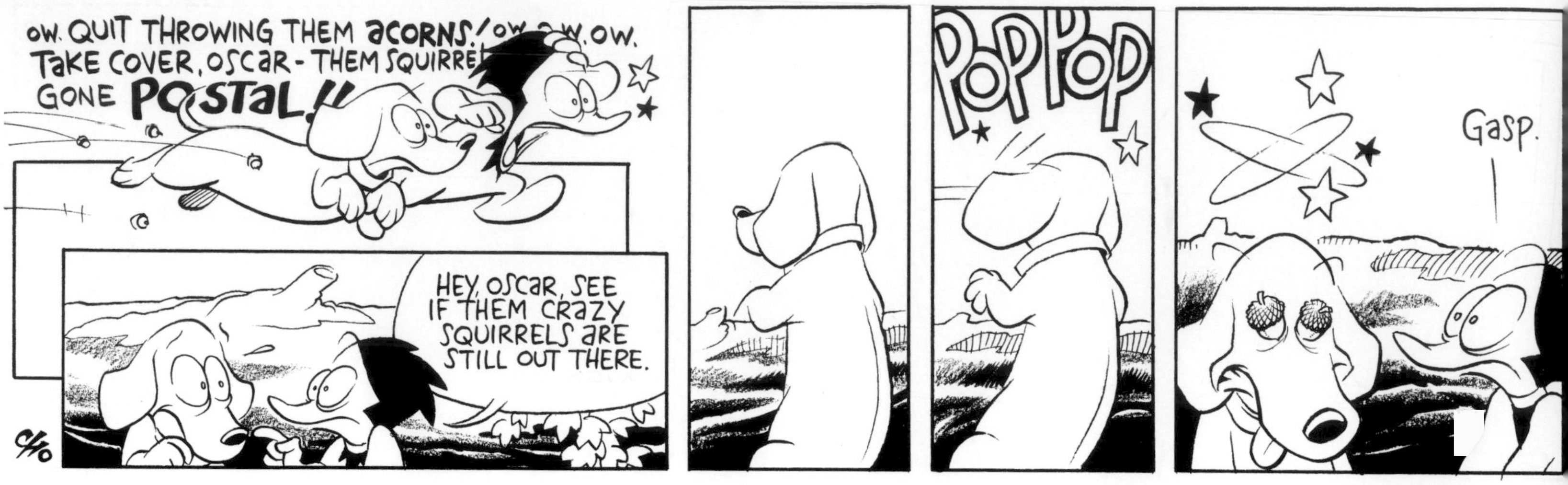
OW. QUIT THROWING THEM ACORNS! OW. OW. OW.
TAKE COVER, OSCAR - THEM SQUIRRE
GONE POSTAL!!
HEY, OSCAR, SEE IF THEM CRAZY SQUIRRELS ARE STILL OUT THERE.
POP POP
GASP.

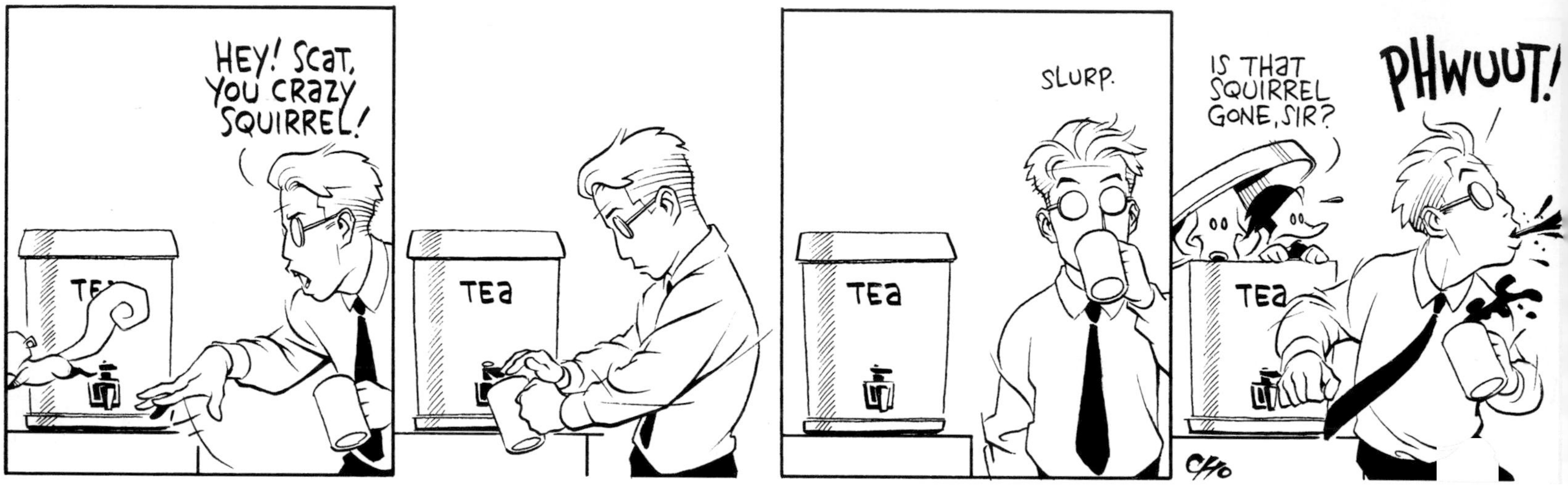
HEY! SCAT, YOU CRAZY SQUIRREL!
TEA
SLURP.
IS THAT SQUIRREL GONE, SIR?
PHWUUT!

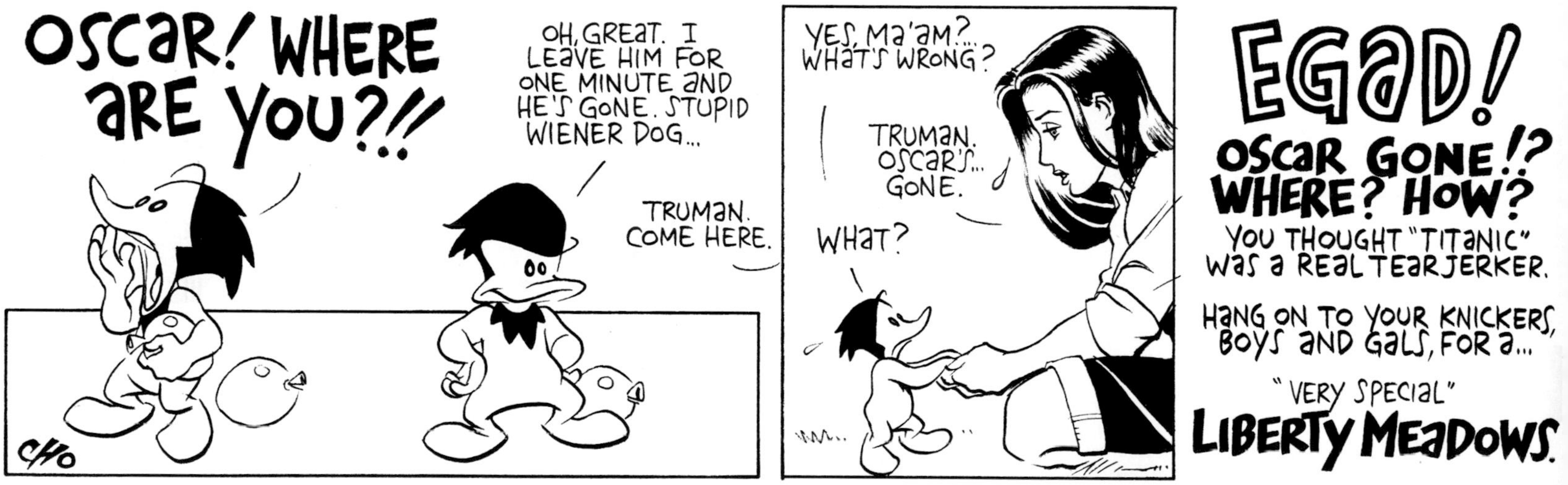
OSCAR! WHERE ARE YOU?!!
OH, GREAT. I LEAVE HIM FOR ONE MINUTE AND HE'S GONE. STUPID WIENER DOG...
TRUMAN. COME HERE.
YES, MA'AM?... WHAT'S WRONG?
TRUMAN. OSCAR'S... GONE.
WHAT?
EGAD!
OSCAR GONE!? WHERE? HOW?
YOU THOUGHT "TITANIC" WAS A REAL TEARJERKER.
HANG ON TO YOUR KNICKERS, BOYS AND GALS, FOR A...
"VERY SPECIAL"
LIBERTY MEADOWS.

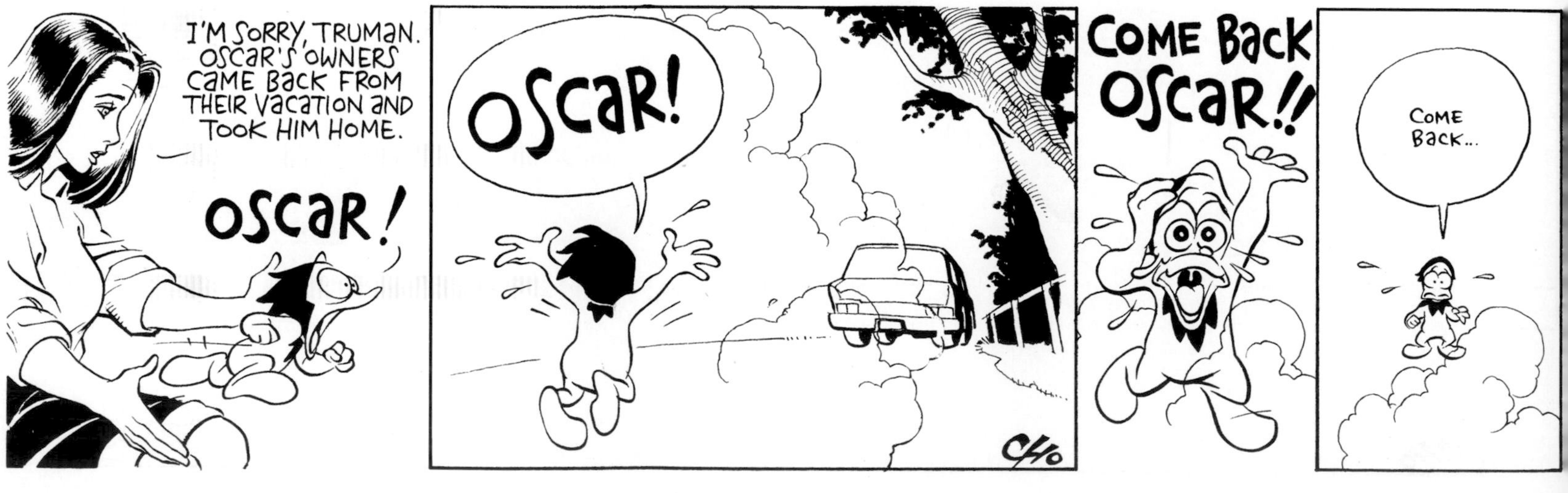
I'M SORRY, TRUMAN. OSCAR'S OWNERS CAME BACK FROM THEIR VACATION AND TOOK HIM HOME.
OSCAR!
OSCAR!
COME BACK OSCAR!!
COME BACK...

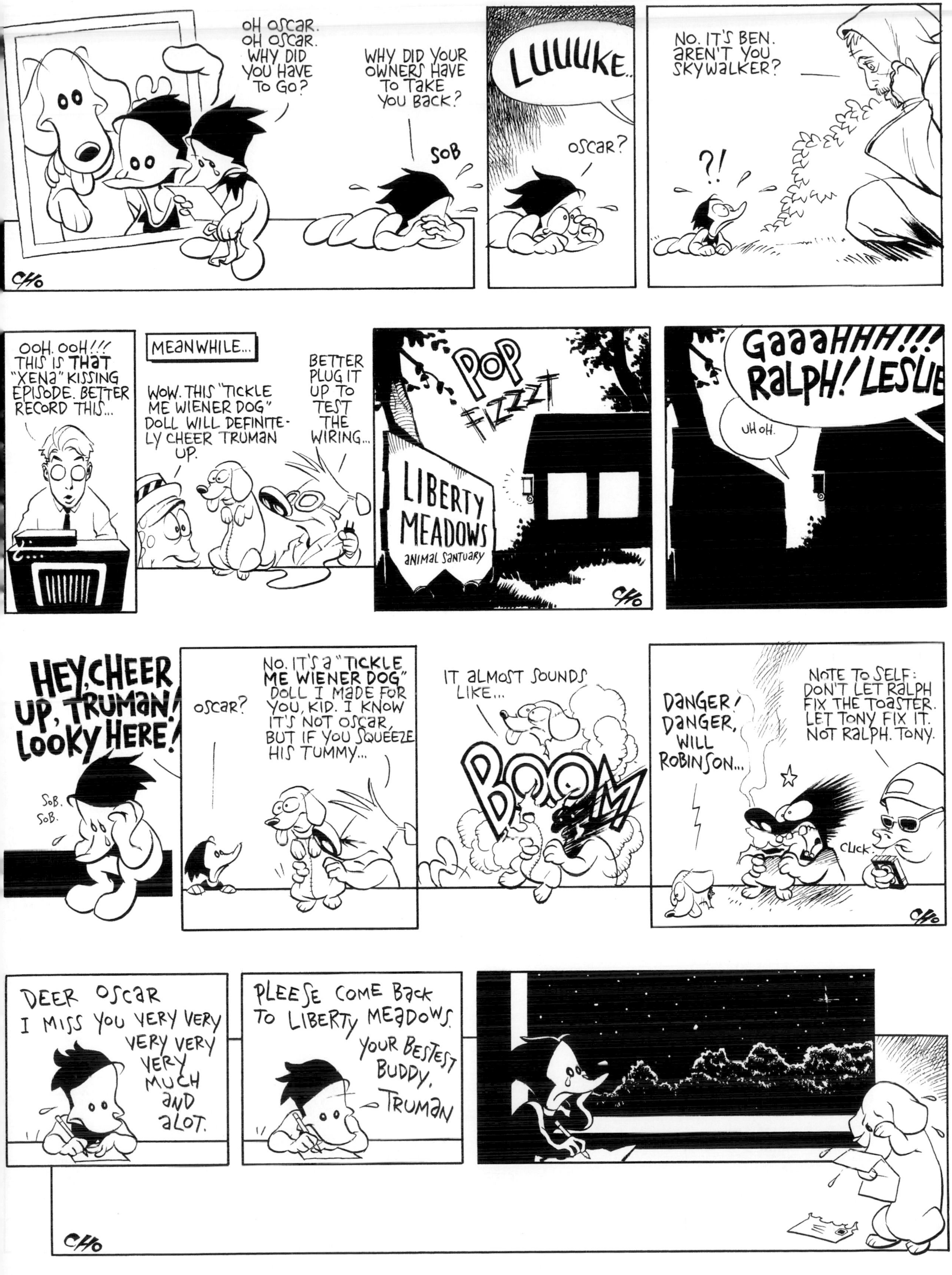
CHO
OH OSCAR. OH OSCAR. WHY DID YOU HAVE TO GO?
WHY DID YOUR OWNERS HAVE TO TAKE YOU BACK?
SOB
LUUUKE...
OSCAR?
NO. IT'S BEN. AREN'T YOU SKYWALKER?
?!
OOH. OOH!!! THIS IS THAT "XENA" KISSING EPISODE. BETTER RECORD THIS...
MEANWHILE...
WOW. THIS "TICKLE ME WIENER DOG" DOLL WILL DEFINITELY CHEER TRUMAN UP.
BETTER PLUG IT UP TO TEST THE WIRING...
POP
FIZZZT
LIBERTY MEADOWS
ANIMAL SANTUARY
CHO
GAAAHHH!!! RALPH! LESLIE
UH OH.
HEY, CHEER UP, TRUMAN! LOOKY HERE!
SOB. SOB.
OSCAR?
NO. IT'S A "TICKLE ME WIENER DOG" DOLL I MADE FOR YOU, KID. I KNOW IT'S NOT OSCAR, BUT IF YOU SQUEEZE HIS TUMMY...
IT ALMOST SOUNDS LIKE...
BOOM
DANGER! DANGER, WILL ROBINSON...
NOTE TO SELF: DON'T LET RALPH FIX THE TOASTER. LET TONY FIX IT. NOT RALPH. TONY.
CLICK.
CHO
DEER OSCAR
I MISS YOU VERY VERY VERY VERY VERY MUCH AND ALOT.
PLEESE COME BACK TO LIBERTY MEADOWS.
YOUR BESTEST BUDDY,
TRUMAN
CHO

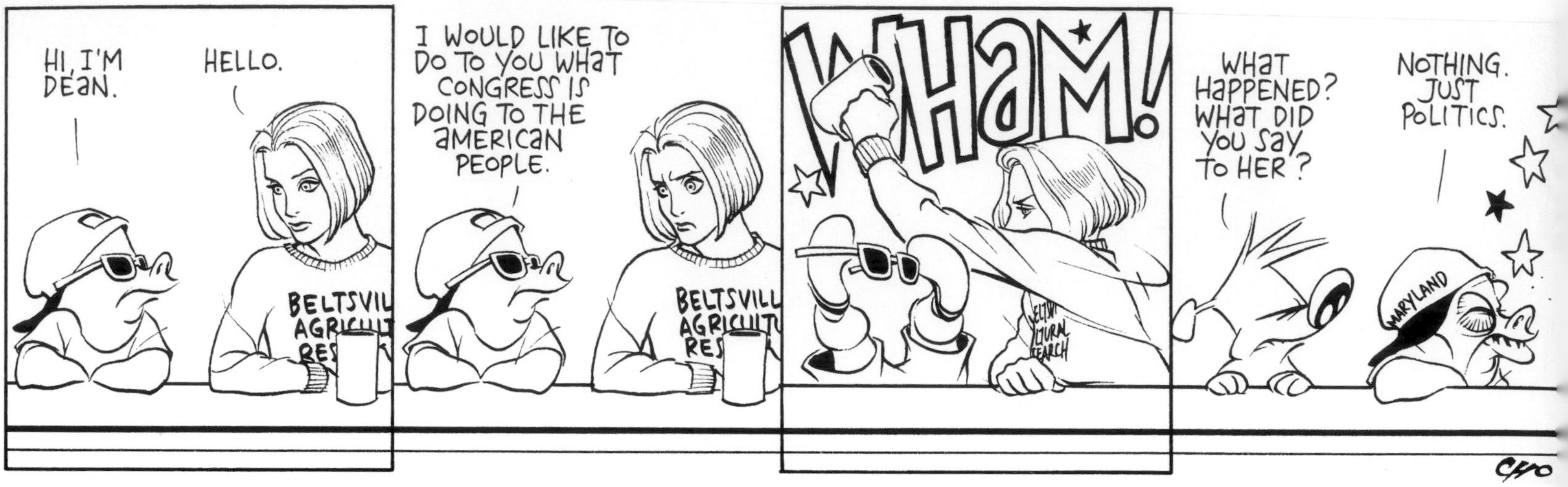
HI, I'M DEAN.
HELLO.
I WOULD LIKE TO DO TO YOU WHAT CONGRESS IS DOING TO THE AMERICAN PEOPLE.
WHAM!
WHAT HAPPENED? WHAT DID YOU SAY TO HER?
NOTHING. JUST POLITICS.
BELTSVILL AGRICULTU RES
MARYLAND
CHO

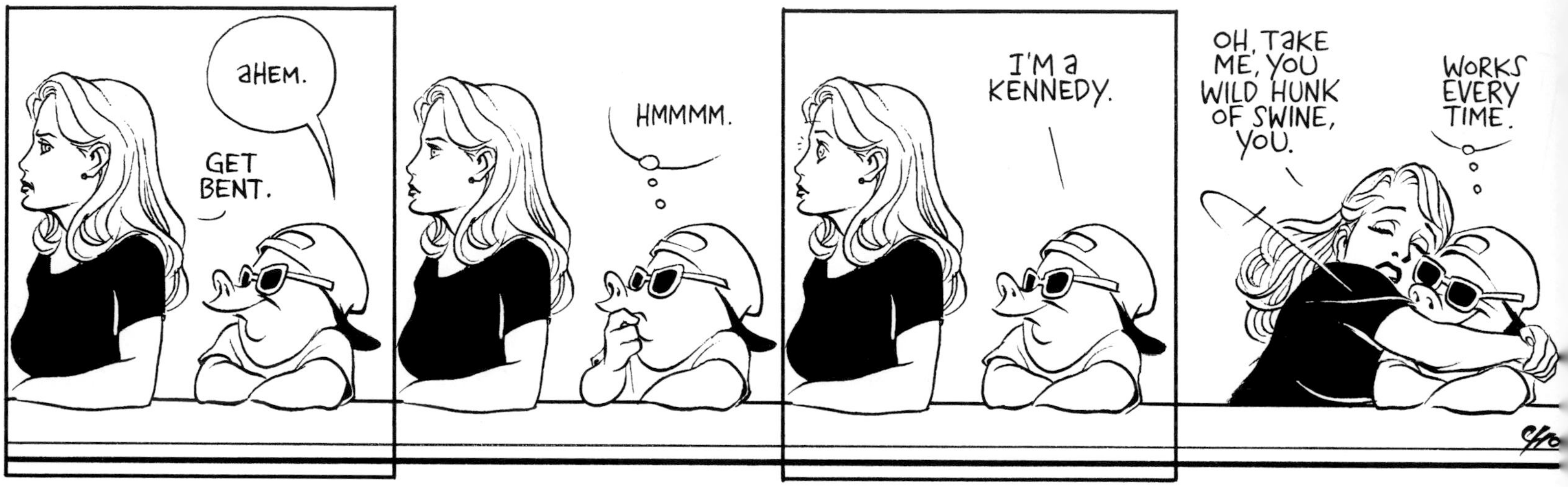
AHEM.
GET BENT.
HMMMM.
I'M A KENNEDY.
OH, TAKE ME, YOU WILD HUNK OF SWINE, YOU.
WORKS EVERY TIME.
CHO

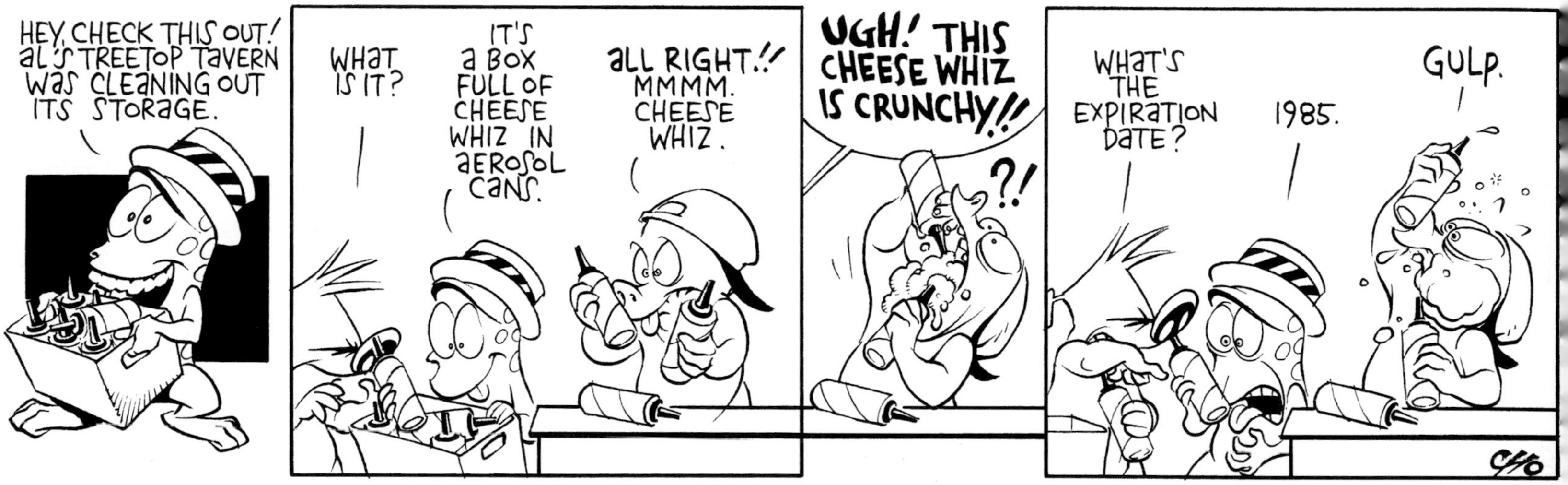
HEY, CHECK THIS OUT! AL'S TREETOP TAVERN WAS CLEANING OUT ITS STORAGE.
WHAT IS IT?
IT'S A BOX FULL OF CHEESE WHIZ IN AEROSOL CANS.
ALL RIGHT!! MMMM. CHEESE WHIZ.
UGH! THIS CHEESE WHIZ IS CRUNCHY!!
?!
WHAT'S THE EXPIRATION DATE?
1985.
GULP.
CHO

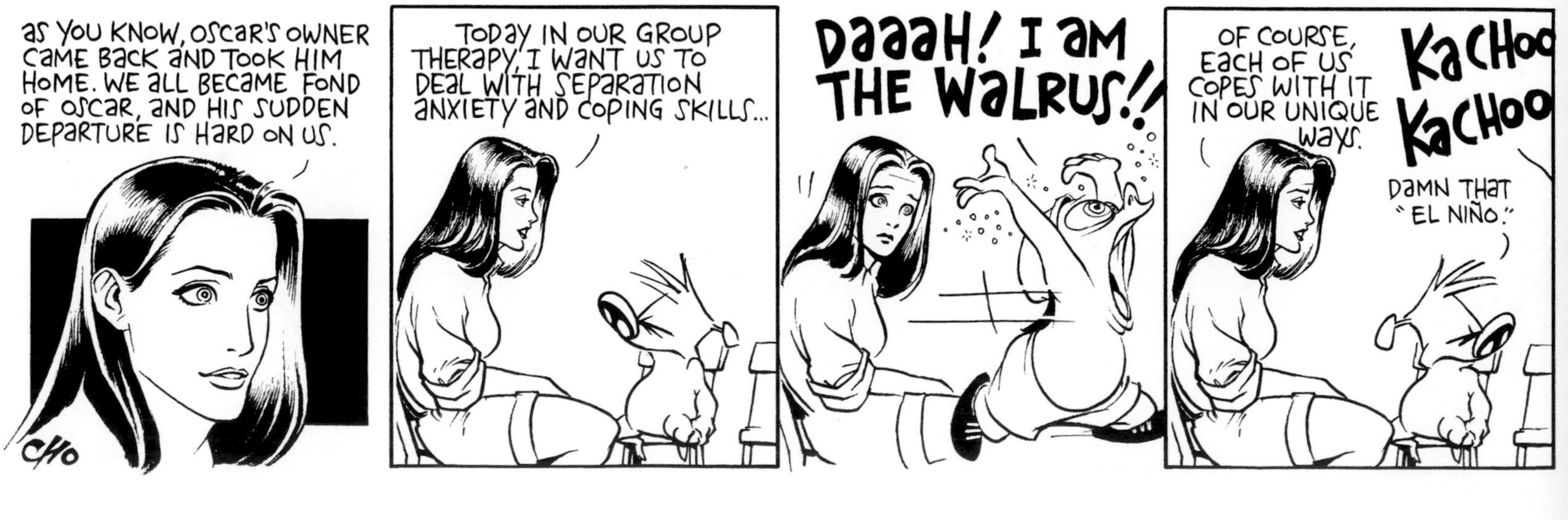
AS YOU KNOW, OSCAR'S OWNER CAME BACK AND TOOK HIM HOME. WE ALL BECAME FOND OF OSCAR, AND HIS SUDDEN DEPARTURE IS HARD ON US.
TODAY IN OUR GROUP THERAPY, I WANT US TO DEAL WITH SEPARATION ANXIETY AND COPING SKILLS...
DAAAH! I AM THE WALRUS!!
OF COURSE, EACH OF US COPES WITH IT IN OUR UNIQUE WAYS.
KACHOO KACHOO
DAMN THAT "EL NIÑO."
CHO

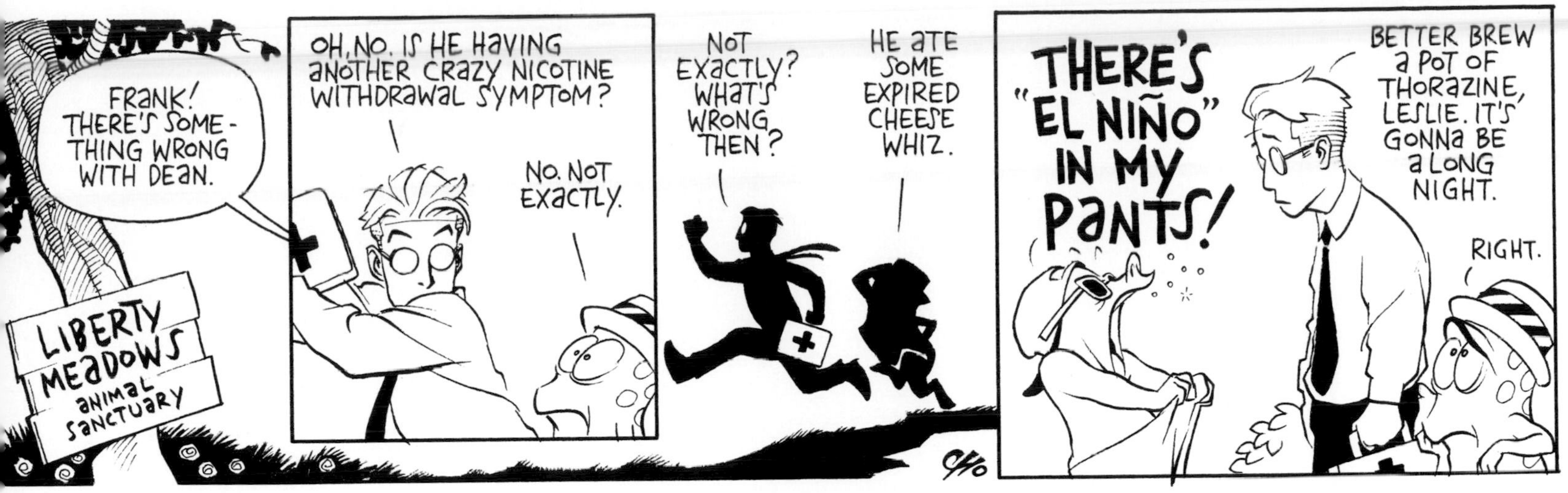
FRANK! THERE'S SOME-THING WRONG WITH DEAN.
LIBERTY MEADOWS ANIMAL SANCTUARY
OH, NO. IS HE HAVING ANOTHER CRAZY NICOTINE WITHDRAWAL SYMPTOM?
NO. NOT EXACTLY.
NOT EXACTLY? WHAT'S WRONG, THEN?
HE ATE SOME EXPIRED CHEESE WHIZ.
THERE'S "EL NIÑO" IN MY PANTS!
BETTER BREW A POT OF THORAZINE, LESLIE. IT'S GONNA BE A LONG NIGHT.
RIGHT.
CHO

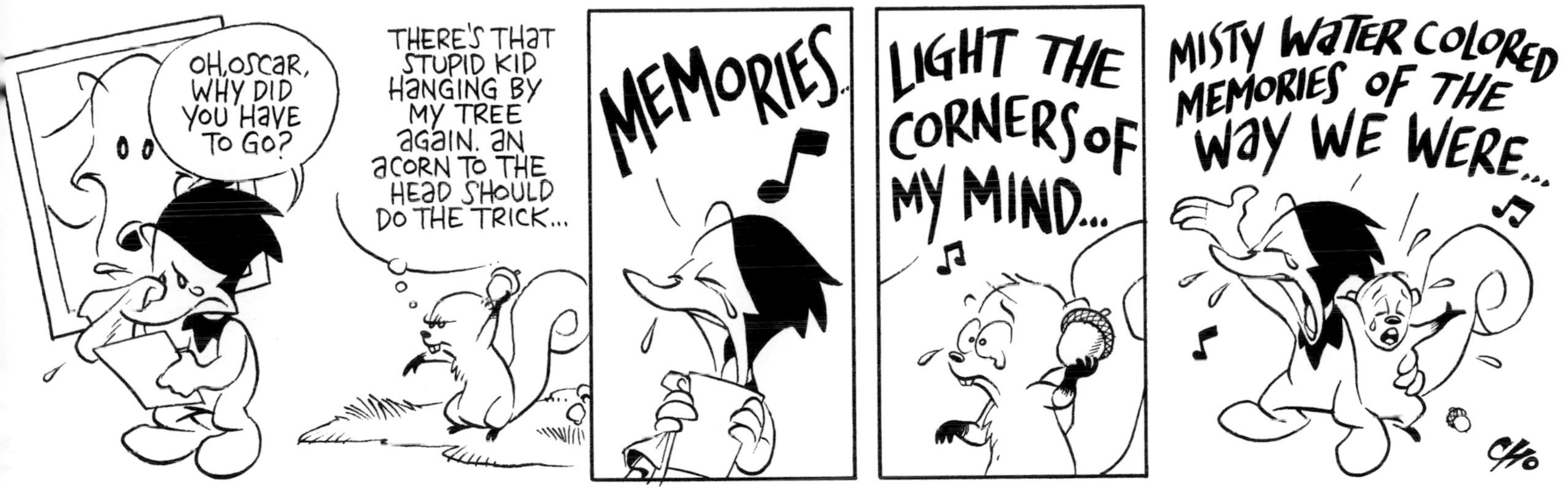
OH, OSCAR, WHY DID YOU HAVE TO GO?
THERE'S THAT STUPID KID HANGING BY MY TREE AGAIN. AN ACORN TO THE HEAD SHOULD DO THE TRICK...
MEMORIES..
LIGHT THE CORNERS OF MY MIND...
MISTY WATER COLORED MEMORIES OF THE WAY WE WERE...
CHO

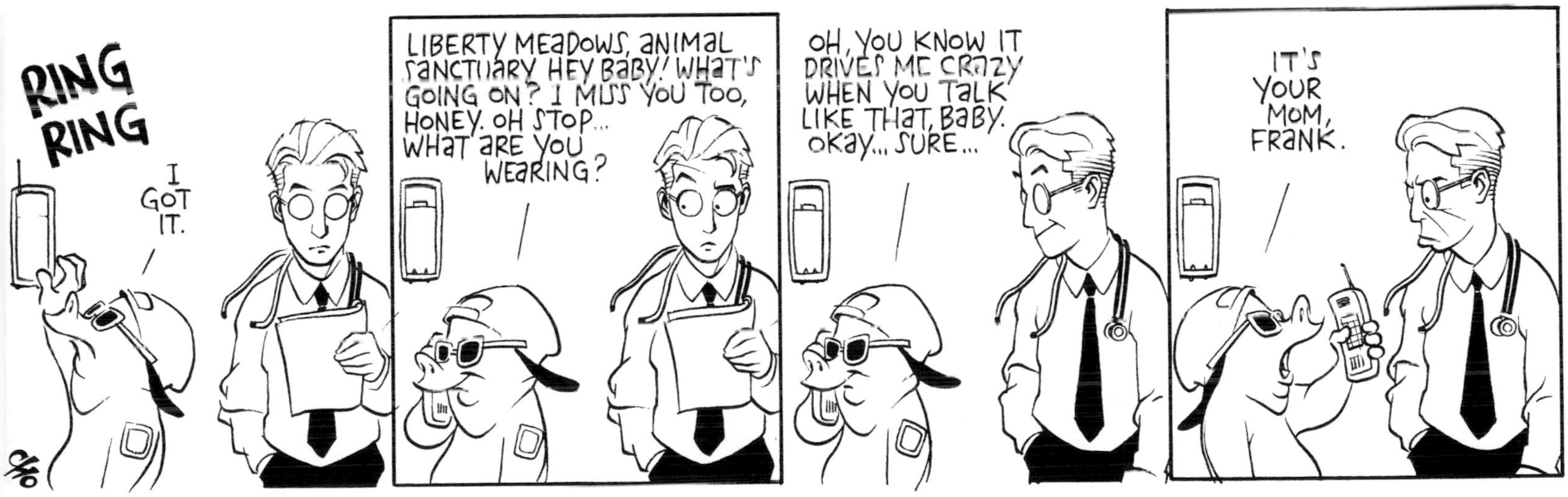
RING RING
I GOT IT.
CHO
LIBERTY MEADOWS, ANIMAL SANCTUARY. HEY BABY! WHAT'S GOING ON? I MISS YOU TOO, HONEY. OH STOP... WHAT ARE YOU WEARING?
OH, YOU KNOW IT DRIVES ME CRAZY WHEN YOU TALK LIKE THAT, BABY. OKAY... SURE...
IT'S YOUR MOM, FRANK.

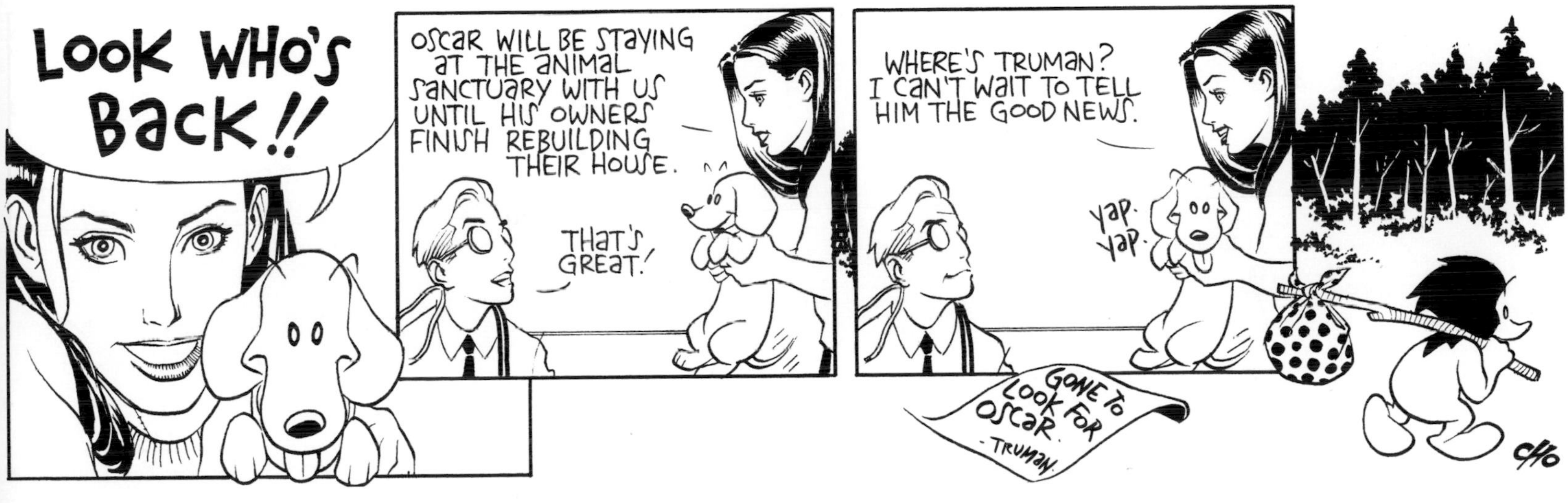
LOOK WHO'S BACK!!
OSCAR WILL BE STAYING AT THE ANIMAL SANCTUARY WITH US UNTIL HIS OWNERS FINISH REBUILDING THEIR HOUSE.
THAT'S GREAT!
WHERE'S TRUMAN? I CAN'T WAIT TO TELL HIM THE GOOD NEWS.
YAP. YAP.
GONE TO LOOK FOR OSCAR. - TRUMAN
CHO

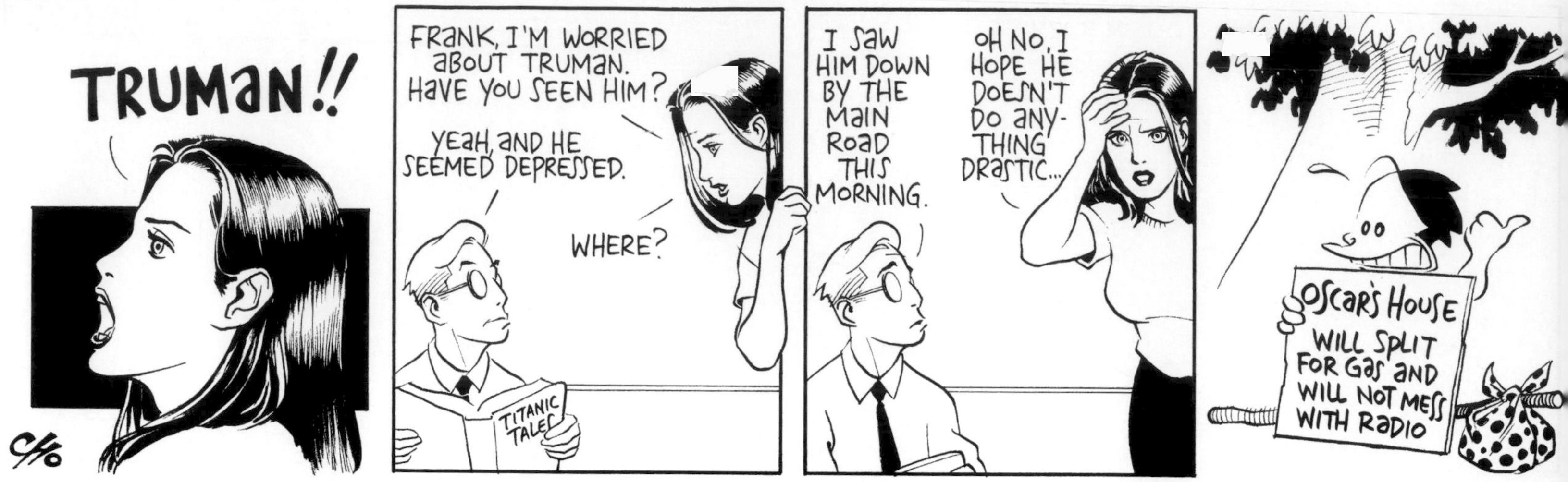
TRUMAN!!
FRANK, I'M WORRIED ABOUT TRUMAN. HAVE YOU SEEN HIM?
YEAH, AND HE SEEMED DEPRESSED.
WHERE?
I SAW HIM DOWN BY THE MAIN ROAD THIS MORNING.
OH NO, I HOPE HE DOESN'T DO ANYTHING DRASTIC...
OSCAR'S HOUSE
WILL SPLIT FOR GAS AND WILL NOT MESS WITH RADIO
TITANIC TALES
CHO

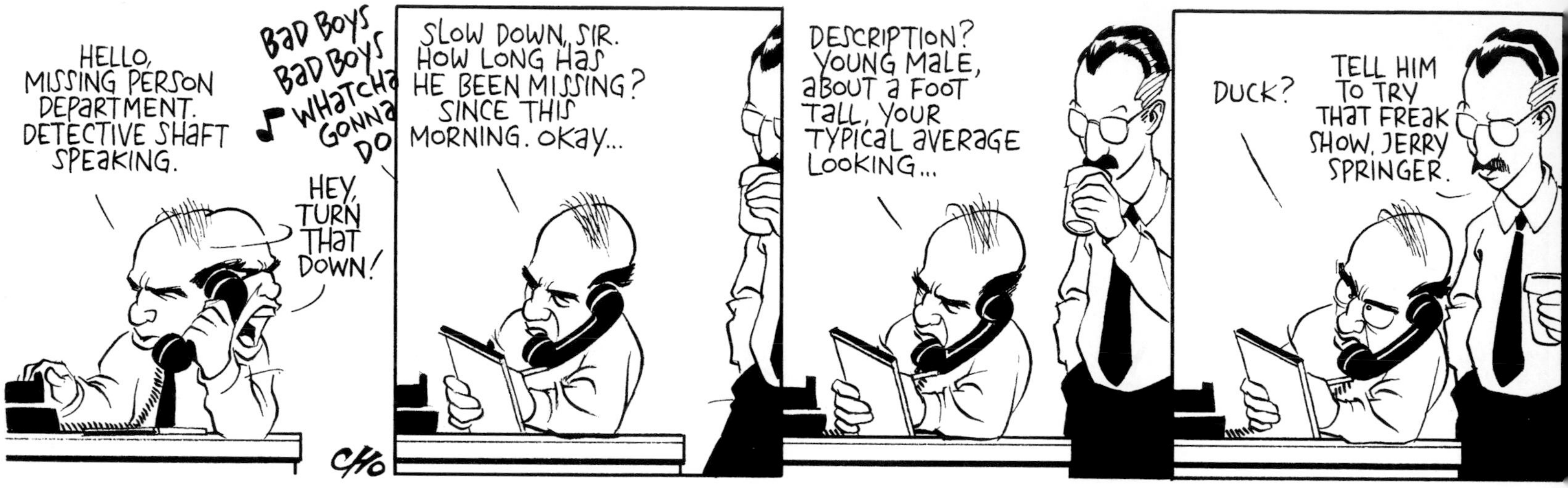
HELLO, MISSING PERSON DEPARTMENT. DETECTIVE SHAFT SPEAKING.
BAD BOYS BAD BOYS WHATCHA GONNA DO
HEY, TURN THAT DOWN!
SLOW DOWN, SIR. HOW LONG HAS HE BEEN MISSING? SINCE THIS MORNING. OKAY...
DESCRIPTION? YOUNG MALE, ABOUT A FOOT TALL, YOUR TYPICAL AVERAGE LOOKING...
DUCK?
TELL HIM TO TRY THAT FREAK SHOW, JERRY SPRINGER.
CHO

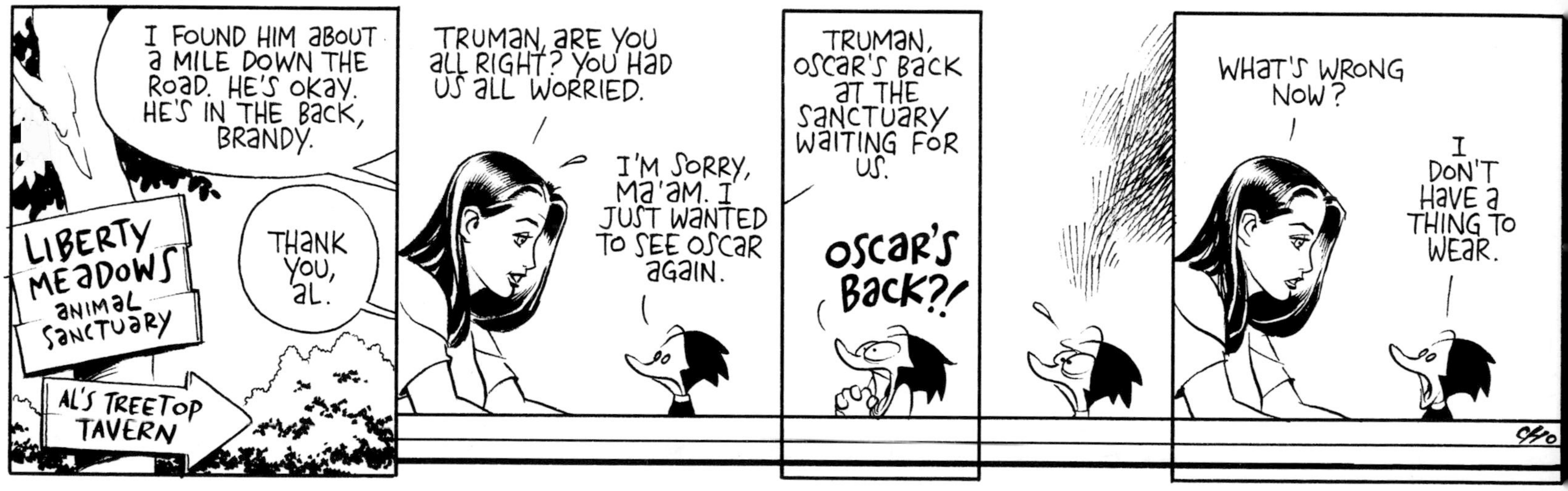
I FOUND HIM ABOUT A MILE DOWN THE ROAD. HE'S OKAY. HE'S IN THE BACK, BRANDY.
THANK YOU, AL.
LIBERTY MEADOWS ANIMAL SANCTUARY
AL'S TREETOP TAVERN
TRUMAN, ARE YOU ALL RIGHT? YOU HAD US ALL WORRIED.
I'M SORRY, MA'AM. I JUST WANTED TO SEE OSCAR AGAIN.
TRUMAN, OSCAR'S BACK AT THE SANCTUARY WAITING FOR US.
OSCAR'S BACK?!
WHAT'S WRONG NOW?
I DON'T HAVE A THING TO WEAR.
CHO

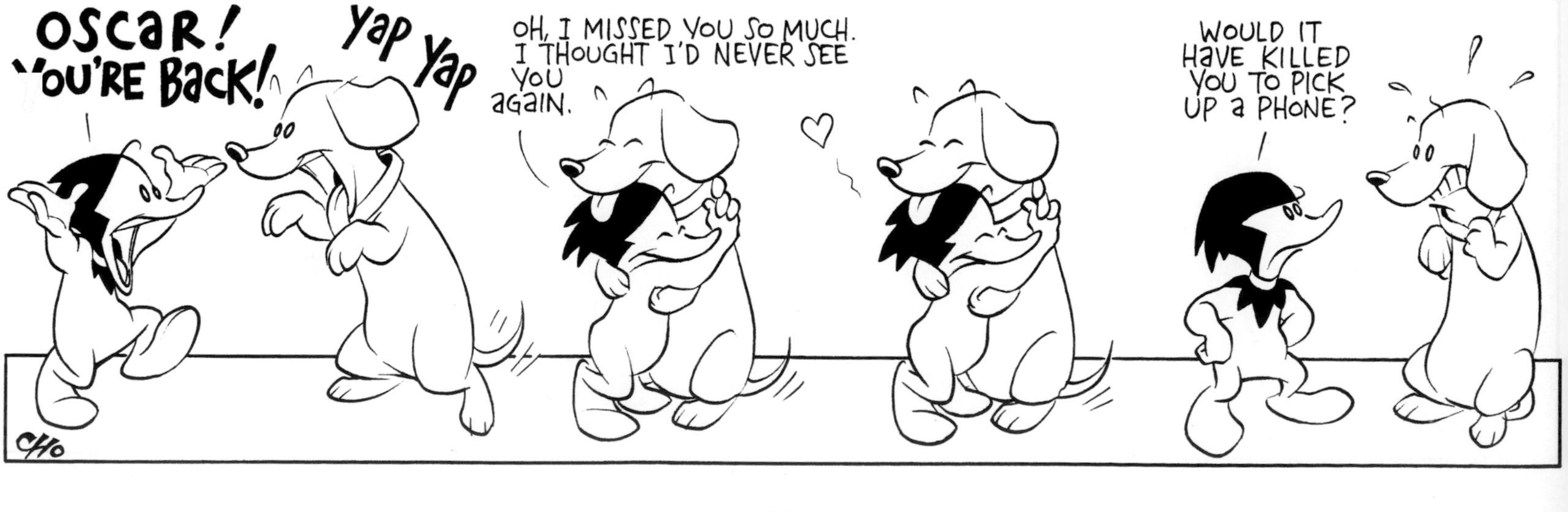
OSCAR! 'OU'RE BACK!
YAP YAP
OH, I MISSED YOU SO MUCH. I THOUGHT I'D NEVER SEE YOU AGAIN.
WOULD IT HAVE KILLED YOU TO PICK UP A PHONE?
CHO

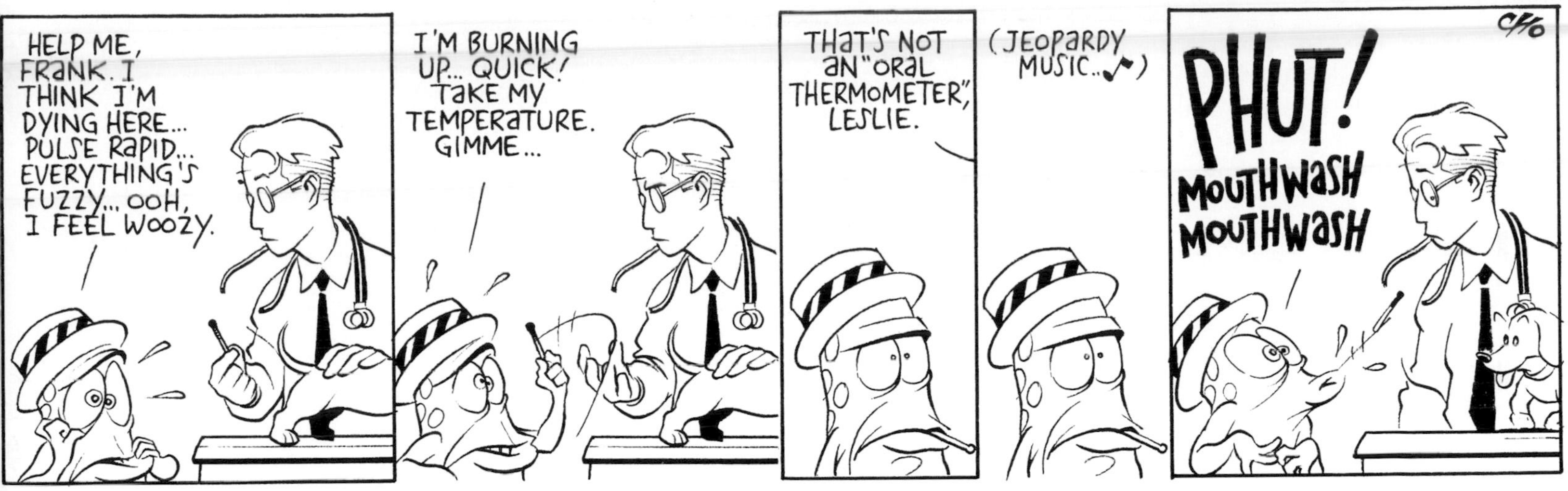
C/HO
HELP ME, FRANK. I THINK I'M DYING HERE... PULSE RAPID... EVERYTHING'S FUZZY... OOH, I FEEL WOOZY.
I'M BURNING UP... QUICK! TAKE MY TEMPERATURE. GIMME...
THAT'S NOT AN "ORAL THERMOMETER," LESLIE.
(JEOPARDY MUSIC..♪)
PHUT!
MOUTHWASH MOUTHWASH

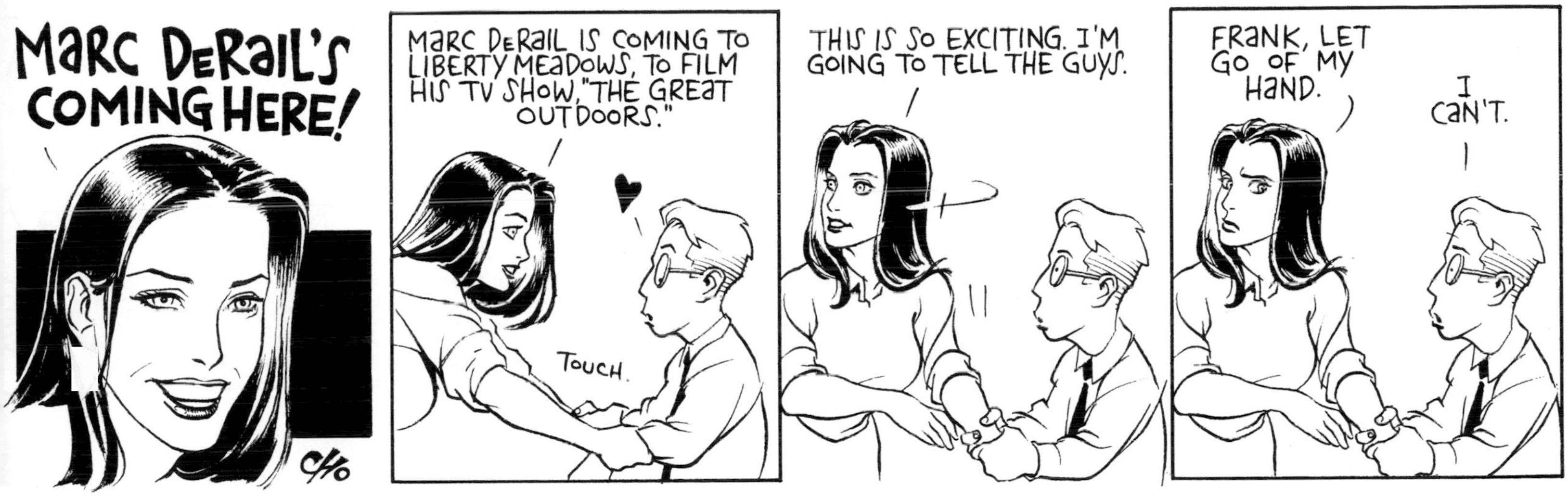
MARC DERAIL'S COMING HERE!
C/HO
MARC DERAIL IS COMING TO LIBERTY MEADOWS, TO FILM HIS TV SHOW, "THE GREAT OUTDOORS."
TOUCH.
THIS IS SO EXCITING. I'M GOING TO TELL THE GUYS.
FRANK, LET GO OF MY HAND.
I CAN'T.

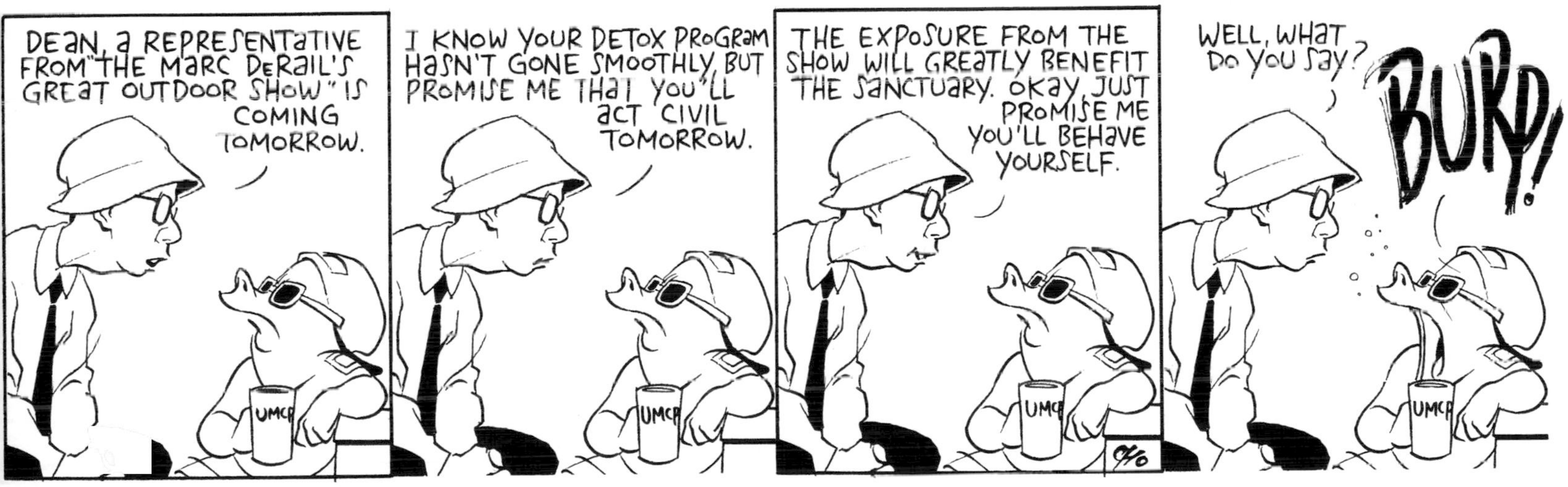
DEAN, A REPRESENTATIVE FROM "THE MARC DERAIL'S GREAT OUTDOOR SHOW" IS COMING TOMORROW.
UMCP
I KNOW YOUR DETOX PROGRAM HASN'T GONE SMOOTHLY, BUT PROMISE ME THAT YOU'LL ACT CIVIL TOMORROW.
THE EXPOSURE FROM THE SHOW WILL GREATLY BENEFIT THE SANCTUARY. OKAY, JUST PROMISE ME YOU'LL BEHAVE YOURSELF.
C/HO
WELL, WHAT DO YOU SAY?
BURP!

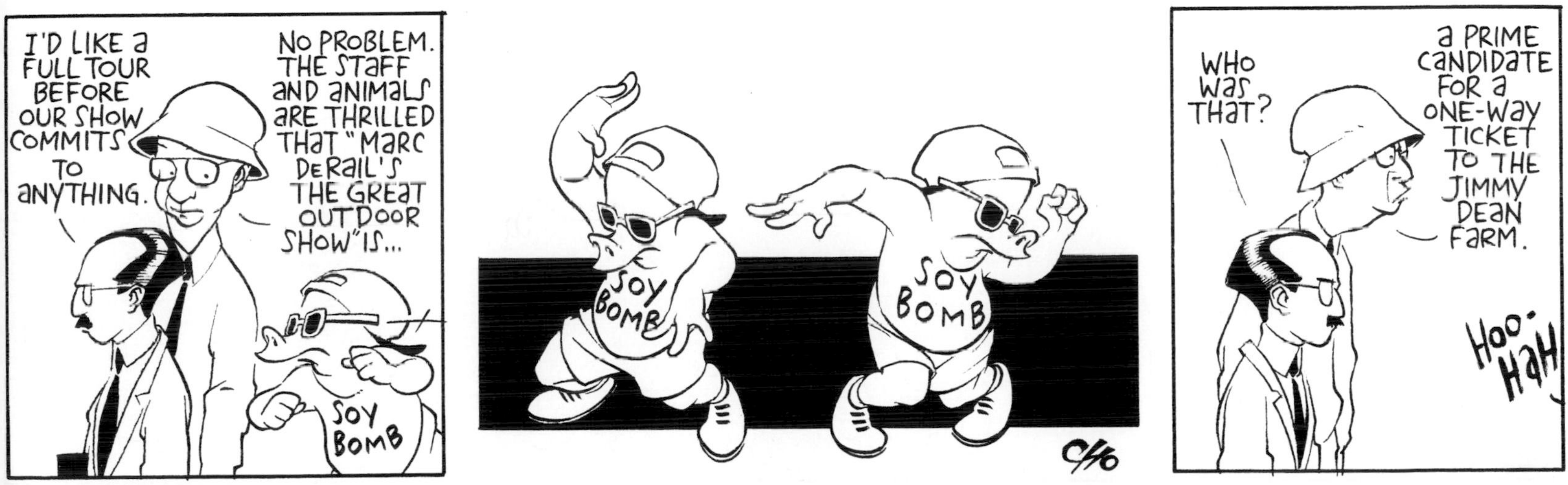
I'D LIKE A FULL TOUR BEFORE OUR SHOW COMMITS TO ANYTHING.
NO PROBLEM. THE STAFF AND ANIMALS ARE THRILLED THAT "MARC DERAIL'S THE GREAT OUTDOOR SHOW" IS...
SOY BOMB
SOY BOMB
SOY BOMB
C/HO
WHO WAS THAT?
A PRIME CANDIDATE FOR A ONE-WAY TICKET TO THE JIMMY DEAN FARM.
HOO-HAH

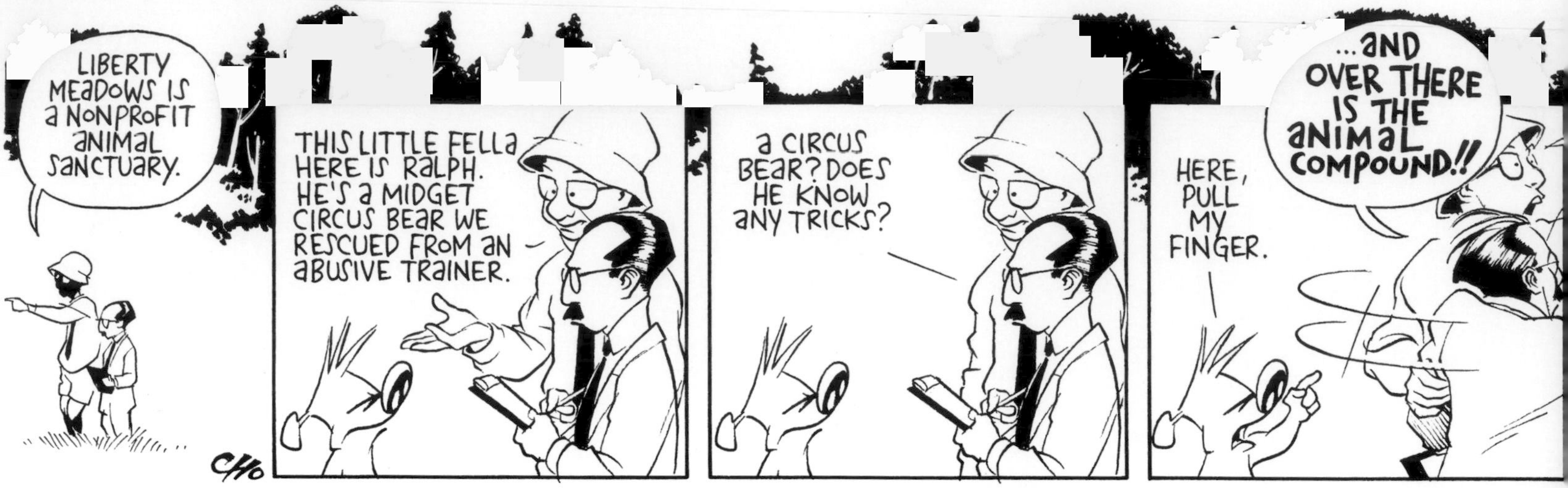
LIBERTY MEADOWS IS A NONPROFIT ANIMAL SANCTUARY.
THIS LITTLE FELLA HERE IS RALPH. HE'S A MIDGET CIRCUS BEAR WE RESCUED FROM AN ABUSIVE TRAINER.
A CIRCUS BEAR? DOES HE KNOW ANY TRICKS?
HERE, PULL MY FINGER.
...AND OVER THERE IS THE ANIMAL COMPOUND!!
CHO

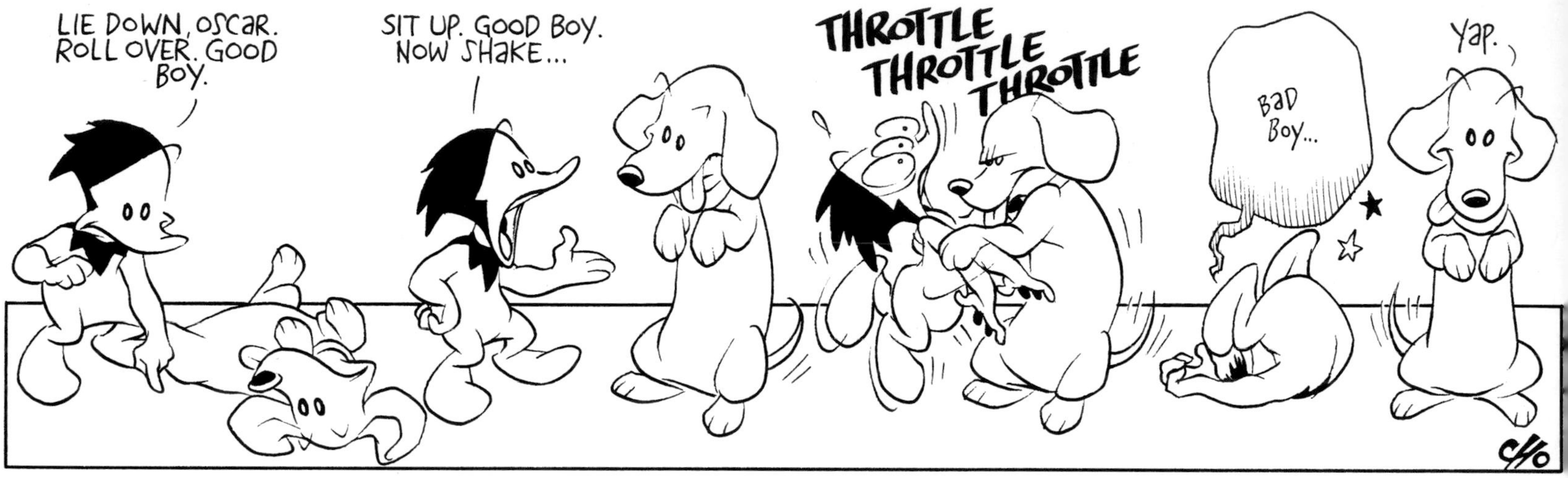
LIE DOWN, OSCAR. ROLL OVER. GOOD BOY.
SIT UP. GOOD BOY. NOW SHAKE...
THROTTLE THROTTLE THROTTLE
BAD BOY...
YAP.
CHO

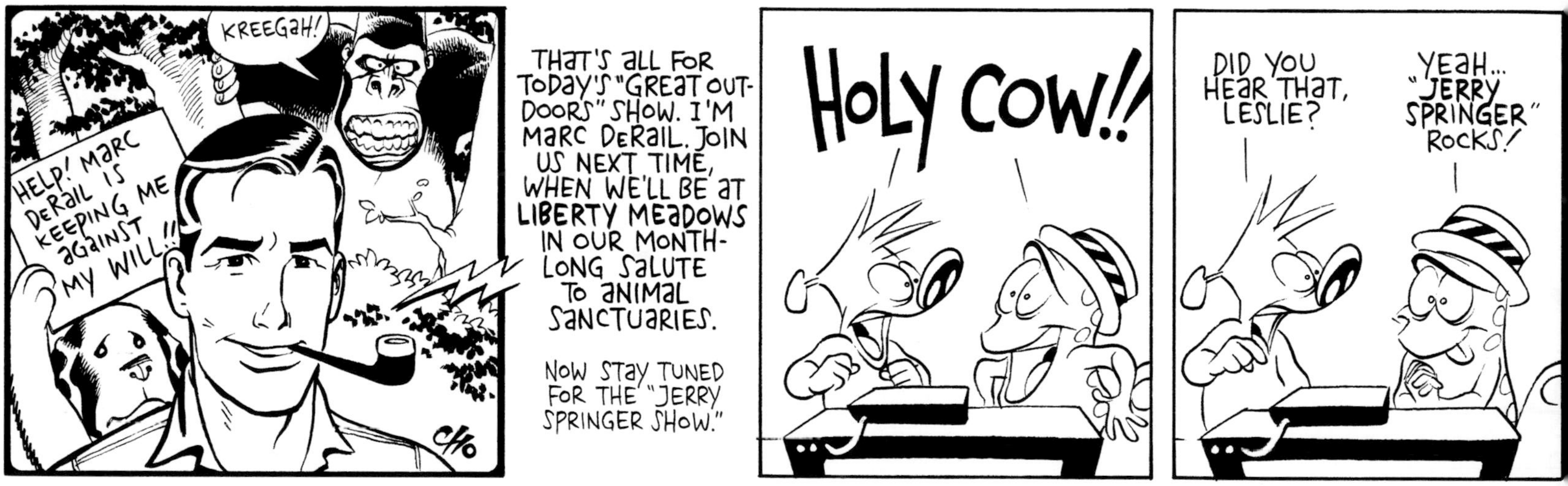
KREEGAH!
HELP! MARC DERAIL IS KEEPING ME AGAINST MY WILL!!
CHO
THAT'S ALL FOR TODAY'S "GREAT OUTDOORS" SHOW. I'M MARC DERAIL. JOIN US NEXT TIME, WHEN WE'LL BE AT LIBERTY MEADOWS IN OUR MONTH-LONG SALUTE TO ANIMAL SANCTUARIES.
NOW STAY TUNED FOR THE "JERRY SPRINGER SHOW."
HOLY COW!!
DID YOU HEAR THAT, LESLIE?
YEAH... "JERRY SPRINGER" ROCKS!

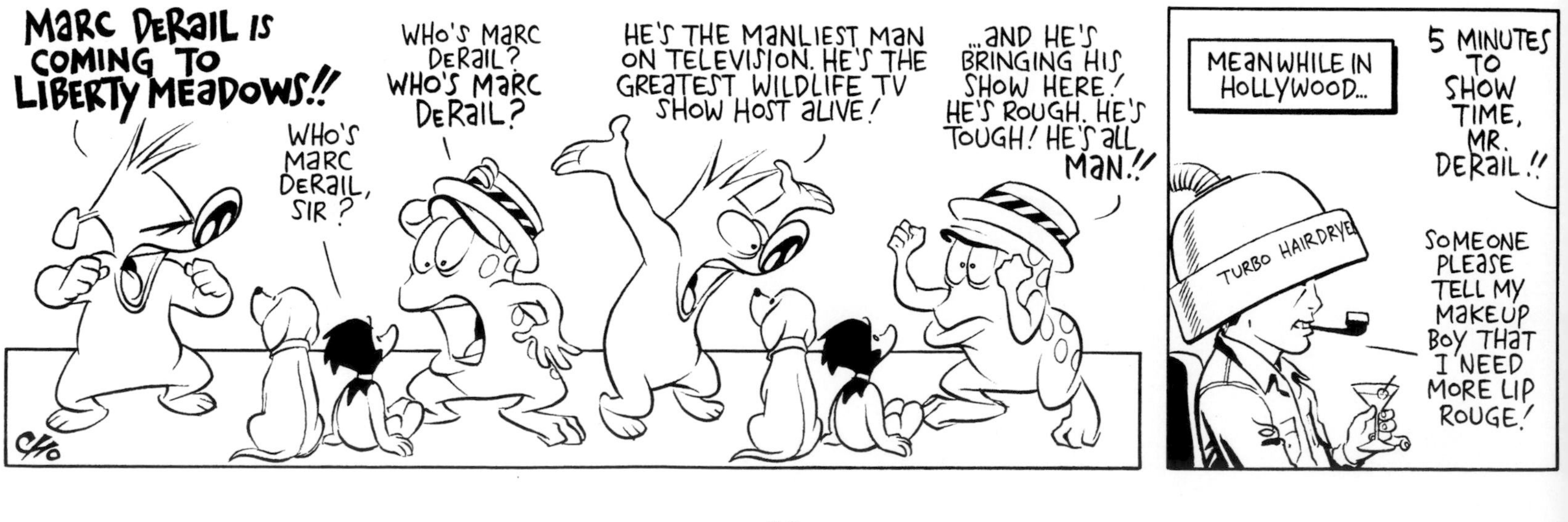
MARC DERAIL IS COMING TO LIBERTY MEADOWS!!
WHO'S MARC DERAIL, SIR?
WHO'S MARC DERAIL? WHO'S MARC DERAIL?
HE'S THE MANLIEST MAN ON TELEVISION. HE'S THE GREATEST WILDLIFE TV SHOW HOST ALIVE!
...AND HE'S BRINGING HIS SHOW HERE! HE'S ROUGH. HE'S TOUGH! HE'S ALL MAN!!
CHO
MEANWHILE IN HOLLYWOOD...
5 MINUTES TO SHOW TIME, MR. DERAIL!!
TURBO HAIRDRYER
SOMEONE PLEASE TELL MY MAKEUP BOY THAT I NEED MORE LIP ROUGE!

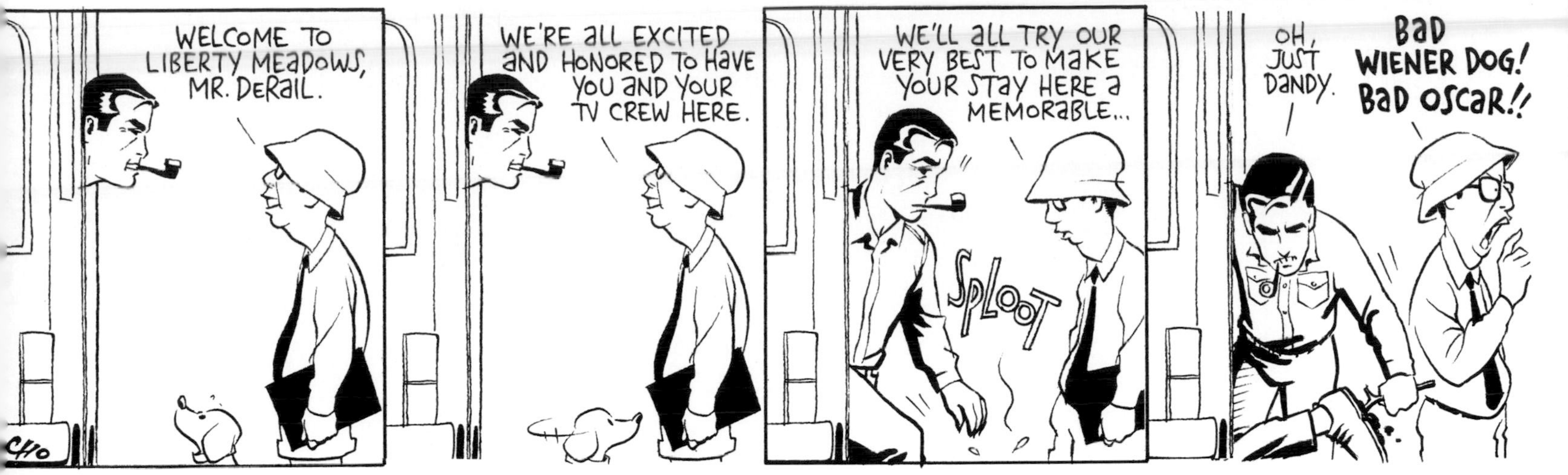
WELCOME TO LIBERTY MEADOWS, MR. DERAIL.
WE'RE ALL EXCITED AND HONORED TO HAVE YOU AND YOUR TV CREW HERE.
WE'LL ALL TRY OUR VERY BEST TO MAKE YOUR STAY HERE A MEMORABLE...
SPLOOT
OH, JUST DANDY.
BAD WIENER DOG! BAD OSCAR!!
CHO

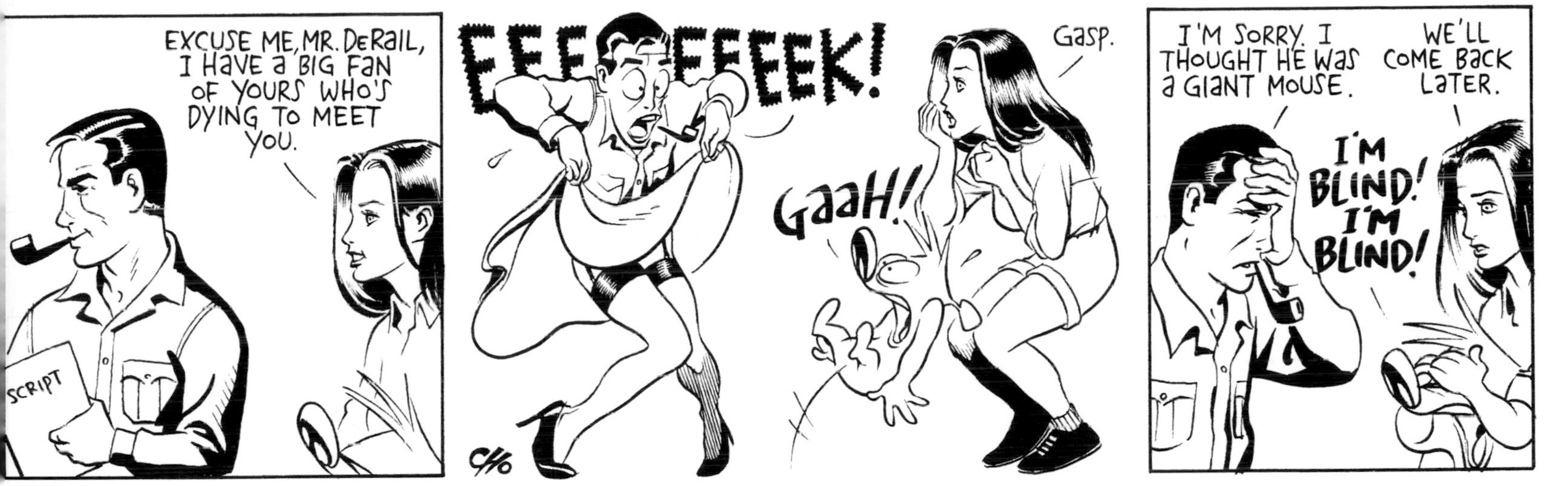
EXCUSE ME, MR. DERAIL, I HAVE A BIG FAN OF YOURS WHO'S DYING TO MEET YOU.
SCRIPT
EEEEEEEEK!
GASP.
GAAH!
I'M SORRY. I THOUGHT HE WAS A GIANT MOUSE.
WE'LL COME BACK LATER.
I'M BLIND! I'M BLIND!
CHO

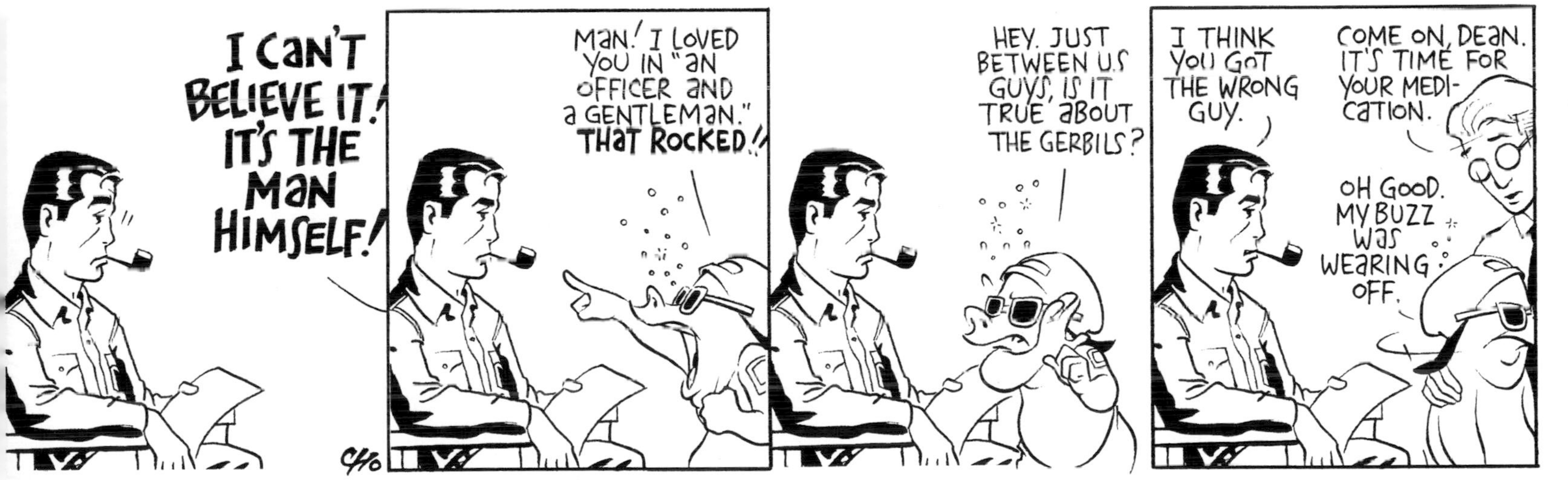
I CAN'T BELIEVE IT! IT'S THE MAN HIMSELF!
MAN! I LOVED YOU IN "AN OFFICER AND A GENTLEMAN." THAT ROCKED!!
HEY. JUST BETWEEN US GUYS, IS IT TRUE ABOUT THE GERBILS?
I THINK YOU GOT THE WRONG GUY.
COME ON, DEAN. IT'S TIME FOR YOUR MEDICATION.
OH GOOD. MY BUZZ WAS WEARING OFF.
CHO

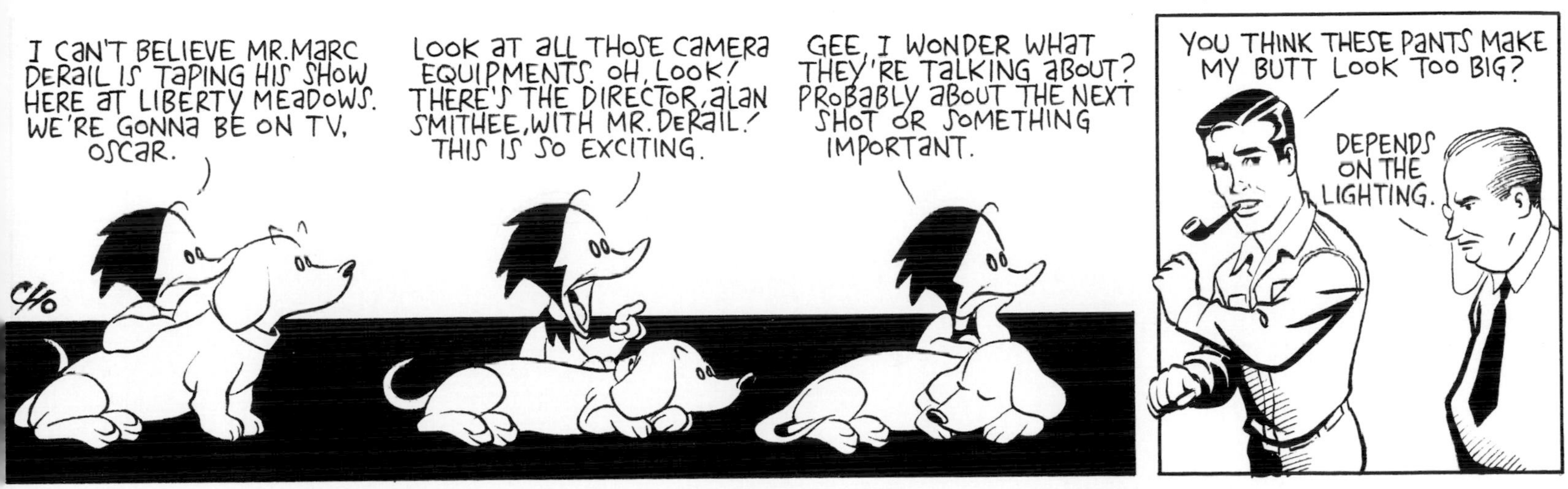
I CAN'T BELIEVE MR. MARC DERAIL IS TAPING HIS SHOW HERE AT LIBERTY MEADOWS. WE'RE GONNA BE ON TV, OSCAR.
LOOK AT ALL THOSE CAMERA EQUIPMENTS. OH, LOOK! THERE'S THE DIRECTOR, ALAN SMITHEE, WITH MR. DERAIL! THIS IS SO EXCITING.
GEE, I WONDER WHAT THEY'RE TALKING ABOUT? PROBABLY ABOUT THE NEXT SHOT OR SOMETHING IMPORTANT.
YOU THINK THESE PANTS MAKE MY BUTT LOOK TOO BIG?
DEPENDS ON THE LIGHTING.
CHO

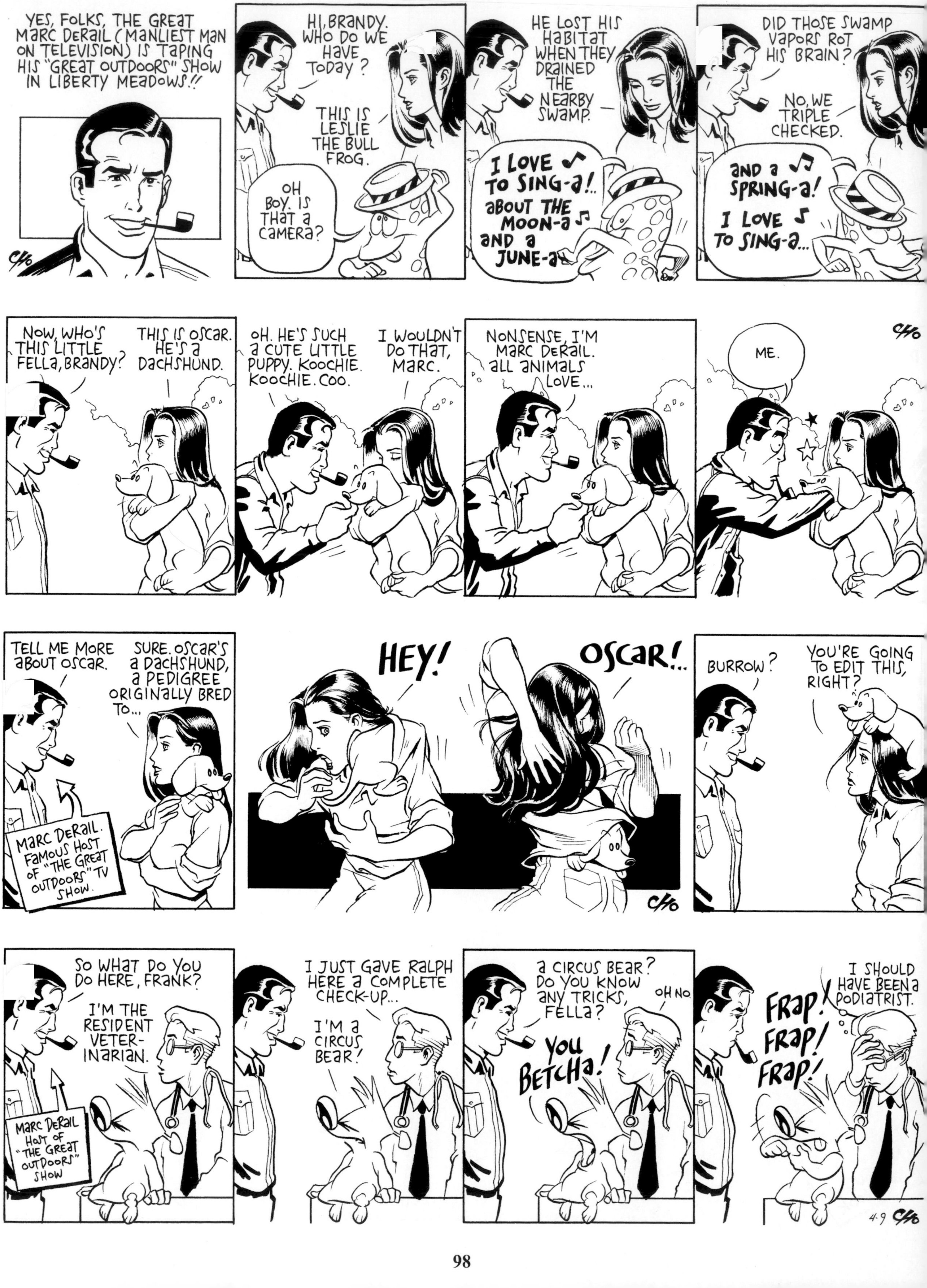

YES, FOLKS, THE GREAT MARC DERAIL (MANLIEST MAN ON TELEVISION) IS TAPING HIS "GREAT OUTDOORS" SHOW IN LIBERTY MEADOWS!!
HI, BRANDY. WHO DO WE HAVE TODAY?
THIS IS LESLIE THE BULL FROG.
OH BOY. IS THAT A CAMERA?
HE LOST HIS HABITAT WHEN THEY DRAINED THE NEARBY SWAMP.
I LOVE TO SING-A!.. ABOUT THE MOON-A AND A JUNE-A
DID THOSE SWAMP VAPORS ROT HIS BRAIN?
NO, WE TRIPLE CHECKED.
AND A SPRING-A! I LOVE TO SING-A...
NOW, WHO'S THIS LITTLE FELLA, BRANDY?
THIS IS OSCAR. HE'S A DACHSHUND.
OH. HE'S SUCH A CUTE LITTLE PUPPY. KOOCHIE. KOOCHIE. COO.
I WOULDN'T DO THAT, MARC.
NONSENSE, I'M MARC DERAIL. ALL ANIMALS LOVE...
ME.
TELL ME MORE ABOUT OSCAR.
SURE. OSCAR'S A DACHSHUND, A PEDIGREE ORIGINALLY BRED TO...
MARC DERAIL. FAMOUS HOST OF "THE GREAT OUTDOORS" TV SHOW.
HEY!
OSCAR!..
BURROW?
YOU'RE GOING TO EDIT THIS, RIGHT?
SO WHAT DO YOU DO HERE, FRANK?
I'M THE RESIDENT VETERINARIAN.
MARC DERAIL HOST OF "THE GREAT OUTDOORS" SHOW
I JUST GAVE RALPH HERE A COMPLETE CHECK-UP...
I'M A CIRCUS BEAR!
A CIRCUS BEAR? DO YOU KNOW ANY TRICKS, FELLA?
OH NO.
YOU BETCHA!
I SHOULD HAVE BEEN A PODIATRIST.
FRAP! FRAP! FRAP!

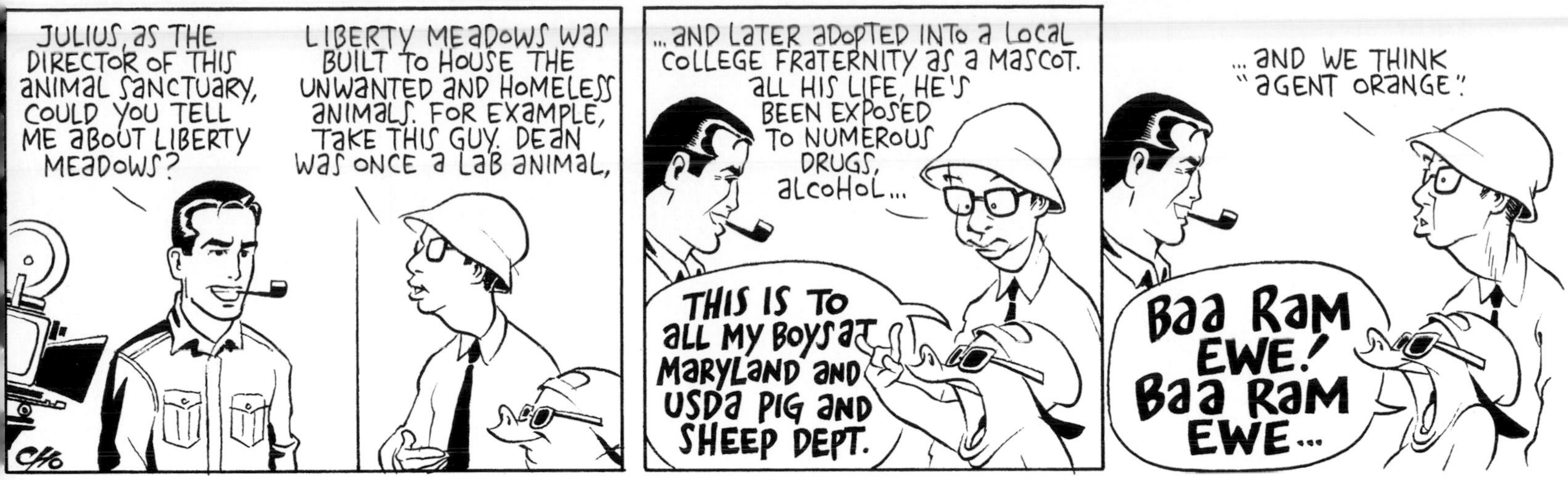

JULIUS, AS THE DIRECTOR OF THIS ANIMAL SANCTUARY, COULD YOU TELL ME ABOUT LIBERTY MEADOWS?
LIBERTY MEADOWS WAS BUILT TO HOUSE THE UNWANTED AND HOMELESS ANIMALS. FOR EXAMPLE, TAKE THIS GUY. DEAN WAS ONCE A LAB ANIMAL,
...AND LATER ADOPTED INTO A LOCAL COLLEGE FRATERNITY AS A MASCOT. ALL HIS LIFE, HE'S BEEN EXPOSED TO NUMEROUS DRUGS, ALCOHOL...
THIS IS TO ALL MY BOYS AT MARYLAND AND USDA PIG AND SHEEP DEPT.
...AND WE THINK "AGENT ORANGE".
BAA RAM EWE! BAA RAM EWE...

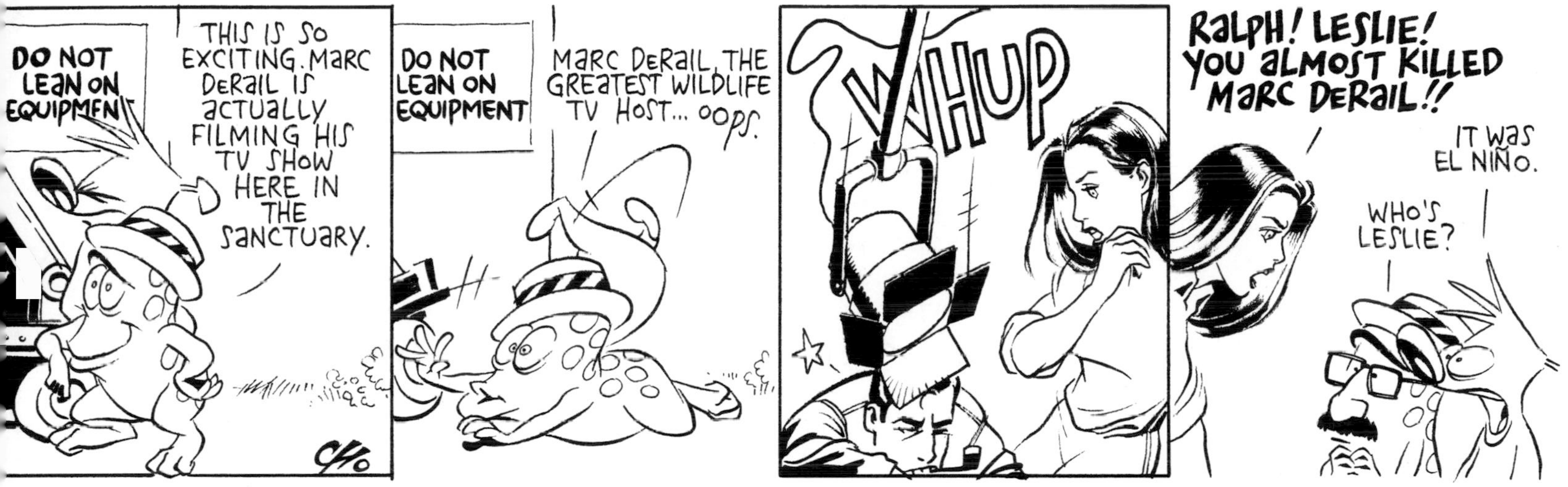

DO NOT LEAN ON EQUIPMENT
THIS IS SO EXCITING. MARC DERAIL IS ACTUALLY FILMING HIS TV SHOW HERE IN THE SANCTUARY.
DO NOT LEAN ON EQUIPMENT
MARC DERAIL, THE GREATEST WILDLIFE TV HOST... OOPS.
WHUP
RALPH! LESLIE! YOU ALMOST KILLED MARC DERAIL!!
IT WAS EL NIÑO.
WHO'S LESLIE?

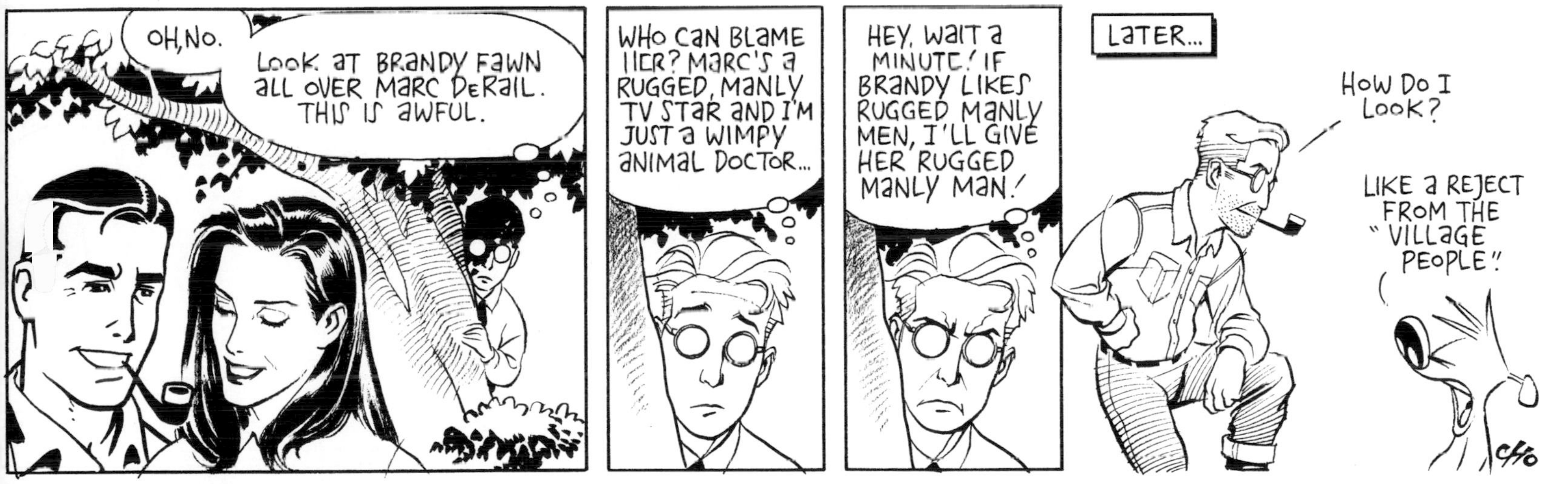

OH, NO.
LOOK AT BRANDY FAWN ALL OVER MARC DERAIL. THIS IS AWFUL.
WHO CAN BLAME HER? MARC'S A RUGGED, MANLY TV STAR AND I'M JUST A WIMPY ANIMAL DOCTOR...
HEY, WAIT A MINUTE! IF BRANDY LIKES RUGGED MANLY MEN, I'LL GIVE HER RUGGED MANLY MAN!
LATER...
HOW DO I LOOK?
LIKE A REJECT FROM THE "VILLAGE PEOPLE".

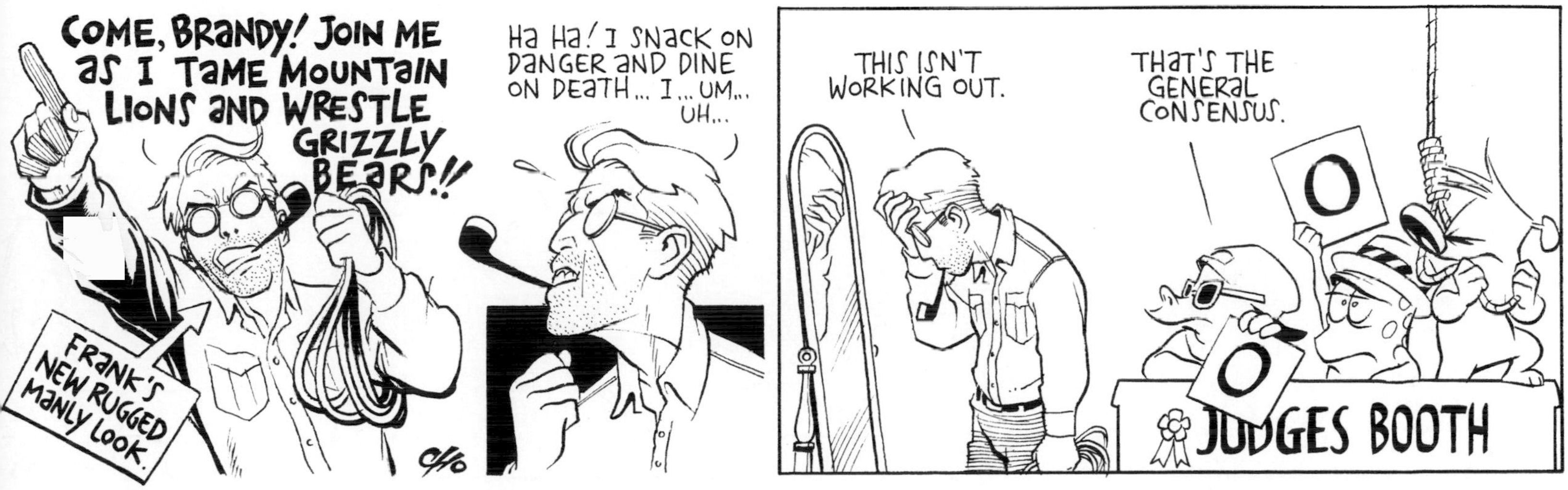

COME, BRANDY! JOIN ME AS I TAME MOUNTAIN LIONS AND WRESTLE GRIZZLY BEARS!!
FRANK'S NEW RUGGED MANLY LOOK.
HA HA! I SNACK ON DANGER AND DINE ON DEATH... I... UM... UH...
THIS ISN'T WORKING OUT.
THAT'S THE GENERAL CONSENSUS.
0
0
JUDGES BOOTH

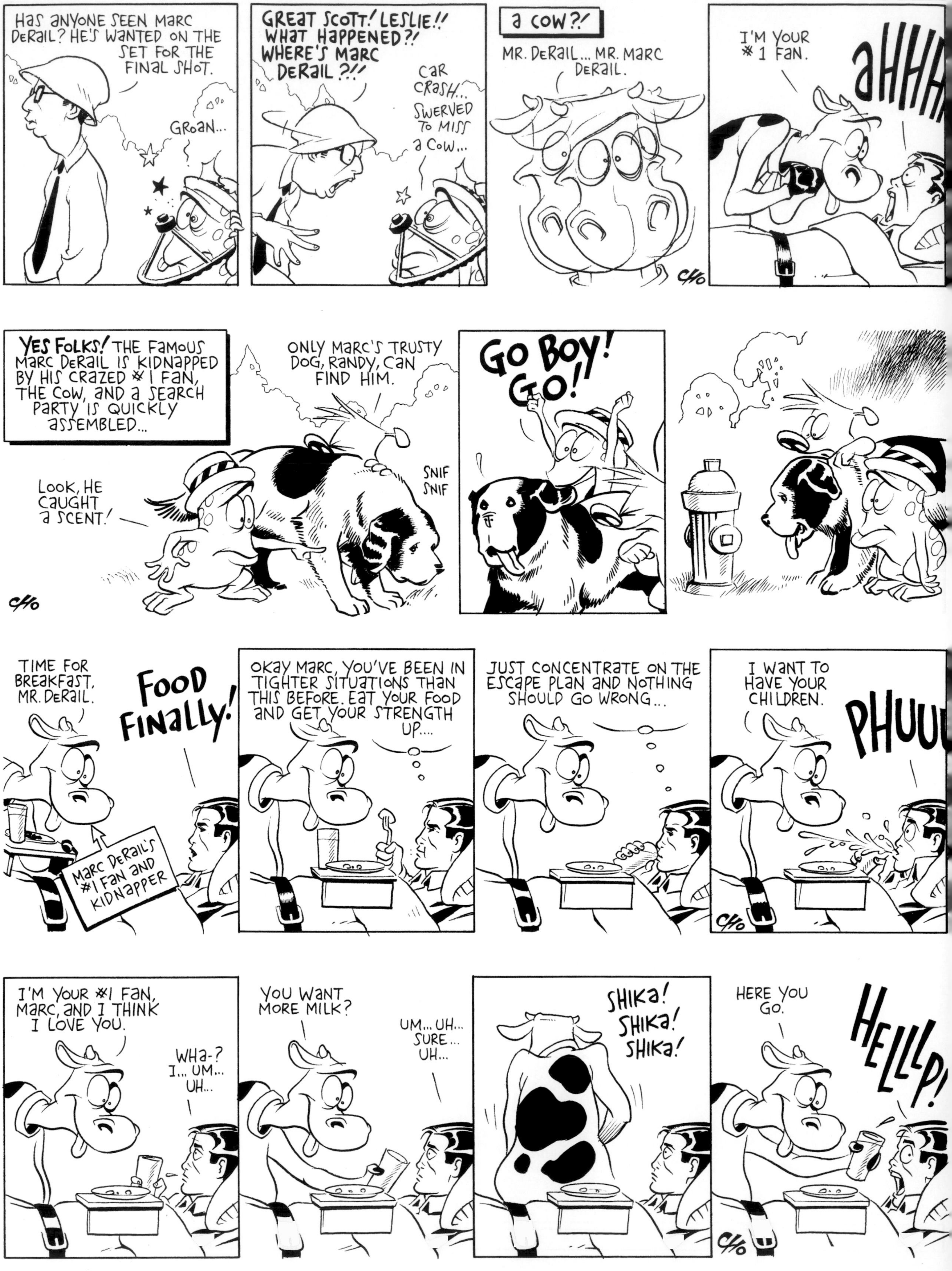
HAS ANYONE SEEN MARC DERAIL? HE'S WANTED ON THE SET FOR THE FINAL SHOT.
GROAN...
GREAT SCOTT! LESLIE!! WHAT HAPPENED?! WHERE'S MARC DERAIL?!!
CAR CRASH... SWERVED TO MISS A COW...
A COW?!
MR. DERAIL... MR. MARC DERAIL.
I'M YOUR #1 FAN.
AHHH
YES FOLKS! THE FAMOUS MARC DERAIL IS KIDNAPPED BY HIS CRAZED #1 FAN, THE COW, AND A SEARCH PARTY IS QUICKLY ASSEMBLED...
ONLY MARC'S TRUSTY DOG, RANDY, CAN FIND HIM.
LOOK, HE CAUGHT A SCENT!
SNIF SNIF
GO BOY! GO!!
TIME FOR BREAKFAST, MR. DERAIL.
FOOD FINALLY!
MARC DERAIL'S #1 FAN AND KIDNAPPER
OKAY MARC, YOU'VE BEEN IN TIGHTER SITUATIONS THAN THIS BEFORE. EAT YOUR FOOD AND GET YOUR STRENGTH UP....
JUST CONCENTRATE ON THE ESCAPE PLAN AND NOTHING SHOULD GO WRONG...
I WANT TO HAVE YOUR CHILDREN.
PHUUU
I'M YOUR #1 FAN, MARC, AND I THINK I LOVE YOU.
WHA-? I... UM... UH...
YOU WANT MORE MILK?
UM... UH... SURE... UH...
SHIKA! SHIKA! SHIKA!
HERE YOU GO.
HELLLP!
CHO

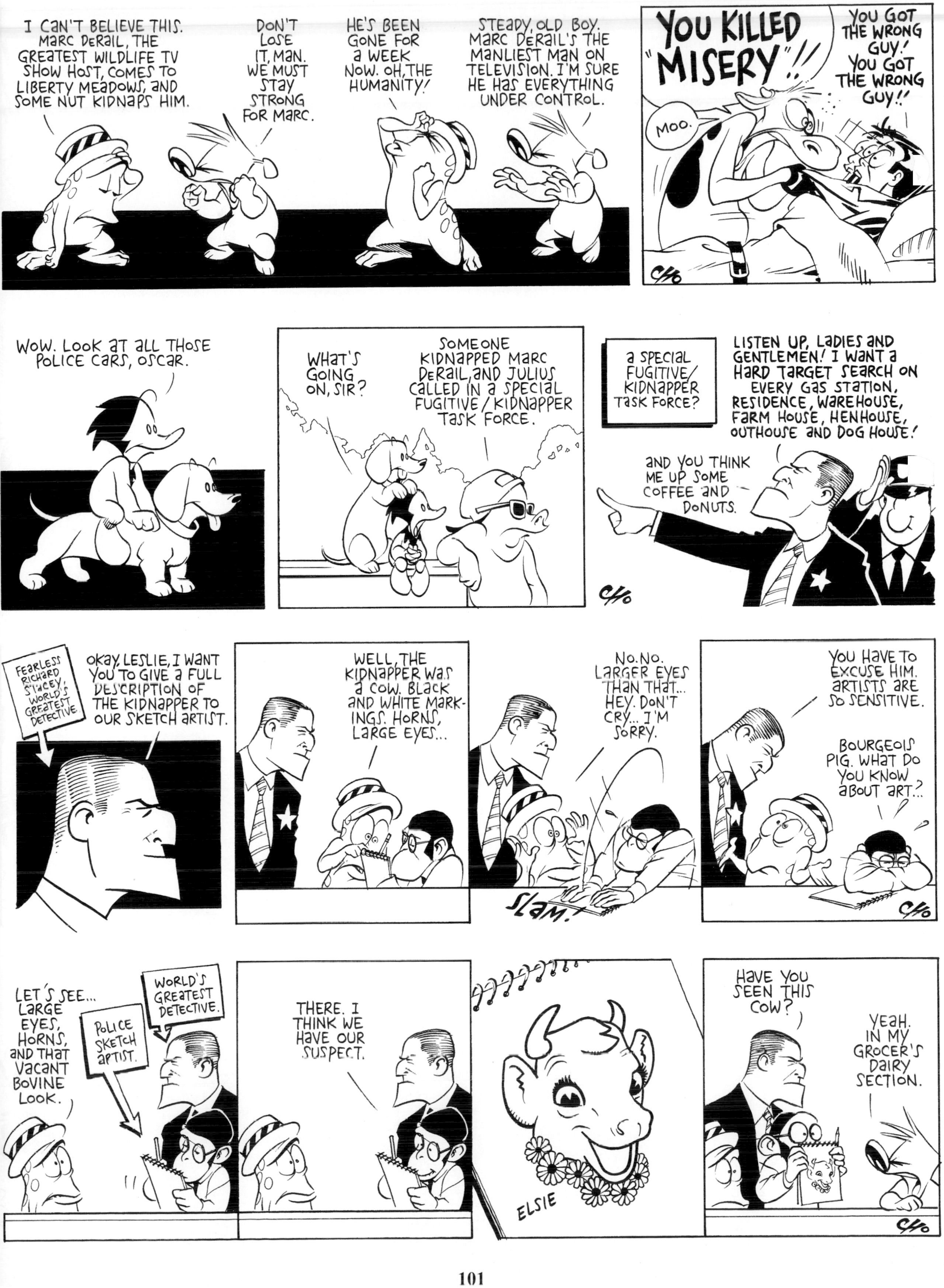
I CAN'T BELIEVE THIS. MARC DERAIL, THE GREATEST WILDLIFE TV SHOW HOST, COMES TO LIBERTY MEADOWS, AND SOME NUT KIDNAPS HIM.
DON'T LOSE IT, MAN. WE MUST STAY STRONG FOR MARC.
HE'S BEEN GONE FOR A WEEK NOW. OH, THE HUMANITY!
STEADY, OLD BOY. MARC DERAIL'S THE MANLIEST MAN ON TELEVISION. I'M SURE HE HAS EVERYTHING UNDER CONTROL.
YOU KILLED "MISERY"!!
YOU GOT THE WRONG GUY! YOU GOT THE WRONG GUY!!
MOO.
CHO
WOW. LOOK AT ALL THOSE POLICE CARS, OSCAR.
WHAT'S GOING ON, SIR?
SOMEONE KIDNAPPED MARC DERAIL, AND JULIUS CALLED IN A SPECIAL FUGITIVE / KIDNAPPER TASK FORCE.
A SPECIAL FUGITIVE/ KIDNAPPER TASK FORCE?
LISTEN UP, LADIES AND GENTLEMEN! I WANT A HARD TARGET SEARCH ON EVERY GAS STATION, RESIDENCE, WAREHOUSE, FARM HOUSE, HENHOUSE, OUTHOUSE AND DOG HOUSE!
AND YOU THINK ME UP SOME COFFEE AND DONUTS.
CHO
FEARLESS RICHARD STACEY, WORLD'S GREATEST DETECTIVE.
OKAY, LESLIE, I WANT YOU TO GIVE A FULL DESCRIPTION OF THE KIDNAPPER TO OUR SKETCH ARTIST.
WELL, THE KIDNAPPER WAS A COW. BLACK AND WHITE MARKINGS. HORNS, LARGE EYES...
NO. NO. LARGER EYES THAN THAT... HEY. DON'T CRY... I'M SORRY.
SLAM!
YOU HAVE TO EXCUSE HIM. ARTISTS ARE SO SENSITIVE.
BOURGEOIS PIG. WHAT DO YOU KNOW ABOUT ART?...
CHO
LET'S SEE... LARGE EYES, HORNS, AND THAT VACANT BOVINE LOOK.
POLICE SKETCH ARTIST.
WORLD'S GREATEST DETECTIVE.
THERE. I THINK WE HAVE OUR SUSPECT.
ELSIE
HAVE YOU SEEN THIS COW?
YEAH. IN MY GROCER'S DAIRY SECTION.
CHO

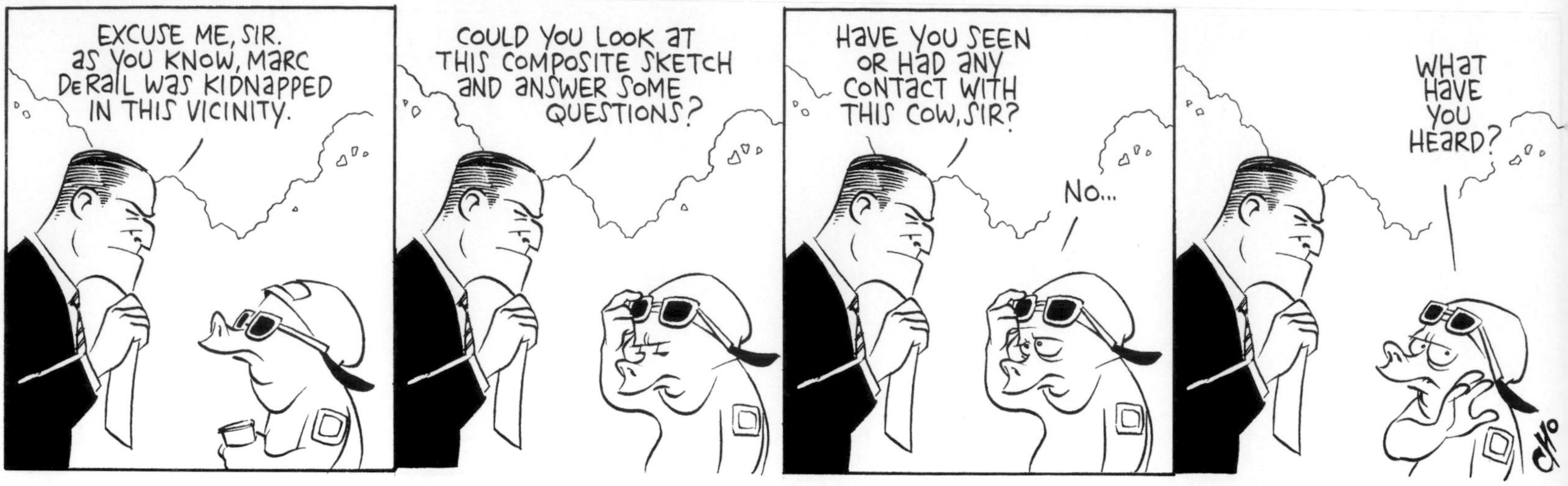
EXCUSE ME, SIR. AS YOU KNOW, MARC DERAIL WAS KIDNAPPED IN THIS VICINITY.
COULD YOU LOOK AT THIS COMPOSITE SKETCH AND ANSWER SOME QUESTIONS?
HAVE YOU SEEN OR HAD ANY CONTACT WITH THIS COW, SIR?
NO...
WHAT HAVE YOU HEARD?
CHO

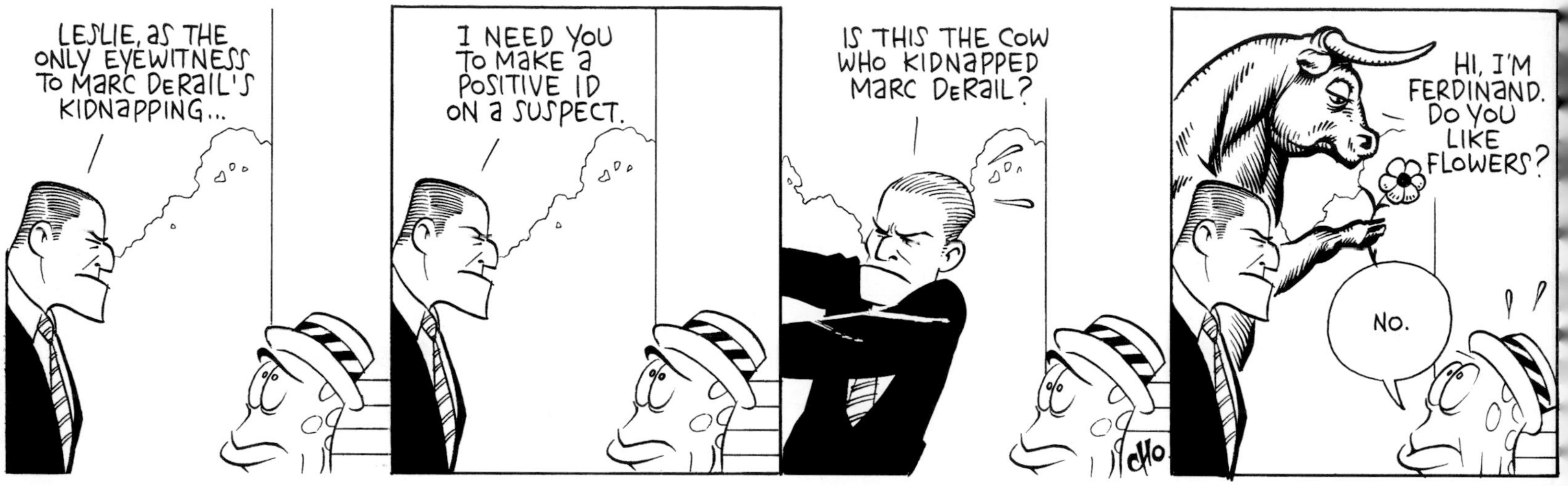
LESLIE, AS THE ONLY EYEWITNESS TO MARC DERAIL'S KIDNAPPING...
I NEED YOU TO MAKE A POSITIVE ID ON A SUSPECT.
IS THIS THE COW WHO KIDNAPPED MARC DERAIL?
CHO
HI, I'M FERDINAND. DO YOU LIKE FLOWERS?
NO.

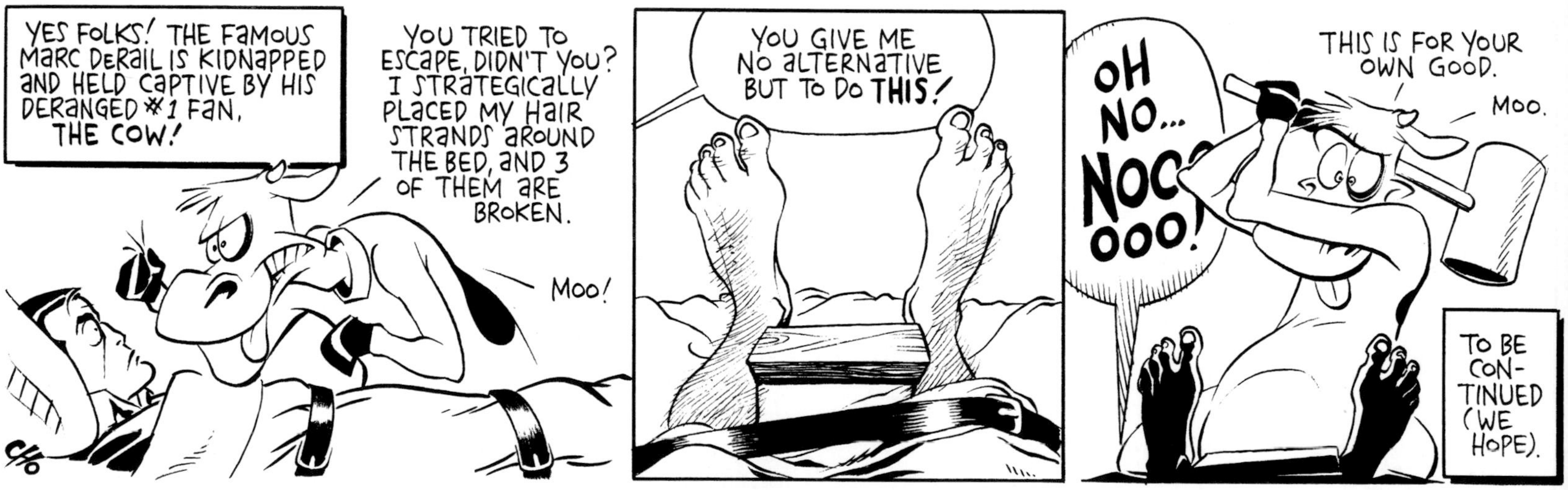
YES FOLKS! THE FAMOUS MARC DERAIL IS KIDNAPPED AND HELD CAPTIVE BY HIS DERANGED #1 FAN, THE COW!
YOU TRIED TO ESCAPE, DIDN'T YOU? I STRATEGICALLY PLACED MY HAIR STRANDS AROUND THE BED, AND 3 OF THEM ARE BROKEN.
MOO!
CHO
YOU GIVE ME NO ALTERNATIVE BUT TO DO THIS!
OH NO... NOOOOO!
THIS IS FOR YOUR OWN GOOD.
MOO.
TO BE CONTINUED (WE HOPE).

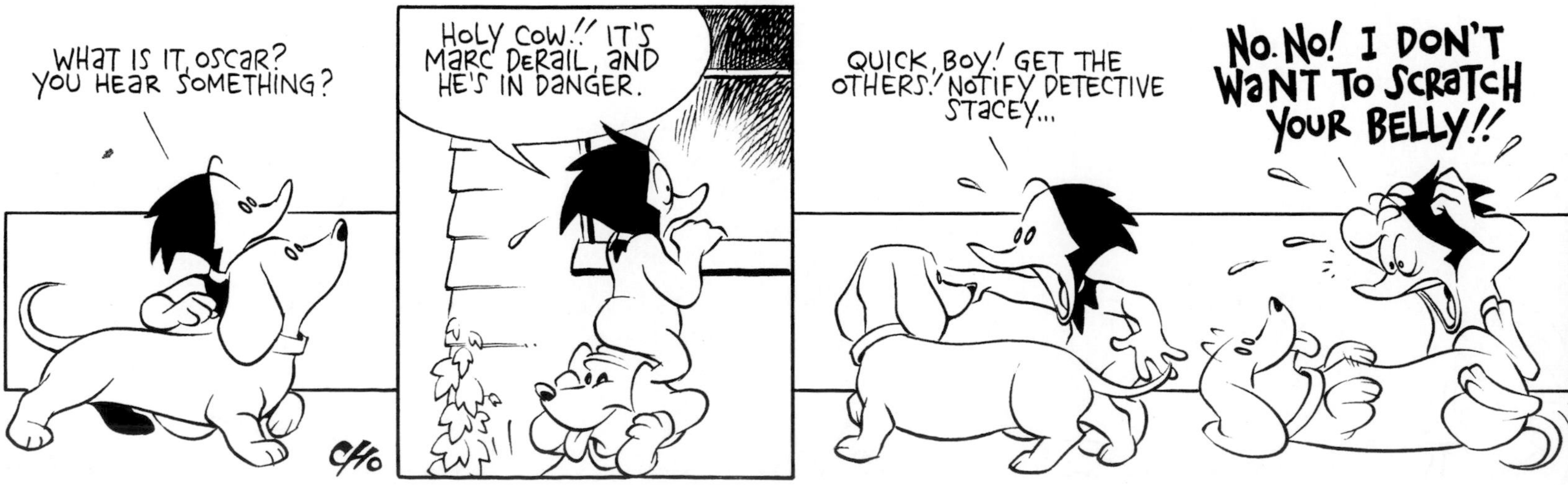
WHAT IS IT, OSCAR? YOU HEAR SOMETHING?
CHO
HOLY COW!! IT'S MARC DERAIL, AND HE'S IN DANGER.
QUICK, BOY! GET THE OTHERS! NOTIFY DETECTIVE STACEY...
NO. NO! I DON'T WANT TO SCRATCH YOUR BELLY!!

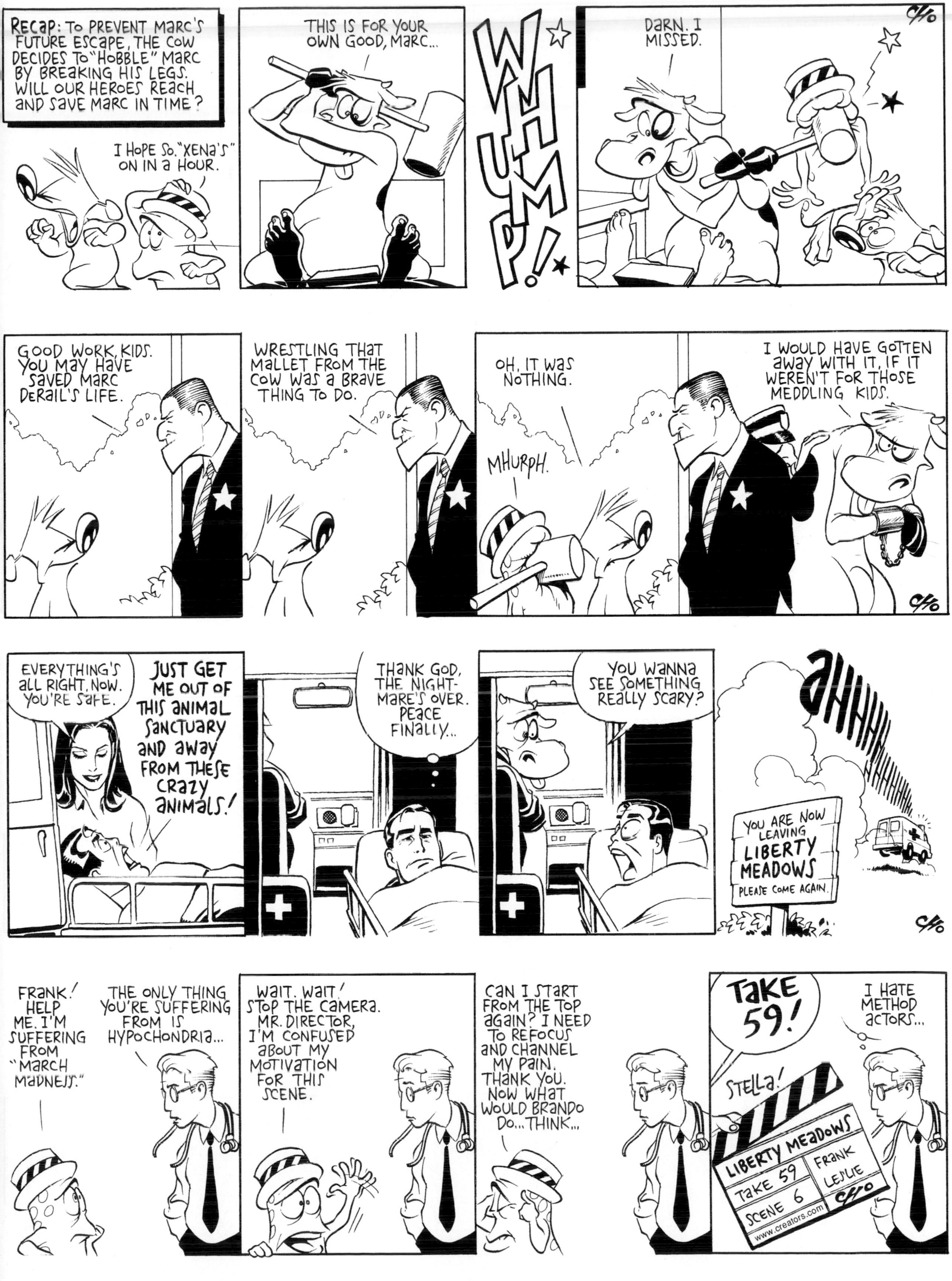
RECAP: TO PREVENT MARC'S FUTURE ESCAPE, THE COW DECIDES TO "HOBBLE" MARC BY BREAKING HIS LEGS. WILL OUR HEROES REACH AND SAVE MARC IN TIME?
I HOPE SO. "XENA'S" ON IN A HOUR.
THIS IS FOR YOUR OWN GOOD, MARC...
WHUMP!
DARN. I MISSED.
GOOD WORK, KIDS. YOU MAY HAVE SAVED MARC DERAIL'S LIFE.
WRESTLING THAT MALLET FROM THE COW WAS A BRAVE THING TO DO.
OH, IT WAS NOTHING.
MHURPH.
I WOULD HAVE GOTTEN AWAY WITH IT, IF IT WEREN'T FOR THOSE MEDDLING KIDS.
EVERYTHING'S ALL RIGHT, NOW. YOU'RE SAFE.
JUST GET ME OUT OF THIS ANIMAL SANCTUARY AND AWAY FROM THESE CRAZY ANIMALS!
THANK GOD, THE NIGHTMARE'S OVER. PEACE FINALLY...
YOU WANNA SEE SOMETHING REALLY SCARY?
AHHHHHHHHHHHHHH
YOU ARE NOW LEAVING LIBERTY MEADOWS
PLEASE COME AGAIN.
FRANK! HELP ME. I'M SUFFERING FROM "MARCH MADNESS."
THE ONLY THING YOU'RE SUFFERING FROM IS HYPOCHONDRIA...
WAIT. WAIT! STOP THE CAMERA. MR. DIRECTOR, I'M CONFUSED ABOUT MY MOTIVATION FOR THIS SCENE.
CAN I START FROM THE TOP AGAIN? I NEED TO REFOCUS AND CHANNEL MY PAIN. THANK YOU. NOW WHAT WOULD BRANDO DO... THINK...
TAKE 59!
STELLA!
I HATE METHOD ACTORS...
LIBERTY MEADOWS
TAKE 59
SCENE 6
FRANK
LESLIE
CHO
www.creators.com

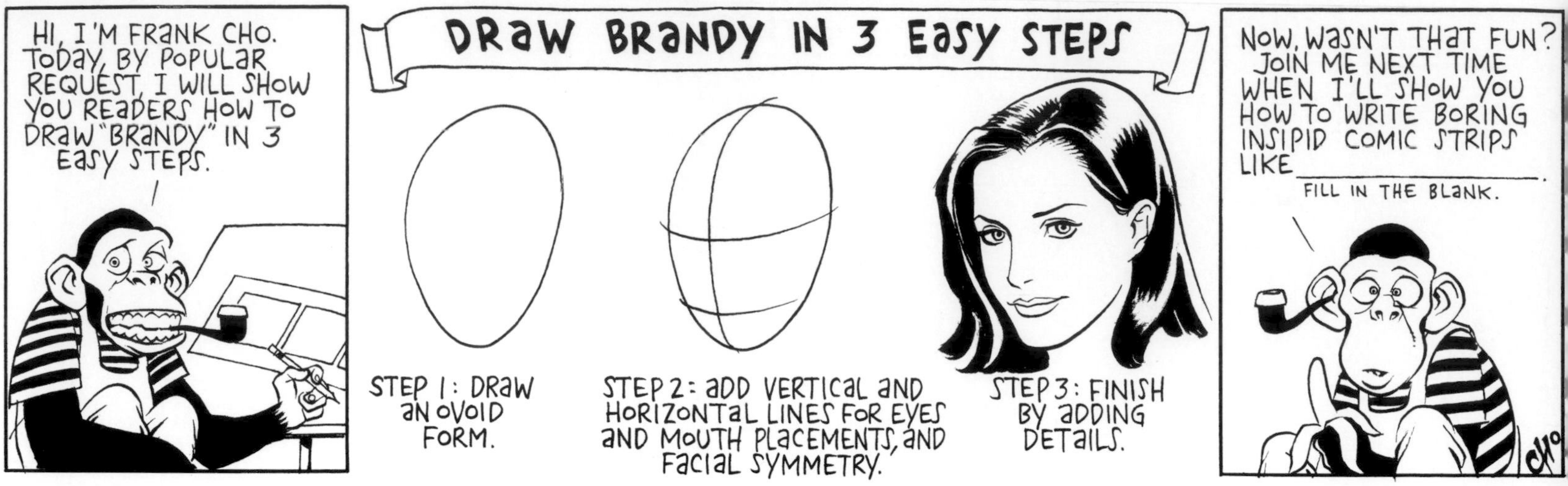
Hi, I'm Frank Cho. Today, by popular request, I will show you readers how to draw "Brandy" in 3 easy steps.
Draw Brandy in 3 Easy Steps
Step 1: Draw an ovoid form.
Step 2: add vertical and horizontal lines for eyes and mouth placements, and facial symmetry.
Step 3: Finish by adding details.
Now, wasn't that fun? Join me next time when I'll show you how to write boring insipid comic strips like ____________.
Fill in the blank.
Cho

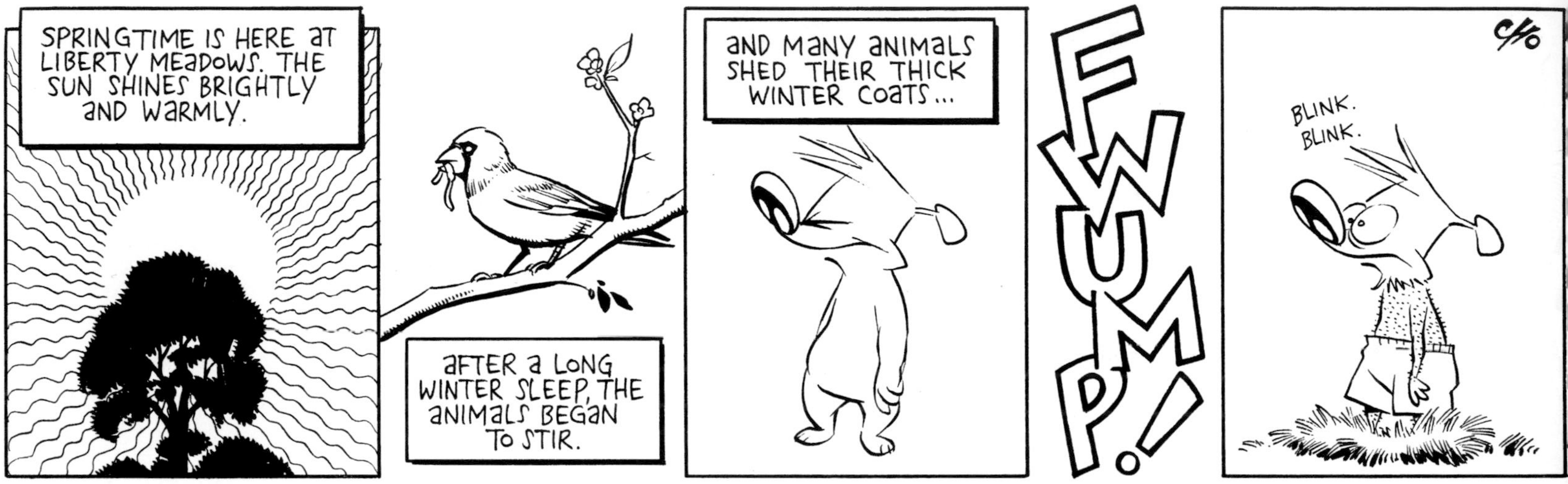
Springtime is here at Liberty Meadows. The sun shines brightly and warmly.
After a long winter sleep, the animals began to stir.
And many animals shed their thick winter coats...
FWUMP!
Blink. Blink.
Cho

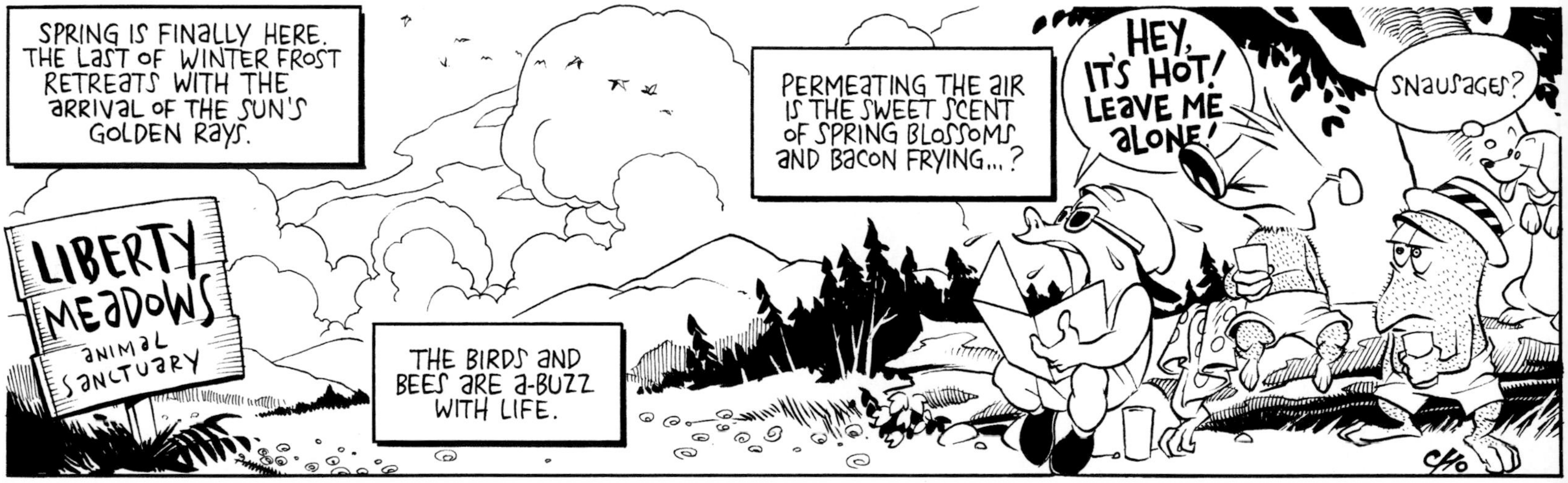
Spring is finally here. The last of winter frost retreats with the arrival of the sun's golden rays.
Liberty Meadows animal sanctuary
The birds and bees are a-buzz with life.
Permeating the air is the sweet scent of spring blossoms and bacon frying...?
Hey, it's hot! Leave me alone!
Snausages?
Cho

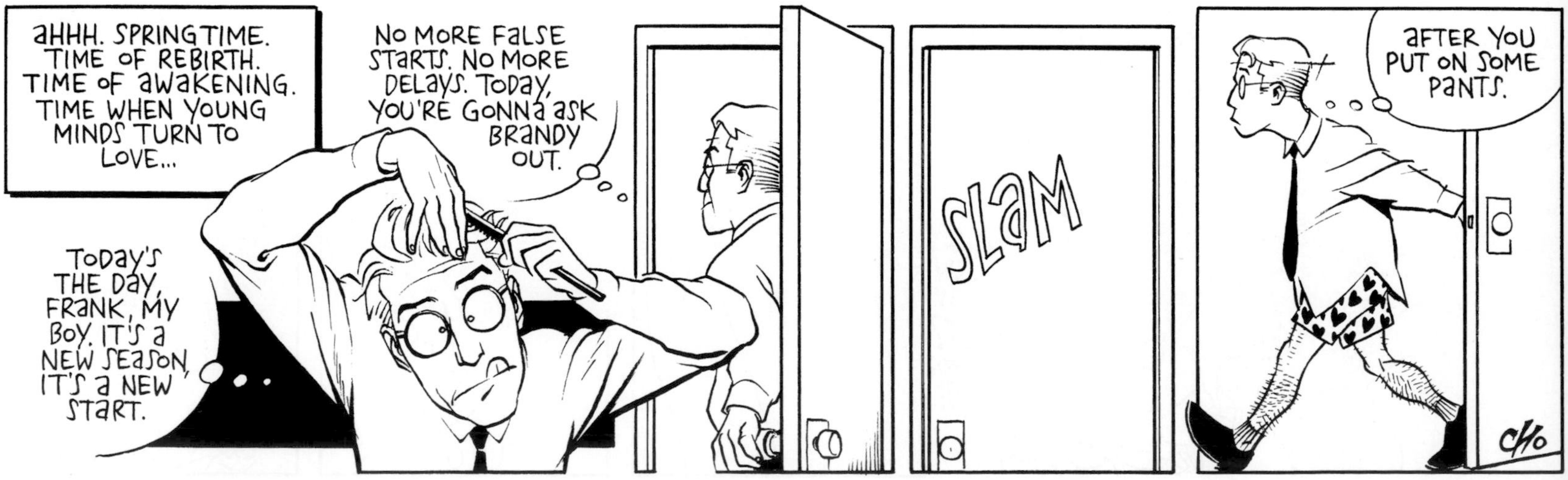
Ahhh. Springtime. Time of rebirth. Time of awakening. Time when young minds turn to love...
Today's the day, Frank, my boy. It's a new season, it's a new start.
No more false starts. No more delays. Today, you're gonna ask Brandy out.
SLAM
After you put on some pants.
Cho

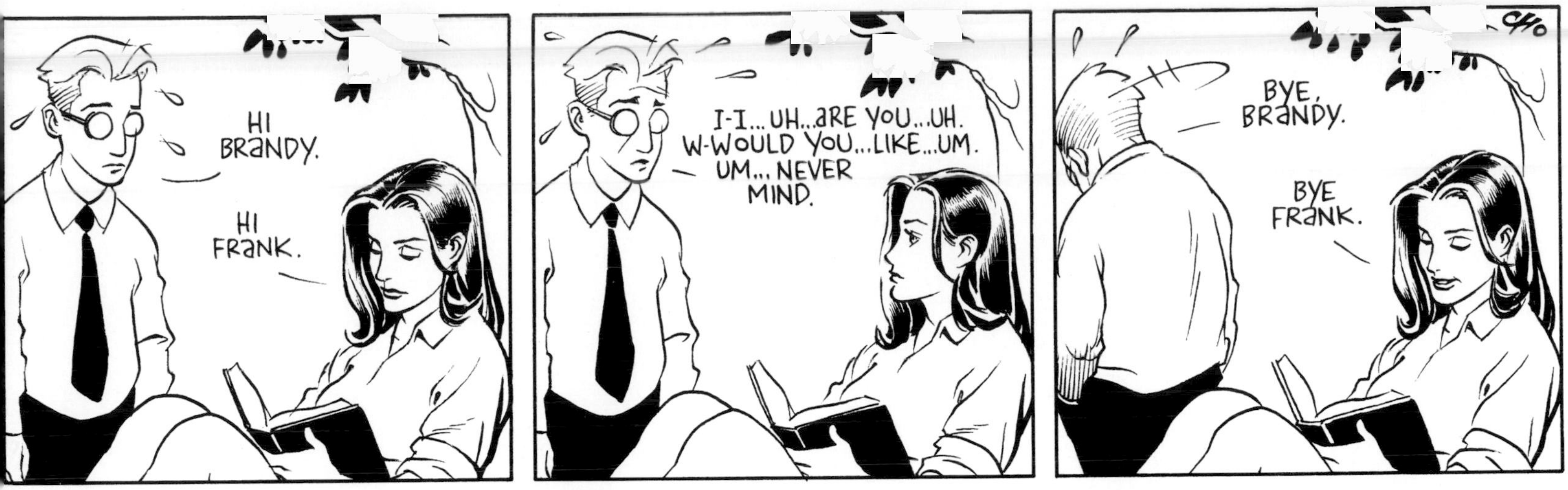
HI BRANDY.
HI FRANK.
I-I... UH...ARE YOU...UH. W-WOULD YOU...LIKE...UM. UM... NEVER MIND.
BYE, BRANDY.
BYE FRANK.

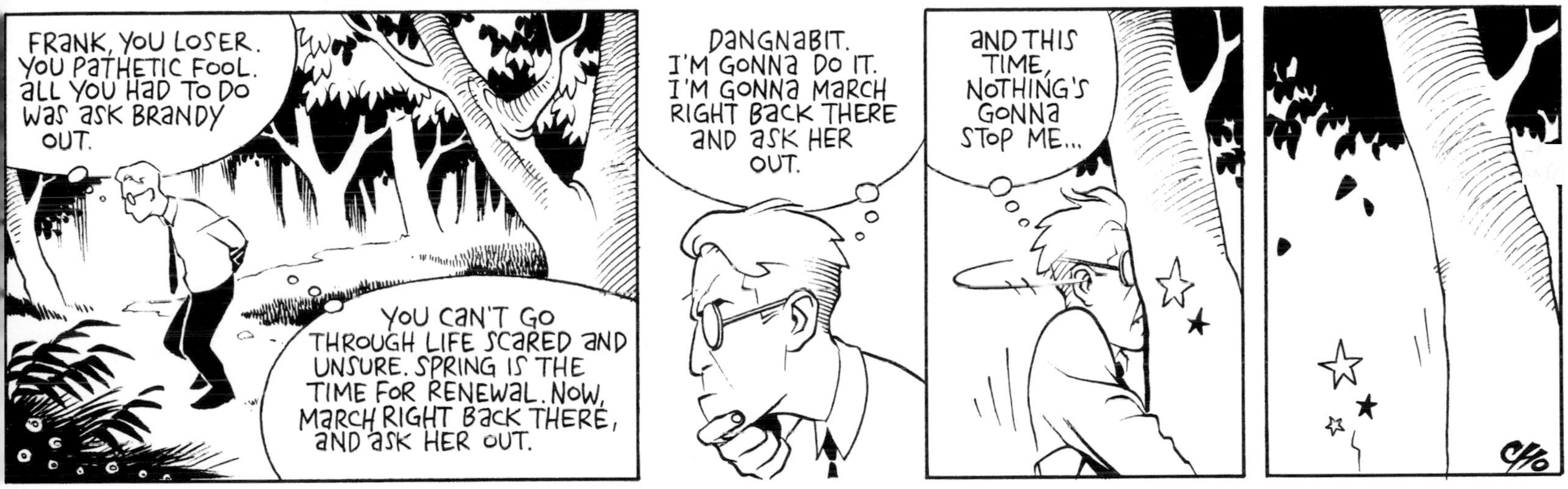
FRANK, YOU LOSER. YOU PATHETIC FOOL. ALL YOU HAD TO DO WAS ASK BRANDY OUT.
YOU CAN'T GO THROUGH LIFE SCARED AND UNSURE. SPRING IS THE TIME FOR RENEWAL. NOW, MARCH RIGHT BACK THERE, AND ASK HER OUT.
DANGNABIT. I'M GONNA DO IT. I'M GONNA MARCH RIGHT BACK THERE AND ASK HER OUT.
AND THIS TIME, NOTHING'S GONNA STOP ME...

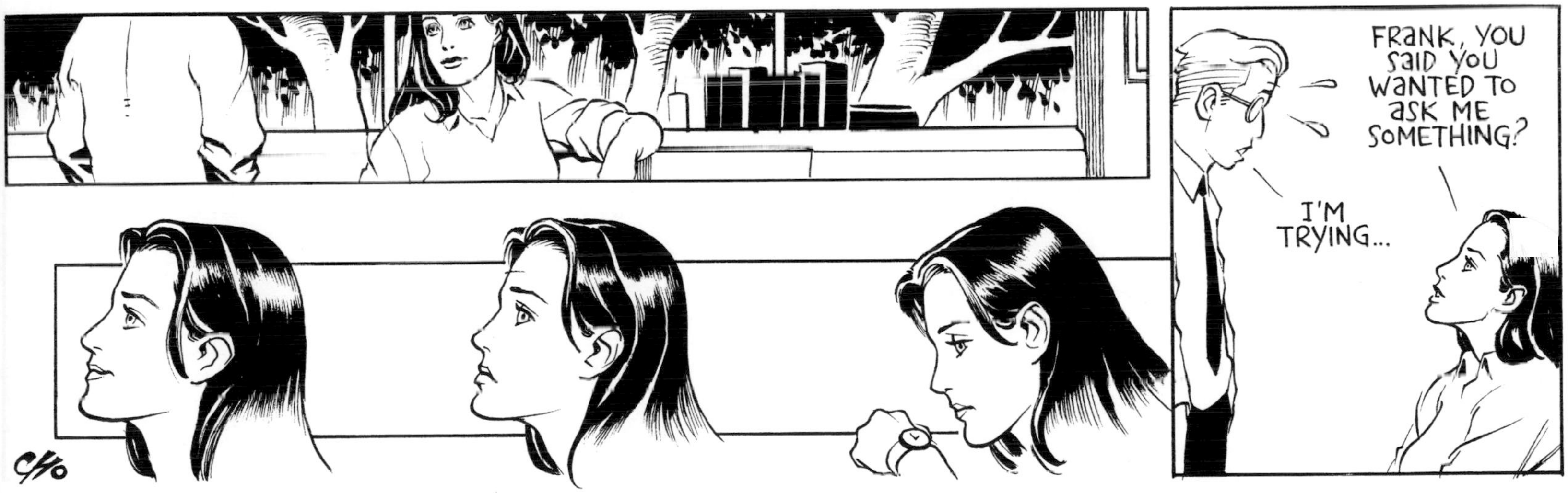
FRANK, YOU SAID YOU WANTED TO ASK ME SOMETHING?
I'M TRYING...

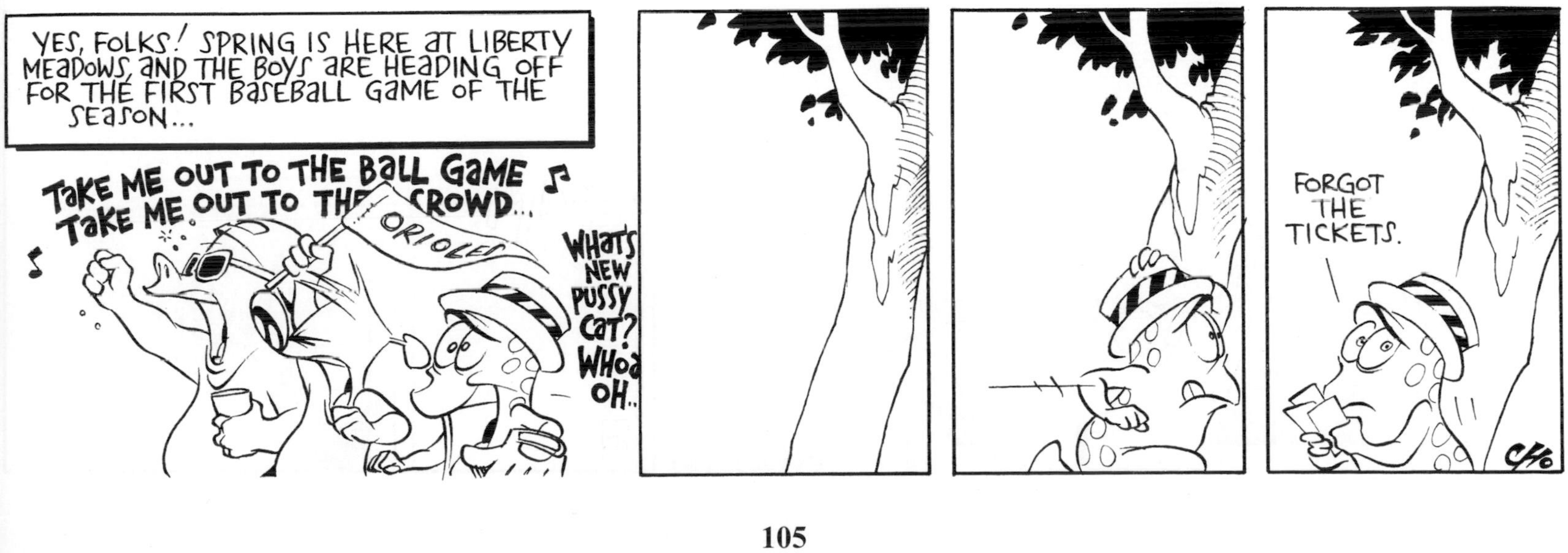
YES, FOLKS! SPRING IS HERE AT LIBERTY MEADOWS, AND THE BOYS ARE HEADING OFF FOR THE FIRST BASEBALL GAME OF THE SEASON...
TAKE ME OUT TO THE BALL GAME TAKE ME OUT TO THE CROWD...
ORIOLES
WHAT'S NEW PUSSY CAT? WHOA OH..
FORGOT THE TICKETS.

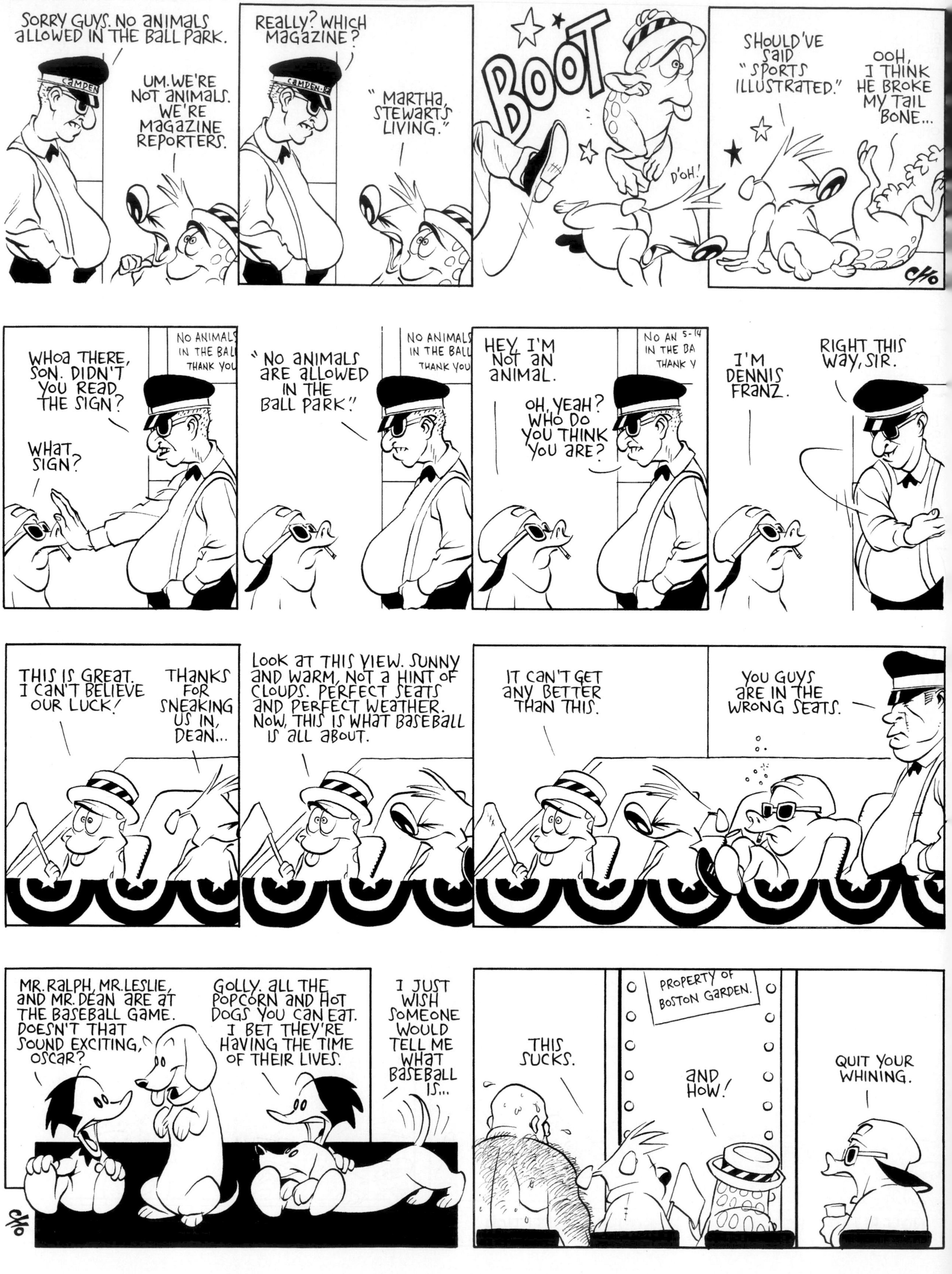
SORRY GUYS. NO ANIMALS ALLOWED IN THE BALL PARK.
CAMDEN
UM. WE'RE NOT ANIMALS. WE'RE MAGAZINE REPORTERS.
REALLY? WHICH MAGAZINE?
"MARTHA STEWART'S LIVING."
BOOT
D'OH!
SHOULD'VE SAID "SPORTS ILLUSTRATED."
OOH, I THINK HE BROKE MY TAIL BONE...
NO ANIMALS IN THE BALL THANK YOU
WHOA THERE, SON. DIDN'T YOU READ THE SIGN?
WHAT SIGN?
"NO ANIMALS ARE ALLOWED IN THE BALL PARK."
HEY, I'M NOT AN ANIMAL.
OH, YEAH? WHO DO YOU THINK YOU ARE?
I'M DENNIS FRANZ.
RIGHT THIS WAY, SIR.
THIS IS GREAT. I CAN'T BELIEVE OUR LUCK!
THANKS FOR SNEAKING US IN, DEAN...
LOOK AT THIS VIEW. SUNNY AND WARM, NOT A HINT OF CLOUDS. PERFECT SEATS AND PERFECT WEATHER. NOW, THIS IS WHAT BASEBALL IS ALL ABOUT.
IT CAN'T GET ANY BETTER THAN THIS.
YOU GUYS ARE IN THE WRONG SEATS.
MR. RALPH, MR. LESLIE, AND MR. DEAN ARE AT THE BASEBALL GAME. DOESN'T THAT SOUND EXCITING, OSCAR?
GOLLY. ALL THE POPCORN AND HOT DOGS YOU CAN EAT. I BET THEY'RE HAVING THE TIME OF THEIR LIVES.
I JUST WISH SOMEONE WOULD TELL ME WHAT BASEBALL IS...
PROPERTY OF BOSTON GARDEN.
THIS SUCKS.
AND HOW!
QUIT YOUR WHINING.

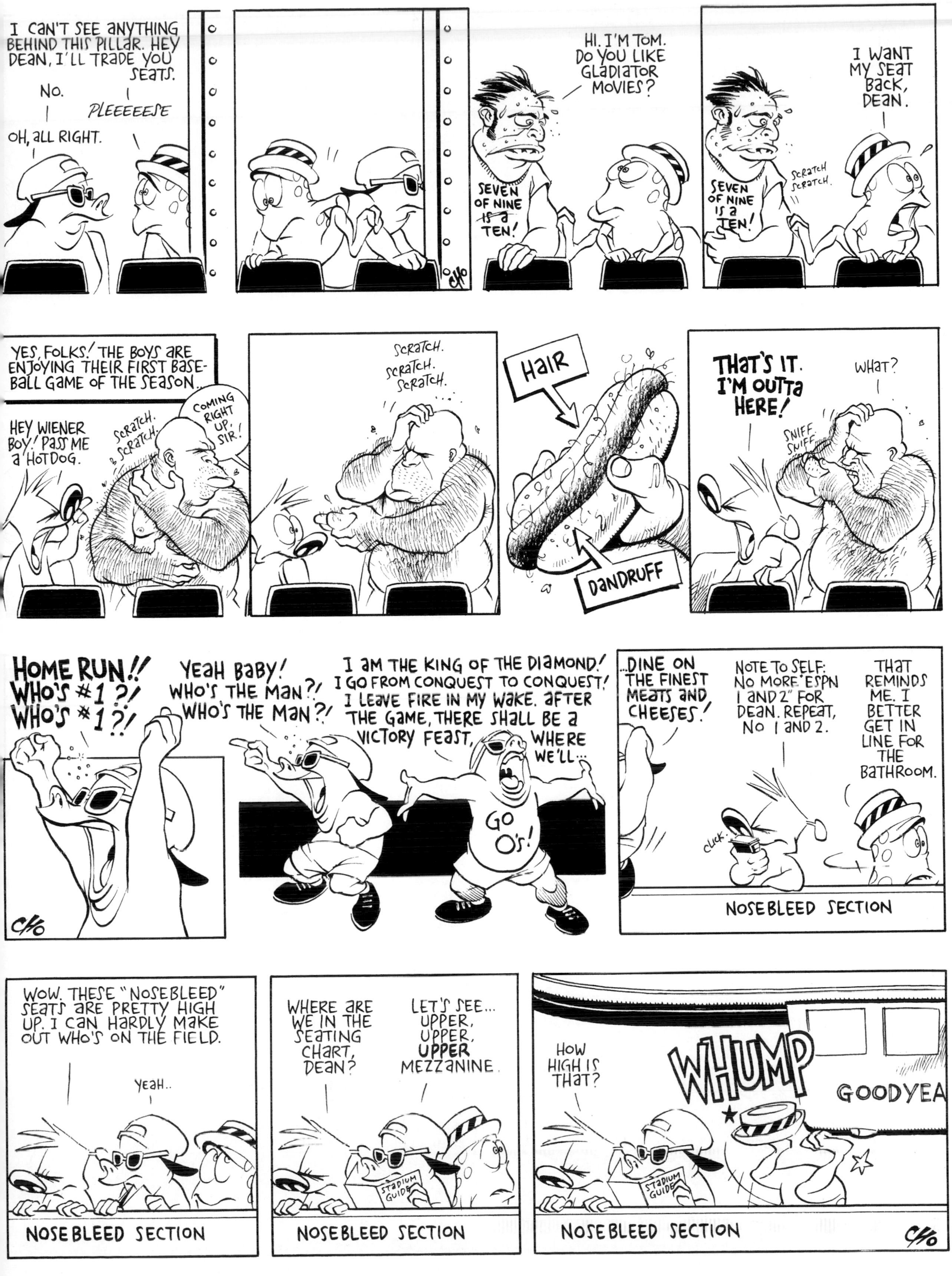

I CAN'T SEE ANYTHING BEHIND THIS PILLAR. HEY DEAN, I'LL TRADE YOU SEATS.
NO.
PLEEEEEESE
OH, ALL RIGHT.
HI. I'M TOM. DO YOU LIKE GLADIATOR MOVIES?
SEVEN OF NINE IS A TEN!
I WANT MY SEAT BACK, DEAN.
SEVEN OF NINE IS A TEN!
SCRATCH SCRATCH.
YES, FOLKS! THE BOYS ARE ENJOYING THEIR FIRST BASEBALL GAME OF THE SEASON...
HEY WIENER BOY! PASS ME A HOTDOG.
SCRATCH. SCRATCH.
COMING RIGHT UP, SIR!
SCRATCH. SCRATCH. SCRATCH.
HAIR
DANDRUFF
THAT'S IT. I'M OUTTA HERE!
WHAT?
SNIFF. SNIFF.
HOME RUN!! WHO'S #1?! WHO'S #1?!
YEAH BABY! WHO'S THE MAN?! WHO'S THE MAN?!
I AM THE KING OF THE DIAMOND! I GO FROM CONQUEST TO CONQUEST! I LEAVE FIRE IN MY WAKE. AFTER THE GAME, THERE SHALL BE A VICTORY FEAST, WHERE WE'LL...
GO O's!
...DINE ON THE FINEST MEATS AND CHEESES!
NOTE TO SELF: NO MORE "ESPN 1 AND 2" FOR DEAN. REPEAT, NO 1 AND 2.
CLICK.
THAT REMINDS ME. I BETTER GET IN LINE FOR THE BATHROOM.
NOSEBLEED SECTION
WOW. THESE "NOSEBLEED" SEATS ARE PRETTY HIGH UP. I CAN HARDLY MAKE OUT WHO'S ON THE FIELD.
YEAH..
NOSEBLEED SECTION
WHERE ARE WE IN THE SEATING CHART, DEAN?
LET'S SEE... UPPER, UPPER, UPPER MEZZANINE.
STADIUM GUIDE
NOSEBLEED SECTION
HOW HIGH IS THAT?
WHUMP
GOODYEA
STADIUM GUIDE
NOSEBLEED SECTION

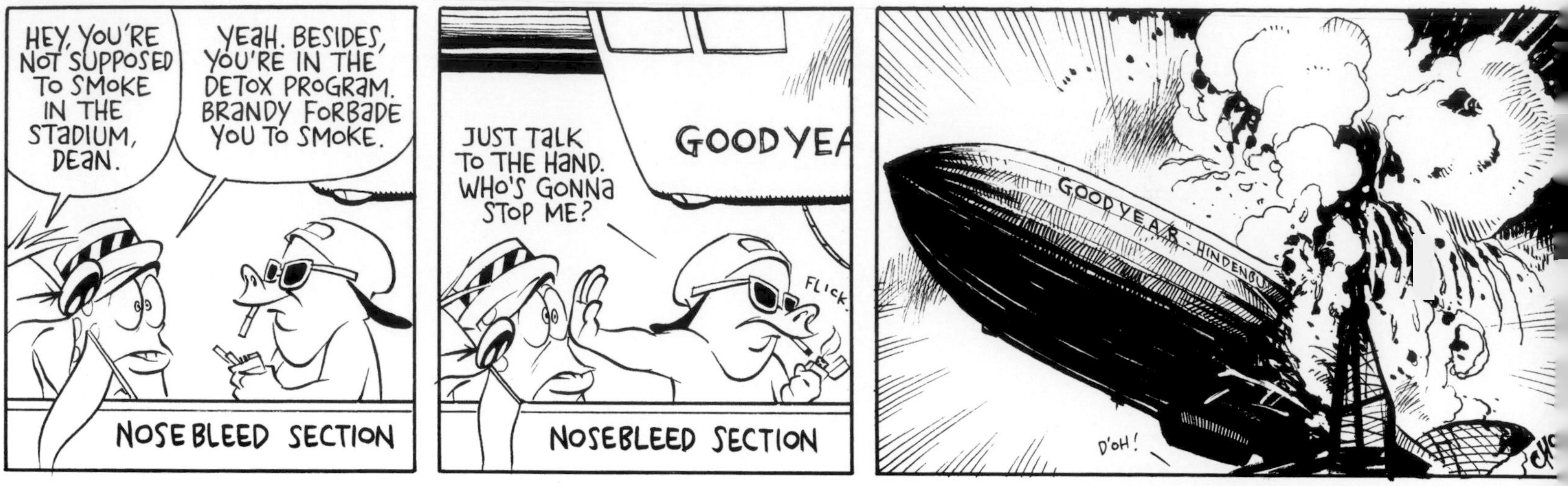
HEY, YOU'RE NOT SUPPOSED TO SMOKE IN THE STADIUM, DEAN.
YEAH. BESIDES, YOU'RE IN THE DETOX PROGRAM. BRANDY FORBADE YOU TO SMOKE.
NOSEBLEED SECTION
JUST TALK TO THE HAND. WHO'S GONNA STOP ME?
GOODYEA
FLICK.
NOSEBLEED SECTION
GOODYEAR HINDENB
D'OH!

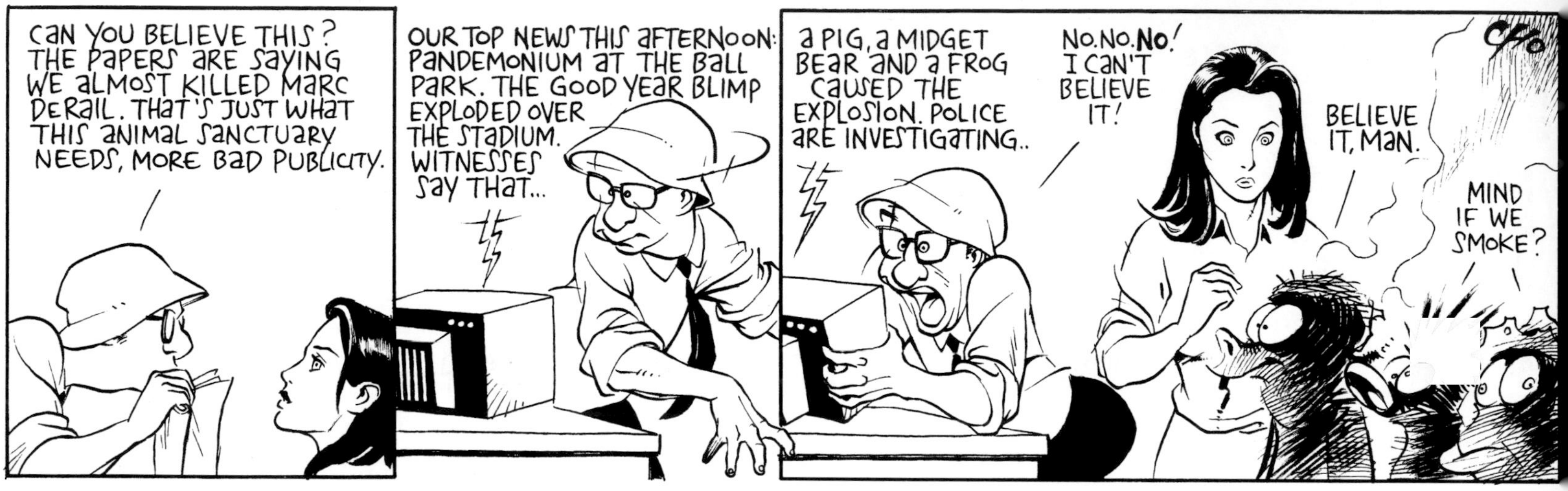
CAN YOU BELIEVE THIS? THE PAPERS ARE SAYING WE ALMOST KILLED MARC DERAIL. THAT'S JUST WHAT THIS ANIMAL SANCTUARY NEEDS, MORE BAD PUBLICITY.
OUR TOP NEWS THIS AFTERNOON: PANDEMONIUM AT THE BALL PARK. THE GOOD YEAR BLIMP EXPLODED OVER THE STADIUM. WITNESSES SAY THAT...
A PIG, A MIDGET BEAR AND A FROG CAUSED THE EXPLOSION. POLICE ARE INVESTIGATING..
NO. NO. NO! I CAN'T BELIEVE IT!
BELIEVE IT, MAN.
MIND IF WE SMOKE?

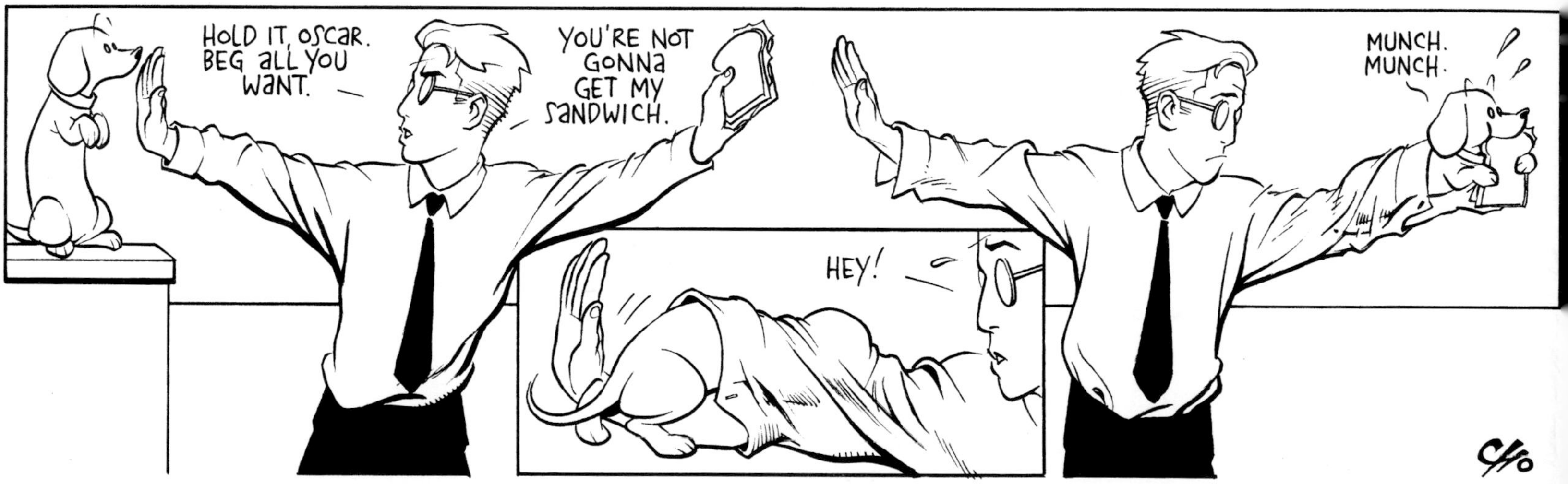
HOLD IT, OSCAR. BEG ALL YOU WANT.
YOU'RE NOT GONNA GET MY SANDWICH.
HEY!
MUNCH. MUNCH.

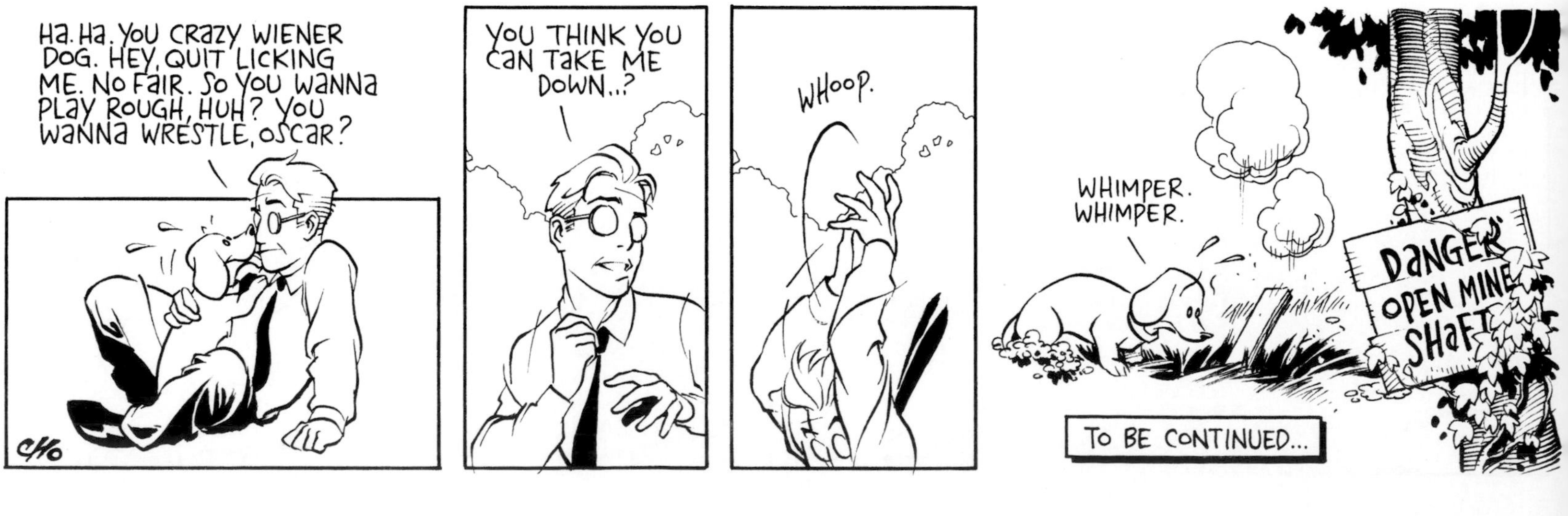
HA. HA. YOU CRAZY WIENER DOG. HEY, QUIT LICKING ME. NO FAIR. SO YOU WANNA PLAY ROUGH, HUH? YOU WANNA WRESTLE, OSCAR?
YOU THINK YOU CAN TAKE ME DOWN..?
WHOOP.
WHIMPER. WHIMPER.
DANGER OPEN MINE SHAFT
TO BE CONTINUED...

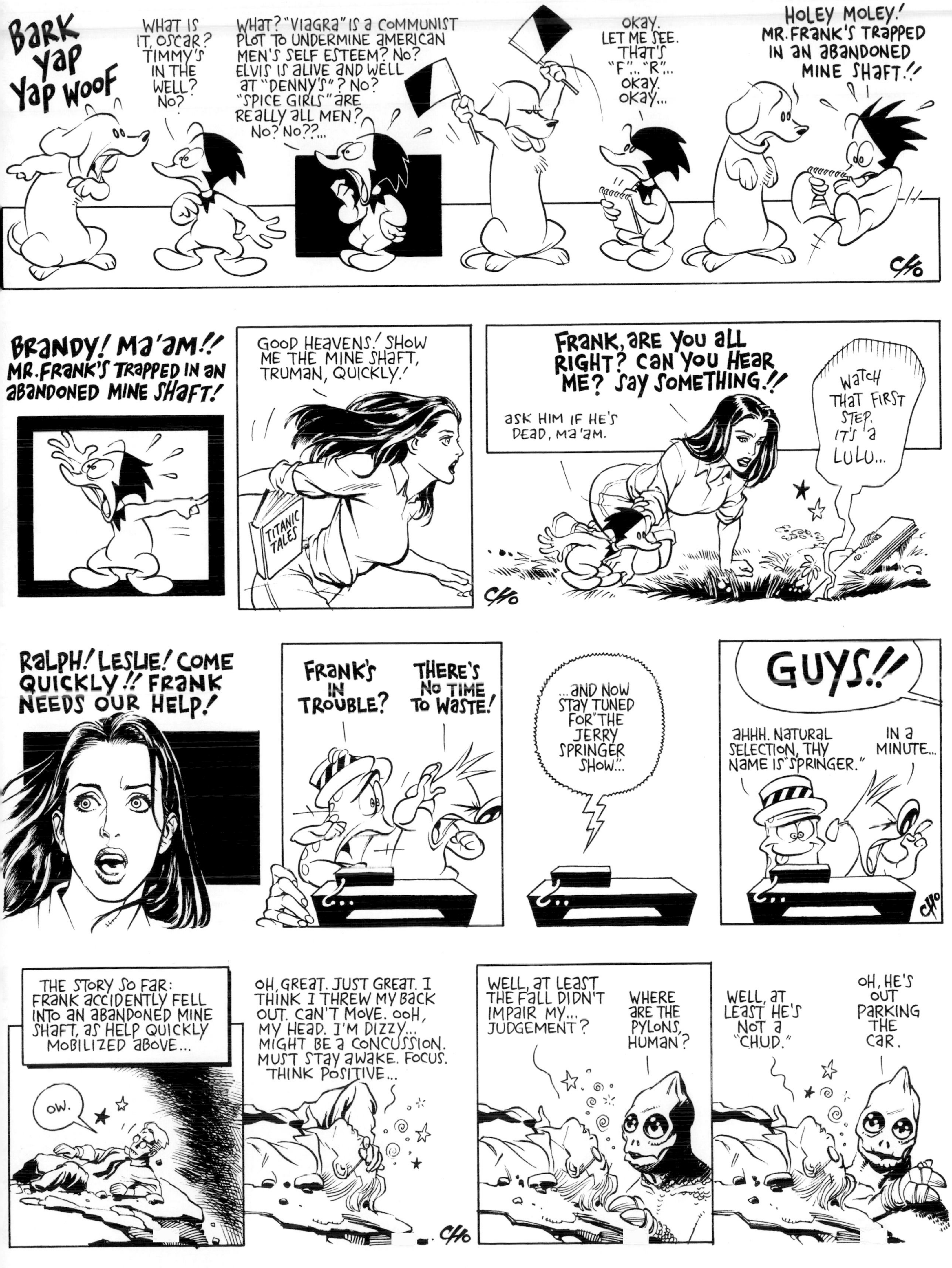
BARK YAP YAP WOOF
WHAT IS IT, OSCAR? TIMMY'S IN THE WELL? NO?
WHAT? "VIAGRA" IS A COMMUNIST PLOT TO UNDERMINE AMERICAN MEN'S SELF ESTEEM? NO? ELVIS IS ALIVE AND WELL AT "DENNY'S"? NO? "SPICE GIRLS" ARE REALLY ALL MEN? NO? NO??...
OKAY. LET ME SEE. THAT'S "F"... "R"... OKAY. OKAY...
HOLEY MOLEY! MR. FRANK'S TRAPPED IN AN ABANDONED MINE SHAFT!!
CHO
BRANDY! MA'AM!! MR. FRANK'S TRAPPED IN AN ABANDONED MINE SHAFT!
GOOD HEAVENS! SHOW ME THE MINE SHAFT, TRUMAN, QUICKLY!
TITANIC TALES
FRANK, ARE YOU ALL RIGHT? CAN YOU HEAR ME? SAY SOMETHING!!
ASK HIM IF HE'S DEAD, MA'AM.
WATCH THAT FIRST STEP. IT'S A LULU...
CHO
RALPH! LESLIE! COME QUICKLY!! FRANK NEEDS OUR HELP!
FRANK'S IN TROUBLE?
THERE'S NO TIME TO WASTE!
...AND NOW STAY TUNED FOR "THE JERRY SPRINGER SHOW"...
GUYS!!
AHHH. NATURAL SELECTION, THY NAME IS "SPRINGER."
IN A MINUTE...
CHO
THE STORY SO FAR: FRANK ACCIDENTLY FELL INTO AN ABANDONED MINE SHAFT, AS HELP QUICKLY MOBILIZED ABOVE...
OW.
OH, GREAT. JUST GREAT. I THINK I THREW MY BACK OUT. CAN'T MOVE. OOH, MY HEAD. I'M DIZZY... MIGHT BE A CONCUSSION. MUST STAY AWAKE. FOCUS. THINK POSITIVE...
CHO
WELL, AT LEAST THE FALL DIDN'T IMPAIR MY... JUDGEMENT?
WHERE ARE THE PYLONS, HUMAN?
WELL, AT LEAST HE'S NOT A "CHUD."
OH, HE'S OUT PARKING THE CAR.

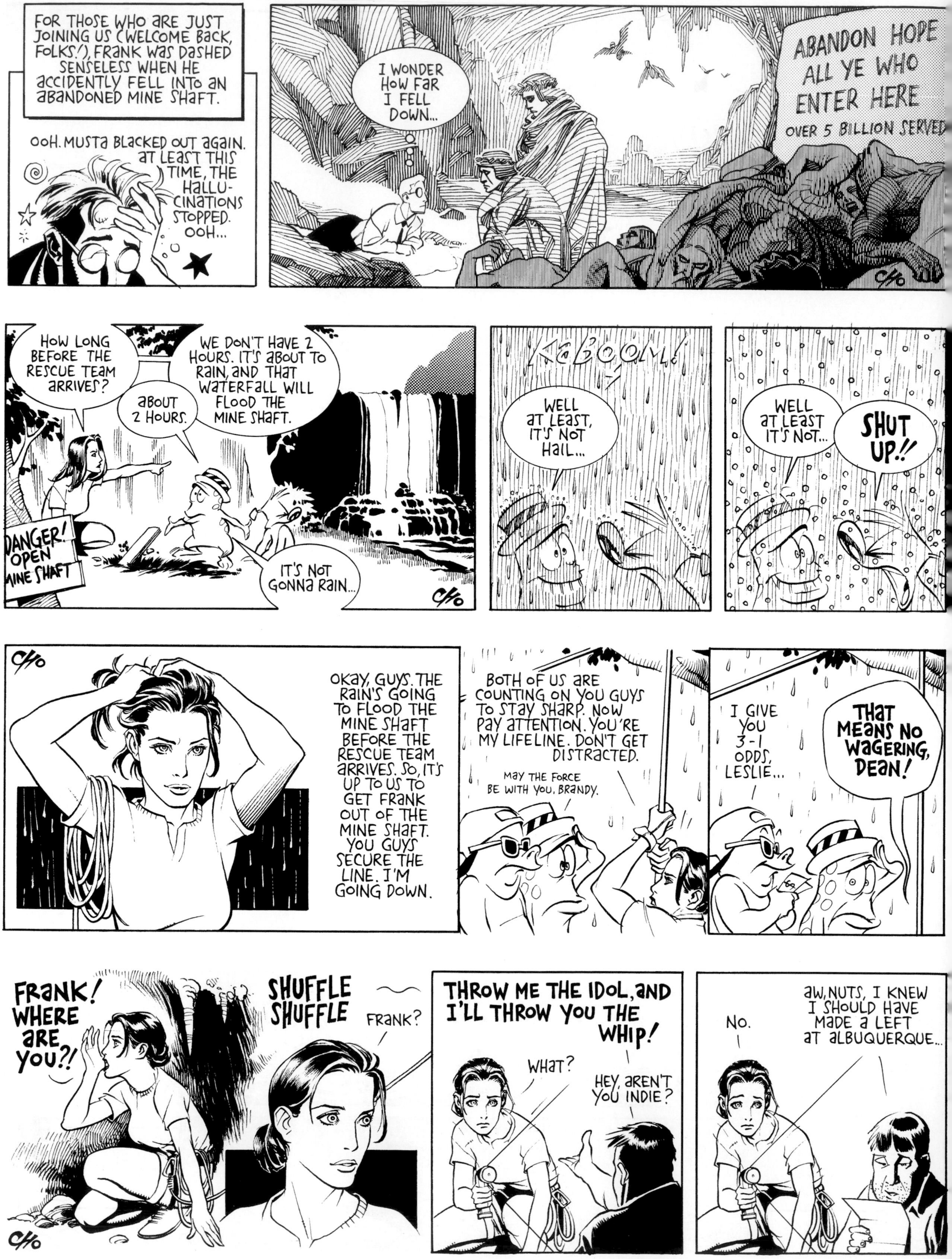
FOR THOSE WHO ARE JUST JOINING US (WELCOME BACK, FOLKS!), FRANK WAS DASHED SENSELESS WHEN HE ACCIDENTLY FELL INTO AN ABANDONED MINE SHAFT.
OOH. MUSTA BLACKED OUT AGAIN. AT LEAST THIS TIME, THE HALLUCINATIONS STOPPED. OOH...
I WONDER HOW FAR I FELL DOWN...
ABANDON HOPE ALL YE WHO ENTER HERE
OVER 5 BILLION SERVED
CHO
HOW LONG BEFORE THE RESCUE TEAM ARRIVES?
ABOUT 2 HOURS.
WE DON'T HAVE 2 HOURS. IT'S ABOUT TO RAIN, AND THAT WATERFALL WILL FLOOD THE MINE SHAFT.
DANGER! OPEN MINE SHAFT
IT'S NOT GONNA RAIN...
CHO
KABOOM!
WELL AT LEAST, IT'S NOT HAIL...
WELL AT LEAST IT'S NOT...
SHUT UP!!
CHO
OKAY, GUYS. THE RAIN'S GOING TO FLOOD THE MINE SHAFT BEFORE THE RESCUE TEAM ARRIVES. SO, IT'S UP TO US TO GET FRANK OUT OF THE MINE SHAFT. YOU GUYS SECURE THE LINE. I'M GOING DOWN.
BOTH OF US ARE COUNTING ON YOU GUYS TO STAY SHARP. NOW PAY ATTENTION. YOU'RE MY LIFELINE. DON'T GET DISTRACTED.
MAY THE FORCE BE WITH YOU, BRANDY.
I GIVE YOU 3-1 ODDS, LESLIE...
THAT MEANS NO WAGERING, DEAN!
FRANK! WHERE ARE YOU?!
SHUFFLE SHUFFLE
FRANK?
CHO
THROW ME THE IDOL, AND I'LL THROW YOU THE WHIP!
WHAT?
HEY, AREN'T YOU INDIE?
NO.
AW, NUTS, I KNEW I SHOULD HAVE MADE A LEFT AT ALBUQUERQUE...

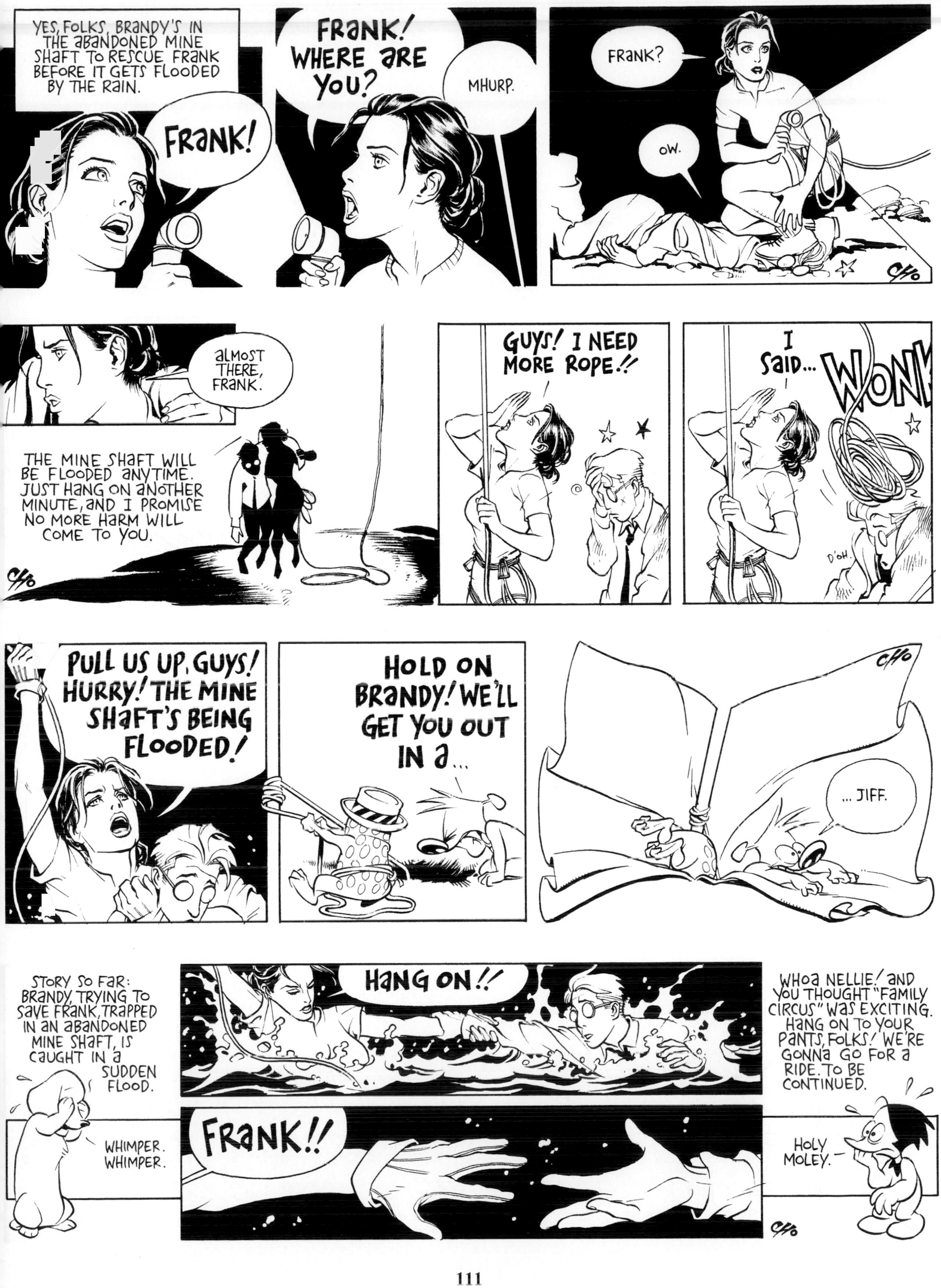
YES, FOLKS, BRANDY'S IN THE ABANDONED MINE SHAFT TO RESCUE FRANK BEFORE IT GETS FLOODED BY THE RAIN.
FRANK!
FRANK! WHERE ARE YOU?
MHURP.
FRANK?
OW.
ALMOST THERE, FRANK.
THE MINE SHAFT WILL BE FLOODED ANYTIME. JUST HANG ON ANOTHER MINUTE, AND I PROMISE NO MORE HARM WILL COME TO YOU.
GUYS! I NEED MORE ROPE!!
I SAID...
WONK
D'OH.
PULL US UP, GUYS! HURRY! THE MINE SHAFT'S BEING FLOODED!
HOLD ON BRANDY! WE'LL GET YOU OUT IN A...
... JIFF.
STORY SO FAR: BRANDY, TRYING TO SAVE FRANK, TRAPPED IN AN ABANDONED MINE SHAFT, IS CAUGHT IN A SUDDEN FLOOD.
HANG ON!!
WHOA NELLIE! AND YOU THOUGHT "FAMILY CIRCUS" WAS EXCITING. HANG ON TO YOUR PANTS, FOLKS! WE'RE GONNA GO FOR A RIDE. TO BE CONTINUED.
WHIMPER. WHIMPER.
FRANK!!
HOLY MOLEY.

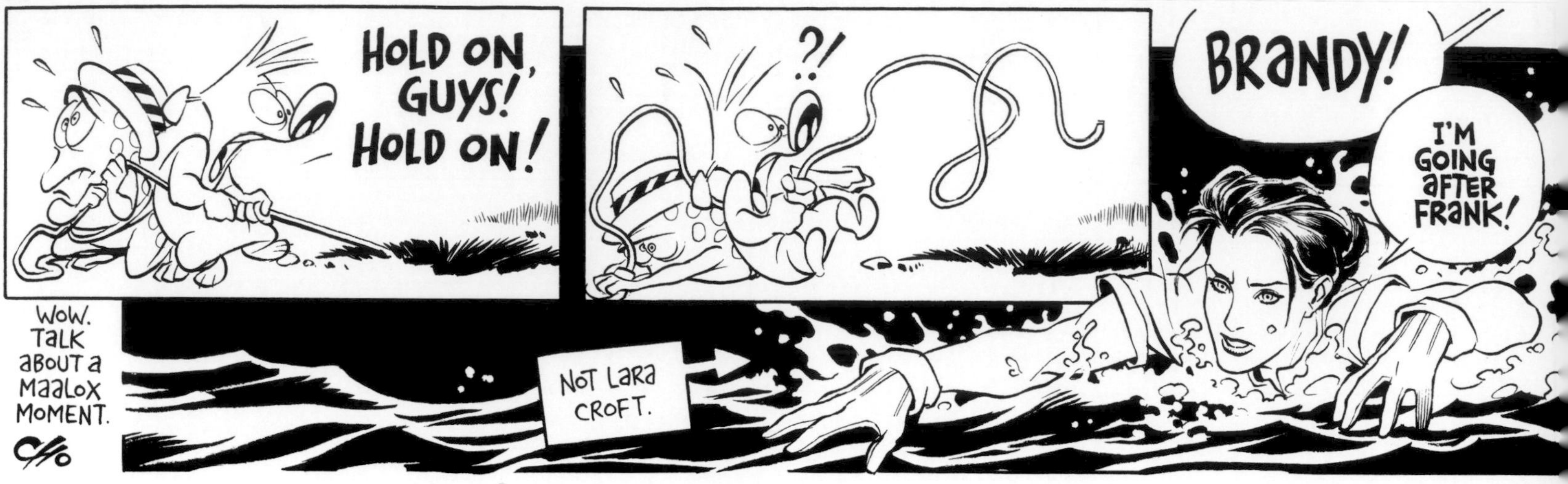
HOLD ON, GUYS! HOLD ON!
?!
BRANDY!
I'M GOING AFTER FRANK!
WOW. TALK ABOUT A MAALOX MOMENT.
NOT LARA CROFT.
CHO

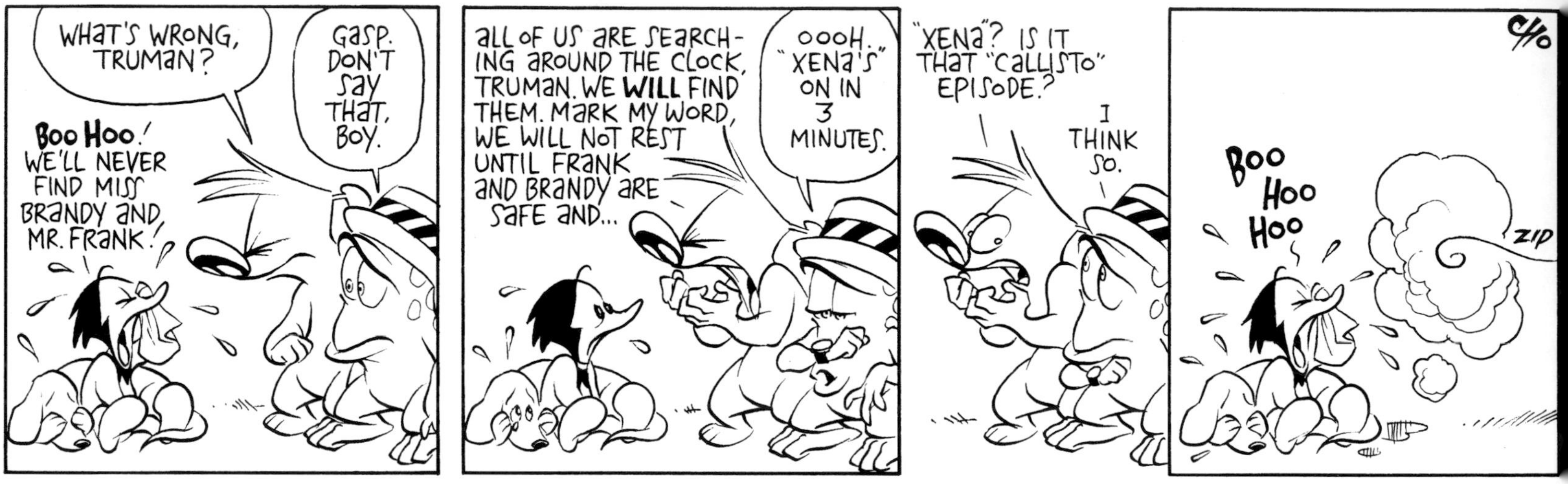
WHAT'S WRONG, TRUMAN?
GASP. DON'T SAY THAT, BOY.
BOO HOO! WE'LL NEVER FIND MISS BRANDY AND MR. FRANK!
ALL OF US ARE SEARCHING AROUND THE CLOCK, TRUMAN. WE WILL FIND THEM. MARK MY WORD, WE WILL NOT REST UNTIL FRANK AND BRANDY ARE SAFE AND...
OOOH. "XENA'S" ON IN 3 MINUTES.
"XENA"? IS IT THAT "CALLISTO" EPISODE?
I THINK SO.
BOO HOO HOO
ZIP
CHO

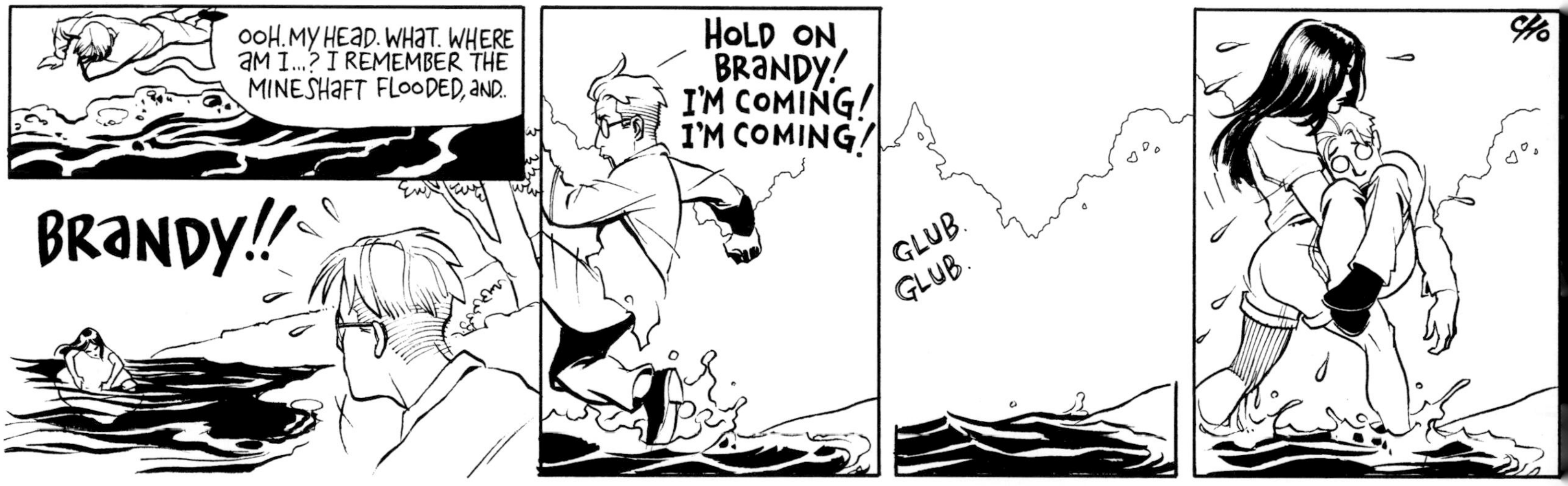
OOH. MY HEAD. WHAT. WHERE AM I...? I REMEMBER THE MINESHAFT FLOODED, AND.
BRANDY!!
HOLD ON BRANDY! I'M COMING! I'M COMING!
GLUB. GLUB.
CHO

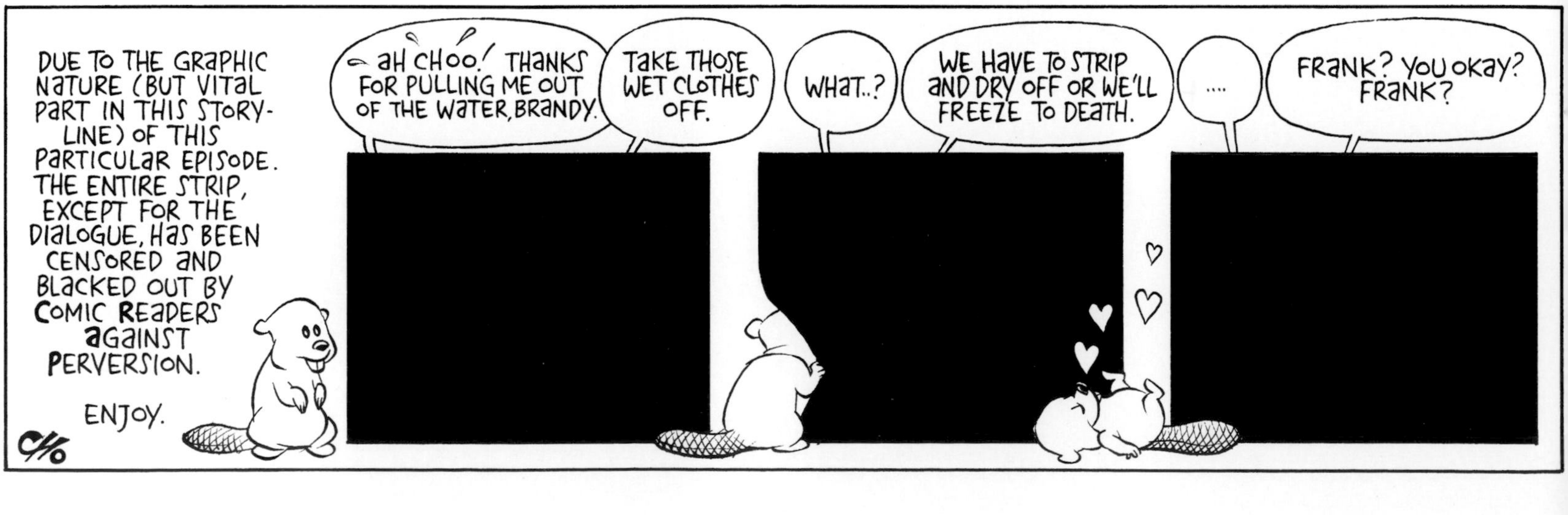
DUE TO THE GRAPHIC NATURE (BUT VITAL PART IN THIS STORY-LINE) OF THIS PARTICULAR EPISODE. THE ENTIRE STRIP, EXCEPT FOR THE DIALOGUE, HAS BEEN CENSORED AND BLACKED OUT BY COMIC READERS AGAINST PERVERSION.
ENJOY.
AH CHOO! THANKS FOR PULLING ME OUT OF THE WATER, BRANDY.
TAKE THOSE WET CLOTHES OFF.
WHAT..?
WE HAVE TO STRIP AND DRY OFF OR WE'LL FREEZE TO DEATH.
....
FRANK? YOU OKAY? FRANK?
CHO

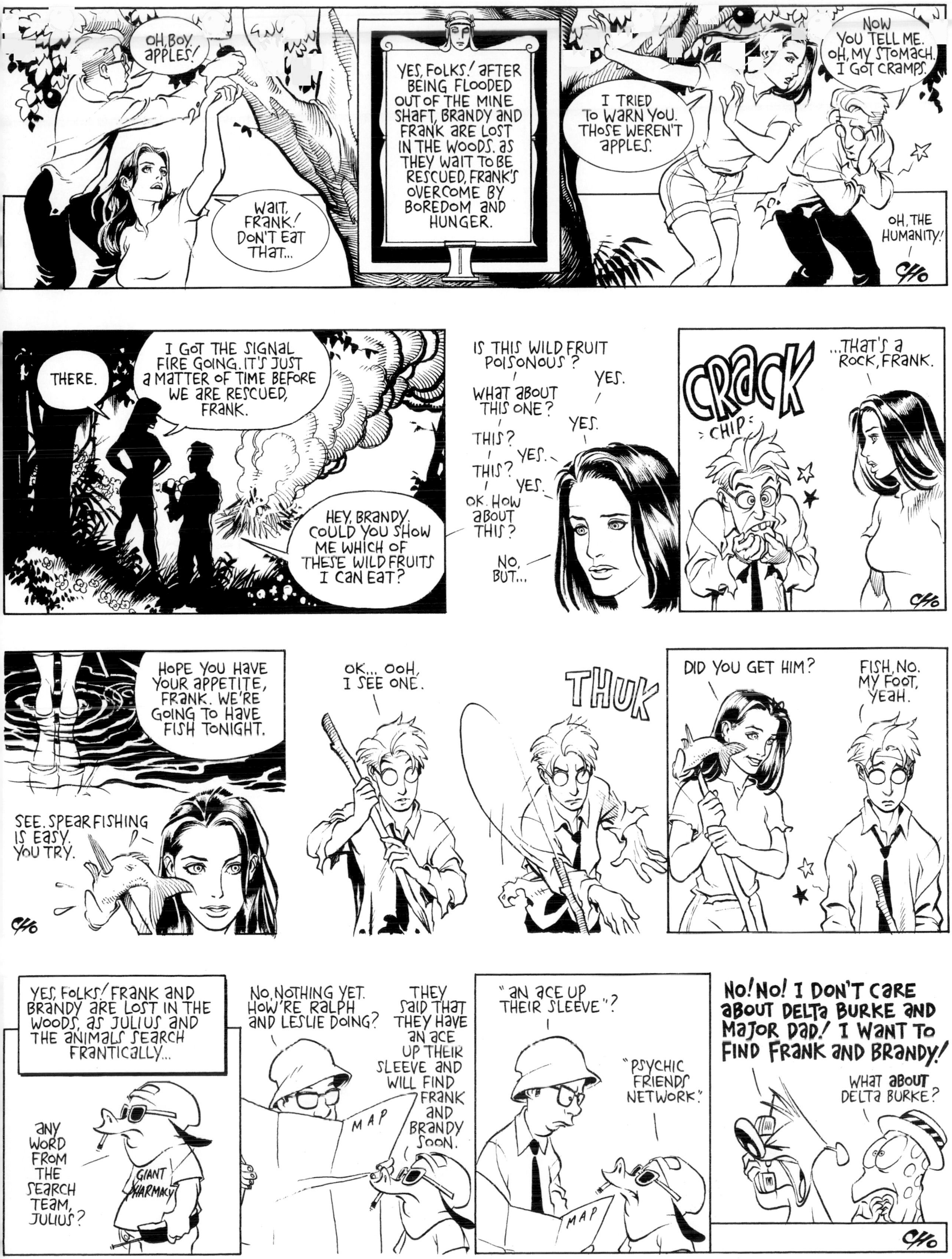
OH, BOY, APPLES!
WAIT, FRANK! DON'T EAT THAT...
YES, FOLKS! AFTER BEING FLOODED OUT OF THE MINE SHAFT, BRANDY AND FRANK ARE LOST IN THE WOODS. AS THEY WAIT TO BE RESCUED, FRANK'S OVERCOME BY BOREDOM AND HUNGER.
I TRIED TO WARN YOU. THOSE WEREN'T APPLES.
NOW YOU TELL ME. OH, MY STOMACH. I GOT CRAMPS.
OH, THE HUMANITY!
CHO
THERE.
I GOT THE SIGNAL FIRE GOING. IT'S JUST A MATTER OF TIME BEFORE WE ARE RESCUED, FRANK.
HEY, BRANDY. COULD YOU SHOW ME WHICH OF THESE WILD FRUITS I CAN EAT?
IS THIS WILD FRUIT POISONOUS?
YES.
WHAT ABOUT THIS ONE?
YES.
THIS?
YES.
THIS?
YES.
OK. HOW ABOUT THIS?
NO, BUT...
CRACK
CHIP
...THAT'S A ROCK, FRANK.
CHO
HOPE YOU HAVE YOUR APPETITE, FRANK. WE'RE GOING TO HAVE FISH TONIGHT.
SEE. SPEARFISHING IS EASY. YOU TRY.
CHO
OK... OOH, I SEE ONE.
THUK
DID YOU GET HIM?
FISH, NO. MY FOOT, YEAH.
YES, FOLKS! FRANK AND BRANDY ARE LOST IN THE WOODS, AS JULIUS AND THE ANIMALS SEARCH FRANTICALLY...
ANY WORD FROM THE SEARCH TEAM, JULIUS?
GIANT PHARMACY
NO, NOTHING YET. HOW'RE RALPH AND LESLIE DOING?
THEY SAID THAT THEY HAVE AN ACE UP THEIR SLEEVE AND WILL FIND FRANK AND BRANDY SOON.
MAP
"AN ACE UP THEIR SLEEVE"?
"PSYCHIC FRIENDS NETWORK."
MAP
NO! NO! I DON'T CARE ABOUT DELTA BURKE AND MAJOR DAD! I WANT TO FIND FRANK AND BRANDY!
WHAT ABOUT DELTA BURKE?
CHO

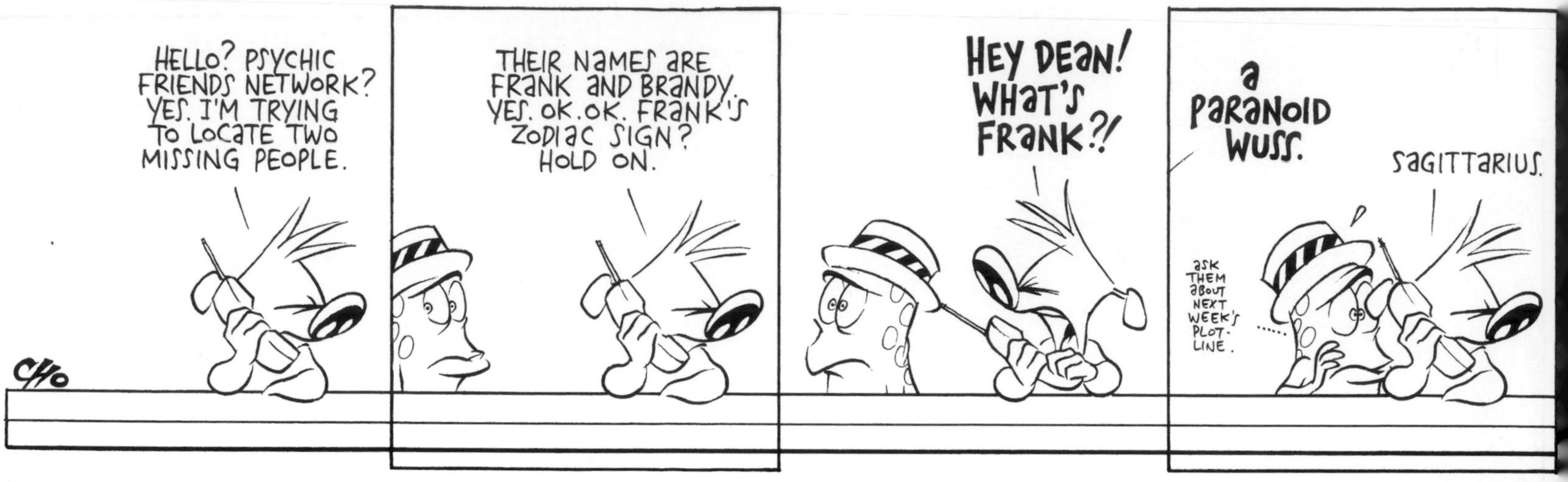
HELLO? PSYCHIC FRIENDS NETWORK? YES. I'M TRYING TO LOCATE TWO MISSING PEOPLE.
THEIR NAMES ARE FRANK AND BRANDY. YES. OK. OK. FRANK'S ZODIAC SIGN? HOLD ON.
HEY DEAN! WHAT'S FRANK?!
A PARANOID WUSS.
SAGITTARIUS.
ASK THEM ABOUT NEXT WEEK'S PLOT-LINE.
CHO

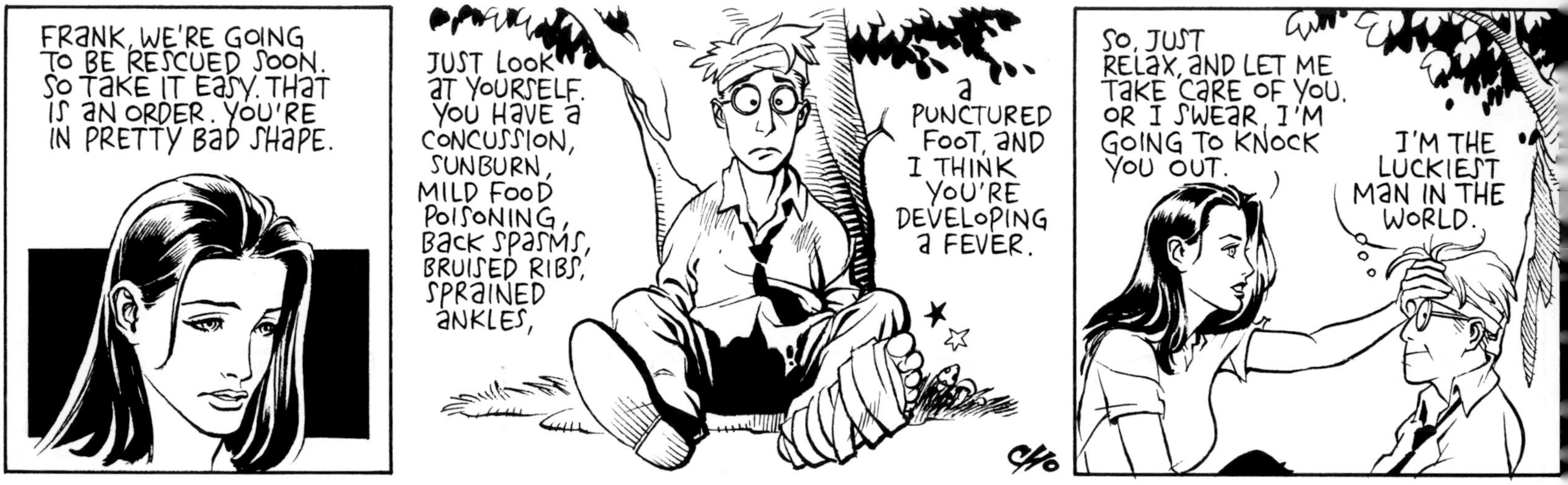
FRANK, WE'RE GOING TO BE RESCUED SOON. SO TAKE IT EASY. THAT IS AN ORDER. YOU'RE IN PRETTY BAD SHAPE.
JUST LOOK AT YOURSELF. YOU HAVE A CONCUSSION, SUNBURN, MILD FOOD POISONING, BACK SPASMS, BRUISED RIBS, SPRAINED ANKLES,
A PUNCTURED FOOT, AND I THINK YOU'RE DEVELOPING A FEVER.
SO, JUST RELAX, AND LET ME TAKE CARE OF YOU. OR I SWEAR, I'M GOING TO KNOCK YOU OUT.
I'M THE LUCKIEST MAN IN THE WORLD.
CHO

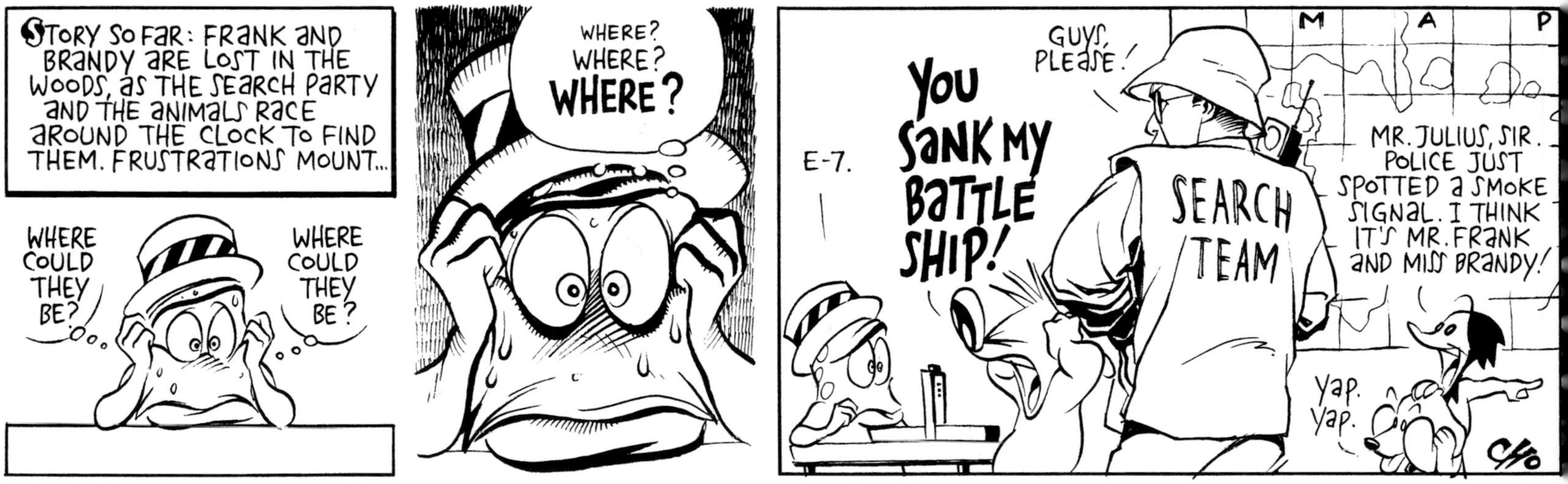
STORY SO FAR: FRANK AND BRANDY ARE LOST IN THE WOODS, AS THE SEARCH PARTY AND THE ANIMALS RACE AROUND THE CLOCK TO FIND THEM. FRUSTRATIONS MOUNT...
WHERE COULD THEY BE?
WHERE COULD THEY BE?
WHERE? WHERE? WHERE?
E-7.
YOU SANK MY BATTLE SHIP!
GUYS, PLEASE.
M A P
SEARCH TEAM
MR. JULIUS, SIR. POLICE JUST SPOTTED A SMOKE SIGNAL. I THINK IT'S MR. FRANK AND MISS BRANDY!
YAP. YAP.
CHO

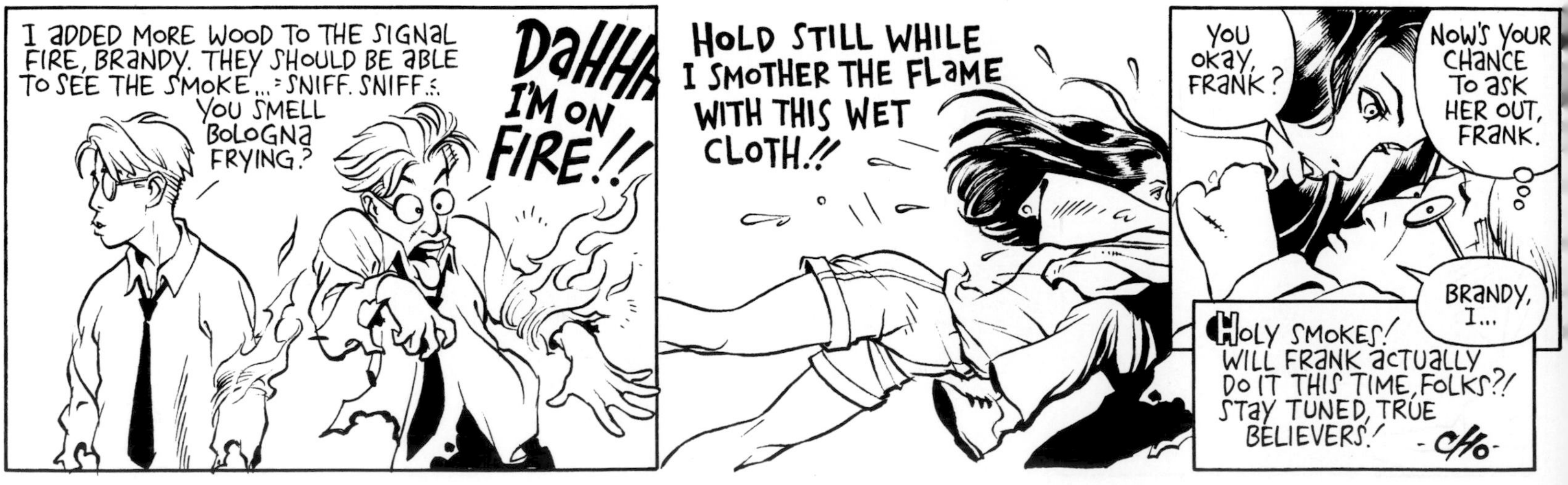
I ADDED MORE WOOD TO THE SIGNAL FIRE, BRANDY. THEY SHOULD BE ABLE TO SEE THE SMOKE... SNIFF. SNIFF.
YOU SMELL BOLOGNA FRYING?
DAHHH I'M ON FIRE!!
HOLD STILL WHILE I SMOTHER THE FLAME WITH THIS WET CLOTH!!
YOU OKAY, FRANK?
NOW'S YOUR CHANCE TO ASK HER OUT, FRANK.
BRANDY, I...
HOLY SMOKES! WILL FRANK ACTUALLY DO IT THIS TIME, FOLKS?! STAY TUNED, TRUE BELIEVERS!
- CHO -

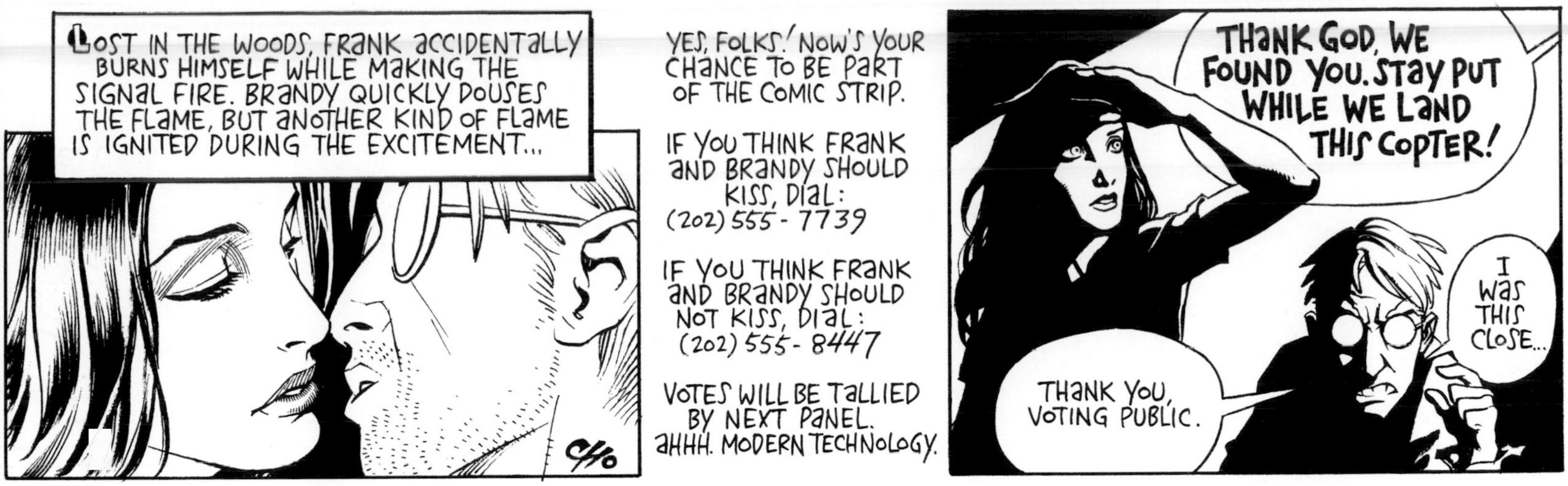
LOST IN THE WOODS, FRANK ACCIDENTALLY BURNS HIMSELF WHILE MAKING THE SIGNAL FIRE. BRANDY QUICKLY DOUSES THE FLAME, BUT ANOTHER KIND OF FLAME IS IGNITED DURING THE EXCITEMENT...
CHO
YES, FOLKS! NOW'S YOUR CHANCE TO BE PART OF THE COMIC STRIP.
IF YOU THINK FRANK AND BRANDY SHOULD KISS, DIAL: (202) 555-7739
IF YOU THINK FRANK AND BRANDY SHOULD NOT KISS, DIAL: (202) 555-8447
VOTES WILL BE TALLIED BY NEXT PANEL. AHHH. MODERN TECHNOLOGY.
THANK GOD, WE FOUND YOU. STAY PUT WHILE WE LAND THIS COPTER!
I WAS THIS CLOSE...
THANK YOU, VOTING PUBLIC.

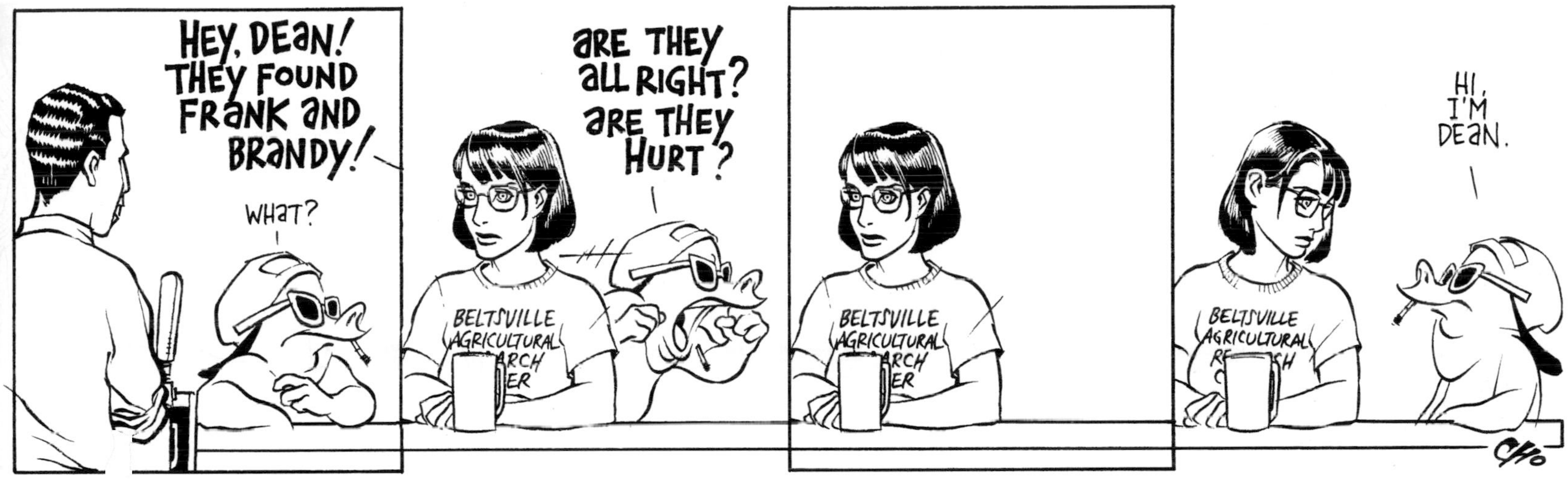
HEY, DEAN! THEY FOUND FRANK AND BRANDY!
WHAT?
ARE THEY ALL RIGHT? ARE THEY HURT?
BELTSVILLE AGRICULTURAL RESEARCH CENTER
HI, I'M DEAN.
CHO

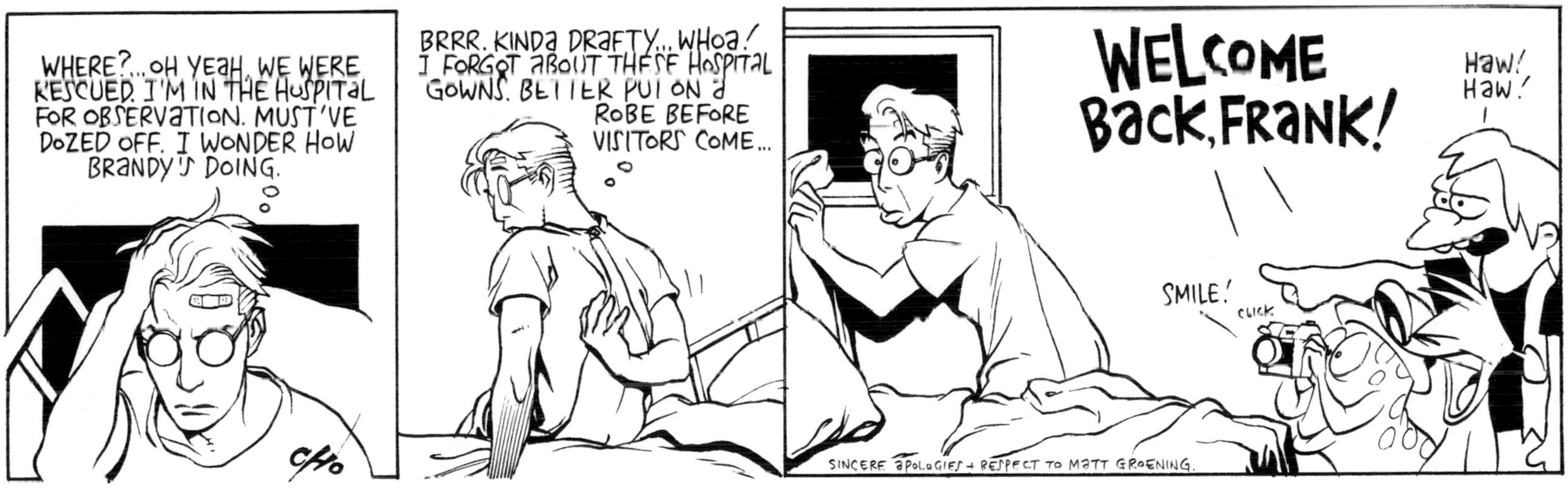
WHERE?...OH YEAH, WE WERE RESCUED. I'M IN THE HOSPITAL FOR OBSERVATION. MUST'VE DOZED OFF. I WONDER HOW BRANDY'S DOING.
CHO
BRRR. KINDA DRAFTY... WHOA! I FORGOT ABOUT THESE HOSPITAL GOWNS. BETTER PUT ON A ROBE BEFORE VISITORS COME...
WELCOME BACK, FRANK!
HAW! HAW!
SMILE!
CLICK
SINCERE APOLOGIES + RESPECT TO MATT GROENING.

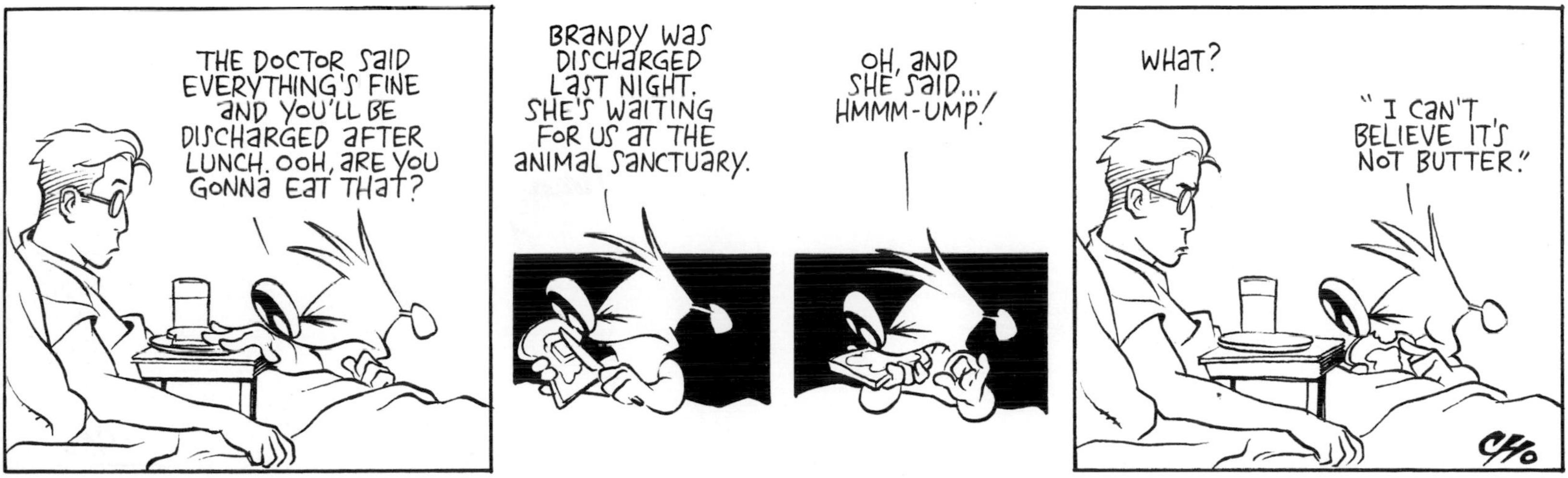
THE DOCTOR SAID EVERYTHING'S FINE AND YOU'LL BE DISCHARGED AFTER LUNCH. OOH, ARE YOU GONNA EAT THAT?
BRANDY WAS DISCHARGED LAST NIGHT. SHE'S WAITING FOR US AT THE ANIMAL SANCTUARY.
OH, AND SHE SAID... HMMM-UMP!
WHAT?
"I CAN'T BELIEVE IT'S NOT BUTTER."
CHO

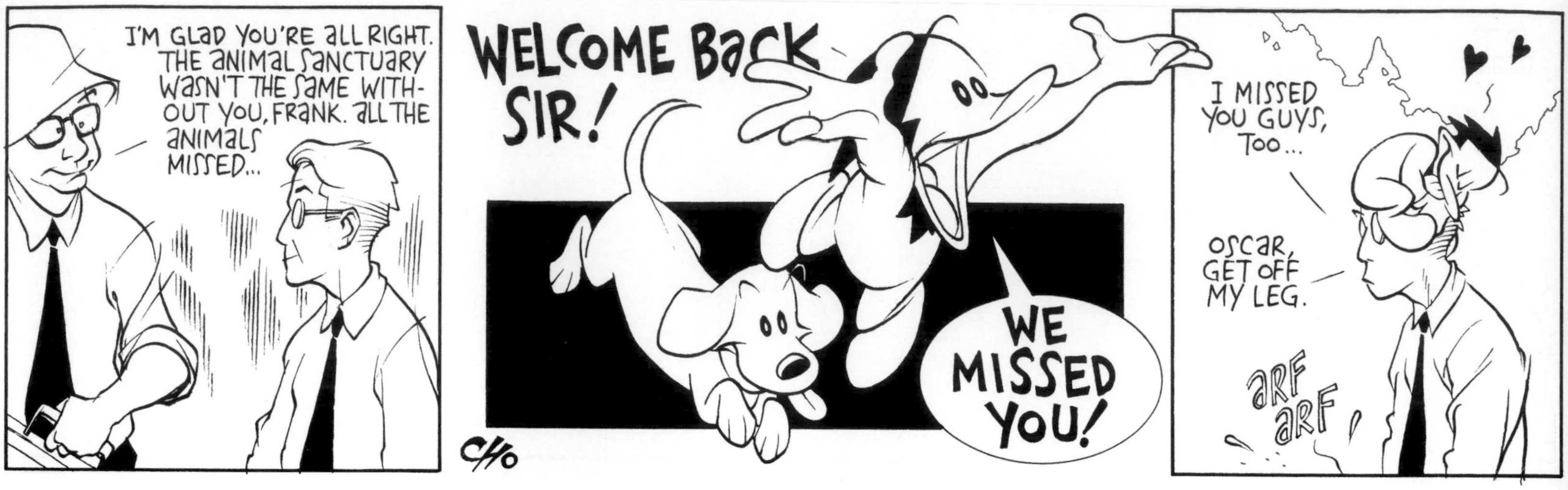
I'M GLAD YOU'RE ALL RIGHT. THE ANIMAL SANCTUARY WASN'T THE SAME WITHOUT YOU, FRANK. ALL THE ANIMALS MISSED...
WELCOME BACK SIR!
WE MISSED YOU!
CHO
I MISSED YOU GUYS, TOO...
OSCAR, GET OFF MY LEG.
ARF ARF

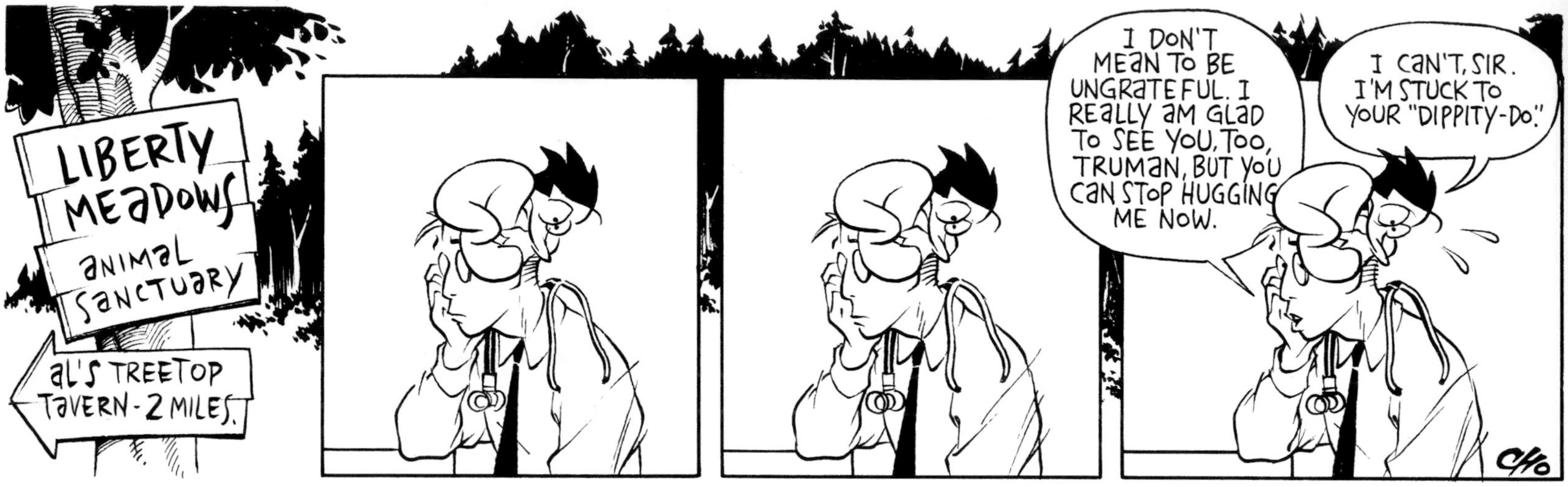
LIBERTY MEADOWS
ANIMAL SANCTUARY
AL'S TREETOP TAVERN - 2 MILES
I DON'T MEAN TO BE UNGRATEFUL. I REALLY AM GLAD TO SEE YOU, TOO, TRUMAN, BUT YOU CAN STOP HUGGING ME NOW.
I CAN'T, SIR. I'M STUCK TO YOUR "DIPPITY-DO."
CHO

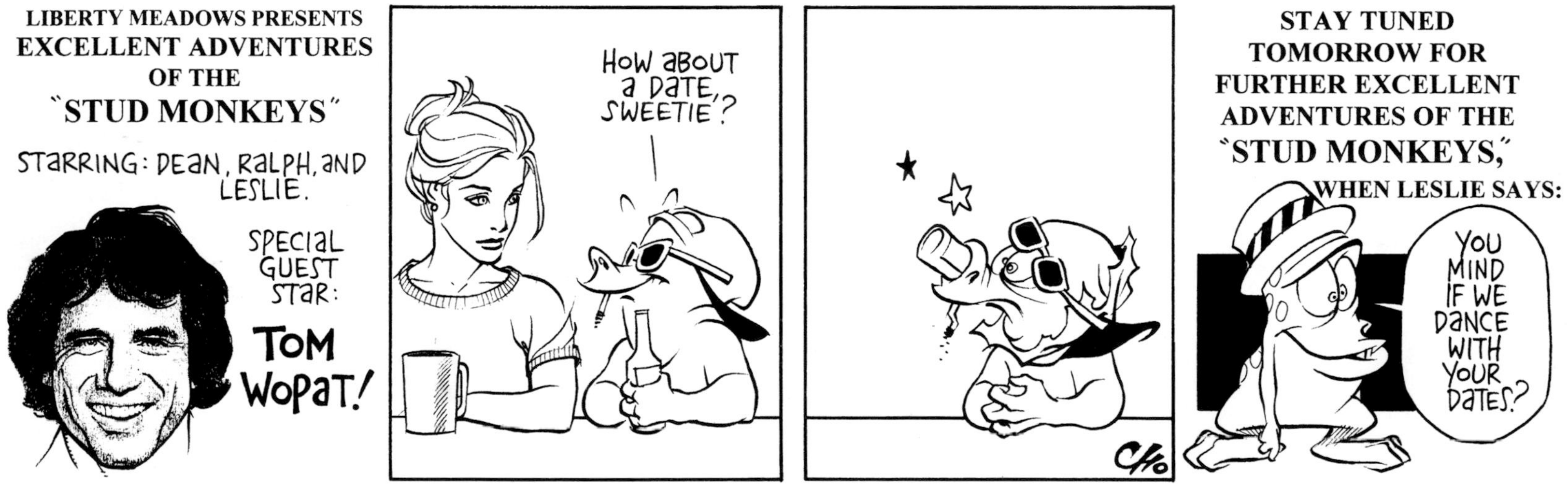
LIBERTY MEADOWS PRESENTS
EXCELLENT ADVENTURES OF THE
"STUD MONKEYS"
STARRING: DEAN, RALPH, AND LESLIE.
SPECIAL GUEST STAR:
TOM WOPAT!
HOW ABOUT A DATE, SWEETIE?
CHO
STAY TUNED TOMORROW FOR FURTHER EXCELLENT ADVENTURES OF THE
"STUD MONKEYS,"
WHEN LESLIE SAYS:
YOU MIND IF WE DANCE WITH YOUR DATES?

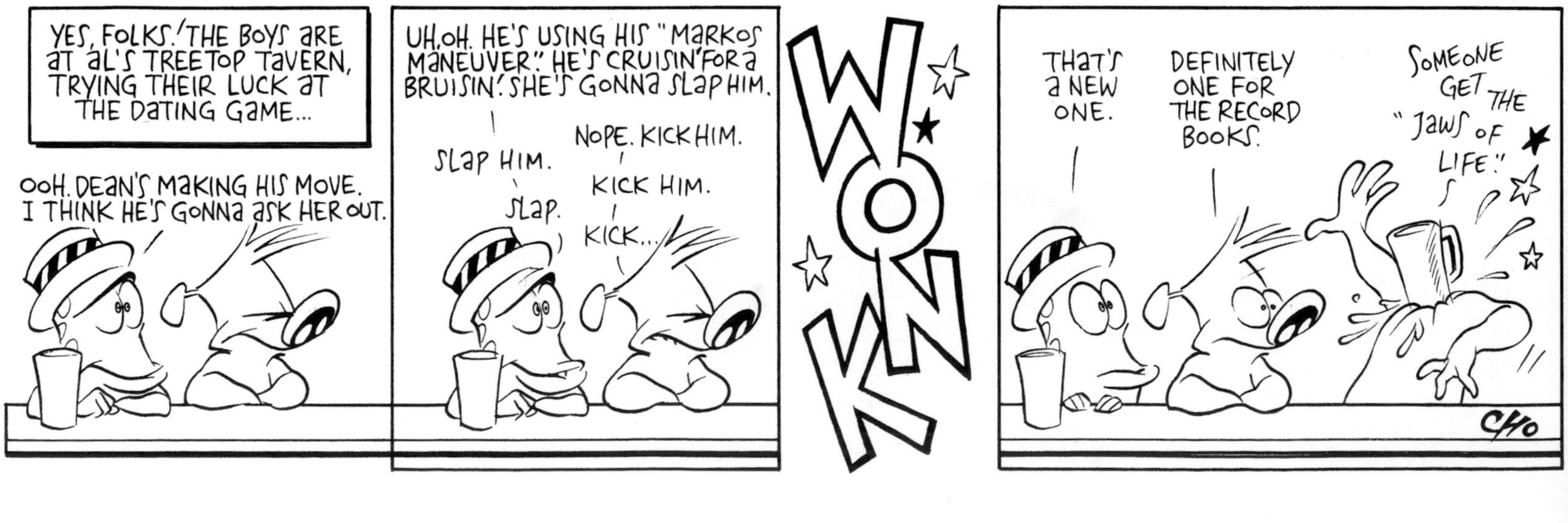
YES, FOLKS! THE BOYS ARE AT AL'S TREETOP TAVERN, TRYING THEIR LUCK AT THE DATING GAME...
OOH. DEAN'S MAKING HIS MOVE. I THINK HE'S GONNA ASK HER OUT.
UH, OH. HE'S USING HIS "MARKOS MANEUVER." HE'S CRUISIN' FOR A BRUISIN'! SHE'S GONNA SLAP HIM.
SLAP HIM.
SLAP.
NOPE. KICK HIM.
KICK HIM.
KICK...
WONK
THAT'S A NEW ONE.
DEFINITELY ONE FOR THE RECORD BOOKS.
SOMEONE GET THE "JAWS OF LIFE."
CHO

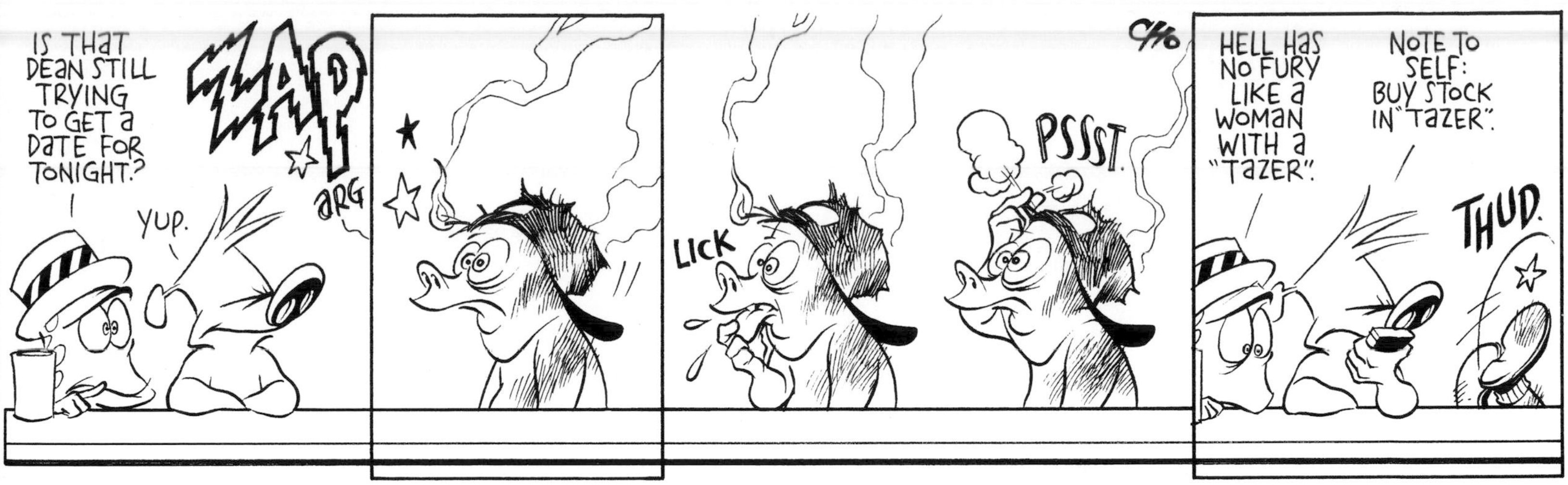
IS THAT DEAN STILL TRYING TO GET A DATE FOR TONIGHT?
YUP.
ZAP
ARG
LICK
PSSST.
CHO
HELL HAS NO FURY LIKE A WOMAN WITH A "TAZER".
NOTE TO SELF: BUY STOCK IN "TAZER".
THUD.

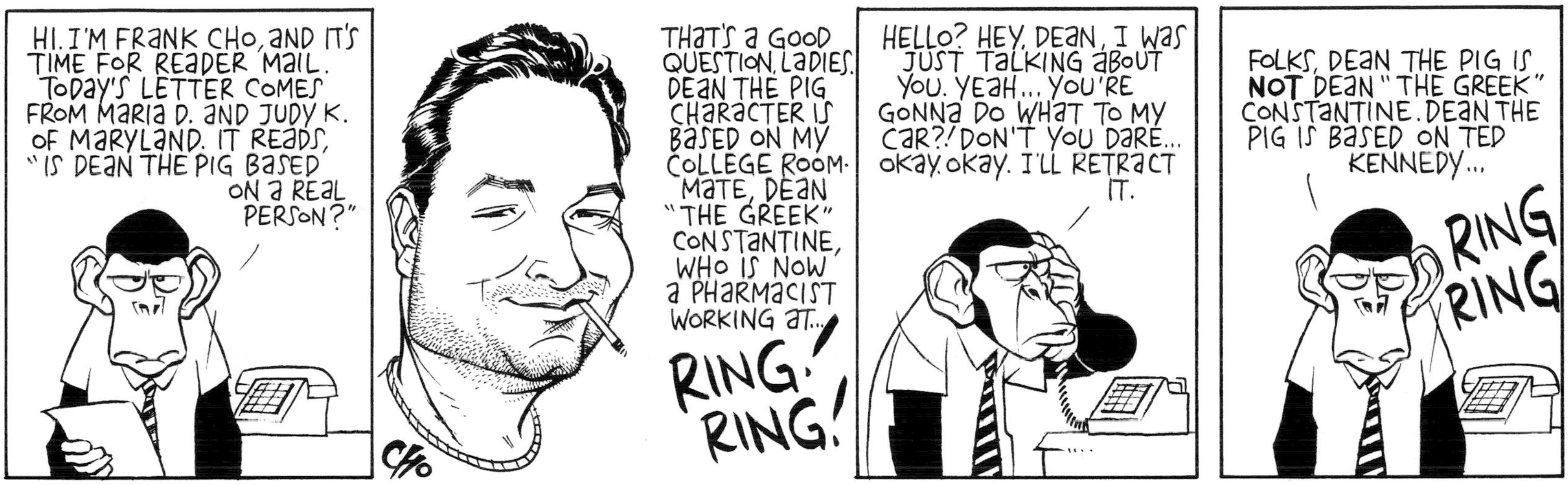
HI. I'M FRANK CHO, AND IT'S TIME FOR READER MAIL. TODAY'S LETTER COMES FROM MARIA D. AND JUDY K. OF MARYLAND. IT READS, "IS DEAN THE PIG BASED ON A REAL PERSON?"
CHO
THAT'S A GOOD QUESTION, LADIES. DEAN THE PIG CHARACTER IS BASED ON MY COLLEGE ROOMMATE, DEAN "THE GREEK" CONSTANTINE, WHO IS NOW A PHARMACIST WORKING AT...
RING! RING!
HELLO? HEY, DEAN, I WAS JUST TALKING ABOUT YOU. YEAH... YOU'RE GONNA DO WHAT TO MY CAR?! DON'T YOU DARE... OKAY. OKAY. I'LL RETRACT IT.
FOLKS, DEAN THE PIG IS NOT DEAN "THE GREEK" CONSTANTINE. DEAN THE PIG IS BASED ON TED KENNEDY...
RING RING

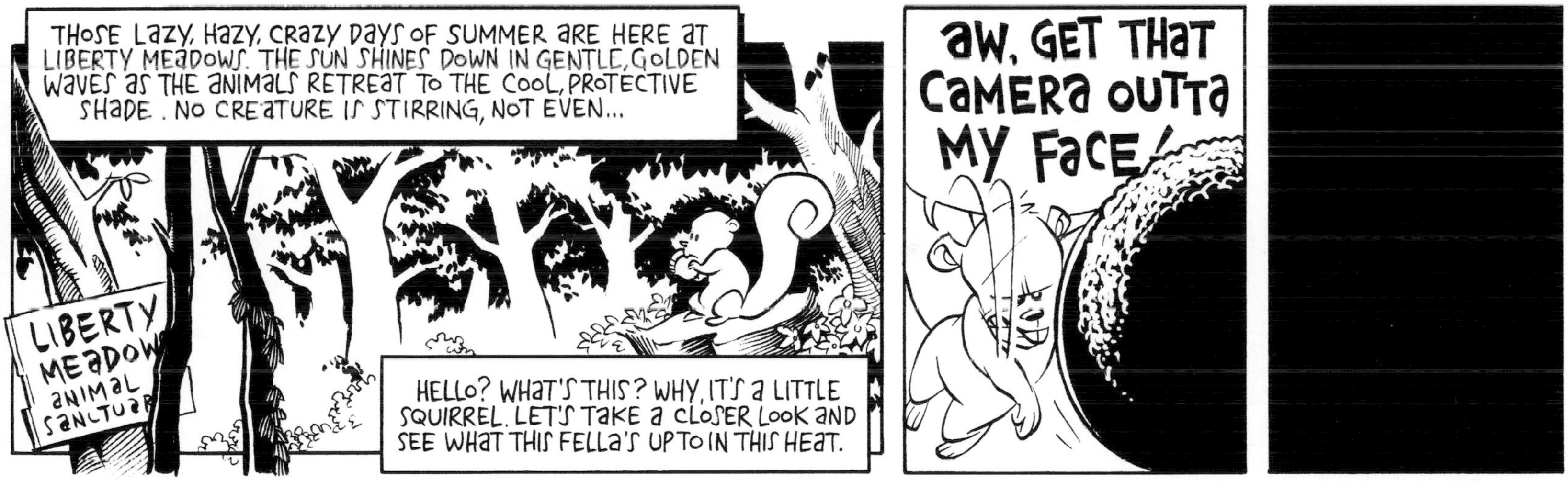
THOSE LAZY, HAZY, CRAZY DAYS OF SUMMER ARE HERE AT LIBERTY MEADOWS. THE SUN SHINES DOWN IN GENTLE, GOLDEN WAVES AS THE ANIMALS RETREAT TO THE COOL, PROTECTIVE SHADE. NO CREATURE IS STIRRING, NOT EVEN...
LIBERTY MEADOW ANIMAL SANCTUAR
HELLO? WHAT'S THIS? WHY, IT'S A LITTLE SQUIRREL. LET'S TAKE A CLOSER LOOK AND SEE WHAT THIS FELLA'S UP TO IN THIS HEAT.
AW, GET THAT CAMERA OUTTA MY FACE!

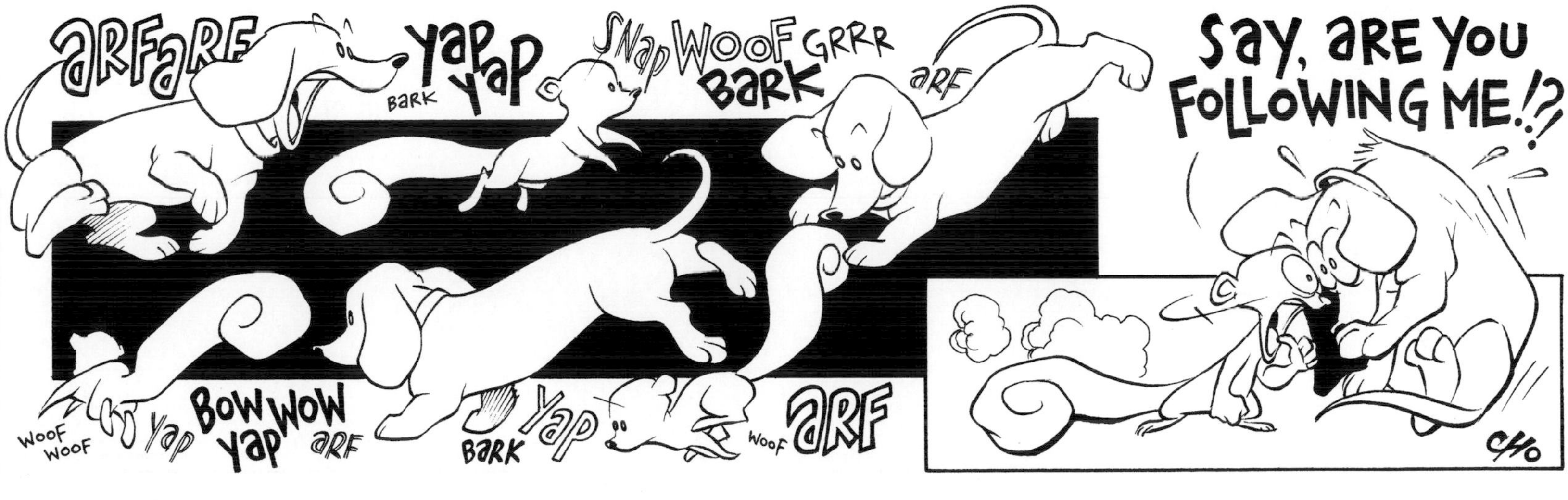
ARF ARF
BARK
YAP YAP
SNAP
WOOF GRRR
BARK
ARF
WOOF WOOF
YAP
BOW WOW
YAP
ARF
BARK
YAP
WOOF
ARF
SAY, ARE YOU FOLLOWING ME!?
CHO

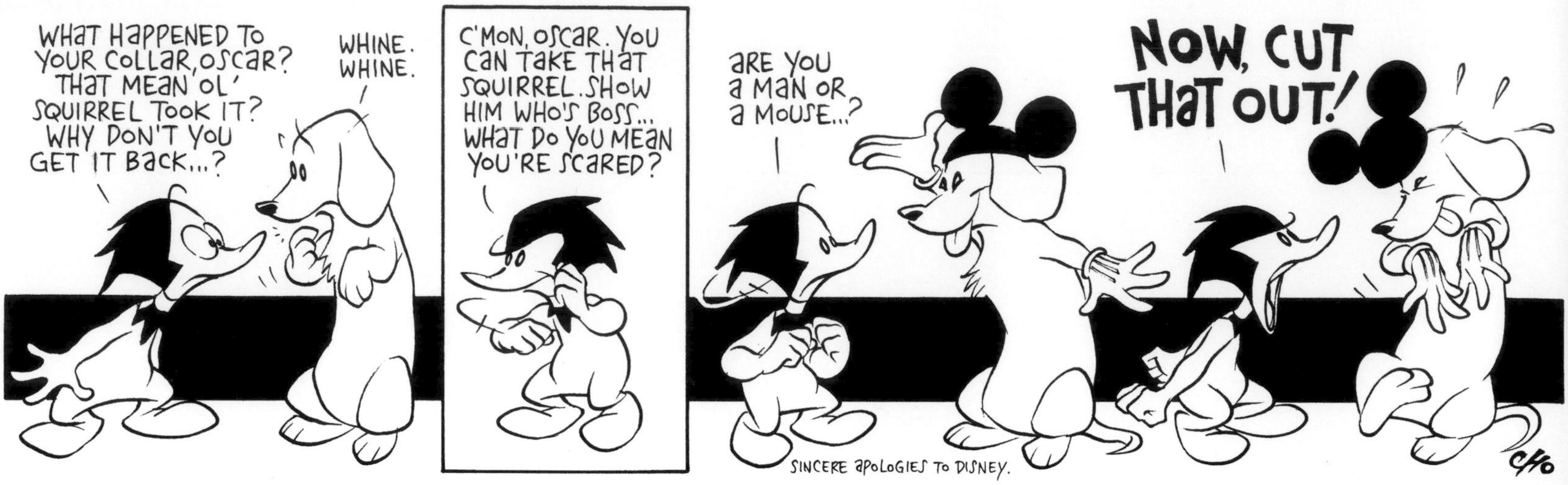
WHAT HAPPENED TO YOUR COLLAR, OSCAR? THAT MEAN OL' SQUIRREL TOOK IT? WHY DON'T YOU GET IT BACK...?
WHINE. WHINE.
C'MON, OSCAR. YOU CAN TAKE THAT SQUIRREL. SHOW HIM WHO'S BOSS... WHAT DO YOU MEAN YOU'RE SCARED?
ARE YOU A MAN OR A MOUSE...?
NOW, CUT THAT OUT!
SINCERE APOLOGIES TO DISNEY.
CHO

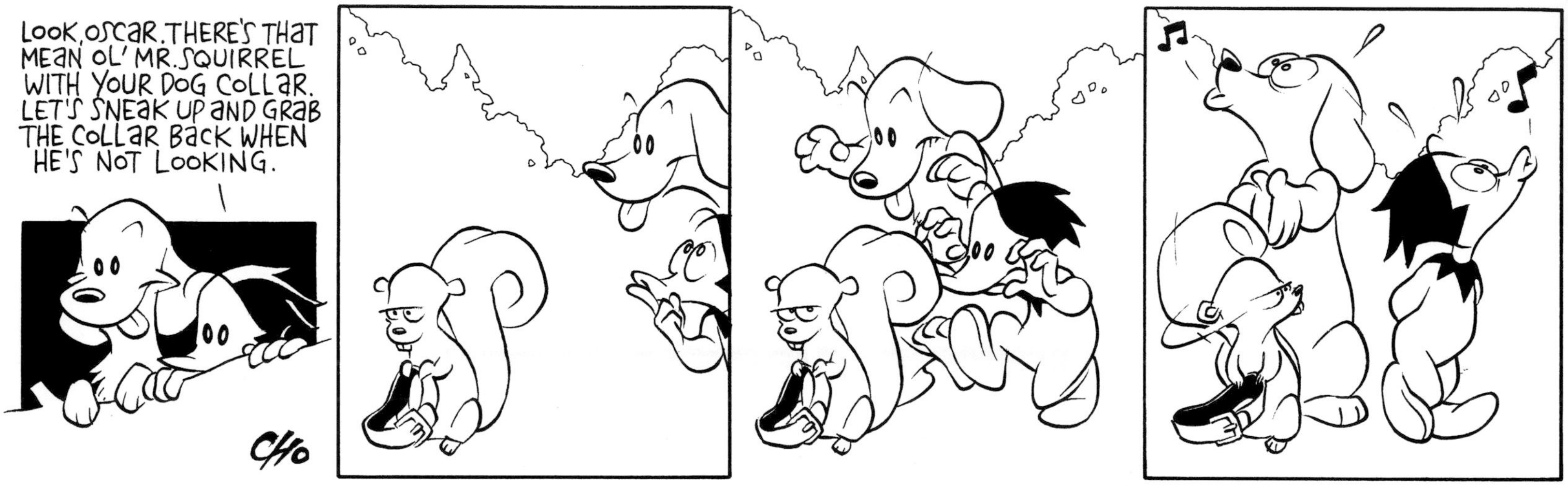
LOOK, OSCAR. THERE'S THAT MEAN OL' MR. SQUIRREL WITH YOUR DOG COLLAR. LET'S SNEAK UP AND GRAB THE COLLAR BACK WHEN HE'S NOT LOOKING.
CHO

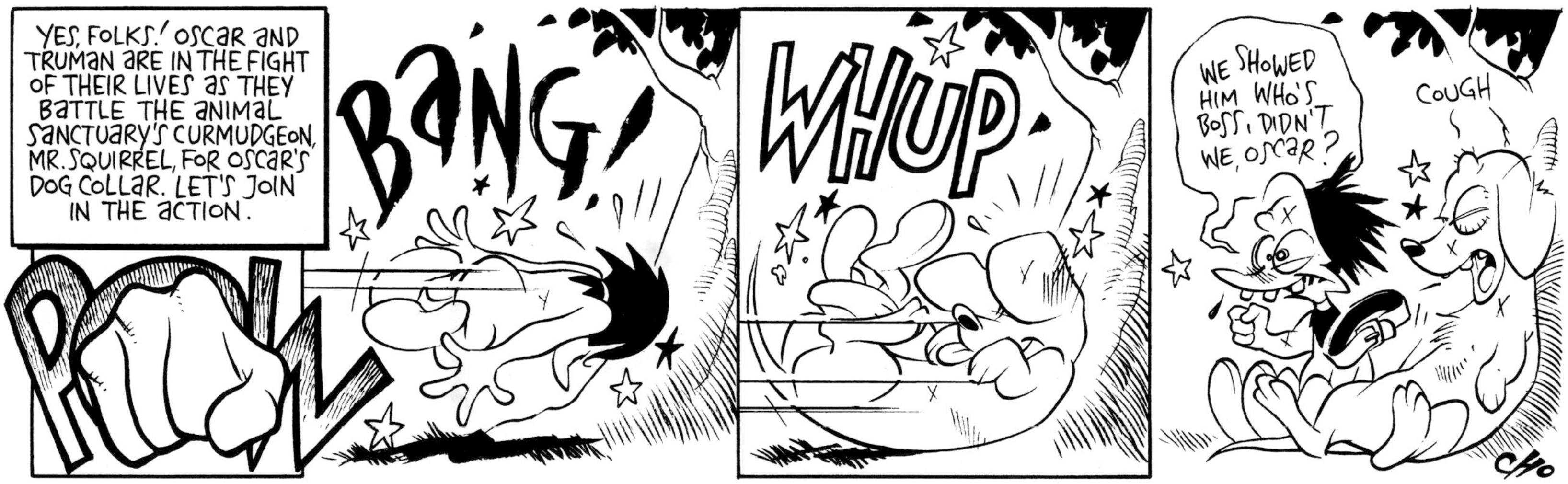
YES, FOLKS! OSCAR AND TRUMAN ARE IN THE FIGHT OF THEIR LIVES AS THEY BATTLE THE ANIMAL SANCTUARY'S CURMUDGEON, MR. SQUIRREL, FOR OSCAR'S DOG COLLAR. LET'S JOIN IN THE ACTION.
BANG!
POW
WHUP
WE SHOWED HIM WHO'S BOSS, DIDN'T WE, OSCAR?
COUGH
CHO

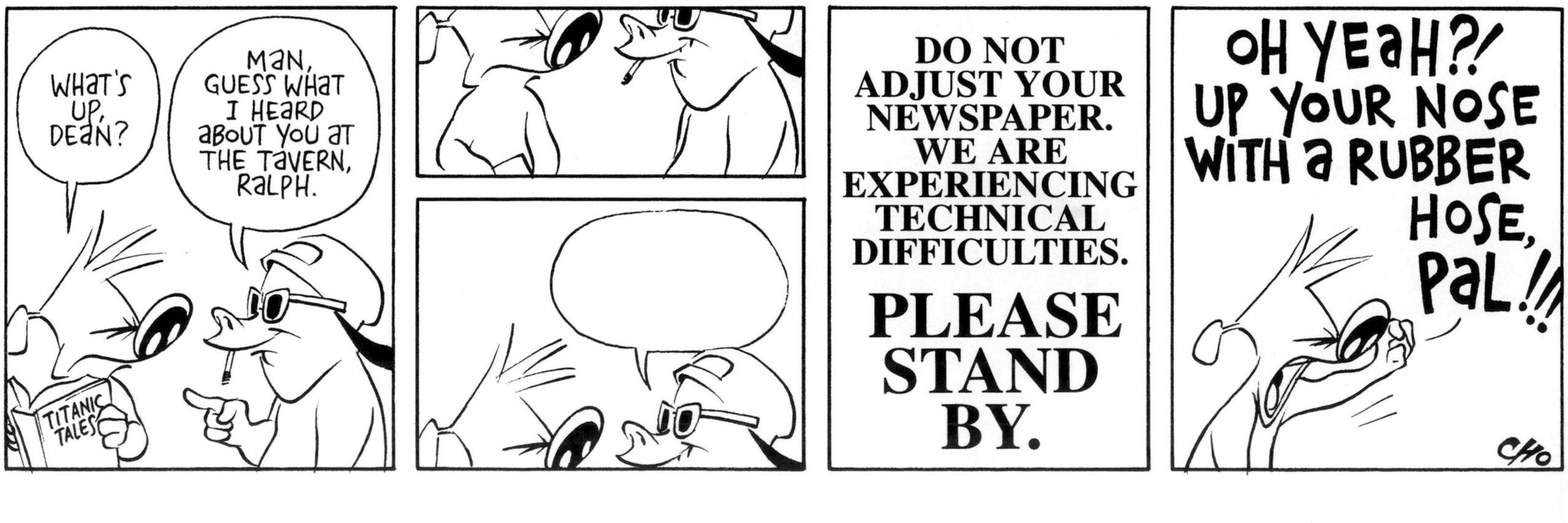
WHAT'S UP, DEAN?
MAN, GUESS WHAT I HEARD ABOUT YOU AT THE TAVERN, RALPH.
TITANIC TALES
DO NOT ADJUST YOUR NEWSPAPER. WE ARE EXPERIENCING TECHNICAL DIFFICULTIES.
PLEASE STAND BY.
OH YEAH?! UP YOUR NOSE WITH A RUBBER HOSE, PAL!!!
CHO

COVER GALLERY

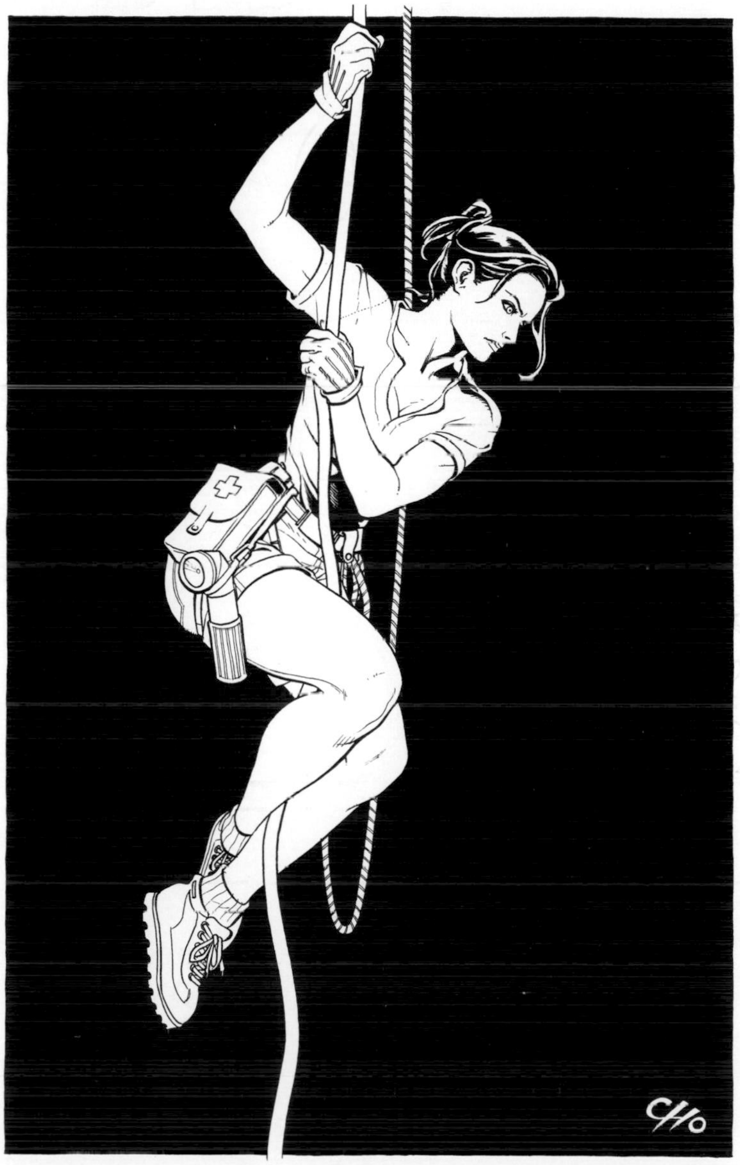
CHO

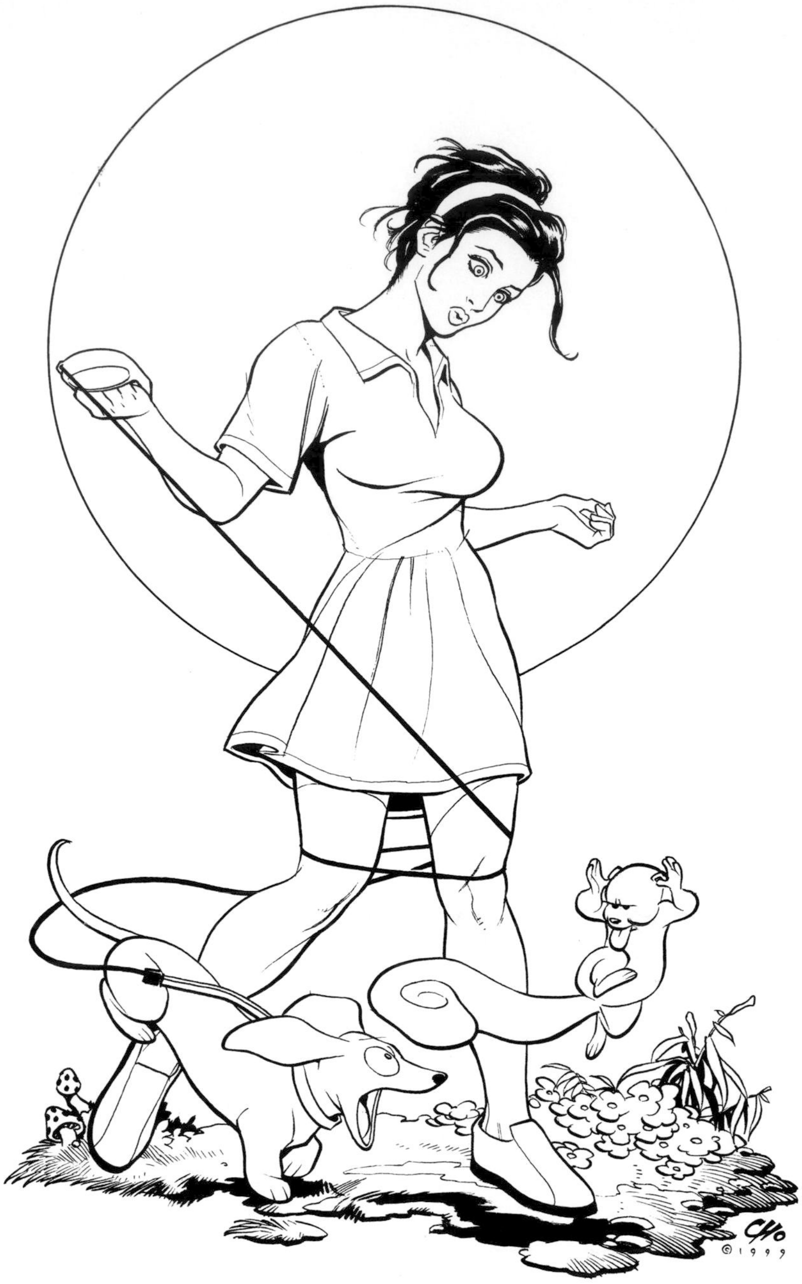
CHO
©1999

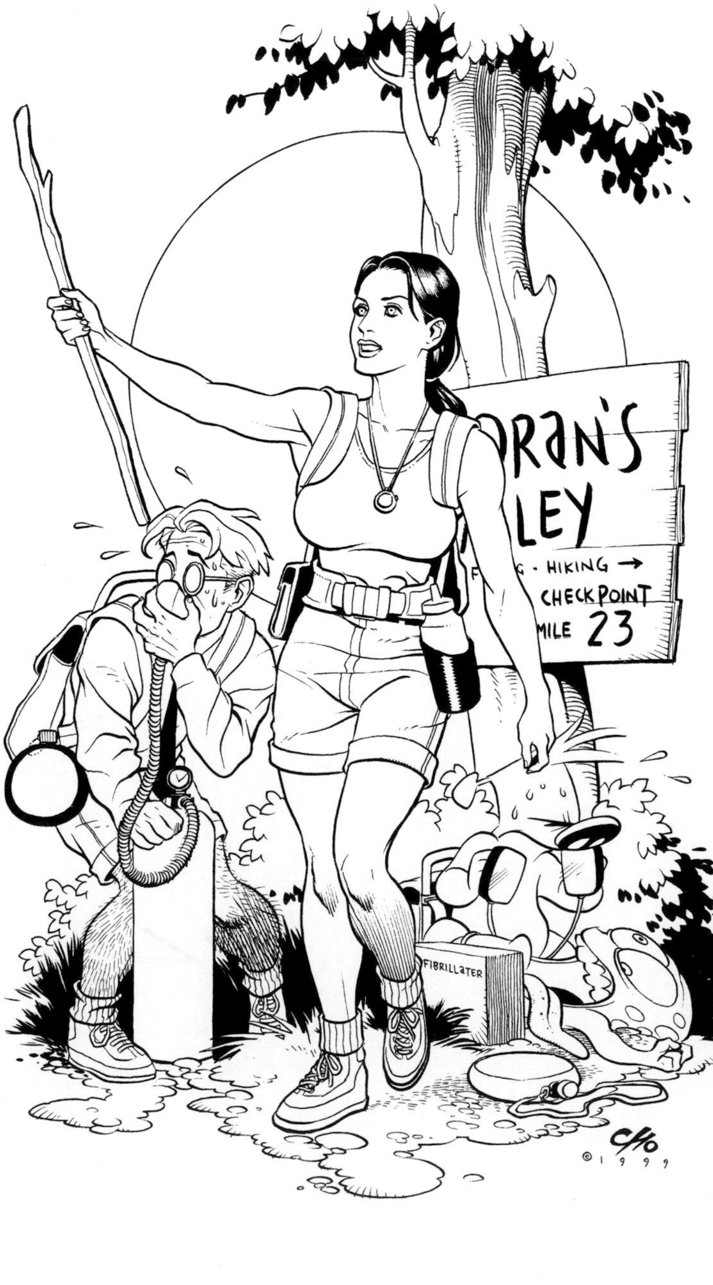
LEY
HIKING →
CHECKPOINT
MILE 23
FIBRILLATER
CHO
©1999

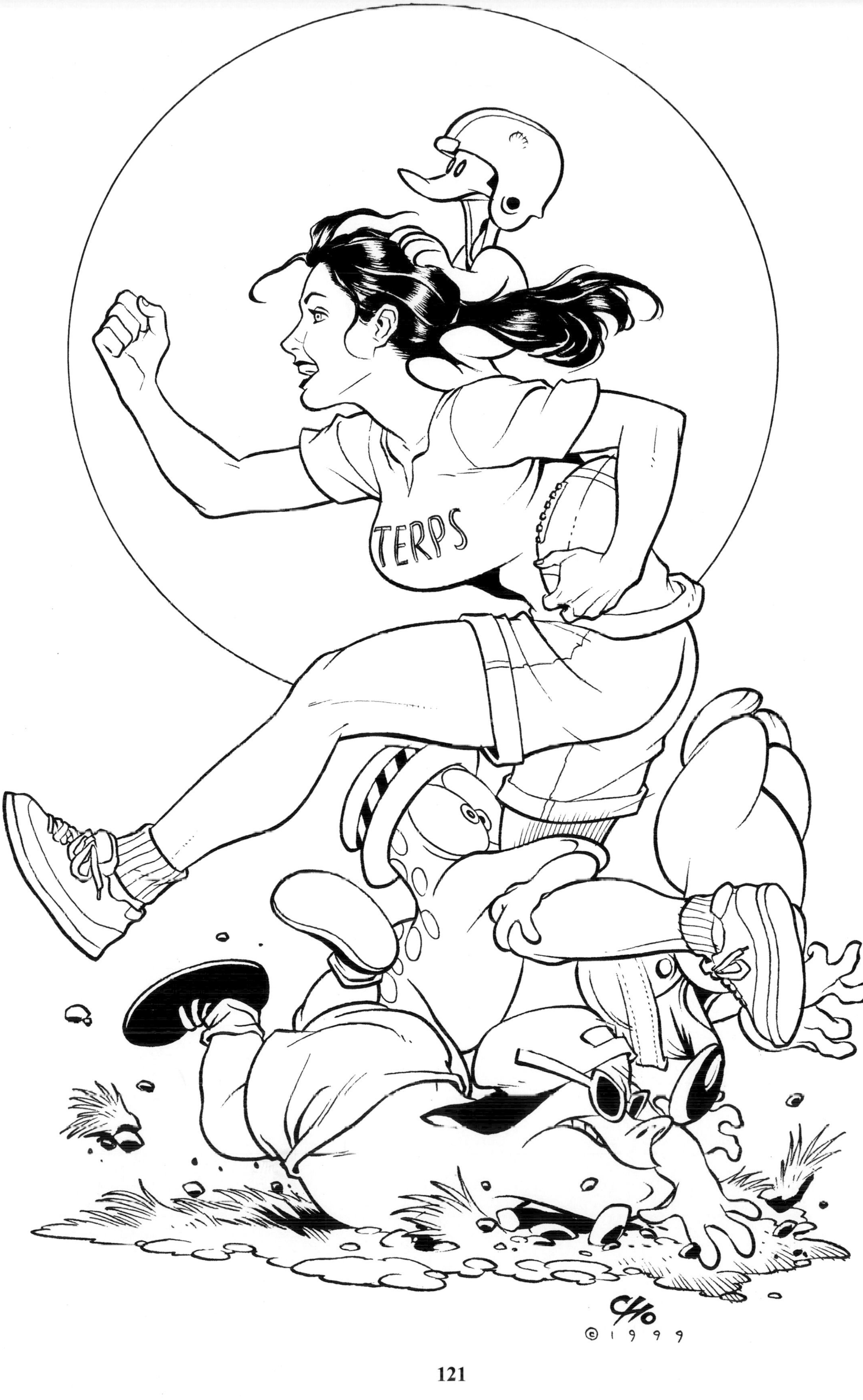
TERPS
CHO
©1999

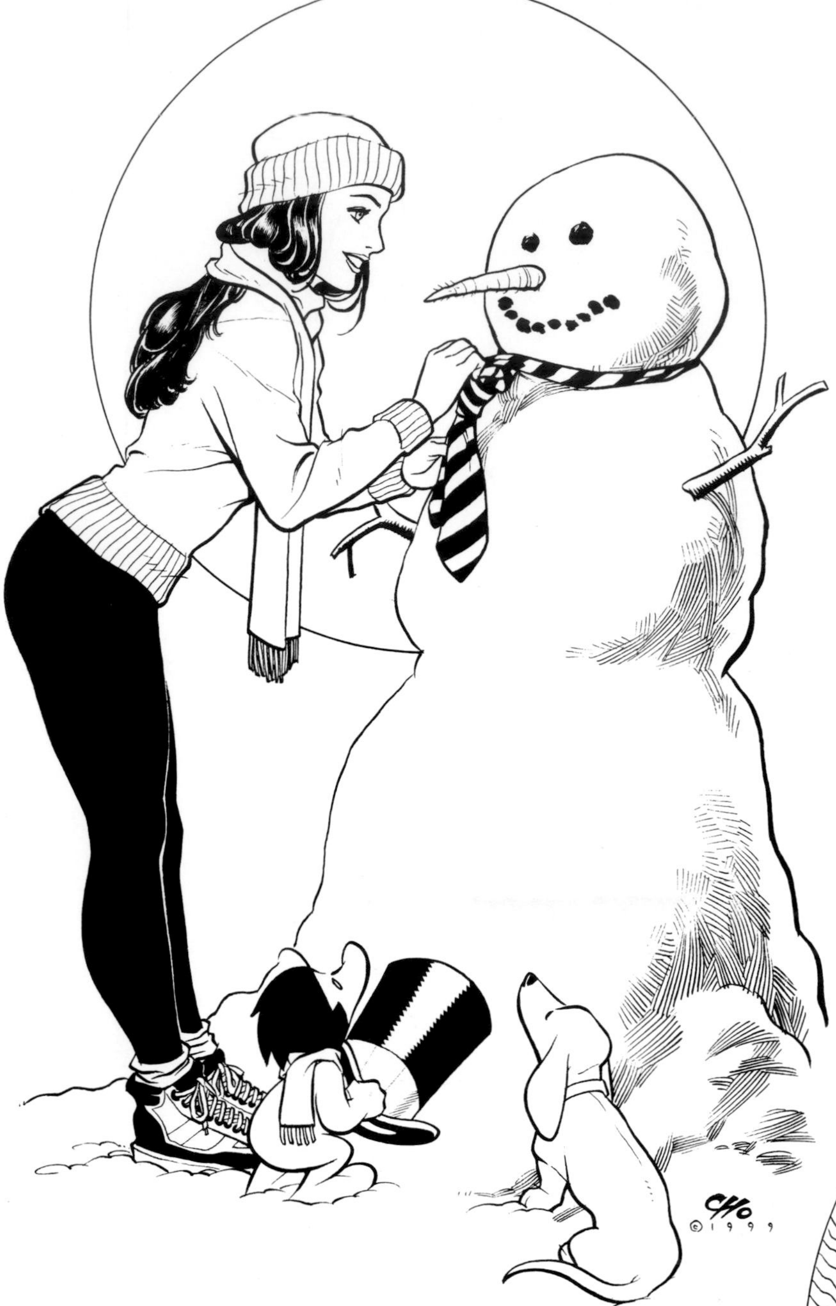
CHO
©1999

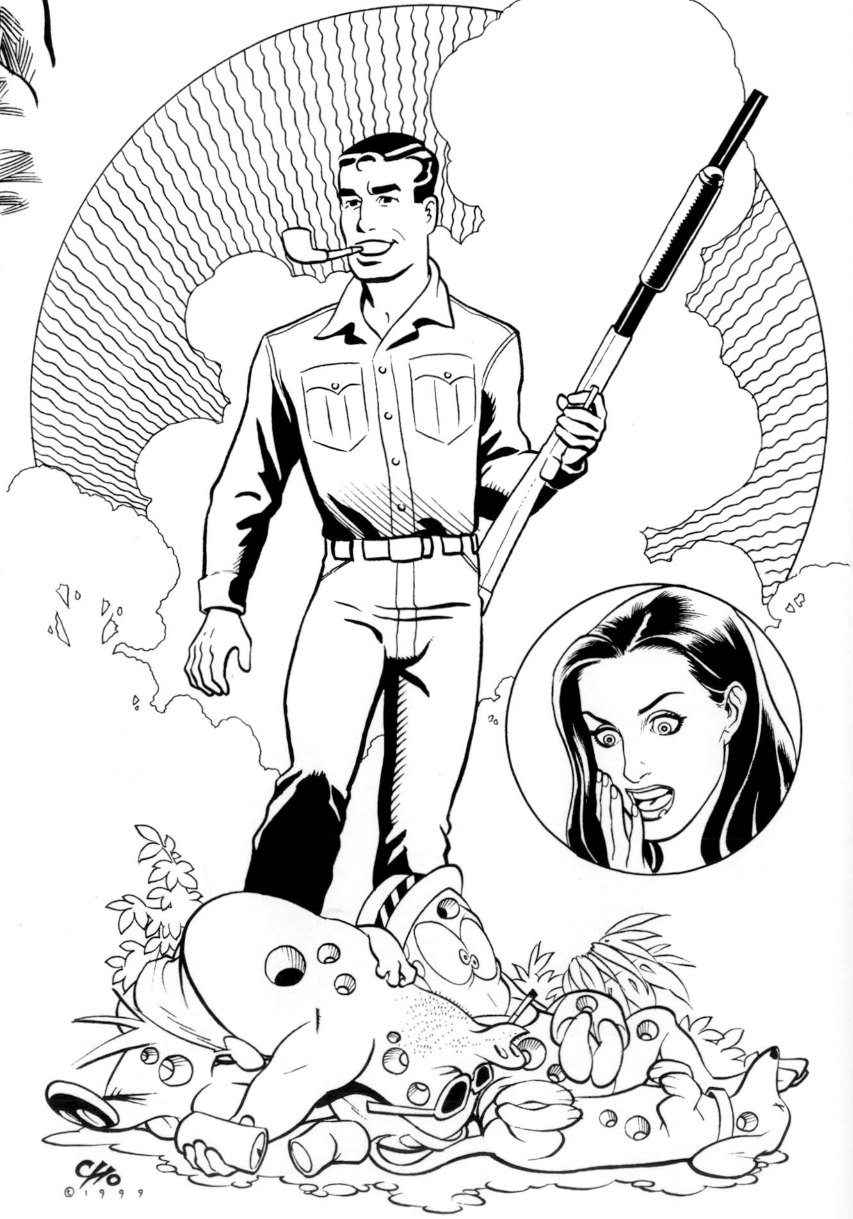
CHO
©1999

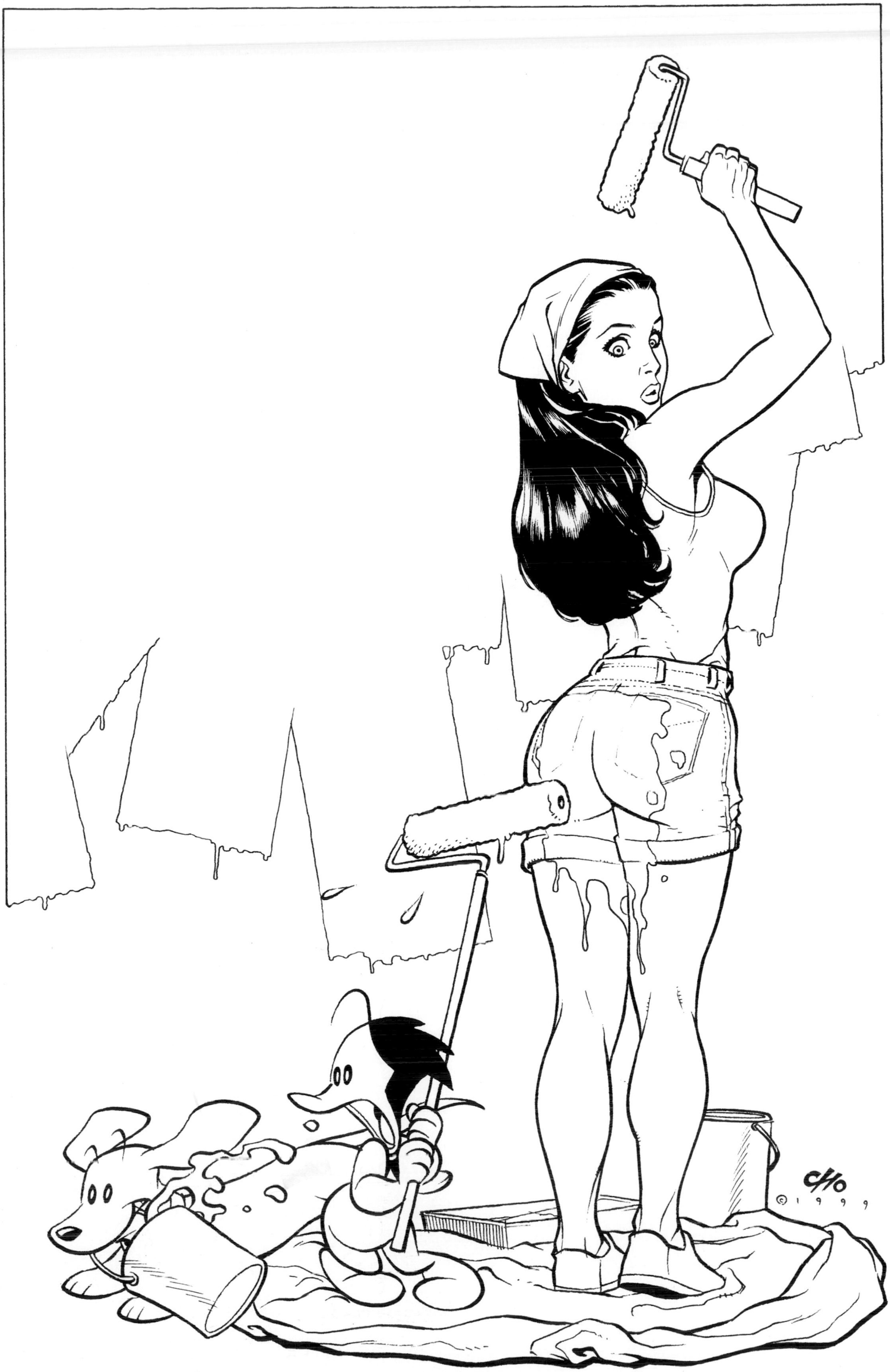
CHO
©1999

SKETCH GALLERY

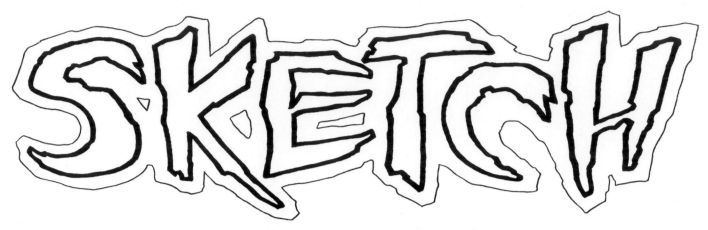

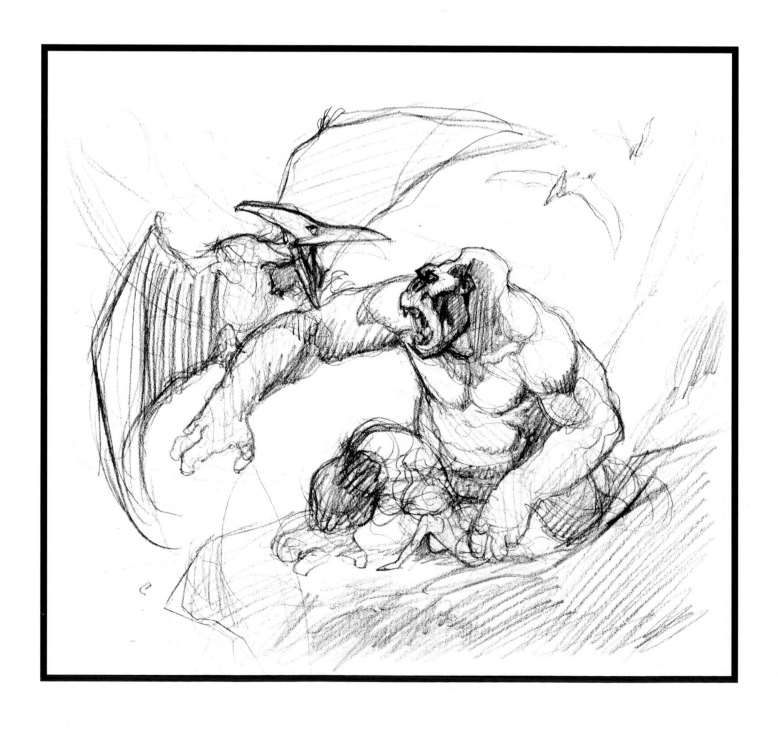

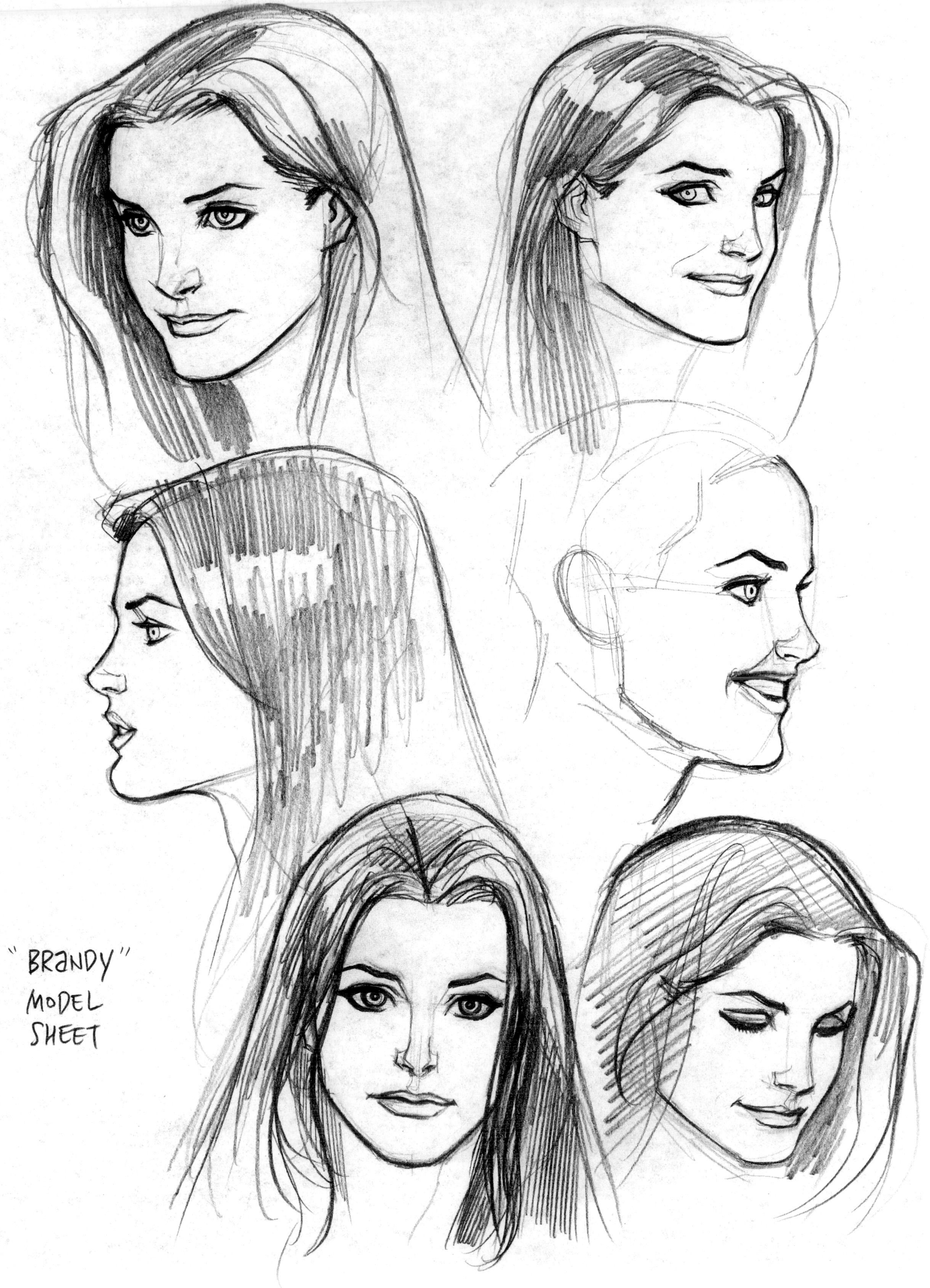
"BRANDY"
MODEL
SHEET

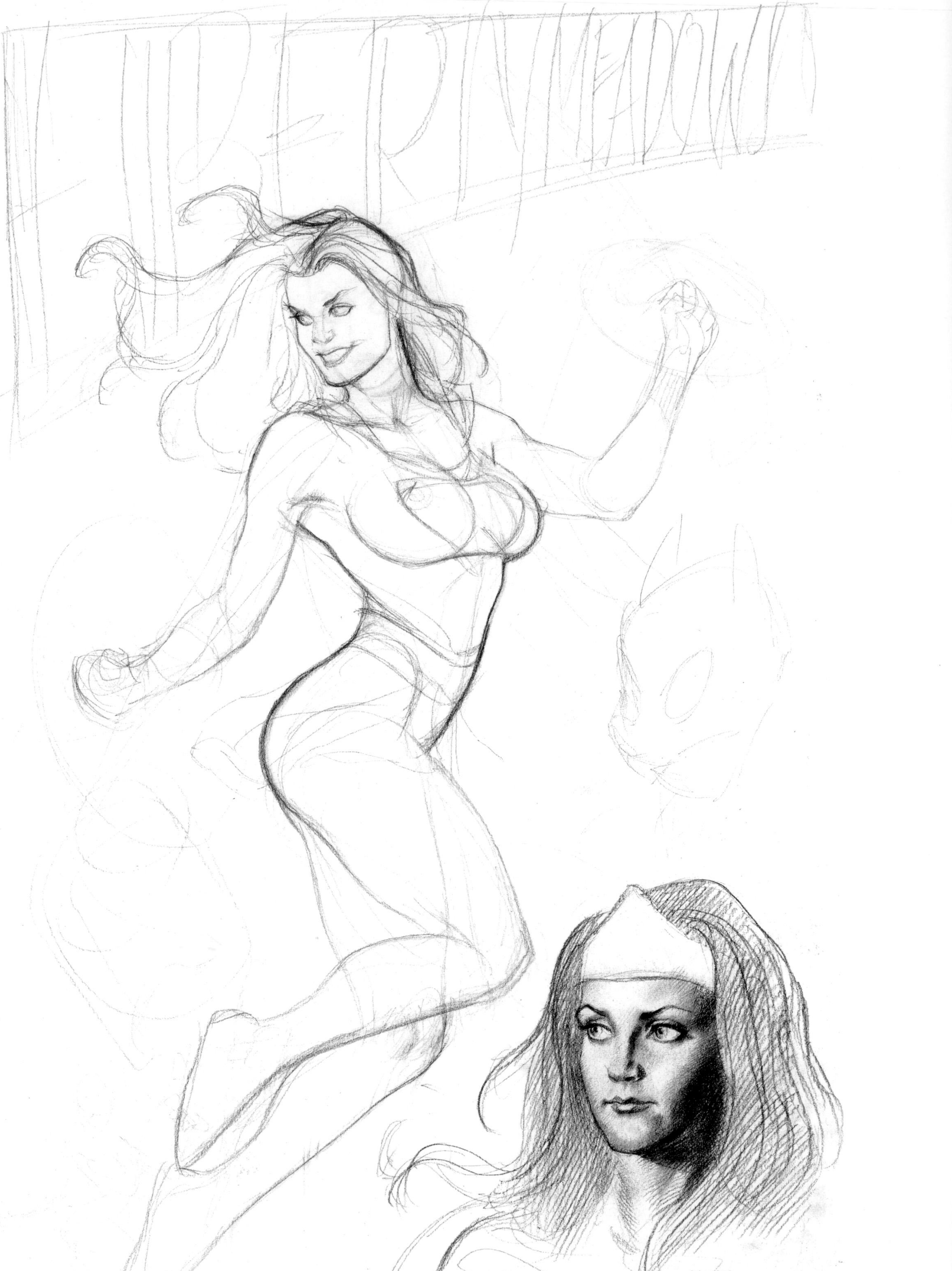
WONDER
BRANDY!

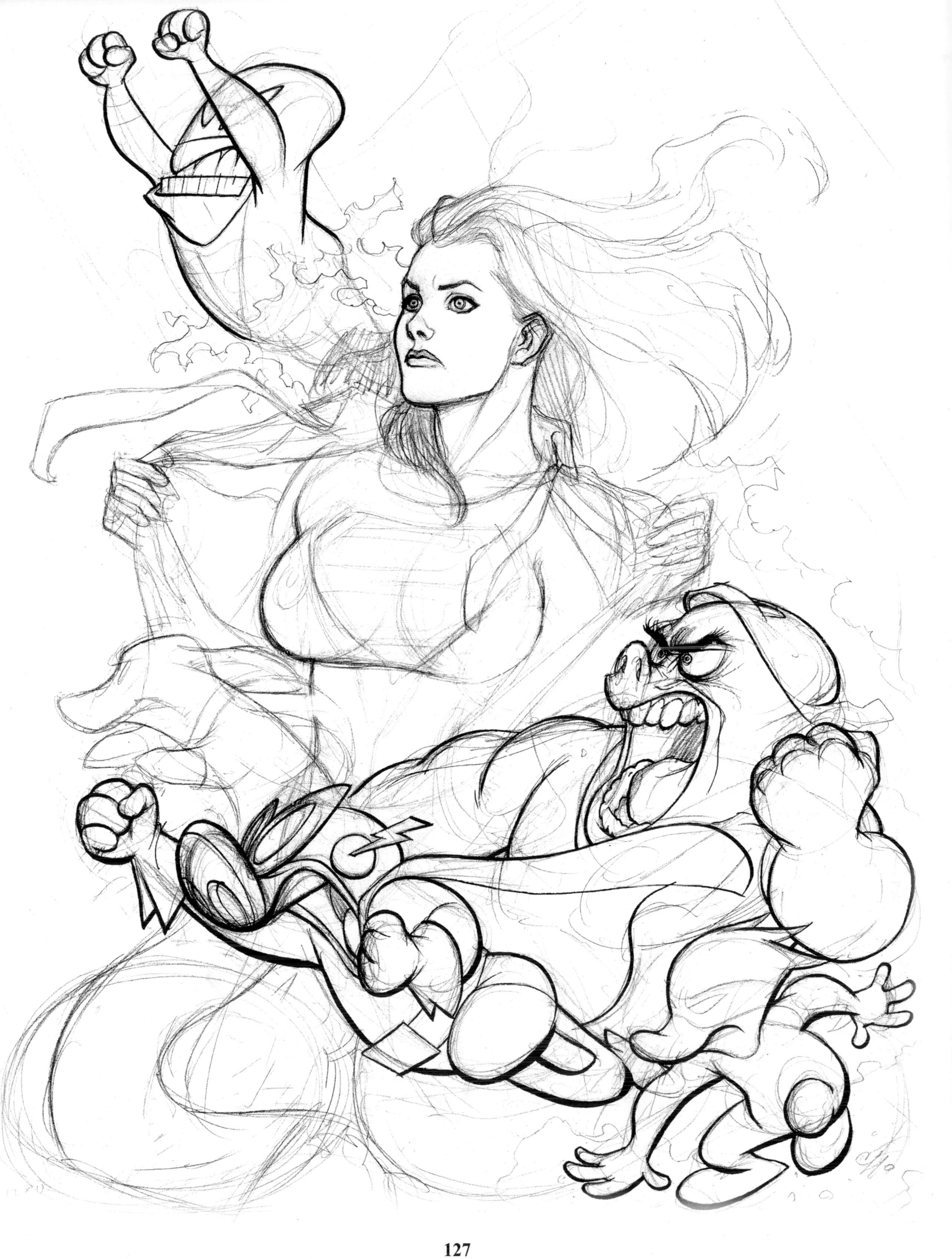

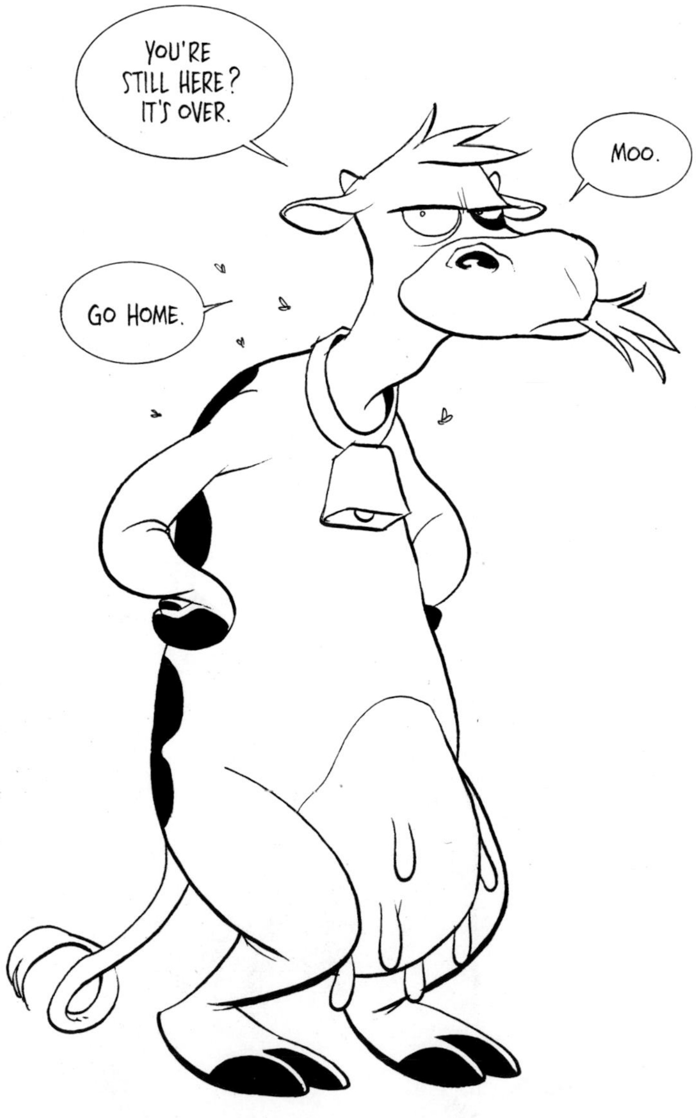
YOU'RE
STILL HERE?
IT'S OVER.
MOO.
GO HOME.